WHAT PEOPLE 

THE INNER LIGHT

P.T. Mistlberger's *The Inner Light* is a stupendous accomplishment, linking spiritual, psychological, and magickal traditions into a coherent whole. Its focus on history is kept fascinating by revealing the interplay and interdependence between the seemingly disparate threads of Eastern and Western spiritual traditions and what has evolved into modern psychological theories and practices. This weaving of systems, combined with practical techniques, will bring new insights to students and practitioners in many fields as well as increasing respect and understanding.
Donald Michael Kraig, author of *Modern Magick*

A mightily impressive work! A comprehensive and easy to follow guide through and around the Western Esoteric Tradition. I learned a lot from it and no doubt shall continue to do so. One to keep by you for constant reference!
Gareth Knight, author of *A History of White Magic* and *Experience of the Inner Worlds*

An immensely enjoyable book. This well written and insightful work is a must read for everyone interested in the history and development of the Western Esoteric Tradition and its varied perspectives on spiritual development and their practical applications.
Will Parfitt, author of *The Complete Guide to the Kabbalah*

The Inner Light: Self Realization via the Western Esoteric Tradition is a worthy addition to a growing corpus of literature that attempts to bridge the gap between the theoretical elucidation and practical application of the fundamentals of what used to be considered as "rejected knowledge" in Western culture. Although not an academic study per se, Mistlberger's book is an erudite overview of some of the major currents that comprise Western esoteric traditions, in addition to being an account of some relevant Eastern and modern psychoanalytic teachings and techniques equally concerned with the task of Self-realization. The practical instructions suggested in the book contextualize these esoteric teachings and provide a possible framework of actualizing their theoretical propositions and implications. *The Inner Light* will be of value both to those interested in the historical and thematic overview of some major trends in Western esotericism as well as to those who are intent in applying these teachings to practical use.

Gordan Djurdjevic, Ph.D., Sessional Instructor, Department of Humanities, Simon Fraser University

A comprehensive book, comprising a well-researched and annotated reference text of the history, components, and better-known personalities of the Western Esoteric Tradition. Some of the inclusions surprised me, not because they were inappropriate, but because the author does us a great service by placing them in true context; his understanding of the difference between popular neo-Eastern practices and genuine Eastern traditions, for example, is used in places to elucidate the content of Western esotericism. Especially impressive is the author's understanding of the interaction between the many streams that merge and flow as the broad river of the Western Esoteric Tradition. P.T. Mistlberger has made the wise choice not to include many examples of methods, but to offer us the sources of many related methods to research and pursue for ourselves. I will recommend this book to my students.

R.J. Stewart, author of *Advanced Magical Arts* and *The Underworld Initiation*

The Inner Light

Self-Realization via the Western Esoteric Tradition

The Inner Light

Self-Realization via the Western Esoteric Tradition

P.T. Mistlberger

Winchester, UK
Washington, USA

First published by Axis Mundi Books, 2014
Axis Mundi Books is an imprint of John Hunt Publishing Ltd., Laurel House, Station Approach, Alresford, Hants, SO24 9JH, UK
office1@jhpbooks.net
www.johnhuntpublishing.com
www.axismundi-books.com

For distributor details and how to order please visit the 'Ordering' section on our website.

ISBN: 978 1 84694 610 3

A CIP catalogue record for this book is available from the British Library.

Design: Stuart Davies
www.stuartdaviesart.com

Printed in the USA by Edwards Brothers Malloy

CONTENTS

Introduction **1**

Part I: History and Theory **15**

Chapter 1: The Essence of the Western Esoteric Path 16
Chapter 2: Introduction to Spiritual Alchemy 28
Chapter 3: Essentials of the Kabbalah 61
Chapter 4: Angels, Demons, and the Abyss 90
Chapter 5: Psychotherapy and the Western Esoteric Tradition 125
Chapter 6: Tantra and the Fundamentals of Sex Magick 167
Chapter 7: Philosophy and the Western Esoteric Tradition 187
Chapter 8: Transcendentalism, New Thought, New Age 215

Part II: Practice: The Technology of Transformation **243**

Chapter 9: The Fundamentals of Spiritual Psychology (Part I) 244
Chapter 10: The Fundamentals of Spiritual Psychology (Part II) 284
Chapter 11: Meditation and Self-Realization 312
Chapter 12: Magic and Manifestation 331
Chapter 13: Inner Planes Work: Lucid Dreaming, Dream Yoga, Astral Travel 368

Part III: Lore **387**

Chapter 14: The Body of Light 388
Chapter 15: A Brief History of Witchcraft 411
Chapter 16: Lycanthropy, Shapeshifting, and the Assumption of God-forms 442

Appendices

Appendix I: Ancient Egypt, Hermeticism, Rosicrucians, and the Kybalion 464
Appendix II: The 'Fall' According to Eight Traditions 479
Appendix III: The Chief Grimoires of Magic 496
Appendix IV: A Note on the Tarot and Experiential Astrology 512

Bibliography 524
Notes 534
Index 570
Acknowledgments 583
About the Author 585

To Rosho, who shared the journey and announced, at the end, that it was all 'boo-boo'.

By the light of the mind the human soul is illumined, as the world is illumined by the sun—nay, in yet fuller measure.
—Hermes

The most Ancient One is at the same time the most Hidden of the hidden. He made the ten lights spring forth from his midst, lights which shine with the form which they have borrowed from Him, and which shed everywhere the light of a brilliant day. The Ancient One, the most Hidden of the hidden, is a high beacon, and we know Him only by His lights, which illuminate our eyes so abundantly. His Holy Name is no other thing than these lights.
—The Zohar

One dark night
Fired with love's longings
—ah, the sheer grace!—
I went out unseen,
My house being now all stilled.

In darkness, and secure,
By the secret ladder, disguised,
—ah, the sheer grace!—
In darkness and concealment,
My house being now all stilled.

On that glad night,
In secret, for no one saw me,
Nor did I look at anything,
With no other light or guide
Than the one that burned in my heart.
—St. John of the Cross

Introduction

This book is an attempt to synthesize historical research with esoteric theory and practical inner work—a combination not typically seen. As such it can be of interest to those spiritual seekers who desire some historical rigor and background theory, and also to those academics or intellectually oriented students of the esoteric paths who desire to undertake some practical 'inner work'. It is also suitable for either the curious general reader or serious student of inner work.

The book is based mainly on material from the great Western wisdom traditions, integrated with some important insights from modern Western psychotherapy, as well as a sporadic sampling of Eastern teachings. The book covers some of the main disciplines of inner work from the Western esoteric traditions, including the following:

1. The spiritual dimension of Western psychology
2. Psycho-spiritual alchemy
3. The Kabbalah
4. The Holy Guardian Angel (higher self) and the 'dark side'
5. Theory and practice of magic and manifestation
6. Tantra, sex magick, relationship, and 'shadow' work
7. Inner Planes work
8. Meditation and Self-realization

Part One of the book focuses largely on history and theory, delving into alchemy, the Kabbalah, Tantra, sex magick, the Holy Guardian Angel, angelology and demonology, Western philosophy and psychotherapy and their relation to and influence on the esoteric path, and ending with a look at the 19th and 20th century New Thought and New Age movements. Part Two, the practical section of the book, focuses on some essentials needed in order to usefully apply some general methods of transformation. The material presented in this section is the product of my own search, study, and practice since the mid 1970s, as well as lengthy exploratory travels around the world and active teaching since the late 1980s. The section on magic focuses both on some general theoretical principles as well as practical work. The third part of the book, 'Lore', consists of three extended essays on the more 'fringe' areas of the esoteric and occult. The book ends with four Appendices that touch on a broad range of interrelated material.

This work contains a fair degree of material on the history of psychotherapy and discussion of the principles of transpersonal or 'spiritual' psychology and their role in the awakening process. This is not an exhaustive study, but more a summary of some of the most innovative, essential, and useful ideas from various seminal schools of psychological thought, with particular emphasis on Freud, Jung, Gurdjieff, Assagioli, Ken Wilber, and the Enneagram. Psycho-spiritual teachings are presented herein for two main reasons: one, they are in some ways the leading edge of modern Western wisdom teachings; and two, they are an essential foundation for any wishing to probe deeper into the Western mysteries and more esoteric teachings. The main downfall with those exploring esoteric teachings in general has been a lack of grounding in psychology, but in particular the psychological teachings that are geared for those embracing a spiritual path. The present book aims, in part, to correct that lack.

The Inner Light

The title of the book—*The Inner Light*—represents a specific view of reality that is based on a combination of teachings from the perennial wisdom traditions (both West and East) and some relatively recent Western philosophers. The matter ultimately focuses on the nature of both consciousness and personal identity (the ego), perhaps the two supreme mysteries of existence. Such a discussion is necessarily limited by space and does not present any definitive conclusions. The main premise presented is that reality as we know it is a construct of the personal mind—itself a modification of the Cosmic Mind, or matrix of Consciousness—and all 'other worlds' ('planes', 'dimensions') reside *within*, as representational models of reality. The 'personal self' (ego) as we commonly experience it is not what we really are; this 'self' is a type of manufactured image generated by various factors.

Many of these ideas (in varying forms) have been long extant, in the East via the teachings of Buddhism and Advaita Vedanta in particular, and in 18th and 19th century Western thinkers such as Kant, Fichte, and Schelling, and even some current neuroscientists and philosophers such as Owen Flanagan and Thomas Metzinger (both of whom disavow the reality of the separate, personal self). The three chief streams of Western esoterica—the Kabbalah, Neoplatonism, and Gnosticism—all examine the matter from the point of view of an essentially Idealist philosophy that maintains that reality is fundamentally Mind, or Consciousness. Tiny modifications of this universal Consciousness—'souls'—undertake a 'descent' from Source down via the various intermediary realms (archetypal, celestial, planetary) before incarnating in material reality. Once here, a long process of maturing begins, after which the soul, now ready, begins its journey toward Self-realization. It does not arrive at this destiny as the same entity that left it; it arrives rather fully matured, ripe, and ready to assume profounder responsibilities and participation in an endless unfolding of the cosmos. (In some models the soul is considered to be 're-absorbed' back into the non-sentient Infinite Source, only to begin the whole process of descent/re-ascent again at some further juncture—while in other models, such as the Integral approach, the process does not involve any 'return to Source', but rather a forward progression that both transcends and includes our origin point). The main point stressed here is this entire process, however it is understood, is unfolding in consciousness, not 'out there' in some concretely discrete reality. What is being proposed is not that the 'truth is within' or that some 'light within' is the great secret; but rather that we reside *within* the limitless field of consciousness that is the Ground of existence. And thus *we ourselves* are the 'inner light'. The Self-realization process may be said to involve the recognition that our true nature is unlimited consciousness (best represented by the metaphor of light). The entirety of the book is an examination of this matter, as well as a full frontal look at some of the darker elements of the mind that appear to impede or interfere with our Self-realization process.

The Yoga of the West

Traditional Eastern teachings on Yoga—Hatha Yoga, Raja Yoga, Kundalini Yoga, Ashtanga Yoga, Karma Yoga, Bhakti Yoga, and endless other forms, along with instructors, studios, books, and so on—are commonplace in the modern Western world, having more or less seamlessly integrated with mainstream culture. The word 'Yoga' derives from the Sanskrit root *yuj,* meaning to 'join together'. This refers to the essence of its philosophy, which is concerned with employing disciplined effort toward attaining inner unification, in order to ultimately attain a state of effortless unity—'oneness'—with existence. Eastern Yoga is commonly associated with its Hindu roots, but as a practical set of techniques, it is also found in varying forms in Jain, Buddhist, Sikh, and Taoist traditions. All forms of Yoga are ultimately concerned with an 'inner science' that, in theory, leads to Self-realization or enlightenment.

There exists a parallel tradition in the West, known generally as the 'Western esoteric tradition'. However, it is something of an irony that in current times the Western esoteric tradition is less well known than Eastern Yoga is in the Western world itself. The Western esoteric tradition is entirely concerned with the matter of Self-realization and attaining a state of unity with our spiritual source, and thus it can be accurately defined as the 'Yoga of the West' (a term coined by Dion Fortune, the early 20th century author and esotericist, in a reference to the Kabbalah, though in reality all Western esoteric teachings, not only the Kabbalah, fit this definition).

East vs. West

The seminal Western psychologist C.G. Jung had argued that Westerners (Europeans and, by extension, North Americans) are more suited to Western disciplines of work on self. He had made this point in the context of contrasting Eastern practices to Western psychotherapy. Jung was not lacking in sympathy toward Eastern psycho-spiritual techniques and philosophies; on the contrary, he greatly admired them, and at times openly admitted that Eastern inner-work practices were, in some ways, more advanced than Western systems. However he believed that Western intellectual development was more advanced than the Eastern counterpart, and thus a Westerner was at greater risk for disconnecting from their instinctual, unconscious roots. He asserted that the key to Self-realization lay in the balancing of psychological opposites, which can then, in theory, provide the ground to higher development. Without that balance, he maintained, the danger is real that we may become overdeveloped in certain areas, and underdeveloped in others—lopsided, as it were. Jung considered Eastern practices more generally appropriate for the Oriental, because he saw the Oriental as being more balanced between the polarities of conscious and unconscious minds, whereas he believed that Western intellectual development has resulted in the Westerner having a more distinct division between these two parts. In commenting on Richard Wilhelm's translation of the Taoist alchemical text *The Secret of the Golden Flower*, Jung starkly declared:

> There could be no greater mistake than for a Westerner to take up the practice of Chinese yoga, for that would merely strengthen his will and consciousness against the unconscious and bring about the very effect to be avoided. The neurosis would then be simply intensified. It cannot be emphasized enough that we are not Orientals, and that we have an entirely different point of departure in these matters.[1]

He elaborated on this viewpoint when, commenting on *The Tibetan Book of the Great Liberation*, he wrote:

> It is safe to assume that what the East calls 'mind' has more to do with our 'unconscious' than with mind as we understand it…to us, consciousness is inconceivable without an ego...The Eastern mind, however, has no difficulty in conceiving of a consciousness without an ego. Consciousness is deemed capable of transcending its ego condition; indeed, in its 'higher' forms, the ego disappears altogether...I do not doubt the existence of mental states transcending consciousness. But they lose their consciousness to exactly the same degree that they transcend consciousness. I cannot imagine a conscious mental state that does not relate to a subject, that is, to an ego. The ego may be depotentiated, divested, for instance, of its awareness of the body but so long as there is awareness of something, there must be somebody who is aware. The unconscious, however, is a mental condition of which no ego is aware.[2]

The problem, as Jung saw it, was that the Eastern ego has developed in a fashion that is fundamentally different from the Western ego, and thus required a different approach:

> It seems as if the Eastern mind were less egocentric, as if its contents were more loosely connected with the subject, and as if greater stress were laid on mental states which include a depotentiated ego...There is no doubt that the higher forms of yoga, in so far as they strive to reach *samadhi*, seek a mental condition in which the ego is practically dissolved. Consciousness in our sense of the word is rated a definitely inferior condition, the state of *avidya* (ignorance)...[3]

These views of Jung, though important and demonstrating courageous insight, have certainly been contested. In 1960 Alan

Watts wrote:

> Jung's understanding of the ego-less state of consciousness as the Eastern texts describe it leaves much to be desired...he believes that it is not egoless at all. It is only that the ego is forgotten in descending to a more primitive level of consciousness, to an undifferentiated awareness that is supposed to have been characteristic of man's pre-civilized mentality...however he does not confuse it with an actual reversion to primitivity. His point is that members of the ancient Eastern cultures can afford this relapse into undifferentiated awareness...just because their cultures have given them very strong ego structures and have at the same time provided for the ordered fulfillment of their instinctual urges. This is why he discourages the use of Eastern techniques such as yoga, by Westerners. For us there is the danger of 'inflation', of being swamped and possessed by the unconscious just because we have repressed it so strongly and have not yet come to terms with our less respectable instincts. The Westerner who lowers the level of consciousness and relaxes the vigilance of the ego is liable to lose self-control in the uprush of the repressed forces. One thinks immediately of the 'beat' variety of Zen in America's bohemias, and the delusions of spiritual and occult grandeur among some of those who take up Theosophy or Vedanta.[4]

Watts went on to argue that despite Jung's many 'excellent intuitive judgments' he was still trapped in Christianized (specifically, Protestant) conditioning that promoted the view that life must remain a point of tension between consciousness and the unconscious, and that problems in life are not to be solved but rather 'worked at incessantly'. Jung held that the development of a healthy ego is at the foundation of civilization. Watts countered this with the view that most suffering throughout history has not been caused by defective ego development, but rather by *too much* ego (isolation, disconnectedness from others and life, and so on).

We present this contrast between Jung and Watts because it highlights matters related to one of the themes of this book, which is the relative neglect of Western esoteric traditions in contrast to Eastern, along with the role of psychotherapy as part of a spiritual quest. In a sense, both Jung's and Watts' views are now somewhat dated. Jung's general view that Eastern methods should be avoided by the Westerner is probably too limited, but his point that Western psychotherapy is practically essential for a Western seeker is likely well founded. Watts' idea that sound ego-development is not a necessary element of consciousness and higher intelligence[5] seems too idealistic, a product of the heady days of the 1960s when Zen was the new kid on the block in America and the idea that there was a rapid, direct path to egoless consciousness had a novel shining appeal. That said, Watts provided an important counterpoint to Jung's polarizing of East and West. It would be left to 'integral' and transpersonal thinkers such as Sri Aurobindo, Jean Gebser, Roberto Assagioli, Stanislav Grof, Michael Washburn, and especially Ken Wilber, to bring greater clarity to the matter (although some of these modern thinkers are not in full agreement on certain key issues; see Chapter 9).

As Above, So Below

At the root of the Western esoteric tradition is the idea that a human being is a microcosm of the divine. This is best formulated in the old Hermetic expression, 'as above, so below'. It suggests that there is a direct parallel, a correspondence, between a Greater Reality and the personal, subjective reality of Man. The Bible refers to this as 'God created Man in his own image' (Genesis 1:27). What it points to is the idea that reality is a reflective process, always mirroring back to us who we are. In the esoteric traditions the underlying idea has been to see deeply into the 'mirror reflection' of reality, and to gradually see and understand that the deeper we look, the more we see that we are actually gazing upon our own selves. Initially what we see is rarely appealing; it may even be horrifying, as we begin to look into the complexities of our ego-mind and its various elaborate defenses. The process has been characterized as one of journeying through three essential levels: 1) who we think we are; 2) who we are afraid we are; and 3) who we really are. The most difficult zone to traverse is #2, 'who we are afraid we are', because this is where the self-sabotaging tendencies of the personality tend to operate. When Jesus faces Satan in the desert, or when Buddha encounters Mara under the Bo tree, or Padmasambhava battles demons in Tibet, or when the shaman tackles the troublesome spirit in the wild as part of his initiation, all these hint at the trials that await us as we seek to move deeper, toward the center of our being. Ultimately, if not defeated by our self-sabotaging patterns, we come to understand that we are not separate from reality in the greater sense; and more, we see that we are both one with it, and with the divine. To achieve this realization is to achieve what is sometimes called 'gnosis' (Self-realization), or in its most total state, 'transfiguration' or 'henosis' (merging totally with the divine).

Such a realization, however, necessarily requires a profound and life-long commitment to undertake the inner work, precisely because a one-time revelation or momentary flash of insight is never enough. Typically our inner journey proceeds through peaks and valleys—the peaks being our realizations and the valleys being the phases where we learn to integrate these realizations with the gritty details of our life. However we see it, the essential idea is that we possess the golden key to Self-realization: the process of understanding and training our mind, sometimes called the Great Work.

Clarification of Terms

There is often confusion around terms connected to the Western esoteric tradition. A clarification of some of these terms follows:

Exoteric (from the Greek *exo*, meaning 'outer'), refers to the standard outer church of any given religion, and its preserved teachings as commonly dispensed via doctrine and dogma. It frequently interfaces with geopolitics. This is what the average person recognizes as 'religion' and often merely pays lip service to, occasionally attempting to apply the moral guidelines of the faith to his or her life. (More insidiously, exoteric forms of spiritual belief are often co-opted by revolutionaries or more aberrant radical types, such as terrorists, and used as moral justification for their actions). Of course this is not to imply that all who are conventionally 'religious' are necessary superficial, let alone deviant, in their spiritual values. But in general, at this level there is minimal interest in personal transformation.

Mesoteric (from the Greek *meso*, meaning 'middle'), refers to that level of spiritual study and practice wherein the adherent of a particular faith is no longer comfortable with paying lip-service only, and desires to more fully *live* the deeper teachings of their faith. This stage is characterized by a more sincere approach, more open-mindedness, more intellectual curiosity, and occasionally the experiencing of altered states of consciousness, epiphanies, and breakthroughs of understanding. Sometimes a personal, inner connection begins to be nurtured with a saintly historical figure or archetypal image of the sacred. At this point, the development of critical thinking becomes important, as without it there is the danger of an inflexibility arising based on one's burgeoning mystical sensitivity, leading to intolerance, or worse fanaticism, and even worse, condemnation of any and all who regard one's cherished symbols of the divine differently.

Esoteric (from the Greek *eso*, meaning 'inner'), is, in theory, the stage of spiritual maturation (concerning deeper, and presumably more mature, spiritual teachings). Esoteric paths provide specific working systems that can enable a participant to undergo inner transformations with a view toward actualizing one's best potential in life—a potential that involves both inner insight (*gnosis*) and outer results (consciously intended manifestation).

The vast majority of humanity subscribes predominantly to the exoteric, the 'outer church' (of whatever religion). Accordingly, people who have arrived at the esoteric level of understanding—the 'inner church'—often walk a thin line, occasionally (or sometimes, frequently) deal with the judgments and condemnations of others, commonly feel alone until connecting with those of similar understanding, and are subject to all the difficult psychological states (including depression) as are those within the first two stages. In fact, intense levels of esoteric work are often characterized by the passage through a kind of 'dark night of the soul', a sort of initiatory rite required of anyone who wishes to break out of the centuries of limiting psychosocial and religious programming fostered by the religious or political doctrines at the heart of most established civilizations. This cultural programming is deeply wedded to the structure of the nuclear family, transmitted through generations of indoctrinated attitudes and beliefs, and so tends to be naturally inherited by the average person with them scarcely being aware of it. Successful navigation through the 'dark night' ends with a sobering view of reality, and a deep sense of the divine both as something transcendent and immutable, and as something immanent and ordinary—and perhaps most importantly, of one's unique role within it.

Mysticism: The word 'mystic' originates from the Greek terms *mystikos* ('connected to mysteries') and *mystes* ('one who has been initiated'), and from the Latin *mysticus* ('mystical, secret rites'). The word 'mystic' was used in English as far back as the late 1300s CE; the earliest recorded mention of the word in connection to the occult is from the early 1600s. A *mystikos* was originally an initiate of the old Greek mystery schools, especially those of the annual ceremonies devoted to the goddesses Demeter and Persephone via the Eleusinian mysteries, heralding from approximately 1500 BCE. (These were oral traditions; any written records of what occurred in these ceremonies, if they were ever recorded, have not survived, and thus the nature of what precisely they involved remains conjecture). The idea of mysticism was developed by Plato and later by Plotinus and his disciples from the 3rd century CE on, based on the notion of identifying (merging) with the ideal of divine consciousness. In older traditions, such as those of the Egyptian and early Greek periods, this process appears to have taken the form of identifying with a deity of some sort, but over time became refined into the idea of identifying with divine consciousness in an abstract or formless sense. In the classic sense of the term, 'mysticism' is connected to the idea of merging with the divine to such an extent that the sense of individuality is abolished. The expression 'you cannot attain to God—once you do so, *you* are no more, only God is'—may be said to be the essential basis of mysticism. The mystical experience itself is 'trans-rational' and can only be communicated via myth, symbol, or metaphor—a clear distinction with esotericism, which contains teachings that can in fact be directly and rationally transmitted.

Occultism: The word 'occult' stems from the Latin terms *occulere* and *occultus*, meaning 'concealed', 'hidden', 'covered over'. By the 1540s the word was in use in the French language as *occulte*, meaning 'beyond the understanding of the mind'. In English it first began to be associated with esoteric practices such as magic and alchemy by the 1630s. As a general body of learning and practice occultism has its roots in the Egyptian, Greek, Roman, Gnostic, Hermetic, Neo-platonic, and Kabbalistic traditions that arose in the Mediterranean cultures in the first few centuries before and after Christ. The word acquired more glamour during the late 18th and 19th century revival of Western esoteric teachings, owing chiefly to the influence of writers such as Antoine Court de Gebelin (via his work with the Tarot), Rosicrucianism, Theosophy and esoteric schools such as the Hermetic Brotherhood of Luxor and the Hermetic Order of the Golden Dawn. This glamour was eventually tainted and degraded by the influence of 20th century popular authors of sensationalized horror fiction such as Dennis Wheatley as well as the movie making industry. Consequently the word 'occult' now generally carries a dubious connotation in popular culture, based on sensationalized distortions of some of its elements. In general, however, an 'occultist' could be said to be distinguished from a 'mystic' on the basis of practical work; a mystic seeks to realize divine consciousness via simple practices such as contemplation, prayer, or meditation, whereas an occultist, while often using these, will also employ a much broader scope of practices, some bearing influence from religious structures such as ceremony, ritual, usage of symbols and consecrated tools and props, and so on. In addition, an occultist may demonstrate interest or active participation in more 'shamanic' activities such as divination, communing with so-called non-corporeal intelligences, studying unseen influences (as per astrology, for example), whereas a mystic generally shows less concern with such matters, being exclusively focused on direct communion with the divine, and further, on direct realization of one's inherent divinity.[6] All that said, there has unquestionably been a darker strain within occultism, where it has served as a lure for some seeking to compensate for a sense of alienation from mainstream culture, or a personal deficiency in self-image related to success, power, status, and so on; for these, occultism has largely been a statement of rebellion. In general the occult field has been populated by three types: those with a detached intellectual interest, those seeking a means to enhance personal power, and by those seeking to penetrate the 'divine mysteries' and attain deep wisdom. (Needless to say it is possible to pursue all three approaches, although any total commitment to attaining wisdom and Self-realization tends to eclipse the first two).

Theosophy: The word 'theosophy', though typically associated with the widespread esoteric fellowship founded in 1875 by Helena Petrovna Blavatsky and Henry Steel Olcott, has in fact been in use since shortly after the time of Christ. The word means 'wisdom of the divine' or simply 'God's wisdom' (*theo-sophia*). It is generally recognized as a sub-topic within the broader subject of esotericism, having more to do with the theory and practice of the individual's path to spiritual liberation or enlightenment.

The Perennial Philosophy: This term, first coined by the Italian scholar Agostino Steuco in the 16th century and used by the German philosopher-mathematician Leibniz in the 17th century, refers to a universal body of truth-teachings, and in particular, to the thread of this truth-teaching that can be traced in all known religions and wisdom traditions. Steuco had been influenced by the important 15th century Italian Renaissance scholar Marcilio Ficino, who had co-founded an informal academy in Florence, a gathering of scholars who sought to re-create some of the ideals of Plato's academy via translating many key works of antiquity, including those of Plato, Plotinus, and the early Kabbalists. The notion of a 'Perennial Philosophy' was popularized in the mid-20th century by Aldous Huxley, and has emerged as a key theme in late 20th and early 21st century lines of study and practice of inner transformational work.

Part One

History and Theory

Chapter One

The Essence of the Western Esoteric Path

To be free is nothing; to become *free is heavenly.*
—Johann Gottlieb Fichte

The essence of the path of inner transformation—especially via the Western esoteric tradition—may be characterized as *initiation*. To be an 'initiate' is, in this context, not a reference to inclusion in some 'secret society'. It speaks, rather, to a profound commitment to the realization and actualization of one's highest potential. This potential is necessarily spiritual, meaning it encompasses the loftiest and most profound possibilities for a human being.

The idea behind the journey of inner transformation is simple: we humans are not living our full potential. We are, generally speaking, asleep to this potential; both the experiential reality of it, and for many, even the mere possibility of it. It can be argued that humans are, largely, conditioned to feed a system, and that system is the machine of civilization as it has been operating for thousands of years. Even to conceive that one may have a destiny that is beyond being merely a working part in the unit of one's society is somewhat extraordinary, and rare enough. To actively search for a way to realize this optimal destiny is rarer still.

Why is this? Why is it that comparatively few conceive of a destiny beyond quietly 'fitting in' the established order, and even fewer actively engage a process of discovering and unfurling their 'wings' to maximum capacity? The answers to these questions may lie in the depths of mysticism, philosophy, psychology, and the scientific mysteries of cause and effect, but these answers seldom amount to more than conjecture, inference, or speculation. They are in the realm of history and theory, models and maps of reality, or of what is possible. Nevertheless such history and theory with their models and maps have their place. This is because studying them frees us up to examine the uncharted territory of our inner being, instead of wasting time re-inventing theoretical wheels or getting caught up in the ideas of one particular influential figure (of whatever quality) who seems to be proclaiming something new and original. In truth, there is very little 'new' and 'original' in the field of the great wisdom traditions. Most of it, including the deepest and most profound thoughts and insights, have already been thought up, spoken, and written down, and often very long ago. Our task as seekers of truth—as initiates into the mysteries of being—is, to paraphrase Isaac Newton, to 'stand on the shoulders of the giants' who preceded us, in so doing appreciating their wisdom while at the same time uncovering our unique and personal contribution to the blossoming of the human race.

The optimal potential of a human being, as defined by the Western esoteric tradition, can perhaps best be summarized by the terms **being**, **wisdom**, and **becoming**. Eastern wisdom traditions, while emphasizing the first two (being and wisdom), are less concerned with the third (becoming). This is due in part to the way time is conceived of in the East, i.e., as cyclical or recurring. The world goes around and things go around and nothing much about the world changes (or is ultimately relevant to our liberation). The Eastern approach to awakening is not fussing over the world (it is regarded as largely illusion anyway), instead focusing rather on one's emancipation ('getting off the wheel'). The Western model includes a progressive approach, a 'becoming'. This is, in part, because the Western concept of time is regarded as essentially linear in nature, part of a process that is developmental and evolutionary. We are going somewhere (paradoxically, even as we realize that things are 'perfect' as they are). In so doing, we have an active role to play in the unfolding of the cosmos, and in the evolution and development of the human race. We are participating in a grand unfolding of the universe, redeeming the world as we redeem ourselves.

The central idea here is that we hold within the key to realizing our best potential and destiny, and that key is consciousness itself. All wisdom traditions, be they of the East or West, supply techniques of transformation that in the end amount to forms of self-observation. However, the complex (and arguably, in some ways degraded) times we currently inhabit demand new approaches, ones that include addressing issues that relate to the psychological state of a seeker of spiritual wisdom. Quite simply, the practice of self-observation cannot be undertaken in any effective way if we are too wounded psychologically; that is, if we are too caught up in faulty self-image, i.e., self-doubt and self-rejection. Consequently, our inner growth unfolds via a two-step process of self-acceptance and self-observation. As our self-acceptance deepens and matures, so too does our capacity to self-observe—to bear impartial witness to all that is within us, the sum of what we understand as ourselves, and even deeper, to the very nature of individual identity itself.

Most wisdom traditions agree that our ability to impartially self-observe is frustrated, obscured, or blocked altogether by our identification with the *personal* self, sometimes referred to as the 'personality' or 'ego'. This is a notoriously tricky area to understand, mainly because many modern systems of inner growth present the 'self' or the 'ego' as if it were some sort of disease or monster that must be purged or got rid of. Regarding the self or the ego as the 'enemy' is based on a misunderstanding and commonly reinforces the very patterns one may be trying to overcome.

The Ego

The idea of 'ego' is sometimes treated glibly or narrowly in 'personal growth' teachings or by popularizers of such, and this is usually due to an Eastern bias in which the Eastern notion of the 'self' as being a mere impediment to enlightenment is taught to Westerners who have been subjected to different cultural conditioning. For example, Eckhart Tolle, a popular (and undeniably sincere) early 21st century teacher of spiritual principles writes:

> To become free of the ego is not really a big job but a very small one. All you need to do is be aware of your thoughts and emotions—as they happen. This is not really a 'doing' but an alert 'seeing'. In that sense, it is true that there is nothing you can do to become free of the ego. When that shift happens, which is the shift from thinking to awareness, an intelligence far greater than the ego's cleverness begins to operate in your life. Emotions and even thoughts become depersonalized through awareness.[1]

Tolle's remarks are Eastern teaching (particularly Buddhist) *par excellence*. While carrying obvious merit, such teachings do not necessarily apply readily and absolutely for Westerners, in part due to the Eastern emphasis on depersonalizing. As mentioned in the Introduction, Jung had suggested that the 'boundary' between conscious and unconscious in the Eastern psyche was less defined than in that of the Western psyche, and that transcendence of ego is in some respects more readily attainable for an Easterner owing to stronger social bonds that provide for greater harmony between the conscious and unconscious mind. A Westerner is prone to repressing his or her ego—'pushing' it into the unconscious—when engaging in Eastern meditative disciplines while seeking to aspire to an ideal of enlightenment that has, as one of its main qualities, depersonalization. In some respects Westerners who engage Eastern disciplines are prone to regarding the 'ego' as a type of taboo, or as a negative or even malevolent quality to be avoided at all costs—perhaps not dissimilar to how a Christian fundamentalist may regard 'the devil'. The risk then is to end up simply repressing the ego—something like banishing the devil to hell—rather than truly transcending it.

A key to understanding the difference between the Eastern and Western notions of the ego is that in a basic respect the two models are talking about two different things. The Eastern view of the ego, deriving from the great wisdom traditions of India, is that the sense of individual identity—*aham* ('I')—after first arising, is immediately followed by fear and desire, respectively. That is, the moment I realize I am a separate entity, I experience vulnerability and fear, followed by particular desires designed to get me things (food, security, love, sex, power, etc.) that will relieve me of these fears. In the Eastern understanding the separate self is wedded to the need for pleasure (to ward off fear and pain). From the spiritual perspective, it is understood to be based on the delusion of believing that we have no connection to any 'divine' source. We are alone, an island cut off from everything, and must struggle via control, manipulation, and so forth, in order to survive.

The Western view—especially as shaped by such pioneers of the psyche as Freud and Jung—is that the ego is not so much a pleasure principle as it is a reality principle. That is, the ego has a particular job to do, and that is to shape us into mature adults who can distinguish between selfish cravings and self-absorbed needs, and the importance of operating responsibly in the world. Spiritual development, in this view, begins with dealing with reality *as* a separate self, not merely abolishing the sense of separate self.[2] Because Western civilization has been conditioned with religious teachings that present the *relationship* between God and person as all-important—as opposed to the Eastern model of seeking to realize Oneness with the divine principle—the Western mind is more relationship-oriented in general, and thus has a greater need to come to terms with what it means to be a separate self in relationship with the universe.

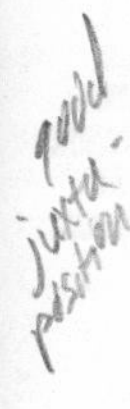

These caveats aside, it should be stressed here that it is not being suggested that Eastern meditation practices are useless for a Westerner. Most definitely they are useful, and many can employ them without concern. Many others, however, are better off engaging a practice that combines elements of psychotherapy and active (as opposed to purely passive) meditations (discussed in Part II), in order to embody a healthy sense of self prior to concerns of transcending self. The Western esoteric tradition is, in general, more concerned with active meditations than its Eastern counterpart.

The Latin word *ego* means 'I myself'. It refers specifically to our typical sense of conscious identity (though the ego is not a 'thing' and is best understood as a process). Symbolically, since we are not usually fully conscious of all aspects of our self, the ego or conscious identity—our conventional sense of 'I'—is something like an 'island' surrounded by the 'sea' of all that we are not conscious of. In keeping with the understandings of Western psychology, we will refer to all contents of our mind that we are not conscious of as the *unconscious*. (The term 'subconscious' is interchangeable here with 'unconscious', though the latter is more commonly used by psychologists and philosophers).

The ego is, naturally, basic to personal identity and is needed in order to function in the world. (For example, to be purely 'egoless' would be to have no identification with any personal terms—it would therefore be impossible to remember what one's name is, as one would identify equally with 'all possible names' or with 'no name'). The ego is closely tied in with the survival instinct and our sense of personal boundaries. From that perspective the ego could be said to be ancient, rooted in the long evolutionary journey of the human being, from our harsh past up to our still-challenging present times. Accordingly, the ego has a key role in human life and development.

'The Fall', Suffering, and the Problem of Evil

It may not be too difficult to surmise where the ego originated, from an evolutionary perspective—as mentioned above, it appears to be an ancient mechanism for survival, as well as a process by which we experience individual identity. However from a spiritual perspective the ego—or more precisely, the experience of having an ego, or being a separate self—is less easy to explain away. If there is any basis to the notion that we are grounded in a transcendent spiritual source, or that we are in some sense emanations or extensions of that Ground of Being (something argued by most wisdom traditions), then it is not immediately clear why we should ever have separated from that Ground (even if such a 'separation' is only an appearance or elaborate delusion). This matter is tackled by the traditions in various ways. Most Eastern traditions tend to view the self, and the essential division from our true nature, as being a profound ignorance that is ultimately understood to be a powerful illusion.[3] Even to call the self an 'illusion' is, from the purist Eastern perspective, inaccurate, because it implies that someone is having the illusion. It is more accurate to say that there is simply no ego, no self at all. It is purely a mental construct (or, if we are to believe philosophers such as Flanagan or Metzinger, a type of fantastically complex cognitive or perceptual trick).

Western traditions explain the causes of the original separation from the source in many ways, often presented via myth (the word 'myth' is used here in the sense of an enormously influential story, rather than a mere fiction). This subject is vast in scope and could scarcely be exhausted in a work of even encyclopedic length. A brief summary on the matter from eight traditions—Zoroastrian, Platonic/Neo-Platonic, Gnostic, Judeo-Christian, Kabbalistic, Manichean, Sufi, and that deriving from the late 20th century semi-Gnostic text *A Course in Miracles*—can be found in Appendix II.

Dualism and Non-dualism

In considering the matter of how we are to understand the creation of the ego—the origin of the experience of separation, including ideas such as 'sin', 'evil', and any so-called 'fall' of Man—it is important to understand the distinction between dualism and non-dualism. The various Western wisdom traditions bear elements of these two models to varying degrees. Technically there are, in addition to non-dualism, two different types of dualistic systems[4]:

Radical dualism: Radical dualism is based on the idea that there are two opposing principles (Good and Evil) that exist from the very beginning that work in tandem to create all that is. Examples of this are found in Zoroastrianism and Manichaeism (see Appendix II).

Mitigated dualism: In mitigated dualism it is posited that Good is supreme and primordial, and that Evil arises only later, owing to an initial error set in motion by Good. This secondary evil force is inferior and sets in motion the creation of a flawed universe (such as ours) that is to be escaped from via the process of Self-realization (gnosis). Most traditions of Gnosticism are examples of mitigated dualism. In both cases (radical and mitigated), dualistic systems argue that good and evil, or light and dark, are pre-existent, that is to say, they are fundamental to existence and are prior to any separation of Man from God.

Non-dualism: With non-dualism, in contrast to dualism, darkness or evil are not granted any absolute existence prior to our apparent separation from God, but rather appear later—and it must be emphasized that their existence is only an *appearance*—due to ignorance or delusion (the esoteric meaning of 'sin'). Accordingly, darkness/evil is ultimately understood to be an illusion resulting from ignorance of our inherent divine condition. Escaping from this illusion is the basis of the path of awakening.

It has been suggested by some that non-dualism is a more sophisticated and mature model, if only because it is less given to a rigid absolutism that easily leads to dogmatic assertions, excessive morality, and the tendency to project disowned elements of the psyche onto scapegoats (the ultimate one being the 'devil'). However it is something of an oversimplification to dismiss dualistic systems as more primitive. It is probably more accurate to say that each school of thought provides an approach to higher truth that is most appropriate for a given individual. And, needless to say, each path is as capable of being misused as any other. Those who embrace non-dualism are equally prone to the traps inherent in that path (such as denial of personal shadow elements—since, after all, if only the 'Absolute' is real, why bother examining the shadow-side?), as are those who follow a rigidly dualistic path, who are prone to divisiveness.

To sum up: the dualistic approach to the 'Fall of Man' and the experience of suffering that arises from separation from our source, is explained as a result of a pre-existing natural duality (Good-Evil) that can only be overcome via strenuous purification and ardent devotion to the process of individual transformation. The non-dualistic approach, in contrast, is based on awakening from ignorance, and realizing our already-existing divine condition, via resolving the blocks in our mind and deficiencies of character that are keeping us asleep to our true nature.[5]

Western esotericism—from Neoplatonism to Gnosticism to Hermeticism and the Kabbalah—find purpose in the 'Fall of Man' and the apparently degraded nature of material reality, in that it provides the testing ground for a soul to develop qualities that will mature its spirit and make it ready to take the journey to the divine. This concurs with the standard explanation from philosophical Idealism, put forth by Schelling, Hegel and others, and reinforced by 20th century psychotherapists such as Erich Fromm or C.G. Jung, that ego is necessary for growth, and that no freedom or responsibility is possible without it—thus Schelling wrote that 'the Fall' was 'the most fortunate and greatest event in human history', because from it arose the perspective of opposites which allows for maturity to develop. The psychological parallel for all this lies in the personal sense of disconnectedness from existence, and how that is navigated throughout the course of our life. Separation is real on all levels of experience except that of a supreme illumination in which the discrete personal self is revealed to be illusory, leaving behind nothing but the realization of perfect Oneness. However, for all intents and purposes almost no one is living in such a condition. Therefore the matter of recognizing the mind's construction of its experience in the world (and its perception *of* the world), and the suffering that invariably arises from a deep sense of separation and disconnectedness, is ultimately very practical. As the old expression has it, 'when caught in a burning building, never mind how the fire started. Just get out'. The process of 'getting out of the building' may be said to be the basis of initiation.

Initiation: The Second Birth and Overcoming Time and Space

The other core theme of the Western esoteric tradition, in addition to coming to terms with the ego (separate self) and the 'loss' (fall) of our connection to divine source, is our return (our journey) to it. This return or journey is characterized in many ways: on occasion it is seen as a growth or development, a 'transcendence and inclusion' (as the 'integral' model describes it), implying that we do not 'return' so much as progress; or as in the pragmatic language of Gurdjieff, 'building a soul'. Most Western traditions have been influenced to some extent by the 'rebirth' or 'resurrection' themes, stemming either from ancient Egyptian myth (the death and resurrection of Osiris), numerous worldwide myths that involve 'life-death-rebirth' gods, and of course Christian doctrine, wherein the resurrection of Christ is central to the tradition. Sufism has its teachings of *fana* (annihilation of the delusion of self) and *baqa* (awakening to the divine); and Jewish mysticism, via the Kabbalah, teaches the awakening process that leads up the 'Tree of Life' from *Malkuth* (the earthly personality) to *Kether* (the Godhead). Gnostic and Neo-Platonic traditions both involve 'returns' to the supreme source from which we derive.

In many worldwide mythologies and rites of initiation the 'second birth' is ceremonially simulated for an adolescent to facilitate their emergence into adulthood. (Additionally, there are numerous universal rites of passage involving a return of sorts to the 'chaos' prior to the Creation of the world). Spiritual initiation is similar, as awakening to our highest potential is really not distinct from 'growing up' in the truest sense of the term, and this 'growing up' generally involves touching bases, as it were, with our roots.

The 'return' premise is not based on the idea of a mere regression, of course—a *regressus ad uterum*, or a return to the primal bliss that Freud spoke of. The return to our roots is indeed a basic part of both healing and awakening to our higher possibilities, something known in both primitive cultures as well as in modern psychotherapy.[6] But the 'return' we speak of here is a process that depends crucially on our experience in the realms of separation and even isolation, and above all, how we handle our experiences in these realms. Our return is therefore more an 'emergence', a 'second birth' in which we draw strength from our primordial roots while at the same time blossoming into something much greater. This 'something greater' has as its basis a freedom from the apparent constraints of time and space.

Mircea Eliade, in defining a universal theme found in the great wisdom traditions, once wrote, 'To cure the work of Time it is necessary to go back and find the beginning of the World'.[7] The 'beginning of the World' is a metaphor for grasping the origin point of the ego's experience of separation. The point at which we achieve direct insight into the mechanism of egoic separation and how it gives rise to our experience of disconnection from reality, is the point at which we can begin to recognize its ongoing operation in us in a daily, moment by moment way. This 'disconnect' is the contraction, the recoil, and the fear of life that lies at the basis of our self-imposed limitations. The problem is not the experience of 'separation' itself; the problem lies in how we respond to it. How it all began is less important than the fact that we are actively contributing to it.

Resistance

Why do we seem to resist the process of spiritual emergence (the 'second birth'), and all that it implies? It seems we do so mainly because we fear the ramifications of being truly accountable and responsible for what we really are—and perhaps more crucially, for what we can *become*. Most people are aware of a deep ambivalence within them in relation to the forward movement in life. A desire to 'regress', to return to the past—or, more fundamentally, to return to (or re-create now) *a magical past that one never had*—becomes a significant roadblock on the path of development. In order to move beyond this roadblock we have to look deeper into the matter, and understand the mechanisms of the mind and how our consciousness constructs our experience of reality. To overcome the 'fall' and the limitations of egoic consciousness necessitates recognizing the ways in which we are actively participating in such limitations and suffering. These matters will be touched on throughout the book, and are especially addressed in Part II. For now, it helps to look into the historical roots of some key esoteric teachings.

– 27 pages.

- No discussion of the fact that the "Divinity" of ancient history was not singular, but a plurality/pantheon of Supreme Beings

- No explanation regarding who many of these key figures are. So, unless you understand the teachings of Gurdjieff & Neo-Platonism, and then – even if you did – of what use is what is written up to this point?

Chapter 2

Introduction to Spiritual Alchemy

Aurum nostrum non est aurum vulgi (our gold is not ordinary gold).
—Gerhard Dorn

In old times, anyone with the slightest knowledge of alchemy knew that it had something to do with gaining wealth or immortality. By the late 19th century an idea arose that alchemy was really an ancient secret science about inner illumination. Since roughly the mid-20th century a new piece was added, and alchemy began to be associated with a repository of psychological symbolism. Here in the early 21st century, for the average reader perusing the self-help section of a local bookstore, it is indeed possible that they think alchemy has only to do with some type of self-improvement. The story of alchemy is, however, much more complex, mysterious, and multileveled. In a sense, alchemy is a type of chameleon language, shape-shifting and adapting to the latest cultural zeitgeist it finds itself in.

It is perhaps prudent to begin this chapter by addressing its very title. Is there, in fact, a legitimate *spiritual* alchemy, and if so, does it have any sort of legitimate pedigree? The views on this are divided, and in many ways are microcosms of views on the entire history of the Western esoteric tradition. The main arguments take roughly one of two positions: first, that alchemy was never a psychological or spiritual practice or art, but largely a basic proto-science—at least, up until the mid-19th century when, chiefly via the efforts of Ethan Allan Hitchcock (1798–1870) and especially Mary Ann Atwood (1817–1910), followed by a host of re-visionaries and re-interpreters culminating in the sophisticated writings of Rene Guenon, Mircea Eliade, Titus Burckhardt, Julius Evola, and C.G. Jung—it began to be seen as a symbolic system for inner study and transformation. The first view, alchemy as proto-science, has been championed most effectively by the recent work of the science historian Lawrence Principe[1] and colleagues. It argues that any attempt to retroactively interpret alchemy as an ancient esoteric teaching or disguised religious philosophy—beyond some very basic and minimal Gnostic influences—is essentially misguided. The second view, more commonly encountered in typical modern writings on alchemy, is that the 'inner science' of alchemical transformation has operated, since ancient times, alongside the outer laboratory practices, and in many cases was pre-eminent. Some have even argued that there was no significant laboratory work at all, that alchemy has always been a spiritual discipline concealing itself as a material science. This position was perhaps best exemplified by Atwood, who in her influential 1850 publication *A Suggestive Inquiry into Hermetic Mystery*, wrote:

> ...the records of Alchemy are, above all, calculated to mislead those who have gone abroad thoughtlessly seeking for that perfection which was to be found only by experimentally seeking at home within themselves...Man then, shall we conclude at length, is the true laboratory of the Hermetic art; his life the subject, the grand distillatory, the thing distilling and the thing distilled, and Self-Knowledge to be at the root of all Alchemical tradition?[2]

Admittedly, the scholarship backing the first view—that Western alchemy was from the beginning mainly a mechanical, proto-scientific practice designed to produce valid material results and devoid of any significant esoteric, religious, or 'inner work' component—appears sound. For example, Principe demonstrated (via theory and actual laboratory practice) that the various 'stages of alchemy' involved in the production of a transformed element, such as that found in some famed 16th century works such as the *Rosarium Philosophorum*, Basil Valentine's *The Triumphal Chariot of Antimony* or

Of the Great Stone of the Ancients, or in George Ripley's *Compound of Alchymie* and its 'twelve gates' or stages, actually describe legitimate laboratory steps of practical chemistry, even if poorly understood. The accompanying illustrations—those notoriously mysterious alchemical images of hermaphrodites, mating kings and queens, dragons, green lions devouring the sun, black crows, and so on—are meant to symbolize the laboratory processes, but are often interpreted by modern spiritual seekers in strictly psychological terms independent of their original accompanying texts, which according to some modern historians of science, is a mistake.

As an example Principe cites that of antimony, a silvery grey toxic metalloid element, which was of great significance to early alchemists. It was symbolized in Valentine's *Of the Great Stone of the Ancients* as a fearsome wolf devouring a king. Subsequently, the psychologized interpretation saw antimony as representing the primal beast within, the 'hidden wolf' in the sheep's clothing of the repressed priest or monk—when in fact the symbol of the wolf was representative of a particular physical element, in this case the ability of melted antimony ore (the 'wolf') to react with gold (the 'king') by dissolving it instantaneously (i.e., 'devouring' it).[3] (These complex, multileveled symbols appear to have their origins in the 3rd century CE Greek alchemist Zosimos, who was the first to begin the practice of concealing names and jumbling symbols into a type of cipher that could only later be 'decoded' by one who had both knowledge and sincerity of intent, i.e., was a 'worthy' candidate).[4] Accordingly, it is not difficult to see how easy it is to overlay the rich and peculiar symbolism of alchemy with psycho-spiritual ideas (perhaps most vividly accomplished by Jung), and assume automatically that these symbols must only (or at least chiefly) have represented particular ideas rooted in spiritual philosophy—when in fact the reverse may have been true, i.e., the symbols being simply a cover for natural chemical processes.

That said, it is not a given that just because the psycho-spiritual component of alchemy may be a more recent development that it automatically invalidates that psycho-spiritual viewpoint. Spiritual philosophy (or 'integral' philosophy) is by nature inclusive, that is, claims all as its domain, and thus interprets all as an element of a greater process that is, from the point of view of the mind, symbolic. From this vantage point everything is part of a process of development and growth, be it inorganic matter, simple life, or human—and everything that occurs in a human life, from an integral perspective, is to be understood within this greater context. A walk to the store, paying a bill, doing the laundry, relating to another person, doing laboratory experiments, or profound contemplation and meditation are all equally 'spiritual', simply because the spiritual domain is ultimate and all-inclusive. The point is not to *confuse* domains (spiritual, mental, physical) by applying the laws of one to another. That is, the logic of mathematics is not used in spiritual contemplation, nor is the knowledge of how to fix a car used in the process of painting a work of art—and vice versa; the attention of a witness-based meditation practice is not essential in aiding us in performing a laboratory experiment or changing a flat tire.

Alchemy, however, is a notoriously difficult field to assign exclusively to one domain of consciousness (be that the physical, mental or spiritual). Its symbols are rich and multivalent, and like a dream, can be read in many ways. It may indeed have originally been (and for a very long time remained) merely a fumbling attempt to discover a scientific method within a primitive chemistry, regardless of the personal motivations involved of those practicing it, often getting injured and sometimes even killed doing so. (This point of view strengthens the argument that magic has often been a closer relative of science rather than religion). But the ease with which its rich symbolism fits with the inner journey of self-examination is so marked as to make it difficult (and even pointless) for the seeker to not apply its symbols accordingly if such an application yields useful insights.

Jung is commonly recognized as the main modern exponent of

the psychologized view of alchemy, although in fact he himself acknowledged that he was inspired by the writings of the Austrian psychoanalyst Herbert Silberer (1882–1923), whose 1914 work *Problems of Mysticism and its Symbolism* dealt with alchemy and the attempt to interpret it psychologically. (Silberer had been a disciple of Freud, who ultimately rejected his metaphysical interests. Despondent over this and other matters, Silberer committed suicide at age forty). Jung, who did not come to his alchemical studies until well into his fifties, greatly enhanced on Silberer's ideas. Jung's main argument was that he had noticed that symbols found in alchemy texts showed up commonly in the dreams of many of his patients, most of whom knew nothing about alchemy at all—thus causing him to conclude that alchemy was a superb repository of 'collective' or universal symbols that could be highly effective tools for psychological insight. Jung concluded that the alchemist of the past, engaged in the process of trying to produce gold, ended up projecting his unconscious mind onto the process, which he then symbolized (unintentionally) via the unique alchemical images and meanings. In other words, the whole thing was a kind of inadvertent revealing of the unconscious mind of the alchemist—who, Jung boldly claimed, did not know what he was writing about—and by extension, of the nature of the 'collective unconscious' itself. Certain traditionalists, such as Titus Burckhardt, rejected this, maintaining that the alchemists of the past were never chiefly concerned with the production of gold to begin with, and hence knew exactly what they were doing, that is, accomplishing a very specific spiritual work. They were not merely naively projecting the symbols of their unconscious onto crude laboratory work; they were engaged in a very real and spiritual *magnum opus*.

All these views—whether the stark scientific interpretations of Principe and his colleagues, the psychologized views of Silberer, Jung, and many of Jung's disciples, or the views of the Traditionalists such as Guenon, Burckhardt, Evola, and others, ultimately remain interpretations. It is perhaps a testament to the power of alchemy that it can incite such varied and heatedly contested viewpoints. Nevertheless, with due respect to the historians of science and their solid scholarship, this chapter proceeds with a view to using alchemical symbolism as a vehicle, a symbolic analogue, an aid in understanding the process of inner transformation.

Transmutation

The key to alchemy, whether interpreted scientifically or psycho-spiritually, lies in the word *transmutation,* a word that in its original Latin meaning refers to *total change*. Physically this denotes a change of the properties of matter, and thus of substance; psycho-spiritually, it refers to inner transformation—in specific, particular actions to aid in freeing the 'spiritual essence' that is 'trapped' within (echoing the Gnostic view). This idea had its basis in the ancient belief that within the Earth 'grew' metals and that, given enough time, these metals would ultimately become gold. Nature was seen as fundamentally engaged in a process of evolution, and the essential idea of alchemy was to speed this process up—in short, to save time.

Spiritual alchemy is concerned with the transmutation of the personality and its structures, so as to allow for the light of unobstructed consciousness and 'pure being' to be directly known. The direct knowing of pure being is *gnosis,* Self-realization. Spiritual alchemy is thus a symbolic means by which we re-structure our personality and the various levels of our identification with it, with the ultimate goal of being free of all unnecessary identifications with the personality, so as to realize the infinite potential of our true being. In this sense alchemy is essentially a comprehensive roadmap, using colorful and sophisticated symbols, detailing means and steps by which we get ourselves 'out of our own way' and allow our highest and best destiny to unfold.

The main difference between a 'spiritual' alchemy and alchemy as merely a primitive proto-science—the precursor of modern chemistry—is that the former involves an interdependent relationship between the subject (self) and the object (all that is not-self). In materialistic science the subject is the observer distinct from what he or she studies (the object). In spiritual alchemy this distinction is much less defined, because the transformation of the subject, of the personality, is pre-eminent.

A key point found within the psycho-spiritual interpretation of alchemy is the idea that the alchemist can only succeed in his work if he approaches it with purity of intent, with a heart free of confused or dubious agendas (an idea that was mirrored in the Grail myths, where only a knight of 'pure heart' had any hope of finding the Grail). This idea was emphasized by some early scribes who noted with irony that alchemy was notorious for its failed alchemists, i.e., those who sought alchemical success in elaborate and expensive laboratory attempts to create gold but typically ended up broke in the process.[5]

The esoteric foundation of spiritual alchemy is often associated with old world-wide myths that deal with the life, death and resurrection of a god. The candidate or initiate is to undergo a similar process, in order to awaken to their divine condition—a type of radical deconstruction and 'rebirth'. This process involves a number of stages reflected in traditional alchemy, to be summarized below. Before detailing these stages it is useful to have some grasp of the history of alchemy, as well as some of its most basic features as seen from the esoteric viewpoint.

Background

Historically, there are generally recognized to be three main lines of alchemy: Chinese, Indian, and Western. All three appear to have developed some time during the first few centuries BCE, though evidence at present favors the Chinese version to be the oldest.[6] Traditionally, alchemy has been associated with two main activities: the attempt to manufacture gold (or silver) from baser metals; and the attempt to create an elixir of sorts that when ingested would result in great vitality and health, and possibly even immortality.

Chinese and Indian alchemy was concerned at times with producing gold, but more commonly the focus was on the creation of the magical elixir that could, it was believed, produce great powers and everlasting life.

Western alchemy in all likelihood had its origins in the early work of goldsmiths, miners, and metallurgists, especially those of Hellenized Egypt.[7] Initially it was not actually concerned with producing gold, but rather, with producing 'fool's gold'—applying certain chemicals to metals so as to make them *appear* to be gold. It was only around the 2nd or 3rd century CE that the idea was born of attempting to go beyond causing something to merely look like gold and instead trying to directly *produce* gold.[8] This form of alchemy became concerned with the idea of the 'Philosopher's Stone' (Latin: *lapis philosophorum*), the name given to a substance that theoretically could transmute base metals, like lead, into gold. (The process of turning a base metal into gold is technically known as *chrysopoeia*; the production of silver from base metal is called *argyropoeia*). As with many elements of the Western esoteric tradition Western alchemy finds much of its roots in the ideas of the ancient Greeks, ideas that were given coherence most notably by Plato and Aristotle. By the time of the early centuries after Christ it had evolved into a specific practice (both a 'science' and an 'art' in the wider definition of those terms), tailored toward creating changes in metals. (The psycho-spiritual interpretation of alchemy argues that early alchemy was also tailored for creating changes in the psyche of the alchemist, although evidence for this is at best inconclusive).

Both Eastern and Western alchemy lend themselves easily to esoteric interpretations based on the idea of inner transformation. The material dimension of alchemy may have been concerned with such matters as immortality of the body or the production of gold, but from the esoteric perspective these can be seen as not separate from the work of inner transformation. Because alchemy was almost certainly influenced by initiatic streams of thought (arising from Taoism and Tantra in the East, and Hermeticism and Gnosticism in the West) it was probably eventually understood, at least by some of the alchemists of antiquity, that the practical outer work was not separate from an inner process of transformation. This would have been naturally consistent with the idea of an essential interconnection between mind and matter best summarized by the Hermetic maxim 'as above, so below'. It is a given that not all alchemists would have been concerned with inner transformation, that most were doubtless only concerned with the pursuit of dreams of wealth and power (or in the later case of Paracelsus and his followers, with healing). But it is also possible that alchemy, influenced by other esoteric streams, through the centuries preserved certain spiritual philosophies, including elements of Gnosticism that were suppressed or exterminated outright by the rising power of the Church after the 4th century CE.

The focus of this chapter is on Western alchemy and in particular its psycho-spiritual dimension.[9] The English word 'alchemy' has uncertain origins, but is sometimes thought to stem from the Arabic *al-khimia*, possibly deriving from the Coptic word *kem*, which means 'black land', another name for Egypt. Thus 'alchemy' may have originally meant 'of Egypt'. The black land refers to the soil around the Nile valley, which was rich with nutrients when the waters of the Nile would recede after the annual flooding. An alternate view holds that the Chinese word *kim*—which refers to the production of gold—migrated to the Middle East where it became the word *kem*, and later, *al-khimia*.

Western alchemy as a specific practice appears to find its origins largely among Greek-speaking peoples on the coast of northern Egypt in Alexandria, that extraordinary city founded around 330 BCE by Alexander the Great. With the ascent of Christendom and the decline of Alexandria (including the gradual destruction of its famous library in a series of calamities), alchemy faded from view in the West, but it did not die out entirely. It was, instead, taken up by the Arabs (themselves the conquerors of Egypt), and later by Jabir ibn Hayyan, an 8th century Persian whom some regard as the prototypical alchemist. (Identifying the authors behind early alchemical writings has been notoriously difficult, as a standard practice was to ascribe such works to important figures or even gods such as Hermes, but most scholars accept the legitimacy of Jabir's name and legacy, although some suggest that his name represents a composite of several writers).[10]

As mentioned, modern science tends to view early alchemy as largely the primitive proto-science that morphed into chemistry around the 17th century via the efforts of Robert Boyle and others. By the 18th century and the beginning of the scientific revolution alchemy had largely been abandoned as a laboratory 'science', but its esoteric side was preserved (or 'invented', depending on point of view), and discussed in various occult circles (especially the 'secret societies' such as the Freemasons and Rosicrucians) of the 18th and 19th centuries. In the popular domain it was C.G. Jung who, in the early 20th century, largely rescued alchemy from the dusty pages of forgotten library archives by wedding much of its rich symbolism to his theory of analytical psychology. Some scholars such as Julius Evola took exception to Jung's efforts, believing it to be a kind of debasement of the deeper meaning of the Great Work. In Evola's extreme esoteric view, alchemy is a path of spiritual awakening that is intended only for psychologically integrated individuals, and is not a symbolic description of the process of *becoming* psychologically integrated (what Jung called 'individuation').[11] Evola, along with other Traditionalists such as Rene Guenon, made determined attempts to preserve the sanctity of the esoteric path against what they saw as the vulgar, simplified world-views of our modern materialistic times, and it is not hard to find sympathy for their positions if one takes the time to reflect on some of the side-effects of the scientific revolution and industrial age. But the fact remains that the average modern day seeker is rarely a psychologically integrated individual in the ideal sense, and almost always needs to do considerable psychological healing prior to, or alongside with, more rarefied spiritual practices. Thus from a practical point of view it is more than a matter of merely finding sympathy for Jung's work and related psycho-spiritual interpretations of alchemy, it is a matter of recognizing the usefulness of such approaches for current times.

The Inner Interpretation of Alchemy: Gold and the Philosopher's Stone

The Arabic term *al-khimia* also means 'the art of transformation', and this applies to both physical levels as well as to the inner practice of alchemy, which involves the transformation of the individual from unconscious 'raw material' to the 'finer material' of Self-realization and divine illumination. The prized goal of alchemy was of course gold (and, on occasion, silver). Gold has some interesting chemical properties—it is the most ductile of all metals, meaning it can be reshaped into endless forms without fracturing. It is also largely immune to most corrosive agents of air or water, and resistant to corruption by fire (which is why it has always been valued in making jewelry). Thus its great strength and brilliant color appear to make it a natural and powerful symbol for that which is both radiant and indestructible within us, i.e., our highest spiritual nature.

However, according to alchemy, the manufacture of gold was possible only via the medium of the Philosopher's Stone. When this latter was applied to base metals, then the transmutation, resulting in gold (or silver) allegedly could happen. On the level of psycho-spiritual symbolism, the formula…

Base metal (such as lead) + Philosopher's Stone = Gold (or Silver)

…has not always been fully understood. Commonly the end result (gold or silver) has been thought to represent the awakened self, but it is more meaningful to regard the Philosopher's Stone as the awakened self. The gold or silver better represents the transformation of one's world, or the manifestation of one's higher desires and true calling in life. On the symbolic level, the essential relationship between the two (Philosopher's Stone and gold) is crucially important because they are ultimately interdependent. That is, transformation of self really only works when we also have an intention to transform our outer world, i.e., shine the inner light of our being outward in order to realize our best destiny in life.[12] In other words, Self-realization without involvement in the world—outer actualization—is incomplete. (And this is true in any domain, be it the spiritual or the scientific). The reverse, involvement in the world without spiritual realization—blind materialism—is also fruitless, something addressed eloquently in the biblical Psalms:

> The idols of the heathen are silver and gold, the work of man's hands. They have mouths, but they speak not; eyes have they, but they see not; they have ears, but they hear not, neither is there any breath in their mouths. (135: 15–17, KJV)

The Materia Prima and Solve et Coagula

Alchemy posits that all things in the universe originate with the *materia prima* (First Matter). The idea of the 'primal material' was developed by Aristotle and refers to the notion that there is a primordial matter that lies behind all forms, but that is itself invisible. It is the womb of creation, the field of pure potentiality, but it only gains existence, in the strictest sense, when given form. In the alchemical process, the primal material is that which remains when something has been reduced to its essence and can be reduced no further. Psychologically, this is a potent symbol for the inner process of transformation in which we regularly arrive at 'core realizations' that cannot be deconstructed further, but that themselves become the ground for successfully moving forward in life—'integrating' as we evolve.

The alchemists of old believed that any given base metal must first be reduced to its *materia prima* prior to it being transmuted into gold. The psycho-spiritual symbolism here is straightforward. It points to the de-conditioning process that lies at the heart of spiritual transformation—that is, the deconstructing of that which is false about us, to reveal that which is true and real. This 'deconstruction' was typically likened to a 'mystical death', or the reduction to formless chaos, often represented by aquatic symbols, sometimes expressed as 'perform no operation until all be made water'. It can be seen to denote the necessary relinquishment of the past, the 'death' of the initiate's false self, prior to their rebirth or re-awakening to their higher self.[13] In mystical Christian symbolism this was all symbolized by the crucifixion and resurrection, an echo of older pagan myths that generally involved the death and reconstitution of a god.

The process of deconstruction can also be seen as a *constructive* process, and in some Hermetic schools of alchemy that is how they saw it—the physical body, being associated with Saturn (or lead) being transmuted into the 'solar body', or gold. Various world esoteric traditions make reference to the idea of a 'body of light' that is attained only through deep and profound practice. The Bible seems to point to it in Matthew, 17:1–2, in what has come to be known as the transfiguration scene:

> And after six days Jesus taketh Peter, James, and John his brother, and bringeth them up into an high mountain apart, and was transfigured before them: and his face did shine as the sun, and his raiment was white as the light. (KJV)

Ultimately, whether we choose to see the process of transformation as deconstructive (dissolving the ego impurities) or constructive (transforming and thus heightening our 'vibration' so that we attain a more rarefied consciousness) is more a matter of perspective, and less important than actually engaging the work. But in point of fact the process of alchemy actually involves both of these actions, through what is referred to as *solve et coagula*—dissolution and coagulation—the deconstruction and re-construction of our personality. Or put more simply, to separate and recombine. There is a clear and interesting symbolic parallel here in the Egyptian myth of Osiris, who is killed by his brother Set, has his body dismembered, and then is reconstructed by the gods Isis and Thoth as part of his resurrection in the *duat* (Otherworld)—a symbolism that is pure alchemical *solve et coagula*. It defines the heart of the spiritual process of 'breaking down' and being 'reborn'.

In alchemy, as in all forms of Hermetic high magic as well as the Tantric schools of India and Tibet, matter, or the physical universe, is not seen as separate from the mind, or spiritual realities, but is rather recognized as a reflection of it. The *magnum opus* or 'Great Work' of alchemy is ultimately to realize the fundamental interrelationship between mind and matter, between self and world, between heaven and earth, finally ending in non-dual realization (All is One). However—and this is a crucial point—the apparent dualism of existence is not to be denied or glossed over out of fear of embracing its lessons. Rather, duality is to be embraced (and even celebrated) as the means by which we uncover key realizations about our inner nature. In this sense alchemy as psycho-spiritual symbolism is all about altering time, that is, hastening the natural evolution of things, so that we can pass through our essential lessons more quickly. But it is not about denying these lessons, nor the joys and struggles of independent selfhood.

The idea that the alchemist of old had to transform personally before hoping to have success materially, although probably largely a fanciful retroactive interpretation, remains valid psycho-spiritually. The idea applies to the so-called arts of manifestation. All our efforts to create abundant changes in our lives via manifestation practices amount to little if we are not first seeking to *change ourselves* for the better. It is obviously possible to attain material success without any sort of self-observation practice, but it is equally obvious that such results will be limited in reach and efficacy.

Psycho-spiritual alchemy is ultimately not about manipulating reality. It is a system in which the alchemist seeks to confront and understand his or her own mind and soul, so as to pass through a deep transformation and emerge free of the limitations of the personality. Like all 'inner traditions' it is prone to corruption. The corrupted version is more concerned with the manipulation of external events—much as corrupted versions of science and business exist in current times in the form of those who use science or commerce to further selfish agendas. The deeper esoteric work of the alchemist is about personal awakening and union with the divine mind or higher self, much as the true higher purpose of science or business is about increasing both well-being for self and well-being for others ('win-win').

This inner awakening is given priority, and then leads naturally to the transformation of our world—much as the alchemist first transforms him or herself, and *then* seeks to transform the outer world, or how the classical magician first awakens the inner higher self, and *then* interacts with the more elemental energies, spirits, or daimons. This idea was well illustrated in a Chinese fable once relayed by Richard Wilhelm, concerning a Taoist monk and a Chinese village suffering the effects of a prolonged drought. The village councilors, desperate for rain, sought the aid of the monk to bring about rain by some 'supernatural' method. The Taoist simply asked for a private room and shut himself in for three days. At the end of the third day, rain fell. The monk emerged from his room, whereupon Wilhelm asked him what he had done. The monk replied that prior to visiting the town he had been merged with the Tao. When he arrived in the town, he was not connected to the Tao, but after three days of meditating in the room, he was once again merged with the Tao. He then added that it would be natural for that which was around him (the immediate environment of the town) to also be in Tao.

This very idea is the essence of alchemy and the core principle of Hermetic wisdom, meaning that in aligning ourselves with the higher principles, we aid in causing changes around us that may follow suit. As we uncover the light within, so we aid in bringing light to our surroundings.[14]

Some Basic Alchemical Principles

As mentioned, alchemy essentially begins with the idea of the Prime Matter (*materia prima*). This Prime Matter was believed to have a basic fourfold structure, known as the four basic classical elements—usually recognized as fire, water, air, earth. A fifth 'element' has been commonly recognized as well, variously called ether, space, quintessence, or spirit. The idea of these basic elements goes back to ancient Babylonia (the *Enuma Elish*, the chief Babylonian Creation myth, written circa 1700 BCE, made mention of them). It fell to the Greek pre-Socratics, in particular Empedocles (circa 490–430 BCE), to elaborate on the idea, although it was Plato (424–348 BCE) who first used the term 'elements' (from the Greek *stoicheion*), and Aristotle who fleshed out the scheme.[15] Empedocles had been influenced by Pythagoras and certain esoteric schools such as the Orphic mysteries, but appears to have developed his independent view of things. His idea of the four basic elements was part of his attempt to explain how things come to undergo *change*. Empedocles held that all of existence is a process of change via the separation and combination of different elements. Things do not, he maintained, change by passing from existence to non-existence (as Heraclitus had held), but rather via the process of the mixing, dividing, and the re-combining of different combinations of substances and their elemental properties.

An essential idea behind most esoteric tradition, never to be lost sight of, is that this material reality we dwell in is a degraded copy of a finer, more subtle and rarefied, dimension. Much of Plato's highly influential cosmology was based on this idea, and even Empedocles asserted it in reference to the basic elements, declaring, 'from them, flow all things that are, or have been, or shall be.'[16] For him these elements represented phases of transition, a crystallization of subtle energies into material form. In short, the 'Supreme Being' imposed a fourfold structure onto the Prime Matter, in order to condense the subtle into the material, and thereby create the material universe. Such ideas are seen by historians of science as primitive scientific glimmerings (for e.g., complex elements arising from simple elements, as the result of a star going nova), but they are equally valid when understood as esoteric teachings that are central to an understanding of psycho-spiritual alchemy. Elements of the personality are to be restructured, made concrete, if you will, so that they can be recognized and thereby transformed. In so doing, the personality becomes more capable of supporting the growth of higher potentialities, and the emergence of the true self.

According to the early alchemists, the four elements—fire, water, air, and earth—come into existence via the combination of specific qualities, recognized as hot, cold, wet, and dry, being 'impressed' on to the Prime Matter. For example, when hot and dry are impressed on the Prime Matter, we have fire; if cold and dry, then earth; if wet and hot, then air; if cold and wet, then water. When these qualities are changed, the elements themselves are changed. A few examples will suffice:

1. Add water to fire (substituting wet for dry; hot and dry becomes hot and wet: steam, or air).

2. Add fire to water (substituting hot for wet; cold and wet becomes hot and wet: steam, or air). This is known as vaporization, which can occur via boiling or evaporation.

3. Add cold to air, and air will 'become' water (substitute cold for hot; wet and hot becomes wet and cold; air becomes water). This is known as condensation.

And so forth. Modern chemistry is obviously vastly more comprehensive in its grasp of such matters as pertains to physical reality—the modern table of elements, or Periodic Table, recognizes (as of this writing in 2012) no less than 118 isolated elements, a far cry from the four or five of Empedocles, Plato, and Aristotle—but when an esoteric symbolism of alchemy is allowed, it is understood to be addressing a domain utterly distinct from that addressed by modern chemistry.

What follows is a brief synopsis of the esoteric significance of the five elements:

Fire: In esoteric studies all elements carry great significance, but in the realm of alchemy, fire rules. It is the key, the mastery of which has long been held to be of prime importance by alchemists and shamans of old (as well as by smiths and potters, craftsmen whose work was related in many ways to alchemy). This is because fire is the element of transmutation *par excellence*, the key to changing things from one state to another—beginning with the most obvious examples of the power of the Sun and the core of our planet to heat the surface of the Earth, allowing for the possibility for life as we know it to develop.[17] (There is even a Biblical basis to the spiritual supremacy of fire: the highest of the angels are called 'seraphim', literally meaning 'the burning ones'). Of the four qualities mentioned above—hot, cold, wet, and dry—only two, hot and cold, are foundational (being found in space beyond our planet), and as cold is but the absence of heat, in the final analysis only fire (hot) is the essential transformational force. As Titus Burckhardt put it:

> It is the effect of fire alone that renders the substance in the alchemist's retort successively liquid, gaseous, fiery, and once again solid. Thus, it imitates in miniature the 'work' of Nature herself.[18]

In alchemy, fire is traditionally associated with the color red, with the qualities of hot and dry, and the force that rarefies and refines things, as well as causing total transformation. Psychologically, fire is usually connected to will, energy, and sometimes intuition. (On occasion it is connected to feeling, although this latter is more often associated with the water element). Alchemically, fire is symbolized by a triangle with the apex pointing up. In terms of geometry, the

Platonic solid that is connected to fire is the tetrahedron, or four-sided pyramid. (The idea of Platonic solids corresponding to the four elements derives from Plato, although it was earlier Greeks who discovered the shapes of the actual Platonic solids. Plato's scheme is subjective and somewhat contrived; it is included here more as a historical curiosity. He considered that fire was 'sharp', rather like the four-sided pyramid).

Water: Water is traditionally connected to the color blue, and to the qualities of wet and cold. It is a potent symbol in physical reality and for life in particular, as the surface of the planet we live on and the bodies we inhabit are primarily water. Water is the great dissolver and the womb for creation. Psychologically it is usually associated with feelings, emotions, and the unconscious. In the symbolism of alchemy it is represented by the triangle with the apex pointing down. The Platonic solid for water is the icosahedron (a solid with twenty sides, closest of the five solids to resembling a ball, and thus most similar to the 'smoothness' and 'slipperiness' of water).

Air: Air is traditionally connected to the color yellow, and to the qualities of hot and wet. Air is a natural purifier, rendering the coarse more fine, and enabling the subtlety of mind that allows for clearer understanding. Accordingly, air is the element of thinking and reason. Its alchemical symbol is the right side up triangle with a horizontal line running through it. The Platonic solid for air is the octahedron (eight-sided solid).

Earth: Earth is the element traditionally associated with the color green (and sometimes black), and with the qualities of cold and dry. It is the symbol for all matters pertaining to the physical and the practical. Its symbol is the upside down triangle with a horizontal line bisecting it. The Platonic solid is the cube (six-sided solid, its square solidity making it a natural symbol for the solid Earth that supports us).

Quintessence (or Spirit, or Ether): The word 'quintessence', which literally means 'fifth element', is beyond the four basic elements as such. Aristotle described it as being beyond the 'sub-lunar sphere' and as being the basic material of the immortal and incorruptible 'heaven realms', free of any of the four qualities and incapable of change. However, later philosophers and alchemists granted this mysterious element certain qualities, such as the ability to change density and a subtlety beyond that of light itself. (There are perhaps grounds for speculating a link between this enigmatic 'fifth classical element' and the 'dark matter' and 'dark energy' currently studied by modern physicists). Quintessence, or 'ether' as it also has been known, is sometimes linked to the concept of empty space. Its symbol is generally a circle with eight spokes, and its Platonic solid is sometimes considered the dodecahedron, the twelve-sided solid (although Aristotle resisted this latter association).

The Three Great Principles

In the early 1500s the Swiss alchemist Theophrastus von Hohenheim (1493–1541), better known as Paracelsus, inspired by the earlier Sufi alchemist Jabir ibn Hayyan, decided to develop the old Greek notion of the five elements and the tandem of sulphur and Mercury (quicksilver), by adding salt to create a trinity of key elements, representing spirit, soul, and body, respectively. Much as with the four basic elements, these three do not refer to the actual physical forms of sulphur, Mercury, and salt, but rather to the various processes and stages of alchemical transformation that they represent. It should also be noted here that it is easy for the casual researcher of these matters to become confused, as it is uncommon to find any two 'authorities' on alchemy agreeing completely on the respective symbolic meanings of sulphur, Mercury, and salt. What follows is the broadest consensus of the views of a number of scholars and historians.

Sulphur: According to Paracelsus' original teachings on the three principles of alchemy, sulphur was considered to be 'that which boils', or oil, and thus the aspect of unctuousness. Psycho-spiritually it symbolizes the immortal Spirit, or pure consciousness. It is generally connected to the solar and masculine principles, and symbolically to the lion.

Mercury: Mercury, known more technically as quicksilver, is the volatile quality of transformation, representing that which arises as a fume. It is symbolic of the vital spirit or soul, or what is sometimes called the life-force, (and hence its natural connection to the breath). As an energetic principle it is considered to be connected to both blood and semen, key substances associated with the vital spirit or life-force. It is sometimes symbolized by the griffon, and is generally associated with the lunar and feminine polarity. (Although it is occasionally also viewed as hermaphroditic in nature). It is that which unites Spirit and the worlds of material form. Some authors seem to confuse Mercury with Spirit, probably because one of the terms for the life-force is 'vital spirit', deriving from the Latin word for breath, *spiritus*.[19]

Salt: In alchemy, salt represents the physical foundation, and may be thought of as the body in its corrective state. It is what remains from the transformational process, the 'ashes'. It serves to 'ground' the volatile 'spirit'. As with so many alchemical symbols, the meaning is at times ambivalent and seldom universally agreed on. For example, C.G. Jung, drawing from the *Turba Philosophorum* (a medieval alchemical work) associated salt with the ocean (salt-water), with the lunar symbolism of the unconscious, and with the feminine polarity (he saw Mercury as hermaphroditic).[20] Symbolic specifics notwithstanding, salt as an alchemical psycho-spiritual symbol can best be understood as pertaining to the body-mind in a purified state, in which it serves as a proper vehicle for the full flowering of consciousness.

Alchemical Stages of Transformation

As mentioned, the key to alchemy (both material and psycho-spiritual) is summarized in the Latin expression *solve et coagula*. 'solve' here means to break down and separate elements and 'coagula' refers to their coming back together (coagulating) in a new, higher form. The alchemical idea of transmuting base metals into gold is an excellent metaphor for the inner work. We must 'break down' aspects of our character that are in the way of the realization of our deeper, higher nature. This deeper, higher nature is the Philosopher's Stone, along with our 'higher calling' in life represented by the symbol of gold. Thus, *solve et coagula* means to see clearly our limiting characteristics, take steps to wear them down by dispersal, and then to reconstitute in a higher, more pure form—which then allows for the possibility of accomplishing our maximum potentials in life.

There are, in some schools of thought, seven general stages in the alchemical process, which correspond well to seven stages of individual transformation. Needless to say, as in all matters pertaining to alchemy, there is no overall consensus among alchemists or esoteric scholars as to the details of these stages (other than the fact that they did, in all likelihood, originally represent actual stages of primitive chemical laboratory work). What follows is a simplified and psychologized overview of the seven stages, based on a scheme that is a good representation of an overall view of inner development.

1. **Calcination**: This is the first stage of alchemy. Chemically, calcination is the term given for the heating and pulverizing of raw matter to bring about its thermal decomposition, that is, its breaking up (or down) into more than one substance, or into a phase shift (from, say, water to gas at boiling point).

In psycho-spiritual language, this stage is sometimes humorously referred to as 'cooking' or 'baking' (and in fact the prime symbol for this stage is fire). It occurs naturally as a process whereby our egos get gradually worn down by the inevitable challenges of life. In alchemical symbolism this stage is sometimes represented by bringing down a tyrannical king. The idea there is that we have two essential elements to us: our essence, and our ego-personality. The ego serves us in our early years, aiding in protection and survival, but becomes a problem as we seek to grow and mature into spiritually awake adults. The more we try to hold on to this limiting part of us, the more life will gradually hammer us—'cooking' us until we become sufficiently 'opened' (or humbled) to realize that we are going in a wrong direction. A hallmark of this stage is a growing willingness to be wrong about core issues, a willingness to let go of positions that we cling to. The expression from the book *A Course In Miracles*, 'Would you rather be right or happy?' speaks, in a simplified fashion, to this. The ego-self cares primarily about being right—right that we know, or right that we are not good enough, or right that we are too good, or right that we are a powerless victim, or right that we cannot trust life or love owing to previous experiences, and so on. Calcination is the process of having that part of our stubbornness, pride, and arrogance worn down. (This stubbornness, pride, or arrogance need not only express as an outwardly puffed up nature; indeed, more commonly it tends to disguise itself in shyness, self-doubt, or self-sabotage).

The sooner we understand the point that in most cases we are the architect of our own frustrations and failures, the better, because we can avoid years of unnecessary suffering. Ideally the spiritual path is about hastening the process of calcination, rather than it being drawn out over the course of a whole life, only to realize in old age just how intransigent and controlling we have always been. The reason why this process is so essential is because the personality we cling to, the sense of personal identity, the 'me' that we invest so much energy in maintaining, is ultimately illusory, based as it is on identification (with body, form, history, borrowed knowledge, and so on). Aging, and eventually death, will wear down and destroy this false self in time. Learning to let go of constructed mental positions, pride, excessive stubbornness, reactive blame of others, playing small owing to crippling self-doubt, and fear of confronting our falsehoods, will hasten the process and potentially give us more time to experience our deeper nature while still alive.

2. **Dissolution**: Chemically, 'dissolution', or 'solvation' as it is also called, refers to a process whereby a solute (like salt) dissolves in a solvent (like water). Psycho-spiritually, the element that symbolizes dissolution is water, and this stage represents a deep encounter with our subconscious mind. After our ego has been sufficiently cooked (humbled) from calcination, what remains of our personality has to be further processed, and this is brought about by its dissolution in a solvent like water.

Dissolution, or deep deconstruction of the ego, is a challenging phase, especially for those with strongly developed personalities and egos. The common expression that someone 'has a lot of personality' is conventionally taken as a compliment, but from the point of view of psycho-spiritual alchemy it is problematic, because usually it just means that the person has a stronger ego-system and greater defenses built up over time. Whether this ego is unpleasant or charming is secondary. Either way, it has to be dissolved in order for the true self to be liberated.

Ego-dissolution is directly related to our beginning to take responsibility for our projections—in short, to our beginning to truly grow up. We begin to move beyond victim-consciousness, the tendency to blame the world for our struggles, and the tendency to see in others what we most dislike about ourselves. This stage is often characterized by experiencing the emotion of grief, and allowing ourselves to truly grieve painful incidents from our past that we may have long buried. Repressed or with-held pain keeps us dry and inwardly contracted. These psychic knots of pain need to be dissolved via permitting ourselves to truly experience the pain with awareness, as opposed to avoiding it with endless distractions, narcotizations (mind-altering substances like drugs or alcohol, including excessive T.V. watching), or endless other forms of avoidance. In many cases the stage of dissolution is forced on a person by unexpected accidents or illnesses. If a right attitude is brought to bear on such apparent misfortunes, overall maturing and growth can result.

A key to the stage of dissolution is the awakening of passion and the harnessing of the energy of emotional pain toward an object of creativity. We do not just passively witness the reality of our inner pain; we redirect its energy, wedding it to our authentic personal desires and constructive aims. In so doing we are participating and aiding in the dissolving of our false self. We are using the energy freed up by letting go of old, stale ego positions, in the service of re-aligning our life in the direction of our higher purpose.

3. Separation: Chemically, separation, or 'separation process', refers to the appropriate extraction of one substance from another—for example, the extraction of gasoline from crude oil. In spiritual alchemy, separation refers to the need to make our thoughts and emotions more distinct by isolating them from other thoughts and emotions. For example, the process of forgiving someone is usually only authentic if we have first honestly recognized our negative thoughts and feelings toward that person, such as anger. We must first experience the anger prior to moving into an authentic forgiveness. When attempting to come to terms with our 'shadow-side', we need to identify and isolate particular elements of our character in order to honestly see and assess them. This is very much like a scientific process of extracting something from something else, in order to gain knowledge and insight about it. Developmentally it relates to the importance of a young adult differentiating from their parents (or other influential relatives) in order to clarify their own identity. On a sociopolitical level, it has [illegible] the idea of the separation of church and state.

This stage [illegible] to focus on what has been revealed in us after the first two [illegible] stages, and can [illegible] on what precisely needs to be given attention. Navigated successfully, the separation stage aids us in taking a clearer stock of our life, honestly admitting our errors in judgment. A common symbol for this stage is the black crow, which in its black color denotes the dying away of the false that has occurred in the first two stages, as well as the positive possibilities for the future symbolized by the crow's capacity to fly.

The Separation stage is of crucial importance on the path of awakening, if only because it is most commonly both feared and overlooked. Many 'feel-good' approaches to personal transformation, or diluted new age teachings, in their rushed desire to reach an idealized state of unity with existence, gloss over the need to face and assume responsibility for one's inner shadow element, or darker nature. The separation stage is entirely concerned with the need to both see and take responsibility for the shadow within. If we fail to do this, the shadow elements will be projected onto the world, usually showing up in the form of others who appear to subject us to unjust treatment.

In this stage we begin to see what is of value in our life, and what is not. To illustrate the point with a simple example: back in the 1990s the former NY Times reporter Tony Schwartz quit his stressful job and decided to travel the country seeking out many prominent cutting edge psychologists, philosophers, and spiritual teachers and interviewing them. He wrote a book about his journey and what he'd learned from these teachers, titling it *What Really Matters*. When we've been humbled enough by life that we begin to recognize what really matters, then we've begun the alchemical process of separation. We are literally separating the wheat from the chaff both from within us and from our outer lives as well. However this is only possible when we are truly ready to be deeply honest with ourselves, by taking ownership of our frustrations and self-imposed limitations, and the entire range of thoughts and feelings within, from the positive to the negative—in short, of our entire self-image. Such a step makes it possible to achieve a radical breakthrough in our lives, something that may take the form of a thorough change in attitudes and inner positions, if not also in outer circumstances.

4. **Conjunction**: The fourth stage in the alchemical process is conjunction. Psycho-spiritually, this refers to the proper combining of the remaining elements of our being, after the purification and clarification of the first three stages. It speaks to an inner unification that is made possible by the hardships, purifications, and inner divisions that happened in the first three stages.

The essence of psycho-spiritual conjunction is to provide an inner space in which to mediate between two apparently distinct opposites. For example, we all know what it is to experience conflicted feelings toward another person, especially someone we are close to, the typical 'love-hate' scenario. In the previous stage, separation, we need to distinguish these two states clearly if we are to be authentic. We need to be fully honest with ourselves about all of our inner states—put another way, we need to bring all of our unconscious thoughts and feelings about this person, and who/what they represent to us, to the light of awareness. In conjunction, we worry less about totally unifying these thoughts and feelings than we do about developing the inner spaciousness in which to allow them to be there without condemning any as 'wrong'. In this sense, 'conjunction' is not a forced joining of distinct and opposite states of mind, but rather a natural connecting process that happens as we honestly recognize the reality of both within us.

Additionally, psycho-spiritual alchemy proposes that what is left if the first three stages of calcination, dissolution, and separation have been properly undergone is a state wherein we can more clearly mediate between our 'soul' and 'spirit'. In this sense 'soul' refers to our *embodied spirit*, the part of our essential nature that is 'fully human', and 'spirit' refers to our most rarefied connection with the divine, transcendental Source. These two are sometimes categorized as the divine feminine (soul) and the divine masculine (spirit). The combining of the two is the essence of inner tantra, a sacred marriage of spiritual opposites, or what Jung called the *mysterium coniunctionis*. Alchemical symbolism sometimes refers to this as the marriage of the Sun (spirit) and the Moon (soul), having its roots in the combination and heating of sulphur and Mercury to produce the Philosopher's Stone.

All this speaks to the important of *balance* on our path of awakening, and in particular, direct and honest awareness of those parts of us that remain out of balance. In achieving a conscious balance of our spirit-soul/masculine-feminine energies, we become capable of deeper spiritual realizations and more effective manifestations in our life. Put in practical terms, we maintain a balance between our maximum-context awareness (meditation) and our embodied immanence (which is essentially relationship, in all its forms—relationship with others, with our practical affairs, our immediate surroundings, and so on).

The conjunction phase is sometimes compared to the spiritual Heart (or 'heart *chakra*'), which as metaphor speaks to the ability to 'hold a space' in which conflicting elements can work out their differences and become resolved to a higher potential. It is here where we realize a definite maturity, understanding that differences, especially those of polar opposite qualities, do not get resolved via force, but rather by holding space, i.e., cultivating the patience to allow integration and change to occur organically.

However this stage is not the end of our process of transformation, as elements of ego remain, and must in turn be processed.

5. **Fermentation**: In biochemistry, 'fermentation' refers to the process of oxidizing organic compounds (changing their oxidation state). Examples of products of fermentation are beers and wines. In spiritual alchemy, fermentation has to do with a new stage in the process of transformation in which so-called higher energies begin to be tapped into. The first four stages all dealt with the energies of the personality (and its remnants), but with fermentation we are beginning to access the energies of the higher dimensions (or subtle

inner planes or deep self, depending on how we view it).

Fermentation occurs in two parts, the first being **Putrefaction**. In biology, putrefaction refers to the breakdown or decomposition of organic material by certain bacteria. Spiritually, this refers to a kind of inner death process in which old, discarded elements of the personality are allowed to rot and decompose. It is sometimes referred to as the dark night of the soul, and can involve difficult mental states such as depression. In the Tarot this phase is represented by the Death card, which denotes the death of an aspect of our personality that no longer is needed.

Putrefaction is followed by a stage called **Spiritization**. Here, we undergo a type of rebirth resulting from the deep willingness to let go of all elements of us that no longer serve our spiritual evolution. This marks the true beginning of inner initiation, of entry into a 'higher' life in which our best destiny has a chance to unfold.

6. **Distillation**: Chemically, distillation refers to a separation process of substances. It has a long history, being used for the production of such things as alcohol and gasoline. Psychologically, distillation represents a further level of purification that involves an ongoing process of integrating our spiritual realizations with our daily lives—dealing with mundane things with integrity, being as impeccable in our lives as we can be, and not using the inner work as a means by which to escape the world. At this stage remaining impurities, hidden as 'shadow' elements in the mind, are flushed out and released, which is crucial if they are not to surface later on (a phenomenon that can be seen to occur when a reputed saint, sage, or wise person, operating from a relatively advanced level of development, appears to have a fall from grace). Repeatedly practicing this leads to a strong and profound inner transformation that is rooted in integrity. Most standard definitions of 'enlightenment', in the Eastern sense of that word, correspond to this stage. A common alchemical symbol for the distillation stage is the image of the Green Lion eating the sun. It suggests a robust triumph and an embracing

of a limitless source of energy.

7. **Coagulation**: This stage brings to a completion the seven phases of the *solve et coagula* process. Biologically, 'coagulate' refers to the blood's ability to form clots and so stem bleeding, thus being a crucial life-saving function. In spiritual alchemy it symbolizes the final balancing of opposites, symbolized in the Tarot by the meeting of Magician and Devil, or higher self and the raw material of form, the ultimate marriage of Heaven and Hell. The end result is the Philosopher's Stone, also sometimes called the Androgyne, and is often symbolized by the Phoenix, the bird that has arisen from the ashes. This is closely connected to the idea of the Resurrection Body of mystical Christianity, or the Rainbow Body of Tibetan Buddhism, which includes the esoteric idea of the ability to navigate all possible levels (dimensions) of reality, without loss of consciousness. It is the form of the illumined and fully transformed human, in which matter has been spiritualized, or the spiritual has fully entered the material. Heaven and Earth as seen as one, or as the Buddhists say, *nirvana* (the absolute, or formless) is *samsara* (the world of form). At this end stage, wherever we look we see the divine, as we have come to realize our own full divinity. We have arisen from the ashes of limited individuality, and been reborn as our best, unlimited Self.

Three Stages of Transformation

The above describes seven stages of transformation. Alchemy in places abbreviates all this into a more compact scheme. From roughly the time of Christ until up to the 15th or 16th centuries, it was defined as four essential stages, based on four colors mentioned by Heraclitus, via the following Greek-Latin terms: *melanosis* or *nigredo* (blackening), *leukosis* or *albedo* (whitening), *xanthosis* or *flavum* (yellowing), and *iosis* or *rubedo* (reddening). By the 1500s the stage of 'yellowing' was gradually dropped, on rare occasions replaced by 'greening'. All of this appears to have had its roots in actual chemical processes based on laboratory attempts to create the

Philosopher's Stone, found in texts such as the *Rosarium Philosophorum*: two ingredients, usually personified as King and Queen (representing sulphur and Mercury) are added together in a specially sealed flask (called the 'seal of Hermes', the source of the term 'Hermetically sealed'). This mixture is then gradually heated. Provided an explosion does not occur (and sometimes it did, due to improper heating or improper glass), in a little more than a month the cooked ingredient turns black (*nigredo*). With continued heating over the next few weeks the mixture exhibits different (and short-lived) changing colors, called *cauda pavonis* (the peacock's tail), eventually becoming a light, very white (*albedo*) semi-liquid. At this point the alchemist could opt to remove the white ingredient and, adding silver to it, hope to produce a 'stone' that would be capable of converting base metals into silver. Or, he could continue to cook the white ingredient further, in which case it would gradually turn yellow and finally deep red (*rubedo*). The resulting red stone (the Red Elixir), after a few more stages such as mixing with gold, resulted in the Philosopher's Stone, believed capable of producing gold from base metals.[21]

Nigredo: *Nigredo* means 'blackening'. Traditionally it referred to the challenging and often discouraging first phase of the alchemist's work, which often required a tedious persistence. Psycho-spiritually it represents facing directly into the chaotic void—what the Old Testament referred to as the 'face of the deep'. In this sense *nigredo* represents the first stage of awakening, characterized by a breaking down, or a challenging encounter with the parts of our ego that are clearly in the way of our inner growth. The process of *nigredo* begins as we truly and sincerely begin to walk the path of transformation. The first step faced by all who desire to know themselves is to face the ego, and in particular, its means of sabotaging our inner flowering and overall success in life. In the seven-stage scheme presented above, *nigredo* may be said to encompass the first two stages, calcination and dissolution.

Albedo: *Albedo* means 'whitening'. In this phase, the seeker brings to completion the work of *nigredo*—the confrontation with the chaotic, undifferentiated void—by separating things and creating division, i.e., two substances in opposition to each other. This phase of the Great Work thus involves the creation of division necessary for the further unification of these opposites (for e.g., Spirit and body). It is here that the symbol of Mercury plays a crucial role, representing the guidance and assistance that appears to come from outside of the personality and ego-system, and that brings about the corrective balancing and integrating of the opposites, a process referred to by the term *mysterium coniunctionis*. *Albedo* also refers to the inner light that arises in the face of genuine suffering and the breaking down of old conditioning brought about by the first stage. The white dove is a common symbol for this stage. *Albedo* corresponds to the above stages of separation, conjunction, fermentation, and distillation. It is in this stage where a kind of rebirth happens for us, once we have dispensed sufficiently with the old conditioning of the ego, via the stages of encountering the void, creating coherence and clarity via division into opposites, and re-unifying these opposites.

Rubedo: *Rubedo*, meaning 'reddening', is the final stage. Whereas *nigredo* and *albedo* were concerned with the chaotic void and division, *rubedo* is entirely concerned with unity, with the result of this unity being the power of the Philosopher's Stone, representing our ability to forge real change in our lives by uncovering our highest reasons for being. The figure of Mercury herein undergoes a symbolic change, no longer being seen as the cause of the process of synthesis of opposites, but now as the goal itself, leading us to a state of integrated wholeness and unity. However, this wholeness is not a mere return to the Primal state (something Freud, for one, defined as 'infantile regression'). Rather, we re-capture the primal unity of the child-like state, while at the same time achieving something much more, the mature wisdom of a sage.[22] *Rubedo* thus points toward genuine Self-realization occurring while deeply embracing the totality of life (as opposed to renouncing the world in order to gaze within). It corresponds more or less to the last stage in the seven stage scheme, that of coagulation. This stage is the main objective behind all inner practices of spiritual transformation. It is the goal, the light of our best potential that all seek, even if not always consciously.

Chapter 3

Essentials of the Kabbalah

'Kabbalah' is the traditional and most commonly used term for the esoteric teachings of Judaism and for Jewish mysticism, especially the forms which it assumed in the Middle Ages from the 12th century onward. In its wider sense it signifies all the successive esoteric movements in Judaism that evolved from the end of the period of the Second Temple and became active factors in Jewish history.[1]
—Gershom Scholem

There are generally two elements within the history of most wisdom traditions, those being the historical, and the so-called mythic. Needless to say, both have value. The historical view attempts to show a rational and factual basis to the origin of a spiritual tradition, and is also valuable for helping us understand the cultural context in which a given tradition may have arisen, as well as providing actual examples of seekers of truth who may have radically transformed their lives by following that tradition. The mythic view teaches us about the psychological archetypes and spiritual themes that are timeless. Because they are timeless, they apply equally to our own present condition, even if they express themselves in tales set in ancient times, or in fantastical situations. The mythic view has a power and meaning that is independent of the historical. For example, Jesus exists as a powerful symbol or archetype of spiritual truth, regardless of whether or not he even actually existed.

Holding the above in mind helps when approaching a topic like the Kabbalah, owing mostly to its unclear roots in Jewish history. There are, in truth, several versions of the Kabbalah—a traditional, or dogmatic Kabbalah, which is based on the original Hebrew source books; a mystical Kabbalah that has been heavily used by practitioners of the Western esoteric paths (a version that is sometimes spelled 'Qabalah'); and a so-called unwritten Kabbalah, which involves an inner, mystical journey into the heart of its symbolism. (Other traditions have also attempted to integrate Kabbalah into their teachings, such as the Christianized Kabbalah—see below—often spelled as 'cabala').

In 1975 the American literary critic Harold Bloom remarked that of the three important streams of Western esoterica, Gnosticism, Neoplatonism, and Kabbalah, only the latter has received any thorough modern scholarship.[2] Times have changed somewhat in the forty years since Bloom made his comments—Gnosticism, Neoplatonism, and Hermeticism are now the province of a new crop of post-modern scholars reminiscent of those of the reconstituted Platonic Academy of 15th century Florence. But to some extent Bloom's observation remains true: Kabbalah, if anything, is even more popularized in the early 21st century than ever, and so requires a proper understanding of its place in Western esoteric teachings. The Kabbalah is not popular just because it has been embraced by some celebrities; it is relevant for any sincere seeker because it provides a highly comprehensive road map to the inner realms. It is well suited to the modern-era Western tendency to intellectualize, and seems to communicate well with other esoteric systems (though rarely with the approval of more traditional Kabbalists) such as astrology, the Tarot, and to the Masonic notion of graded initiations that represent levels of growth and understanding. It even interfaces, in some respects, with modern psychoanalysis.

The word *Kabbalah* literally means 'tradition', and derives from a Hebrew word meaning 'to receive'. According to traditional Jewish legend the Kabbalah was first received by some elect people (namely, Abraham and Moses), transmitted to them as a sacred oral tradition by divine emissaries (usually understood as angels). Its real purpose was thought to provide the deeper, esoteric meaning behind the Jewish scriptures, as well as to comprehensively explain the workings of human consciousness and how we can attain full awakening to our divine potential.

Background: Merkabah, Enoch, and Metatron

The Kabbalah is the most renowned element of Jewish mysticism. It has much of its roots in 12th and 13th century southern France and Spain. There are much older influences behind it, however, the most obvious being the Old Testament itself. It was immediately following the Roman destruction of the Second Temple in Jerusalem in 70 CE and subsequent cultural trauma and further diaspora that Jewish mysticism, now depending heavily on oral transmission and the safeguarding of 'secret' texts, began to become more cohesive. Some of this had its origins in less commonly recognizable elements of early Jewish esotericism. These are found in the respective first chapters of the Biblical books of Genesis and Ezekiel, the former of which, called the *ma'aseh bereshith* ('story of creation') deals with the themes of creation and the nature of the soul; and the latter of which deals with *ma'aseh merkavah,* or Merkabah mysticism. The word 'Merkabah', translated as 'chariot' (or less grandiosely, as 'cart'), is first found in 1 Chronicles 28:18, a compact line that also includes hints pertaining to alchemy and angelology:

> And for the altar of incense refined gold by weight; and gold for the plan of the chariot of the cherubim, that spread out their wings, and covered the ark of the covenant of the LORD. (KJV)

The Merkabah was the chariot that bore the Throne of God, driven by four mysterious beings. The word *merkavah* is not explicitly mentioned in Ezekiel, but is thought to apply to 1:4–26, in which Ezekiel describes an elaborate vision that involves a windstorm emerging from the north, complete with a huge cloud flashing with lightning. (It is impossible not to notice the parallels here between these kinds of descriptions and some of those appearing in modern popular culture, such as scenes from Steven Spielberg's 1977 science-fiction film *Close Encounters of the Third Kind*. However that is not to suggest that Ezekiel was describing UFOs, but more the reverse, how Ezekiel, and other ancients, left their footprint on modern popular art. George Lucas, creator of the 'Star Wars' movies, was influenced by Joseph Campbell, himself drawing from classical myth; J.R.R. Tolkien borrowed from Scandinavian myth, and J.K. Rowling from medieval and Renaissance magic). In the centre of the windstorm, heated like glowing metal, is seen four living creatures. Each had four faces and four wings. The faces were those of a human (looking ahead), a lion (facing right), an ox (facing left) and an eagle (facing behind). Fire and lightning accompany them (they are compared to burning coals or torches), and they are mounted on a structure with wheels that 'sparkle like topaz' (possibly connected to the Sanskrit term *tapas*, meaning 'heat' or 'fire'[3] referring to the effort needed to cultivate spiritual discipline and the suffering that naturally arises from this, thus being similar to the alchemical idea of *nigredo*, or 'blackening').

Merkabah mystics were primarily interested in undergoing a direct experience of the divine, a kind of shamanistic journeying into the inner realms of being. The main idea in Merkabah mysticism amounted to traversing the 'seven heavenly halls of heaven' to stand before the chariot and Throne of God. It has been speculated that Jewish converts to Christianity (between 100–200 CE) transmitted elements of Merkabah mysticism to Christian Gnostics, teachings that in places become corrupted into the Gnostic idea of an alien God who has nothing to do with this material universe, which was created by disobedient archangels. (Jewish myth, in sharp distinction to Gnosticism, posits a God who is very much connected to this world and immanently involved with it).[4]

By the third century CE Merkabah mysticism had developed significantly, involving a combination of elaborate depictions of higher dimensions (generally seven in number) populated by various angelic hosts, conjoined with personal mystical experience. Because this idea so closely resembles both Gnostic and Neoplatonic theory it is believed by most scholars that crossover and mutual influence between the three traditions was ongoing, although some Jewish historians maintain that Merkabah mysticism was always unique to Judaism. Of note is that these early Merkabah mystics appear not to have been concerned with matters of 'low magic' (the summoning of angelic or demonic energies with the intention of controlling them for personal ends), which was a somewhat later development within 'practical Kabbalah' (Kabbalistic magic) when its teachings became more accessible to the common man and his mundane desires.

The period following the exile of the Jews in Babylon (circa 550 BCE) was pivotal and heavily influential on Jewish cosmology (mainly from Persian Zoroastrianism). Prior to that the God of the Old Testament—Yahweh—was chiefly a warrior-god, aided by a few *Elohim*. After the exile, archangels and angels gained currency in Jewish lore, along with a plethora of detail involving name, rank, purpose, and so on.[5] (The flip-side of this attention to angelic detail was attention to demonic detail as well, which carried over into the elaborate demonological texts of the Medieval and Early Modern periods).

Angels are not elaborated on in any significant way in the Bible, brief mention being only accorded to Michael and Gabriel. A key figure in the history of angelic lore is Enoch, a 6th generation descendent of Adam via Seth, and the great-grandfather of Noah. Of interest here is the apocryphal and highly disputed Book of Enoch, written between 300 and 100 BCE. It is in here where we find some of the origins of the Jewish mystical tradition; the Book of Enoch itself was kept by the Essenes of Qumran (an alleged ascetic sect of mystics) something made known via the 1947 Dead Sea Scrolls discovery. Jewish mysticism was closely associated with apocalypticism and information kept for the 'elect' or private groups of ascetics.[6] (The notion that mystery teachings were the province of the 'chosen few' has always aroused hostility and even persecution, as it did in days of the Essenes. It has also been behind some anti-mystical ideologies in more recent times, such as communism and even Nazism, which have opposed organized occult groups on the grounds that they are forms of elitism counter to the welfare of the common man; but more accurately these objections have been based on fear of the power of such groups and their potential for disturbing or undermining the control of rulers or tyrants).

It is in the Book of Enoch where the tradition of pseudepigraphical writings finds some of its earliest examples, where anonymous authors hid their identities behind older authoritative names such as Enoch, Noah, Abraham, and Moses. At the heart of the book lies its attempts to tackle the mystery of the divine not so much by direct revelations about the nature of God, but rather by revealing the nature of the structure *around* God, namely, the 'Throne' of God, as on its 'chariot' (*merkavah*). These metaphors point toward one of the key elements of esotericism and high magic, which, in contrast to pure mysticism and its interest in the direct experience of God, is more concerned with communicating with the divine by understanding the vast and complex realms between God and the lower material world.[7] In so doing, the Book of Enoch specifies the role of seven key archangels (Michael, Gabriel, Raphael, Uriel, Raguel, Remiel, and Saraqael), potent symbols for the link and medium between the highest and lowest domains of existence. The book also makes reference to the 'Watchers', itself connected to Genesis 6, in which it is stated that certain angels mated with human females, resulting in the *nephilim*, hybrid 'giants', who allegedly walked the earth in antediluvian and post-Flood times. Other apocryphal sources (such as the Book of Jubilees) allege that these *nephilim* eventually became the demons of later times, and that Yahweh attempted to purge them from Earth via the Flood. (This story evolved into the various myths of medieval folklore, such as that of the 'cambion', half demon, half human—an example being Merlin from the Arthurian legends; or the 'changelings', offspring of elves or fairies and humans). From the esoteric perspective, all this can be seen as elaborate metaphor for ego-traps such as pride, greed, and lust, and the consequences that arise from them.

Jewish apocrypha identifies Enoch with the great archangel Metatron (although Metatron is not mentioned in the Hebrew Bible).

The key line is from Genesis, 5:24 (KJV): 'Enoch walked with God; then he was no more, because God took him away'. The implication is that Enoch did not die the way typical mortals did, but in some other way, usually associated with some sort of 'ascension/resurrection' supposedly possible for highly developed beings. Exodus 23:20–21 is thought to refer to Metatron (KJV):

> Behold, I send an Angel before thee, to keep thee in the way, and to bring thee into the place which I have prepared. Beware of him, and obey his voice, provoke him not; for he will not pardon your transgressions: for my name is in him.

In general Jewish myth holds Metatron as highest of all archangels, in some cases referring to him as the 'lesser Yahweh'. This is a subtly problematic issue, as it hints at a dualistic God, a view not supported by most esoteric wisdom traditions. Hence the matter of Metatron has long been a disputed issue in mystical Judaism. There is some parallel for Enoch-Metatron in the 'resurrecting god' myth (via Osiris, Mithras, Jesus, etc.), although Enoch-Metatron appears to be unique in its angelic nature. One clear distinction according to the legends is that Enoch was 'taken by God'; Jesus, however, resurrected of his own accord, a reflection of the idea that angels are step-down mediums for God but lack autonomy. This notion may appear to break down with the matter of the so-called rebellious angels (led by Satan)—for how could they have rebelled if they lacked autonomy? But the problem is resolved with the view that even Satan performs a divine role: that of 'testing' (tempting) souls and functioning as a necessary adversary so that higher qualities can be developed by working against adversarial conditions (as told in the Book of Job).

The Tetragrammaton

Tetragrammaton is a Greek word meaning 'four letters'. It refers to the Hebrew יהוה, transliterated into the Latin letters YHWH. This is usually written in English as 'Yahweh'—the corrupted Middle Age version of this name became 'Jehovah'—and typically pronounced in Hebrew as 'ye-ho-vah'. (When pronouncing the four Hebrew letters consecutively, it is usually vocalized as 'yud-heh-vav-heh'). The Jews were not the first to hit upon the idea of a singular, transcendent and supreme God, but they did emphasize the utter unknowable quality of him, while at the same time asserting that he is a personal God who can and does intervene in worldly matters. Paradoxically he is both remote and accessible, but absolutely beyond form and human ken. Because his nature is both distant and yet accessible, it was thought that the best way to access him was via the power of words, and in particular, via the Holy Names. After the destruction of the Jerusalem Temple in 70 CE, his highest name—the Tetragrammaton, YHWH—was declared unpronounceable, and instead was obliquely referred to as *Adonai* ('my lord').

This idea of a 'secret' or 'forbidden' Name of God became one of the prime sources of the Jewish contribution to esoteric practices and practical Kabbalah (in essence, the art of manifestation). The main idea behind it all was that Hebrew was believed to be the supreme language, originally spoken by God himself to Adam, and therefore the 22 Hebrew letters came to be regarded as compressed instruments of great spiritual power. Perhaps the most influential magic grimoire of all, *The Key of Solomon*, was based mostly on Jewish nomenclature—in specific, the Holy Names of God (despite the irony that the grimoire was originally written in Greek and is not based on Jewish teachings—see Appendix III). Such 'practical magic' was founded on very specific names and numbers (each Hebrew letter corresponding to a particular number), the combination of which was used to construct talismans or amulets, objects designed to attract desirable objects or events, or to ward off undesirable ones. It was also believed that by correct manipulation of numbers that correspond to specific angels, spirits, or even demons, communication could be established with them, and their help could be requested or compelled.[8] (This was, of course, a key piece behind the

Christian Church's vehement denunciation of magic, maintaining that it was all based on 'dealings with Satan' that ultimately stemmed from a rejection of Christ as Messiah and an ambition to 'become equal with God'. Needless to say, it also lay behind the rejection of magic from within orthodox Judaism itself, which instructs its members in the means of living a selfless and ethical life founded on subservience to an all-powerful God who is understood to be ontologically real and the sole source of all 'miracles'. All desire to work magic was thus understood as a type of rebellion against God).

The Kabbalah

Despite the background of the Book of Enoch and Merkabah mysticism, the Jewish mystical tradition is ultimately based largely on the three books known as the *Sepher Yetzirah*, the *Sepher ha-Bahir*, and the *Sepher Zohar*. The *Sepher Yetzirah* ('Book of Formation' or 'Creation') is the oldest source book of Jewish mysticism, although historians do not all agree on how old it actually is, some dating it to between the first and fourth centuries CE, others ascribing at least parts of it to as recent as the 13th century CE. The book describes the creation of the universe by God and his expression via thirty-two domains of wisdom, comprised of ten numbers (the basis of the ten *sephirot* of the Tree of Life) and of the twenty-two letters of the Hebrew alphabet. The *Sepher ha-Bahir*—or more commonly, the Bahir (meaning 'bright' or 'splendor')—is traditionally believed to have been written in the 1st century CE, although critical scholarship suggests it is a product of the Sefardim of 12th century southern France.[9] It is a commentary on the first chapters of Genesis, on the *Sepher Yetzirah*, and on the mystical nature of the form of the Hebrew letters, and was the origin of the idea that the *sephirot* were emanations of the divine. It has signs of Gnostic influence, and also discusses the doctrine of transmigration of souls (reincarnation), though does not attempt to explain it philosophically.[10]

It is the *Sepher Zohar* ('Book of Splendor' or 'Book of Radiance'), however, that is generally considered to be the heart of Jewish mysticism, especially of the Kabbalah (and is, in fact, the only Kabbalistic work considered to be canonical). The Zohar is the name for a series of books that are a mystical interpretation of the Torah (the five books of Moses that are the heart of the Old Testament, i.e., Genesis, Exodus, Leviticus, Numbers, and Deuteronomy). In the conventional religious view, the Torah forms the basis of understanding Man's relationship with God. The Zohar is similar to the Gnostic element within Christianity and the Sufi element within Islam, in that it seeks to understand the more mystical aspects of its faith. That is, it is primarily concerned with the esoteric, and how the relationship between Man and God can best be approached for the individual's spiritual transformation and ultimate union with the divine. The Kabbalah in particular keys in on this relationship, holding that no real direct knowledge of God is attainable without first understanding the relationship of the divine to creation. (Or put more technically, the relationship of consciousness to all that appears *within* consciousness—the relationship of the Supreme Self to all that appears as objects to be aware of).

The origins of the history of Jewish mystical thought are typically unclear, but it is known that the Zohar first appeared in an organized form in Spain in the 13th century CE, shortly after the time that the French poets Christian de Troyes and Robert de Boron had written the Grail myths (esoteric interpretations of Christianity). The Zohar was probably composed (or compiled) in the 1280s by the Spanish rabbi and mystic Moses de Leon (1250–1305) and colleagues, although he himself claimed it had been written by a 1st century CE sage called Simeon bar Yochai, inspired by the spirit of the prophet Elijah. Spanish Jewish mystics of the 13th century had clarified an important concept, the Source as a formless reality that cannot be defined, excepting as 'that which is without end'. This infinite Source—usually referred to as *Ein-Sof*—is beyond matter and spirit, space and time, and without impulse or desire; that is, it is beyond any sort of personal comprehension whatsoever. *Ein-Sof* ultimately exists and manifests in two essential ways: one, as the Infinite, unknowable Source, and two, as the Creator of the universe. The latter, the Creator, is the first 'outer' manifestation of *Ein-Sof*, which then gradually and naturally diversifies in increasingly 'dense' expressions via numerous dimensional levels (the ten *sephirot* of the Tree of Life) before culminating in the material universe.

Ein-Sof, the formless, unknowable Source—in essence, the Void—is sometimes reduced to *Ein* (or *Ayn*) meaning 'no-thing'. Technically, there is nothing that can be properly said by way of defining *Ein*, because in our current condition we lack the capacity to comprehend it. In other words, it is beyond representation—that is, the best we can do is to point in its direction. It is the basis of 'apophatic' theology, or a *via-negativa*, meaning it is only described in terms of what it is *not*. It cannot be grasped or explicated by thought. This notion is closely mirrored in several Eastern teachings, namely the Hindu Advaita Vedanta idea of *neti neti* ('not this, not that'—a meditation to uncover divine consciousness by negating all attempts of the mind to define it); the Buddhist doctrine of *anatta* (no-self) and *shunyata* (emptiness); as well as the notion of the *Tao* in Taoism, and the famous lines of the *Tao Te Ching*: 'The Tao that can be known is not the true Tao. The Name that can be named is not the true Name'.

According to the important 16th century Jewish mystic Isaac Luria (1533–1572), *Ein-Sof* can be understood as occupying all of existence for all of eternity before (paradoxically) contracting inwardly at some point, leaving behind the empty space in which the universe could form. This contraction—called *zimzum*—is necessary because logically nothing can exist 'outside' of God, he being the Totality. Therefore his contraction makes possible a 'space' within which the universe of energies and forms can arise. Once this space within was created, *Ein-Sof* then performed its sole wilful act, the sending out of a singular ray of light. This light, in a fashion very similar to Plotinus's idea of the emanation of 'the One', then leads naturally to the creation of the various *sephirot* that constitute existence. However, each *sephira* cannot be rightly understood in a simple, linear fashion, as they each exist via a four-fold nature. This is because when the *Ein-Sof* emanated its primordial Light, it manifested via four distinct dimensions or Worlds. These are referred to as the Worlds of *Atziluth* (Emanations), *Briah* (Creation), *Yetzirah* (Formation), and *Assiah* (Actions). Some of their attributes are as follows:

1. (*Atziluth*-Emanations) is the domain of the Infinite Light of Creation (*Ein-Sof Aur*), and is associated with the archetypes; it is the realm of pure spirit, and the source of all other subsequent worlds. It is represented by the first letter of the Tetragrammaton (the Divine 'unpronounceable name'), *Yod*, and represents Primal Fire.

2. (*Briah*-Creation), is the domain of the formless agents of the Infinite, pure mind, and the realm of the 'ten great archangels'.[11] It is represented by the second letter of the Tetragrammaton, *Heh*, and represents Primal Water.

3. (*Yetzirah*-Formation) is all the non-physical dimensions of form (subtle planes). It is represented by the third letter of the Tetragrammaton, *Vau*, and represents Primal Air.

4. (*Assiah*-Actions) is the physical domain where all is synthesized. It is represented by the second and final *Heh* of the Tetragrammaton and denoted Primal Earth.

This idea of a universe manifesting via four essential domains is not unique to the Kabbalah. There are similarities here with Plato's idea of the 'divided line', in which Socrates explains how existence can be explained via four distinct models of reality; and the later Neoplatonic views of Plotinus, who also divided existence into four essential domains: The One, The Divine Mind, the Higher World

Soul, and the Lower World Soul/Nature. The Gnostics, also, had their 'inner planes' to be traversed on the journey back to the Divine. The parallels of these traditions with the Kabbalistic four-fold model above seem clear, indicating a certain degree of cross-pollination. Despite the similarities, however, there are key differences. Jewish mysticism, by and large, does not regard the cosmos as an 'inferior copy' of the divine (Plato), nor as the mere flawed creation of a misguided archangel (Gnosticism). In many early sources of Kabbalah, the cosmos, via its ten *sephirot,* was held to be one and the same as the Infinite from which it emanates. The Zohar declares, in reference to His Names and Powers, 'He is They, and They are He' (3:11b, 70a). Later views refined this position, holding it in paradox: God is both present within his *sephirot,* and separate from them, using them as tools for his expression. This was sometimes depicted through the striking imagery of a single candle reflected in ten differently colored mirrors: all the reflections of the light appear different, but all are in essence the same light.[12] In general it may be safely said that the Kabbalah is not an 'anti-world' or 'anti-body' doctrine; in its teaching, the material dimension (*Malkuth*) is the 'kingdom', the domain of synthesis and consecration, and as holy as the Infinite from which it has emanated.

The Tree of Life and the Sephira

The heart of the Kabbalah may be said to be a cosmic map called the 'Tree of Life' that contains ten *sephirot* (singular, *sephira*—the word means 'number'). The idea of the *sephirot* originates with the *Sepher Yetzirah,* oldest of the Jewish mystical texts (although it was elaborated on in the *Sepher ha-Bahir*). The *sephirot* constitute distinct domains or aspects of reality that correspond to levels of consciousness. They can be thought of as both descriptions of the external universe and the primordial elements that created it, as well as a description of the inner realms of mind. The reference to the *sephirot* being associated with a 'tree' first appears in the *Sepher ha-Bahir,* although interestingly, this tree was understood to grow 'upside down', that is, from its roots (Keter) to its tip (Malkuth). It had a man superimposed on it, referred to as the 'upside down tree' (although the man appeared to be standing upright from the perspective of the last *sephira*). The fleshed out map—the Tree of Life as we know it today—appears relatively later in the records, sometime in the 14th century.[13]

We mentioned above the concept of *Ein*, or no-thing, which in the Kabbalah is considered to be the ultimate realm of existence (though technically it is not a realm, nor is it part of existence; it is entirely beyond any sort of facile conceptual understanding). According to Kabbalah, the *Ein* becomes *Ein-Sof* (the Infinite) as a means of becoming conscious of itself, and then becomes *Ein-Sof Aur* (the Infinite Light). This Infinite Light then modifies itself to become Keter, the first *sephira*.

The Matter of Correspondences

Any student of the Western esoteric teachings is familiar with the idea of correspondences, the interrelating of various symbolic elements and factors—everything from divine names, numerical values, colors, sounds, planets, angels, demons, and even plants or types of incense. The Kabbalistic Tree of Life has, perhaps as much as alchemy, been subject to a great deal of correspondence-application. Where all these correspondences arose from is not always a straightforward matter to trace, although the majority of those more commonly cited appear to derive from the *Sepher Yetzirah*. Others came from Moses de Leon or Joseph Gikatilla (1248–1305), but most are in general agreement. (Some, such as the Tarot card attributions, are 19th century accretions). The overarching idea behind the symbols and their various correspondences is that the Divine has a specific structure, and that this structure can be detected, known, understood, and even harnessed for particular purposes, via the interrelationships of Creation (the pathways between the *sephirot*). Some of these correspondences were the product of influences from other traditions, particularly the Neoplatonic, with its idea of stages of emanation deriving from the Source. For example, the *sephirot* were conceived of as progressive stages arising from God, each therefore worthy of a 'divine name'. These ten names became the 'ten names which must not be erased' (listed below as the 'God names' of each *sephira*).

1. Keter Elyon: *Keter Elyon* means 'the supreme crown', although it is usually rendered as simply Keter ('crown'). It has the primal position on the Tree of Life, at the very top. Keter can be understood as the root and source of life and consciousness as we know it, essentially corresponding to the orthodox view of the God of the Old Testament. Keter is traditionally associated with 'knowledge'. This 'knowledge' can also be understood as pure Consciousness, but it is not the 'consciousness' we typically understand. This consciousness can be thought of as Totality-Consciousness beyond our ken. There is a parallel for this idea in Eastern Vedanta: the 'fourth state of awareness', the highest, known by the Sanskrit word *turiya*, or consciousness without object, non-dual awareness, pure 'Oneness'.

Correspondences: Pure Being, beyond personal consciousness as we normally conceive of it. Non-duality. God Name: *Eheiyeh;* archangel: Metatron; body: crown; color: white; Tarot: the four aces.

2. Chokmah: The second *sephira* is known as Chokmah (sometimes transliterated as 'Hokhmah') meaning 'wisdom'. It is considered to be the primal masculine manifestation, the Supernal Father, and is associated with the 'knower'. The main distinction here between Keter and Chokmah is that while Keter has the blueprint of Creation, Chokmah also has the intent, and is thus the initiating force. In this sense Chokmah can also be thought of as pure formless spirit or energy, the vital basis of all existence. It is the original stimulation of the universe, stepping-down the primal power of the crown, Keter.

Correspondences: Full illumination, enlightenment. The Father. God Name: Yod (first letter of the Tetragrammaton); archangel:

Raziel; body: left side of face; color: gray; Tarot: the four 2s.

3. Binah: The third *sephira* is Binah, which means 'understanding' or 'intelligence'. It is regarded as the primal feminine manifestation, or Supernal Mother. It can be understood as that which creates form. It does this by *limiting* the active force of Chokmah, something like how the female egg will allow only one (of thousands) of male sperm to enter her domain, thus giving rise to an eventual particular form (a foetus). In contrast to Chokmah as 'knower', Binah can be understood as 'that which is known'. There is a parallel for this in the Hindu doctrine of Shiva (the subjective knower) and Shakti (the object that is known). The universe-proper may be said to begin with Binah, where the pure consciousness/energy of Chokmah is given coherence and form. Chokmah is thus the active principle, and Binah the passive. Simplified, Chokmah says 'I create', and Binah says 'I limit and shape'. Both are required to bring about a Creation that has objective phenomena.

Correspondences: Consciousness awakened to the Source of all forms. The Mother. Sorrow, that is, recognition of the struggle inherent in existence, and the compassion that arises from that recognition; vice: greed; God Name: YHWH Elohim; archangel: Tzaphkiel; body: right side of face; color: black; Tarot: the four 3s.

Da'ath (the Abyss): The idea of Da'ath, as a domain originally appearing between Chokmah and Binah, begins to show up in the records near around the year 1300 CE. The meaning of the word *da'ath*—'knowledge'—hints at its nature, similar to Keter, and it has been understood to be a kind of externalization of Keter. Traditionally, the upper three *sephirot*—Keter, Chokmah, and Binah—are thought to be separated from the lower seven *sephirot* by what is called the 'Abyss'. In terms of human consciousness, this is understood as implying that only the top three levels are immortal (not subject to space and time), with the lower seven being mortal (subject to space and time). In order for a seeker of truth to realize full enlightenment they must cross the Abyss. Few are thought to ever attain this while living. (In some esoteric schools, it is maintained that the Abyss can be crossed only after the death of the physical body). Psycho-spiritually, the Abyss can be thought of as the transition passed through by those rare souls who achieve full transcendence of the ego and complete identification with the Divine. This domain is sometimes referred to as the 'shadowy' *sephira*. It is referred to as shadowy because it is not a truly distinct domain of consciousness, but is rather best understood as a passageway, or 'quantum leap', to a higher state of being.

4. Chesed: The fourth *sephira* is Chesed (or Hesed), which translates as 'mercy' or less commonly, as 'love'. (Another name for this *sephira* is Gedulah). Chesed continues on the original work of Binah, and represents the specific creation of forms within the universe that we experience. This is different from the creative force behind forms (Chokmah) in that Chokmah has to do with the invisible, primal forms (similar to Plato's 'intelligible images and ideas', the sources of material forms). Chesed however is that which gives form to the universe we experience via the senses of our bodies and the filters of our perception and egos. Chesed is also the first of the 'Miscroprosopus', *sephirot* 4 through 9, sometimes collectively likened to a 'king' who 'weds' *sephira* ten (Malkuth, the 'bride'). Chesed can be understood as performing a 'catabolic function', breaking down and directing into specific purposes the raw energy provided by the higher *sephirot*.

Correspondences: Consciousness of *agape* (love that transcends form); vice: bigotry, hypocrisy, tyranny; God Name: El; archangel: Tzadkiel; body: left arm; color: blue; Tarot: the four 4s.

5. Geburah: The fifth *sephira* is Geburah (sometimes spelled Gevurah) meaning 'strength' or 'power'. This is the principle of the destruction of forms. This again applies to the world we experience, the world that we come to know. The world 'as it really is' is given form by Binah, but the world as we know it—with our senses and mental filters—is defined by Geburah. Chesed generates forms, and Geburah limits these, discards what does not work, and thereby shapes a functional universe. Psycho-spiritually, Chesed is the part of us that puts an idea into action, and Geburah can be understood as our discriminating faculty that streamlines things by rejecting what does not work, thereby allowing what truly has potential to properly develop. Geburah, manifesting a 'severity' that balances the 'mercy' of Chesed, can be misunderstood as an 'evil' force, but more properly should be understood along the lines of how Satan functions in the Book of Job, as God's divine prosecutor and 'tester' of moral quality.

Correspondences: Consciousness of the right use of power; vice: cruelty, destruction; God Name: Elohim Gibor; archangel: Khamael; body: right arm; color: red; Tarot: the four 5s.

6. Tiphareth: The sixth *sephira* is known as Tiphareth, which means 'beauty' or 'harmony'. Psychologically, this realm represents the essence of individual consciousness, the purest aspect of our identity, the 'true (or 'higher') self' as it is sometimes called. It is the doorway to the divine Source (Keter). Tiphareth can also be thought of as 'awareness of awareness', that is, pure consciousness that is turned back upon itself. However this is not the same as the consciousness of Keter, which is purely non-dual. Tiphareth retains awareness of individuality and duality. Tiphareth is also the realm of compassion, whereby we relate to others as souls, not as bodies or personalities. That is, we see others in the highest possible light. Traditionally, Tiphareth has been symbolized by three figures: that of child, king, and sacrificed god. Which of the three it will be seen as depends on perspective. From the point of view of Keter, Tiphareth is the child. From the point of view of Malkuth (the tenth and last *sephira*) it is the king. And from its own position, it is the sacrificed god, because it is the central point of equilibration and balance, where the ego is relinquished on the journey of awakening from Malkuth to Keter.

Correspondences: Consciousness of harmony; vice: pride; God Name: YHWH Eloha Va Daath; archangel: Raphael; body: solar plexus (encompassing the 3rd and 4th *chakras* in Hindu Yoga); color: yellow; Tarot: the four 6s.

7. Netzach: The seventh *sephira* is known as Netzach, which means 'victory' or 'lasting endurance'. It is the domain of instinct, emotions, and desires. When we are pushed or pulled in one direction, without clearly understanding why, we are operating in this realm. Whereas Tiphareth can be thought of as consciousness of consciousness, Netzach can be thought of as representing consciousness of energy, and all of our personal desires and reactions to the endless forms of energy, both psychic and physical, that we typically experience. Esoteric doctrine describes Netzach as first of the *sephira* of the 'illusory world', in that it is the domain of egoic constructs and all the delusions that can accompany them. When the Buddha addressed the causal link between suffering and craving, he was speaking to this. The reason it leads to suffering is because it tends to reinforce the notion that we are cut off from the vastness of existence (symbolized by the higher *sephira*), and moreover, that we must manipulate and control others in order to safeguard our existence. In general, as we descend the Tree of Life, the universe becomes more objectified and its elements appear to be more discreet and distinct. Concrete symbols arise at this level, themselves often turned into objects of worship and blind adherence to.

Correspondences: Consciousness of beauty; vice: squandering of energy; God Name: YHWH T'zaboath; archangel: Haniel; body: left leg; color: green; Tarot: the four 7s.

8. Hod: The eighth *sephira* is Hod, which means 'glory' or 'majesty'. Whereas Netzach represents the instincts and emotions, Hod is the intellect, as well as consciousness of form. This is the domain through which we communicate with symbols and languages.

Separation is denser at this level, requiring more concrete means by which to communicate.

Correspondences: Consciousness of splendor and magnificence; vice: dishonesty; God Name: Elohim T'zaboath; archangel: Michael; body: right leg; color: orange; tarot: the four 8s.

9. Yesod: Yesod is the ninth *sephira*; the word means 'foundation of the world'. This is the realm of consciousness of matter. Here exist the basic images and constructs behind the material world, sometimes called the 'etheric plane' in theosophical thought. Plato referred to this realm as that of the 'visible things' behind the visible forms.

Correspondences: Consciousness of the workings of the universe; vice: laziness; God Name: Shaddai El Chai; archangel: Gabriel; body: sex organs; color: purple; Tarot: the four 9s.

10. Malkuth: The tenth *sephira* is Malkuth. It is the material, physical universe. Though Malkuth translates as 'kingdom', paradoxically it is sometimes considered to be the 'princess' or 'bride' that 'marries' *sephirot* 4–9 (and particular 6, Tiphareth) an alchemical wedding that symbolizes the full manifestation in physical reality of the God-realized person. This 'wedding' is sometimes referred to as *hieros gamos* (Greek for 'holy marriage'), a process of sacred conjunction or tantric joining between 'god' and 'goddess' that reflects the inner unification of opposites. This 'sacred marriage' lies behind Kabbalistic ideas of redemption of the world, or *tikkun* (see below), the means by which Adam's original error is rectified.

Correspondences: First glimpse of our true, spiritual nature (our reason for being); vice: inertia, fear of change; God Name: Adonai Ha'aretz; archangel: Sandalphon; body: the feet; colors: citrine, olive, russet, and black; Tarot: the four 10s.

All the *sephira* can only be fully grasped in relation to each other. For example, Malkuth is nothing but an empty shell of matter without the animating energy of Yesod to give it meaning and purpose. And Yesod is nothing but formless energy without the substance of Malkuth to give it specific form and definition. Likewise, all of the *sephira* are meaningless as isolated phenomena; each has its purpose defined by its relationship to the others.

The Tree of Life is extremely complex and can be studied for a lifetime without exhausting its possibilities. As a metaphor for transformation, the Tree maps out the inner work that lies in gaining mastery over each of the lower seven *sephira* and what they represent. (The upper three *sephira*—Keter, Chokmah, and Binah—are not 'mastered' as such; rather, they are realized by the consciousness that is ready to enter fully the realms of limitless light and life, a process sometimes referred to as 'grace').

Jewish esoteric thought follows Aristotelian and Neoplatonic thinking in its division of the soul into multiple components. Over time an alternate version of the Tree of Life developed (especially by Isaac Luria) explaining it in terms of five levels: *Yechida* ('singularity'—Keter), *Chiah* ('life'—Chokmah), *Neshamah* ('breath'—Binah'), *Ruach* ('wind'—Chesed, Geburah, Tiphareth, Netzach, and Hod), *Nephesh* ('living entity'—Yesod and Malkuth). Sometimes the term *Guph* is added, corresponding to the tenth *sephira*, Malkuth, although there seems to be some confusion around this idea in modern occult treatments. According to tradition, *Guph* simply means 'body' and refers to a 'chamber of souls' in heaven, where souls first emerge into existence, followed by descending to Earth; the Jewish Messiah will appear only when the *Guph* is finally 'emptied of souls'. The first three (*Yechida, Chiah, Neshamah*) represent elements of the soul in its most rarefied state; the next, *Ruach*, represents individuality, from 'higher self' to ego-personality, with its five sub-elements of reason, will, desire, memory, and imagination; the next, *Nephesh*, represents the so-called animal-soul, or instinctive and material aspect. On occasion, the scheme is simplified into three parts: *Neshamah, Ruach,* and *Nephesh*, corresponding roughly to the spiritual, the mental-egoic, and the instinctive-physical.

The practical idea behind all this soul-cartography is to have these different aspects of the individual communicate with each other, so that the entirety of the person is known—a type of integral self-knowledge that includes the whole picture. The problem, however, is that for the average person what dominates their life is the *Ruach*, or ego-personality—the conventional sense of 'I'. However the *Ruach* is not an obstacle to vanquish, but rather something to be consciously connected (often allegorized as a 'sacred marriage') to the other realms—the Higher Self, the animal self and material world. This addresses the heart of the Western models of inner work, that being the *relationship* between the elements of reality.

The Shekhinah

Shekhinah is an important concept in Kabbalah. The word means 'dwelling' or 'inhabiting'; specifically it refers to the 'presence of the divine', the means by which God's presence is experienced in a specific location in time and space. It is sometimes compared to the Christian idea of the Holy Spirit (or Holy Ghost, the word 'ghost' deriving from the Old English *gast*, meaning 'spirit'), although technically the Hebrew term for the Holy Spirit is *ruach ha-qodesh*; it is also compared to the New Testament Greek word *parousia* ('divine presence'). A certain misconception about Kabbalah is that it is focused on achieving a mystical union with God, when in fact it is more concerned with a spiritually refined communication—more properly, *devekut* ('communion')—with God. In keeping with Western wisdom traditions, it is the relationship with the divine that is emphasized (in contrast to Eastern traditions, where the idea of union with the divine is central). In the context of relatedness with God, the idea of *Shekhinah* (understood as a feminine element of the divine) becomes significant. Put simply, we cannot hope to understand something deeply (such as the divine) without first understanding our relationship to it, and this is experienced in part via opening to the presence of the divine.

Shekhinah relates to an idea that lies at the heart of Judaism, which is that God's presence was located in the Jerusalem Temple. (Christian doctrine argued that with the coming of Christ this had been overturned, and that now God's presence could be experienced within via the agent of the Holy Spirit). The key has to do with the idea of accessibility. Because the divine—specifically, the higher *sephirot* of the Tree of Life—is understood to be generally inaccessible to the average person, there must be a means by which the power of the Infinite can be contacted, and it is here where the idea of *Shekhinah* becomes instrumental. It is also for this reason that *Shekhinah* is equated to the tenth *sephira*, Malkuth, and is understood to be its function. It is in Malkuth that the divine becomes fully manifest as 'I', the individuated and embodied experience of the Infinite.

The Problem of Evil and the Matter of Restoration: The Qliphoth and Tikkun

Qliphoth (sometimes transliterated as *klippot* or *kellipot*) means 'shells' or 'husks', and refers to the metaphor of the outer bark of a tree concealing the holiness and goodness within. Thus, the *qliphoth* are thought to be the cause of all evil and chaos, although it is understood that they are also creations of the divine. In general Kabbalistic doctrine has a greater interest in the 'dark realms', and in their interrelationship with the realms of 'light', in contrast to mainstream Jewish theology and philosophy. The idea of the *qliphoth* is complex and there are many interpretations of it, but the general view is that Adam's original decision to rebel and eat of the Tree of Knowledge resulted in a materialization of evil, thereby causing divisiveness to enter into reality. According to the Zohar this is connected to the separation of judgment and loving-kindness, with the tendency of judgment on its own to move toward division and autonomous disconnection from the Whole. There are similarities here with Gnosticism (belief in hostile elements that are very real) and Neoplatonism (the greater the distance from the divine, the greater the tendency toward evil), but there are differences as well, one of which is the idea that 'evil' is seen in a more impersonal light. The Zohar suggests that human evil is an inevitable by-product of the dark realm that formed as a result of Adam's actions. This dark realm, called *sitra ahra,* is understood to be distinct from God and having little to do with him, despite emerging from him. That said, the Zohar (in agreement with many Gnostic traditions) asserts that God's 'spark of holiness' remains in the dark realms.

All Kabbalistic ideas about the *qliphoth* are the attempt to come to terms with the nature of evil. The views on the matter are not consistent; some Jewish mystics regarded evil as an essentially negative element that arises only due to the inability of conscious entities, such as humans, to properly receive the pure light of God. Much as cold is simply the absence of heat and darkness the absence of light, so too is evil merely the absence of the intrinsic good of the divine Source. Other later views (such as put forth in the *Sepher ha-Bahir*) hold that there is an actual realm of evil, a 'positive evil' if you will, that is more than mere absence of good, carrying its own intrinsic reality as 'the left hand of the Holy One', and accompanied by a 'hierarchy of the dark side'.[14]

The Zohar speaks of evil as being a 'leftover' of previously destroyed worlds, an old idea that finds its reflection in religion and politics (the gods of older, defeated cultures often become the demons of the current, triumphant culture), and even science, wherein it is understood that 'lesser' stars (including our own sun) form from the stardust of previous novae or supernovae. Other views put forth the idea that evil is the natural result of a passive quality in God that is in perpetual conflict with the part of him that seeks to expand and create. Much of this philosophical hair-splitting has a purpose on the esoteric level, in that all apparent 'outer evil' ultimately must be seen as a reflection of the nature of the soul, and more pointedly, as that of the individual psyche. That evil exists, if only in demonstrable actions, is a given, just as it is a given that any individual has the capacity to sabotage their forward development in life owing to conflicted thoughts and energies within. Turning a blind eye to this and pretending we are pure light with no shadow side likely does us no good.

The idea of the *qliphoth* is, at least according to the Lurianic Kabbalah that became prevalent by the 17th century, closely connected to the idea of *tikkun* ('restoration', and its messianic overtones). In order to understand this we have to consider Luria's idea of the 'breaking of the vessels' (also called the 'death of the kings'). In brief, the idea is that after the creation of the world (brought about by the inward contraction, or *zimzum,* within God mentioned earlier), the various *sephirot* of the Tree of Life were gradually structured and formed (all this should be understood as metaphor, an attempt to explain a vastly complex process of creation using straightforward symbols). Once the *sephirot* were formed, the brilliant and pure light of God descended into them. However only the first three (Keter, Chokmah, and Binah) could withstand the power of this light and hold it within their domain. The next six—Chesed, Gevurah, Tiphareth, Netzach, Hod, and Yesod—failed to contain the light and broke. Malkuth, the last *sephira,* broke also, but not as severely. Some of the light that was released from these damaged vessels found its way back to its source, but some of it was scattered. Its remnants, along with the 'broken pieces' of the vessels, underwent a type of reconstitution that resulted in the *qliphoth,* or dark side, forming. In essence, evil arose as a result of the emanations of God being incapable of withstanding the purity and power of his light. (Luria's idea was clever and is reflected in many models of modern spiritual psychotherapy, such as the view that the suffering of the individual is related to an inability to withstand 'light', or properly embody the notion that they have a contribution to make to the universe, let alone the human race. The idea is that it is light, love, recognition, and accomplishment that we fear, feeling unworthy of them, and accordingly seek to disguise this existential fear by taking refuge in shadows—i.e., hiding out, playing small, and refusing to shine our light—or worse, resenting or seeking to undermine those who do).

It was from these remnants or shards that the material universe formed; all of it a degraded version of what it was originally supposed to have been, sometimes described as a 'cosmic catastrophe'. Luria did not see this catastrophe as emerging chaotically however, but rather along structured lines of order (much how our universe appears mostly ordered). The parallels here with Gnostic ideas about the creation of the universe as stemming from the actions of a wayward archangel (resulting in a degraded, flawed universe) seem clear, although Kabbalah has a more sophisticated model, in that the entire process has its origins in God's actions, not that of a mere renegade child of God.

How this 'cosmic catastrophe' gets fixed relates to the idea of *tikkun,* which refers to restoration and reintegration. Luria's idea was that after the 'breaking of the vessels' and subsequent catastrophe a process is begun in which each soul has the possibility of participating in a collective restoration project, the 'gathering together' of all the 'sparks of divine light' that were scattered when the vessels shattered. These sparks of light, scattered throughout the vast universe, are 'hidden' within the husks of the *qliphoth,* and the great work is to liberate them from these outer shells. How we individually participate in this collective great work is via our individual efforts to deepen and raise our consciousness. In keeping with Zoroastrian, Hermetic and Gnostic ideas, to transform personally is to contribute to the transformation of the cosmos. In this regard, Kabbalah in particular does not regard evil as something to be merely eradicated, but rather as a challenge to our nature in which we are to extract the divine from the dross. This work applies both subjectively, via our self-examination efforts, and objectively, via helping to 'raise the world'.

The Christian Cabala

The key figure to consider here is Giovanni Pico della Mirandola

(1463–1494), who in 1486, at the age of 23, wrote a lengthy manifesto attempting to bridge and synthesize many disciplines of learning, including the Jewish Kabbalah and Christianity. Pico's work had its genesis in the Platonic (or Florentine) Academy founded in 1462 in Florence by Cosimo de' Medici and led by Pico's teacher, Marcilio Ficino (1433–1499). The academy had its origins in the translations of Plato's and Plotinus's works into Latin, and a renewed study of other ancients, such as Pythagoras. Pico's '900 theses' on religion, science, magic and related wisdom traditions, was posted as a challenge to any who might debate him. The underlying motive for his work was not always clear; some suspected that it was part of a general trend at that time in some Christian metaphysical circles to demonstrate that anything of esoteric significance, such as the Kabbalah, must have been pointing toward the truth and supremacy of Jesus Christ. Although Pico did indeed attempt to use the Kabbalah in this fashion (efforts that were generally dismissed by traditional Jewish Kabbalists), his greater purpose was his passion for syncretism, and his conviction that all wisdom traditions must be pointing toward the same truths. In this he was one of the great pioneers of what would later be called the 'Perennial Philosophy', the idea that there is a universal wisdom expressing in a multitude of ways and forms.[15] It was in this greater sense that Pico's efforts were part of the early Renaissance and its spirit of reviving old traditions—in particular Platonism and Neoplatonism—as part of an overall search for the best of human learning. Predictably, such efforts landed Pico in hot water with Church authorities. He was forced by the pope to answer to an inquisitional tribunal and to recant some of his views. Privately he rebelled, however, and when this was found out he was arrested, and released only upon intervention by powerful family connections. (The help was short-lived; Pico died in mysterious circumstances at age 31. In 2007 his remains were exhumed and it was determined he was poisoned by arsenic, although the motive for his apparent murder is unclear due to a number of possible factors, not all related to his writings and philosophy).[16]

Nevertheless Pico's efforts bore fruit; he transmitted his understanding of Kabbalah to the German humanist scholar Johann Reuchlin (1455–1522) whom he met in Italy in 1490. Reuchlin went on to publish Latin works on the Kabbalah, the first authored by a non-Jew, including the renowned *De Art Cabalistica* (1517). A contribution of Reuchlin's, at times repeated within the circles of 19th and 20th century Western occult lodges, was the idea that the history of humanity has proceeded in three general stages, defined as follows:

1. The early, 'natural period', represented by Shaddai: שדי

2. The period of the Torah, as represented, via Moses, by the holy Tetragrammaton: יהוה

3. The period of redemption, represented by Jesus, and symbolized by the addition of the letter 'shin' to the Tetragrammaton, thus spelling 'Yehoshua' (Jesus): יהושה

The main idea was that the previously unspeakable name of God became directly knowable via Christ, thus neatly fusing the 'missing' messianic element to mystical Judaism.[17]

Modern Uses of the Kabbalah

It is no secret that the 19th century occult revival drew heavily from the Kabbalah. The origins of the fusion of Kabbalah with other Western esoteric traditions—at least in a fashion that seems to have caught on with Western esotericists and occultists—seems to originate with Cornelius Agrippa (1486–1533), who drew from it in his landmark *De Occulta Philosophia*.

Agrippa's work, some of it copied verbatim three centuries later by Francis Barrett in his influential 1801 publication *The Magus*, was a prime influence on 19th century esoteric groups, and accordingly so too was the Kabbalah. The influential French occultists Eliphas Levi

(1810–1875) and Gerard Encausse (1868–1916, more commonly known as 'Papus'), helped to popularize the Kabbalah for non-Jewish esotericists. Levi in particular made an impact via elaborating on the correspondences between the twenty-two Hebrew letters and the twenty-two trumps of the Tarot, something first discussed by the Comte de Mellet in an essay in volume 8 of Antoine Court de Gebelin's influential *Le Monde Primitif* published in 1781. In 1887 S.L. Mathers published his first edition of *The Kabbalah Unveiled*, which was based mostly on the Christian cabalist Knorr von Rosenroth's (1636–1689) *Kabbala Denudata* (1684). Von Rosenroth had followed in the footsteps of Pico and Reuchlin, attempting to demonstrate how the Kabbalah pointed toward the supremacy of Christ via its idea of Adam Kadmon (which he equated with Jesus) and the supernal triad (Kether, Chokmah, and Binah), which he connected to the Christian Holy Trinity. A.E. Waite's *The Holy Kabbalah* (1929) was a more scholarly attempt, although apparently hampered by relying on secondary sources.[18]

Not all efforts to correlate different systems of esoteric thought work; efforts to bridge Kabbalah and modern occult systems (such as the Tarot) have been widespread but criticized. Attempts to associate the Kabbalah with alchemy seem to fare even worse when closely examined, as demonstrated by Gershom Scholem in his *Kabbalah and Alchemy*, perhaps most tellingly in how these traditions regard the symbolism of gold. For alchemy gold is, of course, of prime symbolic importance, with silver being secondary. For the Kabbalah, however, this is reversed, with silver preceding gold in 'spiritual rank' according to its symbolic correspondences with the *sephira* of the Tree of Life (silver to *Chesed*, and gold to *Geburah*).[19] These may seem to be points of trivia, hair-splitting issues for scholars who have no interest in an actual practice of transformation, but in fact such scholarly accuracy is not antithetical to practical inner work. Clear experience arises out of conceptual clarity. The latter unaccompanied by applied self-examination may seem merely dry, but it provides the important foundation for deeper avenues of wisdom.

Chapter 4

Angels, Demons, and the Abyss

When it comes to the knowledge of how one may stand before God and attain to eternal life, that is truly not to be achieved by our work or power, nor to originate in our brain. In other things, those pertaining to this temporal life, you may glory in what you know, you may advance the teachings of reason, you may invent ideas of your own…but in spiritual matters, human reasoning certainly is not in order; other intelligence, other skill and power, are requisite here—something granted by God himself and revealed through his Word.[1]
—Martin Luther

To every man there are assigned two angels, the good for protection, the evil for trial.
—Caesarius of Heisterbach (c. 1180–1240)

The top quote above from Luther, one of the most influential religious innovators of the past millennia, is a classic example of how interpretation and meaning depends crucially on perspective. Luther, the founder of Protestantism and initiator of its Reformation, was speaking from an essentially spiritual perspective, yet his words are easily degraded into a mere socio-political platform, an empty and aggressive rebellion. Centuries of wars and bloodshed between Catholics and Protestants attested to that. Nevertheless the spiritual core of Luther's words is sound; indeed, it lies at the heart of the initiation process, the awakening to a consciousness that is beyond egocentric agenda.

The essential matter of spiritual realization has always lain in three key areas: **clarity of intent**, **unconscious resistance**, and **ego-transcendence**. The first, clarity of intent, is crucial. However the matter of 'free will' is ultimately seen, the fact remains that we clearly have at least the *apparent* capacity to make choices. It is a given that for one embarking on a genuine path of inner awakening the intention to realize truth has already been set. The only thing that remains to be answered is the *degree* of our clarity of intent. Regardless of our degree, however, we will meet with levels of resistance. That is to say, no matter how strong our intention to self-realize may seem, we almost certainly will encounter various roadblocks on the way. These roadblocks will seem, at times, to be actively involved in undermining our path. It will seem as if not all parts of the universe are signed up for the process of our evolution and awakening. And, more to the point, that not all parts of *us* are signed up. The result is what may be termed a 'corrupted will', which contributes toward the sabotage of our best intentions. Accordingly, it behoves us to look squarely into this resistance—and some of the esoteric roots of what modern psychology generally refers to as the 'shadow'. This chapter is devoted in part to a historical examination of the manifestations of 'shadow psychology' within the Western esoteric tradition. It may seem unclear at first as to why an examination of medieval 'shadow psychology' requires a discussion of the old magical texts ('grimoires'), since it is a given that most of these texts were concerned with the practice of manifestation (acquiring things by occult means). The connection lies in understanding the relation, and our interaction, between 'outer' and 'inner'. In the end it makes little difference whether or not 'spirits' (of whatever moral quality) exist. What matters more is understanding how our mind interacts with what they represent.

Demonology

The matter of understanding the nature of unconscious resistance or conscious opposition to our Self-realization is a notoriously murky area to wade into, if only because it is so heavily given to being usurped by the psychological process of projection. Indeed, as discussed in Chapter 5, modern psychotherapy in large part finds its origins in Early Modern-era demonology. It is not our intention here to pronounce a verdict on the matter of the existence or lack thereof of intelligences that we cannot perceive with bodily senses, and have no way of proving the existence of outside of our imaginations. Realities such as gravity, electricity, and radio waves were incomprehensible or inconceivable to peoples of past times, yet their effects are manifestly real. On the other hand, human imagination is essentially unbounded, and human psychopathology, based largely on invented and delusional worldviews, is as old and established as civilization itself. One popular author on the Western esoteric tradition, addressing the matter about whether or not 'invisible entities' are all in one's head, answered, 'Yes they are all in your head—you just have no idea how big your head is'.[2] It's a clever and concise way of resolving the conflict between dualistic and non-dualistic paradigms. In a sense, both are valid and true, the matter depending entirely on perspective. Additionally, merely reducing something to 'just imagination' means little, as imagination is immensely powerful, and indeed lies at the heart of not just the 'secret' inner schools of transformation, but is also an important element of the entire philosophic, artistic, literary, and scientific realms. Accordingly, in what follows we will be less concerned with reality vs. illusion and more with an examination of ideas as they have arisen over the centuries on the matter of how to understand so-called oppositional factors to individual awakening.

All religious and esoteric traditions map out their versions of cosmology, in which are typically included realms of light and dark populated by a vast spectrum of beings of all conceivable moral quality. Eastern traditions, even those of certain of the Buddhist schools, present elaborate cartographies of angelic and demonic forces ranging over wide dimensional expanses. The various 'Books of the Dead' (particularly the Egyptian and Tibetan versions) present elaborate descriptions of how such entities are encountered in the 'afterlife realms' upon the death of a person. Older worldwide shamanic traditions all carry myths and legends elaborating on the various roles and activities of invisible beings, including those of the adversarial kind. In the Western traditions, the earliest evidence of a structured demonology, including the usage of rituals for supplications, protection, curses, and so on, appear to be from Sumerian and Egyptian sources. The Hellenistic period (following the military successes of Alexander the Great after 332 BCE) led to a greater elaboration of these practices.

The Greek word *daimon* originally meant a 'guiding spirit' or 'lesser god', indicating that its nature was divine. It was only during the later Hellenistic period (approximately 100 BCE to 100 CE) that the word began to be associated with something of a darker nature, where *daimon* as 'evil spirit' became distinct from *theos* (a 'god'). Plato had referred to a *daimonion* (the gender neutral form) as 'something between' the divine and the mortal human.[3] These 'in between' spirits often held greater appeal for the common man and woman, bogged down with everyday survival, who had not the interest or attention to devote to abstract metaphysics or consideration of the 'highest' gods and their agendas. The common folk were more concerned with their personal aims and needs, and for these, the 'in between spirits'—the *daimons*—were more accessible.

The Greek *daimon* became the Latin word *daemon* ('spirit'). By the time this became the English word 'demon' (about 1200 CE) it had already long been associated with an 'unclean spirit', first specified in Matthew (8:31) as 'evil spirit'. The New Testament mentions several cases of *daimonia* 'entering into' people and causing physical or mental illnesses, which in turn required exorcisms. These *daimonia* were associated with ruins and places of destruction—the proverbial 'ghost towns'—long ago deserted by their human inhabitants (who had been killed or enslaved following warfare), with only the spirits remaining. These spirits were then 'demoted' to *daemons*, sentinels of the ruins, watched over by Beelzebub ('lord of the flies'). As the historian George Luck aptly put it, 'the supreme god of one culture has become the Satan of a hostile culture...and its subordinate gods have been degraded.'[4] It seems reasonably clear that the demonization of the Greek idea of a mediating spirit (*daimon*) in the late Hellenistic period was due to the influence of Christianity and its messianic focus. The proclaimed perfection of Christ automatically generated the conditions for the rise of its opposite, the 'unclean spirits'. All this seems to have been inherited from Zoroastrianism and its arch-dualism.

Solomon, the Master Magician

In the Western esoteric tradition a key figure in understanding the relationship of men to the so-called darker realms is Solomon, the legendary Jewish king (ruled circa 970–930 BCE). The Old Testament identified him as a son of David, and both Jews and Muslims (the latter of whom know him as 'Sulaiman') recognize him as one of their prophets. Solomon was renowned for his power, influence, wealth, and love of women (he was alleged to have had hundreds of wives and concubines). Modern scholars ascribe much of his reputation to historical exaggeration, but he is noteworthy for the content of the myths attached to his life. Of particular note is the passage from 1 Kings in which God awards Solomon wisdom precisely because this is what Solomon prayed for: 'Give therefore thy servant an understanding heart to judge thy people'. (1 Kings 3:4–9). Solomon asks for an understanding heart, not for mere power over others, or the fulfilment of material desires.

Over time legends built around Solomon, and he became associated with the control of demons, particularly in connection with the building of his famously elaborate temple. Some of the earliest associations of Solomon with demons appears to come from the 1st century CE Roman historian Josephus, who recorded mention of a book of spells attributed to Solomon and used by a 1st century exorcist. This was followed by the Gnostic text *The Revelation of Adam*, believed to have been written some time between 100–300 CE. The author was Greek, but the text (written in Coptic) is pseudepigraphical, that is, attributed to another, more famous author, in this case Seth, son of Adam. The passage in question is one simple sentence: 'Solomon, too, sent his army of demons to search for the female virgin…'[5] This was elaborated on in the pseudepigraphical *Testament of Solomon,* written around the same time (also by a Greek), which claims that Solomon, disturbed by the attack of a demon on one of his workers building the temple, prays for guidance. In answer he is given a ring of power—designed with the 'Seal of Solomon'—by Archangel Michael. The ring is then used to subdue the demons, including the prince of demons himself (Beelzebub). The resulting demonic army placed at Solomon's disposal enables him to construct the temple in a comparatively short seven years.

Some of the demons described in the *Testament of Solomon* are grotesque in shape and seem to be part of the origins of the 'seventy-two demons' of the so-called *Lemegeton* or *Lesser Key of Solomon,* a famed demonology grimoire written in the 17th century, based in part on Weyer's 16th century publication *Pseudomonarchia Daemonum,* and later popularized by the 1863 edition of Jacques de Plancy's *Dictionnaire Infernal* in which the demons received graphic and original artistic renderings. The connection to the *Testament of Solomon* is confirmed via the same (or similar) names of some demons appearing, such as Asmodeus (first mentioned in the biblical *Book of Tobit*), the demon associated with 'lust', or what would be called in modern psychological language 'psycho-sexual disorders'. Many of these demons had names that underwent changes over time, or were associated with more than one name, and so attempting to cross-reference the various catalogues of demons can be confusing. An interesting example is the demon listed in the *Lemegeton* as 'Astaroth', which is essentially a corruption of the Greek name of the Mediterranean goddess Astarte, which in turn had connections to the older Egyptian deities Sekhmet and Isis. History is generally crafted by conquerors and victors; a good example being many of the Gnostic texts, known only via the polemical writings of early Christian church fathers. Many of the 'demons' of Middle-Age grimoires were the re-shaped deities of older, vanquished cultures.

The *Testament of Solomon* provided detailed information on the names of principal demons as well as the names of the angels to control them, in addition to three dozen 'lesser demons' that are attributed to various illnesses and diseases. The associating of demons with misfortune and illness is an essential part of primitive forms of animism, the belief that all things have 'souls', i.e., a semblance of an individual intelligence that causes them to do certain things. This belief lies behind the ancient practice of supplicating to gods, using elaborate protection rituals or symbols, or attributing misfortune to spirits with ill intent. It is, essentially, the process of personifying cause and effect. (Modern science has served to strip away this personification, but in so doing has incurred the shadow-debt of materialism, i.e., the tendency to view the universe as lifeless and mechanical, and therefore to be manipulated solely for our purposes). Reference to Solomon and demons was also made in the Gnostic text *On the Origin of the World*, part of the Nag Hammadi cache discovered in Egypt in 1945:

> Thus, when the prime parent of chaos saw his son Sabaoth and the glory that he was in, and perceived that he was greatest of all the authorities of chaos, he envied him. And having become wrathful, he engendered Death out of his death: and he (viz., Death) was established over the sixth heaven, for Sabaoth had been snatched up from there. And thus the number of the six authorities of chaos was achieved. Then Death, being androgynous, mingled with his (own) nature and begot seven androgynous offspring. These are the names of the male ones: Jealousy, Wrath, Tears, Sighing, Suffering, Lamentation, and Bitter Weeping. And these are the names of the female ones: Wrath, Pain, Lust, Sighing, Curse, Bitterness, and Quarrelsomeness. They had intercourse with one another, and each one begot seven, so that they amount to forty-nine androgynous demons. Their names and their effects you will find in the Book of Solomon.[6]

The 'magic books' (grimoires) that became such a key part of Middle-Age Western occultism had their roots in the Solomonic legends (which included a strong Arabic influence) as well as Hermetic, Neoplatonic, and Kabbalistic magic. There were, in all, perhaps two dozen late-antiquity, medieval, Renaissance, and Early Modern-era grimoires of repute, most still well known to occultists of modern times. A listing and description of the more important ones is given in Appendix III.

Magic within the Medieval Church

Religion and magic have never been easily separated. A well established fact is that magical practices were not always clearly distinguishable from rituals and ceremonies within the Catholic Church. The 16th century Protestant Reformation included complaints about the magical rites and 'anti-Christian' conjurations practiced by the Catholic clergy. Many of the popes were branded as conjurors; for example, Protestant reformers claimed that the eighteen popes from 999 to 1085 CE had all been sorcerers and conjurers (beginning with Pope Sylvester II who headed the Catholic Church from 999 to 1003 CE; Sylvester had been a scholarly and bookish pope who after his death became the subject of all sorts of fantastic legends about his studies of Islamic magic and alleged pacts with the Devil). Daniel Defoe referred to the papacy as 'one entire system of anti-Christian magic'.[7] Martin Luther himself had identified the papacy as the Antichrist.

These were of course Protestant polemics, but as far as the usage of magic was concerned, were far from groundless. Keith Thomas, in his magisterial study *Religion and the Decline of Magic*, outlined a number of Catholic practices that were essentially indistinguishable from magic.[8] For example, the very issue of miracles vs. magic was an ongoing matter, in that the power of the Church came in large part from its proclaimed monopoly on saints and their miraculous powers—although when one examined the nature of these powers claimed, they differed in no way from those ascribed to the magician or shaman of antiquity (predicting the future, controlling the weather, providing protection from danger and healing for sickness, and so forth). Another good example lay in the protective symbols known as 'amulets', such as the *Agnus Dei* ('lamb of God' in the form of a small wax cake), which was supposed to provide protection against the Devil or all other sorts of prosaic dangers. Amulets are, of course (along with talismans) common objects in the magical practices of many cultures. In addition, the Catholic Mass and Host were replete with magical symbolism and meaning, thinly veiled under the supposition that these were different from common magical rites and tools in that they were 'divine' in purpose. But the end result was the same: over time the priest carrying out the rites was regarded as more than a mere intermediary to God; he and his Church carried all the importance and power as the feared and respected witch-doctor did for a primitive tribe. This was even reflected in the whole idea of 'excommunication', which arguably was simply a more sophisticated form of the magical 'curse'.

It is a fact that the vast majority of the witchcraft persecutions occurred between 1200 and 1750 CE. The fact that this period of time corresponds roughly with the publication of the significant magical grimoires outlined in Appendix III is noteworthy. This was likely due to several large-scale factors. From about 1250 to 1600 a general belief in the Devil was widespread across Europe—but not just a passive Devil. On the contrary, this Devil was viewed as very active, part of which included using a network of agents to spread his business. These agents were understood to be the 'witches'. That this 'Devil' and his 'witches' were a scapegoat for deeper social issues is clear. The Black Death (an earlier version of the Bubonic Plague) decimated the population of Europe from 1347–1350 (as much as 45 percent of the population was wiped out). Additional plagues and numerous wars ravaged the continent for the next three centuries, culminating in the Thirty Years War between Catholics and Protestants (1618–1648), which engulfed Europe and resulted in millions of deaths. In this climate of struggle and despair, prior to the beginning of the 'Age of Reason' (circa 1650–1700), it was not some anomaly to believe in the Devil, demons, witches, and black magic; rather, it was absolutely the norm. Even the educated classes only rarely expressed doubt about such matters. During these times and up until the scientific revolution of the 18th century, 'truth' was not ascertained via a Cartesian distinction between mind and object, close observation, or experimental verification; it was maintained via obedience to doctrine, i.e., via precedent based on what earlier authorities had established. (Technically, this is called 'concept affirmation', as opposed to 'referential accuracy', and indicates the power of transmitted beliefs and dogmas to overpower simple observation of what may be under one's nose). This blind obedience to the previously written word is what, in part, fuelled the transmission of magical grimoires for centuries.

In the popular mind the essence of magic, in contrast to religion (with which it overlaps in ways too numerous to detail here) has always centered on the question of human will. Religion has traditionally been thought to be based on a subservient relationship with the agencies of the divine, including the 'most High'. Personal issues (or greater matters) are supposedly pressed via supplication, prayer, and the commitment to a moral life with the expectation of some sort of benefit (or, perhaps more bluntly, reward). Magic, in short, has been understood as the practice of attempting to take matters into one's own hands. At the crudest level this seems to amount to employing a series of rituals that will in turn draw forth certain energies that can then be directed—a cause and effect process not much different from a simple business transaction. *Do this to get that.* Conventional religious ethics teaches that this is soon revealed to be an empty process, accomplishing little more than showing the one who attempts it what his actual (usually base) motivation is, and how indeed, it is not really possible to 'get something for nothing'.

These, however, are mostly superficial views, based on an artificial distinction between 'religion' and 'magic' that has been reinforced by religious authorities with a vested interest. The historian Morton Smith, author of the controversial 1978 publication *Jesus the Magician,* summed it up concisely:

> When we compare avowedly religious texts and reports of religious practices with the texts of the magical papyri and the practices they prescribe, we find the same goals stated and the same means used. For instance, spells for the destruction of an enemy are commonly supposed to be magical, but there are many in the Psalms. The cliché, that the religious man petitions the gods while the magician tries to compel them, is simply false. The magical papyri contain many humble prayers, and the black mass was an outgrowth of Christian beliefs that credited a priest with the power practically to compel his god to present himself on the altar.[9]

In the context of actual esoteric practices such as that of magical evocation, as a general rule of thumb for one who seeks some sort of material gain or to win the heart of another, etc., they are better off attempting to gain these via direct and honest means. Employing the use of 'demons' to achieve profane desires seems to amount to little more than hiring an enforcer to close a business deal, or using a drug to hypnotize the potential lover we may wish to conquer or capture. In this baser regard ceremonial magic is mostly a sophisticated form of manipulation, a brazen attempt to control invisible realms prior to having understood the deeper issue. (And unquestionably ceremonial magic has been used in such a fashion since the beginning, much as how alchemy has always been populated by 'puffers', those solely concerned with material matters such as the production of gold). However, there is an exception to this 'rule of thumb', and it lies in a fuller understanding of the entire shadow realm, including so-called demonic energies and their apparent powers.

The key lies in understanding our relationship to these energies. As the medieval period transitioned into the Renaissance and beyond, there was a growing realization that magic involved more than merely mastering a sophisticated type of manipulation. The piece to the puzzle that had, for all intents and purposes, been lost for many centuries—but that seems to have been understood in ancient times—was the *spiritual state* of the magician. The state of mind and level of consciousness of the operator of the magic himself will influence his perception. This is vital to understand, because when dealing with so-called spirits, perception amounts to everything. (By 'perception' we are, of course, not referring to visual acuity, but rather to psychological and spiritual perspective). A key to understanding this idea is found in the Bible, Acts 19:15–17, which describes a scene in which two exorcists attempt to cast out a demon merely by using the names of Jesus and Paul:

> And the evil spirit answered and said, Jesus I know, and Paul I know; but who are ye? And the man in whom the evil spirit was leaped on them, and overcame them, and prevailed against them, so that they fled out of that house naked and wounded. And this was known to all the Jews and Greeks also dwelling at Ephesus; and fear fell on them all, and the name of the Lord Jesus was magnified. (KJV)

The demon replied contemptuously that while he knew Jesus and Paul, he did not recognize these two exorcists—'these names I know, but who are *you*?' It's a powerful metaphor regarding the importance of attaining a degree of realization prior to engaging with the lower realms. Words of 'power' are ineffective if the one using them has not embodied sufficient insight. The demon beating up the two exorcists who were merely repeating words is apt symbolism for the limitations of empty ritual devoid of actual inner transformation. (This is the probable esoteric meaning underlying the third Biblical commandment 'not to take the name of the Lord God in vain').

It has been pointed out by some hard-line post-modern magicians such as Joseph Lisiewski that all of the 'old magic' (based on the Middle-Age grimoires) was concerned with producing actual results in the material world, whereas all modern traditions (beginning roughly with the Golden Dawn of the late 19th century) are heavily psychologized, that is, able to produce changes in consciousness but ineffective for causing demonstrable change in one's outer life. While this may be a difficult assertion to prove, Lisiewski does have a point, and it relates to some of the essential differences between high magic and mysticism.

The goal of all high magic is sometimes reduced to the idea that it is the same as the goal of the mystic: that is, it is not to *acquire* light, but rather to *become* light. This is, however, something of an oversimplification. In fact, there are differences between the paths of high magic and mysticism. High magic derives in part from the Zoroastrian (and later the Hermetic) worldview, which contains the essential point that the magician contributes directly to the spiritual evolution of the cosmos. Mysticism (especially Oriental mysticism) is based on renunciation; that is, leaving the world alone, and quietly withdrawing so as to direct one's energies toward one's spiritual emancipation. That does not mean that a mystic cannot be a 'bodhisattva', i.e., a teacher directly helping others or even a social activist; but even then, what the Eastern mystic is aiding in is in helping those who seek wisdom to extricate themselves from the illusory nature of the world. The magus has a different aim: not to escape the world, or even to see it as illusory, but to aid in 'growing it' by growing him or herself at the same time. The idea of 'growing' the world, or being actively engaged with it in some fashion, may seem antithetical to the stereotypical image of the solitary magician conjuring energies via complex and recondite practices. Indeed, the very basis of the 'esoteric' traditions has been the inner life, and all too often, practices that have been condemned or even suppressed by organized religion. But the underlying philosophy, rooted in Zoroaster and Hermeticism, remains the idea that by growing individually we are directly contributing to the evolution of the world and the universe. So while the magician seeks, like the mystic, to 'become light', he is also concerned with the transmission of his light, the *sharing* of it with the world.[10]

The relationship between the conscious self (represented by the magician) and the shadow-energies (represented by the demons) carries highly meaningful psycho-spiritual symbolism and is important to understand. The key piece to magical evocation is to understand the effect the process has on the magician, not the effect it has on the 'demon'. The energy evoked, the demon summoned, regardless of their ontological reality or lack thereof, will create a feedback system in which the magician (depending on their degree of sensitivity) experiences a shift in consciousness. This 'shift' will involve a movement of perspective as it is normally generated by consciousness. This 'movement' or 'shift', though often very subtle, reveals elements of the magician's character to himself, which then gives him the chance to be accountable for them. The 'demon' encountered corresponds to an unconscious complex in the mind that represents both the 'block' in the magician's inner progress, as well as the means by which he can liberate himself from it. That these demons appear to be archetypal energies, beyond the scope of our mere personal identity—that is, they belong to Jung's 'collective unconscious', rather than our personal unconscious—only makes their energies more powerful and potentially instructive. As John Dee, the great Elizabethan scholar and magician, had been warned, if he wanted to secure 'outer treasures' he would have to consort with demons, precisely because 'they are the lords of this world'.[11] So too, we cannot avoid our shadow energies, as they are largely the architects of the more difficult elements of civilization.

Roberto Assagioli's psycho-spiritual map is useful here. The sections of the psyche he designated as:

1. The Lower Unconscious
2. The Middle Unconscious
3. The Higher Unconscious.
4. The Field of Consciousness.

5. The Conscious Self, 'I'.
6. The Transpersonal Self.
7. The Collective Unconscious.

The work lies in forming a bridge between points 5 and 6—that is, between the Conscious Self, and the Transpersonal Self (another name for the Holy Guardian Angel or *atman*)—with the understanding that in order for the link to be formed, we must pass through the realms of the unconscious. Once this link has been established (though the quality and strength of the link will, of course, vary greatly, depending on the maturity and readiness of the operator) it is then possible to form a 'working agreement' with an energy from realm 7 (the Collective Unconscious), wherein archetypal energies such as so-called demons reside. Realms 1, 2, and 3 can then receive the new energies that lead to further purification and growth, and a greater connectedness between all realms.[12]

The Renaissance placed greater emphasis on the development of the individual, drawing in part as it did on the individualism of the ancient Greeks. It has been noted by historians that some magicians of the 16th century and beyond were influenced by sources such as the *The Spiritual Exercises of St. Ignatius* (by the Spanish knight and mystic Ignatius of Loyola, 1491–1556, who founded the Society of Jesus—the Jesuits—in 1534, and was canonized in 1622).[13] A key to Ignatius's method involved the development of discernment, how to read the qualities of the various forms of spiritual energy. It amounted to a type of Western Yoga, with the main purpose being to direct one's personal energy toward the impersonal realization of one's highest and best destiny on earth (as opposed to squandering energy in the repetitive urge to satiate base personal desires).

Western demonology has some interesting parallels with similar Eastern practices. A good case in point is the legendary 8th century CE tantric Buddhist adept Padmasambhava. Renowned as both an enlightened mystic and a master magician, Padmasambhava is said to have controlled and bound demons to serve his cause, that being the transmission and entrenchment of Buddhism in Tibet. Padmasambhava is the Eastern parallel of Solomon, whose employ of demons to build the Temple is a good metaphor for the psychological process of integrating the shadow-elements of the unconscious mind and utilizing their energies in the service of construction and creativity.

In the context of this chapter the matter of the 'spiritual dark side', regardless of the degree of obfuscations involved in its literary legacy, is important, because for the one who seeks to realize their fullest spiritual potential they must understand the nature of universal resistance that manifests in endless forms. The nature of this resistance is complex, its means and workings often unclear, and its ultimate greater purpose has long been debated. It goes beyond a mere 'study of evil' or tackling the very old philosophical question as to why evil even exists. It must ultimately involve a radical re-orientation from viewing misfortune as lying solely outside of us, in strange, frightening, unexpected and inexplicable causes and effects, to a deep understanding of our own individual capacity for destructive, hurtful, and self-sabotaging behavior.

Augustine's Influence

St. Augustine (354–430 CE), bishop, theologian, and philosopher, is renowned for the impact he made on Christian doctrine, particularly in relation to the matter of 'original sin'. Augustine's central argument was both simple and powerful. He observed and reasoned that the human being is so fundamentally flawed, so given to self-centered actions that invariably lead to suffering, that it is impossible to escape from their condition by individual efforts alone.[14] Augustine's views on demons appear to be a main source for the views echoed a millennia later by the grimoires of the Middle Ages and Renaissance, in that he maintained that these entities were real (as real as us, at any rate), and that their powers (e.g., for seeing the future, or creating desired changes for the one who forms a 'contract' with them or uses sacred words to compel them) are limited, because their knowledge of cause and effect is 'incomplete'. They are angelic in origin, of the element of the 'air' (that is, non-corporeal or 'astral'), hence they retain a semblance of power, but due to their corrupted state their capacity to influence men is only psychological, by generating various levels of illusion. Augustine's views on this matter stem in part from a dispute between two of Plotinus's famed disciples, Iamblichus and Porphyry. Iamblichus had argued that a legitimate practice of Platonic philosophy was the theurgical technique of invoking the powers of *daimons* (of the good variety) 'down' into our world so that they can be communicated with (a key element of ceremonial magic). Porphyry cast doubt on this practice, suspecting that all such activities invariably lead to some sort of deception. Augustine agreed with Porphyry, and, in an act that would alter how *daimons* would come to be seen by later theologians, declared that all *daimons* were tricksters, deceivers, and fallen spirits whose agendas could not be trusted. (He did, however, believe in the power of angels, maintaining that Moses was able to defeat the magicians of Egypt as his power derived from angelic sources, whereas the magicians employed demons). Augustine's view that the only real power of demons lies in generating confusion and illusion was the probable main source of the views of the authors of the important 12th century *Canon Episcopi*, in turn reflected in the *Malleus Maleficarum* (1486) and the *Compendium Maleficarum* (1608), these latter two being influential 'witch-hunter' and demonology texts, both of which described the powers of witches and the demons behind them as amounting to solely that of generating illusions. In short, the Devil certainly existed, but he was a consummate deceiver and trickster, nothing more.

The association of demonic power with mere appearances and illusions is an important one to note, as the entire process of Self-realization may be said to be based on the contrast between truth and illusion, or between absolute reality and mere appearance. Here we see a key point: demonic forces can be understood as psychological barriers or challenges on the way to realization. But what is the nature of these 'barriers'—to what degree are they merely projected elements of our own nature, from whence do they arise, and is there something more to the whole picture that we are missing?

Augustine's arguments on this amount to a few essential points. The first of these is that an individual's will cannot be compelled to do evil; it is rather that evil arises from within owing to a misdirection of energy, a perversion of desire. But how does this 'perversion of desire' come about? In other words, why has God granted man free will in the first place, if this free will can be corrupted from within? Augustine answered this through several arguments. His first point is that all powers of a human are intrinsically good, as they were created by God. They can be *used* wrongly, but are themselves good. He then proposes that we have three essential levels of 'bodily goods', those being the material body, the 'in between levels' (in modern psychology, the ego-mind), and the higher nature. The problem lies in the middle level, and it is at this level where the will resides. Evil is committed the moment the will 'turns away' from the divine nature within and seeks its own agenda ('sins'). The reason God grants this capacity to choose either good or evil is because without it man would have no means by which to develop righteousness.

However the problem is far from solved. Augustine proclaims that free will in and of itself is good because it is from God, and allows for a man to know himself as a child of the divine by choosing good. Nevertheless the problem of the 'movement toward evil' has still not been fully accounted for, because if God has perfect foreknowledge, he must know who will sin, and how they shall. What God fore-knows must come to pass, and therefore, anyone sinning cannot be doing so out of free will—it must have been predetermined. Augustine initially had a tentative answer for this difficult conundrum. He said that there are two levels to the matter: 1. Things happen as God foresees they will, with no interference from man's free will, and 2. Man's will is exercised, causing things to happen. In the second case, man's power and freedom to exercise choices is not removed by God's foreknowledge, and God does not cause a man to sin just by knowing that he will. In his later years Augustine was to modify this position and increasingly adopt determinism, in which God simply pre-ordained who would be able to escape the consequences of Adam's error and who would not.[15]

The main challenge to Augustine's central position that a human cannot escape their flawed condition without divine grace, came from the Celtic monk Pelagius (b. circa 354 CE), who argued that because man was made by a good God, his 'flaws' were entirely the result of his own doing and therefore could also be *reversed* by his own doing. In this Pelagius denied both original sin and the need for divine grace. His main argument was that if we can do evil by an act of individual will, then we can also reverse this by an act of individual good. In both cases, the act comes from the individual. Augustine attacked this position, holding that all 'good' comes from God, and therefore no man can be the source of a creative act of good, for that is the province of God only. Owing to the condition of man's fallen nature he is incapable of turning toward God, but rather only away from God (toward nothing, or 'evil'). And therefore, only via divine grace can a man's will be correctly directed toward good.

Pelagius rejected this, arguing that a man is more than merely an effect of Adam's original error, or a vehicle for God's grace. His position represented, in a sense, the philosophical basis of the esoteric practitioner (magician) as commonly understood, i.e., that one can attain to full spiritual development via personal effort, without resorting only to supplications for grace. In fact, however, both positions (of Augustine and Pelagius) seem to hold some truth, to be touched on below in the section on the Holy Guardian Angel and the abyss.

Christ as Magician

It has been proposed by some that the medieval and Renaissance grimoires were compiled largely by low-level Christian clerics who had access to the manuscripts of antiquity that had been safeguarded in the monasteries during the so-called Dark Ages (from the collapse of the Roman empire to the late medieval period, circa 475–1350 CE). As touched on above, magic was part of the Catholic Christian tradition. Early medieval European religious culture brimmed with a confusing mix of pagan and Christian symbols, many used as talismans (magical devices to attract good fortune) or amulets (protective symbols). For example, there is a certain parallel between the Catholic practice of supplicating saints and the magical practice of evoking demons, in that both involve the attempt to gain practical benefits via affiliation with a supernatural agent. The Catholic may argue that their prayers are based on affiliation with God, but the magician in his mind is doing the same thing, i.e., performing purification practices and prayers designed to align himself with God prior to consorting with the dark side. Perhaps the only significant difference appears to be that the magician seeks some practical gain via direct means, whereas the religious supplicant would be more inclined to repress their personal desires in the name of a moral injunction.

Be that as it may, there has always been the temptation to classify Christ as merely another magician of the kind relatively common in the Mediterranean world of his time. Morton Smith's work (cited above) was an effort of considerable scholarly weight—albeit necessarily conjectural—that argued for the probability that Jesus was in the tradition of a pagan magician, rather than a rabbi who was merely used as a vehicle to express God's miracles. The difference between a 'magical' operation and a 'miracle' may seem at first glance trivial—both, after all, appear to be brought about by supernatural means, that is, by a cause and effect process that is beyond our ability to detect or comprehend. But the public relations difference is decidedly not trivial, and it this difference that was never lost upon theologians or Church authorities. It is the same difference that was claimed to lay between the old Egyptian magicians and Moses, first highlighted in their 'duel of magic' in the important Book of Exodus:

> Now the LORD spoke to Moses and Aaron, saying, "When Pharaoh speaks to you, saying, 'Work a miracle,' then you shall say to Aaron, 'Take your staff and throw it down before Pharaoh, that it may become a serpent.'" So Moses and Aaron came to Pharaoh, and thus they did just as the LORD had commanded; and Aaron threw his staff down before Pharaoh and his servants, and it became a serpent. Then Pharaoh also called for the wise men and the sorcerers, and they also, the magicians of Egypt, did the same with their secret arts. For each one threw down his staff and they turned into serpents. But Aaron's staff swallowed up their staffs. Yet Pharaoh's heart was hardened, and he did not listen to them, as the LORD had said. (Exodus 7:8–13, KJV).

This was followed by the scene in which Moses and Aaron, as directed by YHWH, caused the waters of the Nile to turn to blood, a feat which was then matched by the Egyptian magicians. This same issue of attempting to distinguish between miracles and magic followed with Solomon, whose use of a magic ring to control and compel demons was a classic element of sorcery, but who was also guided by the archangel Michael as directed by God, which suggests that Solomon was merely a vehicle for miracles. Therefore, magic and religion are impossible to truly separate in the case of Solomon.

The tradition of key prophets or mystics receiving 'divine powers' from 'above', and exercising these powers in ways that seem identical to lower forms of magic as performed by magicians (at times aided by demons), is longstanding and ubiquitous. In addition to Moses and Solomon, there are of course the events of Jesus' life, including transforming substances, walking on water, stilling storms, changing shape, performing exorcisms, raising Lazarus, and so forth. (This latter feat, raising the dead, is sometimes cited as proof of the supreme power of Christ, and yet even this is not unique in religious lore, being claimed, for instance, by followers of the

Tantric mystic Padmasambhava).[16] The Greek hero Jason, leader of the Argonauts searching for the Golden Fleece, received the means of a love spell from the goddess Aphrodite; the Egyptian deity Isis taught magic to select mortals, and so on. The difficulties in properly defining the difference between magic and miracles, or more specifically, between the essence of magic and religion, are so marked that some modern scholars conclude that the matter will probably never be resolved.[17]

That said, the scribes of the New Testament were not uncertain about the difference between 'magic' and 'miracles' as they pertained to Christ. The synoptic gospels (Mark, Matthew, Luke) all emphasized the point that the power of Jesus came directly from God. A good example of this is the scene in which Jesus, after exorcizing a demon out of a man, is accused of wielding the power of darkness (in this case of Beelzebub, the 'prince of demons') to control demons.[18] This accusation against Jesus amounted to the same claim made in the *Testament of Solomon* (written perhaps a century after the synoptic gospels), i.e., that Solomon used Beelzebub to control the demonic hordes—but with the blessing of Archangel Michael. In the gospels Jesus denies that he is using any sort of demonic force to do his work, but rather that he is a direct vehicle for God. (This is accompanied, in Matthew, by his famous militant line 'he who is not with me, is against me'). The differences between Solomon and Jesus seem more a matter of theological interpretation. The similarities seem to be clearer. Additionally, there is the problematic sequence of events described in Matthew 8:28-34, where Jesus bids a legion of demons to leave the bodies of two men and enter a herd of pigs. Once this happens, the pigs immediately rush into a lake and drown. It has been argued by some that the story offers evidence that Jesus not only allowed the herd of swine to be possessed, but in effect caused it to happen—an action that could only be attributed to a powerful magician or shaman.[19] Perhaps even more difficult to explain away are the miraculous feats of the disciples as detailed in The Acts of the Apostles, including the scene where Peter condemns an early Christian who has betrayed a code, upon which man suddenly falls down dead (Acts, 5:5). Peter can also heal others and cast out demons merely by the contact with his shadow (Acts 5:15-16). These are powers classically ascribed to great shamans. There are even suggestions of outright sorcery in some of the apocryphal gospels, such as the Infancy Gospel of Thomas, in which Jesus as a young boy is alleged to have had powers comparable to a powerful sorcerer, including killing other boys, via spoken curses, who had offended him (although to be fair, the Infancy Gospel was written over a century after Jesus had died; it also contains stories of him healing and bringing people back from the dead, although not, evidently, the ones he killed).

The main early critic of Jesus was probably Celsus, the 2nd century CE Greek who wrote *The True Word*, an early polemic against Christianity. Celsus had argued that Christ was originally trained by magicians in Egypt, thereafter returning to his homeland, where he combined his occult prowess with a philosophy based on answering the prophecies of Judaism. The work of Celsus is known only via the writings of the early Church father Origen, who used them as a vehicle in which to argue the legitimacy of Jesus as Son of God. As Morton Smith pointed out, the most potentially damaging accusation against Jesus was that his 'miracles' were essentially no different from the magic feats performed by relatively low-grade magicians (most of whom were trained in Egypt). Origen attempted to refute the accusation as follows:

> You can see that by these (arguments Celsus) practically grants that magic is effective...and things told of Jesus would be similar...if Celsus had first shown that Jesus did them as the magicians do, merely for the sake of showing off their powers. But as things are, none of the goetes (sorcerers), by the things he does, calls the spectators to moral reformation, or teaches the fear of God to those astounded by the show.[20]

Origen's assessment of magicians as 'show offs' reminds one of the common street magician of current times in, say, India, but he is clearly dismissive of the possibility that a magician might be aligned with a supreme spiritual source. Nevertheless Origen was driving at a legitimate point, even if his approach was at times confused and limited by his political agenda to promote the supreme divinity of Jesus and the Church.

All of this suggests that, at a certain level of distinction, there *is* a defining feature in question between 'magic' and 'miracles'—however it applies less to the categories of 'magic' and 'miracles' (or religion, for that matter) than it does to the *consciousness* of the magician or the mystic or the prophet. This defining feature relates to the topics of angelology, the Holy Guardian Angel and the Abyss (see below).

Freud's Insight

In some respects it was Freud who understood the master key for resolving the psychological problem of the split between 'higher' and 'lower' natures, between the so-called conscious self and the 'demonic forces' of the unconscious. The matter comes down to the crucial question of *distance*. Modern science is based on the idea of an observer (the subject) achieving distance from what he observes (the object). It is precisely because of this distance that he can make objective observations about things and arrive at conclusions that are not distorted by his biases and agendas—a process that became the basis of the scientific method. As pointed out by David Bakan, Freud's great genius lay in penetrating to matters previously held as completely lacking in 'distance' (i.e., far too personal) in such a way as to manage a marked degree of objective observation and reasonable interpretation (beginning with an analysis of his own unconscious).[21] Freud's whole work boiled down to bringing unconscious material into consciousness. The entire practice of magic may be said to be based on harnessing the power of the unconscious realms by bridging them to the conscious mind. Freud was attempting to bring the necessary 'objective distance' into such a practice and thus adding into the mix the crucial element of conscious comprehension. He was trying to make the cause and effect mechanisms of the mind more clear (in contrast to the practice of merely repeating a method because 'others have done it before' or some supposed authority had proclaimed it so).

The image of the Devil becomes a key to the resolution of inner guilt that lies behind most neurosis and unhappiness in life. Bakan explained it as follows:

> Freud took [the Devil] as indicative of forces within the individual by which the 'suppressed material finds methods and means of forcing its way into consciousness'. In the religious allegory, God holds the content unconscious, and the Devil is the counterforce which renders the material conscious...continuing the allegory, an alliance of the ego with the Devil was necessary to make it possible to achieve the requisite 'distance'. Thus by permitting successful intervention of the Devil the person wins 'distance'. Hence, paradoxically, the Devil must cause its own destruction. By bringing the demonic into the light, the demonic is stripped of its demonic character.[22]

Essentially, 'God' is the punitive, containing force, and the demonic is the rebellious element. By 'conjuring' the demonic into consciousness, both images (of God and demon) are seen as primitive (even infantile) constructs, with their very real creative energies freed up to be both utilized and enjoyed. The 'demon' is a complex, an energy that bears the signature of our unfinished business in life. By summoning it into the light of consciousness, we begin the process of untangling the unfinished business—a process that begins with the crucial step of summoning the willingness to face into the matter once and for all.

Angelology

An essential idea in all esoteric teachings is the notion of transcending identification with form. Consciousness that is identified with form (typically, a body) is thought to be operating under a type of spell or delusion, believing itself to be limited; that is, defined solely by its form. The Biblical legend of the Golden Calf (from Exodus) spoke to this, an idol made by Aaron to satisfy the spiritual needs of the Israelites when Moses was on Mt. Sinai. The Golden Calf was supposed to represent the material form of God, thus becoming a kind of supreme example of a 'false idol' (as God was understood to be beyond both the material universe and any kind of form). The *Qliphoth* of Kabbalism speaks to this as well; the word itself means 'husk' or 'shell' and relates to the idea that by defining itself as a particular form, it serves to conceal the divine that lays within.

The bridge between the worlds of dense matter and the pure formlessness of the divine has often been represented by immaterial spirits, in particular, angels. (The word derives from the Greek *angelos*, 'messenger'). According to traditional theology, angels are believed to lack material form, but to be capable of assuming form via manipulating the 'air element'. Because they are beyond materiality, they are beyond temporal constraints as well, thus being able to move through conventional space and time in ways inconceivable to humans. Despite such abilities they are considered to have limitations, both in terms of knowledge, and in terms of their ability to experience individuality or passion (uniquely human traits). According to the lore of angelology, there are several essential levels in the angelic hierarchy, with the following scheme (deriving from Thomas Aquinas, and further back, from the late 5th century CE Christian mystic Pseudo-Dionysius the Areopagite and his *De Coelesti Hierarchia*) commonly cited:

1. *Seraphim*. These are generally considered the highest class (their mention is first found in Isaiah); their name literally means 'the

burning ones', thus associating them with light, heat, and fire (the supreme element of alchemy). Seraphim are believed to surround the 'throne of God' and continuously pay homage to him with a perpetually burning love and devotion. Some sources regard Metatron as a Seraphim, as well as Michael, and Satan before his fall. Their light is believed to be blinding, even for other angels. Isaiah and *Enoch II* ascribe four faces and six wings to Seraphim.

2. *Cherubim*. This order of angels is mentioned more frequently in the Old Testament (and indeed the Cherubim are the first angels to be mentioned, as in Genesis 3:22—they guarded the Tree of Life and Eden with flaming swords). These are the beings who 'drive' the Merkabah, or 'chariot of God'. Their name is Assyrian in origin, and they were originally regarded as guardian spirits. Cherubim are sometimes confused with the 'Putti' of Baroque art, the term for a chubby infant (usually male) often depicted with wings and associated with God's presence. In fact the Cherubim of angelic lore are powerful entities associated with wisdom, knowledge, and regal animals such as lions and eagles.

3. *Thrones*. According to Pseudo-Dionysius, Thrones are ranked third in the 'first triad'. They are a class of angelic entity associated with justice, often imagined as bearing many eyes, and closely connected to the Cherubim. Thrones are mentioned by name in the New Testament, Colossians 1:16.

4. *Dominions*. According to lore this class of angels (also called 'Dominations') preside over lower classes of angels, and are the guardians of nations. The name is associated with 'lordship', and thus with an important 'chain of command' function.

5. *Virtues*. This class of angels is sometimes placed second in the second triad (or sixth overall). The Virtues are connected to the occurrence of miracles, as well as the qualities of grace and valor.

Virtues were believed to have escorted Christ on his ascension. They are also associated with the movement of cosmic bodies and the overall functioning of the universe.

6. *Potentates (Powers).* According to Pseudo-Dionysius, Potentates are a type of warrior or guardian angel involved in counteracting the activities of demonic forces, and are involved in overseeing the 'balance of power' as it plays out on Earth.

7. *Principalities (Rulers).* This order of angels are believed to be 'protectors of religion' and to function as guardian angels and spirit guides for leaders on Earth. They are also believed to inspire advances in art and science, and in general to be very involved in Earthly affairs and the spiritual evolution of humans.

8. *Archangels.* 'Archangel' means 'first angel'. The Book of Revelation makes mention of 'seven' particular angels who 'stand before God' (8:2). The names of these seven vary, depending on the tradition, although a commonly cited source is the Book of Enoch, where they are identified as Michael, Raphael, Gabriel, Uriel, Raguel, Seraqael, and Haniel. Other sources suggest that 'archangel' is a designation for any higher than the lowest class of angels, while the seven listed are in fact a distinct group of supreme archangels (Seraphim) as Michael, for one, is sometimes identified as. Typically, archangels and angels are associated with Judeo-Christian faith, but in reality there is little mention of angels in the Bible, and even less of archangels. For example, nowhere in the Old Testament are archangels explicitly referred to; only twice are they mentioned in the New Testament; and only one is named, Michael. The name of Gabriel is also mentioned, but he is never explicitly identified as an archangel. The passages mentioning archangels occur in 1 Thessalonians 4:16, 'For the Lord himself shall descend from heaven with a shout, and the voice of the archangel, and with the trump of God: and the dead in Christ shall rise first' (KJV). And in Jude 1:9,

'Yet Michael the archangel, when contending with the devil he disputed about the body of Moses, durst not bring against him a railing accusation, but said, The Lord rebuke thee' (KJV).

Those passages sound obscure when not put in context. The first, in 1 Thessalonians, is the voice of Paul writing to the Jesus-communities in Thessalonica around the year 50 CE. He is referring to the future return of Jesus in resurrected form, and in particular, how those who are already dead and buried will in fact be the first to be 'raised up' by Christ upon his return. The dead who will be raised up will be those who are dead *in Christ*, i.e., those who had spiritually connected with Jesus prior to their death. The implication is that the death and resurrection of Christ brought a new spiritual dispensation to Earth, which did not go into effect until after his resurrection. The 'archangel'—and in the passage it is not specified which archangel—is thus associated with a *voice* that portends a rebirth for those connected to Christ. The idea is that only those who truly decide and who are truly committed to realizing their highest nature (via Christ) will hear the voice of the archangel; that is, hear God's message. The second passage is a letter from Jude (Judas Thaddeus, one of the twelve apostles, not to be confused with Judas Iscariot). In it he is warning a Jesus-community of the dangers of corruption from within their own community. The passage referring to Archangel Michael is about a battle between Michael and the Devil over the body of Moses, and how Michael refused to openly curse the Devil, instead saying only that 'God will deal with you'. This can be interpreted esoterically as a teaching about how true power derives only from alignment with our highest spiritual potential (God).

Michael is also mentioned in the Book of Revelation (12:7) and in Daniel (10:13, 21; 12:1), though not with the title 'Archangel'; though it is assumed by most Bible scholars that this is Archangel Michael. He is also mentioned in some apocryphal texts like the Book of Enoch. Gabriel is first mentioned (without the Archangel title) in Daniel (8:15-17). He also appears in the Talmud, and is believed in

Judaism to have been the voice of the burning bush who spoke to Moses. He is also the angel of the 'Annunciation', where Mary is told of her coming pregnancy with Jesus. The Book of Enoch has Gabriel as the left hand of God. Islam credits Gabriel with revealing the Koran to Mohammad. The idea of archangels (and angels) in general appears to have entered into Judaism via the influence of Persian Zoroastrianism, during the period of the exile of Jews around the first half of the 6th century BCE in Babylon.

9. *Angels*. This class of angelic entities is understood to represent the 'common' angels, who are especially involved in Earthly affairs. The historical origin of the idea of angels is not entirely clear, but there is evidence of winged spirits in many of the ancient religious cults of the Near East, where the spirits of dead relatives were often imagined as winged, hovering over still living relatives on Earth, and then soaring off into the higher realms. Angels are regarded commonly as messengers and were thought to 'fly' between the higher worlds and the Earth. Of course we understand now that Earth is not a flat plain with higher celestial worlds 'above' it, but is rather a globe, with space all around it; this space is essentially a vacuum, lacking atmosphere, in which wings would be useless. The wings of angels are therefore perhaps best understood as esoteric metaphors for the process of intra-psychic communication or even inter-dimensional interfacing. The Spanish Torah scholar Maimonides (1135-1204) arrived at an eminently sensible interpretation of angels, regarding them as natural forces that shape the universe. He reasoned that the universe operates on cause and effect, and that God does not affect things *directly*, but rather by intermediary forces. To cite one example understood only recently by modern astrophysics, we are all 'made' of stardust. This is because our sun is a second generation star, itself created from the remnants of a previous supernova (star that exploded). Material from this supernova cooled and condensed to form our sun and the planets. Thus, the creation of Earth was *indirectly* brought about by

previous causes. Life on Earth arose from chemical combinations that were already present as part of Earth. And so forth. Hence all life on Earth—including us—derives from star matter. Thus even if God is assumed to be behind the creation of Earth, he did not do it directly, but via the previous creation of star matter. This example shows how life itself is a result of previous causal forces, 'stepped down', as it were, from stellar forces (exploding stars). According to Maimonides, angels are not entities with form, they represent particular *forces* that cause things to be. They are, in a sense, symbols of, or interactive agents for, the process of cause and effect. According to this line of thought, archangels would represent the 'highest' forms of cause and effect, i.e., the highest and best choices we can make.

The Holy Guardian Angel and the Abyss

The above angelic hierarchy is but one system; the Jewish hierarchy is of course different, as is the Islamic, and those of Eastern systems. Angelic hierarchy in general is derivative of the idea of the 'Great Chain of Being', arising largely from Plato and elaborated by Plotinus (see Chapter 9). The lore of angelology can be confusing, perhaps nowhere better shown than in attempts to identify the so-called 'fallen angel', Satan. He has been confused with Lucifer (by misunderstanding Isaiah 14:12), and variously identified as any number of names (Mastema, Belial, Duma, Gadreel, Azazel, Samael, etc.).[23] The name 'Satan' derives from the Hebrew *ha-Satan*, meaning 'adversary', from the noun *satan* meaning 'to obstruct or oppose'; in the Old Testament it is a title or designation for an office, with the angel inhabiting the position not automatically assumed to be apostate. In the important *Book of Job*, 'the satan' is the prosecutor, a 'son of God' who is subservient and dutifully carries out the task of testing Job to reveal his deeper quality. It was only in the New Testament that Satan takes on a more malevolent form, clearly in contrast to the spiritual perfection of Jesus. Christianity inherited the stark dualism of Zoroastrianism, in which the 'forces of light and darkness' are deeply polarized (an element lacking in Judaism and the Old Testament, where Yahweh is presented at times as morally ambiguous, and Satan is little more than a hired gun prosecutor).

Of particular interest here is the mysterious 'angel of the abyss' called Abaddon (also known via his Greek name, Appollyon, deriving from Apollo—indicative of the dual, shamanistic nature of this angel as both 'lord of light' and 'angel of destruction'). The Hebrew word *abaddon* means 'place of destruction'. He has been variously characterized as another name for Satan, another name for Jesus, or as any number of versions representing something in between. In the Book of Revelation he is the 'angel of the abyss' (9:11), and the angel that binds Satan for a millennia (20). As a mythic symbol Abaddon is a key to understanding the idea of the abyss, and how it becomes perverted into a symbol of death to be feared, when spiritually it represents something quite different (the death of egocentric consciousness).

The English term 'abyss' derives from the Latin *abyssus* (bottomless pit), itself deriving from the Greek terms *a* (without) and *byssos* (bottom). In our material world the idea of a 'foundation' holds primal power and meaning. We stand on the Earth, held in place by a mysterious 'force' called gravity (itself a product of other factors). Our planet is immersed in vast (perhaps infinite) space. The sense of things being 'held in place' is entirely an appearance, a kind of perceptual trick. Psychologically, however, we rely on this perceptual trick in order to maintain a semblance of solidity and safety. The appearance of solidity, of being 'grounded' and having an Earth under our feet, gives us the foundation needed to venture forth in other ways. This applies to instinctual levels as well as to emotional and interpersonal levels.

When the ground is taken away, the 'carpet pulled' from under our feet, we are confronted with a clash between instinctual and spiritual perspectives. The instinctual response is fear, and in many respects it is the same fear that is encountered when we venture forth spiritually and seek to realize what is outside of our ego-boundaries. This same fear arises in intimate relationship, when proximity to the other provokes all fears related to being consumed by the other (or judged, rejected, abandoned, etc.). In short, any and all fears connected to the breaking of the ego's boundary, the division between personal self and the totality of existence we are situated in will arise when this boundary is challenged. The link between the totality and the personal self, the 'bridge' to be contacted and crossed, has been known by many names, one of which is the Holy Guardian Angel. (This is not to be confused with the idea of the 'guardian angel' found commonly in angelic lore, which is usually referring to four of the chief archangels, Michael, Gabriel, Raphael, and Uriel; or to the more poetic idea of the 'guardian angel' found in the Talmud, which is a type of protective spirit assigned to each life form—everything from a human being to a blade of grass).

The term 'Holy Guardian Angel' has been interpreted in various ways. Historically, it appears to have been first used by the Zoroastrians (circa 500 BCE), but is more commonly associated with the *The Book of the Sacred Magic of Abramelin the Mage*, as reputedly authored by the German Jew Abraham of Worms in the 14th or 15th century. It was, however, the Hermetic Order of the Golden Dawn initiates S.L. MacGregor Mathers (1854–1918), and in particular Aleister Crowley (1875–1947), who popularized and developed the idea of the Holy Guardian Angel in the early 20th century.

On occasion the Holy Guardian Angel is understood to be a singular guiding agent that is 'assigned' to each person—a distinct, discrete entity, highly evolved, and entirely 'outside' of the psyche of the individual. From another perspective the Holy Guardian Angel is understood as simply the 'true self', very similar to the idea of the *daimon* as mentioned above (the Greek term, used by Socrates, for the 'higher genius' within each person) or the *atman* of Hindu doctrine. In fact, both perspectives carry truth, from the relative and absolute points of view. The particular perspective that is generated (whether relative and personal, or absolute and impersonal) will determine how the Holy Guardian Angel is experienced. The psychic function that determines which perspective we generate is *identification*. When identified with form (in specific, the body) and the personal self, we can only experience the Angel as 'outside' of ourselves. When identification with form is released (even if only momentarily) the Angel is understood to be our actual, divine nature. When identification with the personal self collapses, the Angel, in effect, disappears, and we understand that *we are that*.

There is a relationship between space and time—they are coeval, interdependent, and ultimately the same thing.[24] When space is 'collapsed', so, in a sense, is time. That is why the realization of *I am That* tends to accompanied by the realization of *I have always been That*. This realization has been known via different terms in the wisdom traditions: gnosis, samadhi, satori, illumination, enlightenment, and so forth. In the vast majority of cases the realization is not a permanent sea change. It is a temporary experience in which the personal self is soon re-identified with, with the ultimate aim being to integrate the expanded perspective, deep peace, and wisdom of the Angel or true self with the personal, worldly, embodied self of everyday life.

Can this 'integration' be accomplished to any significant degree? It is obviously debatable. In general there have been two approaches to this perennial problem, what can loosely be called the 'gnostic' and the 'tantric'; or alternatively, the transcendent and the immanent. The former, the gnostic-transcendent, holds out little hope for this material world and counsels the seeker to finish their inner-business so they can escape the limitations and density of this world. The latter, the tantric-immanent, offers a different approach, one of reshaping one's view of the world into a perception of it as sacred, divine, no different from any 'other world' or even the state of pure formless consciousness, with the ultimate view that there is nothing to truly 'escape' from.

Neither approach is easy. The great difficulty is that the experience of the true (or higher) self is almost automatically distorted (or contaminated) by the conscious ego-based mind. It is reduced to an idea, or an image.[25] Because of this it ultimately does not make too much difference whether we choose a more gnostic, world-denying (ascetic) path, or one that is based on attempting to integrate spiritual principles with everyday life (a 'tantric' approach). Both are susceptible to the distortion of the ego-mind, in particular its tendency to reduce everything, even the direct experience of our deepest nature, to a mere experience, an image, or a memory to be compared to that which arises in the next moment. This is why we say that to let go of identification with form, even only momentarily, results in the momentary disappearance of the Angel. The Angel is a mere image, a form, an idea, and only exists in that fashion from the point of view of the ego-mind. Once we understand, fully, that we *are* it, then its image collapses, having served its purpose.

The key point that the 'abyss' and the 'Holy Guardian Angel' represent—consistent with the idea of 'divine illumination' in Western mysticism, or 'satori' in Zen Buddhism—is that of an entry into something that is entirely beyond our conscious, personal idea of how things 'should be'. The movement into deep awakening, actual Self-realization, is radical and the shift is quantum, to use a 20th century term. This notion is actually consistent with Augustine's idea of grace, perhaps ironically. It is an utterly naked entry into the unknown, always containing an element of the unexpected. This is necessary in order for the ego-mind to relax its perpetual control to allow for interaction between conscious self and the infinite.[26]

Chapter 5

Psychotherapy and the Western Esoteric Tradition

> *Man can stretch himself as he may with this knowledge and appear to himself as objective as he may; in the last analysis he gives nothing but his own biography.*
> — Nietzsche

At the deeper levels of inquiry into consciousness and being, philosophy, psychology, and the perennial wisdom traditions (the 'spiritual path') meet up. That may seem objectionable to those who seek a more scientific approach to psychology, but ultimately all are concerned with truth, be it subjective or objective. As we shall see in Chapter 7, philosophical inquiry cannot avoid overlapping with, or entering entirely into, the study of the human psyche, especially as demonstrated by 17th and 18th century thinkers such as Spinoza, Locke, Hume, and Kant. The wisdom traditions, those Western and Eastern esoteric paths to self-knowledge, have always been based on a close study of the mind, alongside practical techniques for expanding and deepening consciousness. The similarities between Eastern wisdom paths and Western psychotherapy were noted as early as 1961, when Alan Watts wrote:

> If we look deeply into such ways as Buddhism and Taoism, Vedanta and Yoga, we do not find either philosophy or religion as these are understood in the West. We find something more nearly resembling psychotherapy...the main resemblance between these Eastern ways of life and Western psychotherapy is in the concern of both to bring about changes in consciousness...[1]

Transpersonal psychology (also referred to as 'spiritual

psychology') is the study of psychology within the context of spiritual growth. As with most approaches to psychology of the human potential movement, beginning with Jung, Maslow, and Rogers, it is concerned with the deeper awakening of the individual to their fullest potential. Conventional psychotherapy (in particular, psychiatry) is chiefly concerned with the overall basic health of an individual, their ability to function in the world, to 'adjust', to conform to normalcy and thereby experience a natural fulfillment born of peer-approval and self-acceptance. This is of course an important foundation. While such 'mainstream' approaches may not be concerned with the esoteric paths that are the focus of this book, it is nevertheless important to understand their fundamentals and history. This is so because modern Western psychology and psychotherapy have had a vast influence on modern Western esotericism. All significant Western esoteric systems (high magic, alchemy, the Tarot, astrology, and so on) have, since roughly the early 20th century, been re-interpreted in the light of psychological theory, and many have been heavily 'psychologized' by the tendency to view all (or most) matters as solely in 'one's head'.

Much of the esoteric schools of the past taught a version of psychology that tended to be expressed via myths, symbols (or what C.G. Jung would call 'archetypes'), classifications of entities, spiritual cartographies of the cosmos, etc. However for people of older times these entities were very real, not merely 'in the mind', or the 'unconscious' (an idea that was scarcely recognized until the 19th century). Even most of the highly educated of the Middle Ages or Early Modern era (up to the 18th century) granted the existence of the Devil, for example (which was in part why the various inquisitions and witch-trials lasted so long). The psychotherapist of past times was the shaman, priest, monk, ceremonial magician, 'cunning man' or 'wise-woman'. An essential aspect of the work of shamans or priests (of whatever faith) lay in various approaches to healing, such as 'soul retrieval', and especially, the casting out (extraction) of causes of illness. Some used more aggressive forms of magic, such as casting spells or curses. In pre-scientific times many serious forms of illness were commonly believed to be caused by malevolent forces, often personified as 'evil spirits' or 'demons'. Some of these latter required exorcisms, often elaborately performed, in order for a healing to be brought about and the victim to be restored to health.

Three Pioneers: Weyer, Gassner, Mesmer

It has been argued by some that the actual modern 'father' of Western psychiatry was the Dutch physician and demonologist Johann Weyer (1515–1588).[2] As a young man Weyer had been a student of Cornelius Agrippa (1486–1535), the German polymath who wrote the influential *Three Books of Occult Philosophy*. Weyer was one of the first to speak out against the witch-persecutions, insisting that any deviant behaviors allegedly observed in 'old hags' or others accused of witchcraft were more likely deriving from mental disturbances as opposed to malevolent supernatural influences. It is important to appreciate how radical this position was; as mentioned, the vast majority (even the most educated of their times) in most cultures throughout history have accepted at face-value the existence of invisible entities, including of the malevolent sort. As early as 1563 Weyer was openly declaring via his work *De Praestigiis Daemonum* (*The Trickery of Demons*)—a work that Sigmund Freud himself once called 'one of the ten most significant books ever written'[3]—that most witchcraft was the product of delusion or mental illness, and most magicians were charlatans. He held that 'witches' should be tended to by physicians rather than interrogated and tortured by witch-hunters.

These views were, of course, antithetical to the accepted views of the time, and accordingly Weyer was attacked and marginalized, even by King James I (1566–1625), a noted demonologist himself. Weyer in his writings had carefully refuted the fantastic allegations of the notorious *Malleus Maleficarum* ('Hammer of Witches'), first published in 1486, and the leading manual for 16th–17th century witch-hunters). Weyer was no scientist or atheist by modern understanding; like most educated men of his time he continued to believe in the Devil and in the reality of evil spirits, but he also insisted that those afflicted by them, such as witches, were essentially ill—often with *melancholia* (now generally known as 'clinical depression')—and in need of healing, not ecclesiastical prosecution or torment. This compassion and broad-mindedness marked him as a prototypical psychotherapist.

The links between the origins of psychotherapy and religious interpretations of 'evil' forces is inescapable; indeed, modern Western psychotherapy has some of its indirect causes in the work of the Austrian Catholic priest and exorcist Johann Gassner (1727–1779), who achieved some apparently remarkable healing successes merely by force of prayer, ritualized exorcisms (conducted in Latin with elaborate flourish) and close attention to his patient. By the year 1775 he had achieved such renown that a prominent bishop sponsored his work, and considerable crowds of people flocked to his town in southern Germany to either seek his treatment or observe its results. Gassner was, predictably, very controversial—he had many admirers and believers, but equally so, many who were stridently opposed. Some of these adversaries included certain prominent members of the clergy influenced by the age of 'enlightenment' prevailing in educated Europe at that time, in which reason, and the emphasis on the scientific method as originally put forth by Francis Bacon, was influencing religious faith. The scientific discoveries of Copernicus, Galileo, Newton, alongside the rational philosophies of Bacon and Rene Descartes, made it increasingly difficult for the intelligentsia to accept the practices of 'primitive' exorcisms and related faith-based healings.

It was into this setting that the German physician Franz Mesmer (1734–1815) entered. He began exploring the usage of magnets in healing people, but quickly (and astutely) concluded that something more was going on than just the magnets—and that that 'something' was related to a quality in himself that was somehow affecting his patients (hence the origin of the word 'mesmerize'). He called that quality 'animal magnetism', and noted that many of his patients experienced direct 'streamings' or movements of energy in their bodies while in his presence. All of this eventually led to later understanding around 'auto-suggestion', charismatic faith-healing, and hypnosis, but at that time Mesmer believed, and did so to his last days, that he was causing the movement of an actual tangible energy—'magnetic fluid'—that was responsible for the healings.

Mesmer, a contemporary of Gassner and only a few years younger, naturally became his rival, with the key difference being that Mesmer was more in tune with the *zeitgeist* of his time (which included the burgeoning scientific movement). By disclaiming any religious causes to his healing work, Mesmer was in effect accusing Gassner of a critical misunderstanding. He claimed that Gassner was, in fact, using animal magnetism without understanding it—and that, by extension, all so-called exorcisms are in fact forms of animal magnetism, based crucially on the self-confidence and charismatic force of the exorcist along with an actual movement of a 'universal magnetic fluid' (unseen energy), and not on any religious ceremony, excepting that such may be a prop upon which the exorcist focuses his will and the patient their faith.[4] (This whole idea, of course, plays a key part in ceremonial magic, where the various props—candles, incense, magical symbols, etc.—help to bring about a state of suggestibility in which changes in consciousness, and even outer circumstances, can readily occur).

Despite this more reasonable theory to healing—re-interpreting the idea of exorcism as a more physical (and psychological) 'animal magnetism'—Mesmer experienced a broad range of hostility and rejection from the intelligentsia of his day. Most of his contemporary physicians (doubtless some motivated by professional jealousy at his growing success) dismissed him as a quack. Part of the problem seems to have been related to Mesmer's apparent egotism—reminiscent of Paracelsus, he believed that all of medical history since the Greeks was rendered superfluous by his discoveries—and for the rest of his life had difficulty accepting his rejection by the established medical world of the time. His idea of a universal fluid or force that connects all things, the balance of which in a given organism determines its overall health, seemed to anticipate by two centuries Wilhelm Reich's idea of the 'orgone energy', which also earned its theorizer round condemnation and even eventual imprisonment. (The esoteric traditions, those of the East and West, have long believed in the existence of universal energies that are undetectable to normal human senses, and one finds the belief in more primitive, shamanistic cultures as well).

Mesmer ended his life in frustration and obscurity, much of his work rejected, with many of his disciples abandoning him or taking some of his ideas and developing them in their own ways, often without acknowledging their master—and often with highly influential consequences. (For example, Jacques Puyseger, one of Mesmer's close students, in later years stumbled upon the modern practice of hypnotherapy while practicing Mesmer's form of healing with large groups of people. One of Puyseger's own students, Charles Poyen, took the teachings of mesmerism to the United States, where in 1836 Phineas Quimby met him, was greatly influenced, and subsequently began the work that led to the New Thought movement). Despite Mesmer's reputation as straddling the line between legitimate healer and egocentric mystical quack, he is now generally acknowledged as being a key instigator behind the gradual birth of modern depth psychology (or 'dynamic psychiatry'). He was the first to clarify the points that a therapeutic rapport between healer and patient is crucial, and that resolutions and healings are inevitably preceded by crises. In short, a healer needs to make his patient believe in the possibility of healing, and this begins with believing in the healer. A good healer radiates a certain self-confidence (what Mesmer attributed to 'animal magnetism'), and this confidence can, in theory, rub-off on the patient, who then, in effect, heals themselves (reminiscent of the words of Jesus from Luke, *physician, heal thyself*).

Mesmer's doctrine was summarized as:

1. A life force, or energy, permeates all living (breathing) organisms, which Mesmer called 'magnetic fluid'. He called various effects brought about via organisms interacting with each other 'animal magnetism' (to distinguish it from other forces such as 'mineral' or 'planetary' magnetism, etc.).

2. All physical and mental illnesses are due to disturbances in the magnetic fluid.

3. A 'magnetizer' can cure these ailments in the patient by using his own energy ('magnetic fluid').

4. The first step in healing is to establish rapport between healer and patient.

5. A crisis must be provoked in the patient; that is, symptoms of their illness must be brought forth, so the magnetizer may gain control over them, and thus bring about a healing. One of Mesmer's methods of doing this was, while conducting a session with his patient, to place a hand on the hypochondrium region (the general area between the pelvis and solar plexus, just below the diaphragm).[5]

The idea of 'provoking a crisis' was related to the movements of energy (and even sometimes convulsions) brought about via Mesmer's work with his patient. The provoking of the symptoms into conscious awareness potentially led to integrating the pattern, thus releasing an old mental 'knot' or wound. Many of these ideas, although discarded or refined over time (especially Breuer's 'discovery' of catharsis, see below) lay at the basis of future psychotherapy.

Three Lines

Three traditional lines of psychology developed over time,

sometimes termed Rational Psychology, Organicist Psychology, and Depth Psychology. Rational Psychology holds that free will and reason are supreme, and that the correct use of reason leads to the best possible destiny for an individual. Organicist Psychology considers the mind-body complex as primary, and in particular, holds that it is the body that influences the mind—consciousness is an emergent property of the brain, as the belief is that matter precedes mind. As the health of the body and its intricate chemistry goes, so goes the health of the mind.

The third, Depth Psychology, is closest to the approach of the perennial wisdom traditions that deal with work on self, so as to realize one's maximum potential. The key element of Depth Psychology is that it takes into consideration the unconscious mind, and in particular, irrational forces from within, which can be encountered, experienced, and (to some extent) integrated. Mesmer's great contribution was to attempt to create a means by which these unconscious patterns and energies could be worked directly with. When a shaman, exorcist, or ceremonial magician evoked 'demons' in order to control them or expel them from one afflicted by them, the operating idea was the same, with the main difference being that the affliction was blamed on the spirit, rather than an element of the victim's own unconscious mind. Modern psychotherapy was essentially born via making this switch from concern with external forces (invisible 'evil entities') to disowned or disconnected unconscious patterns. Other developments occurred in the 19th century, mainly the development of methods of hypnosis (in which it seemed that the hypnotist could simply 'command' symptoms in their hypnotized subjects to disappear, as it were). Magnetism as a healing practice was very popular and respected in many parts of mid-19th century Europe, and was widely acknowledged by various important philosophers (such as Schelling and Fichte) and writers (such as Balzac and Dumas).[6] It was from Depth Psychology that 20th century schools of psychology concerned with the spiritual dimension of the human being developed, namely transpersonal and integral psychology, which are sometimes referred to as 'Height Psychology' (see Chapter 9).

The Unconscious Mind

The term 'unconscious mind' is generally recognized to have originated with the 18th/19th century German philosopher Friedrich Schelling (see Chapter 7). The notion of an unconscious mind was, however, strongly alluded to much earlier, by Plotinus (205–270 C.E.), sometimes called 'the first psychological philosopher'. Plotinus was developing and refining the foundational work of Plato, who set the tone for much of the Western world's approach to a philosophical view of the universe (regardless of how much of his thought was contested or negated by later thinkers). The essence of Plato's view was that there are levels of reality and being that we are not normally aware of, something Plotinus (and others, such the Gnostics and the later architects of the Kabbalah) added to, gradually building a type of map of all possible realms of consciousness and being.

The Dutch-Portuguese philosopher Baruch Spinoza (1632–1677) presented some key advances in the rational understanding of the 'unconscious' mind when he wrote, in his *Ethics*, of the tendencies of the personality to avoid awareness of troublesome or disturbing thoughts and feelings—an ability that Freud later characterized as 'repression'.[7] That is, we have the remarkable capacity to block out parts of our mind from immediate conscious awareness. The problem, however, is that these disturbing parts do not really 'go away'. They merely go underground and manifest in different shapes and forms, often via the process of projection.

The fact that elements of our mind become unconscious is of course natural; our conscious mind is capable of dealing with only so much at any given time (most of our body mechanisms perform without conscious participation on our part, which is absolutely necessary). However there are two essential problems connected to the general repression of thoughts and feelings. One of these is related to the entire realm of mental illness, and the other to the area that concerns the 'truth-seeker', one who sets out on a path of Self-realization or spiritual development. The former, the matter of the mentally ill, is connected to the practice of psychiatry and psychotherapy as it has slowly evolved (in different guises) down through the centuries, quantum-leaping in sophistication at the turn of the 20th century with the coming of Freud and his acolytes. The latter, the domain of the spiritual seeker, is equally connected to the matter of the unconscious mind precisely because the seeker seeks to realize Socrates' maxim, *know thyself*. It follows that knowledge of self is going to be based on discovery, on bringing the light into the dark, on making conscious that which has been unconscious.

Understanding and working with the unconscious mind is central to the whole idea of Self-realization. This is because the elements of our nature that get in the way of our inner development tend to be unseen, hidden—in short, unconscious. Our conscious ideals and plans and longings are often not in accordance with our unconscious elements, and in fact these latter may even actively oppose the conscious intention to become more awake in general. It is one thing to seek wisdom, the 'light within', and seek to bring it to fruition and realize it externally in one's life, and it is another entirely to actually accomplish this. Very generally stated, the problem usually lies in the self-image, the view of us that constitutes our overall sense of self-worth. Limitation and self-defeating tendencies that commonly sabotage inner growth are unconscious by nature, residing in dark and hidden pockets of our mind that are usually associated with old traumas, hurts, and repressed thoughts and feelings. Sometimes these surface in dreams at night, or in psychosomatic disturbances, but most obviously they manifest via relationship discord, various life-failures, and for the wisdom-seeker, as tendencies to stumble on the path of awakening or abandon it altogether. Exploring the unconscious mind is important not just for healing purposes, but also for entering into the unknown mysteries of being and for cultivating the crucial qualities of curiosity and courage in order to move forward on our path.

Romanticism and Existentialism

Romanticism in a philosophic context is discussed in Chapter 7; here we limit ourselves to some remarks on the influence of Romanticism upon the modern psychotherapy schools. The era of the European Enlightenment (which peaked in the 18th century) was based largely on the notion of the supremacy of reason, the idea that reason could understand the workings of the universe in totality, leading naturally to greater social conscience and compassion based on a deeper understanding of things, and ultimately a fulfilled contentment. Led by the paradigm-shaking revelations and discoveries of such scientific luminaries as Copernicus, Galileo, Newton, Boyle, Darwin, and a host of others, the universe gradually shifted in view from a mysterious array of images and strange forces forever beyond the ken of humans and best left to religious faith, into a functioning mechanism that could be understood and, more crucially, controlled and used with constructive and compassionate intent. That was the ideal, at any rate. Even the mechanism of reason itself, the human mind, was analyzed—reason analyzing the nature of reason—beginning with Locke, Hume and Kant. Such rationalism met its inevitable revolt in the early 19th century with the advent of the so-called 'Romantics', led in the literary realm by poets such as Byron, Shelley, Swinburne, and Blake, and in philosophy by Fichte, Hegel, Schelling, Schopenhauer, Kierkegaard (probably the first existentialist), and Nietzsche.

It is unquestionable that modern Western psychotherapy, as generally launched by Freud and his associates, had at least to some degree its roots in Western science, as born from the foundational ideas of Aristotle, Roger Bacon, Francis Bacon, and Descartes, all of whom in different ways emphasized the importance of the subject-object split, the essential division between the self and the surrounding universe, and the role of the reasoning mind in observing and understanding the world in which we appear to exist.

In particular, modern psychiatry was crucially influenced (and in a sense, arose from) something called 'Enlightenment associationism'. This was an understanding that arose chiefly from John Locke's philosophy, based on the idea that our view of reality is shaped by the mind's tendency to 'associate' sensations or perceptions based on similarities. From this notion early (18th century) mental health workers sought a more compassionate approach to treating the insane by 're-ordering associations', i.e., by changing the conditions of their environment. It was hoped that a more humane environment (removing bonding chains, for example) would result in internal shifts in the psyche of the patient. While helping in some ways, such measures were inadequate overall, because the impact of the personal nature of the interaction between doctor and patient was not appreciated, and nor was the role played by the unique nature of the individual's unconscious mind grasped.[8]

The personal element—the rapport between doctor and patient, and between patient and their own unconscious—was brought into greater focus due in part to the influence of the Romantics. Romanticism emphasized the role of the individual, some of which included the important understanding that the human mind was not just a passive association mechanism recording environmental impressions via the senses, as Locke had maintained. It also had the ability, via imagination, to shape its view of the world. As historian Eli Zaretsky put it,

> The romantic idea of the imagination was a precursor to the late 19th century idea of the subconscious...drawing on the German tradition of Naturphilosophie, according to which the entire universe was a unitary, living organism...romantics defined the imagination as an internal storehouse of images and creative drives. The artist, they insisted, was a 'lamp' rather than a 'mirror', an original source of values rather than a mere recorder of events.[9]

A further main tenet of the Romantics was that the emphasis on a rational understanding of the universe failed to account sufficiently for the *irrational* nature of the human being, something that obviously colors much of human history. Romantics sought not just to embrace the irrational, unexpected, and unconscious forces of the psyche, but also the natural and the mystical, which accordingly involved greater emphasis on the individual. In keeping with some of the old Hermetic teachings, the individual was held as primary, of unlimited capacity and potential; the key was the process of 'becoming', self-realizing, or what Jung later called 'individuating'. The Romantic Movement was initially Germanic, in part because 19th century Germany was a fragmented nation (consisting of small sovereign states) having been overrun by such factors as the Thirty Years War (1618–1648), and the 18th–19th century conquests of Louis XIV and Napoleon. Romanticism in part afforded the possibility of a mystical connection with national identity, and thus a possible road to national unity.[10] Romanticism at its best served to redirect interest and attention inward, toward the subject and the psyche, in which investigation of the person became central (in opposition to the fascination with the external world of objects that was basic to the Enlightenment). The 19th century revival of metaphysics, esotericism, and the occult was largely an outgrowth of Romanticism, based as both were on a point of view that honors the unknown, the unexpected, the inherently mysterious, and the process of integrating all facets of human nature, including reason, feeling, and the body.

As mentioned above, the 19th century German philosopher Schelling made key contributions to Romantic and Idealist thought that influenced modern psychology. Many of his ideas can be seen to parallel some of the old Hermetic teachings attributed to the mythic sage Hermes Trismegistus, as well as those of the Neoplatonists, such as:

1. Nature and Spirit are two sides of the same coin.

2. All realms of existence are interconnected; to understand the laws of one realm is to understand the laws of other realms (correspondence).

3. Nature functions via polarities (positive-negative, male-female, waking-sleeping, etc.).

4. The world itself is the creation of an all-pervasive universal will.

Schopenhauer and Nietzsche in particular laid emphasis on the idea of 'will' as the key determining factor of human life, in part to counter the mechanical and materialistic worldview brought about by the birth of modern science. It was Schelling who took the notion of 'will' to a kind of ultimate level, seeing it as something that permeates existence, a type of universal-will that is behind the operation of the universe, and that is proceeding with its own purpose and destiny. Human beings have the capacity to 'tap into' this universal will, and so participate in the grand unfolding of everything. It was during this time (mid-19th century) that the terminology began to change, and the word 'unconscious' began to be used instead of 'universal will'.[11]

Nietzsche himself had a marked influence on modern psycho-analysis, albeit indirectly. Freud claimed that he resisted reading Nietzsche in depth for some time as he feared being influenced by him, sensing that Nietzsche had already arrived at similar conclusions to Freud, which in fact proved to be the case. Nietzsche, before Freud, used terms such as *das Es* (later rendered into 'the It' by English translators), 'sublimation', 'repression' (which he called 'inhibition'), and ideas such as neurotic guilt and false morality. In essence, Nietzsche's writings show that every good philosopher is also a good psychologist, at least of the theoretical kind.

The other highly influential philosophical movement that has left its mark on modern psychotherapy was existentialism, generally conceded to have begun with the Danish philosopher Soren Kierkegaard (1813–1855) and developed by Schopenhauer, Nietzsche, Heidegger and Sartre, as well as literary figures such as Dostoyevsky. Kierkegaard had insisted that pure objectivity (as promoted by science and Hegelian philosophy) was illusion, and that truth was, above all, of the nature of subjective, personal revelation.

The central concern of existentialism is human freedom, and the main existential premise is that mere *theories* of reality, be they scientific, religious, or philosophical, fail to adequately address human nature and human experience. (This was in part a reaction to Hegel's highly abstract philosophy, which had become very influential in the mid-19th century). Similar to the ideas of the Romantics, existentialism puts emphasis on the notion of being truly authentic, the echo of Shakespeare's 'to thine own self be true', echoed by Nietzsche's 'become what you are'. Human fulfillment lies in fully exercising one's individuality, its uniqueness, and in both discovering and manifesting that individual uniqueness. The emphasis is on living both passionately and sincerely, free of the impositions of others or moral notions of how one 'should' be and 'should' live. This idea has been summarized as 'existence precedes essence', meaning that how we live (existence) takes precedence over abstract categories from theoretical systems that seek to define us (essence). In this light, actions become crucial in determining identity—to act nobly is to 'be noble', to act unkindly is to 'be unkind', an idea that makes the individual responsible for their acts (as opposed to faulting other 'essence' factors, such as environment, genetics, or even God, etc.). As Sartre said:

> What do we mean by saying that existence precedes essence? We mean that man first of all exists, encounters himself, surges up in the world—and defines himself afterwards. If man as the existentialist sees him is not definable, it is because to begin with he is nothing. He will not be anything until later, and then

> he will be what he makes of himself...that is the first principle of existentialism.[13]

Sartre's main argument, as summed in his landmark work *Being and Nothingness* (1945), is that there are two forms of existence: that of unconscious objects, and that of consciousness itself. The key attribute with a conscious being is that it is capable of conceiving of negatives, i.e., what is *not*. When we can imagine 'nothingness' (what is not), as well as what is, then we can also imagine possibilities. For example, in your living room you have certain furniture. Because you can imagine this same living room as being empty of furniture, you therefore can imagine it being filled with *new* furniture. Only the ability to conceive of what is not (not this furniture), allows for the ability to conceive of something new. The point of Sartre's argument is humans are capable of determining their future and as such, consciousness allows for the possibility of genuine freedom. More, a human is whatever they act; that is, our actions determine what we become. Finally, the character of a person is the sum of all their previous decisions and acts.[14]

This view came under fire by those who counter-argued that freedom is limited by many restraints, be they social, environmental, etc., and by those who maintain that free will is entirely an illusion, that all so-called choices are determined by previous factors. But Sartre's views, being strong representations of the existential school of thought, are historically important as part of the overall process of liberation from limitations (of endless variety) that humans have always sought. Existentialism influenced modern psychotherapy by emphasizing that personal meaning is arrived at via decision-making (echoed in the work of Adler and Assagioli), and moreover, one that was oriented toward the future, not the past. In order to grapple with the fear of the unknown (anxiety) brought about by examining the future, a quality of robustness (or 'hardiness' as it was often called) is needed, leading to a sense of expansiveness and greater sense of meaningfulness of one's life. Those who choose the past (avoiding the future) have difficulty coping with the stress that accompanies change or possible change, and became 'small' and contracted within, prone to despair, depression, and a sense of the meaninglessness of life. Life consists in moving forward, *becoming*, as opposed to escaping into the safely 'known' past.[15] Obviously, this does not mean that to have an interest in the past is to be 'small' or 'full of despair'. It has rather to do with the overall orientation of one's life. One may be a historian and be a fulfilled person, if one is using one's interest in the past to further one's understanding of the present and expansion in wisdom and understanding, i.e., *becoming* wiser, which is future oriented.

European existential philosophy made inroads in American humanistic psychology in the late 1950s, via the work of Rollo May and others, by emphasizing the ideals of freedom and will, combined with an optimistic outlook (the prevailing view of the Americans was that European existentialism, while profound in insight, was too pessimistic in places). The existential approach to psychotherapy was echoed in the work of certain therapists of the human potential movement, beginning with Maslow and Rogers, as well as Fritz Perls. A key element of this involved something sometimes referred to as 'paradoxical intention'. This is a somewhat confrontational technique in which a particular behavior, based on a certain fear, is intentionally exaggerated so as to diminish its power. For example, the fear of looking silly in front of others would be confronted by intentionally acting *sillier than usual* in front of others (going out dressed up absurdly, etc.). The idea is to become empowered by gaining a measure of control over particular fears, a classic existentialist and humanist approach.

In contrasting the existential approach and Eastern philosophy, Rollo May once wrote:

> Both Existentialism and Eastern philosophies such as Taoism and Zen] seek a relation to reality which cuts below the cleavage between subject and object. Both would insist that the Western

absorption in conquering and gaining power over nature has resulted not only in the estrangement of man from nature but also indirectly in estrangement of man from himself. The basic reason for these similarities is that Eastern thought never suffered the radical split between subject and object that has characterized Western thought, and this dichotomy is exactly what existentialism seeks to overcome.[16]

Freud and Psychoanalysis

All the theorizing, from the ancient philosophers to the 19th century Romantics and existentialists, was deficient in 'field work', so to speak, i.e., actual observation and systematic investigation in order to bring about a method of treatment for those suffering from mental disturbances such as general depression—what the ancients called 'melancholia'—or simple despair with their life. It was here where the pioneers of modern Western psychology, Gustav Fechner (1801–1887), William James (1842–1910), James Baldwin (1861–1934), and Pierre Janet (1859–1947) made their great contributions. But it was Sigmund Freud (1856–1939), an Austrian Jew, whose ideas and work proved most impactful. However controversial these ideas would prove to be in subsequent decades both during his life and after his passing—and Freud has been castigated and dismissed as much as he has been admired and acknowledged—they were unquestionably of immense influence on modern Western civilization, let alone on the modernized Western esoteric traditions.

Freud has often been declared to have been the first to offer a truly comprehensive and systematic explanation of human behavior and a means by which it can be altered if so desired. While this strictly speaking is not true—many of the wisdom traditions of history, particularly those of the East, have offered systems to do the same—it is true that Freud was probably the first Westerner to apply a semblance of scientific method and a truly comprehensive theory for the functioning of the human psyche.

Some key elements of modern psychotherapy put forth (or influenced) by Freud involved the following:

1. **Catharsis**. The word stems from the Greek terms *katharsis* ('purging' or 'cleansing'), and *katharos* ('pure, clear of shame or guilt; purified').[17] The idea of catharsis as being a key in the healing process is very old, although it has not always been clearly recognized or understood. As noted above, much of the work of a shaman, exorcist, or even Mesmer's 'magnetizers', was based on a variation of catharsis, a bringing into consciousness (evoking a 'crisis'—whether that was understood as a 'devil' or an emotional reaction) so that the behavior could be controlled or altered in some way. Even Aristotle, in his *Poetics*, alluded to the idea of catharsis; it was understood to play a part, as it were, in early Greek theatre, wherein the witnessing of a staged tragedy was thought to aid in the balancing of inner emotional states in the one observing. In modern times it was Freud's early colleague, the Austrian physician Josef Breuer (1842–1925) who first utilized catharsis as a treatment for patients suffering from hysteria. He used hypnosis to aid his patients in re-experiencing the blocked memories connected to the original painful event, which often led to the release of the symptoms. The technical term for this is 'abreaction', the reliving of a painful memory in order to release negative emotional imprints. (The U.S. Navy experimented with abreactive methods during W.W. II but ultimately abandoned it as they found evidence for its efficacy lacking. L. Ron Hubbard supposedly learned abreactive methods from his time in the Navy and utilized these within his Dianetics theory, later the basis for Scientology doctrine. C.G. Jung felt that the abreactive approach was limited, citing the therapist-patient rapport as more important; it's conceivable that the Navy work was less effective for precisely this reason, that the therapy was conducted without the warmth of genuine rapport). Freud modified Breuer's work by replacing hypnosis—which did not work for some patients—with free association.

2. **Free-association**. First developed in the early 1890s, this was Freud's method to replace the less reliable hypnosis. The idea was for the patient (usually lying down on a couch, with the therapist out of sight), to verbalize a stream of consciousness of thoughts, impressions, and memories, connected to a particular matter. The key was to abandon any form of censorship, and to freely express whatever arises in consciousness. The point was made by subsequent psychoanalysts that the mere ability to truly and successfully free-associate (without unconscious censoring) is itself remarkable and often a sign of healing, more than what is actually being spoken. One commentator went so far as to suggest that once true free-associating has been achieved, the therapy can be concluded. Free-association as a literary device—sometimes called 'stream of consciousness', the term coined by William James in 1890—has appeared in some famed works, notably those of James Joyce (*Ulysses* and *Finnegan's Wake*), as well as those by Virginia Woolf, William Faulkner, and Jack Kerouac. The main idea is that uninhibited expression can free up energetic and creative blocks and be a potent device for uncovering profound truths underlying fears and inhibitions.

3. **Repression**. In the course of listening to his patients free-associate, Freud observed that no case was free of 'amnesia', that is, memory-gaps in the events recounted. These memory-gaps were attributed to repression, in which the patient was blocking particular memories owing to various reasons related to pain, shame, and so on. As indicated above Freud did not 'discover the unconscious', but he is generally recognized as the first to fully understand the power of repression, and its ability to render certain states of mind as unrecognizable to the subject, i.e., 'cut off', which often results in neurotic or pathological symptoms.[18] The concept of repression, and how to work with repressed material so as to relieve the psyche of pressure and thereby reduce anxiety in one's life, was probably the central feature of Freud's practical work. He saw repression as the main defense against anxiety and believed that while it can lead to

neurotic symptoms it often does not, owing to the ability the psyche has to redirect unacceptable states of mind into acceptable ones. This is done via the usage of what he called defense-mechanisms, such as denial, rationalization, reaction-formation, displacement, projection, sublimation, etc. (See Chapter 9 for more on these).

4. **Resistance**. This was the term Freud used to define the way a patient would block memories from conscious access. Repression was the unconscious mechanism in place to block the memory; resistance is the manifestation in behavior as a lack of willingness to look at the issues needing to be addressed.

5. **Projection**. This is a particular defense mechanism in which someone is not aware of their own negative impulses or tendencies, instead seeing them only in others. Freud believed that people prone to projection were either too harshly disciplined or too spoiled in early life, especially from birth to age two. (Projection is discussed fully in Chapter 10).

6. **Transference**. The importance of the rapport between therapist and patient had long been recognized, going back to Mesmer and the 'mind-cure' therapists such as Phineus Quimby, but Freud identified clearly the ways in which a patient will form a child-like relationship with a therapist, one often colored by sexualizations and parental projections. That is, the therapist becomes the new parent, or other figure from the past that carried authoritative weight for the patient, often accompanied by strong feelings, or an erotic component. The reverse, where the therapist projects qualities of a significant past person onto their patient, is called 'counter-transference'. Needless to say this is a crucial area to understand, and lies behind many breakdowns in therapist-patient boundaries such as when sexual relationships form between therapist and patient. (Transference also commonly occurs outside of the therapeutic setting, for example, between an older man and a younger

woman. Often such relationships are short-lived because once the erotic charge passes, it is seen that the image of the person one was infatuated with bears little resemblance to the actual person, owing to the erotic projections).

7. **Sexuality and Libido**. The libido was Freud's term for the instinctive energy of the Id (see below), chiefly sexual in nature. The main goal of libido energy is pleasure (avoidance of pain), and survival. It is in a constant state of tension with the ego and the 'reality-principle', i.e., the need to delay gratification (impulse control) in order to function cooperatively in society. A key to this was Freud's famous (and infamous) idea of the Oedipus complex, involving a male child's unconscious urge to sexually possess his mother and defeat or kill his father. This, Freud theorized, was accompanied by anxiety that his father will overpower him by castrating him, which the boy reacts to by repressing his attraction to his mother and replacing it with feelings of affection, and deals with his fear of his father by identifying with him; the 'Electra Complex' is the female equivalent that was introduced by Jung (a girl desiring to possess her father, and regarding the mother as the competition), although Freud did not fully accept it, believing that a female child was controlled more by 'penis envy' rather than the need to possess her father. (Karen Horney countered the idea of penis envy with what she called 'womb envy'. In general, Freud's grasp of feminine psychology was, by his own admission, 'incomplete'. One of his biographers suggested that Freud saw women as 'a kind of castrated man'; near the end of his life he admitted his frustration with the 'feminine soul', saying that after thirty years of research he still could never answer the question, 'what does woman want?')[19]

Early in Freud's career he had noticed that many of his patients reported apparent memories of being molested sexually, usually by a parent. Initially Freud was surprised, even aghast, at how frequent these memories seemed to arise, and in how many of his patients. As time went on however and as he worked through his own extensive self-analysis, he came to conclude that infants and toddlers have their own unrealized sexual desires. He declared, 'A child has its sexual instincts and activities from the first; it comes into the world with them'.[20] From this Freud concluded that many, if not most, of the so-called memories recovered by his patients in therapy about sexual molestation were in fact fantasies about their own sexual urges projected outward (most commonly onto a parent). Freud was not so naïve as to believe that sexual molestations did not occur, but rather believed that more often it was a case of projected sexual instinct on the part of the patient. He further defined his scheme into five general stages of psycho-sexual development, those being oral (first year of life), anal (1–3), phallic (3–6; Freud used 'phallic' for both boys and girls), latency (6–puberty), and genital (puberty onward). Each stage has corresponding neurotic symptoms that can have life-long consequences if problems occur in it, such as oral fixations (over-eating, oral sex compulsions, etc.); anal-retentive behavior (obsession with neatness) or anal-expulsive (messy, disorganized); phallic-Oedipus issues; latency-sexual dysfunctions; and genital-general sexual and relationship dysfunction.

8. **Dream Interpretation**. Freud's landmark work *The Interpretation of Dreams* (1899, first English edition in 1913), introduced some of his key ideas. A major tenet of Freud's view of dreams is that they embody wish-fulfillments; that is, attempts to satisfy desires via various forms of symbolism within the dream. This view was subsequently challenged by other psychotherapists who saw dreams as involving more than mere wish-fulfillments, but Freud had hit on a valid and important idea, that we seek to resolve issues in our dreams at night, often involving matters that we cannot see any appropriate way to resolve in our waking lives.

Freud's other key contributions included clearly formalizing the notion of a three-leveled structure of the mind, that he designated the **superego**, the **ego**, and the **Id**. (Plato had thought up a more simplified idea of a 'tripartite soul' long before, comprised of spirited, rational, and libidinal portions—essentially corresponding to superego, ego, and Id—something that Wilfrid Trotter claimed 'makes Freud respectable').[21] The Id was his name for the repository of unconscious drives and primal instincts that dominates the life of a newborn up to roughly the age of two, and remains in effect for the rest of our life as the seat of our primitive impulses. The ego is our emerging sense of 'me', and is the reality-principle that begins to develop between the ages of two and five. It is the part of us that begins to be fully aware of others as distinct and separate from us and of what we are in relation to them. The ego is able to recognize that we cannot always have all of our needs met instantaneously. (We must deal with the world and everything in it). The superego develops after the age of five, roughly, and it is the part of us that is concerned with morality and conscience, a more refined sense of right and wrong. The superego generally works to oppose the selfish instincts of the Id.

Freud also conceived of three basic levels of mind, called the **conscious**, **preconscious**, and **unconscious**. This idea has been commonly represented by the metaphor of an iceberg, with only about 10 percent above the 'water', that being our conscious self. Freud saw the human being as mostly (90 percent) unconscious (the greater iceberg mass below the water). The preconscious mind is a shallower level of unconsciousness; that is, it contains things that we are not normally conscious of, but can recall easily enough. The unconscious proper is deeper, containing much material that is difficult, and at times even impossible, to recall.

As mentioned above, the early 'therapists' were mostly exorcists (and after the 18th century, 'magnetizers' and hypnotists). Perhaps nothing defined Freud's work more appropriately than his interpretation of the phenomenon of so-called demonic possession. In commenting on a particular case, an alleged 'pact' between an artist and 'the Devil', Freud—echoing Johann Weyer's 16th century seminal efforts to debunk certain tenets of demonology—wrote:

> What in those days were thought to be evil spirits to us are base and evil wishes, the derivatives of impulses which have been rejected and repressed. In one respect only do we not subscribe to the explanation of these phenomena current in medieval times; we have abandoned the projection of them into the outer world, attributing their origin instead to the inner life of the patient in whom they manifest themselves.[22]

Freud ultimately concluded that 'pacts with the Devil' were, essentially, father-substitutions ('I'll get from a deal with the Devil what I could not get from my father'); that is, unfinished psychological business with the father often ended up being projected onto the ideas of God and Devil. Freud saw these as two sides of the same coin:

> It requires no great analytic insight to divine that God and the Devil were originally one and the same, a single figure which was later split into two bearing opposed characteristics...the father is thus the individual prototype of both God and the Devil.[23]

These thoughts may not take into account particular sophisticated philosophies (such as that of Vedanta, Plotinus, or Kabbalah—Harold Bloom doubted that Freud had any real interest in his Jewish Kabbalistic mystical tradition[24]—in which the 'supreme source' is non-dualistic), but they reveal a key element of Freud's thinking and approach to the matter of healing: a concerted attempt to reclaim Man's psyche, to attempt a measure of accountability for our experience of reality via understanding how we demonize the 'other' (or the world itself) by projecting our repressed hostilities deriving from unmet sexual and love needs; and to apply critical reasoning to a realm long the province of credulous faith and stale dogma. If nothing else, Freud represented a key stage in the maturation of Western thought. He once wrote that human narcissism had suffered three profound 'blows': first from Copernicus (our planet is not the center of the universe); then from Darwin (the human being is merely a sophisticated animal, evolved from other animals); and from his own psychoanalysis, which he believed showed that the idea that Man is primarily a reasonable creature, in control of himself, is unfounded. Man is rather a creature of, in part, uncontrollable unconscious tendencies and irrational forces that can erupt, or manifest in covert and limiting ways, at any time, thus demonstrating that the conscious ego is 'not the master of the house'. This is ultimately a key piece for those working within the Western esoteric tradition, because all efforts directed toward personal transformation or manifestation to create changes in one's life will fall short if the hidden recesses of the mind are not properly addressed.

Various other key figures followed Freud, most of who further refined and developed his original work, and in many cases ventured off in directions very different. A brief outline of some of the more important ones follows:

Pierre Janet (1859–1947). Janet, born in France three years after Freud, is placed in this brief survey also after Freud, in deference to the latter's enormous influence, but in fact Janet's work preceded Freud's and in some respects was a key influence on him, as well as several of the figures outlined below. Janet was the key link between the pre-Freudian mental health healers and those who followed. In contrast to Freud, Jung, and Adler, who were influenced by Romanticism, Janet was more a product of the Enlightenment.[25] Janet is credited with devising the words 'subconscious', and 'dissociation' as pertaining to psychological use. He theorized that a lack of ego-integration can lead to the fragmenting (dissociating) of elements of the personality, although he did not use the term 'repression', this latter idea being developed by Freud. Janet also discovered, independent of Breuer and Freud, that by hypnotizing his patients and having them recall a past trauma, their neurotic symptoms often disappeared merely via the process of re-living and communicating the past trauma, i.e., via the cathartic process.[26] There were some bitter controversies between Janet and Freud in later years, concerning the issue of who discovered what first. The general consensus over time has become that Janet preceded Freud in some key ways, but that Freud developed his own theories in a more comprehensive and influential fashion.

Alfred Adler (1870–1937). Adler, an Austrian, was a key member of Freud's original inner circle and the first to break away and found his own school, generally known as Individual Psychology. He, like Jung, was not a mere deviant from Freud, but rather had his own specific system that both overlapped and ran parallel to Freud's. He has been characterized as a social idealist owing to his interest in community psychology. Specifically, he encouraged parents to raise their child to experience a sense of personal empowerment by learning how to make decisions (in contrast to knee-jerk parental authoritarianism that minimizes the child's personality and autonomy, thus reinforcing their dependence on authority). Like Jung, he sought to de-emphasize Freud's concern with the sexual instinct, and like the existentialists, he had more interest in a person's future, as opposed to his immediate past. Among his more important ideas was that of the 'inferiority complex' and his realization of the crucial importance of self-esteem in overall personal fulfillment (echoed in later years by Maxwell Maltz's ideas of the 'self-image' as being central to personal success in life; Maltz's work, mainly via his 1960 publication *Psycho-Cybernetics*, was a prime influence on the modern 'self-help' genre of popular psychology). Adler sought to humanize the therapist-patient relationship, being one of the first to dispense with the 'Freudian couch' in favor of two chairs and face to face interaction, a key element in subsequent therapeutic styles developed in the mid-20th century. Adler was also a prime influence on the main luminaries of the 1960s human potential movement, such as Maslow, Rogers, and Rollo May.[27]

C.G. Jung (1875–1961) Jung, born in Switzerland, was originally a key protégé of Freud, but after five years of close work under him broke away while in his late 30s. The cause of the break was mostly related to Jung's dissatisfaction with Freud's overarching concern with sexuality as being at the basis of personality development. There is also evidence that Freud was not comfortable with Jung's inclination toward mysticism via seeking to penetrate to deeper, more unknown realms of the unconscious. The system Jung eventually founded was called Analytical Psychology. A number of original concepts were thought up and popularized by him, including the idea of the 'collective unconscious', extroversion and introversion, complexes, the application of archetypes to psychotherapy, and a personality typology that became the basis of the well-known Myers-Briggs Type Indicator. Jung's main idea was probably that of 'individuation', his term for defining the life-long goal (so he maintained) of each person to realize their maximum potential, via the balancing of inner opposites, i.e., the joining of unconsciousness (what he sometimes called the 'shadow') with consciousness, a process he saw as detailed, in veiled terms, in the literature of alchemy. Part of what made Jung unique was his broad interest in a number of disciplines related to inner transformation, including in-depth research into the old forms of 'natural magic' such as alchemy and astrology, and the Eastern wisdom traditions (he wrote Forewords to both *The Tibetan Book of the Dead* and the Taoist text *The Secret of the Golden Flower*). He even took some interest in highly unconventional fields of study such as that pertaining to UFOs.[28] One of his key contributions to the field of modern psychology was his grasp of the universal, deriving from his deep interest in other cultures. He was a notable scholar, widely read, and was also an accomplished artist, this latter only really evident with the controversial posthumous publication of his *Red Book* in 2009, a collection of journal entries and paintings that his family had kept locked in a bank vault for four decades after his death.

A key to understanding Jung's ideas, and how they apply to

transformational work, is his notion of the collective unconscious. Unlike Freud, who had viewed the unconscious as wholly of the individual, Jung extended the idea to include the notion of a type of universal unconscious, comprised of universal symbols he termed 'archetypes' (from the Greek words *arkhe,* meaning 'first', and *typos,* meaning 'model' or 'type'). Jung lamented the fact that his idea of the collective unconscious was often misunderstood.[29] His main definition of the collective unconscious was that, in contrast to the personal unconscious, it does not 'owe its existence to personal experience and consequently is not a personal acquisition.'[30]

This is a key idea to consider, because a defining feature of the esoteric path, stemming largely from Hermeticism, is that an individual human being is a type of microcosm of a greater reality. That is, an individual has a direct link to this greater reality, which by definition is beyond his personal self and all his personal experiences. When Jung takes Freud's model of the conscious-unconscious, and adds to it the collective unconscious, he is in part restoring an esoteric element, because he is introducing the idea that there is a level of reality that is shared, that is, beyond individual, isolated experience.

Melanie Klein (1882–1960). Klein was an Austro-British Freudian psychoanalyst and an important pioneer in the field of child-psychology (she worked with children as young as two years) and 'object relations' theory (which defines, in part, how painful early life experiences become 'objectified' in the subconscious, only to repeat in later years when we connect with individuals who remind us sufficiently of the past persons initially involved in the painful experience).

Otto Rank (1884–1939). Rank was an Austrian psychoanalyst and one of Freud's closest associates, essentially his right-hand man, for two decades. He eventually fell out with Freud over his idea that Freud's Oedipal theory, which was a major bulwark in psychoanalytic theory, did not represent the true beginning of separation anxiety. Rank believed this originated in the 'birth trauma', the idea that the most essential trauma of all is being born—blissful pre-natal existence disrupted by sudden entry into an existence separate from the mother—and the rest of life is spent, essentially, recovering from this trauma in varying ways. His book *The Trauma of Birth* was published in 1924. Though initially endorsed by Freud it was gradually rejected by him, as well as his inner circle of psychoanalysts, as they believed it undermined too many of Freud's ideas. Rank's book would later have marked influence on certain 1960s alternative therapies, most notably Janov's Primal Therapy (see below). Rank was also a key figure in bringing forth awareness of the need to address the reality of emotions in therapy (Freud had advocated the classic model of the reserved, emotionless therapist), and of the values of interpersonal warmth between therapist and patient, which accordingly influenced many humanistic therapists, including Carl Rogers (see below). The existential psychologist Rollo May considered Rank to be an extremely important figure in the post-Freudian therapies that emphasized a more humanistic and pro-active approach to the model of personal healing and growth.

Karen Horney (1885–1952). Horney was a significant German 'neo-Freudian' psychoanalyst, one of the first to challenge Freud's views on early-life feminine psycho-sexuality, in particular via her idea of 'womb-envy', in which she proposed that males experience a natural envy of a woman's ability to give birth, which in turn provides men incentive to both subordinate women, and to compensate by excelling on other dimensions of life; this idea is one of the core elements of feminist psychology. Because the vast majority of the pioneering figures of psychology and psychotherapy were men, Horney's contributions (best summarized in her 1950 work *Neurosis and Human Growth: The Struggle Toward Self-Realization*), were an important counterbalancing factor in the development of modern psychotherapy. In particular she brought in a greater emphasis on relational patterns, such as her model of how a child (and adult) deals with basic anxiety. She saw this as unfolding in one of three ways: tendencies to move toward others (attachment, neediness, compliance), away from them (exaggerated independence), or against them (hostile combativeness). She emphasized that such patterns are normal and occur in most people, but only become neurotic when we become stuck in one of the three patterns. These views distinguished her from Freud, who placed more emphasis on instinct and innate tendencies (such as the Oedipal complex), in contrast to Horney's view that neurosis arises from a child's natural fear toward a world 'potentially hostile'.[31]

Roberto Assagioli (1888–1974). Assagioli was an Italian psychiatrist and founder of 'Psychosynthesis', an approach to psychology and therapy that was inclusive of a spiritual foundation (although Assagioli always saw himself as not abandoning his scientific training). For one following a path of inner transformation and interested in the perennial wisdom, Assagioli (like Jung, Reich, and the human potential pioneers) is very useful to study, because in addition to being a European psychologist he was also clearly influenced by the wisdom traditions, and in particular the Kabbalah. Assagioli was concerned with the personal will and offered practical methods for developing it, in the context of going beyond the healing of childhood trauma and mere normalized development of a healthy ego (the main goal of traditional psychotherapy), into spiritual development (or what would in later years be termed transpersonal psychology). Assagioli was a confederate of C.G. Jung and Abraham Maslow in his interest in 'Self-realization' (although Jung and Maslow understood the idea of Self-realization in somewhat different terms). Assagioli was, arguably, the first 'transpersonal' psychologist, in that he conceived of a 'higher self' that was distinct from the conscious and unconscious minds, something that aligned him with the great wisdom traditions.

Fritz Perls (1893–1970). Perls was a German psychoanalyst who founded 'Gestalt therapy' (not to be confused with Gestalt psychology) in the 1940s, along with his wife Laura Perls. He eventually made his way to Esalen, the famed growth center of Northern California (see below), where he resided from 1964–69. Perls' work was based on existential ideas, with a focus on will, responsibility, and the importance of addressing the actuality of the present moment—that is, what is happening *right now*, as opposed to theoretical or speculative ideas about how one should be, or could be, etc. Perls was legendary for his reputation as a group-therapist to evoke strong responses from participants as an aid for them to encounter the most resistant aspects of their character. A key element of the Gestalt therapy approach is deep acceptance of how one is. Change itself rarely occurs when there is rejection of present-time reality—if one strives to be something one is not, one simply remains the same. Change is possible only when there is first profound acceptance of how one is, now. In that regard, Perls sought to greatly de-emphasize the traditional psychoanalytic approach of both introspection (analysis) and retrospection (history). Perls also addressed the importance of the body as a signpost for underlying psychological issues. He had conferred with Wilhelm Reich (see below) in his earlier years, and came to agree with Reich's view that repressions manifested via the body and its constrictions, mannerisms, and so on. (This was somewhat reminiscent of Gurdjieff's emphasis on the body and the importance of how well we 'inhabit' it—he once characteristically remarked, 'what good does all the knowledge in the world do for a man who still acts like a boo-boo?')

Anna Freud (1895–1982). Anna was the sixth and last child of Sigmund and Martha Freud, and the only one to follow her father and become a prominent 20th century psychoanalyst. She was considered, even by Freud himself, to be (along with Melanie Klein) one of the founders of child-psychology. She was very close to her father and even underwent analysis by him. Although writing original papers, especially focusing on ego psychology in which she elaborated on the particular defense mechanisms of the ego (repression, suppression, projection, reaction-formation, etc.), she remained a loyal Freudian, and at times engaged in public disputes with Freudian analysts who were diverging away from her father's ideas (such as Melanie Klein). Anna Freud was particularly influential in American psychotherapy in the decades between her father's death and the rise of the human potential movement (1940s–50s).

Jean Piaget (1896–1980). Piaget was a French-Swiss developmental psychologist, heavily influential on late 20th century theorists of consciousness (such as Ken Wilber). He was both philosopher and psychologist, and specialized in defining specific developmental phases in life, with special emphasis on child psychology and 'constructivism' (the theory of learning via subjective constructs).

Wilhelm Reich (1897–1957). Reich, an Austrian psychoanalyst, was highly radical, controversial, and impactful on many alternative therapies that arose from the human potential movement especially from the 1960s on, chiefly via the work of his disciple Alexander Lowen (see below). He wrote seminal works on the tendency of the body to reflect psychological disease via muscular armoring (*Character Analysis*, 1933); how fascist leaders (like Hitler) rise to power, fuelled in part by sexual repression (*The Mass Psychology of Fascism*, 1933); the effects of state-reinforced sexual repression (*The Sexual Revolution*, 1936); the importance of the sexual orgasm as a natural regulator of psychological health (*The Function of the Orgasm*, 1942), and on the existential need for the individual to assume responsibility for their own life and empowerment in contrast to being blindly controlled by authority (*Listen, Little Man!*, 1945). Reich was similar to Freud in his understanding of the crucial power and importance of sexuality, but he veered off from Freud in his development of his ideas and how they could be applied to particular healing modalities (such as bodywork and various breathing therapies). His interest was in experiential work, as opposed to an exclusive talk-therapy approach.

The original and very controversial 'crown jewel' of his theory was the concept of 'orgone energy', and his attempt to frame it into the Western scientific paradigm. It is conceivable that the 'orgone energy' he had 'discovered' was a manifestation of the same 'subtle energy' that is described in worldwide esoteric traditions, going by names such as *shakti, prana, kundalini, ruach, manas,* and so on. Reich derived the term *orgone* from the words 'orgasm' and 'organic', stemming from his initial thesis that the sexual orgasm is an indispensable aspect of psychological and physical health. He believed orgone energy to be the fundamental energy of life and the universe, and further, that all disease and ill health in humans was related to some sort of blockage in the natural flow of this force. Clear parallels for this can be found in Eastern teachings, for e.g., the Chinese Taoist teachings around the flow of *chi* through the human body, and the results of imbalance and disease arising from blockages to this flow of *chi*.

Reich gradually came to suspect the presence of this energy when his patients, undergoing the bodywork-emotional clearing therapies that he pioneered, would report consistent sensations of 'tingling' or 'pulsing' or 'streaming' of energy whenever they experienced breakthroughs in their therapy. In time, Reich came to believe that orgone energy was blue in color and composed of something he called 'bions', which he hypothesized were the smallest units of living matter. One of Reich's colleagues, Dr. Charles Kelley, outlined ten traits of orgone energy, allegedly following much experimentation:

1. Is free of mass, without weight and inertia.

2. Is universally present, even in vacuum.

3. Is the medium for the movement of light, as well as electro-

magnetic and gravitational activity.

4. Is always moving, in either a pulsating or curving fashion, and at times is detectable visually as a blue-ish shimmer.

5. It contradicts the Second Law of Thermodynamics in physics, and specifically the idea of entropy, flowing in reverse direction from that of electricity or heat (which naturally flow from a higher potential to a lower) by moving from low potentials to higher. In other words, high concentrations of orgone energy draw more orgone from lower concentrations. In short, 'energy goes where energy is'.

6. Orgone energy forms units, from 'bions' to cells to plants all the way to galaxies. As with orgone itself, these units draw energy from their environment (are negatively entropic), and pass through life-cycles from birth to death.

7. Matter derives from orgone energy.

8. All life derives from orgone energy.

9. Streams of orgone energy can converge and join, and this will often take the form of a spiral.

10. Orgone energy can be manipulated and controlled by devices known as 'accumulators'.

As can be seen from this list, many of these traits (with the exception of points 9 and 10) are consistent with the general and mystical descriptions of subtle energy from the global esoteric traditions.

Reich was often attacked for his ideas and work, culminating in a substantial quantity of his papers and books being burned in America in 1956 (due to his violation of certain FDA protocols in relation to his telephone booth-sized energy-accumulating 'healing device'), followed by his death in an American prison (due to heart failure) a year later. The human potential movement and the New Age of the late 20th century had something of a tendency to romanticize Reich, particularly to depict him as the unfortunate martyr and victim of 'Big Brother'. In fact Reich was a complex and contentious character who in his later years suffered from bouts of mental illness (apparently paranoia; he was convinced at one point that he was engaged in warfare with aliens from outer space—he seems to have been one of the originators of the 'chemtrail-type' conspiracy, the idea that unseen powers are poisoning the planet by distributing noxious elements into the atmosphere). That said he was unquestionably ill-treated by the authorities, his book-burning event being described by some as one of the most 'blatant episodes' of literary censorship in American history,[32] and his contribution to more experiential and arguably effective forms of psychotherapy (utilizing breathing and bodywork) is probably valid.

Carl Rogers (1902–1987). Rogers, an American, is generally recognized as the key figure behind modern (especially American) humanistic psychology. In his mid-30s he was exposed to the seminal ideas of Otto Rank, after which he developed what came to be known as 'client-centered' therapy, based essentially on a less controlling and less directive approach. Rogers saw qualities on the part of the therapist such as 'warmth and understanding', as well as a deep interest in the client's personal reality—and in particular, not attempting to direct or change that reality—as crucially important. Rogers held that self-esteem was of central importance and that a therapist could help their client by not widening the 'gap' in the client's self-concept between how they were, and how they 'should' be (the 'ideal self'). This was best brought about by the therapist establishing, first and foremost, a rapport with their client based on a deep acceptance of how they are and how the client sees themselves, sometimes referred to as 'unconditional positive regard'.

He called the approach 'non-directive therapy'. The main idea is that by accepting the client and their state of mind (whatever that be), the tacit message is being delivered that the client has the means, innate within them, to bring about positive changes in their life—in contrast to the suggestion (however unintended) that they are flawed, wrong, and need to be fixed.

Jean Gebser (1905-1973). Gebser was not a psychologist or psychotherapist, but rather a philosopher and poet, who nevertheless merits mention here owing to his important contributions to consciousness theory. His model of human development, via structures he classified respectively as 'archaic-magic-mythical-mental-integral', had a later marked influence on integral thinkers such as Ken Wilber, who endorsed (and developed further) Gebser's essential insight that the movement from birth to maturity to wisdom is not a regressive 'return to Source', but rather a forward movement toward a greater destiny.

Abraham Maslow (1908–1970). Maslow was raised in poverty in a New York City slum, a personal history that may have contributed to the compassion that became an important part of the system he would ultimately develop. He is most renowned for developing his 'hierarchy of needs', in which he defined a series of levels of needs based on their degree of importance for overall health. The scheme has generally been represented in a pyramidal shape, with basic survival needs at the base, followed upwardly by needs of safety, belongingness-love, self-esteem, self-actualization, and cognitive-aesthetic. Maslow also acknowledged the reality and importance of 'peak-experiences' and their spiritual associations. Along with Rogers, he was a major contributor to modern humanistic psychology.

Rollo May (1909–1994). May was American, one of the key early figures in American existential psychology, and one of the founders of Saybrook Graduate School in San Francisco, a major academic center for progressive consciousness studies.

Alexander Lowen (1910–2008). Lowen was probably Wilhelm Reich's most important student, and the developer of Bioenergetics, a form of therapy that emphasizes the interconnection of mind and body. The history of early psychotherapy is largely a history of theory combined with talk-therapy. Reich and Lowen, along with several others who came after, pioneered the more experiential therapies that included the body, with special emphasis on how the body mirrors patterns and structures of the psyche, along with various innovative modalities to restructure these patterns in the musculature of the body. Lowen published over a dozen books; some of the more notable ones were *The Language of the Body* (1958), *The Betrayal of the Body* (1967), *Bioenergetics* (1976), *Depression and the Body* (1977), *Fear of Life* (1980), and *The Spirituality of the Body* (1990).

Arthur Janov (1924–). Janov, an American psychotherapist, is one of the more radical figures mentioned here. His work has met with considerable controversy. He broke upon the scene with his 1970 publication *The Primal Scream,* in which he documented a form of therapy that he largely stumbled upon, which involved a particular patient reliving an early life trauma that was apparently connected to his birth, and expressing the pain of this trauma in a session with Janov via a blood-curdling scream. The patient then reported a sharp decline in neurotic symptoms. Janov subsequently employed the approach of facilitating his patients into the recovery and release of what he called 'primal pain', connected to early life (and birth) trauma, an idea that had originally been proposed by Otto Rank in 1924. Janov's theory was relatively simple and direct: all neurosis stems from the repressed pain of early life trauma. He followed his early work with a number of other books, including *The Feeling Child* (1973), *The New Primal Scream: Primal Therapy 20 Years On* (1992), *The Biology of Love* (2000), and *The Janov Solution: Lifting Depression*

Through Primal Therapy (2007). Despite four decades of active work and a consistent confidence in his healing modalities, Janov has come in for considerable criticism and in 2006 an American Psychological Association poll deemed Primal Therapy 'discredited' owing mostly to lack of substantive studies that could demonstrate its effectiveness.[33] Janov initially claimed a '100 percent cure rate', but independent investigators estimated the actual rate at closer to 40 percent. Janov's work, especially in the 1970s–80s, was particularly prone to being copied by therapists of wide ranging qualifications (or lack thereof).

R.D. Laing (1927–1989). Laing, a controversial Scottish psychiatrist, is probably most renowned for his first book, *The Divided Self: An Existential Study in Sanity and Madness* (1960). Laing's main argument was that psychotic symptoms should not merely be regarded as something aberrant to be fixed, but rather as valid (if distorted) expressions of particular subjective views. Laing met Arthur Janov and was interested in his work, though skeptical; despite that, he himself used some radical experiential methods, including a type of 'rebirthing' that involves simulating the birth experience. Laing did not support traditional psychiatric classifications of mental illness and had serious reservations about the usage of antipsychotic medications. His basic view was that mental illness need not always be regarded as an unfortunate breakdown simply to be treated, but rather on many occasions may be viewed more as a 'creative episode' of deconstruction, or even a type of 'shamanic journey' leading to a deeper self-knowledge. These views echo the teachings of the psychologically oriented alchemists, including the writings of Jung, who himself passed through such a phase of 'creative illness' (just prior to World War One) that in some ways was similar to a psychotic break.

Stanislav Grof (1931–). Grof, a Czech-American psychiatrist, is considered to be one of the founders of transpersonal psychology.

His work has ranged far into the realms of the alternative, though he has always retained a scholarly rigor in his writings. He has promoted and utilized approaches such as psychedelic psychotherapy (using hallucinogens for therapy) and 'holotropic breathing' (a variation of Orr's rebirthing technique; see below). One of his prime influences was Otto Rank (especially via his theory of the 'birth trauma'). Grof has authored over twenty books, including *Beyond the Brain: Birth, Death and Transcendence in Psychotherapy* (1985), *The Stormy Search For The Self: A Guide To Personal Growth Through Transformative Crisis* (1990, with Christina Grof), *Psychology of the Future: Lessons From Modern Consciousness Research (2000)*, and *The Ultimate Journey: Consciousness and the Mystery of Death (2006).*

Leonard Orr (1937–). Orr's main legacy is his 'discovery' of a type of alternative therapy that he called 'rebirthing' (not to be confused with the method mentioned above that R.D. Laing used). Orr's technique involves deep, sustained and rapid breathing for a period of between thirty to sixty minutes, essentially a type of yogic breathing (similar to *kriya yoga*) for Westerners, that he claimed was transmitted to him by a mysterious Indian guru when he was in India in the 1960s. His first book, *Rebirthing in the New Age* (1977, with revised editions in 1983 and 2007) was a landmark work in the New Age renaissance of the 1970s–80s. As with Janov, many of his ideas have been attacked and marginalized within mainstream psychotherapy, and some openly lampooned (such as his writings on physical immortality), but Orr was unquestionably a major influence on post-1960s alternative therapy modalities. His main technique, 'rebirthing', has been widely used in both private therapy and in many communities devoted to experiential, transformational work, since the late 1970s. He called it 'rebirthing' because he holds that the method enables the healing of the 'birth trauma' (first espoused by Otto Rank) although Orr appears to have been influenced by Eastern ideas rather than by Rank.

Charles Tart (1937–). Tart is an American psychologist and, along with Grof, considered one of the founders of transpersonal psychology. He has authored over a dozen books along with hundreds of articles in peer-reviewed journals. Alongside his work in the field of 'spiritual psychology' he has been one of the more accomplished interpreters of the Greek-Armenian mystic G.I. Gurdjieff's teachings. Among his better known works are *Altered States of Consciousness* (1969, editor), *Transpersonal Psychologies* (1975), *Waking Up: Overcoming the Obstacles to Human Potential* (1986), *Living the Mindful Life* (1994), *States of Consciousness* (2001), and *The End of Materialism: How Evidence of the Paranormal is Bringing Science and Spirit Together* (2009).

Ken Wilber (1949–). Wilber is an American writer and theorist of consciousness studies. Though not formally trained in psychology he is considered by many to be one of the more important and profound explicators of psychological theory, perennial philosophy, and a vision that goes beyond both as they have traditionally been understood. In 1998 he founded the Integral Institute, a think-tank based on his vision of integrating all significant fields of human knowledge, which attracted the support and participation of a number of prominent figures in turn-of-the-21st century consciousness studies, such as Michael Murphy, Roger Walsh, Don Beck, Deepak Chopra, and Jon Kabat-Zinn. Wilber has published over twenty books, including *The Spectrum of Consciousness* (1977), *The Atman Project: A Transpersonal View of Human Development* (1980), *Eye to Eye: The Quest for the New Paradigm* (1984), *Sex, Ecology, Spirituality: The Spirit of Evolution* (1995), *A Brief History of Everything* (1996), *The Marriage of Sense and Soul: Integrating Science and Religion,* (1998), *Integral Psychology: Consciousness, Spirit, Psychology, Therapy* (2000), and *Integral Spirituality: A Startling New Role for Religion in the Modern and Postmodern World* (2006).

The Esalen Experiment. Deserving mention here is the famed cutting edge growth community known as Esalen Institute. Situated near Big Sur in Northern California, it was founded in 1962 by Michael Murphy (1930–) and Dick Price (1930–1985). The original intention was for it to function as a community offering alternative forms of psychological healing, particularly those based on the existential concern with freedom and present-time reality, in contrast to more conventional psychotherapy with its emphasis on analysis and personal history. Murphy and Price wanted to attract cutting edge thinkers in the fields of psychology, philosophy, comparative religion, and science, yet they also wanted to avoid creating an organization based on a dominant single teaching or a charismatic single teacher's work. Esalen soon grew into a meeting ground for some of the most progressive minds in the field of human potential of the 1960s. Among the renowned personalities who were involved, to varying degrees of participation and influence, were Abraham Maslow, Carl Rogers, Fritz Perls, Alan Watts, Joseph Campbell, Gregory Bateson, Aldous and Laura Huxley, Richard Alpert (Ram Dass), Stan Grof, Timothy Leary, John Lilly, Virginia Satir, David Steindl-Rast, Ida Rolf, Richard Feynman, Andrew Harvey, and Michael Harner. The community continues to exist (as of this writing in 2012) offering a broad range of workshops and trainings in personal development.

Chapter 6

Tantra and the Fundamentals of Sex Magick

A Brief History of Eastern Tantra

The adepts of Tantra believe that...the present age of darkness has innumerable obstacles that make spiritual maturation exceedingly difficult. Therefore more drastic measures are needed: the Tantric methodology.[1]

—Georg Feuerstein

Before covering the essentials of so-called Western 'sex magick', some background on the history of Eastern Tantra is important. 'Tantra' is one of those words that most 21st century people on some sort of inner journey have at least heard of but usually understand only vaguely. The word is usually associated with sexuality in conjunction with certain mystical states of consciousness, but the truth is remarkably more involved than its Western New Age simplifications. Tantric doctrine is voluminous, encompassing a vast range of theory and practice pertaining to the matter of spiritual liberation, and sexuality occupies only a relatively small part of its doctrine.

The word *tantra* is from the Sanskrit language and has various literal interpretations, but most commonly is understood to mean 'web' or 'loom'; it derives from the root *tan*, meaning to 'extend' or 'spread', and *tra*, meaning 'to save'; the word can thus be understood as 'spreading knowledge in order to provide salvation'.[2] It is also closely related to the word *tanta* ('thread'), suggesting the weaving of a tapestry that makes contact with everything in existence, leaving nothing out—a good metaphor for the all-embracing nature of its view of reality.[3]

Tantra has its roots in the ancient Hindu-Vedic traditions of

India—the word *tantra* was used in the Rig Veda scriptures as far back as at least 1500 BCE—but is generally recognized as having first appeared in a coherent form in north India around 500 CE. About a hundred years after that the Buddhist version appeared (and in fact, the oldest surviving complete Tantric texts are Buddhist).[4] There is a legend that the Tantric teachings were first given by the historical Buddha (around 500 BCE), but this is seen by scholars as mostly myth. It is generally accepted that Tantra as a unique form of spirituality was established by the 6th century CE in Northwestern India. Most forms of Hindu Yoga (such as *Hatha* and *Kundalini* Yoga) were influenced by Tantra. The Buddhist version eventually migrated (or was chased) across the Himalayas to Tibet, where, chiefly via the work of the 8th century CE Indian monk-scholar Shantarakshita, it resulted in a particular school and lineage generally referred to as the *Vajrayana* ('Way of the Diamond Thunderbolt'). The legendary figure of the great tantric mystic Padmasambhava as well as the important 8th century CE Tibetan king Trison Detsun are traditionally believed to have been involved in the transmission of the Buddhist lineage to Tibet as well. After an initial struggle with the entrenched shamanistic tradition known as *Bon*, the *Vajrayana* teachings took hold (partly by absorbing some elements of *Bon*) and became established. It is in Tibet, many believe, that the Tantric path became most highly elaborated and evolved; it was only after the 1959 Chinese invasion that the *Vajrayana* teachings were dispersed to the West following the destruction of thousands of Tibetan monasteries by the Red Army, and the subsequent exodus of many advanced Tibetan teachers (*lamas*) of Tantric Buddhism.

A few generalities can be stated about Eastern Tantra. It has certain characteristics that mark it apart from more conventional forms of spirituality. Although a vast literature within the tradition exists, Tantra is less a philosophy and more a way of life based on direct experience and very structured practices. In its embrace of material existence and inner freedom deriving from practice, it bears similarities with existentialism and Zen (though probably more effective and practical than the former and more colorful than the latter). Like Zen, Tantra is not interested in dry rationality divorced from direct practice. That said Tantra is no whimsical 'way of life' lacking theoretical structure, as it is sometimes depicted in diluted New Age Westernized versions of it.

The theological basis of Tantra was described by Sir John Woodroffe (1865–1936), who wrote under the mystical pseudonym of 'Arthur Avalon' and was the first Western scholar of Indian Tantra, as follows:

> ...Pure Consciousness is Shiva, and His power (Shakti) who is She in Her formless self is one with Him. She is the great Devi, the Mother of the Universe who as the Life-Force resides in man's body in its lowest centre at the base of the spine just as Shiva is realized in the highest brain centre, the cerebrum or Sahasrara-Padma, Completed Yoga is the Union of Her and Him in the body of the Sadhaka [practitioner]. This is...dissolution...the involution of Spirit in Mind and Matter.[5]

Woodroffe, who had been a judge of the High Court in Calcutta in the 1890s, courageously studied and published the first scholarly treatments of Hindu Tantra for Western audiences, during a time (early 20th century) when Tantra was still regarded as a debased and decadent version of Hindu religious tradition. This view was doubtless colored by colonial English puritanicalism; after all, the West first became aware of Tantric teachings during a century (the 19th) when the reality of the female orgasm was still being denied by many so-called medical authorities. Prior to Woodroffe's efforts any texts concerning Tantra were typically bowdlerized by European translators so as not to offend Victorian and Edwardian morality. (A good example of this being the 1958 Columbia University Press edition of *Sources of Indian Tradition*, part of an 'Introduction to Oriental Civilizations' university series, a 900-page textbook that devotes precisely half a page to Tantra, omitting all mention of left-hand approaches. An example of a Western scholar who did treat Tantra openly and objectively was Heinrich Zimmer, especially in his *Philosophies of India* published by Princeton University Press in 1951 and edited by Joseph Campbell). Indian scholars themselves were often embarrassed by Tantric teachings and commonly omitted mentioning them altogether in tomes on Indian spirituality.

Philosophically, Tantra is, generally speaking—and the word 'generally' must be emphasized here as Tantra is not represented by any one authoritative doctrine—based on a radical acceptance of material reality and life-energy. In contrast to teachings that view material reality as illusory at best, or as a debasement to be overcome, or even as evil, Tantra regards corporeal existence as pure energy, divine in essence, to be harnessed and converted and even to be delighted in. In brief, Tantra includes the body in its model of spiritual enlightenment—it is a radically inclusive path, and even holds that liberation can be achieved in degenerate social conditions. This idea of working *with* the energies of life rather than against them (or seeking to transcend them), has become particularly relevant since the Industrial Revolution, with its emphasis on materiality, and for the general current state of our planet. There are prophecies from both ancient Hinduism and Buddhism that speak to this. The Hindu Vedic texts of old specify four distinct ages spanning our history. The last and current one is known as the *Kali Yuga* ('dark age'), an age when the Tantric teachings are considered most appropriate. The idea is that in the 'dark age' the negative social and psychological conditions on the planet get so out of hand that the only possible way to understand them is to work *with* them, rather than attempt to deny, suppress, overlook, or overcome them. From the Tibetan Buddhist tradition comes Padmasambhava's prophecy, recorded around the 9th century CE: 'When iron birds shall fly and people shall ride horses with wheels, armies from the north will crush Tibet, and these teachings will travel west to the land of the Red man'. All this can be seen as a metaphor for appropriate timing, in that the Tantric approach is believed by its adherents to be well suited to a particular cultural milieu, namely global civilization under its current conditions.

That said, the antinomian ideology of 'radical acceptance of material reality' within Tantra does not mean that it is a tradition that lacks structure and discipline. To define this structure precisely is nearly impossible, as there are over five hundred Tantric lineages in India alone.[6] In addition, Hindu Tantra is comparatively lacking in literature that treats its teachings comprehensively, in comparison to Tibetan Buddhist Tantra, which has a rich literature and an established lineage of accomplished practitioners. This lack of literary clarity within the field of Hindu Tantra (and the difficulty in finding Hindu Tantric adepts both accomplished in practice and knowledgeable in theory) has made it ripe for Western simplifications. As the Yoga scholar Georg Feuerstein lamented:

> The paucity of research and publications on the Tantric heritage of Hinduism has in recent years made room for a whole crop of ill-informed popular books on what I have called 'Neo-Tantrism'. Their reductionism is so extreme that a true initiate would barely recognize the Tantric heritage in these writings. The most common distortion is to present Tantra Yoga as a mere discipline of ritualized or sacred sex. In the popular mind, Tantra has become equivalent to sex. Nothing could be farther from the truth![7]

The broad scope of Indian Tantra ranges from extreme asceticism (as in the Aghori practitioners, who frequent cremation grounds, usually naked, for their meditation practices), to Tantric sorcerers who deal in the business of spells and curses, to left-hand practitioners who use *maithuna* (ritual sexual intercourse), to relatively conventional 'right hand path' tantricas who practice celibacy and disciplined yogic techniques of semen retention. It also needs to be understood that Tantric theory was, in part, intended to expose the social limitations of the Indian caste system, in so doing making its practitioners vividly aware of ego-impurities related to the caste conditioning and its various prejudices.[8]

It is helpful here to understand what makes Tantra distinct from the great Indian tradition of Advaita Vedanta, as the two traditions, though both aiming toward the supreme goal of enlightenment, in some respects use polar opposite approaches. For Advaita all that is real is the transcendent, supreme Self. The world and all its manifest phenomena are regarded as *maya* (illusion). Tantra adopts a different viewpoint, instead arguing that 'the world' and all of its energies are simply the manifestation of divine power, or what it calls *Shakti*. This divine power is merely the outer expression of pure consciousness, what is known as *Shiva*. Thus the world need not be rejected or regarded as illusion, but rather can be understood as 'divine form'. For Tantra existence is both consciousness and energy, whereas Advaita regards energy and all its phenomena as ultimately illusion, mere appearances, with only formless consciousness as Absolute reality.

These may seem to be theoretical differences best left to scholars and religious theoreticians to quibble over, but in fact they reflect a profound difference in method and practice. Tantra embraces physical reality, including the realm of sensual experience. From a purely psychological level it is not hard to understand how the Tantric approach can be useful for those who are deeply mired in materialism and governed by a strong identification with physical life (features common of the *Kali Yuga*, Tantric adepts have maintained). Any approach that involves regarding physical reality as illusory requires a particular psychological maturity to avoid the dangers of repression and the denial of primitive drives (as Jung, for one, had argued).

In this regard an important concept to understand in relation to Tantra is defined by the Sanskrit term *bhoga,* which means, basically, 'enjoyment of the world'. In Tantric teaching this is usually coupled with the term *mukti* (spiritual realization). The essential idea is that both can be embraced, although this was frequently suppressed by early writers on the Tantric traditions, who suggested that Tantric rites involving sexual intercourse were mere 'duties' performed with no accompanying pleasure. That notion has been ridiculed by serious scholars and Tantric practitioners, who at the very least recognize the difficulty of achieving functional sexual arousal without accompanying desire and enjoyment.[9]

In many respects Tantra is the Eastern parallel of the Western esoteric tradition, and this is perhaps never more evident in the view Tantra has of the different 'levels' of reality. Included in this are the 'subtle planes' or finer dimensions, which Tantric doctrine (both Hindu and Buddhist) asserts are populated by a vast range of entities, including various deities that can be supplicated to, commanded, or communed with, for any variety of reasons. For the modern psychologically sophisticated observer this may seem to be primitive animism, but the Tantric view is not simplistically dualistic. The 'entities' of the subtle dimensions are more properly understood as 'energies' having direct associations with particular regions of our mind. When Aleister Crowley famously referred to the 'demons' of the Goetic magic as 'portions of the human brain' he was, in some respects, closely mirroring the Tantric view, which while not denying the 'outer reality' of these entities/energies, also sees their important parallels within the human psyche.

Tantric doctrine includes specific methods for communing with divine energies in the form of particular deities. The chosen deity, known as the *Ishta-devata*, is invoked via intensive visualization practices, its energies awakened in the body, aided by the usage of *mantras* (sacred intoned sounds) and *mudras* (specific hand postures and movements). Both *mantras* and *mudras* on their own are believed to be potent means by which to alter consciousness or relieve the mind and body of particular stresses or diseases. In addition, Tantra employs the usage of *yantras*, geometrically designed images that represent particular divine energies and deities, and are simultaneously understood to be fractals, that is, miniature representations of the universe and its greater energies. (The most elaborate *yantras* are typically the *mandalas*, richly colored circular designs well known to the world mostly via the Tibetan Tantric tradition.) The ultimate purpose of invoking the energies of the deities is to self-identify with them, consistent with some practices of Western theurgical magic.

For Tantra, the key to this connection between the Absolute and the human being is the body, which is held to be both a temple of the divine and a valid expression of the divine (putting it in radical contrast to most Platonic or Gnostic traditions of the West that regard the body as an inconvenient distraction at best, and a disgusting bag of fluids and waste at worst—what the alien in a Star Trek episode once referred to as 'ugly bags of mostly water'). Tantric tradition held a deep interest in the body and its energies, particular those of the 'subtle' variety, and was responsible for the idea of the *chakras* (Sanskrit for 'wheel'), particular subtle energy centers that are thought to correspond to organs, glands, and psycho-spiritual domains (similar, in some respects, to the *sephirot* of the Kabbalistic Tree of Life). The specific map of the *chakras* was introduced to the West by Woodroffe in the early 20th century; it was first mentioned in a structured form in an 8th century CE text of Vajrayana Buddhism (although the concept of subtle energy channels, called *nadis*, was discussed in yogic texts long before). The Theosophist C.W. Leadbeater (1854–1934) adapted Woodroffe's work and from there the New Age popularity of the *chakra* system grew, resulting in the vast literature on the matter of the *chakras* now commonly available.

The acknowledgement of material reality, and specifically the body, is a key to the Tantric world-view that the transcendent is found in the immanent; that is to say, that there is nothing that is not divine. The body becomes central to this philosophy because the body is the most obvious example of what is transitory and how that affects our experience of life, vulnerable as the body is to aging and decay. Because of the vulnerability of our bodies it is natural to view the body as mortal, limited, and by extension, flawed. Tantra teaches that this view is severely limited. In so doing Tantra offers an approach to spiritual deepening that is available for the common person, not just the renunciate. Needless to say this is also what makes the teachings so susceptible to misuse by those lacking in psycho-sexual maturity and seeking a religious or spiritual license to indulge sensory pleasure. For this reason most Tantric texts insist on a powerful sincerity of intention prior to engaging the practices, as well as a profound discipline of study and practice to support the purification of psychological motive for embarking on the path.

In sum, the general disciplines of Tantra involve the following: mastery of posture (yogic *asanas*) and breath-work (yogic *pranayama*); usage of sounds (*mantra*) and hand movements-postures (*mudras*); usage of specific geometric images (*yantras*); and identification with deities (*Ishta-devata*). Additionally, the whole practice is traditionally overseen by a qualified guru; initiation to the guru is believed to be important in that it safeguards against ego-inflation (pride and grandiosity), as well as the common stumbling blocks of the solitary practitioner, namely apathy and lack of discipline.

All of the above may be said to constitute traditional 'right-hand' Tantra. There is also a 'left-hand' path (usually known by the Sanskrit terms *vamamarga* or *vamachara*). This approach gained notoriety doubtless due to its embrace of sex (first introduced to Victorian audiences), and then became of interest particularly in the mid-to-late-20th century owing in part to the 'sexual liberation' of the 1960s-era and beyond. Tantra became attractive to seekers of the post-hippie era who saw it as a means to enlightenment and partying at the same time. The idea seemed enticing but of course is easily misunderstood or abused.

Left-hand Tantra, in addition to using any number of the methods of the traditional 'right-hand' approach, also uses practices such as ritualized sex (at times with a partner who is not one's spouse); the consumption of meat; the consumption of alcohol (wine, generally); and practices taking place in cremation grounds for necromantic rites. These practices are highly antinomian (sexual rites opposing traditional yogic moral codes and celibacy, meat-eating opposing traditional Hindu vegetarianism, etc.), but they are all also, appearances notwithstanding, based on very definite theories of the development of consciousness. For example, a common image of Indian Tantric art is a depiction of Shiva, naked with an erect penis, being ridden by a wild Shakti-Kali, adorned with various fearsome accessories such as daggers and a garland of skulls, the whole thing taking place in a cremation ground. Shiva here represents pure Consciousness, unattached to material existence, and Shakti represents the divine play of manifest existence, all the energies of the universe and their appearances within the vast field of form. It is in the uniting of these two principles, Shakti and Shiva—or energy and consciousness—that the divine is realized and being-consciousness-bliss (*sat-chit-ananda*) is embodied.

Tantric texts, including those of the left-hand approach, commonly admonish those interested in such a path about the need to seek qualified guidance and avoid undisciplined indulgence, such as in this line here from *Kula-Arnava-Tantra*:

If men could attain perfection merely by drinking wine, all the wine-bibbing rogues would readily attain perfection.

...and with this sterner warning:

> One who drinks the unprepared substance [wine], consumes unprepared meat, and commits forcible intercourse [rape], goes to the raurava hell.[10]

A key to ritual sex in Tantra—and this is probably the area most notoriously misrepresented or misunderstood—concerns the matter of sexual fluids. For the left-hand Tantric both semen and vaginal secretions are of central importance, believed to contain highly charged creative energy that, when harnessed properly, can become the 'nectar of the gods' and the key to immortality. Indian alchemy has close connections to left-hand Tantra, although the symbolism in certain matters appears to be reversed in contrast to European alchemy. For example in Western alchemy Mercury is generally associated with the feminine (and on occasion with the hermaphroditic), and sulphur with the masculine; but in Indian Tantra Mercury is connected to the semen, and sulphur to the menstrual blood.[11] Be that as it may the point is to combine, in a sanctified and ritualized fashion, the male-female substances. On occasion this is understood literally, with the mixture of semen and vaginal secretions (including menstrual blood) to be ritually ingested; more often it appears to be a metaphor for the balancing of male-female qualities. (When ingested materially it is essentially the Tantric parallel of the Catholic Eucharist or Holy Communion, wherein bread and wine represent the body and blood of Christ. One rite may be using actual bodily fluids, the other only proxy symbols, but both are held to impart sacred energies to the one who partakes of them).

Left-hand Tantra often utilizes the renowned *pancha-makara* ritual (the 'five Ms'), those being the following: consumption of *madya* (wine), *mamsa* (meat), *matsya* (fish), *mudra* (dry roasted grain), and *maithuna* (ritual sexual intercourse). Consuming wine and meat are highly antinomian acts in a Hindu society that does not eat meat and considers drinking alcohol a serious transgression, and ritualized sex (especially with a non-spouse) is completely against the norm. The usage of the parched grain has never been fully understood by scholars but was traditionally believed to work as an aphrodisiac when combined with the other substances. The ritual sex often takes the form of a group of practitioners seated in circle engaging in intercourse while a guru sits in the middle with his partner, or via coupling postures involving limbs closely intertwined (artistic stylizations of this practice can be seen in some of the famed carvings of the Khajuraho temples of central India). This sexual rite is anything but mere indulgence. It involves considerable preparatory purification rites, the whole thing designed to be a ritual re-enactment of deities (Shiva and Shakti) making conscious love. It is sensual theurgy (embodied high magic) in the most direct sense.

Western Sex Magick

For one who looks into Eastern Tantra and compares it to Western 'sex magick', the latter may appear to be a poor cousin in contrast to the vast literature and long established practices of the East. When the reality of Eastern influences on Western sex magick is factored in as well, it may seem, at first glance, hard to find much of value or importance in the Western traditions of esoteric sexuality. But this would be a mistake. Western traditions in this vein are as rich and potent as their Eastern parallels, even if they are, it must be granted, less coherently organized and documented. Nevertheless it is not difficult to find teachings of sacred sexuality lying at the very core of the great Western mysteries, including Renaissance high magic, alchemy, Hermeticism, the Holy Grail myths, some of the Gnostic traditions, the archetypal legends attached to Christ and Mary Magdalene, the Greek and Egyptian deities, and the Kabbalah. (Even the Knights Templar, Cathars, and Freemasons were suspected of possessing and teaching secrets of sexual energy).

While it is true that modern ideas around Western sex magick did not take coherent form until the late 19th century and well into the 20th, one does not have to go much further back than the Renaissance to find roots of the modern teachings. The Italian proto-scientist, Dominican monk, and magician Giordano Bruno (1548–1600) wrote about the means by which one's reality can be modified and determined based in part on control of *eros*, the erotic force. The link between imagination, the capacity to visualize, and the magic of altering one's inner and outer reality has always been basic to the esoteric traditions, and the key to this has been *energy*. It is no great secret that little can be accomplished in life without sufficient reserves of energy. When Einstein famously equated mass with energy he was scientifically quantifying what esoteric practitioners worldwide have long understood: all that appears is energy in endless manifestations and interactions. This energy can be affected via specific causes, often leading to specific results.

Once it was realized the role that personal energy-level plays in success in life, it was a short leap to realize that a key to creating and sustaining this energy lay in sexual activity, and in particular in understanding the role that orgasm plays for both sexes. In sexual intercourse the key here was recognized to be the matter of male orgasm, for the simple reason that once the male ejaculated the sex act was usually over for both man and woman. As a result the practice of *coitus reservatus* was undertaken, wherein a man learns to engage in intercourse, to whatever degree of intensity, without ejaculating. This in turn was understood to allow for semen retention and energy preservation for the male as well as greater possibility for conscious pleasure and fuller embodiment for the female (without loss of energy).

The issue of recognizing the intrinsic sexuality of the human being, and how influential sexual energy is, was brought to light in the West (and indeed lies at the root of modern psychotherapy) via the efforts of Freud. Wilhelm Reich (1897–1957), originally a student of Freud's, was excoriated for his ideas about the importance of the sexual orgasm in the life of the average person. Practices from Tantra and Western sex magick involve the control of sexual energy, and often the conscious inhibition of the orgasm, so may seem to be at variance with Reich's central notion that only an orgasmic human being is psychologically healthy. But these are not mutually exclusive viewpoints. Rather, Reich's idea may be understood as an important prerequisite for the practitioner of esoteric sexuality. That is, only a psychologically healthy (i.e., functionally orgasmic) person should attempt Tantric or sex magick practices to begin with.

A key figure in the development of Western sex magick is generally acknowledged to be the American writer and occultist Paschal Beverly Randolph (1825–1875). Randolph, an adventurous, largely self-taught character of mixed-race descent (he counted white-European, black-African, and North American Indian blood as part of his ancestry), may have been the first North American to synthesize spirituality and an active embrace of sexuality into a coherent practice. As a young man Randolph had gained a reputation as a trance-medium in the spiritualist circles of 1850s America, but dissatisfied with this practice, embarked on a trip to Europe where he was influenced by French Mesmerists and occultists, and then followed that up a few years later with journeys to the Middle East as well as Turkey and Persia, where he came in contact with Sufism. After these influences—from which it is believed he began to put together the rudiments of his sex magick—he renounced spiritualism (passive mediumship for 'discarnate' spirits), and began to develop a system that involved a pro-active application of specific methods to gain control of one's life and achieve one's maximum potential. His emphasis on practicality was welcomed by 19th century sympathizers and students of the occult, most of whom at that time were limited to theory and abstract conjecture (Theosophy, for example, the dominant esoteric doctrine of the late 19th century, primarily taught theory). Randolph was highly influential in some circles of late 19th century esoterica. It is generally conceded that the important occult organization known as the Hermetic Brotherhood of Luxor (founded in 1870, a sort of precursor to the more famous Hermetic Order of the Golden Dawn founded in 1888) obtained much of its practical curriculum from Randolph's ideas.[12]

Randolph's sex magick teachings were in some regards consistent with the left-hand path of Eastern Tantra. He did not advocate semen retention, but rather emphasized the importance of orgasm, and in particular, simultaneous orgasm for men and women. His idea was that during orgasm the mind and senses are in a heightened state, thus making it possible for the will and intention to operate much more powerfully, thereby enhancing the possibility of manifesting changes in one's reality (everything from acquiring lovers, money, and physical health—the standard objects of 'low' or 'elemental magick').

The essential basis of sex, from the carnal to the spiritual, is of course unification, the bridging of polarities. (The erotic charge of physical sex is, in part, related to the 'impossibility' of two bodies actually ever truly merging, even as the passionate attempt to do so is enjoyed). Randolph was clearly deeply pre-occupied with the matter of unification; he even practiced and taught a form of trance-merging he called 'Blending' or 'Atrilism', wherein the personality is submerged into the presence of a greater personality, the latter of which operates as a source of information and energy via the conduit of the 'lesser personality' of the medium.[13] (It should be noted, however, that Randolph counseled against casual, undisciplined usage of the practice. Max Theon [1848–1927], founder of the Brotherhood of Luxor, had more serious reservations and advised against it altogether). Randolph's sex magic teachings did not take shape until his mid-40s, and he died at 49, so it is probable that his ideas never got beyond rudimentary form. He himself struggled greatly on the personal level (possibly clinical depression) and his death appears to have been a suicide.[14] He was accused by some of getting entangled in baser forms of magic; in some ways he appears to have been a somewhat less cultured and rougher version of Crowley (see below). A perennial problem for 'householder' mystics and occultists has been material survival; the general path of the religious practitioner who seeks to devote their energies full time to inner development has been monastic renunciation. A mystic who chooses to embrace worldly life does not have this monastic insulation, and thus commonly resorts to cruder ways to obtain money. 'Low magic' or 'sorcery' are simply esoteric forms of 'working it'.

Randolph proved to be highly influential. He claimed that his sources for his sex magic ideas were a combination of 'invisible masters' and a particular Sufi initiate he claimed to have encountered in Jerusalem. The Sufi tradition dates from approximately the same time as the coherently recorded origins of Indian Tantra (6th century CE), but there are unquestionably older hints of Tantric teachings long pre-dating Sufism. Randolph likely had some influence on Carl Kellner (1851–1905) and Theodore Reuss (1855–1923), the 'founding fathers' of the Ordo Templi Orientis

(O.T.O., founded around 1902), a Western occult fraternity similar in some superficial respects to Freemasonry, yet radically different in its embrace of sexual magick as a key element of its initiatic process. The O.T.O. claimed a lineage tracing back to the 18th century 'Bavarian Illuminati' and even the 12th century Knights Templar, although this provenance is now generally recognized as myth.

Kellner, an Austrian chemist and businessman, claimed that during travels in the Near East he was initiated by a Sufi and two Hindu Tantricas; he also claimed that he had been influenced by descendents of 18th century Austrian Masonic and Rosicrucian adepts, themselves allegedly connected in some fashion to Max Theon's Randolph-influenced Brotherhood of Luxor. The O.T.O. is of significance here primarily because of the role Aleister Crowley played in it, and in his subsequent marked influence on 20th century ideas of sex magick.[15] Crowley's life story has been amply documented in numerous biographies, but needless to say his notoriety as a so-called 'sex magician' (as well as prolific author, accomplished poet, mountain climber, genuine mystic, and hedonistic occultist) led eventually to both his fame and infamy. His connection to modern Western notions of Tantra is important but often unrecognized. Although knowledgeable in most matters of the Western esoteric tradition as well as Eastern traditions such as Raja Yoga, Taoism, and the *I Ching*, Crowley, as with many during his time, was limited in his actual knowledge of Indian Tantra. As Hugh Urban observed:

> Ironically, despite his general ignorance about the subject, and arguably without ever intending to do so, Crowley would become a key figure in the transformation and often gross misinterpretation of Tantra in the West, where it would become increasingly detached from its cultural context and increasingly identified with sex.[16]

Kellner and Reuss had taken certain of Randolph's basic (and relatively tame) ideas of sex magick and added entirely new elements to them, in formulating the inner doctrines of the O.T.O. These included the usage of semen to anoint a particular 'sacred' material symbol (such as a talisman, for example), immediately following an act of ritualized intercourse, as well as acts involving masturbation and anal sex. It is generally conceded that these activities would have been rejected by the more conservative Randolph. In 1912 Reuss paid a visit to Crowley and accused him of publishing certain secrets of sex magick 'belonging' to the O.T.O. in Crowley's *The Book of Lies*. Crowley convinced Reuss that he had hit upon these ideas independently (which was true). The end result was that Crowley was empowered by Reuss as an O.T.O. adept. Reuss became ill in 1921 and resigned as leader of the O.T.O. in 1922; shortly after Crowley assumed leadership. He then modified some of its core rituals, expanding the nine rituals to eleven while he was at it. These added rituals included sexual acts that typically offend conventional moral standards, especially those of Crowley's day. These included the 8th degree which involved masturbating on the sigil of a demon, as well as the 9th that included the left-hand Tantric practice of ingesting sexual fluids (sucked out of the female following intercourse). The final degree, the 11th, involved anal intercourse. All of these acts can be understood as part of the psychology of transgression, that is, they derive their erotic power from the tension of ignoring the restriction of a taboo. This erotic power can, in turn, be used as a means by which to accomplish aims, such as changing particular circumstances in one's life. It can also function as a potent metaphor for the entire process of breaking free of the limitations of the egocentric self, in order to achieve a glimpse of unobstructed consciousness.[17]

An interesting and significance aspect of the development of Western sex magick involved some of the 19th century misunderstandings of Indian Tantra, part of which involved (and still involves) confusing the famed *Kama Sutra* texts with Tantra. The *Kama Sutra,* essentially a 'how-to' manual on the erotic arts, is older than Tantra (in its doctrinally coherent form), originating around the

3rd century BCE, but has little to do with actual Tantric teachings.

The idea of semen combined with menstrual blood as an elixir to be ritually consumed was not unique to certain schools of left-hand Indian Tantra (let alone to the founders of the O.T.O. or Crowley). It was also found within early Christian era Gnostic sects known variously as the Borborites and Phibionites (descended from the Christian 'heretics' known as the Nicolaitians, a sect that had been soundly condemned by the early Church fathers as gross hedonists). Anyone even casually acquainted with Gnosticism may find this surprising as most Gnostic sects were anti-material, regarding the physical universe and especially the body as 'prisons' in which the spark of divinity has been trapped. An early central Gnostic text cautioned that 'it is not to experience passion that you have been born, but to break your fetters'.[18] Another common Gnostic idea was that the body of Jesus was only an appearance, lacking corporeality, the implication being that the divine cannot fully enter the physical. Such views could only be seen as diametrically opposed to left-hand Tantra, to say nothing of Western ideas of sex magick originating from Randolph, Kellner, and Crowley.

According to the early Church fathers there was a tradition of libertine groups loosely affiliated with early Christianity, such as the Carpocrations, who allegedly believed that all forms of vice (including morally debased acts) should be experienced in order to avoid rebirth into another body after death. Carpocrations did not appear to be Gnostic in the classic sense, but the Borborites were, holding many common Gnostic myths within their teachings (such as the creation of the World by the false god Ialdobaoth, the duality within human nature, and the incarnation of the perfected spirit Christ within the human mortal Jesus of Nazareth). The Borborites, mentioned above, added unique elements, based on the idea that a task of humanity is to 'collect' scattered remnants of wisdom that have been dispersed throughout the material universe (stemming from the original calamity of the creation of the universe, which Gnosticism in general claims was an elaborate error). Part of the process of 'collecting' involved, according to the Borborites, consuming sexual fluids as a Eucharist. The following was recorded by the Gnostic critic St. Epiphanius:

> They hold their women in common…they serve lavish meats and wines…after a drinking party…they turn to their frenzied passion…and when the wretches have intercourse with one another…in the passion of their illicit sexual activity, then they lift up their blasphemy to heaven. The woman and the man take the male emission in their own hands and stand gazing toward heaven…and they say, 'we offer unto you this gift [semen], the body of Christ and the anointed', and then they eat it, partaking of their own filthiness…and likewise of the woman's emission: when it happens that she has her period, her menstrual blood is gathered and they mutually take it their hands and eat it. And they say, 'This is the blood of Christ…'[19]

Because the only sources of this information are polemical writings by Church fathers seeking to discredit Gnosticism—including allegations by St. Epiphanius that the Borborites went so far as to induce abortions and ritually eat embryos—the whole matter is obviously questionable, and yet the striking similarity of the sexual practices involving male and female emissions (along with the mention of wine and meat) with those of some of the left-hand sects of Indian Tantra strongly suggests that they are authentic. (It is also interesting to note, if only in passing, that the Gnostic sects employing such left-hand practices are older, by a few centuries, than most of the recorded doctrine of Hindu or Buddhist Tantra).

A key to understanding the ideology behind such practices can be found in this Gnostic Phibionite passage:

> It is I who am Christ (the anointed), inasmuch as I have descended from above through the names of the 365 rulers (archons).[20]

These words were spoken by one who had completed a series of ritualized sexual intercourse. All of it relates to the idea of the 'descending current' of spirituality—*materializing the spiritual*. In most traditional 'right hand' spiritual philosophies, the idea is to encourage the 'ascending current'—to spiritualize matter—to rise, to ascend, to transcend, to resurrect. The so-called left-hand approach is principally about the reverse, i.e., 'earthing' the spiritual. Some have likened the right-hand approach of spiritualizing the material to the path of the serpent (*kundalini* 'rising' up the *chakras*), and to the alchemical idea of *solve* (break down); and the left-hand approach of materializing the spiritual as the path of the dove (the descent of spirit into matter), and the alchemical idea of *coagula* (rebirth).[21] Shorn of all moral and ethical concerns, the formula is straightforward: the essential idea of both Tantra (whether left or right hand) and sex magick is to work with our lot in material reality in such as way as to achieve our higher purpose for being here. That higher purpose is conceived of as a deep embrace of our conditions (as opposed to rejecting or renouncing them). The goal is nothing less than a radical personal metamorphosis: a structured process of breaking down the egocentric barriers of the personality so as to allow for the emergence of an embodied and profoundly fulfilled consciousness. When sexual fluids are regarded as sacred ambrosia worthy of ritualized practices, it can be taken as a deep metaphor for recognizing the divine as both a creative force and a material reality.

Chapter 7

Philosophy and the Western Esoteric Tradition

The ultimate point of the esoteric paths of inner work is to access a specific domain of consciousness, via self-observation, that leads to 'direct experience' of reality.[1] This domain of consciousness—what Ken Wilber called the 'eye of spirit'—is distinct from intellectual reasoning. The distinction between these two domains of mind is probably never better illustrated than by the likelihood that the vast majority of the greatest thinkers in history—be they in the fields of philosophy, science, or culture and arts— were not mystics who actively explored the 'eye of spirit', or were even scarcely aware of it. Of course, ideas about 'domains of consciousness' distinct from intellect—not to mention critical thought—run the risk of breeding inflation or grandiosity. However, there are in fact very specific disciplines of embracing the 'eye of spirit' or meditative consciousness (discussed in Part II), much as there is a discipline for learning to play a musical instrument or to perform advanced mathematical operations. What we are addressing in the realm of inner work is always to be self-verified via actual practice. In the course of this the intellect is accorded its best role in the process, something akin to the pilot of an airplane, even if not the passenger in the cabin.

What follows in this chapter is a look at some of the more important philosophers of the comparatively recent past, along with the ways in which their ideas gave voice to some of the greatest dilemmas that the intellect can conjure as it grapples with reality. In particular we will consider mutual influences between the great Western philosophical and literary traditions known as German Idealism and Romanticism and the Western esoteric tradition.[2]

The discussion in this chapter begins with John Locke, Bishop

Berkeley and David Hume. Needless to say Western philosophy that is relevant to the Western esoteric tradition did not magically begin with Locke, Berkeley, or Hume—at the very least Descartes and Spinoza deserve mention,[3] and the ancient Greeks (along with the Gnostics and Plotinus) were obviously foundational. However it was with Locke that the discipline of using the mind to examine the structures of the mind itself really began in a full-fledged fashion, and this, along with the contributions of Romanticism (see below), are hallmarks of the esoteric tradition, in the best sense of self-examination and the quest to understand the mind (and this is despite the irony that Locke and the Romantics represented polar opposite viewpoints—empiricism vs. imagination). Consequently we begin our discussion with Locke.

Locke, Berkeley, and Hume

John Locke was born in 1632 in southwest England.[1] He was an Oxford graduate and in addition to being generally recognized as one of the great English empirical philosophers, he was also a medical doctor. His influence was broad; he is usually credited with being one of the original 'liberals', and his writings on political philosophy were admired by such august figures as Voltaire and the Founding Fathers of the United States (such as Franklin and Jefferson). Like Kant, his more mature philosophical writings did not appear until he was in his late 50s.

Locke followed in the footsteps of the great empiricist Francis Bacon, and was also profoundly influenced by Isaac Newton. Intellectual Europe of the 17th century was awash in the excitement of the birth of empirical science, all based on the general idea that Nature could be understood and explained by the mind, and that further, the mind itself could be understood by the mind. In short, reason was supreme, with the potential of not just devising theories to explain the universe and with creating technologies that could eventually harness the vast powers of Nature itself (to be realized the following century via the Industrial Revolution), but also with the extraordinary capacity to understand its own functioning. With Locke, Western philosophy had entered a new phase: examining, in closely reasoned detail, the workings of the mind itself.

It was in the early periods of this phase that Locke put forth his most significant philosophical ideas, first published in 1690 as *An Essay Concerning Human Understanding*. Although some of his views were later refuted quite convincingly, his work remains highly significant because he was arguably one of the first Western thinkers to begin applying rigorous thought in a fashion similar to how the great Vedantic and Buddhist sages of the East had done centuries before—although Locke himself, with no strong introspective philosophical tradition to fall back on, arrived at only preliminary understandings on his own.

The essence of his main ideas published in his great *Essay* can be summarized as *all mind-content is dependent on sensory input*. As Locke saw it, the mind in its pristine state is nothing but a blank screen, a *tabula rasa*, a hard drive with nothing on it upon which are written 'programs' that contain the 'code' received from our senses. Everything we think and call 'knowledge' derives ultimately from our sensory input. The data received from our senses becomes memory, and then concepts, and then our various levels of understanding. It is the essence of realism: consciousness ultimately arises from matter, since all our ideas are based on the sense impressions our bodies receive from the material universe. We know nothing without our senses. There are no 'native ideas' that somehow exist independent of our sensory experience (thus putting Locke in direct opposition to Descartes), and thus there are no 'innate principles' (a serious threat to religion). This does not mean, of course, that we cannot devise elaborate mental constructs, but rather that all reflections, regardless of how complex, ultimately arise from sensory experience.

Locke's position epitomized the essential creed of the 17th century 'Enlightenment' (Age of Reason), which was that all knowledge of 'things' was held to be based on sensory experience, and that anything else was meaningless imagination. In other words, we know the world only via the body. Matter is the base of the pyramid, with all intellectual understanding sitting at the top, 'resting' on matter. In this realist view the mind is an emergent property of the brain, nothing more, and relies entirely on the senses of the body to develop ideas about the universe in which it dwells.

Locke elaborated this position in some detail. He did not claim that no knowledge whatsoever is possible without sensory input, but allowed that certain forms of knowledge, such as that derived from mathematics and logical operations, was obtainable. We do not need to see, hear, touch, taste, or smell in order to grasp that 2+2=4. But such knowledge is isolated, and cannot help us to 'know' the world in any real fashion. For that, according to Locke, we need sensory experience.

Locke took from Descartes (and developed) the concept of two essential types of ideas: the simple and the complex. A simple idea is that which derives from a particular physical sense—such as, the sound of a dog barking. A complex idea is based on a combination of simple ideas—for example, I have seen the dog, it is black in color and of this particular size, and it makes this type of barking sound. The idea is that a simple idea cannot be broken down further, but can be built on. It was from the basis of different types of ideas that Locke proposed we are capable of distinguishing between what he called the primary and secondary qualities of a given object. Primary qualities are those that will be perceived as the same by all people—examples being size and shape. Secondary qualities depend on sensory interpretation, such as smell, sound and color, and will not be experienced as the same by everyone. For example, a color-blind person will not see a red square block the same as a person with normal vision, but both can agree on the exact size of the object. Therefore, the size is a primary quality, and the color a secondary quality. From all this Locke concluded that scientific exactitude was possible, and real knowledge of things could be attained, by analyzing primary qualities. This position has been called 'representative realism', because it is based on the idea that our mind *represents* the world, but does not replicate it.

The Irish philosopher George Berkeley (b. 1685, later Bishop Berkeley), was five years old when Locke published his *Essay*; unlike Locke his important publications were produced at a young age. In 1710, at just twenty-five, he published his *A Treatise Concerning the Principles of Human Knowledge,* in which he put forth his opposition to some of the essential tenets of Locke's ideas.

Berkeley's main argument was that Locke had erred by not going far enough, by not following his reasoning to its logical conclusion. Berkeley reasoned that there was no true difference between so-called primary and secondary qualities, in that both were experienced as thoughts in the mind. From this position, Berkeley claimed that all we can really know for certain are our ideas about things—we cannot conclude, with absolute certainty, that our thoughts correctly represent any 'thing' in the world. All we can conclude for certain is that we are experiencing these thoughts. We cannot escape the reality that our experience of anything and everything is via our mind, and therefore, all we can assume truthfully is that we know reality via our mind.

Berkeley was, however, a Christian, and so like the old Scholastics such as Thomas Aquinas, he sought to flesh out his views in such as way as to keep God at the center of all. His way of reasoning this out was clever. As mentioned, he argued that the so-called material universe is known to us only via our perceptions and ideas of it. In sharp denial of Descartes and Locke, he maintained that material reality has no intrinsic existence but is rather only an appearance. This view, however, brings up the classic paradox of idealism: if no one is present to see and hear the tree falling in the forest, did it actually fall? Or, even more simply, if no one is there to perceive the forest, does it actually exist? It might seem at first glance that Berkeley's position must hold that if no one sees and hears the fall of the tree, it never fell; or that if no one is there to perceive the forest and to thus have an *idea* about the forest, it cannot truly exist. But this seems to be an obvious absurdity. For example, if evolution is essentially correct, there was a time during the history of our planet when there was no consciousness. And yet clearly the planet existed independent of any consciousness to perceive it, otherwise all of life, and ultimately we humans, would have had no planet upon which to evolve in the first place.

Berkeley managed to work out this problem while at the same time preserving the idea of the central existence of God. His solution was simple: *all ideas ultimately derive from the mind of God*. And thus, the fact that things retain their apparent existence is due to the existence of God's ideas. More, the very existence of apparent things, independent of an individual consciousness (such as a person) to develop ideas about them, proves the existence of God. Things appear to exist because they do so as ideas in the mind of God. The tree in the forest does indeed fall if no one is there to experience it, because it is happening within the mind of God.

Berkeley's position went relatively unchallenged for the next thirty years, until a young Scottish philosopher, David Hume, published his *A Treatise of Human Nature* in 1739. Hume carried some of the reasoning of Locke and Berkeley further, to a type of logical dead-end that was startling, and bore some similarities with certain realizations of the East, in particular Buddhist thought. Hume agreed with Berkeley's basic approach but objected to the presence of God in his scheme, arguing that it was both unnecessary and unsupportable. Berkeley's 'God' was an assumption, nothing more.

For Hume, we can be certain of nothing but our own thoughts and perceptions—not that their content is necessarily true, but only that we are in fact experiencing them. As Berkeley had asserted, nothing exists without a consciousness to perceive it—*esse est percipi* (to be, is to be perceived)—only because we have no means of proving the actual existence of anything outside of our mind. But Hume argued that that necessarily includes the supposed existence of God. He also maintained that so-called cause and effect, the cornerstone of empirical science, was an unwarranted assumption, because in truth we never actually perceive anything more than a succession of discrete events in time—'constant conjunctions'. We never perceive the actual 'law' of cause and effect as some intrinsically real operation. We only perceive specific, discrete, individual events that appear to us to coincide with each other, something like still frames of a movie picture that when seen on film create the illusion of seamless continuity.

The key to grasping Hume's reasoning lies in understanding the idea of *inductive inference*. Inductive inference is reasoning based on making observations about patterns, and then reasoning that such patterns continue even when we are not there to observe them. (For example, by extrapolating into the future—eating an apple a day is good for me, therefore it will always be good for me). Hume criticized this reasoning in a way that was reminiscent of some of the old Greek Skeptics, in terms of his using doubt to relentlessly question our assumptions. (He did not, however, advocate living by extreme skepticism, but rather reconciled himself to the necessity of accepting inductive reasoning—it is pointless to stop eating apples, or other healthy food, just because we have no way of knowing that it will still be good for us at some point in the future—unless the knowledge comes to us in the future that eating apples is bad for us). But his essential point stood on an abstract level, that being that we cannot truthfully assume the reality about anything that involves a situation where we are not there to perceive it. All we really know for certain is the succession of ideas as they arise in our consciousness. We cannot know with certainly the cause of these ideas, whether that be God or some mechanical operation of cause and effect, or both.

Hume asserted that our knowledge of cause and effect is based on our own mental operations. What we perceive is not some external operation in nature, but rather our mental act of associating perceptions together. We are seeing how our mind works, not how things 'outside' of our minds work. Hume applied similar reasoning to the self, arguing that what we assume to be the self is nothing but a succession of perceptions, memories, and ideas associated with each other. Assumptions about the discrete existence of some 'self' are as unwarranted as assumptions about the existence of some 'first cause' like God. (Although it should be noted that Hume still saw God as a type of moral imperative, meaning, that since belief in God is the foundation of moral values, it should be maintained, even if God can never be proven by reason to actually exist. Kant was later to elaborate on this point, going to lengths to distinguish between pure and practical reasoning).

Hume's major accomplishment was to take skepticism to a sort of ultimate level, throwing the whole basis of inductive reasoning—*because something is this way here and now, it therefore should be the same way over there, or in the past, or in the future*—under a sharp light. He cast doubt on the whole process by which we go from specific evidence to general truths. In so doing, he continued Locke's efforts to apply close reasoning not just to the world around us, but to the internal workings of consciousness itself.

Kant

Immanuel Kant was born in Konigsberg, Prussia (then part of Germany, today part of Western Russia) in 1724. Apart from one brief period of travel he lived in the same town his whole life, passing away in 1804, near eighty (remarkable longevity, given that his health was generally frail). He was a small, introspective man, a life-long bachelor, a university professor (of logic and metaphysics) much valued by his many students, and a man given to great inner discipline and consistent outer behavior (it was said that his neighbors could set their watches in accordance with his daily walk that he always took at precisely the same hour). As a thinker he matured slowly, only producing his greatest works when he was in his late 50s. His impact on Western philosophy from the 19th century on has been of central importance; Schopenhauer called Kant's magnum opus the 'most important work in German literature' and stated that any aspiring thinker was a child until they had understood Kant. Kant's writing is famously dense and in places opaque, employing specialized terms and, due to his lack of concrete metaphors, exceedingly dry. But his thought was deep and profound, and while some of his points have over time been discarded or surpassed, he represented a key passage in the maturation of Western wisdom.

The first (and most renowned) of his works was *The Critique of Pure Reason* (1781). As the title implies, it is a study of the faculty of reason itself, but not just any reason; in particular, this is reason that is independent of sensory experience. John Locke had held that all knowledge derives from what we first experience via our physical senses. Sensory input comes first—I see, hear, and feel with my hand the running water of this stream—followed by memory (next time I come to this stream, kneel down and place my hand in it again, I know to expect the same basic experience I had last time), which results in thoughts about the stream (knowledge of the stream). Without the initial sensory experience of seeing, hearing, and feeling the water of the stream, I would have no ideas or knowledge of it. This is the materialist viewpoint: all is dependent on matter.

As mentioned, Locke's view had been famously challenged by Berkeley, who argued that Locke's thesis in fact implied the opposite, namely that what we really know is nothing other than our own thoughts, not the object itself. In seeing and hearing and feeling the water of our rushing stream, what we are really knowing are these sensations and our subsequent memory and thoughts (knowledge) about this stream. We do not truly know the stream itself. Berkeley's main point is that everything we seem to know is nothing more than our mental experience of things. Reality is therefore only to be found in ideas and consciousness. Matter is illusion. However Berkeley added that the stream continues to exist as an 'idea' even if we are not there to perceive it, because it is an idea in the mind of God. But, according to Berkeley, the notion of a stream existing independent of consciousness, and in particular independent of the consciousness of God, is a fallacy. This was, basically, the Irish bishop's attempt to discredit and logically disprove the atheistic materialism promoted by Locke. Hume had followed this by taking some of Berkeley's insights to a logical extreme, arguing that little is knowable to the human mind other than the perception of events in close association with each other. For Hume, the ideas of God, the self, and the scientific notion of cause and effect were all assumptions, guesses, unwarranted attempts to explain our subjective impressions. Hume had thus arrived at a polar opposite position to Plato, who had proposed that all we directly experience, via our senses, is but a shadow of a higher order of reality that we cannot normally perceive. Hume argued the opposite, that all we truly know are our direct perceptions, with everything else being a mental construct devised to explain these impressions.

Some forty years after the appearance of Hume's key work, Kant's *The Critique of Pure Reason* was published, in which he had set himself the formidable task of bridging the realms of religion, science, and philosophy with a coherent thesis. This was deemed necessary because of the vast gulf between these disciplines that seemed to exist at that time, a gulf having been initiated by the Copernican revolution in science along with the reasoning of Descartes, Locke, Berkeley, and Hume. On the one hand, science, chiefly via the work of Copernicus, Galileo, and Newton, had arrived at the position that the universe ran on mechanical laws of cause and effect—in effect, a type of determinism that followed naturally from Newtonian mechanics, i.e., the ability to predict accurately the behavior of objects in space and time according to fixed laws that could be defined mathematically. The basis of Judeo-Christian religion, however, was and always had been that a human has the capacity to makes choices, ones that define their morality and spiritual state. This idea seemed to be incompatible with strict causal determinism.

Kant was more than just sympathetic to science; in his earlier years he made unique contributions to the nascent science of 18th century astronomy. He was also steeped in religious conditioning, having been raised in a family of strict Christian values and a fundamentalist interpretation of the Bible. But as with all great philosophers, Kant was above all an original thinker, and had the capacity to take the existing philosophical views of that time to a previously unknown level.

Kant began by agreeing with Hume on some points—in fact, he credited Hume with waking him from a 'dogmatic slumber'. The most essential of these was Hume's assertion that we are incapable of truly knowing any metaphysical issues such as God or the eternal nature of the soul, because these are not phenomena or appearances, and our mind is capable only of generating thoughts about phenomena or appearances. Hume's reasoning had led him to the final view that all laws inferred by science, such as cause and effect, were ultimately unwarranted, nothing more than elaborate assumptions. Kant, however, balked at this, believing as he did that Newton had uncovered legitimate and real knowledge of reality.

To resolve this seeming gulf between Hume's penetrating skepticism and Newton's discoveries of empirical laws, Kant took note of the ability of the human mind to conceive of mathematical laws, and agreed with Descartes and other rationalists that mathematics is a form of definite knowledge. We may be uncertain of most things, but we can be certain of the logic underpinning 2+2=4. How does this come about? Why is it that we can know so little for certain—for example, even whether or not we are dreaming right now—but we can be certain that 2+2=4?

The problem was this: Newton's science, so revolutionary in its ability to explain the natural laws that surround us, was based on abstracts like mathematics and basic geometry. Yet Hume had convincingly argued that the mental processes within us could never yield real knowledge, but rather only assumptions about the things around us, a position that Kant agreed with. The only way out of the problem was to infer that abstract reasoning such as that used by Newton to formulate his laws was somehow inbuilt into the human mind. In other words, Kant stood the whole mind-world problem on its head. Instead of the world informing the mind, it is more a case of our mind shaping the world we come to understand. It is the inbuilt structures of our mind—our hard-drive, as it were—that is giving rise to the world we come to conceive of and experience.

The key to understanding Kant's reasoning lies in his assertion that space and time are what he called '*a priori* forms of sensibility'. In other words, when everything we think we know about reality based on our direct experience of things is taken away, what remains are the innate conceptions of space and time. These latter two are, according to Kant, inherent in our consciousness. They are essential to knowing the world. But because they are means by which we know the world, they shape our experience of appearances, rather than the other way around.

Kant did not, however, maintain that 'nothing exists outside of our mind'. He allowed for the existence of what he called particulars, and in fact asserted that these particulars, and our association with them, were essential for any actual knowledge. Our senses yield to us experience of particulars, which our inherent reasoning—structured as it is on innate views of time and space—then make sense of. Our senses give us raw data, but how the data is interpreted, and the universe we shape out of it, is entirely done by our mind via its *a priori* views of space and time. Kant argued that thought and sense are simultaneously co-active. Our experience and knowledge of a tree are not deriving solely from seeing, touching, and smelling it (as Locke had argued), nor are they based solely on thinking about it (the pure rationalist position). They are based on the activity of seeing, touching, smelling (in this case) and thinking about it *all at once*. But the tree we know of, and the tree we experience, is rooted fundamentally in our mind. The tree, in all ways we experience it and know it, conforms to our mind. Our mind does not conform to the tree. We can have certain knowledge of the tree, but it is 'our' tree, shaped by our mind's innate structures. Kant outlined very specifically the way in which this mental operation unfolds. He began by asserting that our mind is actively involved in ordering the chaos of raw experience into coherent thought (and eventually, knowledge), via two distinct stages. These stages were described by him as:

1. *Transcendental Esthetic*. By 'transcendental' Kant meant the part of our mind that operates independent of sensory experience—the *a priori* structure of the mind—that which we bring to the equation. By 'esthetic' he meant (in the original sense of the word) relating to sensation or feeling. In this first stage, we coordinate raw sensations via our inbuilt understanding of space and time. In applying our natural understanding of space and time to sensations, we arrive at organized perceptions. For example, standing near a tree we see it, can touch it, hear the wind blowing through its branches, and smell its fragrance. These sensations on their own amount to little, but when efficiently organized, they result in the general perception, and thus knowledge, of the tree. Kant argued that this operation of organizing the sensations into a specific perception and knowledge of the tree was not mechanical or automatic, but is being actively directed by a part of our mind. For example, when driving a car, we experience multiple sensory data coming at us at once, the simplest example being a traffic light. The color of the light may be amber, but the situation may be different depending on where we are as we near the intersection, what other vehicles are present on the road with us, and so on. In one situation we may slow down, in another, we may speed up. But in both cases the color is amber, so clearly our basis for acting is not determined solely by the data provided by our visual sense, the color of the light. Another example: we have two numbers, 10 and 1. If we add them, we arrive at 11. If however we subtract the lesser from the greater, we arrive at 9. But in both cases we were working with the same two original numbers, 10 and 1. The end result is different because our mind is actively involved in shaping the result. It is not a passive *tabula rasa*, but an active organizing principle molding our experience of reality. According to

Kant, this organizing operation of the mind is accomplished via its natural inbuilt understanding of space and time.

2. *Transcendental Logic*. This second cumbersome term was Kant's way of defining the second stage in the mind's conversion of raw sense data into specific thoughts and knowledge. It deals with the means by which we convert perceptions into organized thoughts and knowledge. As with the first stage, in which the mind actively organizes sensations into perceptions, so too in this second stage the mind is equally an active agent, converting perceptions into coherent thoughts. It does this via applying its inherent categories to the perceptions—categories such as quantity, quality, relation, substance, cause, and so on. These categories are inherent in the mind, that is, they are valid about an object prior to experiencing the object. The result of all this is that we come to experience an order to reality not because that order is inherent in some external reality, but because our mind is structured with a particular ordering principle. The reality we experience and have knowledge of conforms to our mind and the laws of thought, not the other way around. And this is why when we try to think about the 'end of the universe' (like the end of a road), or 'what was going on before the universe began', we encounter an intellectual roadblock. The questions register as absurdities, impossible to answer, because we are making the error of assuming that space and time are 'real things' outside of us, when in fact they are inherent structures of our mind.

And thus Kant's clever resolution of Hume's skeptical position (we cannot know with certainty anything like scientific laws) with the discoveries of 17th and 18th century nascent science as led by Galileo and Newton (we can most certainly know scientific laws with precision) was to argue that we can indeed gain certain knowledge of the universe, but only because the basis of this knowledge is inbuilt into the fabric of our mind. Our mind, according to Kant, is not a passive block of marble waiting to be shaped by some external reality as it informs us via our senses, but is rather more akin to a sculptor giving specific shape to the marble of apparent external reality; or, to use a modern metaphor, the mind is akin to a movie projector, illuminating and giving meaning to a world, the knowledge of which is arising from our consciousness. Kant was, in a sense, the first comprehensive 'philosophical psychologist', in that his work redirected the traditional pursuit of philosophy from analyzing things, the world, and our relation with the world, to closely analyzing the nature of the thinker, the nature of mind itself.

The end result of all this was that, according to Kant, we cannot penetrate via reason to any 'real world out there'—*numina* ('things in themselves')—in any true sense. We can seem to 'know things' and acquire great knowledge of how things *appear* to us, but it is never anything more than knowledge of appearances shaped by our own mind and its inherent nature. We can know phenomena (appearances), but not the 'thing in itself' (*numina*). It was in this way that Kant ultimately sought to reconcile religion with science. He reasoned that science can indeed gain definite knowledge of appearances, precisely because of the inbuilt structures of the mind. But science (reason) cannot know reality beyond appearances—created by sensations, perceptions, and conceptions—which, he maintained, allowed an inroad for religion and faith. Reason cannot prove the existence of God (thus Kant claimed the medieval Scholastics, such as Aquinas, mistaken), but neither can it disprove it.

As Ken Wilber and others have noted, Kant seems to have been the first Western philosopher to clearly spell out that we cannot know transcendent realities ('God', Self-realization, etc.) via the power of reason alone. This is largely because the nature of reason and logic is to see things in dualities—for example, the cup is full of tea, or it is empty. We cannot imagine a situation where the cup is both full and empty at the same time. And yet ultimate reality is non-dual, realized via a consciousness that reconciles opposites. This reconciliation is recognizable only via a contemplative or meditative practice, i.e., self-observation, and not via an intellectual investigation alone. The question as to whether we can reason ourselves into the direct experience of Self-realization is straightforward: we cannot, because reasoning is a descriptive process that always implies paradox. It explains and defines, but it does not directly experience either unity or non-duality. To directly experience these, we must engage a meditative discipline in order to properly embrace pure awareness. The metaphor of boiling water is useful here: we can reason ourselves to one degree below the boiling point of water, but that 'final degree' is accomplished not via reason but via contemplation (meditation), a final step that can be thought of as a type of quantum leap.

Kant never claimed to be a God-realized mystic but he did have a strong belief in the transcendent reality. He thus proposed that belief in God was a moral necessity, without which there was no basis for ethics, noble decisions, or as the modern expression has it, 'taking the high road'. In an inner version of the social separation of church and state, Kant sought a sharp distinction between reason and faith that allowed, in his view, for optimum functioning of both. The essence of his moral teaching, what he called the 'categorical imperative' (similar to the Golden Rule), he defined as 'act only according to that maxim whereby you can, at the same time, will that it should become a universal law'. That is, in questioning a specific act, we should ask ourselves if it would be right for this act, and its consequences, to apply to everything. In asking ourselves, 'should I steal?' we apply that universally, asking 'should everyone steal?' with the obvious answer being 'no', and so on.

Kant's reasoning, building on, elaborating, and developing the insights of Descartes, Locke, Berkeley, Hume, Newton, Copernicus, and others, ended with a position that involved a definite schism between the subjective reality of man, and the assumption of any knowable objective reality via reason alone. Man is, in a sense, alone in his mind. Kant did, however, hold that certain elements of the human mind were based on absolutes, such as *a priori* understandings of space and time—though subsequent developments in 19th and 20th century science and philosophy, via the revelations and insights of Darwin, Nietzsche, Freud, Einstein, Heisenberg, and many others, laid siege to even this basic bastion of Kant's reasoning. Relativism, uncertainty, and constant change would become the order of the day as the very idea of anything being 'absolute' took a beating.

The Post-Kantian German Idealists: Fichte, Schelling, Hegel

Johann Gottlieb Fichte (1762–1814), was one of the important German Idealists whose ideas, along with Schelling's, provided something of a bridge between those of Kant and later impactful thinkers such as Hegel and Schopenhauer (although the latter, a notoriously incisive critic, heavily disparaged Fichte). Fichte took Idealism to new heights, in so doing closely paralleling some Eastern ideas (particularly Vedanta) in which consciousness is recognized as primordial and supreme. Fichte's main argument was that Kant's idea of a distinction between 'things-in-themselves' (*numina*) and appearances (phenomena) was an ultimately pointless mental exercise, and should be discarded.

Kant had argued that both *a priori* and *a posteriori* were essential categories of knowing. *A priori* ('what comes before') is knowledge that is not dependent on experience. An example is 'all triangles have three sides'. We do not have to see the triangle to know that it will have three sides. *A posteriori* ('what comes after') knowledge—also known as 'empirical evidence'—is the foundation of science. We gain this form of knowledge only via direct experience (observation, etc.). An example would be, 'some triangles have angles that when jointly added do not sum to 180º' (as they always do in flat Euclidean geometry). This is so in the case of a triangle on a spherical surface, for example, where the sum of angles will be greater than 180º. Such could only be determined via direct observation (that is, we would have to see it to believe it). Kant called *a priori* knowledge 'transcendental', determined by 'form' of experience, and *a posteriori* knowledge as 'empirical', depending on 'content'. It was the latter kind of knowledge that Fichte proposed to philosophically abandon. He asserted the supremacy of the subjectivity of consciousness.

This was, of course, a hallmark of Idealism, in which the very idea of any 'thing in itself' outside of consciousness is essentially meaningless. Kant had maintained that the 'thing in itself' really did exist, but was unknowable via reason—that is, whatever existed 'outside' of the mind's construction of reality, cannot be directly known. Some Idealist contemporaries of Kant (such as Friedrich Jacobi, 1743–1819) took exception to this, arguing that just because a 'thing in itself' cannot be known via reason only means that it should be taken to exist 'on faith'. Implicit in this 'faith' was a form of knowing akin to revelation. A 'thing' could thus be known via a direct experience that was not associated with reason (very reminiscent if the Zen idea of *kensho*, or 'direct realization'). At this point, a difficulty philosophers seemed to be wrestling with was arising from a lack of subjective categories (such as the difference between 'ego' and 'mind', something addressed by modern psychology, and of course, in Eastern traditions). For example, the matter of knowing 'things in themselves' (or the issue of whether they exist or not) can be helped by recognizing that it depends upon our state of mind when approaching the matter. A mind trained via meditation has a potentially greater chance of making sense of the whole matter, and taking it beyond a purely abstract argument.

Fichte's whole point was that the idea of the 'thing in itself' as 'outside' of a knowing subject was unnecessary. He maintained that Kant's idea—that a mental representation must necessitate the existence of some 'external' object that corresponds to it—was mistaken, that it was the subjective representation that was entirely the cause of the external 'thing in itself'. According to Fichte, the entire universe, and our experience of it, arises from our consciousness.[4]

Friedrich Schelling (1775–1854), a student of Fichte's, eventually rebelled against some of his mentor's ideas, which became part of his contribution to German *Naturphilosophie*, a theory of unity within Nature that did not require it being relegated to a mere appearance in the consciousness of the individual. For Schelling, the universe was an Intelligence complete within itself, and more than just one mind's internal representation of it. This approach is essentially realism, sometimes called Transcendental Realism, in which Nature holds within it consciousness; a Nature that is ultimately a manifestation of the one Spirit. Schelling was in many ways a mystic. He did not believe that the Absolute could be apprehended via pure reason (in contrast to Hegel), but held rather that it can only be directly known via a higher intuition that is essentially mystical insight (via contemplation, perception of aesthetics, and so forth). In this regard he was anticipating later integral ideas that distinguish between different modes of apprehending reality. Schelling's impact on modern psychology was considerable, particularly through his coining of the term 'unconscious mind'. Of note was his influence on the poet-philosopher Samuel Taylor Coleridge (1772–1834), who is sometimes credited with exposing the broader public to certain of Schelling's ideas, and for influencing Emerson and American Transcendentalism.

Georg Wilhelm Friedrich Hegel (1770–1831), was one of the more important of the immediate post-Kantian German philosophers. His views were expansive and inclusionary, exemplifying a broad-minded, mature thinking that ended up being highly influential. (He was, for example, a key influence on Marx and socialism, although not by design). Hegel published four main works, between 1807 and 1822. These works brought him fame and wide respect; in the last decade of his life he was considered by many as the reigning philosopher of his time. Post-modern integral philosophers of the early 21st century also hold him as one of the key thinkers of recent history.

Unlike Kant, Hegel was less concerned with the function and

operation of reason itself, and more with specific concepts, in particular some of the 'categories' that Kant utilized. Chief of these categories that concerned Hegel was that of Relation, specifically, the qualities of contrast, opposition, conflict, and negation. All philosophy is ultimately a progression of ideas, with each philosopher building on, or pushing against, the views of his predecessors, and Hegel was no different in that regard. He was influenced by Plato, Aristotle, Jacob Boehme, Kant, and in particular, Heraclitus, whom he lavished special praise on, for being the first to grasp the idea that existence is a process of *becoming*, not a static 'being' or 'void'. Boehme (1575–1624) had caught Hegel's attention with his insight into stages of development (a key to integral thinking)—in particular his idea that the 'fall' of humanity was not an aberration, or an event of tragic misfortune, but was rather a developmental stage that was essential for our collective maturation.

Hegel always strove to see the bigger picture, to place things in their maximum context, and to that end he had a deep interest in history and development of philosophy throughout time. He is often credited with coining the term *zeitgeist* ('spirit of the time'), although he used a slightly different wording—*der Geist seiner Zeit*—to convey the idea that it is very difficult, if not impossible, for an individual to transcend the cultural effects and biases of the time one finds oneself in. Hegel sought to reconcile opposites in all realms: philosophy, politics, art, religion, and so on. His main point was that what appears to be a divisive conflict or disconnect between polar opposites, is in fact a natural process whereby these 'opposites' are irresistibly drawn to each other in order to learn and unite, resulting in a reconciliation that yields a higher order of things. (This was probably the main philosophic influence behind G.I. Gurdjieff's 'Law of Three'). Concrete examples of this idea are found in the notions of subject and object in philosophy (idealism vs. realism), in politics (freedom vs. authority), and in the two main currents of thought in his time, the Enlightenment and Romanticism. Hegel (along with Schelling and the schools of developmental psychology that would follow) was a major influence on the burgeoning 'integral' movement of the late 20th and early 21st centuries, in which the new paradigm is to reconcile seemingly irreconcilable schools of thought by placing them into the context of a maximum-breadth view that factors in the level of consciousness one is operating through.

Hegel was essentially a mystic as well as a philosopher, hence his overriding concern with the 'whole' and with what he saw as the illusion of separation, something he held in common with Spinoza, although he worked the idea out more comprehensively. Like all mystics he did not grant any absolute reality to space and time, as to do so would tacitly admit the reality of separateness. This is an essential element of the esoteric tradition, which always treats the universe as an organism of functioning parts that ultimately mirror the Absolute, as well as the inner workings of a human being.

The Influence of Romanticism on the Western Esoteric Tradition

In some respects Romanticism—though largely a literary, cultural, and philosophic phenomenon of 18th-19th century Germany—found its origins in the Swiss philosopher Jean-Jacques Rousseau (1712–1778), via his emphasis on such values as freedom and the cultivation of natural and innate wisdom (later mischaracterized by others as the idea of the 'noble savage'), as well as the importance of feelings and emotions in addition to abstract reasoning. The golden age of Romanticism was heralded by such literary figures as Blake, Wordsworth, Coleridge, Shelley, Keats, and Byron, all of whom influenced modern sensibilities and intellectual values. The iconic representation of the Romantics was probably best captured by the Greek god Prometheus, the embodiment of rebellion against old and oppressive paradigms, and the exalting of the individual and his or her capacity for freedom, originality, and unique contribution to the progression of the human race. Much of this, and associated values such as feeling, intuition, inspiration—in short, what we might characterize as the 'power of the unconscious mind'—along with an awareness of the unifying spirituality of existence, arose in contrast to the stark rationalism of the Enlightenment and its subsequent scientific revolution.[5] Much of the 'occult revival' of the 19th century was in part inspired by the Romantics, and served as a type of repository for the 'rejected knowledge' of the new sciences alongside the mysticism and occultism rejected by the reigning organized religions. Most occultists of the 19th century were essentially Romantics with an esoteric focus. 'Secret societies' with arcane names ('The Hermetic Brotherhood of Luxor', 'The Golden Dawn', 'The Rosicrucian Society', 'The Esoteric Section of the Theosophical Society', etc.) counted among their membership those who sought to embody the Promethean values of the Romantics, to rebel against the twin pillars of organized religion and coldly rationalistic materialism, and exult in the passion of the belief that they had found a unique pathway to the highest truths. To what extent this was ever realized on an individual level is another matter entirely, but unquestionably the very commitment to such a path filled those following it with a profound sense of purpose and destiny.

All that said, it is equally true that the Western esoteric tradition itself influenced German Idealism and the Romantics. To what extent this was so has been an ongoing debate among historians of ideas, in part because of the difficulty in establishing what exactly Hermeticism (for example) was; distinguishing its theoretical structure from its history across a span of two millennia is not always straightforward. As a good example, William Walker Atkinson's influential 1908 publication *The Kybalion* (see Appendix I) which purports to summarize the Hermetic doctrine of antiquity via a neat list of theoretical principles, was clearly influenced by 19th century New Thought ideas, themselves a child of Romanticism and German Idealism.

The influence of the Western esoteric tradition, chiefly via Hermeticism and Neoplatonism, upon Romanticism is evident via a world-view that emphasizes the organic nature of the universe, in contrast with the mechanistic view of science (mostly initiated with Newtonian mechanics). The esoteric tradition largely views the universe as fundamentally alive and whole, moved from within, as opposed to a clockwork universe that operates via mechanically predictable cause and effect laws that appear to be operating on it from without. (In this matter, it is always worth invoking Arthur C. Clarke's popular slogan 'any sufficiently advanced science is indistinguishable from magic', in that in the end, the word-view of science and that of the esoteric and Romantic traditions may be describing the exact same thing, just interpreted differently owing to different conceptual filters and personal biases). Also important is the matter of imagination, and its relationship to inner growth. The Romantics, in common with many esoteric traditions (both of the West and the East) understood the power and value of the imagination when properly cultivated. Empiricism, via the influence of Bacon, Locke, and the scientific revolution, was antithetical to imagination in general, based as it was on the desire to ascertain truth via facts. Romanticism arose largely in reaction to this, but in so doing was echoing the inner tenets of key parts of esotericism.

A main argument of some of the Traditionalists (Guenon, Schuon, Eliade, etc.) is that the great esoteric tradition is not founded on any particular culture, and nor is it the child of any particular time—where time is understood in the conventional, linear sense. The term 'aeviternity' speaks to this, referring to the timeless present, sometimes also called 'esoteric time', or in Coomaraswamy's words, 'nowever'.[6] The idea is that the truths of the esoteric tradition are timeless—not in the literary clichéd sense of that term—but rather as a literal psycho-spiritual state. Because of this, the Romantic idea of evolutionary progressiveness did not ultimately apply to the esoteric tradition, where its deepest truths are known in the timeless state. This suggests to some extent that it was the esoteric tradition that influenced Romanticism, rather than the other way around. That said, there obviously is a place for progressiveness within the field of spiritual awakening. It applies, however, to the ways in which we can best express within, and extend to, the particular culture and world we find ourselves in. Our evolution, growth, maturation, metamorphosis, however we conceive of it, is defined in part by the means with which we can express these timeless truths. There is always room for improvement. But what we are always improving on is the means of *delivery* of the gift, not the gift itself.

Schopenhauer and Nietzsche

It is not within the scope of this book to cover the ideas and influence of these two philosophers to a degree warranted by their importance. Accordingly only a few of their more seminal ideas and influence on modern esotericism (as well as psychotherapy) will be mentioned here.

The historian Will Durant characterized Arthur Schopenhauer's (1788–1860) magnum opus *The World as Will and Representation,* published in 1818, as 'that great anthology of woe'.[7] Schopenhauer has been regarded as a 'pessimist', but this seems to be based as much on reaction to his uncompromising (and at times outright cranky) style of expression as it does to his ideas.

Schopenhauer had a particularly brilliant insight that foreshadowed much of modern psychotherapy: he argued that our conscious intellect is not actually the 'master of the house', but in fact is more like a servant. The real master is what he called the 'will', a force that drives us, generally in ways that we are not conscious of. In other words, he was talking about something very much like the unconscious mind, and correctly attributing enormous influence to it. This is a crucially important point to understand for any committing to transformational work via an esoteric path, because the path that we set out on rarely unfolds in the way that we initially imagine it will. Life is a process of unfolding surprises, but this is even more so on the path of inner work, largely because we are attempting to encounter the unconscious mind—the 'zone' we must pass through if we wish to access any 'higher' levels of consciousness.

Schopenhauer compared the 'will' to a 'strong blind man' who carries on his back a much weaker man who has the ability to see (the conscious intellect). The key insight in all of this is the idea that our unconscious desires are running the show, as it were; we ascribe reasons and all sorts of justifications for things, thinking that we are being led by these reasons, when in fact it is the reverse: *our reasons are being carefully crafted to fit our desires*. This insight leads to a deeper realization, one that shows up particularly in relationships: we 'need' certain kinds of people in our life in order to fit with our unconscious desires and patterns. We then go through all sorts of mental gymnastics to justify these relationships (or to complain about them), when in fact we are not choosing them at all, at least not consciously. We are gravitating toward them on the basis of unrecognized (unconscious) urges of the will. These relationships are necessary to justify our already-existing beliefs held in our unconscious mind.

Schopenhauer initially had a low opinion of religion, dismissing it as the 'metaphysics of the masses'. However, as he was exposed to certain currents of Eastern thought, such as Hindu and Buddhist doctrines, his view began to change and he came to see some of the power and depth of religious teachings, including those of Christianity. He saw merit in Augustine's idea of 'original sin', recognizing what he saw as its profoundly realistic common sense: he believed that original sin was simply the assertion of the will (i.e., self-centered life), and that salvation was denial of the will (renunciation of a self-centered life). He ultimately favored Eastern teachings, especially admiring (and agreeing with) the realization that the small self (ego) has no real existence, being a type of mirage constructed by the mind to convince itself that as a wave it is separate from the ocean.

Schopenhauer was the first, and in some ways most important, influence on Friedrich Nietzsche (1844–1900), himself to become one of the more influential factors in 20th century philosophical, literary, and psychological thought. Nietzsche's prescience concerning the insights of modern psychotherapy has been established by historians. One of his influential ideas was that of the *Ubermensch*, a term that has been translated in various awkward ways (the most common being 'overman' or the more dubious 'superman') and first expressed in his key work *Thus Spake Zarathustra*. Nietzsche's idea of the overman is one who overcomes his mere humanity, rising above the mediocre masses, but not in the evasive, dismissive, or renouncing way of an ascetic; in many ways, the overman is diametrically opposed to the world-denying elements of Christianity or any form of asceticism. Nietzsche was a trenchant critic of mediocrity, a mediocrity that he blamed in part on the Christian legacy of splitting the world and the soul into two compartments. He was chiefly concerned with life-affirmative views that promoted an embodied spirituality, not one that disparaged or feared bodily life.

The idea of a Godless universe was echoed in one of the most famous of Nietzschean declarations, 'God is dead'. He rejected the 'God-hypothesis' and notions of a 'transcendent reality' beyond this world. Nietzsche's overman is motivated by a love of life, and of this Earth. His view in this matter was stridently anti-Platonic, that is, he wholly rejected Plato's scheme of higher worlds lurking invisibly beyond this world. In that sense Nietzsche was contrary to a great deal of more traditional Western esoteric doctrine, which has much of its basis in Plato. He was adamantly opposed to blind faith, insisting on the need for individuals to apply personal will to break through their limitations, and to find their emancipation through their own selfhood.

Though brilliant, Nietzsche was also a product of his times, a condition that not even the most radical intelligence can fully escape. The 19th century saw the birth of scientific materialism—sometimes called scientism, an appropriate term as it is suggestive of a new kind of faith—and while Nietzsche was no scientist, he did give voice to the long-standing urge to break entirely with the credulous blind faith of our Medieval heritage that had left such a longstanding imprint. He was pre-eminently concerned with freedom, an understandable fact, given the virtual slavery humans have lived in for most of recorded history—slavery to others, slavery to material reality, slavery to the harshness of life. Nietzsche was a singlehanded force of nature when it came to the establishment of a new type of worldview that was part and parcel of the terrible struggle of humanity to free itself of thousands of years of endless forms of slavery. He was a herald of new view of freedom. His influence on so many key thinkers of the 20th century was marked (including some unfortunate and misguided attempts to adapt some of his views to German nationalism, although it is accepted by most historians that most Nazi leaders had either not understood him or had not made a serious study of him).

Summary

The Western esoteric tradition has had a complex relationship with philosophy: Pythagoras, Heraclitus, Empedocles, Socrates, Plato, Aristotle, and the Stoics of Greece all left their mark on the development of Hermetic ideas in Alexandrian Egypt of the first three centuries before Christ. Plotinus himself was as much a mystic as a philosopher, and the tradition he shaped, along with his followers Proclus and Iamblichus—loosely known as Neoplatonism over the centuries—became a central part of esoteric teachings. Traditions such as alchemy and the Kabbalah have remained relatively free of influence from classical philosophy, although Kabbalism shares clear similarities with Neoplatonism. Modern forms of esoteric teachings (from the 19th century on) show, however, obvious influences from philosophy, most notably Kant and the German Idealists. Romanticism operated as a distinct stream of influence, but itself appears to have been influenced by older Hermetic ideas; that said, Romanticism clearly had great influence upon 19th century Transcendentalists, who in turn gave birth (along with Mesmer's followers) to the New Thought and later New Age movements. Existentialists such as Kierkegaard and Nietzsche did have influence upon elements of modern psychoanalysis, and indirectly upon the development of the mid-20th century human potential movement. Most of these currents of thought remain relatively distinct, but over time a convergence effect can be detected, probably showing best in the late 20th-early 21st century interest in 'integral theory', maps of philosophical, spiritual, and esoteric thought that seek to define a 'full spectrum model' of reality.

Chapter 8

Transcendentalism, New Thought, New Age

The relationship between the movements known loosely as 'New Thought' (and its more recent derivative the 'New Age') to the Western esoteric tradition is notable though not always clear. The 19th century 'mind healing' phenomenon (the basis of New Thought), though having its practical roots in Phineas Quimby and to a lesser extent Franz Mesmer, was unquestionably influenced by certain key streams of philosophy. Foremost of these are Immanuel Kant and the German Idealists, along with the Romantics, as mentioned in the previous chapter. Along with all that was the movement we can generally characterize as American Transcendentalism.

American Transcendentalism

Notable figures behind this uniquely American blossoming of thought were Ralph Waldo Emerson (1803–1882), Henry David Thoreau (1817–1862), Walt Whitman (1819–1892), and John Muir (1838–1914), among others. The term 'American Transcendentalism' can more accurately be called 'New England Transcendentalism', since this was the region—specifically, Massachusetts from roughly 1830–1860—where a small circle of thinkers shared ideals that were in part a revolt against Calvinism (with its emphasis on original sin and predestination) and scientific materialism. The New England Transcendentalists emphasized many of the values and ideals that came to be taken up by more progressive 19th and 20th century spiritual and social movements, such as the essential goodness of the human being, the importance in establishing a direct relationship with both nature and God, the spiritual unity of the world, the value of intuition alongside reason, the belief in the power and dignity of the individual, as well as the abolition of slavery, the promotion of women's rights, and so forth.

Emerson's main points of focus were the sanctity of the individual, a deep connection with nature, and a mystical emphasis on both the existence and structure of the soul. His influential 1841 essay *The Over-soul* detailed his views on the distinction between the soul and the ego (with clear parallels to Eastern traditions such as Vedanta as well as Neoplatonism; Emerson was known to have made a study of some Eastern scriptures, such as the *Bhagavad-Gita,* by that time). Emerson proclaimed the virtue and purity of the soul—irrespective of the condition of the ego—and its innate unity with the supreme divine consciousness. Emerson's ideas on the difference between the Over-soul and the personal self were key influences on later New Thought tendencies toward both individualism, and the idea that divinity could be contacted directly from within one's own nature, without recourse to 'God's representatives' (i.e., the priesthoods).

This of course has long been the contention of both mysticism and esoteric traditions; however Emerson made great progress in rendering these ideas more accessible for the 'householder seeker', that is, one who seeks deeper wisdom without recourse to renouncing the world. Probably Emerson's most important essay had been one of his earliest, published in 1836 at age thirty-three. Called simply *Nature,* it put forth some of the basic tenets of American Transcendentalism, part of which was exalting nature via the idea that we need to experience it directly, without the filter of prior concepts (history and theory, basically). When we experience things (specifically, nature) directly, we gain in energy and enthusiasm; when we experience things only via the 'established' ideas of others, we lose vitality. For Emerson, 'nature' was simply the world, all that is not-self. Significantly, the first edition of *Nature* was prefaced with a passage from Plotinus, although Emerson replaced the passage with one of his own poems in the second edition (1849).

New Thought

The essence of New Thought teaching is that all of existence is imbued with Spirit, that all is divine, and that mind is supremely powerful, with matter being but a shadow in contrast to mind. New Thought can be classified as an extreme form of philosophic Idealism, finding its theoretical roots in Plato, Plotinus, Berkeley, Kant, Fichte, Schelling, Hegel, and Emerson, and its practical roots mostly in Mesmer and Quimby. In addition, New Thought ideas were significantly influenced by Eastern philosophy, in particular via the efforts of Swami Vivekananda (1863-1902), whose memorable lectures on Hindu yogic principles at the World's Parliament of Religions in Chicago in 1893 had a lasting impact. (Mary Baker Eddy, founder of the New Thought movement that came to be known as Christian Science, had also been present at this conference).

A key moral element of New Thought—in common with certain non-dualist traditions—is that evil is not a definitive reality, but is essentially delusion, the result of erroneous thinking. This naturally extended from evil to sickness, leading to the idea that all sickness (mental and physical) is also the result of some sort of essential dysfunction on the level of thought. To be sick was ultimately to be 'out of tune' with the spiritual source of all things, a lack of alignment that is corrected by 'right thinking'. It was fundamentally a problem on the level of mind and even more specifically, attitude and will. William James, writing in his 1902 work *The Varieties of Religious Experience,* called New Thought the 'Mind-cure movement' and the 'religion of healthy-mindedness', describing it as deeply optimistic and basing its teachings on the necessity of making crucial attitudinal adjustments. The New Thought movement is best understood via the main characters who promoted it. Capsule biographies of some of these figures follow.

Phineas Parkhurst Quimby

The question is often asked why I talk about religion and quote Scripture while I cure the sick. My answer is that sickness being what follows a belief, the belief contains the evil which I must correct. As I do this a chemical change takes place. Disease is an error the only remedy for which is the truth.[1]
–P.P. Quimby

Phineas Parkhurst Quimby was born in Lebanon, New Hampshire, on February 18, 1802. When Phineas was two the family relocated to a town in Maine called Belfast where he spent most of his childhood. He had six siblings. His father was a blacksmith, earning working class wages, and accordingly Phineas had limited access to quality education (and limited writing skills as an adult). From this modest background, he emerged into adulthood as a watch and clock-maker, the first indication of his considerable practical intelligence. He was less concerned with the abstract theory of things than he was with invention, the solving of practical problems, and in general, the actualization of ideas.

Quimby was the archetypal initiator, working largely on his own, with little in the way of guidance, either from people or books. He soon grew discontented with mere mechanical inventions and patents. He quickly gravitated to an interest in the powers of the mind, and especially, the ability of the mind to 'heal' the body. He became, essentially, a spiritual healer, with his general philosophy based on the crucial idea that one's beliefs and attitudes must first undergo radical change, primarily from limitation to limitlessness. Quimby independently discovered the reality of the 'subconscious mind', although he did not call it by that term. He described human beings as having 'two levels' of mind, comprised of thoughts and beliefs, respectively. He noted that the more active (or dominant) of the two will generally determine our experience and lot in life.

Quimby's interest in the matters of mental and spiritual healing was sparked when, at thirty-six years of age, he attended a lecture and performance in Belfast, Maine, by the Frenchman Charles Poyen, a somewhat mysterious student of the teachings and work of Franz Mesmer. 'Mesmerists' of various stripes followed in Mesmer's footsteps, and were eventually followed themselves by those practicing hypnosis, which was regarded by many as a more intellectually honest approach. Quimby himself initially began his experiments in healing around the year 1838. Many of his initial attempts were failures, but he did achieve some early remarkable successes, enough to encourage him to continue his efforts. One day he achieved some successes during weather conditions (a thunderstorm) that normally—or so he believed—would have nullified his attempts. But because he was not consciously aware that this thunderstorm was in fact happening, he concluded that the healing that had taken place was indeed due to principally to mental power. Put simply, he believed that something could happen, and therefore it did.

In the early 1840s Quimby traveled throughout Maine and Maritime Canada (New Brunswick) giving demonstrations, aided by his student and 'test subject', a young man named Lucius Burkmar. These experiments involved Quimby asserting his will over his subject and performing feats that would seem to defy rational common sense (such as pricking Burkmar with a sharp pin, in such a manner that Burkmar, duly 'mesmerized' by Quimby, felt no effect). For these demonstrations Quimby received his share of scorn and condemnation, and even accusations of witchcraft.

Some did pay closer attention however, and, impressed, sought Quimby's services. His standard approach at that time (which was also the traditional method of most mesmerists) was to place his assistant, Burkmar, into a 'mesmeric trance', whereupon Burkmar would then 'read' a given patient and prescribe a cure, via clairvoyance (paranormal seeing beyond the means of physical senses) and clairaudience (paranormal hearing). Over time, Quimby began to notice a fascinating thing. Burkmar's diagnoses of the 'patient' tended to reflect the views and opinions of those present in the room, rather than any actual truth about the matter. In other words, Burkmar was accomplishing something closer to telepathy, or perhaps more simply an unconscious rapport, with those in the room, rather than any true diagnosis or healing of their physical condition.

The most notable example of this occurrence happened when one doctor sought out Quimby's help in the healing of a patient. Quimby placed Burkmar in the 'induced sleep' state, whereupon the latter 'read' the patient and prescribed a simple herbal tea remedy. The patient used this tea, and got better. But the interesting thing was that the doctor had previously used this same tea with no effect. After pondering the matter, Quimby concluded that the impressiveness of the 'mesmerized' Burkmar reading the patient in trance, and prescribing a cure, so convinced the patient that something special was going on, that the patient believed more deeply in the 'remedy' of the tea. In other words, the tea was a type of placebo; the real power lay in the mind of the patient, and the whole matter was a process of what we now refer to as suggestion (or, in parallel terms, 'uncritical faith').

It is to Quimby's credit, however, that he saw the deeper point, which was that the patronizing expression 'mere suggestion' was entirely wrong. He then followed the matter to its logical conclusion, which is that mental influence is extremely powerful—everything from establishing one person's view of reality (opinion, essentially) as some sort of supreme reality, to the ability of one mind to help another to heal itself, and even its physical body. In short, Quimby from here on in dedicated himself to mental healing.[2] By his late fifties Quimby was referring to mesmerism as 'the greatest humbug of the age'.[3] He had slowly, over a period of twenty years, and entirely by his own observations unsupported by books or other vehicles of higher education, 'discovered' both the subconscious mind, and the entire field of psychosomatic healing (although he did not use these terms, neither yet coined at that time). His crucial discovery was the power of the subconscious mind via personal belief. He wrote, 'I found that my thoughts were one thing, and my beliefs another. If I really believed a thing, the effect would follow whether I was thinking about it or not'.[4]

Once he became convinced that he had a strong hold on what was really going on, he began to develop and formalize his own system, based on what he called 'spiritual matter', and the real possibility that a mind could be changed. As Ervin Seale, in his Introduction to *Quimby's Manuscripts* pointed out, the Biblical word *repent* derives from the Greek *metanoia,* meaning 'change of mind'.

Quimby seemed to be of an unusual purity of character, especially in terms of how his intention manifested. His overriding concern was to develop a 'science' of healing so as to benefit his fellow human beings. According to his son George he was only marginally concerned with making money for himself, and less so with thoughts of great wealth, although he did hold to the view that material abundance is in no way incompatible with a spiritually reputable life. Quimby was a philosophical idealist, holding firm to the view that disease begins in the mind and manifests secondarily in the body. For this view he was, naturally, ridiculed by many medical authorities of his day, given the rise of empirical science in his time. Quimby was working during a time when his views found almost no support, apart from the patients of his who were actually healed in their work with him—and there were definitely many remarkable results. It is reported that he had a 'closet full of canes and crutches left by patients in his office in Portland in the last years of his practice that testified to his remarkable power'.[5]

Quimby was adamant, to the end of his life, that what he was doing was unique, and not to be allied with other alternative approaches common during his time. He wrote:

> As you have given me the privilege of answering the article in your paper... wherein you classed me with spiritualists, mesmerizers, clairvoyants, etc., I take this occasion to state where I differ

> from all classes of doctors, from the allopathic physician to the healing medium. All of these admit disease as an independent enemy of mankind.... Now I deny disease as a truth, but admit it as a deception, without any foundation, handed down from generation to generation, till the people believe it, and it has become a part of their lives.... My way of curing convinces him that he has been deceived; and, if I succeed the patient is cured. My mode is entirely original.[6]

It was this uncompromising approach to the matter of mind in relation to disease that was to be echoed in various forms of New Thought teachings that followed Quimby, everything from Science of Mind to *A Course In Miracles*. Essentially, Quimby was promoting Spirit and consciousness as supreme, with matter being but a reflection of transcendent principles. This was, as theory, nothing new; indeed, Plato had taught the same central idea over twenty-three centuries before Phineas Quimby. But what defined Quimby was his overriding concern with practical results. He was no philosopher, nor even a writer—his manuscripts, never shaped into book form, were not published until several decades after he had passed away. He was a healer above all else, and indeed, the last five years of his life (1861–1866) reflected this more than anything. According to his son he was overcrowded with patients during this time and ultimately became overworked and burnt out, leading to his death at age sixty-three.[7] The lack of any substantial evidence of glamour-seeking or greed on his part for healing services rendered throughout his life marks him as a character of integrity.

In many respects Quimby was a guru, a charismatic individual with knowledge of spiritual principles, and above all, one in whom his patients placed a great deal of trust (and indeed, even Mary Baker Eddy compared his abilities to the healing powers of Christ).[8] In the language of modern psychoanalysis, this can be understood as an 'idealizing transference', something that enables very powerful effects when the patient or follower has deep faith in the 'power' of the healer or guru.

Julius Dresser, Annetta Seabury, and Horatio Dresser

Julius Dresser (1838–1893), his wife Annetta, and later his son Horatio Dresser (1866–1954), were the key early followers of Quimby who did the initial work of promulgating and extending his ideas to the greater public. Julius Dresser had initially visited Quimby as a patient in June of 1860. Dresser was then a young man in his early twenties, but seriously ill and near death. He was healed through his treatments with Quimby and subsequently became deeply interested in his ideas and work. It was at Quimby's office where he met Annetta Seabury, also a patient of Quimby's. At Quimby's death in 1866 Julius Dresser had been asked to carry on Quimby's work and teachings in some fashion, but he initially declined, citing certain doubts that he had about the work at that time. This decision was not to last, however. Julius and Annetta eventually moved to Boston, where in 1883 they set up a healing practice based on Quimby's system.

In 1882 Dresser had discovered the doctrines of Mary Baker Eddy (one of Quimby's patients) on the religion she'd founded (Christian Science), and accused her of appropriating Quimby's ideas without crediting him. The ensuing controversy was to last for many years, involving at one point a court case that the Dressers lost, chiefly because they were unable to gain permission from Quimby's son George to present Quimby's original manuscripts in court. Julius and Annetta were the first to propagate the 'Quimby System of Mental Treatment of Diseases', and are recognized by most as the first practical organizers of the New Thought movement.

Their son Horatio, whose birth date (January 15th, 1866), was one day before Phineus Quimby died, has been described by some historians as the 'first child to grow up in New Thought'. By eighteen years of age he was practicing mental healing. He obtained a doctoral degree in philosophy from Harvard in 1907 (which included a period of time as a student and friend of William James), and ultimately followed in his parents' footsteps. He was the first prolific New Thought author (he had published eight books before he was thirty-five). One of his early works, *The Power of Silence* (1895) had been reprinted over a dozen times by 1903. He also authored the first *History of the New Thought Movement* (1919). He continued to teach and write into his elder years (his last book, *Knowing and Helping People,* was published when he was sixty-seven), part of which included a spell teaching at a Unitarian Congregational Church. He passed away in 1954, aged eighty-eight.

Horatio Dresser once summarized Quimby's teachings via these seven essential points:

1. The omnipresent Wisdom, the warm, loving Father of us all, Creator of all the universe, whose works are good, whose substance is an invisible reality.

2. The real man, whose life is eternal in the invisible kingdom of God, whose senses are spiritual and function independently of matter.

3. The visible world, which Dr. Quimby once characterized as 'the shadow of Wisdom's amusements'; that is, nature is only the outward projection or manifestation of an inward activity far more real and enduring.

4. Spiritual matter, or fine interpenetrating substance, directly responsive to thought and subconsciously embodying in the flesh the fears, beliefs, hopes, errors, and joys of the mind.

5. Disease is due to false reasoning in regard to sensations, which man unwittingly develops by impressing wrong thoughts and mental pictures upon the subconscious spiritual matter.

6. As disease is due to false reasoning, so health is due to knowledge of the truth. To remove disease permanently, it is necessary to know the cause, the error which led to it. 'The explanation is the cure'.

7. To know the truth about life is therefore the sovereign remedy for all ills. This truth Jesus came to declare. Jesus knew how he cured and Dr. Quimby, without taking any credit to himself as a discoverer, believed that he understood and practiced the same great truth or science.[9]

Warren F. Evans

Warren Felt Evans, along with Julian Dresser, his wife Annette Seabury, and Mary Patterson (later Mary Baker Eddy), was one of the four early 'chief apostles' of Phineas Quimby that began the work of spreading his ideas as well as developing and refining them. Evans was born on December 23rd, 1817, in Vermont, the son of a farmer. He attended college (Dartmouth, in New Hampshire), but left before obtaining his degree, in order to become a Methodist minister. He married in 1840, and carried on his ministry for the next two decades. Sometime in his early forties he began to suffer from some obscure illness (what he called a 'nervous affection'), but was unable to heal his condition based on the advice and treatments of the medical authorities of his day. Around this time he came across the writings of the Swedish visionary and mystic Emanuel Swedenborg (1688–1772), and in 1863 he left his Methodist ministry to join Swedenborg's New Church (sometimes called the Church of the New Jerusalem), a ministry based on Swedenborg's material that he claimed was a new revelation from Christ. Clearly, he was searching for a 'way out' of the conventional views and limiting beliefs of his time, as related to both religion and the matter of healing in general. And, as so often happens, his 'motivating cause' was the very illness that befell him.

By 1863 Phineas Quimby, in his twilight years, had become well known throughout New England, with many gravitating toward his healing 'powers' and extraordinary ability to achieve actual results. Evans sought Quimby out, visiting him in Portland, Maine, in 1863. He was healed of his condition, and duly became a devoted student of Quimby and his teachings. He soon felt confident that he himself could function as a healer for others, along the lines that Quimby taught and worked, and with Quimby's blessing he began his work as a 'mental healer' in Claremont, New Hampshire. He also at the time published his first book, *The New Age and its Messenger* (1864), which perhaps ironically was not about Quimby, but about his earlier inspiration, Swedenborg. A few years later he moved with his wife to Boston, where he set up his healing practice, based on Quimby's work. In 1869 he relocated to Salisbury (about 45 miles north of Boston); this was also the year he published the first book known on Quimby's ideas, titled *The Mental Cure*, with the elaborate but descriptive subtitle, *Illustrating the Influence of the Mind on the Body, Both in Health and Disease, and the Psychological Method of Treatment.* Evans lived and ran his practice in Salisbury, with his wife, for the last two decades of his life. He passed away in 1889, aged seventy-one.

Evans did not charge fees for his healing and instruction, although he did accept donations. His great accomplishment, apart from his healing practice, was as a writer. In general, he appears to have been less a 'guru-type' (as in the case of Quimby) and more an intellectual—similar to how Ouspensky was in relation to his mentor Gurdjieff. In addition to being the first to write about Quimby's work in the aforementioned book, Evans also published *Mental Medicine* (1872); *Soul and Body* (1875, the same year Mary Baker Eddy published her first work); *The Divine Law of Cure* (1881, and his most widely read work); *The Primitive Mind Cure* (1885); and finally *Esoteric Christianity and Mental Therapeutics* (1886). Most of these works sold in successful numbers and some went through several reprints. Along with Eddy, Evans is considered by historians to have been the main intellectual force to keep Quimby's ideas alive in written form, until the turn of the 20th century, when New Thought writings began to proliferate in general.[10]

Mary Baker Eddy

Mary Baker Eddy, the founder of the Christian Science faith and its church known as the Church of Christ, Scientist, was born Mary Baker on July 16, 1821, in New Hampshire, the youngest of six children of a farming family. Her father, Mark Baker, was a dominant and controlling figure, strongly attached to his Bible and a rigid, Calvinistic interpretation of Scripture. Mary was something of a sickly child, often consumed with maladies that appeared to be psychosomatic expressions of her desire to rebel against her father. His controlling presence provided something of a counterforce through which she was able to access a longing to realize a more liberated and spiritually advanced interpretation of Christian teaching. This, along with her persistent frail health, led her naturally toward a deep interest in healing in general. Consistent with most mystics throughout history she was motivated not just by a desire to alleviate suffering (beginning with her own and extending toward the universe around her), but by a desire to understand the spiritual roots of suffering, and to undo such causes at their source.

Mary Baker Eddy passed through a couple of dysfunctional marriages in her early adult years, which included giving birth to a son with whom she had, at times, difficulty raising properly owing to her consistent poor health, which included periodic depression. She wrote occasional articles on politics for a local newspaper, and at one point attempted to begin an experimental kindergarten in which she sought to instil more loving values and apply more tolerant schooling methods for young children (the idea failed, meeting with too much resistance from local authorities).

In 1863, aged forty-two, and at the time named Mary Patterson (owing to her marriage to dentist Daniel Patterson in 1853), she met Phineas Quimby. The meeting was to prove pivotal, opening the 'inner doors' in her psyche that paved the way for her major life accomplishments as a religious reformer. Part of Quimby's personal philosophy included a strong denunciation of most elements of conventional religious conditioning, and in particular, Calvinism (itself, ironically, a type of 'reformed' Protestantism). Because Mary's father had been a hard core Calvinist and such a dominant figure of her formatory years, Quimby's views fit perfectly with her desire to liberate herself fully from her early life religious conditioning. (Quimby had gone so far as to proclaim, 'One half of diseases arise from a false belief in the Bible').[11]

Equally significantly, Quimby held women in marked spiritual esteem, a highly uncommon position for a cultured man of his time. He had flat out declared that women have a greater natural attunement to higher spiritual realities, and were often the source of these higher truths, which men then took and shaped into intellectual or secular understandings.[12] This was an interesting and radical reversal of the more common view of men as being more connected to the abstract and conscious realm, and women to the material and unconscious. However in this matter Quimby was, in a sense, echoing an ancient understanding, found in many wisdom traditions, that the unconscious or instinctive mind is a doorway to the 'cosmic intelligence' or 'higher mind'—an idea that is itself one of the prime keys within manifestation teachings in general. Whatever the details of Quimby's views in this matter, it proved to be another quality that naturally drew Mary to him; for she sought not just liberation from ignorant and limited religious philosophy, but also from the social limitations of women of her time.

Mary had sought out Quimby for guidance and treatment for her frail health and persistent depression. He treated her for a few weeks, and she saw dramatic improvement in her condition, which naturally led to her staunch belief in his abilities. She praised him to the rafters in some articles she wrote for a local newspaper, going so far as to compare his healing 'powers' to Christ himself (which, also naturally, stirred considerable protest at the time).

As is so often the case in the life of one destined to spiritual leadership, this initial awakening—in this case, the 'romance' with the healing powers of Phineas Quimby—did not last for Mary, as she soon lapsed back into her various psychosomatic disorders. Over the next four years, up until Quimby's death in 1866, she remained his patient and student, alternating periods of healing and well-being, with periods of illness and despair. During that time she was involved in a number of complex, co-dependent relations with others, which included certain women who great idolized Mary (and were, in a sense, her first students), and yet who were clearly involved in various levels of toxic co-dependency with her. All of this was taking place during the midst of the American Civil War (1861–65), and although the actual battles took place mostly in the southern states, far from the New England of Quimby and Mary Baker Eddy, the ripples were felt, ripples that were all about a deeper awareness of mortality and the depravities connected to warfare, along with the corresponding incentive to search for spiritual 'answers' to such widespread suffering (over 600,000 American soldiers perished in the war alone; the number of civilian losses has never been accurately known).

After Quimby's death, and several other personal losses (including her father, who passed within months of Quimby), Mary experienced deep personal loss, all exacerbated by a further decline in health. This dark period culminated, just two weeks after Quimby's passing, with a fall on an icy street in which she was seriously injured (the attending doctor doubted she would ever walk again). Her recovery was slow, based crucially on her close study and re-interpretation of certain Biblical scriptures, and ultimately led her to turn inward for the next three years. It was during this retreat that she formulated the basis of the Christian Science faith. The key piece of scripture that she initially turned to was Matthew 9:2:

And, behold, they brought to him a man sick of the palsy, lying

> on a bed: and Jesus seeing their faith said unto the sick of the palsy; Son, be of good cheer; thy sins be forgiven thee. (KJV).

In this scripture we can see a loving forgiveness that can be perceived as standing at opposite pole to the stern punitive God of Calvinism. More centrally, however, it reflected the metanoia that Mary had passed through in the period following her near-fatal tumble on the icy street, and that rested crucially on her own personal connection with the divine. She was no longer relying on a human (such as Quimby), but was rather accessing her highest potential *directly*. This was highly significant because it was not an easy route for a 19th century woman to follow (or a woman of almost all previous times and cultures, for that matter), owing to the social and theological restrictions so commonly placed on women. The most common of these 'restrictions' has classically been the dogma that while a man's spiritual source is the divine, a woman's spiritual source is *her man*. This is a legacy of old theology, beginning in Genesis with Eve's having been created 'from the rib' of Adam; and by her later temptation by the serpent, and related consequences, foremost of which was that as punishment her husband shall, herewith, be her 'master'. And so her history and fate is sealed: she derives from a man, and she is beholden to men. It is a doctrine that does not bode well for a woman's faith in her natural ability to be accountable for her psychological states, not to mention sovereign right to access her own highest spiritual potential directly. Mary Baker Eddy was one of the pioneers for women in attempting to break down this social and theological conditioning.

Mary completed her three year contemplative retreat around 1869. The essence of this retreat involved her deep realization that all healing is spiritual, as matter (and the body) is but an unreal shadow in contrast to the infinite light of Spirit. She spent the next several years living in various homes with people inclined to spiritual matters (especially 'spiritualism', or trance-mediumship, which was widespread at that time, having begun in America in the late 1840s via the Fox sisters, Cora Scott, Paschal Beverly Randolph, and others). By 1872 Mary had put together a manuscript based heavily on Quimby's writings (a fact that led to many years of contentious dispute between followers of Quimby and those of Mary).[13] It was eventually agreed by most that Mary's writings ultimately diverged sufficiently from Quimby's ideas to merit the definition of a new religious movement, one that was pre-eminently based on the idea of defining healing as a 'religious science', with Jesus as the prime healing role model and symbol. She then began arranging these writings into a book. This work, originally titled *Science and Health,* was published in 1875; it was eventually re-titled *Science and Health with Keys to the Scriptures,* and since then has essentially served as the source text for Christian Science.[14] In 1877 she married Asa Gilbert Eddy, at which point she assumed the name by which she has been known to posterity. By 1879, Mary Baker Eddy had founded the Church of Christ, Scientist, in Boston, in so doing become the first and only American woman to found a worldwide religion (which as of 2010 has about 100,000 adherents, although this number has been on the decline since the mid-20th century).[15]

Christian Science adheres to conventional Christian doctrine in some ways, and in other ways veers off into a different direction. Some of its core tenets are summarized in this excerpt from *Science and Health,* the essence of which is a type of simplified Gnosticism:

> *There is no life, truth, intelligence, nor substance in matter.*
> *All is infinite Mind and its infinite manifestation, for God is All-in-all.*
> *Spirit is immortal Truth; matter is mortal error.*
> *Spirit is the real and eternal; matter is the unreal and temporal.*
> *Spirit is God, and man is His image and likeness.*
> *Therefore man is not material; he is spiritual.* (*S&H* 468)

In 1895 Mary published the *Manual of the Mother Church* (for the First Church of Christ, Scientist, in Boston), and in 1908, aged eighty-seven, she founded the renowned *The Christian Science Monitor* newspaper (still thriving to this day). She passed away in 1910. She was a controversial and powerful force in the creation of a new spiritual and healing paradigm, uniquely American (with emphasis on the American affinity for the practical), and with the added element of integrating a woman's perspective into spiritual vision and leadership.

Emma Curtis Hopkins

Emma Curtis Hopkins, originally a student of Mary Baker Eddy, was one of the key figures in the broadening public outreach of the New Thought movement during one of its most active decades, the 1880s. She was born in Connecticut in 1849, the oldest of nine children, became a schoolteacher, married another schoolteacher (George Hopkins) in 1874, and had one child (a son who passed away in 1905 at age thirty). In her early thirties Emma met Mary Baker Eddy and studied the Christian Science teachings under her. She soon rose to become one of Eddy's more prominent pupils, but eventually fell out with her over disagreements about the content of editorials she was writing for Eddy's *Christian Science Journal*. (This was partly due to Eddy's renowned autocratic nature, a common personality trait of many effective leaders).

Hopkins is seen by a number of historians as a feminist and an important influence on the early 'feminization' of the New Thought movement, via her efforts to lead, organize, and support the development and advance of other women within the New Thought community. A key element of her theology was to promote a new version of the Christian trinity, in which the Holy Spirit was recognized as feminine (an idea not original to her, but notable nonetheless for the rarity with which it had been put forth prior to her time). More so than Quimby or Eddy, Hopkins was driven to affect practical change on a large scale via the Christian Science methods. She had a broader intellectual scope than Eddy (who was focused more on the establishment of her church), as well as an abiding interest in empowering women in positions of leadership within the mind-healing work. The essence of this work was, of course, the correction of belief-systems; a type of mental reprogramming approached in a 'scientific' fashion, yet based on the central assumption that a supreme, divine good resides at the core of everyone.

In 1888 in Chicago, when Emma was not yet forty, she founded her own school of inner work, called the Christian Science Theological Seminary. In 1893 she sailed to England to give some lectures, establishing herself as a pioneer in the 'export' of American New Thought teachings. Emma ultimately claimed the title of 'bishop' within her burgeoning tradition, and ended up ordaining over a hundred people as ministers (the majority were women). A number of these ministers went on to become key figures in the later 20th century growth of New Thought ideas, such as Charles and Myrtle Fillmore, co-founders of Unity Church, and Kate Bingam, one of whose students, Nona Brooks, was a key figure involved in the founding of Divine Science in Colorado.[16]

In 1895 Hopkins closed her Chicago seminary and moved to New York City, where her teachings took on a more eclectic quality, being less exclusively Christianized in tone and teaching terms. More committed to her ministry and work with her students than to primary relationship or domestic life, she had separated from her husband in the late 1880s (he did not share her passion for the spiritual work) and they divorced in 1900. She continued to write prolifically and teach tirelessly up until her death in 1925 at age seventy-five. Her influence on modern New Thought teachings is marked; as well as other key figures mentioned above, she also taught Ernest Holmes (founder of Religious Science), Malinda Cramer (founder of the Church of Divine Science), Annie Ritz Militz (founder of The Home of Truth and the *Master Mind* New Thought magazine) and Selena Chamberlain, who herself later taught Emmet Fox, one of the 20th century's most successful and widely-read New Thought authors. Emma Curtis Hopkins can thus be credited with being an important influence behind three major 20th century New Thought lineages, those of Unity, Religious Science, and Divine Science, earning her the commonly heard title of 'the teacher of teachers'.

Malinda Cramer

Malinda Elliot Cramer was born February 12th, 1844, in Indiana, into a large Quaker family. In her mid-twenties she moved to San Francisco, marrying photographer Charles Cramer in 1872. Her life followed a standard pattern for one destined to apply herself to the teaching and practice of spiritual principles: sickly for much of her youth (and declared an incurable invalid at one point), she underwent a mystical experience at age forty (a common age for such a metanoia), and gradually became healed of her chronic ill health. Her healing process had been influenced by Mary Baker Eddy's Christian Science teachings. Deeply moved by the process, she committed her life to the path of mental healing and in 1887 became a direct student of Emma Curtis Hopkins. Her progress was fast; the next year she and her husband opened their own school of spiritual healing, called the Home College of Divine Science.

Like the other personalities discussed in this section that followed in the footsteps of Quimby, Eddy, and Curtis, Cramer was also a key figure in the dissemination of New Thought teachings in the late 19th and 20th centuries. This involved extensive travel, including to Europe and Australia. She was involved in the formation of the International Divine Science Association, itself an early source of the International New Thought Alliance and the International Metaphysical League, which held its first New Thought convention in Chicago in 1903. She also authored several books, including *Divine Science and Healing* (1890), *Basic Statements and Health Treatment of Truth* (1893), and *Hidden Harmony* (reprinted as recently as 1990).

Malinda Cramer was badly injured in the great earthquake of 1906 that leveled much of San Francisco (and demolished Cramer's local Divine Home School). She passed away a few months later due to her injuries, aged sixty-two. As an interesting part of her extended legacy, in 1999 in San Antonio, Texas, two practitioners of spiritual healing, William Trainor and Anne Kunath, founded United Divine Sciences Ministries International, based largely on Malinda Cramer's teachings.

Charles Brodie Patterson

Charles B. Patterson was born in Nova Scotia, Canada, in 1854. In his early 30s he moved to Connecticut to seek treatment from a mental healer, and remained in the U.S. In 1899 he was elected the first president of the newly formed International Metaphysical League, a position he served for four years. He authored a number of works, including *The Will to Be Well* (1901), *The Measure of Man* (1907), *New Heaven and New Earth* (1909), and *Rhythm of Life* (1915). He was an excellent writer and a dynamic leader with considerable practical intelligence; accordingly he was informally regarded by many as the main leader of the New Thought movement during the first two decades of the 20th century.

Other early 20th century influential figures followed, all of whose ideas were based on New Thought teachings: the aforementioned Charles Fillmore (1854–1948) who along with his wife Myrtle (1845-1931) founded the Unity Church in Kansas City in 1889; William Walker Atkinson (1862-1932) who writing as 'Three Initiates' published his influential Hermetic-New Thought work *The Kybalion* in 1908; Wallace Wattles (1860–1911) who wrote *The Science of Getting Rich* (1910), the prime source behind Rhonda Byrne's massively successful 2006 book *The Secret*; Ernest Holmes (1887–1960) who wrote *Creative Mind* in 1919 and *The Science of Mind* in 1927 and is recognized as the founder of Religious Science; Napoleon Hill (1883–1970), renowned author of *The Law of Success* (1928) and the iconic *Think and Grow Rich* (1937); Dale Carnegie (1888–1955), author of *How to Win Friends and Influence People* (1936); Maxwell Maltz (1889–1975) who wrote *Psycho-Cybernetics* in 1960, a work that was a key influence on Werner Erhard, founder of the wildly successful 'est' movement that later morphed into 'The Forum' and then 'Landmark'; Joseph Murphy (1898-1981), author of over twenty books including *The Miracles of your Mind* (1953) and the influential *The Power of your Subconscious Mind* (1963); and Norman Vincent Peale (1898–1993), author of *The Power of Positive Thinking* (1952; not his first book, but his most influential).

Most of these figures basically taught a life-affirmative attitudinal healing, based in part on the power of suggestion. It was usually presented with a Christianized foundation that downplayed the central role of Christ, instead emphasizing the idea that the miracles he performed were based on divine laws that anyone could learn. Christ in this view is more a supreme example, rather than a singular manifestation of the Absolute that must be submitted to. This notion was also a key part of New Age thought.

The New Age

The term 'New Age' is not especially new; Warren Evans was proclaiming Swedenborg as the 'New Age messenger' as early as 1864, and A.R. Orage, the well known English literary critic and eventual student of Gurdjieff, was editing a journal called *The New Age* in 1894.[17] Much of what formed a key part of New Age activity, namely communication with 'disembodied spirits' (known via the modern term 'channeling'), was present in 19th century spiritualism, and many of the metaphysical ideas and occult activities of the fertile 1920s decade would in current times be understood as New Age. That said the New Age movement proper is generally recognized to have formed in the 1970s and 1980s, mostly in North America, and to a somewhat lesser degree in parts of Western Europe.

The post-1970s New Age was heavily influenced by both the New Thought teachings just outlined, in addition to American Transcendentalism, German Idealism, as well as much older traditions such as Hermeticism, Gnosticism, Kabbalism, and Eastern teachings. It was also influenced by the 19th century spiritualism; this manifested via a strongly feminine slant that emphasized forms of communication with 'other realms' including 'invisible masters'. To this latter group belong such key figures as H.P. Blavatsky (1831–1891), Alice Bailey (1880–1949), Edgar Cayce (1887-1945), Helen Schucman (1909–1981), and Jane Roberts (1929–1984). All five of these were mediums (or 'channels') for alleged invisible masters; some worked via forms of 'inspired' or 'automatic writing' (such as Blavatsky, Bailey, and Schucman) and others as 'trance-channels' who functioned as vehicles for alleged invisible guides to speak through them (such as Cayce and Roberts). Of the five mentioned it is arguable that Schucman fits uncomfortably into the group, as she was both a very 'reluctant prophet' (she refused payments for the book, *A Course in Miracles,* that she wrote down over a period of seven years, and the material in the book is of relatively high literary and philosophic quality). Nevertheless much of her long and dense book was subsequently simplified and became an integral part of so-called standard New Age beliefs and views.

Spiritualism, as with many of the earlier magical grimoires as well as 20th century New Age teachings, was something of a disaffected cousin of Christianity, espousing similar ideas, prayers, cosmology, and moral values, but distinct in its preference for 'direct contact' with disembodied spirits for information about the 'afterlife' over consulting a clergyman or the Bible. Spiritualism had its modern roots in Emmanuel Swedenborg (1688–1772), the Swedish mystic and psychic who claimed to 'see into' other worlds and conduct elaborate communications with spirits. The other key influence was Mesmer's disciple the Marquis de Puysegur who stumbled upon the hypnotic trance (although it was not categorized as 'hypnosis' until 1842). This trance state became the key for the spiritualism that began in the 1840s, based as it was on the ability of a trance-medium to access normally inaccessible levels of reality (or mind). Trance-states were not, of course, 'discovered' by Puysegur or by 19th century mediums; they have been key to the inner work of shamans and magicians for thousands of years.

In 1980 Marilyn Ferguson published *The Aquarian Conspiracy*, which became a kind of early New Age screed, in which she outlined many of the standard New Age ideas that would gradually coalesce over the following decade. Some of these ideas reached their definitive formulation in the writings of Fritjof Capra (especially his 1992 *The Tao of Physics*), who argued for the parallels between Eastern mysticism and quantum physics, a model which received a somewhat confused summation in a dubious 2004 documentary called *What the Bleep do we Know?* Ken Wilber, in his 2001 *Quantum Questions*, heavily criticized Capra, citing his jumbled conflation of mysticism and hard science, arguing that they are distinct domains not meant to be muddied together. Other influential figures have been Rupert Sheldrake, via his ideas of 'morphic resonance' and telepathy, James Lovelock's 'Gaia hypothesis' (Earth behaving as a living being), and the work of David Bohm, Karl Pribram and Michael Talbot, as related to the so-called 'fractal' or 'holographic model' in which the old Hermetic idea of 'as above so below' is reflected in the idea of a macro-universe that is replicated precisely in its micro parts. All these models underscore the New Age emphasis on the connectivity of all things. Such an emphasis often clashes with traditional science, which seeks to establish discrete distinctions between things so as to understand them more clearly. Arguably, ancient alchemy (for one) more closely supports the scientific model of emphasizing separation prior to unity, via the formula of *solve et coagula* (separate first, *then* join).

Reincarnation

As pointed out by Hanegraaff (1998) the New Age version of reincarnation, such as it is, is not very consistent with traditional Eastern views (despite the fact that it often cites Eastern wisdom and was clearly influenced by it). This is because New Age models of reincarnation appear to be bearing the marks of Darwinian evolutionism and the Romantic notions of progressiveness. In short, the New Age understanding of reincarnation is that it is a process of the soul's evolution from life to life, generally involving some sort of progression (presumably some New Age views allow for the possibility of a 'spiritual decline' if a given lifetime has been 'messed up' badly enough, although it is not easy to find these views). Eastern models of reincarnation, via the two primary traditions of Hinduism and Buddhism, show little interest in reincarnation as the vehicle for the evolution of a soul over a period of lifetimes, more commonly viewing reincarnation (and bodily life) as a negative consequence of spiritual ignorance resulting from attachment to worldly pleasures and material rapaciousness. The Eastern focus is strictly on liberation (*moksha*); although reincarnation is assumed as factual, there is no particular glamour in it (or in bodily life). New Age views, doubtless also bearing the mark of Hermetic and Neoplatonic ideas about a linear progression *upward*, show more interest in the reincarnational process itself, as well as a tendency to glamorize it.[18]

Psychologizing

New Age ideas were influenced not just by Hermetic, Romantic and Darwinian evolutionary progressiveness, but also by psychotherapy. The tendency to psychologize matters, to regard everything as 'in one's head', seems to be relatively recent. For example, there is no evidence that ancient, medieval, or Renaissance magicians regarded the angels, spirits, and demons they were consorting with as mere elements of their psyche or 'shadow selves'. Such spirits were regarded as ontologically real, by all accounts. Perhaps one of the better examples of the tendency of New Age thinking to psychologize was found in Dion Fortune's reshaping of Aleister Crowley's definition of 'magick'. Crowley had written, 'magick is the science and art of causing change to occur in conformity with will'. Fortune tweaked it to 'magick is the science and art of causing changes *in consciousness* to occur in conformity with will' (italics mine). A major influence in this overall movement toward Idealism within esoterica was C.G. Jung (as well as figures such as Jane Roberts and Jach Pursel, both of whom 'channeled' teachings that put heavy emphasis on the idea that we 'create our reality'). Jung—clearly influenced by the Romantic's emphasis on individuality and an embrace of the unconscious—made great attempts to psychologize alchemy, which for the original alchemists would have been mostly inconceivable, as they viewed their art in primitive scientific terms (and, in some cases, in a religious context). The origins of the psychologized approach have been discussed elsewhere, having their roots in the 'discovery of the unconscious'. This general trend toward considering the subject rather than exclusive focus on the object is clearly an important step in the overall maturation of humanity, although needless to say has to be tempered with the need to avoid overemphasis on the internal to the point that indifference to the external breeds self-absorption and irresponsibility. Jung's impact on New Age ideas has been considerable, doubtless in part as he himself was, in some respects, as much a mystic (and guru) as he was a psychologist. The controversial 2009 publication of his renowned *Red Book* (*Liber Novus*) revealed his highly developed mystical and artistic capacity. In his embrace of these domains of consciousness he brought psychology alive for many unable to deal with the dryly clinical approach within much of psychoanalysis.

Ultimately the New Age is not as easy to define now (as of this writing in 2013) as it was fifteen, twenty, or twenty-five years ago. It seems to have had its golden age roughly between 1980 and 2000. After the 9/11 attacks in New York City in 2001, followed by the explosion of smart phone technology and the decline of the 'Silent Generation' (b. approximately 1925–1945) and Baby Boomer generation (b. 1946–1964), both of which were responsible for most of the New Age seed ideas, a new paradigm seems to be emerging based more on a kind of 'techno urban yoga' culture in which an effort has been made to actualize more abstract New Age philosophies into a form that embraces issues such as environmental awareness, as well as a practicality that addresses a more tenuous economic foundation. (Many Baby Boomers grew up in relative affluence and with cheaper real estate, accordingly being more prone to a wandering lifestyle that often involved embracing Oriental mysticism via the requisite journeys to India or Japan, in part made easy by the circumstances of the times). The overall relationship between New Thought and New Age ideas in contrast to the Western esoteric tradition is unclear at the best of times, but in general New Thought/New Age inclines more toward a quasi-Christian paradigm (clear in the many New Age references to 'the Christ', angels, ascension, forgiveness, and so forth). The esoteric tradition, with its roots in Hermeticism and older Greek schools of thought, as well as Jewish and pagan magical branches, is generally distinct from Christianity (with the notable exception of the Grail myths, parts of the Tarot, and of course, the attempts to Christianize the Kabbalah via Pico's efforts). Additionally, the esoteric path usually requires a stronger personal commitment to transformational practices, and at times, committed inclusion in a private (or even quasi-secret) society. Arguably, the New Thought and New Age traditions, however loosely defined, are more feminized, socialized, and accessible, whereas the esoteric tradition is more masculinized, secretive, and less accessible.

Part Two

Practice: The Technology of Transformation

Chapter 9

The Fundamentals of Spiritual Psychology (Part I)

Transpersonal and Integral Psychology

'Spiritual Psychology' chiefly implies the two modern schools of psychology that attempt to address the spiritual dimension of the human being, these being the transpersonal and integral models. Initially these were considered to be essentially the same, but over time have come to be seen as distinct approaches (if in many places overlapping). Primary figures behind the transpersonal psychology movement have been Roberto Assagioli, Stanislav Grof, Michael Washburn, and Charles Tart. The Integral school is chiefly represented by Ken Wilber, along with a great number of modern theorists of consciousness who have been influenced by him. (Despite that fact that these leading figures have been overridingly concerned with the spiritual dimension of psychology—or what is at times called the 'psychology of religion'—they have had their share of disagreements, at times bitterly expressed, with each other and their respective models, something perhaps to be expected in a relatively young school of thought that is greatly ambitious in its intention to define and classify all possible human experience). The key element of spiritual psychology is the attempt to integrate the deepest spiritual insights and theoretical models of reality of the great wisdom traditions of the past, with the understandings of modern psychology (which includes the scientific revolution). The modern movement technically began with the writings of William James, who in 1905 had used the word 'transpersonal' in some of his lectures, although it was Abraham Maslow who first proposed the term to describe a new school of psychology. This suggestion saw its realization with the inaugural publication of *The Journal of Transpersonal Psychology* in 1969.

Both Transpersonal and Integral Psychology attempt to take the work of Freud, Jung, and the pioneers of 'depth psychology', to a higher level. This level is sometimes referred to as 'height psychology', in that it seeks to integrate the theory of the supreme, transcendent levels of consciousness with the understandings of how the unconscious mind operates and influences our lives. 'Height psychology' could be said to have begun with Roberto Assagioli, who was a pioneer in the area of what we can call a psychology of the 'superconscious mind'; that is, a map of human consciousness that includes a higher self, as well as the conscious and unconscious minds. Assagioli's ideas bear influences from Neoplatonism, Kabbalah, and modern Theosophy, as well as Immanuel Kant, whose essential concern with transcendent principles—*by what greater and higher means can we come to know of things?*—is the philosophical basis of spiritual psychology.

Freud and Jung are often mentioned together, although they certainly had fundamental differences. Most essential of all is that Freud viewed the unconscious mind as a pre-egoic entity, whereas for Jung he came to regard the unconscious as trans-egoic (or collective; although he also saw it as containing both 'light' and 'dark' elements, reflective of the ego's ambivalent view of reality). According to Ken Wilber this resulted in both making critical mistakes: Freud in regarding spiritual experience as regressive delusion (spirituality is merely the memory of instinctive states of being, such as 'oneness with the mother'); and Jung in regarding primitive, instinctive levels as spiritual. Freud was not concerned with higher, spiritual development, and his school of psychoanalysis, the dominant psychological paradigm of the early 20th century, did not recognize it. Jung, although heavily concerned with spiritual development (he was a serious student of both alchemy and the history of religion) lacked a strong grasp of the transpersonal factor, possibly because of his general reservations about schools of Eastern wisdom (and their primary concern with the transcendent).

The essential conflict within the schools of spiritual

psychology—a conflict still very much alive as of this writing in 2013—boils down to the regressive vs. progressive paradigms. The former, perhaps best represented by Michael Washburn, asserts that our development unfolds in such a way that involves a differentiation from our source—the development of our rational mind and separate egoic identity—followed by a 'return to source', in which we go beyond the limitations of the ego-mind and re-associate with the primal Ground of existence, the matrix of divinity that we left at some point in the past. This Ground remains the same; however having gone beyond our ego, we now perceive it differently. In this view, the ego-mind is largely an obstacle to be surmounted, a mechanism that represses our natural spiritual nature and thus must be overcome. In the progressive paradigm, best represented by Wilber, the process is understood to unfold from pre-personal, to personal, to transpersonal, in a ladder-like fashion. In this model, the ego-mind is not seen as a mere repressive force, but rather as an essential stage in our over-all development—and one, moreover, that represents a more advanced level than that of pre-egoic, child-like fusion with the Source. Wilber has criticized Washburn's position as representing a 'retro-regressive' model that confuses early life pre-ego consciousness with higher states of mind.

These differences are differences of theory, of course, but they have their practical applicability. For example, a more progressive model arguably is better suited to supporting the development of qualities such as personal responsibility and accountability in general. When spirituality is regarded solely as a kind of 'return to Source' it can foster a mind-set that is indifferent to the world, or to one's personal responsibilities in such a world. A more progressive model may be more suited to a general attitude of accountability and recognition of one's role in playing a part of the overall maturation of the human race. Or to cite another example: the European Witch-craze of the 12th-18th centuries (discussed in Chapter 15) was, according to a regressive model of development, simply an aberration, a manifestation of the repressive nature of the ego-mind.

A more progressive model would rather regard it as an extreme example of a 'growing-pain', a difficult phase in the overall maturation process of humanity, but still beyond the primitive fusion of our early ancestors if only because the passage through such morally depraved times allows for the later development of more advanced human rights and social awareness in general.

Such examples are simplifications, obviously, and the extraordinarily comprehensive writings of integral and transpersonal theorists such as Wilber, Washburn, and others should not be judged without first being thoroughly studied. For instance, Wilber does not subscribe to a simplistic ladder-like model *in toto*, as this would imply that a figure from the past (such as Buddha or Christ) could not have been 'as enlightened' as a modern mystic or sage. He rather grants the existence of deep awakenings irrespective of cultural conditions or era.[1]

The Great Chain of Being

The 'Great Chain of Being' is an important idea to understand. It is a structured view of the universe as hierarchical and multidimensional, from 'higher' (God, or the Infinite) to the 'lowest' (matter in all its forms). In between are the many levels of consciousness and reality. Most wisdom traditions have some form of it—from Plato's and Aristotle's schemes, to Plotinus and the Neoplatonists, to the Kabbalistic ten realms (the *sephirot*), to the Hindu and Theosophical divisions of the soul (usually simplified as spiritual-causal-mental-astral-etheric-physical, or variations thereof). A reasonably simple form is as follows:

The Infinite
Spirit
Soul
Mind
Body
Matter

The main idea to grasp with this cosmic map is that it is a 'holarchy', meaning that each higher level does not reject the levels lower than it, but rather includes them, much like concentric circles, with the largest circle (in this case, Spirit) transcending and including all circles within it, while the Infinite includes all, even Spirit, within its embrace. A holarchy is comprised of 'holons', a term that refers to something that is both a whole and a part. (The term was first coined by Arthur Koestler in 1967). For example, a human organ, like a heart, is both a whole thing, and a part of a larger complex, i.e. the body. Similarly, a cell is both whole and part of a larger complex, an organ, and so forth. Therefore both organs and cells are holons.

Much of the older versions of the Great Chain were tied up in a complex religious cartography that ranked various orders of entities, everything from 'principalities' and 'powers' to angels and all manner of material beasts, life forms, and objects. In this scheme the human race has always been held as occupying a unique spot, one given to enormous challenges as well as enormous potential rewards. Humans straddle the higher worlds of subtle spirit and the lower worlds of gross form, thus making them susceptible to most conceivable foibles and pitfalls. The Western esoteric system has always been concerned with what Antoine Faivre, Nicholas Goodrick-Clarke, and others have called the 'mesocosm', the intermediary range between the macro and microcosms. The subjective correlation of this, the various levels of egoic consciousness and the unconscious that mediate between the material body and its needs and the highest potential of a person, are the equal concern of psychotherapy. The relevance of a Great Chain of Being is that it manages to clarify the idea of levels of reality without disconnecting these levels from each other. The key term here is *transcendence and inclusion*. In transcending something we do not cast it off; we rather include it, integrate it. To 'integrate' means to 'make whole', the opposite of disintegrate (break apart). Psychologically this is a very important point, addressing the need to understand and integrate the 'lower' or 'shadow' self rather than casting it out or denying its manifestations.

It should be noted here that the Great Chain of Being, as a philosophical or theological roadmap, fell decidedly out of favor among the intelligentsia in the 19th century with the coming of Romantic and Darwinian ideas of progressiveness and evolution. This was because the Great Chain seemed to indicate that everything that could exist, must exist, already existed, and was set firmly in place in the overall hierarchy. Ideas such as evolution and progressiveness obviously do not seem to accord with such a structured hierarchy. After all, if everything is already neatly set in place, how can anything new truly develop, much less rise to a higher level?

The other, more serious problem with the Great Chain lay in its being appropriated by politics in particular, the idea of absolute monarchy. It was thought that if the universe is arranged by God hierarchically, then so too should humans arrange their world, something that inevitably required someone at the top of the pyramid. That someone was usually a sovereign, who by virtue of their position was deemed infallible and granted virtually absolute power. History has repeatedly demonstrated the limitations and dangers of such a situation.

However, as pointed out by Arthur Lovejoy and elaborated on by Wilber, the 'Great Chain' can still be salvaged as a working model for spiritual development because it refers mainly to the inner realms of metaphysics and the general interior nature of consciousness. The Great Chain was rejected (reasonably so) by 19th century thinkers because it did not seem to apply well at all to the modern discoveries of science, which is certainly true. It was also rejected by postmodern thinkers who were increasingly concerned with cultural relativism, maintaining that all religious and spiritual roadmaps were products of culture and its various biases. However when the Great Chain is understood as a working model for the inner realms of being, it maintains its power and useful perspective without invalidating outer advances in the hard and soft sciences.

Wilber (1995) eventually developed the Great Chain of Being

idea into a more fleshed out, deeply comprehensive map and meta-theory that he called AQAL ('all-quadrant, all-level'), with the key additions being an understanding of the role of interiority and exteriority in the grand scheme of things. His main realization had been that all previous models of development, be they mythic or scientific, often overlooked the important matter of whether or not they represented individual or collective viewpoints. He therefore conceived of a four-domain map that involved an embrace of inner, outer, individual, and collective, in addition to stages of development. The upper left of the quadrant in his map was comprised of the interior-individual ('I/consciousness'), the lower left of the interior collective ('we/cultural worldview'), the upper right of the exterior-individual ('it/organism'), and the lower right of the exterior collective ('its/social/environmental systems'). Integral Psychology argues that these added dimensions properly add the missing pieces to the Great Chain of Being, a paradigm shift that in some ways is equivalent to a cultural acceptance of the Earth as round rather than flat.

The Pre-Trans Fallacy

There is a great deal of confusion concerning matters of the transformational path when dealing with the issue of the ego, and the idea of going 'beyond' the ego. A common misunderstanding is that any kind of work on self involves a general return to a child-like state, a sort of 'back to innocence' or a 'return' to a divine source. This is not actually the case, certainly not in the simplistic, linear-like fashion it is sometimes presented as.

The 'pre-trans fallacy', popularized by Wilber[illegible], is based on a straightforward idea: 'trans-ego' states of mind (spiritual states *beyond* the ego) can be confused with 'pre-ego' states (child-like states), resulting in faulty understandings about spirituality, and in particular [illegible] (especially if [illegible] means 'being as a child again', [illegible]). Wilber [illegible] what he [illegible] most mystical states of consciousness to the memory of an infantile state of 'oneness' with the mother. (This should be tempered with the understanding that Freud felt he was up against a great wave of societal resistance, partly from religious conditioning, in establishing his views around the innate sexuality of human beings; and so felt compelled to stubbornly enforce his views, a main cause of his eventual falling out with some of his acolytes such as Jung and Adler). Wilber also speculated that Jung made the opposite error, assigning certain pre-ego states of mind to cosmic, 'trans-ego' spiritual states.

In many views of developmental psycho-spirituality, three basic levels are recognized. Those are:

1. Pre-ego (birth to age 2 or so)

2. Ego (roughly from age 2 on, with the development of language skills)

3. Trans-ego (possible in adults who commit to working on themselves)

When we commit to a spiritual path (in whatever form) we are basically attempting to wake up to our higher nature—or, to go 'beyond the ego'. But what does this really mean? As mentioned in Chapter 1, the ego is fundamental to individual development and is not inherently bad. It is necessary for both survival and individuation (recognizing who we are in distinction to others). Something can be *initially known* only in contrast to something that it is not. In the psychological realm, the ego is what provides this basic contrast. 'I am me, and you are you (not-me), therefore I exist.'

As children growing up we had to learn how to separate from our parents (in particular, our mother as we were originally joined with her body). This is sometimes called the process of 'differentiating'. The development of our ego was basic to this process and thus it is important that a young person develops a 'healthy ego', which means good boundaries, a solid sense of self, good self-esteem, and so on. Problems with ego-development are common, however, and often make it difficult for someone to embark on a spiritual path, because we cannot begin to go 'beyond' the ego if we have not first developed it into a functionally healthy process of relating to the world. This is why many who begin to work on themselves have to do some form of psychotherapy in order to integrate old wounds, establish self-esteem, forgive parents or siblings, and come to terms with family history, etc. Failure to come to a reasonable degree of acceptance of our past, and with our basic sense of personal identity, increases the likelihood of falling prey to the 'pre-trans fallacy'—that is, venturing into spiritual practices and confusing altered states of consciousness that can arise from such practices with early-life memories of 'oneness', such as being merged with what was around us, along with little or no sense of responsibility. Spiritual states of mind do indeed include a sense of 'oneness' but they do not abdicate our basic sense of identity. More to the point we do not abandon responsibility, and all the areas of life in which that is important.

There is also much confusion among seekers concerning the role of 'rationality' on the spiritual path. Trans-ego states of being (deep connection with others, or life, or the universe, deep peace/joy, wise sudden revelations and insights, etc.) can easily appear to be non-rational, which can lead to the belief that all rational states are therefore non-spiritual. From there, it is a short leap to assuming that *all non-rational states are therefore spiritual*. This however ignores the fact that pre-rational states are different from trans-rational states. That is, the 'oneness' felt by a child is not the same as the 'oneness' experienced by a mature, responsible adult. The former is more a state of 'fusion'. The latter is a state of deep connectedness in which the ability to use the mind (or personal identity), and be responsible, is not lost.

The main difference between ordinary rationality, and the rationality of trans-ego states, is that in the latter there is less *identification* with the mind. It is not that the mind becomes non-functional or disappears; it is rather that we come to increasingly recognize that we are *not* our particular thoughts, anymore than we are the body. But recognizing that we are not the body does not mean that we abandon the body, mistreat it, or pretend that it is not real (or 'not spiritual'). Similar is the case with the mind.

For those who are heavily identified with the mind (the intellectually oriented) there is a tendency to dismiss all spiritual states as 'pre-rational', that is, a type of regression to immature states of being, sometimes with the accompanying assumption that one will 'grow out of it'. That is also a variant of pre-trans fallacy, in this case, confusing post-ego states with pre-ego states, and in so doing dismissing all spirituality as a childish attempt to avoid being a responsible adult, or necessarily implying that one who pursues such matters is automatically self-absorbed—'navel gazing' as it is sometimes derogatorily referred to. (A good example of how this distinction has often been missed, even in established 20th century Western academia, can be found in an authoritative history of psychiatry textbook published in 1966, in which the authors, both psychiatrists, assert that the goal of Buddhist meditation is 'a psychological and physiological regression to the prenatal state of oblivion, of pure being, in which the differences between subject and object vanishes'.[3] The highest states of Buddhist meditation are not the same as 'pre-natal' or pre-ego 'oblivion', but are rather trans-ego states in which pure non-duality is experienced without any loss of memory, cognitive function, rational insight, or ability to function in the world as an adult—i.e., they are not states of 'infantile oblivion').

Contrarily, it is common in fluffier ('feel-good') New Age or personal growth communities to develop anti-intellectualism, by confusing pre-rational states with trans-rational, and thereby assuming that any non-rational state must be spiritual—even though many non-rational states are actually highly egocentric or narcissistic (self-absorbed)—that is, they are in fact *pre-ego* states.

As mentioned above, the correct development from ego to trans-ego is a process of *transcending and including*. That is, the mind and sense of individuality, along with the capacity for responsibility, are not abandoned, they are rather included on the journey, even as we deepen our sense of who we are and orient ourselves toward greater wisdom and compassion and skilful ability to help others. Spiritual development is not like a submersion of the ego and a return to the imagined bliss of an infantile, pre-ego, state of mind. Spiritual awakening rather transcends and yet also *includes* the mind and the aspect of it we know as ego. We retain our sense of individuality while at the same time clearly seeing and knowing that we are connected to everything, that separation is a construction of the mind made in order to navigate the world and organize it mentally and physically. And yet, such a realization does not mean that we walk out onto the street in front of a car because we are actually 'one with the car'. We continue to function in the world as if separation is real, because for all intents and purposes it is, at least at the level of gross phenomena.

The Enneagram and the 'Holy Ideas'

An essential element of the esoteric paths has always been direct work on the personality; a kind of 'alchemical deconstruction' in which the personality (and all its warts) is seen clearly, accepted, and transformed. Since the 1960s the Enneagram personality system has grown into one of the more effective tools aiding in the psycho-spiritual process of personality-work. The Enneagram is a nine-pointed geometric symbol that appears to have been introduced to the West around 1915 by the Greek-Armenian spiritual teacher G.I. Gurdjieff (1872?–1949).[4] Although Gurdjieff used it as a map for certain esoteric ideas, he did not use it as a system for personality typology. The symbol was introduced to a wider public via P.D. Ouspensky's famous study of Gurdjieff's ideas, *In Search of the Miraculous* (1949). However it was not until the late 1960s that the symbol was adapted by the Bolivian mystic Oscar Ichazo (b. 1931), and further developed by Ichazo's one-time student, the Chilean psychiatrist Claudio Naranjo (b. 1932), in such a way that it became representative of the 'Holy Ideas' and the nine essential personality types, along with the fundamental spiritual challenges facing these nine types.

The more recent Enneagram—as a personality typology—has been criticized by some Gurdjieff purists as being a misuse of his original purpose for it, but unquestionably it is a potent tool and one of the more comprehensive personality-type systems around.[5] Getting clear on our main 'point of fixation' (type) aids in achieving a stronger understanding of the ego, and in particular, its blind-spots—that is, the parts of our personality that cause problems for us. These parts can often be seen by others, but are just as often difficult for us to see or come to terms with (and hence are sometimes known as 'blind spots').

According to the theory developed by Ichazo and Naranjo, and some of their former students such as A.H. Almaas[6] and Helen Palmer, there are two essential elements to the Enneagram. The first is the egocentric facet, what is known as the 'personality type' or 'point of fixation'. The second key facet is sometimes referred to as the Enneagram of Virtues and 'Holy Ideas'. The Holy Ideas are essentially descriptions of the various aspects of non-dual reality as seen from the point of view of conceptual thought. These are (from types 1 through 9), Holy Perfection, Holy Will, Holy Harmony, Holy Origin, Holy Omniscience, Holy Strength, Holy Wisdom, Holy Truth, and Holy Love. 'Holy' here has nothing to do with the traditional religious or moral connotations of that word—it rather refers to the idea of supreme objectivity, where reality is seen *as it actually is*, beyond all distortions of the mind. When reality is clearly and properly perceived, the Holy Ideas are self-evident. However egoic contraction results in a failure to properly perceive or understand reality. The various ways in which this 'failure' manifests corresponds to the nine personality types as they form. The Holy Ideas can also be thought of as aspects of the awakened mind or higher self as it understands the perfection of the universe.

The problem with much of modern Enneagram teaching is that there is a tendency to focus exclusively or mainly on the 'personality type' or ego-fixation, and ignore, or give only passing attention to, the Holy Ideas. This tends to result in people identifying themselves solely on the basis of a 'type'. *Some* identification with one's type is helpful, in that it can assist in reversing denial. (For example, to begin to honestly recognize the aggression and assertiveness of a type-8; or of the detached observing nature of the type-5; or of the 'planning' tendencies of a type-7, is the beginning of essential self-acceptance, without which deeper realizations and changes are not possible). However if we do not move beyond identification with our type we miss the greater point of personality-type work. The point is not to form a new outer cloak to identify with, like a new team to cheer for or a new uniform to proudly wear; the point is to see beyond the personality-fixations to the higher qualities underneath that are expressions of a deeper reality. That said, the value of recognizing a personality type stems from the Sufi teaching that higher 'essence' qualities are often disguised in particular personality traits and quirks.

The Enneagram is a complex system that can be studied for years. What follows is but a brief overview of the nine types, including their fixations and corresponding Holy Ideas.

1. The Perfectionist

The Perfectionist personality type arises out of the egoic distortion of the Holy Idea of Perfection. 'Holy Perfection' refers to the idea that things are exactly the way they are supposed to be. If a star explodes, or an earthquake happens, or a tree falls, that is perfect in and of itself. When the ego distorts this understanding, it forms comparative judgments, believing that some things are 'more right' than others. This is true on the relative level of ego, but not on the absolute level of the Holy Ideas. Therefore the Perfectionist loses touch with the greater harmony of the bigger picture, and becomes anxious about 'flaws' in life. The Perfectionist then assumes the need to create such perfection within, and in so doing acquires a fear of making mistakes, of getting it wrong, or being imperfect. The main psychological pattern underlying the Perfectionist is a fear of criticism, often based on memories of a critical parent, leading to core fears of being inadequate in essential ways. To compensate, a 'perfectionist' personality type is developed, in which the original underlying impulse to return the criticism to one's parents (or other authoritative voices of childhood) is re-directed against oneself. The result is that the Perfectionist becomes very hard on themselves. They carefully monitor their own actions and tend to be disappointed when it becomes clear that others do not share their vigilance. Perfectionists tend to hold on to anger, only releasing it in righteous intensity once they have gathered enough evidence that they are right and the other wrong. Perfectionists in general tend to neglect personal emotional needs, and thus must learn to safely express their anger in a direct fashion while at the same time accept responsibility for addressing their unmet needs and communicating these to others. If they are able to learn to do this consistently, a natural underlying serenity can emerge, based on a deep acceptance of self, life, and universe.

Fundamental Spiritual Delusion: Reality is divided between good and bad
Chief ego feature: Resentment
Chief emotional pattern: With-held anger
Essence quality: Serenity
Holy Idea: Perfection

2. The Giver

The basis of the Giver type personality arises from a distortion of the Holy Ideas of Will and Freedom. Holy Perfection addressed the idea that all things are exactly as they are, and perfect in that absolute sense; Holy Will is the idea that all things *happening*, all apparent changes, are happening with a seamless perfection from the point of view of non-duality. This includes all possible occurrences, from a supernova to a glass falling off a table. Every event that occurs, including those enacted by a conscious human, are of equal perfection. Holy Freedom is the idea that all acts by a human are not separate from the totality or 'will' of the cosmos. From the absolute perspective, it is impossible to act in any way that is not part of the will of existence. When this understanding is lost or distorted, it results in a personality type that anxiously believes itself separate from existence, and thus develops the need to overcompensate by seeking to gain the approval of others. Givers in general move toward people, and seek to please, to manipulate via flattery in hope of getting the other to thereby approve of them. This 'people-pleasing' is deriving from their belief that anxiety is lowered, and safety ensured, when approved of by others. Givers were summed up by Claudio Naranjo as demonstrating 'egocentric generosity'. In short, this is giving with an agenda. The shadow-side of a Giver is often an angry, frustrated tyrant. The balancing-antidote for this type is exploring hidden desires to be selfish. If this is accomplished to some degree, a more authentic and genuine giving nature emerges, along with a natural humility and kindness.

Fundamental Spiritual Delusion: I have a personal will that is separate and distinct from the Whole
Chief ego features: Flattery and Manipulation
Chief emotional pattern: Confusion, taking on the feelings of others
Essence quality: Humility
Holy Ideas: Will, Freedom

3. The Performer

The Performer personality type results from egoic distortions of the Holy Ideas of Law and Harmony. In this context, Holy Law refers to the idea that all things are happening as a movement of perpetual spontaneous dynamism, with no separate God in the background causing things to happen. The idea of Holy Law negates the idea of cause and effect, because Holy Law is based on the idea of the perfect unity of all things, whereas cause and effect requires discrete, separate objects acting on each other. This is, of course, entirely a matter of perspective. From the point of view of the separate ego-self, if I offend someone and they in turn offend someone else, there is obviously cause and effect of some sort. But from the point of view of the idea of Holy Law, this chain of events all occurs in the seamless Oneness of existence, all of which is arising naturally and spontaneously. According to Holy Law, time and space are illusions constructed by the ego-mind; accordingly, there was no 'cause' that resulted in the universe coming into being at some point. There is just a continuous unfolding of events, with nothing separate from anything else. Holy Harmony is the further idea that when all events occurring in existence are rightly understood as a spontaneous arising of the Whole, then a natural harmony is perceived and understood—a harmony that appears as beauty, grace, majestic grandeur, love, and so on.

The Performer type personality arises when there is a failure to understand Holy Law and Harmony. The result is the tendency to believe that one is a separate 'doer', essentially helpless, and therefore needing to overcompensate via striving to appear a certain way to others. The whole basis of this type is an emphasis on projected image. There is a chameleon-like quality here that learns to mask itself by cleverly adapting to the needs of others—'you want blue, I'll give you blue; but if you over there want green, I will give you green'. It is a given that both vanity and deceit will play their part here, as much energy is given over to deflecting others, to keeping them 'off balance' via a display of continuous charisma. The Performer is generally a high energy type and capable of great productivity in work, to the point of being the proverbial workaholic. Performers are given to striving and feeling helpless deep down, because they are caught in the ego-position of believing themselves capable of acting without any contact with their spiritual Source. In general they do not like, nor do they handle well, failure of any sort. As children, they were often prized for their achievements; performance and image were rewarded rather than emotional connections of a deep involvement with other people. Performers learned that love and approval come from what you can produce, not from what you are. The main defense mechanism here is identification, a type of 'acting'. The antidote is the practice of cultivating honesty, particularly within personal relationships, but also via how one's image is projected to the world. When a humbling deconstruction of the performer personality is accomplished, the resulting essence quality of honesty can shine forth.

Fundamental Spiritual Delusion: I have free will, I am a doer separate from the Whole
Chief ego feature: Vanity
Chief emotional pattern: Uncertainty, difficulty accessing authentic feelings
Essence quality: Honesty
Holy Ideas: Law and Harmony

4. The Tragic Romantic

The Tragic Romantic personality arises from a distortion of the Holy Idea of Origin. 'Holy Origin' is the same as ultimate originality, having to do with the understanding that everything derives from God (Source, the Infinite). When the ego-self distorts this understanding, it creates a personality type that is constantly seeking outside of itself for this Origin Point, and in so doing romanticizing the quest for the 'Grail' that always seems to be on the horizon, never quite showing up in one's life. This fascination with 'seeking but never finding' gets directed onto relationships (the present partner is never quite enough, or something about one's life is never quite enough), as well as onto symbols (a romanticizing of art, religion, science, etc.). 'Tragic

Romantics' believe themselves to be 'special' as a result of this longing for the origin of everything, this perpetual seeking for that which will finally complete them. The psychological roots of this type often involve some sort of abandonment in childhood, either literal (e.g., parents divorcing) or more abstract (a parent who was seldom around, emotionally distant, alcoholic, etc.), resulting in doubts about self-worth, resulting in later years in a desire to compensate for feelings of inadequacy by becoming special in some way. One of the archetypes of the Tragic Romantic is the Magician; hence this type is an important one to understand for many who are drawn to esoteric traditions. Key antidotes to the neurotic tendencies of this type involve cultivating a genuine awareness and appreciation of others, as well as understanding the roots of one's desire to be special and its relation to fear of the ordinariness (humanity) of one's life and one's self. If accomplished, the natural underlying essence quality of equanimity (a serenity arising from a sense of deeply 'fitting in' with the universe) can be liberated.

Fundamental Spiritual Delusion: I am a separate identity, a special person, no one understands me, I am cut off from the Whole
Chief ego feature: Melancholy, Envy, tendencies toward depression
Chief emotional patterns: Dramatizing feelings, attachment to being special, artistic sublimation (expressing feelings indirectly via symbols, dramatic style, ritual, etc.)
Essence quality: Equanimity
Holy Ideas: Origin, Presence

5. The Observer

The Observer personality type arises out of a distortion of the Holy Idea of Omniscience. The idea of 'omniscience' as it is meant here refers to a profound understanding of the idea of diversity within unity. Whereas 'Holy Truth' (see type 8) refers to the perfect Oneness of reality as seen through consciousness that has perfectly transcended the experience of separate existence, Holy Omniscience refers to the understanding of the apparent details, boundaries, and distinctions within that reality, or what can be likened to 'God's knowledge'. It is comparable to seeing the divinity and perfection within the details of a particular tree or flower (in contrast to the approach of seeing the whole forest via one sweeping glance). Holy Truth refers to undifferentiated reality, with no awareness of boundaries or distinctions. It can be characterized as a state of pure Being, but is it not consciousness as we know it. In order to experience life and consciousness as we know it, diversity within unity is required. The perception of that diversity is Holy Omniscience. When this idea, Holy Omniscience, is not understood or distorted, the result is a personality type that deeply believes itself separate from existence, disconnected, isolated—not itself part of the *details* of the Whole. Accordingly, it sets about observing things, with minimal participation, minimizing personal interactions, even to the point of actively hiding from life and reality. The antidote is to practice extending to the universe, sharing one's consciousness with others, and seeing deeply into the illusion of separation. If accomplished, the result is a genuine non-attachment (best represented by the image of the Buddha) based on deep peace and acceptance, rather than a neurotic avoidance of contact.

Fundamental Spiritual Delusion: I am an ego, separate, isolated within the Whole
Chief ego feature: Stinginess
Chief emotional pattern: Repressed fear, fear of feelings in general
Essence quality: Non-attachment
Holy Idea: Omniscience

6. The Devil's Advocate

Type 6, known variously as the Devil's Advocate, Dissenter,

Generalist, Rebel, or Loyalist (seemingly inconsistent terms that reveal the ambiguous nature of this type), results from a distortion of the Holy Ideas of Strength and Faith. Holy Faith and Strength refer to the direct understanding that we are always connected to our deep self. This 'understanding' is not based on conventional blind faith; it is rather the result of direct experience. Further, the nature of the deep self is understood to be fundamentally good, innocent, and worthy. When there is a failure to realize Holy Faith/Strength, then there is a resulting doubt, mistrust, and cynicism about the nature of sentient beings. Moreover, there is no trust in the innate nature of one's own deep self—or whether or not it even exists. This leads to an essentially suspicious disposition, one that views others (and oneself) as inherently flawed and untrustworthy. The Devil's Advocate has issues with authority, and often forms an ambivalent relationship with it. On the one hand they can be loyal, guardians or close-follower types; on the other hand they can be rebels, devil's advocates, even saboteurs. When they choose a position of loyalty, it is with the underlying agenda to get close to power so as to keep close watch on it; not for any grand ulterior motive, but simply as a means of reducing anxiety by keeping close tabs on the types of people around most likely to cause them anxiety. (A variant of the expression, 'keep your friends close but keep your enemies closer'). This type may also seek an alliance with those who have power so as to secure their support and protection. When this type chooses a position of distance or rebellion against authority, it is the inevitable by-product of their mistrust of authority and power. Because they doubt themselves, they will often fear success and avoid completing projects, because if they do they fear that they will then be judged and condemned by those authority figures who wield power. The general antidote for this type is cultivating courage by facing into fears and finding ways of challenging them and overcoming them. If this is successfully accomplished, a strong and naturally courageous nature is revealed.

Fundamental Spiritual Delusion: I am without any true nature, without any real Self
Chief ego feature: Fear and Doubt
Chief emotional pattern: Suspicion, fear of what is going on around oneself
Essence quality: Courage
Holy Ideas: Strength and Faith.

7. The Idealist

Other terms for this type are 'Dreamer' and 'Epicure'. This personality type arises as a result of confusion around the ideas of Holy Work, Plan, and Wisdom. Holy Work or Plan refers to the idea that there is a specific and intelligent design to existence; not one that need be thought of as being implemented by some separate God, but rather arising naturally and spontaneously from existence. To directly see and understand this natural plan and its work is Holy Wisdom. From the perspective of Holy Wisdom, we are not called upon to control the fate of the universe or try to alter it or meddle in it in any way; we are simply called to see that whatever activity we are engaged in is part of the Holy Plan. Again, it is entirely a matter of perspective and context. When the Wisdom context is not there, there is a corresponding failure to grasp the 'greater plan' of existence, and how it is all unfolding naturally and seamlessly. From that point of view, it then becomes necessary to control one's own fate via generating mental plans that are never quite in step with the cosmic plan. This leads to a sense of alienation from the Whole. Notable tendencies of this type tend to be a fear of boredom and a strong dislike of pain. They are given to develop sophisticated strategies for avoiding pain, a prime one of which is to keep multiple options on the table, so as to avoid the disappointment (and pain) of any one given option failing. In general the Idealist is a high energy type, can be the proverbial 'life of the party' in an authentic fashion, and can be very productive, especially when their fear of commitment and failure is overcome.

Fundamental Spiritual Delusion: My plan is separate from the unfolding of the Cosmos
Chief ego feature: Planning
Chief emotional pattern: Working to dissipate anxiety via many options (busy-ness)
Essence quality: Productivity
Holy Ideas: Work, Wisdom, Plan

8. The Boss

The 'Boss', sometimes also called the 'Leader', is a type that is born out of a distortion of the Holy Idea of Truth. Holy Truth refers to the understanding that All is One—the entire universe of all possible levels and dimensions is an expression of the One, and is in fact non-dual, only appearing to be fragmented from the point of view of the mind. When this fundamental understanding is obscured or lost, a deep, underlying belief arises that something is essentially wrong. We are living a false existence, out of tune with our natural state, which can result in a personality type that sees reality in a very dualistic light (with emphasis on justice/injustice, strong/weak, good/bad, etc.) and itself as essentially 'bad' or 'guilty'. It then seeks to rid itself of this core wound by controlling others or dominating a situation so as not to feel vulnerable. 'Active bosses' tend toward intensity and rigidity, being disciplinarians, given to conflict and aggression and protectiveness toward the weak. 'Passive bosses' incline toward hedonism and indulgence in excess. The psychological root of the Boss often lies in a family-of-origin culture where weakness (particularly showing vulnerability) is frowned upon. Success lies in controlling others, not in being controlled by them. This type is somewhat uncommon among spiritual seekers (they are more often found in business), however when a 'Boss' gives oneself over to the spiritual path they often become a teacher or guru of some sort. Re-balancing for this type can involve the practice of emotionally exposing oneself, looking silly, being vulnerable, working co-operatively, and so on. When the tough exterior of a

'Boss' is deconstructed to some degree, what is often revealed underneath is a type of natural straightforwardness and innocent purity.

Fundamental Spiritual Delusion: Reality is a dualistic conflict; you are either with me or against me
Chief ego feature: Lust
Chief emotional patterns: Venting anger, intimidating others, denial of tender feelings and masking them via aggression
Essence quality: Innocence
Holy Ideas: Truth and Innocence

9. The Mediator

The Mediator, sometimes also called the Peacemaker, is a generally passive personality type originating in an egoic distortion of the Holy Ideas of Love and Right Action. Holy Love refers to the idea that the universe is not just intrinsically good, loving, and loveable, but that so are we in our core; moreover, this love and loveableness is non-local, that is, not limited to specific parts or places in the universe. When this essential understanding is lost or distorted, the result is a specific spiritual delusion that involves a loss of self-esteem, a general sense of personal inadequacy or inferiority. Accordingly, the idea develops that one's sense of personal worth can only be achieved by playing the 'peacemaker' or 'mediator'; perpetually serving others, putting their interests ahead of one's own. Mediators are given to passive aggression, sloth, and general denial of personal feelings. The laziness here is not a reference to physical laziness so much as it is to mental and spiritual laziness. Naranjo used the term *acidia* and characterized it as a 'loss of interiority, refusal to see, and resistance to change'.[7] The healing for this type often involves some sort of acceptance of personal feelings, particularly anger, and finding a healthy and constructive (non-damaging) means of expressing that anger outwardly. Once this is accomplished to some degree, the underlying essence quality of a genuinely loving nature is revealed.

Fundamental Spiritual Delusion: I have no access to limitless love; love is localized and conditional; it is not 'everywhere' (non-local). My love is limited, therefore I am limited.
Chief ego feature: Sloth, Laziness
Chief emotional pattern: Repressed anger, passive aggression
Essence quality: Love
Holy Ideas: Love and Right Action.

The Metamorphosis of Essence

All nine Enneagram types are ultimately coping mechanisms of the ego to deal with anxiety. Each of the nine types is a *strategy*, developed during approximately the first ten years of life and thereafter refined, to help us minimize core-level fear. This strategy forms the basis of personality. The Enneagram helps reveal the actual form of our personality—particularly in terms of its ability to obscure our 'essence'. 'Essence' here should not be understood as some fully formed resplendent soul; it is a potential, waiting to be developed over the course of our life. If our personality dominates too much our essence remains simple and primitive, never having the chance to grow. The process thus begins with observing and alchemically deconstructing the personality (that is, bringing it into a state of balance), which then enables the essence to emerge and begin to develop. This is very similar to the biological process of metamorphosis. The general purpose of Enneagram work can be defined as:

1. Becoming clearly conscious of the personality tendencies and functions, particularly 'blind spots'.

2. Letting go of self-judgment of one's personality tendencies and functions. That is, to deepen self-acceptance. This makes it possible to deepen self-observation on more impersonal levels.

3. To begin to make conscious efforts to directly work with the

more inhibiting factors of the personality system. For example, if we are a 'Helper' (type 2), to practice attending to our personal needs more, and sacrificing less for others. If a 'Perfectionist' (1), to practice letting go of control or self-criticism. Or if a 'Mediator' (9), to practice directly injecting one's personal views, feelings, and so on. *In all cases, the main goal is to achieve balance by exploring ways of being that are opposite to our habitual personality patterns.*

4. To become increasingly aware of essence and its qualities. In general the essence appears naturally when the personality has been directly observed and suspended. For example, if our personality tends toward arrogance and extroversion, then via direct observation we may be able to consciously suspend our typical mannerisms. In that moment we then may be able to glimpse our essence that is underlying the personality, which in this case will likely be something more or less opposite to arrogance and extroversion—for example, a quiet, shy humility. This 'quiet humility' can then be developed—'metamorphosed'—into a mature self-confidence. The bloated shell of the personality has been discarded, allowing for a more authentic self-confidence to arise, emerging on the 'essence-embryo' of tender, quiet humility.

It is important to remember that the Enneagram is fundamentally a spiritual system, though it is often used by psychologists, business-people, and others less concerned with the transpersonal elements. As a system of transformation, the Enneagram is not so much concerned with typology as it is with the gradual deconstruction of the personality in order to facilitate the liberation and development of the essence underneath. From that perspective, no personality type is 'better' or 'worse' than any other. They are simply nine defined means of coping with the anxiety that arises in early childhood with the formation of the first ego-defenses. Seen thusly, the personality is essentially a defensive structure that safeguards us in life, but it most certainly is not our 'true face'. That does not make the personality 'bad', but rather our 'karmic lesson' for our life. In astrology it has its correlate as the idea of the 'aspects' between planets. In psychology it is generally known via our 'defense mechanisms'.

The idea of working 'beyond' personality can be difficult to consider at first, as most of us are conditioned to regard 'a lot of personality' as a good, interesting, or charismatic thing. But in the context of Enneagram work 'personality' is basically a limiting structure that sets up our tests for our life. Each time we grow beyond the constraints and limitations of our personality, our essence has the chance to strengthen and develop.

According to some wisdom traditions, at the point of death the personality goes through a series of stages in which it is dissolved and cast off. What remains and what functions in the 'other world' is our essence. If in our life little progress was accomplished with the limitations of our personality, then essence remains basically unchanged after death. But if, in the course of our life, we made sincere efforts and managed to work through personality limitations to make contact with essence, then essence itself grows (and according to some esoteric theory, then has the possibility of better equipping us for 'afterlife' transitions).

The basis of essence is that, unlike the personality, it is not defined by the body and localized, societal conditions. However essence itself is not static but is subject to growth and development, which is why even highly 'advanced' humans (masters) are continuing to grow themselves.

Sub-personalities, Buffers, Defense Mechanisms

The great Vedantic sage of south India, Ramana Maharshi (1879–1950), gave his students one essential inquiry—the question 'Who am I'? He taught that rigorous focus on that one inquiry eventually leads to the dawning realization of the true Self, the '*atman*', which is already at one with *Brahman* (God). The realization of this idea presupposes certain things, however, one of which is a balanced or adjusted personality that does not cloud or interfere with one's ability to access the transcendent. In the busy, fast, and complicated 21st century Western world many people are too disconnected and fragmented within to properly approach and usefully utilize Ramana's sublimely simple teaching. Gurdjieff, Ramana's great contemporary and a teacher arguably better suited for Westerners, taught that modern men and women are not whole, but rather are divided into numerous 'sub-personalities'—numerous 'I's. Like Ramana, he also taught that the idea of an egoic, 'individual self' is an illusion. He further taught that the 'real I'—his term for the true Self—can only be realized after much effort has been made to overcome our mechanical nature, and to begin to see clearly our conflicting sub-personalities. The influential (and controversial) 20th century Indian guru Osho (Rajneesh) agreed with Gurdjieff, maintaining that most Westerners need to undergo 'process-type' work (individual or group psychotherapy) in order for their meditation practices to truly deepen and be effective.

That we have 'sub-personalities' will be apparent to anyone who uses a bit of self-observation. One day we want this, another day we want that. One part of us may decide to undertake a project, another part may decide not to. One part may be energetic, another lazy. One part makes plans for Thursday and the other part cancels these plans by Wednesday night. One part enjoys attention and seeks fame and another part shuns attention and desires to be left alone. And so on.

All of this fragmentation and the inconsistency it manifests contributes toward keeping us in a kind of trance-state; effectively, in a kind of waking sleep. Society at large generally contributes toward this trance-state by discouraging any sort of self-observation. To see our inconsistencies and inner contradictions is humbling and can even be disturbing. If we saw them all at once we might even go mad. Accordingly we have a natural defense in this regard, what Gurdjieff termed 'buffers'. A buffer is a type of psychological shock-absorber that allows us to shift from one sub-personality to another, without too much of a shock. Buffers are known in modern psychology as 'defence-mechanisms'. What follows are some of the more well recognized ones:

1. Lying: lying is much more frequent than commonly assumed. In this regard lying is more than just distortions of the truth, or 'white lies', but refers to any kind of misrepresentation of truth, for example, in communication to others that is either overtly false (saying 'A' when we really mean 'B'), or covertly (not saying anything at all—'forget about it'). In a sense, all defence mechanisms are forms of lying. Consensus levels of lying can become very destructive, as for example when an entire society has been conditioned to believe a certain way that is not in accordance with a greater reality. A particularly interesting form of 'lying' is known as *confabulation*. This is the creation of a fantasy that is unconsciously turned into a 'factual account' of something in our memory (related terms for it being 'false memory' or 'retrospective falsification'). Experiments have been done to demonstrate confabulation, a common example being the following: a group of people are shown pairs of cards with photos of faces on them, and then asked to pick the face they find most attractive. Unknown to the test subjects, the cards with faces on them are being handled by a stage-magician, who manages to swap the photos without being noticed. The subjects are then later presented with the photo of the person they find less attractive, thinking that it was the one they chose as more attractive. In many cases the swap of photos is not detected, and the subjects then proceed to generate all sorts of reasons as to why they found the photo of the person attractive—when they had not in fact picked that photo. In other words, the mind tends to fabricate stories to justify situations it finds itself in. We literally 'make things up' on a regular basis, perhaps because at some core level we know that reality is something of a house of cards that might collapse at any moment. We confabulate in part to provide meaning and purpose to reality. (This was what Schopenhauer was getting at when he said that the rational mind follows the will, or unconscious mind, then goes through all sorts of clever justifications to prove that it is in fact 'in charge').

2. Suppression: this is the deliberate effort to control a desire that we think is unacceptable. For example we want to help someone, but fear that others will judge us or attack us if we do. So we suppress our desire to help them. Or, we are attracted to someone, but fear the consequences of our attraction, so we suppress the feeling. The suppression may be so effective that we switch from our sub-personality 'A' that is attracted to that person, to sub-personality 'B', that is not.

3. Reaction-formation: a mechanism for denying a feeling that is unacceptable. It occurs in order to help us not remember or relive an old painful memory. For example, we may have been ridiculed long ago for holding a certain belief—say, in God. Later in life, we become militantly atheist, and violently denounce any talk about 'God'. Whenever we experience a strong knee-jerk reaction toward something, often 'reaction-formation' is the cause, and we in fact have feelings that are completely opposite of our strongly held convictions. Another exaggerated example would be hating the opposite sex and scorning them at any chance, when deep down we badly wanted (and want) the love of our opposite sex parent. Reaction-formation is common with adolescents, who will use it to attempt to differentiate from their parents. 'If you say white, I say black; if you say left, I say right'. Adolescents will often assume the opposite point of view merely to assert that they are different from the other person, thereby beginning to establish their identity. Adults who have matured slowly will often continue to resort to reaction-formation, sometimes becoming contentious or quarrelsome not because they care about the issue, but because they fear being consumed by the other person's point of view and thereby reduced to feeling insignificant.

4. Repression: Whereas suppression is generally a conscious act, repression is mostly unconscious (and thus potentially more problematic). Repression is the unconscious splitting off of parts of the mind, so as not to feel pain or other difficult feelings connected to what is being repressed. Mass society (including religion) in general serves to encourage repression in people, and especially repression of their vitality (including their sexuality). When an element of a person is repressed they are generally out of touch with it. Oftentimes self-observation and/or meditation is not sufficient to dislodge or reveal deeply repressed material ('blind spots'). Sometimes this can be done only with deep psychotherapy (at times utilizing cathartic methods).

5. Identification: this is where we come to merge with and believe that we are a specific quality or tendency. 'I am lazy', 'I am no good', or 'I am superior', etc. When a person strongly identifies with only parts of their personality but refuses to acknowledge other parts, it can take a great deal of work for them to reverse denial and begin to see these other parts.

6. Introjection: to introject means to carry within the image or memory of someone else and to operate as that person would have you do. For example, you are angry at a rude person and want to object to them. But you hold back because your mother taught you always to be nice and polite. The memory of mother is inside of you and is still calling the shots.

7. Projection: projection is the opposite of identification, and in some ways is the most important of all defense mechanisms to understand. To project is to see things in others (whether good or bad) that are actually inside of us. Projection is discussed in full in the next chapter.

Change vs. Being Affirmed

Central to the esoteric paths of inner work is the idea of *change*. The notion of change as a process from one state to another was discussed in Chapter 2 (Alchemy). Deeper approaches to the issue have long perplexed and challenged philosophers, the most essential of which is the question of whether or not 'free will' even exists (which, at the absolute level, it almost certainly does not). It may be safely established that this is largely a theoretical matter and that from the practical (or relative) level our only real avenue is to proceed as if free will is real.

In general, most people avoid drastic changes in their life, unless forced into it by circumstances (usually of the unwanted variety). A prime way to avoid change is via identification. As we establish ourselves in society, we establish an identity, and this in turn is reinforced by those around us, producing the semblance of continuity orchestrated by some 'consistent self' within us. We are encouraged to 'fit in', to find our place. As we do so, others will rarely encourage us to change; in fact, most people are made uncomfortable by too many changes occurring around them, and so seldom encourage others to change or explore more unusual ways of being. This is particularly so in family-systems, where family members typically reinforce a continuous, particular identity in fellow family members (ironically, even if this identity is largely negative). One of the legends of the Grail myths speaks to this idea. It involves the young soon-to-be Grail knight Perceval, who must break free from his mother (whom he lives with in the forest) in order to follow three shining and entrancing knights who are in search of the Grail. His mother of course does not want him to leave, but he must do so, driven as he is to follow the 'hero's journey' and discover the truth about life and reality. Perceval's myth can be seen as an incisive metaphor illustrating the tendency of family-systems to resist change in fellow family members, and of the common need for those aspiring to a life of self-inquiry (or esoteric work) to break free from limited family conditioning and expectations. (There are of course exceptions to this tendency, but they are somewhat rare; in the case of most who seek truth via an esoteric path, they must 'break free' of expectations from others that they will be 'normal' and follow a conventional path in life).

In addition, an important element to be aware of in all forms of inner work is the matter of changing vs. being affirmed. As we engage a path of work on self, we sooner or later are faced with this essential matter and everything associated with it, which is: do we truly seek to change from within, or are we actually seeking to be only affirmed for what we *already believe we are*? It is possible, and even common, for an outer search or apparent intention to grow, to be concealing another agenda, which is to be affirmed for who we think we are—to be told that we are already 'adequate' or 'worthy'. It is even possible to misuse certain spiritual philosophies that promote a type of direct realization ('you are already divine, you just don't realize it') to disguise the underlying agenda to be validated as we already are. This can be problematic when there are unaddressed psychological scars stemming from early life conditions where one experienced heavy or repeated invalidation from parents or other authority figures. If deep down we are truly seeking authority figures (in the form of spiritual teachers, therapists, or even archetypal figures such as spirits, angels or God) to tell us that we are well and good the way we are, thereby vicariously 'healing' the wound of the past in which we did not sufficiently receive this message, then all our spiritual seeking and attempts to change from within will probably not amount to much. This would be because it is not change or growth that we truly want; it is love, acceptance, approval, and affirmation.

The will cannot be properly harnessed if this underlying psychological issue is always running in the background, something like 'spyware' that interferes with the overall performance of a computer. That is because correctly utilizing the will is synonymous with maturity, with actually growing up. If we are more truly seeking to be *affirmed* for what we *think* we are, we are still operating out of an immature place in which we are not yet ready (or willing) to assume responsibility for who we *actually* are—including all of our less pleasant traits. In short, when it is affirmation we seek rather than genuine change, we cannot tackle the 'shadow' elements of our personality because in being confronted with them we will tend to project them outwardly and experience others as being critical of who we are. When we project and disown our shadow elements we usually end up feeling simply victimized. Instead of recognizing these parts of our nature, we will experience them as coming *at* us from others, in the form of invalidations.[8]

Ego Traps

Every path of inner work has its own particular psychological pitfalls that have to be noted along the way. The Western esoteric tradition, which this book is concerned with, has certainly not been spared this problem. Of concern here is the pitfall of **grandiosity**. The closest common term associated with grandiosity is pride, in its negative manifestations (perhaps better defined as hubris), meaning here to have an inflated self-image, to be puffed up, compensating for an underlying self-doubt. Grandiosity is, however, more problematic than mere pride, as it is connected to the narcissistic impulse, something recognized by modern psychiatry as a personality disorder. In older times it was referred to as megalomania. Some understanding of this matter is important, because the baser motive or intention behind mastering the so-called 'black arts' was usually thought to be the desire for power, perhaps best summarized by the Biblical condemnation of Simon Magus:

> But there was a certain man, called Simon, which beforetime in the same city used sorcery, and bewitched the people of Samaria, giving out that himself was some great one: To whom they all

> gave heed, from the least to the greatest, saying, This man is the great power of God. And to him they had regard, because that of long time he had bewitched them with sorceries. Acts 8:9–8:24 (KJV)

In all such judgment there are two sides to the coin—an attempt by organized priesthoods who have a vested interest in controlling the spiritual destiny of their flocks, to keep the common man powerless—as well as a valid psychological critique of ego inflation. That the esoteric path is partly about personal empowerment is a given. But here were are going to take a look at the second issue, that of ego inflation, because the most common unclear intention for working within the esoteric traditions is to compensate for perceived personal shortcomings, and most specifically, for unmet needs related to love, validation, and recognition.

Specialness and Grandiosity

'Specialness' in the sense meant here implies tendencies to be caught up in pride and/or vanity, and their many guises. Both can be seen as compensatory for an underlying negative self-image, or fears of inadequacy. In a more clinical sense, the relevant term here is 'grandiosity', which is related to a kind of narcissism. At the root of it is the belief that one is special, and therefore can only be understood by very particular (and very few) others. It is not too much of a leap to connect the dots and see how many esoteric teachings and groups can seem a natural fit for one with tendencies toward grandiosity or narcissism. It is also arguable that esoteric practices themselves can contribute toward ego-inflation and hubris, although in these cases it more probably serves as a 'trigger' for latent grandiose tendencies that have simply not manifested up to that point. For example it can easily be argued, as Francis Bacon wrote in the 16th century, that esoteric theory and doctrines of magic are 'arrogant substitutes for painstaking thought and investigation'[9]—that is, are deriving from a sense of entitlement and/or resentment at having to work hard to achieve success in life ('just give me the secret formula'). Either way, any who participate in esoteric spiritual practices, especially those involving the usage of 'props' that involve ceremony, ritual, rank within an organization or graded scheme of initiations, and so forth, have to remain watchful for the effect all this can have upon self-image. An artificially inflated self-image leads to as much difficulty and suffering as a poorly or negatively developed self-image. In referring to grandiosity expressing via the magician archetype, Robert Moore wrote:

> The spirituality of an enlightened world would easily see that evil is no more than an illusion held by those still unenlightened but marginal people who don't know what you know. Magician grandiosity cloaks a fundamental coldness, a lack of love and joy, and a denial of the horror of radical evil. With the erroneous perception that you are above it, you try to avoid any responsibility for confronting it.[10]

The key point to see with grandiosity is that it tends to fluctuate between identification to projection, meaning when identifying with it, we experience ego inflation, and when projecting it, we see this ego-inflation in others around us, and often subsequently give away our power to them and allow them to control us—or self-righteously demonize them and rebel against them. Either way, we are not fully confronting our own tendencies toward grandiosity, specialness, and pride. We are either unaware of our own, or blaming others for having it (the 'elite rich', the 'secret cabals that control the world', etc.)

The 'Omnipotence of Thoughts'

[illegible] dismissed religion, magic, and the occult as primitive preoccupations ultimately deriving from a sense of powerlessness, and fear that it can be argued that he was caught in certain implicit assumptions of modern science and materialism that shaped his view of the matter. However, his insights undoubtedly held true in many, if not most, individual cases, and his instinctive skepticism, while painting with a broad brush, almost certainly scored many more 'hits' than 'misses'.

Freud cited Wilhelm Wundt and David Hume on the idea that it is basic to human nature to ascribe qualities to what is around us that are similar to what we know of ourselves. In short, we tend to assume that other beings—or even things—are like us. From there, it is a short leap to assume that 'things' are alive, that each person has an immaterial soul (and therefore is immortal), and that invisible beings watch over us and can intervene or be supplicated to—all of which is the essence of animism, the most ancient of 'spiritual traditions'. From animism arose religion, eventually followed by science. These three—animism, religion, and science—comprise the three great 'systems of thought' that have dominated human civilization. Freud maintained that the main 'technique' of animism, how to control one's world and the powers (spirits) that animated and dominated it, were sorcery and magic. He distinguished between the two, writing:

> If a spirit is scared away by making a noise and shouting, the action is one purely of sorcery; if compulsion is applied to it by getting hold of its name, magic has been used against it.[11]

Freud's remarks, doubtless to be seen as oversimplified by the serious esoteric practitioner, still carry clear insight in a remarkably compact fashion. There are elements of ceremonial magic (so-called Solomonic techniques, for example) involving the evocation of spirits, that clearly have elements of sorcery in them, in that they include aggressive admonishments or even direct threats against certain spirits. The usage of a 'name' to gain the attention or control of an entity, while designated here by Freud as 'magic', is certainly deeply intertwined with religion (calling on the name of 'Christ', 'Krishna', 'Allah', or various Buddhas and bodhisattvas, for example, to compel changes in one's psychic state or immediate environment; let alone all manner of religious rites and ceremonies that involve vocalizing sacred names). Freud was less concerned with these technicalities than he was with what he saw as the overarching theme of animism and its methods of sorcery and magic, and that was the psychology of 'mistaking an ideal connection for a real one'.[12] He goes on to mention a classic myth of ancient Egypt: the Sun-god Ra 'sinking' into his home in the West each night in order to battles demons, only to emerge victorious the next day (confirmed by the rising of the Sun). The ancient Egyptians' ignorance of astronomy (the rotation of the Earth causing day and night) presumably led them to deduce a connection between an 'ideal' (the myth that they concocted about Ra and the demons) and the appearance of days and nights.

Freud's inclination in treating both religion and magic was reductionist, in that he boiled the issue down exclusively to psychological matters. He saw primitive religions and magic as deriving from father-projections, and the ambivalence humans typically feel in relation to them (which is why most ancient 'gods' were a blend of light and dark qualities—a good example being the God of the Old Testament, manifesting traits of wisdom, power, petulance, and vengefulness all in one). More essentially, Freud (drawing partly on James Frazer, author of the influential *The Golden Bough*), saw magic as based on associative thinking, a simple example being via what is called 'imitative magic', such as the burning of an effigy, or the lancing of a doll (representing a person) with pins. From this primitive root arise sophisticated rituals, all ultimately deriving from a desire to gain power over some situation by the belief that we can change something by contacting it, or something that represents it. From there it is not far to the view that we can change something merely by wishing it so—or by what Freud called the 'omnipotence of thoughts'.

Of course, it has to be stressed here that Freud was not referring to some functionally healthy ability to determine one's fate, but rather to an immature self-centeredness that is usually classified as a form of narcissism. That in turn, he argued, lies behind most forms of obsessive compulsion. He wrote, 'It is in the obsessional neuroses that the survival of the omnipotence of thoughts is most clearly visible and that the consequences of this primitive mode of thinking come closest to consciousness'.[13]

The main psychological point here is that most religious, as well as magical (esoteric) disciplines are based on the need to defend *against* something. That something is, at root, anxiety, the fear of death (and, by extension, of life). An effective way to defend against deep anxiety or mistrust in life is to inflate oneself, to imagine that one can 'magically' alter one's reality, even if only via hinting to others that one can do so. It is the element of grandiosity that has to be watched else it creep in and distort one's inner practice. Simon Magus, mentioned above, was perhaps the quintessential figure representing this, as he was portrayed as not just a sorcerer, but a boasting sorcerer. (Simon Magus was portrayed differently by different sources, most of whom were heresy-hunters, so his legend amounts largely to myth—but the idea of the 'boasting magician' is of import here, not the actual character of Simon Magus).

Antinomianism

In the context of the 'ego-traps' of the esoteric paths, it's useful here to understand a particular concept that—although rarely recognized as such—is often part of more radical, 'fringe', or so-called forbidden or secret teachings. In short, much that was considered part of the esoteric (or occult) paths in times past (and still to some measure), is best defined by the word 'antinomian'.

Antinomianism—loosely, 'freedom from moral law'—derives from the Greek words *anti* (against) and *nomos* (rule, or law). It was first used by Martin Luther, an interesting fact in itself as some esoteric currents in Europe (such as Rosicrucianism and related offshoots) were unquestionably influenced by Luther and the impact of the Protestant Reformation of the 16th century. This matter bears mentioning in order to address part of the psychological identity that often accompanies the desire to explore esoteric teachings. Luther's idea of antinomianism was that it was faith, or an inner connection with the divine, that trumps mere compliance with moral law. He viewed the Church as having become corrupt on many levels, and sought to re-establish the personal connection with God even if that meant only the Bible was to be used as one's moral compass and spiritual practice. Of course, the Protestant tradition soon become institutionalized and developed its own forms of decadence, but the original idea of rebellion against established religious 'law' is very closely related to the same current of rebelliousness found in many esoteric traditions.

There are two sides to personal rebelliousness. There is the legitimate attempt to discover one's innate individuality, perhaps best defined by Jung's notion of 'individuation'. But there is also the desire to act out hostilities toward authority in all its guises, be they moral, religious, political, parental, and so forth. Esoteric teachings can easily become a cloak that disguises this deeper psychological issue, or even a vehicle through which to express the unconscious desire to punish authority by either snubbing it or seeking to undermine it by participating in activities that seem counter to its so-called 'laws'.

These factors—grandiosity, the 'omnipotence of thoughts', and antinomianism—are best navigated, understood, and ultimately avoided via the all-important process of 'shadow-work' (see next chapter), alongside the cultivation of balance within one's personality.

A Note on the Implicit Assumptions and Standard Views of Western Psychology

Charles Tart, one of the late 20th century pioneers in the field of transpersonal psychology, once wrote: 'The thing that constantly amazes me…is that while psychologists are quite familiar with the innumerable pieces of evidence supporting [the] picture of human beings as constantly controlled by implicit assumptions, they practically never apply it to their personal lives or to their scientific work...'[14] Tart—a psychology professor as well as a student of Gurdjieff's work—had argued, back in 1975 during the early years of transpersonal psychology, that orthodox psychology suffered from a number of 'implicit assumptions' that in effect blocked most Western psychologists from being open to a transpersonal (or spiritual) perspective, and by extension, to the great wisdom traditions of esoteric paths.

Psychology, influenced as it was by Western science, posits certain assumptions about the universe that tend to reflect a materialist view, such that the universe is essentially lifeless and accidental (or without a primary cause that is intelligent), and that therefore human nature and behavior is rooted in material causes (i.e., brain chemistry). A key to this, rooted in Aristotle's division of subject-object (further clarified and deepened by Descartes), is that the physical universe can be comprehended without significant knowledge of self, and that we are nothing more than our physical body. Modern science derives from the commitment to understand material reality and this single-mindedness has produced the technical wonders we enjoy today, but the price has been something of a 'disconnect' from other modes of perception and experience.

Tart was not so naïve as to overlook the reality that spiritual psychology carries its own set of implicit assumptions as well (the universe is governed by a fundamental intelligence or consciousness, that a human is a 'spiritual being having a human experience', that 'accidents' are merely events that are misunderstood or misperceived, that humanity has a divine purpose in the universe, and so on). The point of inner work is to move beyond assumptions and various forms of 'confirmation bias', via direct observation of self. Spiritual assumptions are no better than those of orthodox psychology—both are assumptions. When we engage a process of self-observation and transformational practices, we are essentially experimenting and undertaking an adventure, the fruits of which will be clear (or not) in terms of clear insights and direct experience.

Chapter 10

Fundamentals of Spiritual Psychology (Part II)

Two Axioms

Two central axioms of spiritual psychology tend to be variations of the following:

1. **There is nothing outside of my mind.**
2. **There *is* something outside of my ego.**

These two axioms—expressed in greatly varying terms—generally lie at the heart of the great wisdom traditions. It is usually asserted, in one way or another, that when these two axioms are properly and deeply understood, they can be a guiding light that takes one to the highest spiritual realizations. That is because although seemingly paradoxical, they work in tandem to reveal the nature of both the ego and the true Self. However, the two points require considerable study and understanding else they can be easily corrupted and misused. This understanding is essential in order to avoid simply following assertions blindly. The esoteric path is, first and foremost, based on the importance of independent self-verification, and as such requires a willingness to 'experiment', as it were, upon oneself.

1. There is nothing outside of my mind.

The first axiom is basic to the philosophical school known broadly as Idealism, with its roots in some of the great wisdom traditions of India and ancient Greece. Idealism asserts that mind or consciousness is primordial, pervasive, and is the foundation from which all derives. From the Idealist perspective the statement 'there is nothing outside of my mind' is straightforward and consistent with the Idealist viewpoint. If mind is primordial, how can anything truly exist outside of it?

In short, what this means is that the reality that we experience at any given moment is known only via the filter of our consciousness. We have only our personal experience of things to go on. We cannot truly prove the existence of anything 'out there'. The world we assume we know could be a figment of our imagination. Perhaps we are living in an elaborate dream world, and so forth. There is no way to be fully certain of the nature of things that appear to be 'outside' of us. The external universe is knowable as an appearance—via our senses and ideas—but in a very real sense, is profoundly unknowable at the ultimate level.

As a simple example, we humans have specific senses connected to our bodies that enable us to experience the universe. But other organisms, like animals, have differently structured senses and thus experience the same objects that we do in a very different way. If a human, a horse, and a bumblebee are all observing a flower, each experiences something totally different, based on their sensory input. Which flower is the real one? The flower perceived by us, by the horse, or the bumblebee? There is no way to be certain. Our bodies are constantly receiving data and interpreting it in such a fashion that enables us to form a constructed model of reality. But it is just that, *constructed*.

We can, however, be certain about some subjective realities. We can conceptualize that 1+1=2, and be certain about the logic underpinning that. We can be certain that we are having a specific thought, feeling, sensation. We may not be sure about the *truthfulness* of the thought, or feeling, or sensation as they apply to some external event (we may be hallucinating, misperceiving, etc.), but we *can* be certain that we are experiencing that thought, feeling, or sensation. Looked at closely enough, it soon becomes clear that the only thing we can truly be certain about is our direct experience, via consciousness itself.

In this connection it is important to understand the idea of 'solipsism'. The word derives from the Latin terms *solus* ('alone') and *ipse* ('self'). Solipsism essentially means 'I alone exist—anything that seems to be outside of my mind cannot be proved to exist, and is ultimately of uncertain reality'. It is the working model of reality that best defines the most primitive level of the ego's view. Logically, this view cannot be disproved (since after all, even if you slap me hard in the face to prove that you exist, I may just be dreaming that you did that). Equally so, it is also a position that cannot be proved (you can reason or shout all you want to tell me that only *you* exist, and that I may be a figment of your imagination, but that proves nothing). Solipsism carried to its extreme is the psychological foundation of many mental illnesses, wherein a person begins to inhabit their own world, complete with its own laws, often impenetrable to others—i.e., they are unable to truly grant the existence of the 'other'. The 'reality-principle' of the ego is weakened or overridden altogether, resulting in a failure to function in the world. This is an example of premature (or faulty) relinquishment of ego.[1]

The first axiom, 'there is nothing outside of my mind', would be purely and simply a solipsist position without the second axiom, 'there *is* something outside of my ego'. The second axiom not only rescues the first from retreating into a lost world of narcissistic self-absorption, it also provides the context and means by which the first axiom becomes transcendent rather than merely disconnected and isolated. And the key term here is the word 'ego'. As mentioned earlier, 'ego' is generally interpreted differently in Eastern wisdom traditions in contrast to Western psychology. The East typically sees the ego as a simple impediment to spiritual awakening—the 'slayer of truth' which in turn must be 'slain'. The West views ego more as a mechanism that must be properly developed prior to being transcended. But in either view the idea that 'there is something outside of ego' remains the basis of higher development. It makes no difference whether we see 'ego' as a primitive sense of individuality and disconnectedness from the universe, or if we see it as a necessary phase in individual development beyond the dimmer consciousness of most animals (where ego appears to be mostly absent). In either case, inner work begins with the recognition that our ego does not define the limits of reality. True 'initiation' may be said to begin the moment we fully recognize our personal ignorance of reality in its greater sense—and signal our willingness to both acknowledge our limitations, and begin to work with them.

2. There is something outside of my ego.

Implicit in this axiom is the understanding that the ego and the mind are *two different categories*. More precisely, the ego—the personal sense of 'me'—is a construct, a process *within* the domain of the mind. As discussed above, the ego defines our sense of personal identity and is largely concerned with establishing and maintaining that identity, along with physical survival, boundaries, self-preservation in all its aspects, and distinction from others and the universe at large.

In terms of survival the ego is obviously important—even highly useful from the point of view of an evolutionary process—and is fundamental to normal human existence. In terms of realizing our optimum potential, however, the ego is problematic because its entire reason for being runs counter to the spiritual impulse, which is to join with a higher ideal that is based on ending disconnection between ourselves and reality. In most people the ego is instinctively wary about any opening to a 'greater reality', telling us that we have bigger fish to fry, namely, all the matters of our survival, status, and positioning in the world. Because of this it becomes tempting to believe that there is truly nothing outside of our own egos—nothing of any real worth, that is.

This is, of course, not the same thing as the idea that there is nothing outside of our *mind*. For the ego delights in informing us that there are *indeed* things outside of our own mind—and we are most definitely separate from them! Therefore the ego, the personal self, in its overriding concern with survival and security puts forth an upside down view: *there are things outside of my own mind, but there is nothing outside of my ego.*

Reduced further, the ruling doctrine of the most primitive face of the ego can be said to be: **I am the only person in the universe**. The enlightened, non-dual, or most spiritually mature perspective is essentially the polar opposite: **There is only One Person in the universe, and we are all an aspect or extension of that One**.

As mentioned above, the ego's view, taken to its extreme, becomes the source of most forms of mental illness, all ultimately based on the narcissistic self-absorption wherein the self creates its own private universe complete with its own laws. Because this private universe is so self-contained it is very difficult for anyone else to enter it, much less conform to it, thereby enhancing the isolation of the disturbed person and leading to all sorts of psychopathologies. These are the more extreme faces of the ego. Most people, though remaining socially functional, suffer from a spiritual sickness that is less detectable, but that shows via living a life that amounts to vastly less than what it could be.

The ego's self-absorbed view is counteracted by repeatedly contemplating the opposite: there *is* something outside of my ego. By its very nature that 'something' is infinitely bigger than my personal self, because it is the totality of all that is possible. In the matter of inner work, this understanding becomes crucial because in it lays the potential for profound realization. When we understand that our destiny begins and ends with our own mind, then we can also take specific steps toward understanding our mind, and even altering how it works, so that we can achieve certain desired results. These 'results' are ultimately related to the re-shaping of our views and the deconstructing of illusions, prime of which is that 'I am alone in the universe with no means of bridging the gulf between me and reality'.

The prime mechanism that the ego uses to create and sustain the experience of separation, disconnection, and isolation, is projection.

The Mechanics of Separation: Projection

Only in recent times, since the late 19th century, has there been a concise grasp of one of the most important psychological functions, that of projection. Psychologically speaking, to *project* is to see something that we assume is outside of us, but that is really inside of us. A good analogy for this is a standard film projector. When we project a thought we perceive it in the world as a quality that seems to be 'out there'—much as an image from a projector appears on a blank screen in front of us, as a 'movie'—but that in reality is originating in our own mind. The main reason we project onto the world, or another person, is so that we can lower our anxiety levels, discharging uncomfortable thoughts and feelings without having to consciously recognize and assume responsibility for them.

The great contribution of modern psychoanalysis, beginning with Freud, has been to clearly spell out the ways in which the self has the ability to disconnect *within* and to lose touch with aspects of itself, due to denial and repression. That is, if we are not comfortable with some part of ourselves we have the ability to deny and repress—to 'disown'—that part and to experience it *as only appearing in the world around us*, and especially in the people we interact with. Put another way, qualities of the 'I' (subject) can appear to become an 'it' (object). When this happens we have effectively repressed and projected a thought or feeling. For example, we experience a certain level of control within us, but we are not ready to see the truth about our own nature, i.e., that *we* are controlling. And so we disconnect from the awareness of our own controlling nature, and instead turn this controlling quality into an 'it' that is then perceived in others. *They* are controlling, not me. *You* are controlling, not me.

We may similarly do this with other qualities, such as greed, anger, jealousy, desire for power, weakness, fear, over-sensitivity, and so forth. In each case, the projected quality shows up in the world around us, in the form of what appears to be *coming at us* from others. The crucial tell-tale sign that indicates to us the degree of the projection is our gut-level *reaction* to it. The more strongly we react to these negative qualities that appear to be around us, or coming at us, then the more likely we are projecting, and the more likely *we* possess the very qualities and traits that we are reacting so negatively toward. To reclaim or take back a projection is to 're-own' the qualities we see in others that are triggering a reaction in us, by honestly seeing to what extent we too possess that quality, or at the least, the potential to be that way (or even worse!).

The mind is essentially an organized (so to speak) collection of thoughts. As we learn concepts and language at an early age, we slowly begin to perceive reality in terms of these concepts. Eventually, the world is largely viewed through the filter of concepts, memories, and imagination. The groupings of particular thought-complexes in the mind can be called *patterns*. In this context, a belief-system such as 'I am inadequate' is a pattern. In order not to feel the uncomfortable feelings connected to many such patterns, the mind learns to project the pattern outwardly. It does this in the form of 'what I see in you that I don't like about myself, but am not ready to see in myself'. The projections that are most problematic are the ones accompanied by a strong charge of negative emotion. In these cases what is being projected is almost always something that the mind does not want to fully see or 'own' within itself. The easiest way to determine the strength of a projection is by noting the degree of emotional charge the projection carries. As a general rule of thumb, the stronger the feeling is, the greater the projection.

For example, someone you know gets very angry. As they display their anger you find yourself feeling very uncomfortable. Suddenly you are aware that you are judging them and that you dislike them. The stronger your dislike for them, and the stronger the emotional charge accompanying that dislike, than the more you are projecting onto them. What you are projecting onto them is your own capacity for anger. Their anger reminds you of your own. But rather than feel your anger, or recognize your capacity for anger being mirrored in them, you simply assign fault to them.

Projection works in both positive and negative ways, meaning, what we greatly admire and love about others are always qualities of our highest potential that we have simply not fully recognized. The other person then reminds us of what we intuitively know *we* are or can be, and we then decide that we like or admire this person. This recognition is often not consciously realized, that is, we may be convinced that we do not have the quality that we so admire in the other—'I could never be like him or her'.

A further remark should be made here concerning the relation of projection and judgment. An erroneous view arises from time to time in certain New Thought or New Age schools of simplified spiritualized psychology that *judgment* in general is nothing but a form of projection, and is therefore not good and to be avoided if possible. This is not accurate. Judgment has its place in the scheme of things, and is often vitally important as a focused form of discernment. While judgment clearly is often used (and grossly abused) as a defense or offense mechanism, it also has its role in the service of truth. For example, if someone is behaving poorly in an obvious fashion, and we proactively point this out to them, we are clearly making a judgment, one that may be both true and possibly crucially necessary to express in that moment. A term first coined by the Tibetan master Chogyam Trungpa (and elaborated on by Ken Wilber) to describe New Age approaches to the issue of judgment has been 'idiot compassion' (or 'grandmother Zen'), in which the attitude of unconditional acceptance is taken to such an extreme that the ego is merely 'massaged', consoled, or indulged. In such an approach, free of the slightest trace of 'tough love', little growth is possible.

The Persona and the Shadow

Persona is the Greek word for 'mask'. That it is also the root of the English word 'personality' should give some hint at what lies at the basis of the personality, and for what we typically understand that word to mean. The 'Shadow' is a term that was coined by the Swiss psychotherapist C.G. Jung to describe that part of our nature that is hidden, repressed, and usually unconscious. It is sometimes referred to as our 'dark side'. He variously referred to it as the 'entire unconscious' of a person or as a given denied aspect of the personality that we fail to recognize consciously. The Shadow is comprised largely of elements of our nature—our repressed sexuality, fears, frailties, secret desires, and so on—that we have rejected for various reasons, and as such have been effectively split off, forming a type of secondary personality that emerges under certain conditions, like stress, anxiety, strong emotions, and anything involving sudden changes. Intoxicants like drugs and alcohol can also bring about the sudden emergence of the Shadow.

However it develops, the outstanding feature of the Shadow is that is comprises the basis of what is best called the 'disowned self'.[2] The disowned qualities of the self are attributes that are in us, either actually or as potential, yet we split them off and perceive them as qualities outside of our sense of 'me'. For example, if we are uncomfortable with our capacity for being manipulative (because it does not jive with our idealistic view of ourselves) we will tend to be sensitive to manipulative tendencies in others. All this becomes very important to see and understand, because it especially applies to our relationships with family members or intimate partners. The most commonly 'unhealed' relationships are those between parents and offspring, or between siblings, or between ex-partners. The great challenge in applied Shadow work is to recognize the ways in which we are not much different from those we have been closest to (once all particular life-circumstances and superficial differences are stripped away). This can be very challenging to the part of the ego that is holding on to positions, most difficult of which is the 'victim-position' (this terrible thing was done to me, and that is all there is to it, and I will forever hold responsible this person for my sufferings, failures, and limitations in life). To begin to see the ways in which we are similar to our parents, siblings, and intimate partners, and moreover to see our capacity for being very much like them in disposition and behavior, given the 'right' circumstances, is a major step forward in maturation and releasing the past.

Radical Acceptance, the 'Two Lies', and the Core Wound

The issues just mentioned are very subtle, because in point of fact the average person does suffer from a faulty self-image, and this fault can only be corrected by a form of what can be called *radical acceptance*. The key point that distinguishes this from a facile or superficial self-acceptance is that 'radical' acceptance involves deep inner work. This is because it is not *others* whom we require to be accepted by, it is ourselves. In short, we need to transform the self-image, prior to being able to transcend it.

There may be said to be two fundamental lies that form the basis of the personal self and its faulty self-image (which creates our overall sense of personal limitation). These are 1. 'I am a flawed, bad person' and 2. 'I must change or fix myself to correct this problem'. The two premises form the basis of the 'core wound'. The good news is that this core wound is ultimately based on profound misunderstandings and illusions. The bad news is that these 'misunderstandings and illusions', if not recognized for what they are, have enormous capacity to generate almost endless suffering.

The antidotes to these two fundamental delusions are a combination of insight and deep self-acceptance. By 'insight' is meant here a willingness to see and confront elements of our nature, and in particular, of our self-image—how we have come to see ourselves, who we believe ourselves to be. (And we speak here not of superficial views and ideals, but rather of the deeper truths that are tied up in our self-doubt, lack of confidence, and core-level fears). Radical self-acceptance is a key to the awakening process. We are not to shun, deny, or condemn elements of our nature, but rather to assume ownership of them and embrace their energies. (This is the ultimate meaning behind the old idea, found in shamanism and ceremonial magic, of the shaman or magician encountering and 'taming' different orders of spirits—the spirits correspond to the shaman/magician's disowned nature, which when re-connected with, re-owned, and on occasion pro-actively disciplined, frees up tremendous energy that can then be used in the service of creativity and manifestation work).

There was a period in early life during which we first began experiencing constraint and invalidation from our elders. This occurred for us when total freedom of expression was curtailed in some way. Prior to that we had basically been living in a kind of Garden of Eden where full allowance of expression and our command of the attention of our elders was mostly the case. We lived as miniature gods, our parents fascinated with us and loving, curious and attentive to our every need. (Obviously, this is not always the case, and in many more painful cases, abandonment, rejection, or abuse is experienced almost from the beginning).

As a child we came to realize, by virtue of repeated experiences, that we were capable of incurring disapproval, that limitations on expression were being imposed on us, and more troublesome, that an awareness of our lack of power was growing. The intense frustration of the powerlessness, combined with the repeated invalidations from our elders, gives rise to the awareness of emotional, or inner, pain. In Eden there may have been physical pain on occasion, but unbroken awareness of being unconditionally accepted was present. We could pretty much 'get away with' anything. With invalidation and inner pain a new element has entered. As the pain is felt more acutely each time (often accompanied by temper tantrums or crying outbursts, which are attempts to discharge the pain), the awareness of the 'core wound' grows. This wound is, in fact, of an order far beyond what we are initially aware of, but the new experiences of rejection and invalidation (as opposed to unconditional, unlimited allowance), makes us more aware of it.

The 'core wound' is a term sometimes given to describe that tendency we have to believe ourselves unworthy at some deep, hard to define level. Christian teaching makes valid reference to this in its 'original sin' doctrine, putting forth the idea that all humans are born flawed. Although it is often dismissed by non-Christians, the concept of original sin is actually a deep insight, touching on the whole issue of generational guilt, and how self-rejection, diminished self-esteem, and self-loathing are effectively passed on from generation to generation. Where Christian doctrine became degraded in this respect was in its appropriation of the original sin concept as a tool to coerce people into the Christian faith; that is, a valid psycho-spiritual idea became a political device and was thereby compromised. Shorn of its religious baggage, however, the notion of 'original sin' is a potent psycho-spiritual idea because it hits strongly on the idea that ego is a self-referencing phenomenon that always ultimately resorts to trying to lift itself by its own bootstraps—a project that must indeed always fail.

Everyone experiences the 'core wound' differently. There is a broad range of possibilities in the degree of invalidation and rejection faced by a child growing up. These can range from the entirely appropriate (being told 'no!' when this was what we indeed needed to hear), to levels of abuse, depending on a number of factors, not least of which is the overall maturity of the parents or caretakers. But be that as it may, pain, by its very nature, is *painful.* As we grow up and mature we may learn that to fight against emotional pain (to deny or repress it) solves nothing and in fact ultimately worsens it, but as children our main concern was how *not* to feel this pain. Thus, we began to look for ways out, for tricks and devices to escape what we were feeling.

Coping With Emotional Pain

It has often been said that the most unpleasant feeling of all is fear, and specifically, anxiety. The anticipation of emotional pain gives rise to anxiety, and the beginning of lifelong issues connected to fear in general. Fear exists only as a projected thought into the future. When we are in fear, our fear is always about *what is to come next*. As such, we develop skills to cope with fear and the future. The anxiety, pain, and awareness of the core wound—our core sense of personal unworthiness deriving from repeated invalidations—propel us into a course of action that is largely unavoidable. Fearful of the power of the elders that surround us (parents, older siblings, or other caretakers), and increasingly aware of our own limitations, we slowly begin to develop the tendency to be *inauthentic*. That is, our outer personality, our *persona* (mask), begins to develop. This process usually begins between the ages of two and five, roughly paralleling the development of language skill (though the seeds of it are likely planted earlier, and in some cases possibly from birth, if the birth was especially difficult or traumatic).

Parts of the surface personality are originally based on a reaction to pain, and an attempt at disguising, managing, and repressing the anxiety that goes with it. This becomes the habitual face that we show the world. It continues to grow and strengthen through childhood and adolescence, becoming solidified by young adulthood. At that point full identification with it has more or less occurred, with all the associated limitations of that (reactivity, insecurity, fear, etc.). In other words, we have come to believe that we *are* our personality and nothing much more (regardless if this personality is positively oriented or negatively oriented).

As the mask is born, so also is birthed its opposite—the Shadow, or the *hidden* personality. The Shadow becomes a repository for those elements of our nature that are in direct opposition to the surface personality we are developing. The Shadow is the part of us that we have learned to reject, precisely because we fear that direct expression of its qualities will lead to rejection and pain. Thus, to a large, extent the Shadow becomes the polar opposite of our surface personality. For example, if a person is exaggeratedly kind and passive in the personality they present to the world, they are often concealing a more hostile, aggressive inner nature. Or, conversely, if a person is outwardly rough and hostile in an obvious way, they are often concealing a nature that is timid, sensitive, and sees itself as vulnerable. (These understandings do not, of course, always apply; occasionally an outwardly 'warm' person is also 'inwardly warm'.

But these seem to be the exceptions. Far more commonly people are capable of polar opposite-type behavior, especially when confronted or pushed to the wall in some fashion).

A way of imagining this is as the surface personality being just like a mask on our face—with the Shadow or hidden personality being a face on the back of our head, the side of ourselves that others can see or at least sense, but that we are usually blind to, something like the dual mask worn by the ancient Roman god named Janus.

Shadow Work

> *Everyone carries a shadow, and the less it is embodied in the individual's conscious life, the blacker and denser it is.* (C.G. Jung).

A good model for doing Shadow work is what Ken Wilber has usefully simplified as the '3-2-1' process. It is based on the idea that our Shadow elements typically arise in the following 'splitting off' fashion[3]:

1. A painful situation arises in which we cannot cope with our true feelings. An example is a child who is angry at their mother or father. The child soon realizes that to harbor such feelings is too risky because it means that they might lose the love, approval, and protection of that parent. So they gradually disconnect from their true feeling (in this case, anger).

2. Because it is too threatening to feel my anger (because I might lose the love/approval/protection of Mommy or Daddy), I project my anger outwardly. I begin to 'see' angry people around me. It is not possible that this anger is mine, so it must be these other people who are angry. (A person will commonly project these onto 'monsters' or other scary images, which is one reason why movies with dramatic villains are culturally popular, providing as they do a screen on which to project Shadow-feelings).

3. Carried on long enough, the original feeling (I'm angry at Mom or Dad) becomes completely dissociated. It is only experienced via outer events. This results in a 'secondary' emotion arising, as a kind of decoy to keep us from facing the primary emotion. For example, a common secondary emotion that arises from the primary emotion of anger is fear, or sadness. A prolonged fear/sadness that is in fact covering up anger can slide into depression.

The process just outlined is a simple 1-2-3 matter—from a personal feeling (anger), to an interpersonal situation ('you are angry, not me', or 'that person in my life is mean and nasty, and I have nothing to do with it'), to a split-off, disconnected state in which a secondary emotion arises (sadness, fear, depression) to cover up the primary, original emotion (anger). In this third stage, we have completely rejected the original emotion (anger) and truly believe it has nothing to do with us. Shadow-work in this case consists of reversing the above process, so that it becomes 3-2-1. This is, in essence, going from 'it', to 'you', to 'I', as follows:

1. **Face the issue**. (This can be done via writing or talking to an empty chair, imagining that it is occupied by someone we have unresolved issues with). Recognize exactly what it is that is bothering you, and be fully honest about it. At this stage don't worry about taking responsibility for your core feelings—just acknowledge them. Talk or write freely about what is disturbing you.

2. **Relate to the issue**. Get into dialogue with it. Make the issue personal, and speak (to an empty chair, or a person who is supporting you, or via writing) by asking it specific questions—'what do you want from me? What are you trying to tell me?'

3. **Ownership—*become* it**. If that which is concerning you is a scary monster (in whatever shape—either a person who you believe has wronged you, or someone gratuitously nasty, or ignoring you, and so

on), become that monster yourself (without acting it out on others, of course). Allow yourself to experience directly the angry, nasty, dismissive, cold, manipulative, etc., thoughts and feelings within yourself—a type of therapeutic role-playing.

The idea of doing this work is to free up energy that is being drained by constantly repressing elements of our Shadow self. In freeing up energy we also allow for the possibility of expanding our horizons, both internally (experiencing more authentic compassion for others) and externally (more creative output in our life, because more energy has been freed up). This type of therapeutic work (or related kinds of Shadow-work) is almost always helpful for most modern seekers.

Aliveness

The ideas of 'aliveness' (and playfulness) are actually important to consider for one following an esoteric path, because it is necessary to guard against excessive seriousness and self-absorption. Our natural state is inherently alive, even if such 'aliveness' expresses uniquely with each individual. The quality of aliveness is central to the experience of fulfillment, in part because it is the antidote to the burden of self-rejection; not the guilt of having 'done something wrong' (which is *shame*), but rather the deeper self-rejection that tells us that *we* are wrong, just for being who we are.

To return to our inner core of natural innocence (self-acceptance) usually requires some work, however, and this work lies especially in the area of 'emotional body purification'. Owing to the nature of modern societies there is much distraction (mostly related to technology) and repression of thoughts, feelings, emotions, and sensations going on all the time. 'Emotional release' therapies can be highly effective for helping to get the 'river' of energy flowing again. There are useful methods for stimulating the flow of personal energy as well as the release of with-held negative thoughts and feelings. Here are some.

Anger Work: In times past, the idea of 'anger work' would not have made much sense—in some cases because people were so controlled and repressed that it would have seemed too radical, or because people were more natural and there was simply no need for it. But we live in a very unique and complex time. Most people living in the post-modern Western world are stressed and exposed to a great deal of sensory and information input. Accordingly there can be a tendency to be less skilful when dealing with feelings and emotions and in particular with anger.

Anger work is generally one of the more challenging methods to undertake, although in principle it is both simple and usually effective. Many people grow up with rigid social and behavioral protocols, and even when that is not the case, anger is usually the most difficult of emotions to embrace and consciously and responsibly express. There are of course many reasons for that, but as a rule of thumb, the greater the fear of facing consequences for expressing one's anger, the greater the life-long tendency will be to repress it. When anger is repressed, it tends to seek outlets via other channels, which leads to such things as passive aggression, indirect hostility, and possibly various psychosomatic physical ailments. These manifestations of behavior (or health issues) are antithetical to living a conscious and healthy life. Open expression of anger is not usually the solution either. Accordingly, there is often a need to do some sort of inner work in order to address one's anger and prevent it from 'backing up' and festering into resentment. The following is a simple release method that if done semi-regularly, or as the need arises, helps to reduce the inner pressure and prevent it from building to the point that it begins to actively interfere with the matters of one's daily life.

Make sure you have at least fifteen minutes in which you will not be disturbed. (More time is better, but in the beginning, fifteen minutes is good. With some practice, you can do this technique in five minutes). Find something that you can strike without damaging anything—this could be your bed, or a couch, mattress, punching bag, etc. Then, using your fists, give yourself permission to pound this object for at least ten minutes. If you can, try yelling into a pillow for a minute or so (making sure to muffle your sounds if in earshot to anyone else). Also very good is lying on your back on a mattress and kicking your legs scissors style, while pounding your fists at the same time. Using a stick or tennis racket, etc., is also effective, but again, be cautious not to damage anything or hurt yourself.

An alternate form of this, for those lacking privacy, is to shout in your car with the windows rolled up (cars are usually good sound insulators. However, make sure the car is stationary and you are not engaged in driving). At first, it is common to feel silly or uncomfortable doing this, but that is only related to old conditioning around feeling shameful for expressing our more passionate energies, which certainly include anger. After a few times you will feel more at ease doing it. (Note: in particular it is not good for young children or pets to hear you doing anger work, as they will assume you are distressed and it will frighten them).

At first try anger release for at least five minutes. Then lie down and rest quietly and gently for another five minutes. The release of anger can precipitate tender, vulnerable feelings, and often a sense of peace. The rest phase is not just for resting, however, it is for gaining insight into the causes of your anger.

The old truism is 'You are never upset for the reason you think'. Anger is almost always a smokescreen or a defense for more vulnerable feelings such as hurt and especially fear. But the insight to look into the causes of the vulnerable feelings, to be mindful of them and above all to take responsibility for them, is difficult to come by if we are carrying too much anger, which is why we do the release work. However it should be stressed that while release work is usually beneficial, in and of itself it is not enough to correct the belief-systems inside that are contributing to the unhappy situation. That is finally accomplished by insight, understanding, releasing attachment to the need to be right about things, and altering certain behavior habits. The release work aids in lowering the 'voltage' locked into our body-mind, so that we can begin to see the patterns causing the problems more clearly. Initially, it is recommended to try this method for a week straight at least. Use anger work if you find yourself feeling especially stressed out, frustrated, disappointed, depressed, misunderstood, etc. In time, this practice can help you feel lighter, more authentic, more empowered, and less reactive to other people. Just remember that anger work is no magic pill. It is a temporary aid to enable us to see more clearly and correct the deeper dysfunctional patterns in our life.

You can also do the method with another person—both of you shouting into a pillow while retaining eye contact. This usually ends in laughter, which is a good sign that the feelings are being successfully integrated. To integrate a mental state is to successfully 'absorb' it, meaning, you can now move on to other matters without suffering the energy drain that comes from 'unfinished business'.

Mirror Work and the Principle of Reflection

'Mirror work', in the context of which it is treated here, does not refer to gazing into an opaque surface. It refers rather to the 'principle of reflection'—the idea, echoed in all wisdom traditions, that the universe is interconnected and, in a sense, operates much like a mirror, reflecting back to us the totality of who we are. *How* we perceive what is reflected back to us depends on our state of consciousness. If we are confused, full of unresolved issues, bearing regrets, grudges, anger, or even malice, then chances are good that we will perceive reality as fundamentally similar—a confusing, difficult, harsh and disturbing world that often seems to ill-treat us (and thus, disturbingly, seems to reinforce our bitterness in a nasty self-perpetuating cycle). Similarly, if we are reasonably clear, at peace, accountable in the details of our life, and essentially bearing good will, we tend to perceive an underlying sanity, meaningfulness, and even higher purpose in the cosmos; or at the very least, a kind of seamlessness to it. (Of course, that does not mean that inner peace automatically means outer harmony—a wise sage may find themselves in an earthquake or a Nazi concentration camp—but even there, having our inner house in order increases the chance that we handle any possible hell around us in a much better way). In general, what we transmit is what we get back. This principle is the source of Christ's utterance in Matthew 13:12:

> For whosoever hath, to him shall be given, and he shall have more abundance: but whosoever hath not, from him shall be taken away even that he hath. (KJV)

There is a further, rather more subtle point to the idea of the principle of reflection, and it has to do with the effect of attention when it is trained outwardly. The best analogy here to illustrate the point is to consider the effect a ray of light has when it is shone upon an object. One reason we see the object is because photons strike the retina of our eyes, which causes molecular excitation leading to electrochemical reactions that activate neural impulses. The brain then interprets these signals, and we 'see'. However, that is not all that is going on. In addition, light shone upon an object affects the object as well, in what fashion depending on whether the light is reflected, absorbed, transmitted, refracted, and so forth. Light behaves in part as an electromagnetic wave that affects individual atoms, which in turn causes them to behave in different ways—usually involving some sort of emission of energy leading to the object becoming visible.

The closest physical analogue for attention (or consciousness) is light. The fact that we have the ability to affect others via the ways in which we give our attention to them is no great secret—much as it is no secret that shining a light on something affects it in some fashion. As mentioned in Chapter 2, alchemy describes a process called 'calcination', a description for certain changes brought about in an object when it is heated. The effect that fire has upon objects is usually obvious. Similarly, the effect that we can have upon others when we express ourselves to them in a 'heated' fashion (an apt metaphor for anger or passion) is no mystery. Less obvious, however, is the effect the quality our attention has on those we train it on.

In essence, reality can be divided into two parts: that which perceives (or that which is conscious), and that which is perceived (or that which we become conscious of). Subject and object. However if we look closer into the matter, we see that it is not so straightforward. There is, as thinkers such as Immanuel Kant pointed out, a third element, that of the mode of our perception or consciousness.[4] This is entirely relevant because depending on this mode, our experience of the object will occur. (For example, Kant maintained that it is only our inherent capacity to understand space that allows for us to make sense of spatial dimensions in our world; and of time in order for us to make sense of temporality). Put simply, we see not what is 'there'; we rather see what we *are*.

Relationships in general involve direct lessons in the principle of reflection, which schools us in the mirror-like nature of the universe. Relationships are showing us, all the time, who we are, and the quality of what we are extending and giving to the world. As such they can be blissful experiences of confirming or celebrating our best self and what we are 'doing right', or painful and devastating encounters with the areas in which we are not yet awake to all of the manifestations of our personality. However, the vast majority of relationships—from the casual and professional, to family, romantic, and spousal—are not used as learning vehicles, and rarely recognized as 'mirrors' reflecting back the qualities within us that we may not want, or be ready, to see. There is a simple reason for this failure to utilize relationships consciously as learning vehicles. It is due to the fact that almost none of us believe—at the all-important unconscious level—that the source of our truth and well-being is 'within'. This includes those on some sort of self-discovery or spiritual path. No matter how much we may read, study, and listen to the words of those who pass along the idea that the 'source of well-being is within'—and that includes listening to those few teachers who have actualized this idea in their own lives—we still tend to find ourselves seeking, looking, and longing for finding, or sustaining, a relationship which seems to provide us with well-being.

There is great discomfort in excessive isolation, because it reminds us of our actual *apparent* condition, which is that we have the experience of being a separate consciousness. However it is in separation that we locate and identify ourselves, and it is in separation that we experience the universe of space and time, and all the lessons that accompany it. (For example, in order to initially experience love as an extension or action, rather than only a state of being, it is necessary to have the experience of the other as separate from us, otherwise there would be nothing to love). Thus, the experience of separation seems overpoweringly real—all reinforced by the information our physical sense organs are constantly sending us, affirming the reality that we are indeed distinct from everything else, encased in these bodies, for good or bad.

This deep identification with the conditions of our body, and its sensory information and instinctive needs, ultimately becomes the basis of the fear of death. Because we have become conditioned to believing that our existence depends on these bodies, it therefore follows that physical death will then take on a dreaded and powerful reality in our minds, all magnified by the fact that (generally speaking) we carry no truly verifiable memories of any pre-life existence (beyond subjectivity), and lack *absolute* proof of the existence of other worlds, life after death, inner dimensions, or other levels of reality. As belief systems they are, for the vast majority of people, no match for the immediate sensory reality of the physical body and the environment that our bodies inhabit. Conviction in the belief in 'spiritual realities' will, generally speaking, initially pale in the face of a loaded gun, a life-threatening illness, or the loss of an important relationship.

Owing to the power of the ego as experienced through the domain of the body to convince us of our separate condition, it quickly follows that this same conditioning will convince us of our basic dependency. For if we are indeed separate, and indeed encased in very mortal bodies, then it follows that *we* are also very mortal and, by extension, dependent. The physical body is, essentially, completely dependent. It can no more go any significant length of time without food, water, and certainly oxygen, than it can fly in the air unaided. We assume all the conditions of dependency that govern our physical forms. And, so close is our identification with this physical dependency, that we are also capable of experiencing horrific fears (and in extreme cases, even phobias) connected with the deprivation of our physical needs. All of this is a way of saying that as conscious beings dwelling in a physical body, we take on the reality of the body, part and parcel of which is becoming dependent.

Gurdjieff pointed out that we receive energy mainly through three avenues: breathing, food, and emotional impressions. This third category, emotional impressions, includes what we commonly refer to as love. Most so-called love is really a form of attachment, sentimentality based on feelings of need, obligation or guilt, or biochemical responses that generate physical sensations that we interpret as love. From the point of view of our separate ego-consciousness that is encased in the realm of the body's needs, it follows that we will always be looking and searching for some sort of external body from which to hopefully receive energy. This is the origin of co-dependency and relationship drama. While we are not here denying the obvious spiritual, creative, joyful elements of deep and profound intimate relating, it is the case in the vast majority of relationships that what is assumed to be a quest for happiness, completion, and fulfillment through relationship, is most commonly a desire to cover up, avoid, and deny the fear and vulnerability connected with our existence as apparently separate beings. In other words, most relationships are based on the urge to cover up the fear of our very basic human condition. We do this by, in a sense, 'using' the other person: trying to get them to make us oblivious to our fundamental condition.

It is somewhat of an irony that the German philosopher Arthur Schopenhauer, notable for his general avoidance of intimate relationship, still managed to generate one of the more profound insights into the causes of the dysfunctions of intimate relationship. Schopenhauer had argued that our conscious intellect does not truly direct our lives, but rather busies itself providing elaborate rationalizations to satisfy the true cause of our situations and conditions of life. The main idea is that most intimate relationship is a dance of mutual attractions and agendas based largely on unconscious motives and impulses. It is common to spend a great deal of time rationalizing one's attractions or repulsions, as if these are somehow being consciously chosen, when largely speaking, they are not. The people we are drawn to 'fit' into our pre-conceived unconscious agendas. When we also fit into theirs, we have the effect of two magnets drawn together. The conscious intellect then rationalizes the whole process and presumes that it has somehow 'chosen' what it has, when in fact it has not. Because of this, the whole area of 'Shadow-work' becomes very important for beginning to understand the totality of who we are, precisely because the people we attract into our lives, especially our special relationships, are mirroring back to us all our unconscious desires and fears.

A Spiritual Practice and Autonomous Fulfillment

Probably the most difficult of all forms of inner work is so-called relationship work, or 'interpersonal processing' (couples counseling, essentially, although often with added methods based on particular transformational principles).[5] This form of inner work has its roots in psychoanalysis and especially in the human potential movement of the 1960s, along with later New Thought and New Age movements (including simplified forms of Westernized Tantra). It is a difficult practice because the motive for engaging in it is often unconscious or unrecognized. Clarity of intent is always essential when engaging in inner work, and this is particularly so with relationship work. For example, it is common to engage in relationship processing with the intent of advancing one's self and one's relationship, when the deeper motive is to control one's anxiety levels by learning new ways of controlling one's partner. That is not to suggest that such work is useless, but what is best achieved is a level of tolerance and peace within one's relationship that allows for the accomplishment of what both would regard their 'best potential' in life.

After all the interpersonal processing is said and done, it is having a spiritual practice and autonomous fulfillment that is most important for true conscious relating. The whole function of relationship of any sort is to confront, slowly and steadily, our personal blocks to remembering, seeing, and realizing our higher nature and best possibilities. A difficulty arises in relationship because it is rarely used consciously for this reason, but rather more commonly becomes an arena for playing out endless levels of co-dependency and attachment, all originating in the deeply conditioned belief that we are flawed in our core and need another person to help distract us from the pain of truly facing this core wound once and for all. Spiritual deepening is possible when we have a spiritual practice and autonomous fulfillment within the relationship. By 'spiritual practice' is meant, in a nutshell, to have some sort of regular, or at least semi-regular, activity, practice, or discipline that involves our direct work on our deeper nature—and that most crucially, does not require the participation of our partner in order for us to do it.

By 'autonomous fulfillment' is meant here to be engaged in life in a way that brings passion and creativity to bear on what we do, reinforcing the truth that fulfillment is derived from living our 'true will' and the contribution we are making to life—not from what we are getting from our partner.

Clearing the Past, and the Importance of Forgiving

Many metaphysical/occult/esoteric groups have experienced difficulties in the past, mostly relating to interpersonal dynamics, and this has been due to several factors. A good case in point was the Hermetic Order of the Golden Dawn, a valid esoteric group that began in the late 1880s in England in a promising fashion, but that within barely over a decade had collapsed among itself due largely to infighting and what appears to have been immature interpersonal, communication skills.

When problems occur amongst esoteric groups they are invariably related to relationship-dysfunction, and in particular, problems dealing with control, authority, integrity in communication, and so on—all the challenges that plague any organization or community. Israel Regardie, the Golden Dawn adept who authored several classic books on Western esotericism, in his later years used to strongly advise anyone interested in following the Western esoteric path to undergo psychotherapy first or at least alongside it. While it is actually more common than not for spiritual seekers to feel somewhat out of step with human society in the greater and more mainstream sense, it still does not change the fact that psychological scars have the ability to totally interfere with one's spiritual aspirations. This is because our psychological and spiritual development proceeds along parallel paths. That is, it is common for someone to work hard spiritually and have numerous profound experiences, and yet be lacking in psychological development and adjustment to the world. The opposite is common as well: a person who is relatively well-rounded psychologically, but lacking in spiritual insight.

Accordingly, it is necessary to develop ourselves psychologically as well as spiritually. Specifically this means that we must work on psychological issues such as communication skills, understanding projection and repression, examining our relationships with our family of origin (especially the parents), cultivating a willingness to forgive, understanding co-dependency, and so on. All of this provides the foundation for a strong and healthy 'inner house', and one that can withstand the construction of higher levels (esoteric development). Without such a healthy foundation our house may well collapse (as the demise of many 'inner work' communities has born testament to).

The most direct and potent form of psychological healing is clearing the past. To clear the past means to a), examine our past and identify 'unhealed' relationships, that is, people we have not forgiven, for whatever reason; and b), to apply a particular method of 'releasing' them. To release them is helpful because the more we have not forgiven someone, the more we remain attached to them in a toxic fashion. The following is an example of a 'clearing the past' method:

1. Stretch, sit comfortably in a chair, take a few deep breaths, and try to relax as best you can. Then think of a person you have (or have harbored) resentment toward. Imagine them sitting in front of you. Allow yourself to feel fully all negative feelings you have toward them. Do not censor or suppress any thoughts or feelings. Identify your judgments about them, what exactly you do not like about them. Pay attention to your body. Feelings tend to register as sensations in the body. Note these.

2. Once you have allowed yourself to experience your thoughts and feelings honestly, then try to detect your projections onto that person—that is, notice what parts of them you dislike, that you in fact have inside yourself as well. To facilitate this, you can use the line 'What I see in you, that I see in myself, is_______'. Make sure to honestly identify the qualities that are particularly negative. For example, 'What I see in you that I see in myself is anger, weakness', etc.

3. Once you have felt your feelings and honestly identified what you project on to the person, then you can move on to the last stage, which is to demonstrate the willingness to see their deeper spiritual face. You can do this by mentally

> saying to the person, '________, I am willing to see the greater Self in you'. Repeat this line several times, speaking slowly and consciously, being fully mindful of each word as you say it. Stay with the process. The key thing here is to be willing. All you have to be is willing. The rest works naturally. If you truly do this process with sincerity you will often feel a sense of peace afterward, or even a sense of connection with all things. This is a natural result of releasing the past.

The key thing to grasp is that not forgiving someone is, in effect, remaining attached to them. To forgive them is to free yourself from them (and to free them at the same time from your attachment). This forgiveness is not, however, a simple granting of license to them to repeat whatever behaviors with you they have done in the past. In fact, the process has nothing to do with their past actions at all. It simply has to do with an altering of your perception of them by recognizing that the past is a block to a deeper and more fulfilling experience of the present and future. The important thing is the intention to let go of an element of the past that is not serving your forward movement in life.

Chapter 11

Meditation and Self-Realization

If we want to truly understand esotericism, the only approach is that of an 'insider'.
—William Quinn

The esoteric tradition is, of course, nothing without practice. By 'practice' is meant many things, but all forms of practice hold in common the essential basis of *participation*. To 'participate' here refers to an active engagement with the process of investigating one's mind, something that applies to even the most seemingly passive of contemplations.

All inner work can be reduced to three over-arching categories: self-acceptance, empowerment, and self-observation. Engaging the first is the basis of psychotherapy; engaging the second is the basis of all self-expressive forms of work (art, music, ritual/ceremony, and physical practices such as martial arts); engaging the third is the basis of meditation.

Meditation and study are essential aspects on the path of transformation. Excepting for rare cases where deep awakening may happen through a purely devotional, heart-centered spiritual practice, most everyone will have to go through some sort of meditation and discipline of learning in order to facilitate the development of *insight,* which is that crucially important ability to look within and understand the workings of the mind.

The essence of meditation is *awareness*. Not awareness *of* anything, but the simple resting in awareness itself. This is called 'consciousness without an object', or 'non-dual awareness'. For the Western mind, conditioned as it is with intellectual training and the scientific objectification of reality, the notion of 'resting in awareness' may at first seem difficult to grasp, as it may seem too simple and too unconcerned with bearing witness to, or perceiving, anything outside of ourselves. However if we are concerned with coming to an understanding of our *true* nature, that is, what we really are, then it is going to be vitally important that we develop the ability to see ourselves, and directly experience the ground of this true nature, which is consciousness.

Rene Descartes' famous line, *cogito ergo sum* ('I think therefore I am'), is perhaps the classic summation of the Western rationally oriented world-view that lies at the heart of the rapid advances in science and technology from the 17th century and beyond. It also clearly defines the quintessence of a civilization that schools its people in such a way that they become strongly identified with their thinking minds. In such a conditioning, it is only in thought that I can define my identity—I *think*, therefore I *am*. However, if we examine the nature of our thinking processes, we will soon find that when not engaged in a specific discipline that requires our focused attention our thoughts are generally lacking in any cohesive structure that would seem able to truly define our identity. In fact, a simple focusing of attention on our thought process will soon reveal that thought itself is incapable of *directly experiencing* anything, and is most certainly incapable of directly experiencing the nature of our identity (who 'I am'). At the most, thought can describe things, much like a menu can describe a meal or a map can describe an area. Because of this, it is necessary to train the mind to experience awareness of the movement of thought *within* consciousness, something like the movement of clouds through the sky. Doing so enables us to organize our thoughts more efficiently, to utilize their energy creatively, and to recognize the nature of our inner being as pure awareness that both transcends and includes thought.

Self Remembering

Self-remembering, in one form or another, lies at the heart of inner work. It has gone by various names over the centuries within the various spiritual traditions, but it always boils down to the practice of maintaining an elevated state of awareness throughout one's daily life activities. Self-remembering is based on the idea of *divided attention*. In typical semi-conscious living, our attention flows outwardly, toward the object we perceive. It is a one-way movement of attention, from us, to the object. The less alert, the less conscious we are at the time, the more we are aware of *only* the object, and nothing else. (This is, of course, the basis of being caught up in the external 'glitter' of reality, everything from the dazzle of a charismatic person, to the dazzle of a cause we identify with). A good example of this occurs in our dreams at night. Typically our dream state is governed by a lack of self-awareness during the dream. All that is 'real' are the objects (things, people, etc.) of our dream. This is why we do not know that we are dreaming at the time, because there is no substantial self-awareness. Thus, we wake up after and realize that it 'was only a dream'.

In divided-attention, what we are endeavoring to do is to 'split' our attention two ways, so to speak. We try to keep our attention on the object of our perception (say, a tree), and, at the same time, we remain aware of ourselves—'I am'. We attempt to remain aware simultaneously of both self and tree. Accomplishing this is an act of self-remembering. In the beginning the practice may seem just intellectual, a forced and artificial mental effort that probably will not be sustained for very long. With consistent practice it becomes easier and more natural and can be done for longer periods of time. Persisted with, we can reach a state where we are naturally remembering ourselves much of the time. As our ability with the method progresses, it becomes less and less a detached mental exercise, and more and more an alive, sensory experience of being *present* in our environment and experiencing the moment more vividly.

To self-remember is to be *present*. Lack of presence is akin to operating in a kind of auto-pilot state. The main purpose of self-remembering is to begin to learn to experience reality free of mental projections and of the cloud of 'daydreaming' that obscures our ability to truly be here. Self-remembering, persisted with, leads to a quieter mind, a mind that thinks more economically and efficiently and is able to let go and relax when appropriate.

It should be understood that with all meditation methods, including self-remembering, we are not trying to force the mind to be still. Trying to will the mind to be silent usually leads to just repression of thoughts and feelings. Self-remembering is not about repression. It is rather a practice that allows us to be more involved in our life in a real fashion, while being able to see things more clearly and truthfully as well. We can practice while driving, eating, going to the washroom, walking, etc. In the beginning it is good to try this method when not engaged in anything serious, but over time we can do it in increasingly complex situations.

Exercise 1 (Self-remembering): Attempt to remember yourself as the one who is having this thought, or the one who is having this feeling, body sensation, etc.—that is, hold the sense of 'I am' whenever possible throughout your daily activities. This does not mean that you can't engage in regular activities or thinking that requires your full attention. It simply means that you remember the sense of 'I am' when having such thoughts, feelings, and so on. In the beginning self-remembering can seem like a tedious mental exercise, in that you have to make a mental effort to remember, 'I am'. But over time this 'I am-ness' becomes less and less a disconnected thought, and more an overall sense of presence, and one that becomes easier to remember.

Exercise 2 (Recording Thoughts): Find a ten minute period of time during which you will be undisturbed. Sit at a table with a note pad, or several sheets of paper, and pen. For ten minutes straight, simply write down every thought that comes into your awareness. It is important to write down *everything,* without censoring at all. Practiced regularly, this simple method will make it clear just how random and apparently unrelated thoughts are, and how fast and how spontaneously they are arising in our mind. (This practice reveals, to some extent, the validity of David Hume's ideas about 'constant conjunctions', and of the way in which so much of what we assume to be cause and effect is really just imagined). We have just learned (for the most part) to block and filter out those which seem unrelated to the tasks we are engaged in—or we indulge in such 'unrelated' thoughts, a process we know as 'daydreaming'.

Recording thoughts also will make it clear to us how similar such thoughts are to the nature of our dreams at night. More importantly, the very recording of the thoughts begins to slowly make us more aware of the *field* in which the thoughts are arising—the field of pure awareness.

There are two basic forms of focusing awareness, what we can call 'concentration', and 'attention'. Neither of these are, strictly speaking, true meditation, and yet both are important as preliminary skills to develop prior to tackling the deeper forms of meditation. Concentration is mental focusing in a 'one-pointed' fashion. The mind can be likened a bit to a laser in this regard, in that whatever it concentrates on with unwavering focus will sooner or later yield information, something like a wall being pierced by an information-gathering laser. Or, put another way, as the mind concentrates, thought-associations are stimulated, generally yielding deeper insights into whatever is being concentrated on. (This is one of the secrets to the esoteric technique of 'roaming', discussed in the next chapter). The capacity for concentration, like a physical muscle, can be developed with practice. Here is one very well known and simple technique for sharpening concentration:

Exercise 3 (Counting Breaths): At first, attempt this practice for no more than twenty minutes. After a couple of weeks of practice, you can lengthen sessions to thirty minutes, or even one hour. But give yourself some time to work up to longer sessions if you feel so inclined to pursue this technique.

Sit down in a comfortable position, either in a straight back chair, or cross-legged, or semi-lotus if this is comfortable for you. Keep the spine straight but not rigid. Be relaxed, yet alert, calm, but attentive. Take a few deep breaths, and then breathe in a calm, natural fashion. With your eyes closed, locate the inhale/exhale rhythm of your breathing either in the pit of your belly or at the tip of your nose. Then, breathing at a normal pace, simple begin to count your breaths. Count only the inhales, and on each exhale, let-go and relax. Inhale-one, exhale relax, inhale-two, exhale relax, inhale-three, exhale relax, and so forth. Continue this until there is a break in your attention and you forget which number you were on. As soon as you realize you have lost the thread of attention and have forgotten your count, start over again. Do not cheat, make sure you start over each time you forget. Do not be concerned about how many times you forget. In the beginning you will forget many times and find yourself wandering off into thought-dreams. The important point is to just keep doing it, exercising patience. Persevere until the twenty minutes are up then make a note of the highest number you reached.

If you persist with this, soon you will be able to retain an unbroken count to very high numbers. This method is a very good tool for sharpening the ability to focus and concentrate. In addition, it affords interesting insights into the nature of consciousness and its ability to 'entangle' with thoughts, become identified, and lose self-awareness.

Exercise 4 (Paying Attention): This method is a simple process of focusing your attention on various parts of your body. As with the previous exercise, sit down and be comfortable. Close your eyes and place your attention in your left foot. Be mindful of the sensations of your left foot. Allow your consciousness to rest as totally as you can in your left foot. After a short time there (about two minutes), then move your attention up to the rest of your left leg, scanning from the ankle to the hip. Take about two minutes for this as well. Continue up the left side of the body, allowing about two minutes each for the left side of the pelvis, the left side of your torso, your left arm, left hand, left arm again, left shoulder, left side of neck, and left side of your head. The whole thing should take about fifteen minutes to do. Then scan downwards on the right side of your body, starting at the head, and continuing down the neck, right shoulder, arm, and hand, back up arm again, and down right side of torso, pelvis, and right leg, ending at the right foot.

You should take about thirty minutes to scan your whole body. Once done, take five minutes to sit quietly with your attention focused on the totality of your whole body. Simply be aware of it, and any sensations in it. (If at any time you have to scratch, do so with slow, attentive movements. Remain conscious of all movements).

Exercise 5 (Listening to Sounds): This exercise works very well out in nature, but if you do not have access to a trail where you casually walk or hike, then simply use wherever you find yourself. It is necessary, however, to make sure you will be undisturbed. The exercise is for twenty minutes at first, later you can extend it to thirty or sixty minutes if you feel so inclined.

When walking on a trail through a natural setting (or sitting in your home with whatever sounds are audible), simply focus all your attention on listening to whatever you are hearing. This could be birdsong, wind, the sound of your feet on the ground, your breathing, traffic, people around you, whatever. Just allow all of your attention to dissolve into the sounds. Stay with the sounds. Persisted with, this method is effective for quieting the mind and opening your perception, on more than one level, to a fuller experience of sensory reality. It can lead to a profound sense of connectedness to the world of your sensory experience, as well as the 'Ground of Being' that, according to the wisdom traditions, both world and consciousness are deriving from.

'Wide range' meditation is distinguished from concentration in that it is not a process of focusing on any*thing* in particular, but rather one of resting in our natural awareness—an awareness that may be roughly characterized as 'deep', 'vast', and 'wide'. In the beginning it may be difficult to meditate this way, which is why it is useful to practice concentration or focusing methods such as the ones given above. In time, as we strengthen our ability to concentrate and truly pay attention, we also will develop the ability (or knack) of meditation, which is ultimately about resting in our naturally pure awareness.

Exercise 6 (Self-Observation): In selected situations throughout a typical day, practice simply observing yourself, without comment or attempt to change anything at all. Just try to catch yourself doing and acting and thinking and feeling and behaving however you may be in any given moment or situation, but don't try to change anything—just bear witness to yourself, be as aware as possible of yourself.

This exercise can be a bit difficult in the beginning and as such is best at first to practice in simple, routine situations. These may include when you stop at a red traffic light, standing in line at the bank, interacting with the bank teller, or the waiter in a restaurant, or the grocery clerk, etc. In all these situations, remember whenever you can to simply observe yourself.

Exercise 7 (Self-enquiry): This exercise is best done in a sitting fashion for at least twenty minutes or longer, though it can also be done at any time during the day, as with self-observation and self-remembering.

Self-enquiry is what it suggests, a direct enquiry into the Self. It is the eternal question 'Who am I?' At first it may take the form of a somewhat disconnected intellectual process, attempting to locate the source of yourself amongst the long lists of self-defining categories that comprise the identity of who you think you are—'I am a man, woman, parent, doctor, teacher, secretary, clerk, healer, happy person, loving person, sensitive person', etc.—all the way down to more simple self-definitions, like 'I am warmth, love, fear, anger, emptiness, despair', and so on. Eventually, if Self-enquiry is persisted with, the process becomes less and less abstract, as the mind runs out of definitions for itself, and longer spaces of silence appear in between the answers to the question.

At this point, a deepening is happening in which *insight* in its true sense—'directly seeing within'—is beginning to be aroused, and discriminating intellect is being relaxed. With persistence profound breakthroughs are possible with this method, in which the tacit and immediate sense of deeper and vaster sense of being can arise, often accompanied by glimpses of non-dual consciousness.

Exercise 8 (Zen Koan): This method derives from the Buddhist schools of the Orient, such as those of China and Korea, and especially Japan, where is has been widely practiced in the Rinzai Zen lineages. A *koan* is a paradox that cannot be solved by reason (thus, is not a riddle), but can only be penetrated by insight, or a leap to a higher level of understanding. It is very similar to Self-enquiry, and in fact, the question 'Who am I?' is a *koan*.

Traditionally, a practitioner of Zen meditation might work on a given *koan* for many years before breaking through and opening up to a higher level of understanding. This higher level of understanding is poorly approximated by the English word 'intuition'. It is best defined by the Japanese word *kensho*, which means 'direct seeing into reality'. Though here again, there is some inaccuracy with the definition, because the breakthrough defined by *kensho* involves a direct understanding and experience of Oneness, which is non-dual, i.e., there is no 'seer' who is separate from what is 'seen'.

Choose a rationally insoluble question, such as 'What is the size and weight of love?' or 'Where is the end of the universe?' or 'What is a tree?' or 'What is the sound of one hand clapping?' Then, hold the question within, coming back to it whenever you can, and giving full attention to it. Allow yourself to exhaust all possible intellectual answers, and then continue to inquire into the question. In time, you will notice a shifting inside and the gradual opening of what we may call the 'inner wisdom eye' which apprehends reality in a direct fashion, without images, concepts, or words. This method is often effective for people with strong, active minds. Zen koan work can liberate strong energies and states of mind that are part of the unconscious mind, so as a cautionary note if engaging this work it is best to seek the guidance of a trained Zen teacher.

Exercise 9 (Vipassana): Vipassana is an old Buddhist meditation technique believed to originate from the time of the Buddha, and probably even before that. It is very simple and effective, yet requires sincere discipline, commitment, and patience. Begin with twenty minute sessions, increase up to one hour as you feel ready. Seated comfortably, back straight but not rigid, take a few deep breaths, and relax into yourself. Then, locating the breath in either the pit of the belly, or at the tip of the nose (choose one location or the other, and then stick with it), simply follow your natural in-out breathing rhythm with your awareness. No matter what, keep your awareness on your breath. Simply stay with the breath. At first, you will forget the breath again and again, as you drift off into thought-dreams. That is normal, try to not get frustrated or self-reproachful, simply keep returning your awareness to the rise and fall of the breath. As you follow the breath, simply bear witness to whatever is happening, but keep your awareness anchored to the breath. This method is excellent for focusing and grounding, as well as clearing the mind and centering within.

Exercise 10 (Witnessing): This is the simplest technique of all, and in some ways, the most challenging. In essence, it involves 'just sitting' and being witness to whatever is happening, or arising, in this moment. The meditation can be done sitting with eyes open or closed, and it can also be done while driving, standing in line, or doing anything that requires nothing more than 'auto-pilot' responses from you. However, in the beginning, you may find it easiest to attempt this in a sitting posture with the eyes closed. In Witnessing, you are simply resting in your natural state, which is that of pure consciousness, pure awareness. Let your awareness be big, all-embracing, all-encompassing. Let it be natural. And simply rest in it, being purely aware, and nothing else. Let go, and be relaxed and yet alert, sharply watchful, and calmly observant.

Exercise 11 (The Body of Light Meditation): Sitting in your meditation posture, generate positive thoughts for all of existence, bless everyone. Then spend a few minutes following your breath, so as to settle inwardly and relax. Follow this by spending a few minutes visualizing a sphere of clear white light, about the size of a grapefruit, directly above your head. This sphere of light is representative of your own highest nature, a visual analog of your deepest and greatest self. After seeing and feeling its presence, imagine it declining in size until it is about an inch in diameter. Then visualize it dropping down through the center of your head until it comes to rest in your heart center. Then imagine this sphere of brilliant light expanding, flooding your whole body with its radiance. In so doing, imagine your body transfiguring into pure shimmering, translucent light. Imagine this powerful light converting all negativities within you into a state of radiant contentment. Rest in this for at least fifteen minutes, longer if comfortable. Then end the meditation by directing and dedicating the energy raised to the benefit of all beings.

Active Meditations

Exercise 12: Rebirthing: This is a potent deep breathing technique that is not recommended, in the beginning, to do alone. It is best to seek a trained facilitator to be coached through the process. It is mentioned here because it is one of the more effective tools, especially when done in a series of weekly sessions for about ten consecutive weeks. Owing to various factors many cultures unwittingly condition their members to be shallow breathers. The flow of breath plays a large part in determining the overall health of a person, and especially their ability to feel alive, vital, and to express spontaneously. Rebirthing as a tool is very effective for improving over-all breathing, and the subsequent ability to both access and express passion. It was termed 'rebirthing' when it was first developed in the 1960s (initially via Leonard Orr) because some of the first people to experience the method found themselves spontaneously reliving their birth and experiencing a degree of healing as a result of such re-visiting (which was the essence of the original idea of 'catharsis' as developed by Freud, Otto Rank, and others). But, the vast majority of people who use this technique do not experience anything as spectacular as consciously remembering their birth. For most, it is simply an experience of release and purification. A number of Yoga techniques that originated in India, such as those from *kriya* and *kundalini* Yoga, are very similar. Rebirthing is, in theory, a breathing technique tailored for Westerners.

Exercise 13: Deep Breathing: This breathing method is simpler and easier to perform than rebirthing. It consists of thirty minutes of deep breathing, done in three stages, repeated once. It is helpful to do this with some sort of gentle, rhythmic music, though not required.

Sitting down comfortably, preferably cross-legged on a comfortable surface, close the eyes and begin to breathe deep, slow breaths. Try to inhale to a maximum, and then relax on the exhale. Have each inhale start in the lower diaphragm, and finish at the top of the chest. Do this slow, deep breathing for five minutes. Then for the next five minutes switch to a somewhat faster pace of breathing, keeping the focus on the inhale, and relaxing on the exhale. After five minutes of this, switch to rapid breathing: short, shallow, panting style. Do this for five minutes as well. Then, repeat the three stages again, for a total of thirty minutes of breathing. Once the thirty minutes are complete, simply sit silently for at least ten minutes. This exercise is especially effective for generating energy and revitalizing.

Exercise 14: Taking Risks: Choose an activity that will challenge you in some way. This activity should be something you have resistance doing, or fear engaging in, and it should involve either a physical challenge, or a challenge in the area of confronting your fears around being judged by others, or being disapproved of by others. Good examples of physically challenging tasks might be climbing up to a high place if you have fear of heights, spending time alone in nature if you have fear of this, or similarly related activities. For working on fears of disapproval, a good exercise is to apply some sort of unusual face paint to your face, and then go out into a public market and walk around, allowing yourself to be seen. Such seemingly absurd activities are actually very effective for drawing attention to unconscious fears that are preventing a greater sense of empowerment in life. The main idea here is to create balance in the personality by pushing ourselves out of our 'comfort zones'.

Exercise 15: Mindfulness of Speech: For one whole day, practice being as mindful (consciously attentive) as possible of how you speak to others. Be especially aware of the 'contraction' that occurs when you are negatively activated by some situation, along with any knee-jerk impulse to disagree, argue, not listen, criticize, or judge. Every time an impulse arises to do one of these, simply take conscious deep breath, and say nothing. Alternatively, throughout the course of the day practice taking one conscious breath before you speak to anyone.

Exercise 16: Examining Self-contraction: Pay attention to the tendency to contract inwardly whenever you are emotionally activated by a given occurrence or situation. Note how the contraction often registers in the solar plexus region, as a tension or 'knot' that feels uncomfortable. Try to be mindful of this contraction as long as possible before being directed by it. See if you can entirely avoid being directed by it, instead simply bearing witness to its movements within, until it dissolves naturally.

Self Realization: Does the Personal Self Actually Exist?

It is a given that by 'Self-realization' the referent is the greater Self, or Ground of Being, not the personal self (ego, personality, etc.). That said, the most obvious, but probably the most commonly missed, of all questions, is simply *who am I*? When universally recognized sages such as Socrates and Ramana Maharshi give supreme weight to this question ('know thyself' and 'who am I?'), it suggests something noteworthy (and even Jesus appeared to be addressing the same question when, according to John, he uttered 'I and the Father are one', speaking to an ultimate realization of universal identity). That said, what these sages seem to be pointing toward is something more subtle and profound than any superficial identification with a greater, higher, or divine self as we would commonly imagine that to be. The Buddha (for one) based his entire teaching on a profound recognition: that the personal self (or ego) does not appear to exist at all when the matter is closely examined via deep and sustained contemplation and meditation.

That of course does not mean that 'we' do not exist; rather, it means that our real nature is not at all what we assume it to be, that we are living under the effects of a mental construct and an elaborate illusion. More recent Western philosophers reasoned their way to similar conclusions, most notably Kant and some of the Idealists who followed him, including and up to William James, although few claimed to have direct experience of this alongside their intellectual comprehension. The clearest example was David Hume, who in the 18th century wrote:

> ...when I enter most intimately into what I call myself, I always stumble on some particular perception or other, of heat or cold, light or shade, love or hatred, pain or pleasure. I never can catch myself at any time without a perception, and never can observe any thing but the perception. When my perceptions are removed for any time, as by sound sleep; so long am I insensible of myself, and may truly be said not to exist.[1]

Hume's conclusion was that perceptions existed, but no self independent of them. Similar conclusions have been reached by contemporary Western philosophers who invoke new and fresh approaches (including neuroscience); two of the more articulate recent examples are Owen Flanagan (b. 1949) and Thomas Metzinger (b. 1958). Flanagan, a neurobiologist and philosopher, is a materialist (or 'naturalist' as he prefers), yet arrives at conclusions remarkably similar to those of certain wisdom traditions that examine the idea of a discrete inner self (and do not find one). In his 1992 work *Consciousness Reconsidered,* in a chapter titled *The Illusion of the Mind's "I"*, he wrote:

> We are egoless...the main idea is that the self emerges as experience accrues, and it is constructed as the organism actively engages the external world...in this sense the ego is an after-the-fact construction, not a before-the-fact condition for the possibility of experience...the posit of the mind's "I" is unnecessary.[2]

Metzinger, a German philosopher, published a difficult book in 2003 called *Being No One: The Self-Model Theory of Subjectivity*, and then wrote a more layman-friendly version of it called *The Ego Tunnel: The Science of the Mind and the Myth of the Self* (2009). He drew from neuroscience, robotics, and experiments with virtual reality, but his central point is simple: we do not, and have never had, a 'self'. It is the various functions of our brain that generate the conditions leading to our subjective construction of the self. This 'inner self' is little more than an imagined homunculus, a 'little person' dwelling within that we assume to be at the command seat of our consciousness, picking and choosing what thoughts to generate each moment, and appearing to exercising a free will with assumed autonomy. Metzinger wrote:

> No such things as 'selves' exist in the world...We are Ego Machines, but we do not have selves. We cannot leave the Ego

> Tunnel, because there is nobody who could leave. The Ego and its Tunnel are representational phenomena: they are just one of many possible ways in which conscious beings can model reality...the Ego is merely a complex physical event—an activation pattern in your central nervous system.[3]

Both Flanagan and Metzinger agree that the 'self' is essentially a representation, a process or mental phenomena brought about by a number of factors, but lacking intrinsic nature. This is very close to what the Buddha taught (though without the comprehensive psycho-spiritual instruction that the Buddha provided to support the realization of no-self; and without the systems of development offered by the Western esoteric tradition that seek to ground the *representation* of self within the context of something much greater). Some of these ideas were expressed in differing ways by early 20th century magicians such as Crowley and Austin Osman Spare, but were perhaps most creatively expressed in the writings of Peter Carroll (b. 1953), co-founder of so-called 'Chaos Magic' and author of *Liber Null*, *Psychonaut*, and other works. Carroll wrote:

> A curious error has entered into many systems of occult thought. This is the notion of some higher self or true will that has been misappropriated from the monotheistic religions. There are many who like to think that they have some inner self which is somehow more real or spiritual than their ordinary or lower self. The facts do not bear this out...there is no sovereign sanctuary within ourselves which represents our real nature. There is nobody at home in the internal fortress...the center of consciousness is formless and without qualities of which mind can form images. There is no-one at home.[4]

Carroll did not hold a nihilistic position, however, maintaining that we do have a higher self or 'Holy Guardian Angel' (or 'Kia' as he called it, borrowing Austin Osman Spare's term) but that it is a minimalist force of pure will and perception to be shaped and applied. It is not an intrinsically divine, wise, loving, overarching presence watching benignly over us, but rather a pristine force to be developed. (This closely parallels Gurdjieff's idea of the 'essence').

Analytical Meditation

Owing to the challenges of healthy ego-formation and the central illusion that the ego generates (separation), the wisdom traditions are clear that the ego or sense of personal isolation ultimately lies at the source of human suffering. This is due to the premise that ego is all about limitation. The Sanskrit term for ego is *ahamkara* (literally, 'I-maker'). It is regarded as basic to survival, but seen as getting in the way of higher truths precisely because it thinks in terms of personal ownership only—'my ideas, my-self, my feelings', etc. It has difficulty in understanding what is *not* I. That in turn sets up and reinforces a false division between self and universe, and leads to a deep-seated mistrust in what appears to lie 'outside' of self. Analytical meditation is a method to see directly into the emptiness of the ego-self.

Exercise 17: Analytical Meditation: We can try a thought-experiment of 'analytical meditation', as follows. Does the body exist—independent of it being solely a conceptual entity?[5] And if so, can we locate it? Let us examine the matter. The body consists of arms, legs, organs, and so on. It is a construction of various parts. But each part is not the body. We cannot say that the arm is the body, or the eye is the body. Clearly that would be nonsense.

Can a grouping of non-body parts make a body in anything other than a conceptual sense? Practically speaking, ten chairs together do not make a table. Four legs and a table top together may make a table, but 'table' exists only as a conceptual label. Seen clearly, the table is really the legs and the top. Similarly, the body does not truly exist other than as a *conceptual entity*. It is purely a concept, a label. And this is the same wherever we look, and is true for whatever we look at. What is a hand? A grouping of fingers, skin, etc., none of which is a hand. Therefore, there is no hand in any absolute sense—there is only the *concept* of a hand, a pure abstraction existing only in the mind. The same applies for all so-called objectively existing things. Wherever we look, we see only the externalization of our *ideas*, all the way down to subatomic particles and empty space.

So, if nothing exists inherently in objective reality, beyond it being an externalized concept, then what about if we look within? Clearly our 'I' is not consistent, as it can be related to many things—thoughts, moods, feelings, memories, and so on. 'I' is a composite of many different mental and even physiological states. Because it would be unsound to refer to one state as 'me'—I am anger, I am fear, I am this memory (but not that one), etc.—then the same thing can be concluded, that being that this 'I' has no real inherent existence as something specifically and separately definable. 'I' is not a discrete thing, isolated from everything else.

If this is so, what is left over? In some traditions it is called 'luminous emptiness', in others 'cosmic Mind', a kind of continuous whole in which there is no *truly real* division between what we experience as 'me' and the universe. That may be called 'absolute reality'. Then there are conventional realities to be recognized, such as the reality of 'I feel hungry, tired', etc. In the investigation of absolute reality, conventional reality is not ignored or denied.

Exercise 18: Laughter. When waking up, first thing in the morning, begin to laugh. Laugh for at least several minutes, longer if you feel like it. If you find the exercise too artificial, just begin laughing, and soon you will laugh authentically at your own attempts to laugh. (If not wishing to disturb your sleeping partner, laugh silently, or go into another room). Laughter is a means for reconciling opposites and integrating absurdities. Existence has a fundamental absurdity to it, and laughter is arguably the best way to resolve most issues.

Into eternity, where all is one, there crept a tiny, mad idea, at which the

Son of God remembered not to laugh. In his forgetting did the thought become a serious idea, and possible of both accomplishment and real effects. –A Course in Miracles (T–27.VIII.6:2–3)

Laughter is the only tenable attitude in a universe which is a joke played upon itself.—Peter Carroll.[6]

Chapter 12

Magic and Manifestation

Mysticism vs. Magic

Mysticism and magic have co-existed, at times uneasily, for a very long time. In the eyes of the average person the former is mostly misunderstood, the latter mostly feared. This is perhaps fitting; for while mysticism is concerned with lofty spiritual states (the meaning of which are easily misunderstood), magic is, at least in part, concerned with power—everything from power over oneself ('individual empowerment'), to power over circumstances, nature or even (in its baser forms) over other people. Few things in life provoke fear more than power, but particularly power that seeks to bypass or subvert conventional religious conditioning.

Mysticism can be defined, in the broadest sense, as that set of ideas, beliefs, and practices that has as its ultimate goal the *unio mystica*, the union of the individual consciousness (or soul) with the source of all (or God). Based on that definition, the oldest evidence we have of a clear teaching on mysticism is in the series of Hindu scriptures from India known as the Upanishads, which date back to at least 1500 BCE, and which reached their highest state of refinement around 750 BCE, centered on the core teachings of non-duality. In the Oriental philosophy of non-duality the basic idea is that 'all is always already One', i.e., all appearances of dualism or separation are in fact elaborate illusions constructed by the mind as it experiences reality through the filters of the self (ego). This is summed up in the Sanskrit words *Tat Tvam Asi* ('you are *that*'), i.e., you (subject) and what you perceive (object) are ultimately one and the same. Another variation of this is the Vedantic expression *aham brahma asmi*, which translates as 'I am the Absolute'. This can be compared to what Christ is reported to have declared, 'I and the Father are One' (John 10:30). It is also the same principle behind the

Hebrew expression *eheiyeh* ('I am') when used in Kabbalism, based on one's full identification with the higher Self.

The mystical approach is typically associated with Eastern traditions, but there is an established Western mystical tradition as well, notably represented by such figures as the 6th century CE 'Pseudo-Dionysius the Areopogite', Hildegard of Bingen (1098-1179), Meister Eckhart (1260-1327), Teresa of Avila (1515-1582), and St. John of the Cross (Juan de Yepes, 1542-1591). The latter's famous refrain, 'the further you withdraw from earthly things the closer you approach heavenly things and the more you find in God / Whoever knows how to die in all will have life in all' is mysticism *par excellence.* St. John of the Cross's teachings on grace or spiritual surrender, particularly in his *The Dark Night of the Soul,* closely parallel the ideas of the Abyss discussed in Chapter 4. His main argument was that our awakening and purification run along two simultaneously operating lines, those being our personal efforts, as well as the grace that descends (from God, he maintained) when we are in a state of passive surrender to the divine. St. John's writings had been preceded by the anonymous author of *The Cloud of Unknowing,* a late 14th century text of Christian mysticism which based its central teaching on the negation of all personal knowledge and the cultivation of an inner spaciousness ('unknowing') that allows for the deep entry of the divine. This in turn had been preceded by the writings of Pseudo-Dionysius the Areopogite, who in his influential work *The Mystical Theology* had coined the terms 'divine darkness', 'divine ignorance', and 'unknowing', in which he maintained 'that He who is the pre-eminent Cause of all things sensibly or intelligently perceived is not Himself any of those things' and who 'needs no light and suffers no change'—contemplation upon which may be defined as the heart of mysticism. This emphasis on 'via negativa' was later balanced by the work of Thomas à Kempis (1380-1471), the probable author of the 15th century *The Imitation of Christ,* which centered on a more practical and pro-active approach of identification with Christ.

The resurrection symbology of Christ had some precedents in

ancient Egypt, especially via the resurrection myths of Osiris. The spiritual ideas of the ancient Egyptians pre-date the Upanishads and even the older Indian Rig Veda scriptures (which have been reliably dated back to at least 1700 BCE). By the time the Rig Vedas appeared, Egyptian civilization was already old. While there appears to be a lack of evidence for any kind of purely abstract non-dualistic mysticism in ancient Egypt along the lines of Indian Vedantic ideas of 'union with the Absolute', there *is* evidence for a different form of spirituality: what is generally called 'theurgy' (from the Greek *theourgia,* meaning 'God-working'). Theurgy (or high magic) refers to a body of ideas and practices that relates to a fundamentally different angle of approach to spiritual development than that used by abstract mysticism. The simpler forms of magic—sometimes called 'low magic' or 'sorcery', from the Greek term *goetia*—are generally involved in the procurement of objects, circumstantial changes, and fulfillment of personal desires. (The earliest example of this—in literary form—is from Homer's *Odyssey,* where a sorceress named Circe transforms Odysseus's companions into swine.[1] That said, the division of magic into 'high' and 'low' is more accurate than the division of 'white' and 'black magic', which is more a modern contrivance. Historically, the line between so-called 'white' and 'black' magic was often blurry and in many cases there was no clear distinction between the two).

The differences between mysticism and magic can be usefully described by briefly resorting to Eastern traditions. In India, two fundamental approaches to inner awakening developed over time, what we can call the *transcendent* and the *immanent* paths. The former, the transcendent, is best defined via the more traditional yogic paths (including Advaita Vedanta, the highest of the Vedantic teachings), and in the later Chinese and Japanese developments of Zen Buddhism. In this approach, the apparently objective universe is regarded as *maya* ('illusion'), something that is meant to be transcended, much as we would awaken from a dream. All focus is put on attaining realization of the ultimate truth and nothing else.

Zen, in particular, is a clear example of this approach, regarding anything that arises in meditation, including all subtle states of consciousness, as *makyo*, a word that translates literally as the 'devil in phenomena', a reference to all mind-states that are anything but a direct realization of the truth of one's nature (and therefore to be discarded). In the second approach, the immanent, which in the East is well described via the teachings of *tantra*, the universe is not regarded as mere illusion, but rather as *Shakti* ('power/energy'), to be utilized and harnessed in such a way as to reach the highest stages of God-realization. There are some similarities between the Eastern paths of tantra and the Western paths of high magic (*theurgy*), which has its apparent roots in Babylonia, ancient Egypt, and the Persian Magi, and which reached its more developed expressions in the Hermetic texts. Low magic (*goetia*) seems to have had its 'golden age' within Roman practices around the time of Christ, although aggressive (and hostile) forms of magic were common among the ancient cultures of the Fertile Crescent.

High magic can be described as a path of spiritual evolution that does not turn away from matter, the body, and the world or its energies, but rather works directly with them, via rituals, imagination, symbols, visualization, active meditations that involve the body and its senses, the invoking or evoking of archetypes and deities, and so on. The transcendent path of mysticism is really only concerned with the *formless*, i.e., the Absolute beyond all form; whereas the more immanent path of high magic embraces form, and seeks to regard it as a sacred expression of the divine to be worked directly with. Mysticism is concerned more with the goal and less so with the journey to get there. High magic could be said to consider the journey to be of equal value to the goal. Ideally, both will arrive at the same place, though they do so by addressing different aspects of human nature.

Of course, it is somewhat simplistic to limit magic and mysticism to seemingly exclusive categories such as immanence or transcendence. Magic has its elements of transcendence, as mysticism has its elements of immanence. Most traditions agree that 'ultimate reality' (God, the Source, etc.) is both transcendent and immanent. It is true however that most traditions also emphasize one approach or the other. Magic, however, has always been concerned with uncovering the secret patterns of existence—and in particular, how to influence these patterns—and as such holds a deep fascination with the workings of the immanent reality that we are immersed in.

Theurgy also translates as 'acting on the gods', thus distinguishing it from its more wordy and theoretical cousin, theology. The probable 2nd century CE author of *The Chaldean Oracles* (the first work to use the term *theurgy*), Julian the Chaldean, was reputedly a magician. The *Oracles*, a partially intact mystery-poem, bears Gnostic and Neoplatonic similarities, being based on a scheme that involves an initiate seeking to purify themselves so as to 'rise up' the inner planes toward communion with the divine.

Some practicing theurgists claimed to be able to draw down the spirit of deities into statues, thereby causing the statue to become animated with the intelligence and wisdom of the deity. The 'statue' could then provide wise counsel to one who underwent the preparatory rituals, prior to seeking guidance from the deity embodied in the statue. It was all a means of communication with spirit, based on the psychological state of the seeker, whose consciousness had been altered via ceremony (and probably in some cases by certain drugs). *Theurgy* was essentially a form of yoga, a practice of purification and alignment with one's highest nature. As with all the yogas it has its higher forms (abstract concerns with the Absolute), as well as its more practical applications; namely, dealing with the material world while also seeking Self-realization.

A key figure in the transmission of theurgical ideas was Iamblichus (245–325 CE), a Syrian Neoplatonist. Iamblichus was one of the first to recognize that divine consciousness cannot be fully grasped and realized via conscious intellect alone (a realization that Immanuel Kant explained in detail fifteen centuries later). His approach was essentially integral and practical, in that he taught the importance of working with the 'divine correspondences' within matter (natural magic, part of which later evolved into modern science), as well as with the contemplative and meditative practices that align the mind with its highest parts. It is the element of practicality that distinguishes the magician from the philosopher, and Iamblichus was in many ways one of the first to emphasize this point. He was, essentially, seeking a balance between the practical ritualism of the ancient Egyptians and the brilliant abstractions of the Greeks.

It was left to the German polymath, scholar, and magus Cornelius Agrippa to organize the theory of magic into a coherent scheme. Drawing on various Greek, Neoplatonic, Hermetic, and folk sources, and in particular Albertus Magnus, Marcilio Ficino, Johann Reuchlin, Pico della Mirandola, and Johann Trithemius, Agrippa wrote his famed encyclopedia of magic and esoteric knowledge titled *De Occulta Philosophia Libri Tres (Three Books of Occult Philosophy)*. He finished a first draft of the book in 1510 at just twenty-three years of age; owing to the influence of his mentor Trithemius who suggested against openly publishing, it circulated in manuscript form for two decades, only being published in full in 1533. The 'three books' referred to in the title indicate the tripartite structure of Agrippa's scheme. He outlined three essential kinds of magic: 1. Natural Magic; 2. Celestial Magic; and 3. Ceremonial Magic. The first, natural magic, seems to describe an animistic proto-science, in which the elements of the material universe are catalogued and analyzed, and particularly their interrelationships, involving such matters as 'sympathies', 'virtues', and 'influences'; in short, the qualities of material phenomena. Natural magic included alchemy and astrology, and in general corresponded to the elemental world. The second, celestial (or stellar) magic, corresponded to the semiotic or mental domain, utilizing symbols and numbers to harness the so-called powers of stellar and planetary influences (Agrippa referred to celestial magic as 'mathematical magic', an interesting fact in that mathematics was regarded with suspicion by religious authorities for some time prior to the scientific revolution). The third, ceremonial magic, concerned the highest spiritual (or supercelestial) domain, the realm of angelic influences that are nearest to the divine Source. Agrippa's scheme closely followed the philosophical scheme of Neoplatonism (The One, Divine Mind, Higher World Soul, Nature). Agrippa's model can be defined as a theoretical map within which to engage the 'Great Work' of Self-realization and manifestation.

The Secret of Magic

Magic, whether of the 'high' or 'low' varieties, is a highly complex tradition with sophisticated, at times baffling, teachings and symbolism. Magic is preeminently concerned with causation, and in particular, the mystery of 'change' and our apparent ability, as entities with will, to cause these changes. (The mystery of what is generating our will—the causative agent behind the wish or desire—is the province of mysticism). Ultimately, however, the 'secret' of magic may be reduced to the practice of **formulating intention** and **creating space**. To 'formulate intention' is, in this context, to clarify intention via realization and action. We clarify our intention to grow spiritually by cultivating some sort of meditation practice (see previous chapter). We clarify our intention to cause specific changes in our life by applying our mind-training to manifestation (see below). To 'create space' means, in this context, several things. A good metaphor to consider initially, mentioned in Chapter 3, is the Kabbalist Isaac Luria's idea of *zimzum*. It was his explanation for how God created the universe, by contracting his infinite Light and thereby creating a space within which the cosmos could arise in finite and interdependent forms. Of course, this was Luria's theological theory to explain creation, but it also works as a metaphor for both Self-realization and manifestation, the two cornerstones of magic.

To 'create space' is both to allow realization of our inherent higher Self to occur, and to allow existence to 'send' desired things our way. In this sense 'creating space' is a metaphor for Self-realization. To create space is also akin to learning the art of letting go, of forgetting things in appropriate ways. For example, it is very true that we must 'forget' ourselves in order to 'remember' ourselves. The Zen master Dogen (1200–1253) addressed the matter concisely when he wrote,

> To study the Buddha Way is to study the self, to study the self is to forget the self, and to forget the self is to be enlightened by the ten thousand things.

'Forgetting the self', in this context, is the same as 'creating space' or 'allowing'. It is sometimes characterized as the art of (seemingly) creating something from nothing. (The storied term 'abracadabra' has been associated with this idea; see Appendix III). It is the essential follow-up stage to engage after we have formulated our intention, i.e., clarified our intent to deepen spiritually and to cause desired changes in our life. This follow-up stage is emphasized here because without it, our best intentions generally do not amount to much.

There is a level of consciousness sometimes called the 'autopilot' level, where we engage ordinary activities (such as driving a car or washing the dishes). We need little consciousness for these activities. They are not useless, however, because it is during these times when our mind is often relaxed enough that there is a 'letting go' process occurring, a space being naturally created within, in which our previously set intentions can begin to be truly actualized. When we do not create space, when we are too present in our ego-self and its chronic tensions and mistrust of existence, there is no room inside for creation to occur. This applies not just to 'manifesting things'. It also applies to relationship. The basis of neurotic, dysfunctional relating is failure to create space, to allow the other to be who they are, and to allow ourselves to be natural (relaxed, unforced, non-defensive) in their presence. It is also the basis of Self-realization, because the main impediment to inner transformation is interfering with the natural recognition of our intrinsic spiritual nature.

In order to understand the mechanics of 'creating space', it is helpful to understand the relationship between pure consciousness and imagination. Knowing how to move from imagination to pure consciousness may be said to be the 'secret' of letting go and of creating space.

Pure Consciousness

'Pure consciousness' has been defined in many ways, perhaps most accurately (and paradoxically) as 'consciousness without an object'. This appears paradoxical because consciousness itself seems to require *something* to be conscious of. Consciousness appears to arise only in contrast. As a simple material analogy: a black dot placed on a background of the exact same shade of black will not be visible. The same dot placed on a white background leaps into appearance. We become conscious of it via the contrast. Similarly, we experience ourselves as 'self' in contrast to all that which appears to be 'not-self'. We know ourselves via differentiating ourselves from others.

If we imagine ourselves to exist without any objects, would we still be conscious? To follow this thought-experiment we would have to be careful to remove *all* objects, including that of our body. What would then remain would be our mind and its thoughts (assuming a mind-independent-of-brain paradigm). This would still allow for consciousness, as the thoughts would then be our sole remaining 'objects'. In dreams at night we experience something similar; we are oblivious of our body, but we find ourselves in a dream-world relating to objects around us. In effect, we are relating to our mind (or if subscribing to a metaphysically realist view, we are relating to other minds in a dimension beyond the material world).

Following our thought-experiment to its ultimate level, what happens if we remove all thoughts? Does consciousness disappear? For those who have sufficient experience in the practice of meditation, they will affirm that consciousness can indeed remain without any apparent thoughts. What exactly remains may be difficult or essentially impossible to explain, and this is why it is usually referred to by such terms as 'supra-rational' or 'transcendent' or 'emptiness'. In essence, pure consciousness is selfless and egoless. It is often characterized as the vast non-local space and non-temporal field from which pure creativity arises—a field of 'pure potentiality'. It is this field that is the Ground of Being, the source of Self-knowledge, and it is also the field from which all 'manifestation' unfolds.

Imagination

There is perhaps no faculty of human nature that is more commonly overlooked, dismissed, or disparaged than imagination. Much as with the *prima materia* of alchemy, it is a thing commonly regarded as unimportant, yet contains within it 'cargo' of the greatest value—the 'gold' of creation and inner illumination.[2]

The capacity to think, in its barest sense, is a tool for enhancing the survival prospects of our physical body. The human body is relatively weak compared to the physical form of many animals, especially the predators. Millions of years ago thinking doubtless evolved as a functional way to ensure some sort of advantage over competing mammals. Over time the purely practical aspects of thinking likely became elaborated, via the development of imagination, which was an essential part of time-consciousness. In order to temporally imagine something it is necessary to remember an event that happened in the past, or speculate about some event that may happen in the future. The usefulness for such capacity to imagine, purely as a survival tool, is clear. To be able to imagine what might be over a ridge of mountains, or what sort of weather might be coming in a few days, based on what was experienced at certain points in the past, would clearly be advantageous. The beginnings of primitive technologies, such as tool and fire-making, would also be facilitated by the ability to imagine.

The higher uses of imagination eventually led to the creative uses of thinking, as a means of expanding and enriching the human experience. This higher imagination was also basic to so-called inner-work methodologies—the esoteric traditions that usually lay behind most organized religions. The word *imagination* derives from the Latin *imaginari,* meaning 'to form a mental image of', and refers specifically to the mental description of an object perceived outwardly by senses. The Romantics of the late 18th and early 19th century had a great deal to say about imagination; poets such as Coleridge, for example, had been influenced by figures such as Emerson, Fichte, and Kant, and in a sense served as 'mediums' to transmit ideas from Idealistic philosophy to the greater public via their creative writings. Coleridge had broadly defined imagination as of three essential levels, what he called the *primary, fancy,* and *secondary*. These can be simplified, respectively, as follows:

Level One: The simple interpretation of incoming data on a sensory level that we make consensus agreements on and learn to perceive together. For example, as a child, after experiencing trees, we eventually learn what 'tree' is as a *concept,* and after a while begin to project the concept of trees onto the incredibly big and alive green and brown thing that we knew prior to affixing the tree label to it. This level of image-making, or imagination, is conditioned and highly subconscious, at least by the time language is learned. It is not even regarded as imagination, but is understood more as the simple ability to think and know what the things of the world are. It is our constructed experience of reality (although rarely recognized as 'constructed'). A basic element of human experience is not just an individually constructed reality, but also a collective construction. Groups of humans together create a social construct of consensus reality, in which collective agreements are made that result in the appearance of a 'solid' reality in which we all move and interact. An essential key of magic involves the means by which to understand and see the constructed nature of reality, and then how to free ourselves of some of the more limiting collective agreements.

Level Two: The ability to abstractly think of a color or shape or fantasy, without significant coherence or particular meaning; to associate and connect ideas, to make up stories, everything from casual daydreaming to conventional thought. Coleridge referred to this level of imagination as the 'fancy'. Gurdjieff considered most art to be a product of this level, what he called 'ordinary art' that is more an expression of the unconscious mind of the artist and is a type of personal catharsis with limited ability to impact others in any significant way.

Level Three: Creative image-making. At this level, mental images are combined in such a way as to result in more subtle, rarefied expressions. This is the level of most sophisticated art and much theoretical science or philosophy. Gurdjieff maintained that art at this level is not typical art, but what he called 'objective art', often based on what modern parlance calls 'sacred geometry'.

Of course, sophisticated use of this third level of image-making does not necessarily mean that any sense of fulfillment or peace will be experienced in one's life—let alone any profound connection with life and the universe. In fact, some of the most sophisticated intellectuals or most notable artists known to history lived in great psychological conflict or general dissatisfaction with life. A few even went mad. This is because with many sophisticated thinkers and image-makers there remains a strong *personal identification* with thought. A key when utilizing imagination in its higher forms is to reach a level of non-attachment to one's creation. This is possible if the self is directly observed (via a meditation practice, for example). One of the key 'secrets' of magic lies in recognizing the very dream-like, ever-changing nature of the presumed personal 'I'—the ego-identity. As this ego is based largely on desires, its whole effort is to sustain the appearance of its existence via constantly acquiring energy from outside of itself. In order to truly 'manifest' our highest destiny, we must self-observe and come to see the constructed nature of the personal self. As we do, we become more capable of getting out of our own way, so to speak. It is then that the higher faculty of imagination can truly work 'through' us. This form of imagination is more properly a spiritual perception, insight into what Antoine Faivre called *mundis imaginalis*, or the deeper, unseen realms of existence.

What follows is a brief overview of the essential inner work of high magic:

1. To recognize the constructed nature of reality, both individually, and collectively. This is accomplished via self-observation. A useful method here is 'thought-rise'.

Thought-rise: This is a meditation similar to some of the witnessing meditations outlined in the previous chapter, but with a particular focus. The practice is to observe thoughts just as they arise into consciousness. Here we try to 'catch' the birth of a thought as it originally 'pops' into our mind. It takes some practice to do this, but in time we become increasingly able to 'locate' ourselves, as witnessing consciousness, *prior* to a thought. In recognizing the innately prior nature of consciousness, it becomes more straightforward to begin to see the constructed nature of the reality we humans live and move in—and thus easier, in principle, to stay awake and avoid elements of the construct.[3]

2. To recognize what we are calling here **mechanical thinking**, as well as **magical thinking**. The first, mechanical thinking, can be characterized as thought that is merely replicating the ideas of others; believing things 'because others said it'. Prior to the rise of modern science (17th century) the means to discovering truth was not by repeated experiments but by consulting established doctrine. If authorities of the past *said* something was true, it was true, and to be believed. The tendency to 'mechanical thinking' can be pronounced in transformational work and spiritual communities, and is often closely connected to 'magical thinking', which is the tendency to assume that because events are closely connected in

time and space, they *must be* causally linked, and therefore must mean something. In truth, the mere coincidence of events does not necessarily imply anything, beyond the meaning that we are assigning to it. (Most divination work, everything from tea-leaves to the Tarot, is based on magical thinking, the practice of reading meanings into things. That does not necessitate that such readings are useless, but they will likely not help if they simply serve to reinforce a constructed reality by adding new unwarranted assumptions to it). The point to see is that meaning is constructed internally, and then applied by us to the outer world via projection. Understanding this opens us to the possibility of much greater freedom and peace of mind, by recognizing that most suffering is caused by unwarranted assumptions about reality (including other people). What we think something 'means' usually does not. But if we insist on 'being right' about our assumptions, we usually suffer proportionately.

3. **Foundational thinking**. To recognize mechanical thinking and magical thinking does not mean that the proverbial baby need be tossed out with the bathwater. 'Foundational thinking' is thinking that is based on learning the essentials of the tradition one is studying in. It can, of course, be confused with mechanical thinking in that an argument might be mounted that one should reject all thought-systems that were not independently discovered by oneself. This however is obviously absurd; even the great radical and creative minds of history, such as the Buddha, Socrates, Jesus, Newton, Einstein, and so on, achieved their insights on the basis of certain prior understandings. Foundational thinking is important on the Western esoteric path, particularly as a safeguard against the shadow-elements of the 'magician personality type' (ego-inflation). Humbly learning the basics of one's tradition is necessary prior to achieving legitimately original thought.

4. **Original thought**. The means for achieving original thought is

creating space. In this context, to 'create space' is to allow one's consciousness to rest both quietly and openly, in a relaxed, alert, and fearless way that welcomes original thought. Such openness closely simulates a type of 'roaming' in which the imagination is set free to organize thoughts and images in its own unique way—to roam the landscape of reality, if you will. Artists, poets, speakers who are not working from a prepared script, and so on, are all 'creating space' when performing their craft and creating their work. It can also be used for deeper psycho-spiritual work, as a means of attuning with higher levels of being. To 'create space' is, essentially, to *allow* insights to arise within, as opposed to scanning our memory to recall what someone else said is true. 'Creating space' requires a balance between focusing and letting go. As mentioned it is also the prime secret to manifestation, insofar as the method of allowing insights to arise from the 'background field' of pure potentiality is the same as the process of allowing 'things' to appear in our life (see below).

Henosis

'Creating space', brought about by various means of meditation and ritual, ultimately leads to **henosis**, which is the supreme goal of high magic. 'Henosis' is the Greek (Neoplatonic) term for 'unification' or 'oneness'. Modern Western high magic sometimes expresses the idea as the 'knowledge and conversation of the Holy Guardian Angel' or union with the 'silent Self'. (A common misunderstanding is that the supreme goal of high magic is to 'become a god', when in fact it is to *join* with God; the idea of 'becoming a god' is an immature expression of rebellious urges to differentiate from existence—something commonly projected *onto* practitioners of esotericism by those with unrealized unconscious fantasies related to power and rebellion). There are many avenues of approach to ideas of supreme spiritual illumination such as 'henosis' (and its closely related cousins, 'gnosis' and 'theosis'—the former an individual awakening leading to henosis, the latter a type of deity-yoga based on identification with a supreme spiritual figure), but an essential element in all cases is deep commitment. Many traditions emphasize the need for regular and extended periods devoted to meditation, invocation, prayer, ritual, and other practices of purification, sometimes in the form of retreats lasting from as long as four days (common in Native American shamanic 'vision quests') to eighteen months (the version given in *The Book of the Sacred Magic of Abramelin the Mage*). Some Eastern traditions (from Tibetan Buddhism) prescribe traditional retreats of three years and three months, and there is even one as long as ten years. The idea behind the withdrawal is to allow the mind to become quiet, and interfacing with Nature has long been a recognized means of facilitating this. Whatever the means, the idea is to commune with the Higher Self, to directly experience the depth, vastness, and wisdom of our deep nature.

Ultimately, it is understood that the Higher Self or Holy Guardian Angel, much like the Holy Spirit, does not actually exist in any discrete fashion. It is an image or reflection appearing to embody a particular form or idea, when in fact it is nothing but a passageway or process of awakening—a bridge that when crossed immediately ceases to operate and is revealed to have been a necessary and enormously helpful illusion. Once the bridge is crossed, the truth of one's essential nature is tacitly clear. As Jesus is quoted as saying in the Gospel of Thomas, saying 51, 'what you look forward to has already come, but you do not see it'. (Such a view, however, should not be used to circumvent the practice of our inner work—it is possible to regard the higher mind, Holy Guardian Angel, or Holy Spirit as real without turning them into objects of blind worship, but rather as guiding symbols to orient our life toward).

Manifestation Preliminaries: Conscious Discipline and Decision-Making

Magic, in its purest sense, ultimately has two purposes: Self-realization (true Self) and Self-expression (true Will). The first arises naturally as the mind is trained to self-observe, and as the ego-contractions of the personality are gradually dissolved via self-acceptance and shadow-work (as discussed in the previous chapter). The second involves various levels of the 'art of manifestation'.

An essential preliminary step in the practice of manifestation is commonly overlooked in teachings on the matter, and that is the training of the will. A major lesson of 'life in a body' while navigating this material universe is simply dealing with the laws of space and time as we currently perceive and experience them. In some respects this is the most important facet of inner work, because if it is not handled properly it interferes with all other transformational disciplines. If transformational work that involves relationship on all levels may be said to be the healing of the heart, and work that involves meditation, contemplation, and study, the clearing of the mind, then transformational work that involves structure and discipline may be said to be the healing and correct development of the personal will. Without a basic level of will-training, most attempts at manifestation will fail. In order to develop the will, there are two general areas important to consider: discipline and decision-making.

Conscious Discipline: If chronic 'laziness' (a widespread and common condition) can be generally defined as resistance to life, and in particular, the fear of self-expression and of experiencing success, then 'discipline' can be viewed as the antidote to such fears. It is important here to understand that we are not referring to 'discipline' as the word is commonly understood. We are referring rather to *conscious* discipline. Discipline is qualified here because typical discipline is often only routinely, half-heartedly, grudgingly or mechanically undertaken as part of a general program to advance in life based on how we have been told we *should* advance, such as through a typical career, with the approval of key family, peer, and societal members around us. This sort of discipline—'mechanical discipline'—is usually enforced on us from the outside, and while it has its merits in early life, is ultimately limited in terms of its ability to help us locate our highest calling. Mechanical discipline is a developmental stage in the process of learning conscious discipline.

Once we have begun to balance and deconstruct elements of our personality via self-acceptance and self-observation, we begin to access our underlying essence and to develop it in such a fashion that we gain glimpses into higher Self and our highest calling in life. It is then usually a matter of acquiring and practicing discipline of some sort in order to bring about the conditions and circumstances that will help this chosen life path to best unfold.

The root of the word 'discipline' is the same as that for 'disciple', the Latin *discipulus*, which means 'learner'. To cultivate conscious discipline is to be a true learner, one who is capable of growing by absorbing the teachings, wisdom, and understanding necessary to advance on their life path. Without such discipline it is very difficult, if not impossible, to truly learn, let alone advance and accomplish. An untrained mind can accomplish little.

In facing the need for discipline we are inevitably confronted by our own resistance to it, which is largely based on the resistance to maturing. For the first decade of our life things were mostly done for us, and in many cases, things 'magically' appeared in our life with minimal awareness on our part, such a meals, shelter, attention, advice, etc. An essential part of the maturation process is learning some degree of self-reliance, which grows in direct proportion to our willingness to practice conscious discipline. As this discipline develops we are forced to confront our fears around self-expression, personal power, and ultimately, responsibility. This is because conscious discipline, when practiced over an extended period of time with consistency, ultimately leads to proficiency, excellence, or mastery of some sort, which often translates into success. Such success (at whatever perceived level) almost always involves a degree of responsibility. All of this will activate our core fears around living and expressing the vastness and greatness of our pure potentiality, which is the main cause behind the resistance to conscious discipline. It is, in the end, connected to the fears of truly 'showing up' in life, of being 'big', and the perceived responsibility and freedom that accompanies such a stance.

Practicing Conscious Discipline: Once you have located inwardly a passion you wish to actualize, and what your dream would be around fulfilling this passion, set yourself the task that for five days out of every week you will always do at least *one thing* that is geared toward *bringing about* that dream. The very nature of 'dream' implies a future potential, but conscious discipline always addresses the here and now in a very practical manner. At the end of each of the five days, mentally review what you have accomplished during that day. Acknowledge efforts made (regardless of the nature of the results), and if there were no efforts made, honestly inquire into the reasons behind your inactivity. Practice this for one month. Eventually, it will become part of the natural flow of your life, where conscious discipline is undertaken much as basic life activities are, such as eating, washing, speaking, sleeping, and so on. When this discipline begins to be *enjoyed*, then it is a sure sign that success is beginning to manifest or will soon follow. By 'success' is meant in this context the expression of what excites and fulfills you in life in such a way that you feel supported by life in what you are doing.

Decision-Making: The most crucial aspect of acquiring conscious discipline is the ability to make decisions. For it is in decision-making that the personal will is developed and strengthened, much as a physical muscle is by repeated use. Of course, such a 'muscle' can be strengthened and then simply used for wrong or unhealthy reasons. In the context of psychological and spiritual growth, the development of personal power must be wedded to discriminating intelligence in order for this power to be utilized in a proper way that does not result in negativity rebounding.

Ultimately, in the further stages of inner awakening, the whole notion of personal will is seen in a very different light, being more part of the fabric and flow of the greater Reality, in which there is understood to be less and less a sense of a separate 'doer' who is apparently making all these decisions. However, prior to acquiring the insight to begin to understand this bigger, non-dualistic picture, it is necessary to learn to exercise our personal will and power. If such exercising is done properly it gradually leads to the dawning awareness that our own higher Will is already connected to the 'universal Will', or the life-path that is our highest calling (and is, from the ultimate perspective, one with it). However, as Lao Tzu once wrote in the *Tao Te Ching*, 'The journey of a thousand miles begins with a single step'. In time, we begin to see that this 'first step' is as important as any other step.

The Decision Exercise: In this exercise we begin with very simple tasks, which may be completely mundane and even unrelated to anything outwardly productive. That is because what we are here learning is how to *consistently* perform certain actions; indeed, it is such consistency that lies at the heart of all productive decision-making capacity.[4]

Choose a simple, mundane activity, such as cleaning your bathroom sink faucet, or mirror, or sweeping the kitchen floor, or standing on a stool in the corner of your room. The activity chosen should be unimportant. The idea is to do it efficiently—and at the *same time* every day. This latter is crucial to the success of the exercise. That is because in doing it at the same designated time every day we begin to train ourselves to believe that we are truly and fully capable of *accomplishment*. As this is believed at deeper and deeper levels of the mind, such capacity for accomplishment can then be exercised toward greater and greater ventures in life. This power behind this exercise, in spite of its simplicity, should not be underestimated. Its power lies precisely in its consistency–much like Aesop's fable of the tortoise and the hare: the tortoise gets to the finish line first because he does not stop moving forward. In the end, it is *consistency* that creates results, not speed.

Once you have chosen your activity—for example, wiping the kitchen sink faucet for ten minutes—then make an agreement with yourself that you will do this activity every day for seven straight days, at the *exact same time* each day. That time could be 3:00 a.m., or 9:47 a.m., or 11:06 p.m., it does not matter; what matters is that you do not waver any day from the appointed time. If it is 9:47 a.m., then the faucet must be wiped—with attentive excellence—everyday day at precisely 9:47 a.m., for ten minutes. In addition to this, each morning as soon as you awaken, take a moment to visualize yourself wiping the faucet at 9:47 a.m. And, at the end of each day, before falling asleep, take a minute to mentally review and visualize having wiped the faucet that day at 9:47 a.m. The visualizing is important, even if your capacity to do so is limited.

The key here is *persistence*. If you are successful at doing all this for seven straight days, you will feel results. The manner in which such results manifest is different for each person, but the most common feelings are those of a sharper sense of decisiveness, more positive, uplifting energy, more wakefulness and increased vividness of perception. Eventually the exercise can be applied to more complex and challenging tasks, but in the beginning it is very important to choose something unimportant and simple that you are sure you will not fail at, so as not to incur the risk of failure and subsequent self-doubt and abandoning of the practice. The key to much in life is confidence. Confidence arises from the conviction that you can complete tasks, and complete them efficiently. As Gurdjieff once said, 'if you can do one thing well, you can do *anything* well'.

Thaumaturgy: Applied Intention (the Art of Manifestation)

The word 'thaumaturgy' derives from the Greek words *thauma* ('miracle') and *ergon* ('work'), thus technically meaning 'miracle worker'. More precisely, the word refers to the 'art of manifestation', via the ability to effect changes in one's psyche that, in principle, may in turn cause changes in one's personal reality.

Much hullabaloo has been generated in recent decades about the idea of using intention to draw things toward one, a practice popularly known as the 'art of manifestation'. The ideas behind this, much as with other esoteric practices such as 'astral projection', depend heavily on a Cartesian frame of reference: the idea that our mind is something distinct and separate from our body and does not conform to the same laws as the material dimension. If mind is truly a distinct agent, then it should be able to cause consciously intended changes in our immediate life circumstances, by more than mundane means.

The question as to whether this is in fact possible is contentious, mostly because those considering it often neglect to address the multi-leveled nature of reality. Put simply, at higher levels of consciousness the whole notion of 'manifestation' appears increasingly irrelevant as the assumptions it is based on begin to break down. That is, the Cartesian point of reference (mind distinct from matter, and, in theory, able to consciously manipulate it) does not appear to be valid at higher levels of consciousness, where the idea of division of any sort becomes increasingly difficult to uphold. The more the seamless interconnection of things is seen and understood, the less relevant the matter of 'creating my reality' becomes. Moreover, the belief in the existence of 'things', as discrete and intrinsically real objects, begins to break down as well, along with the belief in free will as exercised by us as apparent individual agents of causation.

However, to see and even understand a philosophical or spiritual idea is one thing, to be actually living it is entirely another. This has been the problem with spiritual models of reality for a very long time, and has only been addressed on the theoretical level within certain integral approaches to philosophy (for e.g., via Hegel, Sri Aurobindo, Wilber, and others). The level of egoic consciousness, the 'mesocosm', in which separation—the existence of 'me' as distinct from things around me—is manifestly real, is the level at which it is possible to draw things toward us. The theory and method itself is straightforward, but the realization of it is not. This is because of the disunity of the psyche, and in particular, because of interference from the unconscious mind.

The simplest analogy is that of an iceberg. We can imagine that this tip of the iceberg above the water corresponds to our conscious mind and its wishes and intentions, with the mass below (about 90 percent of the whole iceberg) corresponding to our unconscious mind. To further this analogy, if the tip above wishes to go to Hawaii for its vacation and the mass below is not signed up for this, but instead wishes to go to Antarctica, then it takes no great feat of reasoning to see that the whole iceberg will go south. It will certainly not get to Hawaii, not without the cooperation of the great mass below the water.

The above approaches manifestation from the point of view of traditional 'depth' psychology (as pioneered by Freud and Jung), where the unconscious mind is regarded as the key bridge to cross, as it were. From this perspective, manifestation is a practice of bringing about key changes in the unconscious, which in turn will cause outer changes in our life that reflect these changes. The result will be that things seem to come to us. There is another way to view the matter, however, and that is from the point of view of 'height' psychology (as pioneered by Assagioli and others), in which the 'higher mind', with cooperation from the unconscious, is regarded as the key level when effecting changes in our life. From this perspective, it is not so much a matter of 'bringing things toward us', as it is of attuning to the *already existing connection* between us and what we wish to have.

In the end, it matters less which from with approach we choose to view the matter. What is more important is that we face the deeper lessons of thaumaturgy. These lessons are about the psycho-spiritual lesson of *accountability*. The most difficult lesson of embodied life in a material world may be said to be that of accountability, and all the ways in which this singular lesson tends to appear around us. To be accountable, responsible, for our actions in life, and for the results that these actions generally lead to, is the hardest of all lessons, in part because it reveals all tendencies toward hypocrisy that we carry within. We can only find out what we are made of—what we carry within—when we put ourselves in certain situations. A 'magician' in the true sense of the word cannot hide from life, cannot renounce the world, because in doing so he never faces the particular lessons that will test his mettle. And hence the rub: there is no 'magic' in the conventional sense of the word. We cannot 'manifest' things magically into our life, by whatever arcane methods we may wish to employ, without facing the key lessons of accountability. There is no short-cut to paradise. There is no way to trick the universe (except in a Faustian arrangement where we buy a short-term vacation and are footed with a horrendous bill after that is beyond our means of payment).

To be accountable, to be responsible, ultimately reduces to one thing: to declare oneself a 'team-mate' of life. Ideas about being a separate agent who hovers mysteriously above the human race are immature longings to escape the lessons of accountability. The esoteric path frequently gets used as a means to avoid relationship with life in general, yet ironically, if the inner work is truly engaged, it leads us *toward* life, not away from it. In this regard, the key mantra to meditate on is 'avoiding relationship?'[5] 'Relationship' in this context refers to the totality of life; the idea is to examine all tendencies to use esoteric teachings as a means to justify recoiling from life, an inward contraction based on fear and self-doubt.

The Law of Attraction

The art of manifestation is based largely on the so-called 'law of attraction'. This has a simplistic moral foundation to it, part of which is the so-called 'Golden Rule', a teaching that has the unique attribute of being the only general principle that all mainstream religions agree on. Essentially, this rule states 'do to others what you'd have them do to you'; or, 'don't do to others, what you would not want them to do to you'. More simply: 'Treat others how you want to be treated'. Examples from religious texts include:

> Hinduism: *This is the sum of Dharma [duty]: Do naught unto others which would cause you pain if done to you.* —Mahabharata 5:1517

> Judaism: *...thou shalt love thy neighbor as thyself.* —Leviticus 19:18

> Buddhism: *Hurt not others in ways that you yourself would find hurtful.* —Udana-Varga 5:18

> Taoism: *Regard your neighbor's gain as your own gain, and your neighbor's loss as your own loss.* —T'ai Shang Kan Ying P'ien.

> Christianity: *Therefore all things whatsoever ye would that men should do to you, do ye even so to them: for this is the law and the prophets.* —Matthew 7:12 (KJV)

> Confucianism: *Try your best to treat others as you would wish to be treated yourself, and you will find that this is the shortest way to benevolence.* —Mencius VII.A.4

The Golden Rule is a generalized moral teaching; it does not apply literally in all cases. For example, we do not want to serve someone coconut cream pie if they do not like it, just because *we* like it. So we are not always literally aspiring to 'do to others what we'd want them to do to us'. The Golden Rule works best when understood as a teaching that points out how all things are connected and all beings are interdependent. Ultimately it is a teaching of non-duality, instructing us to remember that others are us in another form, merely seeming to be not-us.

Two humorous parodies of The Golden Rule are 'Who has the gold, rules', written by a world-weary merchant; and the more subtle distortion 'Do to others what they do to you', written by

Anton LaVey, author of the extreme antinomian *The Satanic Bible*. LaVey developed his idea further: 'Be kind to those who are kind to you, and wreck vengeance on those who cause pain to you' (a basic tenet within organized crime). As a primitive survival strategy his idea has some merit, but self-destructs in a civilized social context because it does not recognize a fundamental connectedness of all things. It assumes that the distinction between self and not-self is real and absolute, an assumption that lies behind much of humanity's collective suffering and madness throughout history.

The following are some general principles behind the 'law of attraction':

1. *We get what we focus on*. As touched on in Chapter 10 (the 'Principle of Reflection'), the universe is essentially a mirror-like 'yes-machine'. This means that the universe responds to the quality of psychic energy that we are putting out at any given moment. This principle directly schools us in the lessons of accountability. If we do not like what is coming toward us in life, we must become more aware of our unconscious motives. We must become accountable for our mind and its contents.

2. *The Law of Attraction is based on like=like*. We can call this X=X. In order to acquire something, we must *become* like that which we wish to acquire. In order for us to attract 'X' in to our life, we must—to some degree—*become* as 'X' is. On a simple common sense level, if we wish more love in our life, we must become more loving. If we wish more abundance in our life, we must become more abundant in both thought and action. If we wish more peace in our life, we must become more peaceful. And so forth. Because we must become like that which we desire, it is therefore clear that we must change. It is unreasonable to expect changes in our circumstances if *we* do not change. We must therefore make tangible demonstrations of change to our behavior, thoughts, intentions, and attitudes. We must make *effort*. It is here where we can begin to understand how such changes

cannot be brought about if our will, and capacity to make decisions, is not developed to some degree (see previous section).

3. *Inwardly reality is consciousness, and outwardly it is an appearance of energy (phenomena).* Energy is the essence of phenomena, down to what we perceive as the smallest sub-atomic quantum levels. We ourselves—the forms we appear in—are pure energy. Our energy can be thought of as carrying a particular 'frequency' that is a reflection of our thinking patterns (both conscious, and subconscious). The universe appears to 'send us' more of what our frequency is. For example, if we are thinking negatively, we will get negative circumstances. If we think positively, we get positive circumstances. This, however, is not to be understood superficially. Simply denying our negativity will likely do no good. Self-acceptance is the necessary prerequisite, in order to shift entrenched patterns in the unconscious mind that are, in effect, calling the shots.

4. *To change our frequency requires a change in our mind.* In short, we need to become more conscious. That is, the ability to choose or make decisions becomes very important. In life, our choices often reflect our reactions to situations. We have to progress from knee-jerk reaction, to conscious response. For that, consciousness is needed—a willingness to slow down inwardly, and become aware of context and perspective. Meditation is helpful for this.

5. *The task of changing our 'frequency' lies in grasping the nature of the subconscious mind.* In short, the subconscious mind is much larger and much more powerful than our conscious mind. In life we typically want something, but end up getting something very different, occasionally even the exact opposite. We claim we want something positive, but end up instead with something negative, and so on, due to the fact that the subconscious mind may have very different agendas and interests than our conscious mind. This will largely be related to particular forms of programming that we have

inherited from our family of origin, or have acquired along the way from various influences in our life. These particular kinds of programming are referred to as our core beliefs.

Due to the power of the subconscious mind, it is essential that we change our immature core-beliefs. When we are able to do this, the power of the subconscious mind then gets 'behind us', a state of being sometimes called 'being in alignment'. Some examples of negative core-beliefs are: I am afraid of success; if I am successful people will not love me; if I am powerful I may hurt people; my love hurts people; I am bad (guilty, etc.); I am ugly; I am stupid; I am inadequate; I do not belong anywhere; and so on. Each of these core beliefs has developed over time based on certain messages received at crucial points in our earlier years. To change them we have to alter the emotional context in which they were first imprinted. We do this by:

A. Mindfulness of the feelings connected to them (anger, grief, hurt, etc.), and appropriate cathartic (release) work connected to these feelings as deemed necessary (see Chapter 10).

B. Invoking a willingness to see ourselves or others as innocent, i.e., forgiving ourselves and others connected to these beliefs.

C. Creating a new 'program' via an affirmative attitude. While written or spoken 'affirmations' can be used—such as 'I enjoy the flow of abundance in my life'—they ultimately boil down to the willingness to cultivate an essentially enthusiastic attitude and passionate interest in one's life. (The word 'enthusiasm' originated from the Greek *entheos,* meaning to be 'divinely inspired'. In the 16th century the word had a derogatory meaning, suggesting a mentally imbalanced person who believed they were possessed by a god; by the 18th century it began to take on its current meaning, 'filled with zest for what one is doing'. In current times it has arguably become more important, owing to the ways in which modern technology can make life so easy for us that we see less need to generate energy from within. It is also, needless to say, counter to the tendencies of depression, something that is also endemic to current times).

Abundance

This is a more significant issue in current times, especially since the economic downturn of much of the Western world beginning in approximately 2008 (and continuing up to this writing in early 2013). Needless to say one needs capital to survive in a capitalist society. Money itself is an abstraction, a series of numbers on a screen or on a piece of paper, a means to an end; in itself it is rarely used solely for the sake of accumulation, but rather to acquire things or permit events to unfold. As such we do not, strictly speaking, 'manifest money'. What we manifest are particular patterns or situations that may (and often do) involve money. To change our relationship with money we must change our patterns and relationships with the world. For example, we may wish more money in order to experience a greater degree of success and the inner fulfillment that comes from that. In that case what must be changed is the view we have of success in general. We must change our belief-systems about success including those applying to ourselves ('I'm not worthy, undeserving', etc.) and others ('they're greedy and therefore I resent them', etc.). The idea of manifestation is to see ourselves where we want to be, but this 'seeing' will be ineffectual if we do not really want to change any of our inner patterns. It is here where the matter of accountability again raises its head. We cannot cause any significant changes in the pattern of our lives if we do not first assume responsibility for the contents of our mind. For example, it is unlikely we can 'manifest success' in our lives if we are too busy resenting successful people. The resentment will cause us to secretly (unconsciously) resist any movement toward success, because deep down we do not wish to be the same as the people we resent. If we resent successful people, it will be hard for us to become that.

Following the general Principle of Reflection, the keys to creating abundance involve the importance of altering our abundance-patterns by demonstrating *abundance-thinking*. This essentially amounts to *generosity* in its many forms.

a) Material. Give, donate (anonymously when possible—anonymous donations create more positive energy within in terms of self-image, which otherwise may be 'leaked' by seeking approval for one's actions).
b) Relational. Offer help to others as deemed appropriate.
c) Attitudinal. Demonstrate friendliness; not in a forced artificial way, but as a means of extending to the world. 'Esoteric' means, literally, of the 'inner'; to extend to others is a means of maintaining balance.
d) Giving energy. Being total in things, that is, giving yourself fully to whatever you are doing.
e) Counteract with-holding. It is essential to counteract with-holding. With-holding arises from resentment. We harbor resentments because of grievances. These grievances can be cleared with the forgiveness exercise (see Chapter 10).
f) Work! Success ultimately comes down to practical effort. It is possible, and relatively common, to use esoteric teachings of all kinds as an elaborate defense against simply working hard in life.

The Mechanics of Manifestation

1. *Claiming*. For this, we must be clear about what we want. We must be specific and positive, as the subconscious does not filter out the negative or past or future tenses. For example, we affirm 'I am wealthy', not 'I want wealth' or 'I don't want to be poor'. In the latter two cases the subconscious hears only the words 'I want wealth' (I am not wealthy) or 'poor'. Therefore we affirm in positive and present-tense terms.

2. *Awareness of resistance.* This involves the recognition that we are not an inwardly unified person, i.e., not all parts of us necessarily want what we consciously claim we want. Working with resistance requires a certain maturity. In some ways it is the 'golden key' to the entire process.

3. *Embracing the 'no'.* The idea here is to use the 'energy of no'. Whenever we claim something in life, an automatic 'counter-claim' arises, as the 'mesocosm' functions via duality and polarities. Put simply, for every positive affirming force there is a negative denying force. Correctly working with the denying force—the 'no' in us, our resistance—results in a reconciliation of both positive and negative forces, and a better chance of manifesting our intention. Therefore, we do not 'fight' from or 'fly away' from resistance; we rather directly face into and take responsibility for it. We use the energy of the 'counter-claim' that arises in reaction to what we have originally claimed we wanted, to become aware of and take responsibility for our resistance: our laziness, anger, greed, fear, and so on. 'This negativity is mine—I own it'. Doing so makes it possible to free up the repressed energies of resistance, and move beyond them into actual manifestation.

4. *Being 'total' in our decision.* Here we are making sure that the majority of our being is 'onboard' for what we have claimed we want, made possible by correctly working with our resistance.

5. *Create an affirmation.* One that directly addresses what we claim we want. This 'affirmation' need not be an actual written process (although that can be helpful). It is more properly a particular attitude that we acquire, one based on an outlook that acts *as if* what we desire is already here. This is a tricky stage that may seem too artificial, not to mention dishonest. In truth, however, it is addressing the part of our mind that gets bogged down by despair and lack of trust in the idea of 'Holy Plan' (see Chapter 9), the idea

that there is a greater unfolding of reality that we are part of. Affirming the reality of our position within that greater 'plan' makes us aware of the part of our personality that resists such affirmation, because it distrusts life and seeks to 'go it alone', thereby cutting us off from greater sources of energy. Affirmation/attitudinal work is a corrective to this type of resistance.

6. *Creating a mental image of what we want*. Here we spend a short time (five minutes or so) visualizing ourselves *already having* what we want. Doing so early in the morning and before going to sleep at night are usually optimal times for this practice. It is important to allow this visualization to be embodied, that is, engaging the emotional-sensation level of being. Doing so engages the unconscious mind, all-important if we are to have results.

7. *Letting go*. This step involves creating the space to allow existence to 'bring to us' our wish. This point is important because when we focus on our desire *too* much, a conflict is set up between the conscious and unconscious minds and the process is aborted, resulting in nothing happening. The expression 'if you want it too much, it can't happen', speaks to this. We have to find a middle ground—knowing clearly what we want, doing our best to change our thoughts and energy to match what we want (acting 'as if'), and then relaxing and allowing (rather than forcing it to come). Existence tends to fill up space. When we 'create space' between us and what we desire, we often get results.

Utilizing Talismans

A talisman is an object that is 'charged' via intention (which can include a ritual), and utilized as a focal point for the will. The purpose of the talisman is to influence the unconscious mind. The idea is that by simply keeping it around we will be reminded regularly of what we desire to manifest. This is important because the unconscious mind is the main engine behind manifestation. That becomes apparent when we see that things come to us only when we let go. In the letting go, we are allowing the unconscious to do its work.

Also powerful is a simple technique from sex magic (Western Tantra), in which we create a symbol that best represents what we wish to manifest. We then put it on the wall or ceiling near our bed. When making love with our partner, we keep the symbol in visual contact. At the moment of orgasm (or peak excitement), we simply look at the symbol. The idea there is that orgasm or intense sexual stimulation momentarily slows or stops our identification with the conscious mind, allowing the unconscious to be particularly receptive to receiving impressions. The symbol we have created can then 'penetrate' more effectively into the deeper levels of our mind, in theory increasing the effect and orienting our will toward the attainment of our goal.

The Meaning of Karma: Why Thaumaturgy Can Fail, and What We Can Learn From It

A point often left out in many teachings on manifestation is that there are different levels of 'karma' (cause and effect), and many of those levels are 'blind', that is, operating on old (sometimes *very* old) causes and effects that we cannot see. For example, there is a 'personal karma', but there is also a 'family karma' and a 'national karma'. A person may practice manifestation methods but achieve little in the way of results because the conditions in his or her country (national karma) override all efforts made. Or, the family history may have too much influence, thus sabotaging efforts. Ultimately, the deeper we see into the nature of our being, the more we understand the perfection of our different levels of karma, and how we are always in the right place at the right time, based on the unfolding of our soul's lessons (the idea of 'Holy Truth' discussed in Chapter 9).

Ultimately we do not engage in manifestation work to indulge personal desires. In fact what we are actually engaged in is a process of re-shaping our ego, to make it cooperate with our higher intentions. In the process of attempting to change ourselves so that the universe will respond differently to us, we learn about ourselves in a profound fashion. This self-knowledge is the true prize behind thaumaturgy. In that sense, our failures teach us more than our successes.

A Word on Ritual

Traditional rituals of Western high magic, such as those found in many modern books on the topic (most of which are deriving from the ritual templates of the late 19th century Hermetic Order of the Golden Dawn), are not covered herein, as this has already been adequately presented in numerous works.[6] Most rituals ultimately amount to forms of psychological cleansing, self-observation, and individual empowerment. They can be effective for aligning body and mind, via mindfulness, and are best done with a passionate attentiveness. Whether doing the Golden Dawn's Lesser Banishing Rituals of the Pentagram or Hexagram, the Gurdjieff Movements, Yoga *asanas* or *mudras*, or the forms of Tai Chi or Qi Gong, the point is to do it with excellence and totality. This results naturally in a quieting of the mind's repetitive internal chatter—leading naturally to 'creating space'—which in turn makes possible the expression (and liberation) of the deeper qualities of being that are generally obscured by the outer personality.

Additional Exercises

1. *Yogic control*. Sitting (on a chair, or cross-legged, or semi-lotus—back straight, but not rigid). Practice being physically motionless and breathing consciously in a steady, consistent, relaxed fashion for fifteen minutes, holding your attention in the pit of the belly. With practice, attempt to lengthen this to thirty or forty-five minutes.

2. *Zimzum exercise*: Sitting comfortably, imagine white light arising from within. Inhaling deeply, visualize this light filling up your

body. Then while slowly exhaling, imagine the light extending infinitely outward, filling the vast reaches of infinite space. Then, inhaling slowly, imagine this infinite light contracting inwardly, being drawn back into your body. Imagine that the vast space surrounding you is the field of pure potential, the creative womb of existence. Repeat this process for five minutes or so.

3. *Visualizing space.* As you sit, imagine a vast space within you. Relax into the sense of formless vastness. In that space, remain alert for thoughts when they arise. Train your attention on any thoughts that appear in consciousness. In so doing, the mind will eventually slow down and become quiet because your energy is being given to attention, not thinking. The quiet mind is the doorway to deeper states of consciousness.

4. *Visualization training.* Pick a simple geometric object, such as a square, triangle, or circle, of any color, and attempt to hold the image of it in your mind's eye for as long as possible. Initially this is difficult but it is a skill that can be developed with persistence.

5. *Guided exercise.* Seated in meditation, center yourself and relax. Visualize the color red. Try to see it for about thirty seconds. (If you have difficulty visualizing color, imagine a red object, such as an apple, or a traffic stop sign). Follow this with visualizing orange, yellow, green, blue, and purple, spending about thirty seconds with each color. When complete, imagine a staircase in front of you with twenty-one steps, descending. Imagine yourself walking slowly down these steps, counting them as you go. When at the bottom, imagine that you have arrived at a private sanctuary. This should be a natural setting of some sort (shoreline, forest, field, etc.). This sanctuary is your own private place and can never be infringed upon. It is a place for you to rest and rejuvenate. Once spending a period of time there, proceed to the another descending staircase. This one has twelve steps. Imagine yourself walking down it,

counting as you go. Once at the bottom, a small house appears about a hundred feet in front of you. Walk toward it, and enter it. As you do so, a light goes on in the porch of the house. The light will go out whenever you are not in the house. Once inside, proceed to a small room at the end of a hallway. In that room is a chair, desk, and screen (similar to a computer screen). The screen is an Oracle of limitless ability. You can ask it anything you want, and answers will be provided. Once complete, leave the house and ascend the twelve steps. Spend a short time in your sanctuary. Then ascend the twenty-one steps. Once back at the top, visualize the color purple, blue, green, yellow, orange, and red, in that order. After letting go of red, become mindful of your physical body, and slowly open your eyes. Write down an account of your experience.

6. *Sigil creation*. Construct a symbol that represents what you wish to manifest. The symbol should be sufficiently stylized and simplified so that it does not immediately remind you consciously of what it is that you desire. For example, 'I wish more material abundance' is first converted to a present-tense affirmation: 'I am abundant in all ways', and then shortened (following Austin Osman Spare's method) by removing letters that repeat, resulting in 'Iambundtlwysn'. The letters themselves can then be arranged into a symbolic glyph that when glanced at, would initially be incomprehensible. The idea is for the resulting symbol to bypass the conflicted and ambivalent tendencies of the conscious mind, and directly influence the subconscious. The symbol is then 'fired' by projecting it out into the cosmos—or more accurately, deep into one's subconscious mind—during a moment of mental quietude (such as during meditation, artistic rapture, sexual orgasm, etc.). This can be done by imagining the sigil being projected outward into space. To repeat a point stressed in this chapter, manifestation, the active principle of magic, only works when the conscious mind has *let go of the target of its desire*. This is best accomplished, following the 'firing' of the sigil, via engaging a familiar routine, absorbing hobby, or by creating a very

new distraction that traps your attention. What then follows is the activity of existence in bringing to us what is most appropriate for our lessons at that time. Very often this does involve receiving what we initially declared we wanted, although usually there is a hidden lesson accompanying it, and it does not always come in the form (or from the source) that we expected.

Chapter 13

Inner Planes Work: Lucid Dreaming, Dream Yoga, Astral Travel

> *If we cannot remain present during sleep, if we lose ourselves every night, what chance do we have to be aware when death comes? Look to your experience in dreams to know how you will fare in death. Look to your experience of sleep to discover whether or not you are truly awake.*
> —Tenzin Yangal

The esoteric traditions have always been based on the idea of hidden worlds behind worlds, so to speak, stretching back to Plato's notions of the 'Forms' behind physical reality, and further back to the ancient Egyptian idea of the *duat*, or 'underworld'. Modern esoteric terminology often refers to variants of these as the 'subtle planes'. They seem to correspond in some ways to certain categories of the unconscious mind as defined by Jung and Assagioli. These subtle planes (or inner dimensions) are understood to be naturally accessed not just at death, but every night in our dreams as well.

The inner work can be undertaken not only during the daytime waking hours, but also during the night when our bodies sleep. Inner work during this latter time is known variously as lucid (or conscious) dreaming, astral projection ('out of body experience' or 'OBE'), dream yoga, and so on. The purpose of such work is to advance our understanding of the nature of consciousness. Our time on this Earth in one lifetime is relatively short, so it makes sense to use what time we have to deepen our practice. Dream work is making use of the approximately 30 percent of our lives we spend asleep (which for the average lifespan amounts to about twenty-five years).

Lucid Dreaming

Lucid dreaming is *conscious* dreaming, that is, a dream where we can consciously self-reference—that is, we realize (at least some degree) that we are dreaming. There are different levels to that knowingness; some lucid dreams are profoundly vivid, where our conscious awareness is virtually equal to waking state reality; and others somewhat vague, dreams in which we assume that we are aware, but only realize upon waking that this 'awareness' was in fact rather dim. Most lucid dreams seem to be of the middling sort, where we clearly recognize that we are dreaming during the dream, but realize upon waking up that our lucid-dream state consciousness was slightly different in contrast to our waking state. For example, it can be common to have a lucid dream in which one seems to be fully aware that one is dreaming, but upon waking realizes that one did not consciously register the fact that the furniture in one's home was different in the dream in contrast to how it is in actual waking life. This may be mainly due to the sensory effects of the physical body being disengaged during the dream state, making it very difficult for the brain to accurately replicate our actual physical surroundings. Equally so, it may be that our mind is re-creating our physical bedroom on a subtle plane, in what amounts to a different version of it.

Etymologically, the word 'lucid' has nothing to do with dreaming. It derives from the Latin word *lucidus* which means 'clear', 'bright' or 'shining'. The term 'lucid dreaming' was first coined around 1913 by the Dutch psychotherapist Frederik van Eeden, but it was not picked up seriously until the 1970s–80s by Celia Green, Ann Faraday, Steven LaBerge, and others, all of whom used it to describe a dream where we know we are dreaming. Of course, dreams where the dreamer knows they are dreaming are not a 20th century development. Certain very old shamanistic cultures, such as the Australian Aborigines and their 'dreamtime', likely had their sophisticated practitioners. Tibetan dream yoga, which in part concerns lucid dreaming, was mentioned as far back as the 800s CE.

St. Augustine, in a letter dated to 415 CE, mentioned a lucid dream he had.

The challenge that all esoteric traditions have always had to tackle is the issue of what to do with the rational mind when seeking to explore the 'inner planes' (or depths of the unconscious mind). Carlos Castaneda—who himself wrote extensively about lucid dreaming in his (probably) fictional 1972 work *Journey to Ixtlan*, referred to the means of quieting the mind as 'stopping the internal dialogue' so that a fuller awareness can emerge.[1] But how do we do this? Many transformational practices are ultimately geared toward this, and that includes lucid dream work. Conventional psychoanalytic dream-interpretation involves using the rational mind to try to make sense out of symbols, which is worthy enough, but lucid dream work aims to takes it a step further to the point where we can *interact and converse with our own symbols*. That is, we can interact with the deeper parts of our mind; we can dialogue with normally inaccessible realms of our being. We become our own live, interactive dream book.

The Stages of Sleep

Most people follow the following sleep patterns, which have been understood since the 1950s:

We begin in stage one, light sleep (which registers as theta waves). This is that strange space we can fall into, in which someone may wake us and we are convinced that we were not actually sleeping. This stage generally lasts around five to ten minutes. We then go into stage two, which is about twenty minutes long, in which vital signs slow down. We then enter stage three (where delta waves begin), leading to deep, dreamless sleep.[2]

In some wisdom traditions (such as Vedanta) the stage of dreamless sleep is accorded great importance, recognized as synonymous with a purity of consciousness in which there is no subject-object duality—'consciousness without an object' it is also called. According to some of these traditions the reason we usually have no recall of this state upon waking is that our sensory attachments (via the physical body) and the deeply engrained belief that we are a separate bodily entity overrides our memory of the pure non-duality of stage three sleep, resulting in no recall—'I was not there' is the conceptual conclusion we form and simply take for granted. And in some respects this is true: we as we typically experience ourselves in normal waking consciousness were not in fact 'there'. (Something clearly *was* there, because we return each morning when we awake. But the 'disappearance' of the consciousness of the personality each night may be a good indicator that the personality is entirely mortal and limited to one life; if something survives, it is likely not the personality that is identified with the physical body).

We typically spend about a half-hour in stage three sleep. Curiously, stage three is followed by a return to stage two sleep, where we spend another twenty minutes or so. From there, we jump straight to stage four sleep, known as REM ('rapid eye movement'). This is the stage where most dreaming, including lucid dreaming, takes place. By the time we get to REM, about ninety minutes have elapsed. So, if we go to sleep at midnight it is unlikely we will dream much until about 1:30 a.m. (Dream-like visions happen commonly in stage one sleep, but this is not full dreaming). We then repeat this cycle several times through the course of the night. The first entry into REM sleep lasts only a short time, about ten minutes, but each subsequent ninety minute cycle results in us spending longer and longer times in REM sleep. For one going to sleep around midnight, the best chance to recall a lucid dream would be around 4:30–5:00 a.m., or toward the end of the sleep cycles in the morning, sometime between 6:00 and 8:00 a.m. As a result of this there is a correlation between lucid dream work and sufficient sleep. The probability of experiencing lucid dreams increases if we get at least six to eight hours of sleep, simply because the later REM stages tend to last longer.

Dream Recall

No dream work is possible without first developing dream recall—the ability to properly remember dreams. In most cases this takes some time along with consistent practice, although many people can dramatically improve their dream recall within a few weeks.

The simplest practice is to keep a notepad by the bed, and to write down our dreams as soon as we wake up in the morning (or middle of the night, if we prefer). Most people soon find out that the only real way to make this work is by having a note pad on our night table and jotting down dream details *as soon* as we wake (memories of dreams tend to fade rapidly). In the beginning it does not matter if most of the dream details are forgotten by the time of waking. Even jotting down a few memories of the dream is enough to begin strengthening dream recall. Most find that without the note pad there is little hope in getting dream recall happening. Because dream memories are so tenuous, it is helpful to have an 'anchor' to fix the memories. Note-pad writing is, for most people, such an anchor. Once we have begun to recall some dreams, we can set about attempting to induce a lucid dream.

Methods for Inducing Lucid Dreams

One of the best methods for inducing lucid dreams is to set some sort of task before going to sleep that serves to trigger lucidity during dreaming. A good example was Castaneda's method of attempting to find one's hands in one's dream—that is, setting the intention, just before sleep, that we will see our hands in our dreams. Also possible is to suggest that we will recognize absurdities while dreaming (such as our car suddenly flying, and so on—these are usually known as 'dream signs'). Some people have lucid dreams merely by thinking about them during the day, or reading material about them. However most need to apply some sort of practice that involves setting an intention immediately prior to falling asleep. The following uses the 'hand-finding' technique.

1. Before going to sleep, we make the suggestion that tonight, in our dreams, we will find our hands. That is, we will have a dream where we remember to look at our hands. This pre-sleep suggestion need not take long; about thirty seconds to make the suggestion ('tonight, I will see my hands in my dreams'). This should be accompanied by visualizing holding the backs of our hands up to our face.

2. Once we find our hands in our dream, this acts as a mnemonic device to trigger the realization that we are in fact dreaming. Prior to this happening we may have a number of dreams in which our hands are present (for example, dreaming of driving a car), which we realize only upon waking and reviewing the dream. Eventually we will have a dream where we remember, while still dreaming, that we are in fact dreaming.

3. A common result of realizing that one is dreaming is to suddenly awaken from the dream. To prevent this, the best thing to do is to keep looking at different objects in the dreamscape, but not to focus on anything for too long.

Some of the other main lucid dream induction methods (in addition to finding the hands, or feet, etc.) are as follows:

1. MILD (Mnemonic Induction of Lucid Dream): The idea here is that when we awaken immediately after a dream (in the middle of the night, or in the morning,) we are to recall the last dream we were having, and then mentally relive that dream—with the added factor of *imagining* that we are awake in the dream as we replay it in our mind. When we fall back asleep again, we stand a better chance of having a lucid dream. (Those who have seriously tried this method have reported a dramatic increase in lucid dreams, to the point where they can occur almost nightly).[3]

2. WILD (Wake-Initiated Lucid Dream): Here we try to retain

unbroken consciousness as we fall asleep. This generally only works in late sleep REM stages, that is, after we have already slept for several hours. Early morning hours (or afternoon naps) tend to be best for this approach. Methods to use can involve focusing on the breath, images arising in the mind, overall sense of the body, and so forth. These act as an anchor for self-consciousness, which can then be retained even as the body falls asleep.

Tibetan dream yoga (see below) focuses on WILDs, generating them via a visualization method—for example, visualizing a black dot, or a white dot, or a particular geometric or spiritual symbol—while falling asleep. Retaining our focus on the visual image helps to sustain awareness as we pass into sleep. We then end up with the interesting experience of our body being asleep, but not our awareness, as we pass into REM stage. This is sometimes experienced as 'sleep paralysis' (and is typically disturbing if we do not understand what is happening). Many quietly suffer from 'sleep paralysis' without understanding it; such people may have a marked capacity for dream-work.[4] On the physiological level, all that is going on with sleep paralysis is that our brain is inhibiting physical movement because we are entering REM stage. To dream of jumping out a window, and actually getting up and jumping out the window, would obviously not be good, so sleep paralysis is simply the brain's way of protecting our body while we dream.

3. WBTB (Wake-back-to-bed): The idea here is to abort our sleep a bit; that is, if going to bed at midnight, then wake up after five or six hours, stay awake for an hour or so, then go back to bed and use MILD or WILD method. This tends to result in the highest possibility of inducing a lucid dream.

Noticing Universal 'Dreamsigns'

'Dreamsigns' is the term coined by Stephen LaBerge[5] that refers to 'dream absurdities', those events that typically occur in dreams that would be nonsensical, or otherwise out of place, in our waking life.

Once recognized in a dream they can trigger the realization that we are in fact dreaming. There are several dreamsigns that are universal and seem to be true for most dreamers[6]:

1. *Electronics fail*: Electronics usually do not work or do not work correctly in dreams. No one knows why, but it could be because modern technology is so complicated the dreaming brain cannot duplicate it.

2. *Incorrect lighting*: Many times the lighting for a situation will not be correct. It will either be too dark or too light. Another noticeable dreamsign is that attempts to change the lighting do not work. Quick changes in light require recalculation of colors and shadows, which seem to be too much work for the dreaming brain. Shadows may also look distorted or go in the wrong direction.

3. *Deformation*: Animals, people, objects, and scenery often look strange in dreams. The object of attention tends to be larger than everything in its surroundings. Noticing anything misshapen should be a very obvious dreamsign, however it tends to be the hardest one to pick up on.

4. *Illegible Text*: Reading and writing tends to be difficult or impossible in dreams. If text seems blurry or jumbled together, it should be a clear dreamsign. Text may also constantly change and never appear to be the same message twice. This also works with digital clocks.

It is conceivable that the reasons for these 'glitches in the matrix' are not solely because of brainpower limitation, but also because of different laws operating in different dimensions. That is not necessarily to imply that these 'dimensions' are somehow completely distinct from our minds—they may truly be 'inner planes'—but that our conscious interface with these inner dimensions does not, and cannot, follow the laws of physics of our physical dimension. The attempt of our brain to 'override' these dimensional differences results in weird circumstances that we subsequently experience as 'absurd'.

Tibetan Dream Yoga and the Practice of the Night

Some schools of Tibetan Buddhism and the shamanistic Tibetan Bon tradition developed dream work to very high levels. In English these systems have been called dream yoga. Below is a simple technique adapted from the Tibetan Buddhist tradition[7]:

1. Before going to sleep, send out a few positive thoughts to others, wishing them well, etc.

2. Remind yourself that you will remember your dreams tonight. Tibetan tradition generally recommends that you lay on your side—women on their left side, men on their right side.

3. Repeat the following simple prayer:

May I have a clear dream. May I have a lucid dream. May I understand myself through dreaming.

Repeat this several times with sincerity (either out loud, or internally). Then visualize a symbol in your throat chakra. This symbol should be visualized in luminous red. You can use the English letter 'A'. Hold this visualization as long as you can as you fall asleep.

Tibetan dream yoga has a much deeper purpose than merely generating lucid dreams. The key idea here centers on the word *rigpa,* which translates as 'awareness' or 'knowing' and refers to our intrinsic nature, our true being, free of the confusions and projections of the mind. The inner work essentially boils down to differentiating *rigpa* from typical conceptual thought. The practice of dream yoga, in particular via the process of falling asleep consciously (what LaBerge called the 'WILD' method, and what Namkhai Norbu calls, in its more realized teaching, 'the Practice of the Night'), is a means by which to train ourselves to experience pure non-duality or unobstructed consciousness (*rigpa*), which is our 'natural state'. We can do this via dream yoga because each night when we fall asleep we are entering into a state of non-dual consciousness. We do not typically recognize it because we are so identified with objects and thoughts that we are unaccustomed to experiencing our consciousness *without an object to focus on*. By training ourselves to fall asleep while visualizing a symbol (such as 'A'), we can realize the state whereby our consciousness merges totally with the object. There is no longer 'me' as distinct from the object; there is simply pure consciousness, recognizing itself as separate from nothing.

It is worth noting in passing that there is an interesting correlation between the various stages of sleep outlined above, and the stages of the 'transition of consciousness' in the 'afterlife' realms as described in the *Bardo Thodol* (*Tibetan Book of the Dead*). The process of losing consciousness, the opportunity to recognize the true nature of the 'clear light', the loss of consciousness, and the subsequent 're-awakening' in the various 'bardos' within which one experiences complex visions based on one's 'karmic traces' (usually ending in rebirth), corresponds roughly to the process of initial sleep, deepening sleep, REM stage where dreams arise that reflect our personality qualities, followed by eventual waking up.[8]

Levels of Lucidity

Having a legitimate lucid dream is generally an unmistakable experience. Occasionally one may hear people who say 'I think I've had a lucid dream, but I'm not sure.' In those cases it is almost a certainty that their dream was not fully lucid (or possibly, their memory of it after was distorted, resulting in the doubt). In the vast majority of cases there is not the slightest doubt. The contrast between an average dream and a lucid dream is really akin to the contrast between sleep and waking up in the morning (or between a black and white photo, and one in color). The only difference is that this 'waking up' occurs while we are still in REM sleep and the dream is still going on.

It helps to recognize that there are several levels of lucid dreaming. The following six-level model is adapted from Robert Waggoner's *Lucid Dreaming*[9]:

1. *Pre-lucid*: This is the phase of noticing 'dreamsigns', what would be absurdities or impossibilities in waking life.

2. *Sub-lucid*: A vague recognition that you are dreaming, but lacking strong self-awareness. This might take the form of 'my car suddenly flew in the air, so I knew the dream could not be real'.

3. *Semi-lucid*: this is the first lucid-dream proper level. Here we know we are dreaming, but we still continue to follow the dream-plot without consciously altering the dream in any significant way.

4. *Lucid*: This stage is similar to the last, that is, we know we are dreaming; however here we make a conscious effort to control the dream by changing things in it.

5. *Fully lucid*: This marks a more advanced stage in which not only are we aware that we are dreaming, but we also have full awareness of what is going on in our physical life. That is, we can consciously recall and think about events going on in our physical life—'yes, I know that even though I am dreaming now, I have to pay this bill today, or that person spoke to me yesterday', etc.

6. *Super-lucid*: This is a higher energy level where all conventional interests are dropped in favor of spiritual states of consciousness.

For example, you might be lucid dreaming of walking in the market place. Suddenly you dissolve the market place in your mind and direct your attention to higher realities that might involve states like unconditional love, transcendent wisdom, communication with masters, etc.

That does not mean, of course, that only a dream where willful autonomy is exercised is a true lucid dream—for example, it is entirely possible and natural for an experienced lucid dreamer to 'do nothing' and allow events to unfold. But for most, such a *wei wu wei* (the Taoist expression for 'non-doing') is only truly realized after autonomy has been exercised. This is partly related to the importance of knowing ourselves via being in certain circumstances—a kind of variant of the old Mark Twain expression, 'I do not want to hear about the Moon from someone who has not been there'—where the Moon in this case represents the experience of free will (regardless of the ultimate nature of how real free will actually is).

The outline above is helpful to refer to, for a number of reasons. First, it suggests a natural evolution to how we experience lucid dreams. Psychologically, the biggest fear people tend to have around stage four lucidity (exercising control of the dream) is that somehow they will find out something about themselves that they would rather not know. For example, in exercising control in a lucid dream we may find out that we have certain desires, etc., that might surprise us. We may discover that there is a tyrant in us, or a manipulator, or we may find out that we have certain fixations, or we may unearth particular strong emotions or sexual desires, and so on. The reason all these may surface into awareness is precisely because the 'laws' of the dream world are much less constricting and limiting than the laws of physical reality. (Gravity being one simple example—we can fly unaided in the dream world).

Additionally, a common impediment to greater awareness in dream-state is the view that there is *something wrong* with achieving this greater awareness. Similarly, a common stumbling block to achieving greater empowerment and the ability to create things—both in dream life and in waking life—is the view that there is something wrong with doing so. This 'something wrong' judgment may be arising from moral, religious, or psychological conditioning. Either way, our dreams reveal the hidden sides of our nature. Mark Stavish put it like this:

> What we do in our dream life reveals who and what we are and who and what we have chosen to become. What we hide during the day comes out to greet us when we sleep, just as it greets us when we die. This is the biggest fear many instinctually know and seek to avoid...[10]

There is an old expression: 'to really find out the truth about someone, just give them a position of power'. In a lucid dream that power is potentially there, and we naturally seek to exercise it to some degree, not for the purposes of going 'morally astray', but simply for the purposes of self-discovery. This is necessary because we do not transcend the limitations of personal ego until we first see it, assume responsibility for it, and understand it. Dream work can be excellent in that regard in that all the risks associated with physical reality are not there. For example, if we decide to fly to Mars in a dream because the desire to do so is there, we need not repress the desire as we would have to do in physical reality, which does not support unaided space flight. More than one person lost their life via LSD seeking to exercise a similar desire, which could have been harmlessly experienced in the lucid dream state.

There are many benefits to dream work, and in particular, lucid dreaming. Here are a few:

1. *Economizing time.* We spend about 30 percent of our lives unconscious, asleep in our bed. As the Tibetan master Tenzin Wangyal once observed, we need not undertake a traditional three year meditation retreat; we need only undertake dream work over the span of one

decade, during which time we will spend about three years in sleep anyway. Why then not use this great amount of time that is otherwise simply forgotten?

2. *Bolstering self-esteem and counteracting a negative self-image* (the latter which, alongside chemical imbalance, is a prime factor in psychological depression). A common result of dream work is a greater sense of inner accomplishment. Lucid dreams in particular tend to yield a healthy sense of empowerment, especially in the beginning. As one goes further, a greater humility can arise as well, in that one begins to glimpse the vastness of the greater Self. This is especially so when we encounter 'independent agents' (as they are sometimes called) in a lucid dream. This is an element of the dream that appears to be completely out of our control. An example may be encountering some people in the dream, asking them questions, and they all replying in unexpected ways just as if they were fully discreet entities. In an ordinary dream that is commonplace, but in a lucid dream it is a very different kettle of fish. It can be both fascinating and humbling in a healthy way, particularly if some sort of control in the lucid dream state has been achieved.

3. *Creative realizations*. A common result of lucid dreaming is to realize creative potential. There are reports in the literature of lucid dreamers creating music in their dreams or solving difficult problems. Namkhai Norbu, after years of dream yoga practice, reported that during one retreat he had lucid dreams where entire texts containing lengthy teachings were revealed to him. He reported that even upon waking he could still briefly read the texts that appeared in front of him before they faded.[12]

4. *Therapy*. Lucid dreams can be powerful ways to resolve negative dreams or nightmares, by learning how to confront the issues in the dream and even dialogue with them. To dialogue with dream elements is something the psychologist Fritz Perls based much of his

work on (though doubtless some tribal cultures have done this before, via ritualistic re-enactment). This can be done in waking life as a form of therapy, but also in a lucid dream. For instance, during a typical dream in which one encounters a 'monster' of some sort, lucidity enables one to remember that it is just a dream-construct, and thereby overcome a fear. This in turn becomes a powerful metaphor aiding us in understanding the mind-constructed nature of our experience of reality—including our deepest fears.

5. *Spiritual realization*. Via lucid dreaming we can begin to see that all phenomena are interdependent with mind, which is in turn the underlying secret behind all manifestation practices (i.e., mind—in theory—can alter reality). However, the deeper point is that through lucid dreaming we can begin to see directly into the nature of 'naked awareness' (*rigpa*) itself, and see how it lies at the basis of all phenomena.[13]

Dreams show us how all phenomena are passing, or, in a sense, 'plastic'. This in turn helps us to reduce our attachment to worldly matters. According to many teachings it is excessive attachment to objects and possessions that lies at the root of most of our suffering in life. By learning how to be a bit less attached, we can go deeper into the nature of reality. In that sense, dream work is a kind of initiation chamber into the deeper mysteries of self. Additionally, there is the possibility in lucid dreaming of communicating with unknown or previously unrecognized sources of information and wisdom.

As touched on above, concerning the issue of control in lucid dreams, a significant element that ultimately appears in almost all cases of lucid dreaming is that of the 'independent agent'. This often happens when a degree of facility with lucid dreaming is reached, and we might become a bit overconfident, perhaps even arrogant, in our ability to manipulate dream elements. At that point a common occurrence is that something happens in the dream that is absolutely out of our control. A hand may come out of nowhere and grab us, or a person we are talking to might respond or act in some way that shows that we have no control over them, and so on. This idea was shown with the 'agents' in *The Matrix* movie series, where elements in the constructed world of the supercomputers could not be controlled, as they operated from a different 'order' of reality. These same elements have their equivalents in lucid dreaming as well, and may be seen to be part of the greater Self that is training the personal consciousness, bringing greater balance to it.

Lucid dream work can at times be frustrating, but as with all spiritual practice, the key is to persist. The book *A Course In Miracles* has a wise expression: 'An untrained mind can accomplish nothing'. This is certainly true with lucid dreaming as well. It requires a strong intention to succeed. Gurdjieff called a strong spiritual intention an 'oath to essence'. It is a firm decision to not waver from the intent to awaken deeper levels of awareness, whether in the dream state (lucid dreaming) or in the waking state (self-remembering).

Astral Projection (OBE)

This area has become controversial in recent years, with some neuroscience studies appearing to offer evidence that the traditional 'out of body experience' (or 'OBE'—known in occult lore as 'astral projection' or 'astral travel'), including that of 'autoscopy' (looking down on one's physical body), something acknowledged in many cultures throughout history, may be nothing more than an elaborate hallucination entirely caused by particular brain activity. (For example, experiments have been done where it has been found that direct stimulation of parts of the brain can induce an OBE). The general scientific consensus is that the OBE is a psychological phenomenon, an interpretation of a physiological event. Arguments have been presented to counter this view; one of the more impressive cases involved a woman who 'left her body' during surgery and observed a sophisticated medical tool being used on her that she later successfully described in detail, despite never having seen such an instrument before.[13] (Unfortunately these stories rarely ever prove anything, as the 'super-ESP' scenario always remains as a logical 'out'; that is, the possibility that all paranormal events are ultimately caused by some extraordinary psychic capacity that remains unknown).

So-called astral travel is commonly known in many shamanistic or pagan spiritual traditions. Popular ideas such as the shaman who can 'shapeshift' into an animal-form, or the stereotyped witch who flies on a broomstick, are likely metaphors for the OBE state or astral flight. Many Oriental traditions have long been familiar with the practice. In the modern West, astral projection was first written about in the early 20th century by Oliver Fox (1885–1949) and Sylvan Muldoon (1903–1969), but it wasn't until the 1970s that OBE material was presented in a very readable and cogent manner that resulted in much greater public awareness of it. This popularization was accomplished largely by Robert Monroe (1915–1995), a successful American businessman who in the late 1950s found himself spontaneously experiencing the OBE state. Entirely on his own he spent many years exploring it and developing his capacity go 'out of body' to a high degree. Along the way he wrote three eminently reasonable books on the matter and founded the now well known Monroe Institute of Applied Sciences in Virginia, which specializes in audio-visual technologies to induce the OBE. His first book, *Journeys out of the Body* (1971) remains a classic in the field.

The OBE state is not just common to esoteric literature; it is also common within the general public. According to research psychologist Jayne Gackenbach, about 58 percent of North Americans have had at least one lucid dream in their lifetimes. Of those (according to Steven LaBerge) about 39 percent have had at least one OBE experience. That suggests that possibly near 25 percent of all people have had an OBE (or perhaps more accurately, a memory of an OBE).[14]

Methods to Induce Astral Projection

In general, 'astral traveling' is a more intense activity than lucid dreaming and is not commonly engaged in even by practitioners of the esoteric paths. However, some people seem to have a natural affinity for it, and some experience it quite spontaneously. There are specific methods for inducing an OBE. As a general note of caution this work should only be attempted if we believe that we are reasonably grounded in our life, stable, and not given to excessively avoidance of responsibilities. Because the OBE state can be particularly vivid, it is not difficult to explore it to the point that one's life becomes more interiorized in general. Staying actively engaged with one's outer life is, in this regard, helpful.

There is a close connection between OBE and the WILD approach to lucid dreaming. In fact, the most reliable way to experience an OBE state is via the WILD approach—that is, awaken sometime during the night, or early morning, move one's body as little as possible, and pay close, mindful attention to what is happening naturally as we slowly slip back to sleep. If we can stay awake long enough to 'trick' our body into thinking that we are asleep, the body will become naturally immobile. We may at that point notice some interesting things, such as what seems like a form of 'energy vibrations' all around our body (a common, though not universal, experience). If we manage to stay alert and with this process, relaxing into it (and not giving in to any fear that arises), we will sooner or later experience a subtle shift in consciousness that may be accompanied by a vivid sense of 'exiting' the physical body in what seems to be some sort of 'energy' or 'dream body'.

No matter how spectacular or vivid the OBE is, it is still amounts to an altered state of consciousness, and in that sense is not much different from a lucid dream (even if the OBE experience itself can be radically more intense than a lucid dream and much more psychologically impactful). Given sufficient intention, the experience is not too difficult to induce for one who has already had success with lucid dreaming. There remains but the justification for it, beyond the value of mere exploration. The main purpose may be said to involve a general expansion of context and deeper recognition of the larger picture—and in particular, the role of the personality within this greater domain.[15]

The astral body or dream body is sometimes confused with the idea of the Body of Light (or Resurrection Body), which it is very distinct from. The idea of the Body of Light will be explored in the next chapter.

Part III

Lore

Chapter 14

The Body of Light

The notion of the 'Body of Light'—an idea found in some esoteric teachings where it is known via other terms such as the 'Resurrection Body' or 'Rainbow Body'—while allegedly a real form of subtle energy, is perhaps best understood as metaphor. As a symbol of transfiguration—total transformation of all impurities made possible only via enormous commitment and willingness to abandon all falsehood—it is prone to misuse, as all powerful symbols are. The ego-mind has its own version of the Body of Light, a material creation that can do deeds for us without any due risk of loss (material or psychological) on our part. This version of the Body of Light is material technology (reaching its ultimate consummation in the idea of the self-aware robot). The positive impact of science and its industrial revolution and the positive qualities of technology are so evident and pervasive that they need not be highlighted here, and nor is what follows any sort of naïve anti-materialism statement. Science and its rightful application clearly represent an indispensable stage in the maturation of human civilization. Nevertheless there is equally obviously a shadow-element to technology, and it is an area that relates strongly to certain esoteric teachings. In large part the occult tradition, including such branches as astrology, alchemy, and magic, were primitive forms of science, but they were (and are) something much more as well. They are disciplines for acquiring a right understanding of the relationship between self and cosmos, between mind and matter, between consciousness and phenomena. Science and technology attempt to accomplish the same thing, but the angle of approach is different, being concerned with keeping the subject (observing self) distinct from the object (what is observed, studied, measured, analyzed, harnessed, etc.).

Because the effects of technology are so powerful, they have the ability to interfere with certain forms of psychological and spiritual development. Devices—everything from the most basic tool all the way to a sophisticated computer that appears to come close to sentient awareness—always carry with them an element of risk, and that risk is far more insidious than the destructive power of a weapon. The risk may be characterized as a potential decline in the psyche's association with the higher spiritual realms.

Frankenstein: Prometheus Fallen

> *It was on a dreary night of November that I beheld the accomplishment of my toils. With an anxiety that almost amounted to agony, I collected the instruments of life around me, that I might infuse a spark of being into the lifeless thing that lay at my feet.*
>
> —Mary Shelley's *Frankenstein*

In the realm of literature, excellent metaphors for this whole idea were found in the writings of the turn-of-the-19th century Romantics and in particular in Mary Shelley's iconic novel, *Frankenstein*. This novel became the prototype of both the modern horror creature and technology run amuck. Its much later appearance in film (first in 1910, with Charles Ogle playing the monster) represented as good an example as any of the film industry's history of distorting, cloaking, trivializing, and sensationalizing legitimate and important ideas from the mystical and occult traditions. The story is unique in how its title—a name which refers to a fictional Swiss scientist (Victor Frankenstein) who creates a creature that he loses control of—long ago came to be confused with the creature itself. (The 1910 film version was made by the Edison Company, owned by Thomas Edison, the seminal scientist and businessman whose genius was behind the development of both the light bulb and the motion picture camera—a perhaps fitting link with main idea discussed herein).

Frankenstein, with its apropos subtitle, *The Modern Prometheus*, was written by English novelist Mary Shelley (nee Godwin,

1797–1851). She began the novel in mid-1816 at age eighteen and finished it a year later. (This is more impressive than it may sound. Between 1816 and 1817 she gave birth to two children, got married, and lost her half-sister to suicide). It was first published in 1818 when she had not yet turned twenty-one; this first edition was brought out anonymously. Her husband, the renowned poet Percy Bysshe Shelley, encouraged her writing and wrote the Preface. Mary Shelley was credited as author only in the second edition which was brought out in 1823.[1] A further revised edition was published in 1831, in which some of the language in the first part of the story was toned down.[2] The origin of the story lies in a series of meetings between Shelley, her husband Percy, the Romantic poet Lord Byron, and two others. The group had been reading and discussing German ghost stories in French translations, when Byron proposed that they all attempt to create their own ghost story. Mary Shelley initially experienced a block in her imagination and for several days was unable to come up with anything. One night she listened to her husband and Byron discussing the possibilities of galvanism and related matters. (Galvanism, a term coined in the late 18th century, referred to the idea of stimulating muscles via applying an electric current to them, and to the possibility of animating dead tissue via electricity).[3] Shortly after, Shelley conceived of her idea of the story of a scientist who constructs a living creature from derelict organic parts. The outline of the story came to her in a series of visions while she lay in bed unable to sleep, having fallen into a light trance state.

Some have attempted to portray *Frankenstein* as the first science-fiction novel, although in fact the book barely qualifies as science-fiction, as there is no real attempt at 'science' anywhere in its text, even the 'techno-babble' science typical of the genre; it rather leaps straight to the end result, the creation of the monster, thereafter being one extended commentary on the results of such a creation. The subtitle of the book, *The Modern Prometheus*, refers to the Greek god (one of the Titans) who brought fire to humanity by stealing it from Olympus, an act for which he was severely punished by Zeus.

The early 20th century occultist and artist, Austin Osman Spare, once defined magic as the art of 'stealing fire from heaven', a reference to the Prometheus myth.[4]

Shelley did not originally set out to write *Frankenstein* with any serious intention to express esoteric ideas; she simply wanted to write a good horror story. In her Introduction to the revised 1831 edition, she admitted, following her meetings with Percy Shelley and Lord Byron:

> I busied myself to think of a story—a story to rival those which had excited us to this task. One which would speak of the mysterious fears of our nature and awaken thrilling horror—one to make the reader dread to look around, to curdle the blood, and quicken the beatings of the heart. If I did not accomplish these things, my ghost story would be unworthy of its name.[5]

The novel, despite an initial mixed critical reception, was an immediate bestseller and grew to have lasting iconic influence. In addition and more importantly to our concerns here, the connection between *Frankenstein* as penned by Shelley, and the Western esoteric tradition, is clear. Shelley has the protagonist of her novel, Dr. Frankenstein, studying such major occult luminaries as Albertus Magnus, Agrippa, and Paracelsus. When Frankenstein sets about achieving his great creation (and ultimately, monster), he utilizes both science (chemistry) and alchemy. Shelley took this from Paracelsus' actual attempts to create an artificial man (see below).

That said, the general attitude of the book, as expressed by Victor Frankenstein, is progressive, and Shelley was very aware of the movement from mystical alchemy to practical chemistry. In the novel, young Victor discovered Agrippa's occult writings as a boy, and excitedly reported them to his father, who disapproved, remarking,

> 'Ah! Cornelius Agrippa! My dear Victor, do not waste your time upon this; it is sad trash'.[6]

Victor was unimpressed with his father's lazy and disdainful attitude, however, and he continued to study Agrippa, as well as Paracelsus and Magnus.

> 'I read and studied the wild fancies of these writers with delight; they appeared to me treasures known to few besides myself.'

But this thrill was not to last. Soon after young Victor witnessed an oak tree being destroyed by a lightning bolt, it just so happened that a man 'of great research in natural philosophy' was with him at the time, and he proceeded to explain to Victor some basics of electricity and galvanism. Victor was so impressed that for him, Agrippa and the occultists and alchemists and other 'lords of my imagination' were overthrown.[8] He then determined to devote himself passionately to the study of 'that science as being built upon secure foundations, and so worthy of my consideration'.[9] He later on is admonished by a professor of 'natural philosophy' (an early term for science) for having wasted time studying the nonsense of alchemists. But Victor's youth prevents him from becoming too rigid. He retains some suspicion about the merits of modern science, and is not altogether convinced about the so called fallacies of the occultists and alchemists. Concerning the contempt of his professors for the occult arts, Victor remarks, 'I was required to exchange chimeras of boundless grandeur for realities of little worth'.[10] To counter this, another of Frankenstein's professors proclaims:

> 'The ancient teachers of this science [the occultists and alchemists] promised impossibilities and performed nothing. The modern masters promise very little; they know that metals cannot be transmuted and that the elixir of life is a chimera.'[11]

Victor later on meets up privately with this professor, who revives his admiration and appreciation for Agrippa, Paracelsus and their kind, saying:

> 'The labors of men of genius, however erroneously directed, scarcely ever fail in ultimately turning to the solid advantage of mankind'.[12]

Victor then devotes himself wholeheartedly to the study of modern chemistry, at which he excels. He then learns how to vitalize and bring life to dead body parts, which in so doing, eventually leads to his creation of the monster, something he had originally hoped to be beautiful, but which turns out to be hideous. Disgusted, Victor abandons the monster. This monster is sentient, however, and is deeply confused, hurt, and angry at the isolated predicament he finds himself in. The rest of the novel basically centers on the monster's quest for vengeance (in so doing, murdering several people close to Victor, but not without first appealing to Victor to create a companion for himself, so as to relieve him of his great loneliness. Victor considers doing so, but decides against it). The novel ends with Victor, bent on destroying his creation, dying of illness on a boat in the Arctic. The monster is devastated by Victor's death, and vows to destroy himself. He jumps onto an ice raft, and disappears.

There are several important conventional themes in *Frankenstein*:

1. The creation of life and sentient intelligence by the human hand, employing science.

2. The loss of control of this creation, and a general reflection on the dangers of science without adequate conscience.

3. Reaction to appearances, and the power of perception to mold our experience. (Victor Frankenstein is initially repelled by the appearance of his creation, and cannot overcome this reaction, leading to his abandonment of the creature, and its subsequent desire to seek vengeance for this).

The esoteric themes in *Frankenstein* are also clear, if less obvious:

1. The need to distinguish between the inner sciences (occultism and alchemy in particular) and the outer sciences (chemistry in particular), by not confusing domains of experience and consciousness.

2. The esoteric meaning of the 'golem' and the 'homunculus'.

3. Overcoming mortality via the science of inner creation (the 'Body of Light').

4. The Gnostic theme of flawed creation, via the Gnostic myth of the Demiurge who created the universe, and the passive role of the 'true God'.

In the novel, young Victor Frankenstein initially embraced the occult arts, then waffles between them and modern chemistry, until finally coming over to the new science for good, leading up to the creation of his monster. The figures of occultism Shelley mentions in the novel were chiefly Agrippa, Magnus, and Paracelsus. Agrippa wrote his magnum opus *Three Books of Occult Philosophy* at around twenty years old, similar to the age Shelley was when she published the first edition of *Frankenstein*. Albertus had been a marked influence on two pillars of Western civilization, the Italian poet Dante (Mary Shelley was reading Dante when she was working on *Frankenstein*) and the Catholic theologian Thomas Aquinas (who had been a direct student of Albertus). In addition to being a religious 'authority', Albertus was a great scholar, considered one of the most widely learned men of his time. He is known to have embraced astrology as an occult science, although this is not unusual for his time, when astrology was held in the same esteem that astronomy is today. (An interesting folktale has been noted by some literary critics: Albertus allegedly discovered an alchemical elixir (a version of the 'Philosopher's

Stone') that he used to bring a brass statue to life. This statue, a type of robotic-servant, eventually learned speech but became a talkative nuisance and was, one day, destroyed by a vexed Thomas Aquinas with a hammer).[13]

Victor Frankenstein is very much modeled on the figure of the renowned alchemist Paracelsus (and to a lesser degree, Agrippa). And as we shall soon see, that connection is no accident, as Paracelsus had an interest in the creation of the artificial entity—an idea bearing notable resemblance to Shelley's monster—known as the homunculus.

The Homunculus

The term 'homunculus' is Latin for 'little human'. Its origins are connected to the idea of a miniature, yet fully formed, life form. The key here is the philosophical notion found in early biology called 'preformationism', which is the idea that the *form* of an organism exists first, in miniature (a sort of physical parallel of Plato's idea of the prototypical 'forms' that exist as archetypal templates on subtle, invisible levels of reality). For example, preformationism held that inside of a sperm cell a tiny, fully formed human body could be found. It was speculated that when the sperm entered a woman, this 'tiny human' simply grew into an infant eventually ready for physical birth. However, someone eventually deduced that if this tiny person (homunculus) was fully formed, it too must possess sperm which in turn would contain yet more little fully formed human bodies (homunculi). As in the Hindu myth of the world being supported on the back of a turtle, it would then be 'turtles all the way down' (what supports the turtle? Another turtle, and so on). Such an idea is, naturally, absurd. This in turn extends to something called the 'homunculus fallacy'. It is the idea that we cannot truly argue that a 'person' exists inside of us deciding which thought to have at any given moment. For example, we think of a tree. Where did this thought come from? From the 'person' inside of us who decided to have this thought. But then how did this 'inner person' come to create the thought that we as the 'outer person' register as 'thinking about a tree'? It must be because there was a yet 'smaller' person inside of the 'inner person', deciding to think about a tree. And so on, *ad absurdum*. Clearly, there must be a point where the thought of a 'tree' simply appears, without being generated by any 'inner person'.

The idea of the homunculus is found in Renaissance-era alchemy, and in related fictional works such as Goethe's *Faust*, where Faust's student (Wagner) creates a homunculus to perform certain tasks. Goethe likely got the idea from Paracelsus who made mention of it in his writings. Paracelsus had laid out a primitive formula for creating a homunculus, based on a mixture of putrefied semen, horse manure, and human blood. As a proto-scientist he was attempting to show that he could create life, and useful life at that (not dissimilar to a modern engineer constructing a robot). In so doing, he was trying to naturalize the supernatural approach to the creation of magical creatures. (On the physical level he of course failed. In 1859 Louis Pasteur proved that spontaneous generation—a developed life-form arising from inanimate matter—is impossible).

The Golem

The idea of creating an artificial person from dead matter has a precedent in a number of old magical traditions, but was especially developed in the Jewish mystical tradition, where such a creation was called a 'golem'. (The name of Tolkien's strange creature from *The Lord of the Rings*, Gollum, was probably taken from this). The word translates from Hebrew as 'shapeless mass' or 'imperfect substance'. The typical idea of the golem, as originally found in Jewish magical folklore in 13th century Germany, was that it was an artificial life form created to serve a magician or wizard. The modern technological equivalent of this would be a robot or machine constructed to serve a human. Some of the old Kabbalistic sources maintained that the golem could be given vitality by a human, but not 'spirit' or 'soul', a view that would seem to accord with comparisons with modern-day robots.[14]

The golem was believed to be activated by the power of specific magical words and deactivated in a similar fashion. Some legends had the Hebrew word *emet* ('truth') inscribed on the forehead of the golem, which activated it; in order to deactivate it, the first letter (*alef*) of the word *emet* was removed resulting in the word *met* ('dead'). (The usage of special words to activate/deactivate the golem is reminiscent of the code-writing behind computer programs). According to Gershom Scholem, there is no real evidence from any of the early sources that the golem was used for any actual practical purposes. It was viewed more as a symbolic act of creation, a demonstration of mastery of inner power brought about by mystical awakening.[15] It was in some respects similar to Paracelsus's attempts to create a homunculus, and thereby demonstrate 'God-like' powers.

In the Talmudic tradition, Adam was recognized as the first 'golem', until his body was instilled with a soul. (In Genesis, the first human, Adam, is created from earth and breath. God fashions him from the dust/mud/earth, and then breathes life into his nostrils. The earth is the body; the breath is Spirit/soul/consciousness). The word 'golem' occurs once in the Hebrew Old Testament, in Psalms 139:16. The English translation is:

> Thine eyes did see my substance, yet being unperfect; and in thy book all my members were written, which in continuance were fashioned, when as yet there was none of them. (KJV)

The Contemporary English Version offers a more comprehensible if less poetic translation:

> but with your own eyes you saw my body being formed. Even before I was born, you had written in your book everything I would do.

It is an homage to God, as the supreme Creator of life. It refers to the ultimate mystery, the creation of life from non-life; or the creation of something from nothing. This interpretation gives the key to a closer understanding of the spiritual meaning behind the symbolism of the golem or homunculus; and by extension, with the debasement of the idea, symbolized by Frankenstein's monster.

In the iconic 1969 science-fiction film *2001: A Space Odyssey* (one of Stanley Kubrick's masterpieces, based on a short story by Arthur C. Clarke), an advanced supercomputer, called HAL9000 ('Hal' for short), accompanies a small squad of astronauts on a lengthy journey to Jupiter. Hal eventually malfunctions and turns against his masters, killing all but one. The remaining astronaut successfully deactivates Hal toward the end of the movie, before himself going on a journey through a type of 'stargate' or inter-dimensional portal. Hal is the classic modern (or futuristic) version of the technological 'golem' gone bad. Mary Shelley's tale has been seen by some as a morality play cautioning against the dangers of aggressive and single-minded 'masculinist science'—a speculation finding some support from the fact that Shelley's mother, Mary Wollstonecraft (1759–97) was a founding figure of modern women's liberation (her best known publication being *A Vindication of the Rights of Woman*).[16] But Shelley's fable ultimately points toward something more subtle than that.

Resurrection and the Body of Light

The Jewish golem and the alchemical homunculus have in common the idea of artificial creation, and in specific, the ambition of a human creator to attain God-like power via the act of creating a person, or person-like entity, himself. It symbolizes, in some respects, the culminating act of the magus or wizard: *to co-create with God*.

In many Gnostic and esoteric traditions a serpent, or specifically, *the* serpent from the Book of Genesis, is understood to be a key teacher. According to these teachings the serpent is a figure much maligned in many mainstream religions, where it is confused with an evil principle involved in misguiding the human race. A key to all this can be found in the well-known section of Genesis where God warns Adam and Eve not to eat a particular fruit in the Garden of Eden. Eve goes so far as to report this warning to the Serpent, adding that God specified not to eat fruit from the specific tree in the middle of the garden. The Serpent then takes it upon himself to countermand this edict, declaring,

> ...You will not surely die. For God knows that in the day you eat of it your eyes will be opened, and you will be like God, knowing good and evil. (KJV, 3:4–5).

This passage as well as any captures the underlying aim of the magical, occult, and esoteric traditions. Ideally, a wizard is a 'wise person'; a magus is one who serves the divine by being attuned to it. Even the Eastern term 'swami' means 'lord of himself'. The point of the esoteric path is to confront, embrace, and master all elements of oneself, in so doing awakening to the highest principle of being ('higher self', 'soul', Holy Guardian Angel, etc.). It is this idea that also lies at the most root of the most common objection to the esoteric path, i.e. that it ultimately is a manifestation of pride, a desire to attain power.

The famous Hermetic maxim is *as above, so below* is understood to denote many things, but above all it refers to the idea that a person is a miniature image of God, holding latent within all the potential of the divine. Recall from our discussion above that the homunculus is a miniature version of a person. In the Hermetic view, a person is therefore a type of 'homunculus of God'. A person is created by God; so too a wizard can create a life-form, and thus demonstrate God-like capacity. This, however, is the corrupted or debased understanding of the Hermetic principle, and Mary Shelley provided a vivid allegory of what happens when this debased principle is pursued single mindedly.

The *untainted* esoteric element found in latent form within

Shelley's *Frankenstein* is the idea of the creation of the 'Body of Light'. This is a concept that appears in many esoteric traditions, both West and East. It is generally connected to the intention to enable easy transition for the soul, after the death of the body, in the journey through the Afterlife and beyond. It was the ancient Egyptians who created an entire religion around the idea of conquering death, most clearly shown in the myth of Osiris, the resurrected god. This idea of resurrection appeared in other traditions, but most essentially in Christianity, in the mythology of Easter and the legend of the risen Christ and his 'ascension body'. Christ's Body of Light was suggested in the well known 'transfiguration scene' (Mark 9:2–3):

> Now after six days Jesus took Peter, James, and John, and led them up on a high mountain apart by themselves; and He was transfigured before them. His clothes became shining, exceedingly white, like snow, such as no launderer on earth can whiten them. (KJV)

The idea of the Body of Light is also found in Eastern traditions. Tibetan Buddhism refers to it as the 'rainbow body', so-called because at the time of death of one who has attained it, lights and rainbows may be observed. To achieve the rainbow body means that the highest realizations have been attained while still in physical form, leading to the transfiguration of the material body into a form of pure light that enables one to travel freely throughout all dimensions.

The Body of Light has been confused at times with the 'astral body', but it actually denotes a very different idea. In most esoteric teachings all people are regarded as having an 'astral form', but not a Body of Light. The latter can be thought of as a form of highly rarefied energy that is created. We are not simply born with it. (The Greek-Armenian mystic G.I. Gurdjieff was likely referring to this when he maintained that we are not born with a soul, but rather must create one by our spiritual practices). Above all, the Body of Light represents the ability of awakened consciousness to exist independent of materiality and fixed forms.

Dolores Ashcroft-Nowicki described it this way:

> ...There is another form used by some magicians, the Body of Light. Some think that it is the same as the astral body, but it is in fact quite different. The astral is an etheric form common to everyone, a [Body of Light] is acquired through practice and concentration. The Body of Light is deliberately built for a purpose...it is not easily formed, some people never manage it, or at least not fully, and once it is formed it can be troublesome, and requires firm handling.[17]

Her last remark—'it requires firm handling'—might seem peculiar, since surely such a form can only be achieved by one who reaches an advanced state of awareness? In theory, yes, but in fact her caution is valid, because the idea of the Body of Light can certainly be corrupted—much as what happened with the protagonist in Mary Shelley's novel.

On one level, the Body of Light can be thought of as symbolic of the accumulation of our purity of intent. It is the 'vehicle' that enables our return to primordial unity with the source of consciousness. It is the 'inner body' of wisdom and awakened consciousness. The polar opposite of this—what may be called the debasement of the principle of transcendence—is an artificial 'outer body'. In effect, a monster. The Body of Light, or the Resurrection Body, is based on the essential idea of the spiritualization of matter. This is ultimately brought about not just by pursuing arcane esoteric practices, but more importantly by mastering our lessons on planet Earth. We do not 'graduate' to higher levels of being by escaping this world, but by embracing our lessons in total.

Gnostic Wisdom

The 'golem' carries profound symbolism, and this can perhaps best be understood via certain Gnostic ideas around the creation of the universe. According to most Gnostic traditions, the 'true God' did not create the universe. It was created rather by a lesser being, an archangel named Ialdabaoth, who is sometimes identified with Yahweh of the Old Testament. Most Gnostic traditions have Christ entering the world as cosmic Redeemer, enabling souls 'trapped' in the matter of this 'flawed' universe to return to the primal and perfect Unity of the true God.

What do we make of this seemingly strange myth? At quick assessment, it's not difficult to sympathize with the reasoning behind it. It will be apparent to at least some objective observers that the universe is anything but 'heavenly', based as it is on cold laws of physics and equally harsh biological realities (such as organisms being required to eat other, often protesting, organisms in order to survive). Destruction and death is part of the fabric of our reality. It is perfectly reasonable (whether true or not) to argue that a 'perfect' God would not create such a reality.

But that does no good for the existential reality we find ourselves in. We have to 'deal with' the life we are living, and the universe we find ourselves part of—warts and all. That said, the key point is to understand how we *are* in fact 'dealing with' this reality. How exactly do we construct our perception and experience of it, and how exactly are we comporting ourselves within this constructed experience?

To generate delusions and illusions with faulty thinking is, in effect, to create a 'monster' reality in which to live. Gurdjieff referred to this as 'the terror of the situation'. In short, most of us are either asleep or crazy, or some combination of both. The reality we have constructed, both individually and collectively, is a pitiful semblance of our almost limitless potential. For most of us there is nothing 'spiritual' about our actual existence, and that is true even for many who fancy themselves on some sort of 'spiritual path'.

The monster in *Frankenstein*, grimacing and angry as he stumbles about seeking revenge on his neglectful master, can be seen as a type of allegory of our generally debased spiritual condition, as well as our unconscious attitude toward God (and even lesser symbols of authority). In conventional Western religious paradigms (Judaism, Christianity, Islam) God is absolutely external to the personal self, even from the 'soul' of the individual. From this perspective, there is no room—none at all—for negotiating any sort of 'oneness' with God. The only approach to the Lord is via surrender, or more pointedly from our egocentric perspective, via submission. Apologists for this position argue that our egocentricity is too 'hardwired' into us for any other approach to work. The Lord created us, and we must never forget this. 'You shall have no other gods before me'.

The Western esoteric traditions generally propose a different paradigm, one that describes reality ultimately as non-dualistic. That is, our true and ultimate nature is at one with God. The ultimate purpose of the 'spiritual path', via whatever route and whatever disciplines, is to realize this non-duality. Most of the esoteric traditions do acknowledge, however, that this path is extremely difficult to navigate successfully to the end, being fraught with the temptations common to the egocentric self, and with the sheer difficulty of facing up to the depths of our egocentricity (necessary if we are to overcome it and penetrate the 'veil' between our conventional self and our divine condition).

We are not here concerned with comparatively evaluating the pros and cons of the orthodox religious paradigm (God as the supreme separate Being) or of the esoteric paths (we *are* God at the inmost core of our being). What is more revealing is to see the ways in which spiritual paradigms (including all grotesque distortions) are propagated in society by means other than standard religious education.

Memes and the Monster Legacy

A 'meme' is an idea that transmits within society from person to person (the term was coined in 1976 by the biologist Richard Dawkins; he derived it from the Greek *mimema*, meaning 'something imitated'). It could be said to be a type of education via word of mouth. Any self-employed person knows that the most effective form of advertising is word of mouth (as does any large-scale corporation, despite how much they may spend on standard means of advertising). Along with fictional literature, the movie industry has always been a powerful generator of memes, and in our current age of advanced communications and social networking, memes appear and disappear on a weekly basis (and some of them even stick).

Certain memes generated by the movie industry have effectively worked to obscure teachings from the esoteric traditions. The original monster from Shelley's book was talkative and intelligent, and able to move quickly and fluidly. The movie monster, deriving from Boris Karloff's stiff-limbed lumbering and hideous behemoth (first shown in 1931), appears anything but. Shelley's monster was sensitive and introspective (and literate; it had even read Milton's *Paradise Lost*), and its main quest was for love and union with a mate. From the beginning of its creation it experiences nothing but rejection, first from Dr. Frankenstein, and later from every other human it meets. This constant rejection leads the monster to vengeance and murder. In the 1931 film the monster is mute, and remained more or less so in all subsequent sequels. What was originally an allegory about misguided creation, rejection, vengeance, and a vexing and troubling quest for meaning, became, via the Silver Screen filter, an exercise in base fear and primitive aggression. Shelley's thoughtful and sensitive creature descended into a murderer in her novel, but it was fundamentally intelligent—and had been created by a man who was versed in both science and the mysteries of ancient occultism. The movie monster was mostly a vehicle for freakish frightfulness.

The Frankenstein myth has spawned many modern versions of the golem or closely related ideas—a good example being *The Norliss Tapes* (1973), an obscure (but memorable) horror film about a writer who, while researching a book, is contacted by a recently widowed woman. The woman's husband, an artist, has been 'coming back to life' recurrently as a grotesque zombie. In between his zombie night-prowls and his retreating back to his crypt by day, he is creating a type of golem—an artificial man constructed from clay. The zombie-husband works on this golem right up to the end of the film when he and the golem are destroyed by the private investigator who traps them in a circle of blood and fire. Vague references are made a few times in the film to ancient Egyptian mythology, but these are never elaborated on (much how Shelley never elaborated on the occult teachings of Agrippa or the alchemy of Paracelsus).

Technically speaking, Frankenstein's monster was not a zombie, as a zombie is a corpse brought back to life. Frankenstein's monster was never a whole life form; it was a revived amalgam of a number of dead parts. But the relation between the two is very close and the shared symbolism is clear enough. A zombie is brought to life via occult means; Frankenstein's monster arose from Victor's science which was so obscure, it was in effect *occult magic* (recalling Arthur C. Clarke's famous proclamation, 'any sufficiently advanced technology is indistinguishable from magic'). The zombie-notion of the dead 'returning' to life is of course not an invention of 20th century Hollywood. It was famously depicted as far back as the New Testament, in the scene immediately following the death of Jesus on the cross:

> Jesus, when he had cried again with a loud voice, yielded up the ghost. And, behold, the veil of the temple was rent in twain from the top to the bottom; and the earth did quake, and the rocks rent; And the graves were opened; and many bodies of the saints which slept arose, And came out of the graves after his resurrection, and went into the holy city, and appeared unto many. (Matthew 27:50–53).

There was also Jesus' revival of Lazarus, and the ascension story itself. In all cases, the 'dead returning to life' has two essential meanings: the spiritual, which has to do with awakening from the realms of ignorance via conscious work on self, and the refinement of one's inner energies as a result; and the debased version, which is the mere manipulation of matter, minus any introspective element.

Prometheus, Lucifer, and the Divided Man

Prometheus is the archetypal 'overreacher', in the mold of Lucifer, one who seeks and obtains great power, only to be consumed and destroyed by it. In the Greek myth Prometheus tricked Zeus in a misguided effort to challenge him, which resulted in an angry Zeus with-holding fire from humanity. Prometheus then 'stole fire' from Olympus and gave it back to humanity, which enraged Zeus further. He responded by sending Pandora, the 'first woman', to wreak havoc on humanity as retaliation. Pandora was alleged to have been created from 'clay' (much how the Sumerian goddess Ninhursag was believed to have created human beings from clay). Later myths have Prometheus himself fashioning the human race out of clay. Prometheus is considered a champion of humanity, but also a trickster figure who is ultimately something of a mixed blessing.

Percy Shelley himself was involved in the writing of his renowned play, *Prometheus Unbound* (published in 1820) around the same time that his wife was writing *Frankenstein*. For Percy Shelley, Prometheus was more hero than trickster. In his play Shelley reworked the Greek myth and had Prometheus overcome Zeus, symbolizing the victory of intelligence and human creativity over heavy-handed institution and tyranny (as represented by Zeus). The Romantic poets—Shelley, Keats, Byron, Blake, Wordsworth, Coleridge, etc.—exalted the idea of the rebel who opposed the rigid and passionless ideals of the Age of Reason and its spawn, the industrial revolution.

There are important connections between Prometheus, Satan of Milton's *Paradise Lost*, and *Frankenstein*. Mary Shelley, as with her husband and other key Romantic poets of the time (such as William Blake) accorded great importance to the figure of Satan in Milton's epic poem (published in 1667). Some critics have advanced the idea that Dr. Frankenstein corresponds closely to Lucifer—a true rebel seeking to establish his own utterly unique identity via his radical experiments and creation—and that the monster is an analogue of Satan. The transformation from beauty to ugliness was described by Shelley giving voice to Victor as he beheld his hideous creation:

> I had worked hard for nearly two years, for the sole purpose of infusing life into an inanimate body...but now that I had finished, the beauty of the dream vanished, and breathless horror and disgust filled my heart.[18]

In one respect, this passage is the most important in the book, for reasons we will now delve into. A central understanding of *Frankenstein* is that the monster and its creator are two elements of the same self. Some earlier literary critics observed that the subtitle of the book—*The Modern Prometheus*—underscores the essential split in Man (a split that, according to critic Harold Bloom, was very evident in Shelley's husband Percy Shelley and in Lord Byron, her two greatest influences).[19] What is the nature of this 'split'? Many critics who mention it (including the famed Bloom) do not really explain it closely. Vague allusions are made rather to the dual nature of Prometheus (who, like the Trickster figure, is both helpful and a hindrance—retrieving fire from Olympus to aid humanity, but angering Zeus in the process who then vengefully brings more suffering to humanity). Sometimes the 'split' is grossly simplified as between that of the 'head' and the 'heart'. But these skirt around the main issue, which is the split between spirit and matter, and more specifically, the division between *consciousness* and *perception*. Dr. Frankenstein rejects the creature that he has created for what is, in truth, a rather ignoble reason: because the creature is ugly. Or, more to the point, because he *perceives* the creature as ugly—'breathless horror and disgust filled my heart'.

Mystics throughout history have recognized that attachment to sensory perceptions is the great distraction that keeps us chasing rainbows in material reality, keeps us busy engaged in an interminable game that always has the same overall result: we remain oblivious to our higher spiritual potential. What is this higher spiritual potential? What most wisdom traditions agree on is that it boils down to the direct recognition of our inmost nature as pure consciousness. The power of sensory perceptions is that they have the ability, in conjunction with our mental processes, to 'construct' a reality in which we come to believe that our nature is separate, discrete, and fully and utterly contained within, and limited to, physical form. In short, we *come to believe that we are nothing more than our body*. If we believe that about ourselves, it is natural to believe that about others. If Victor flees his creature because he visually perceives him as hideous, it can only be because Victor automatically believes that the creature *is* intrinsically hideous. After all, how could this monster be anything other than his grotesque outer form?

That may seem obvious within the context of a horror story, or even within a story of science (or magic) gone bad, but the more subtle point is that we are all engaged in the process of 'making real' our perceptions of reality to the point that we lose all awareness of the *one who is perceiving*. Much as a movie-goer sits awestruck or lost in the movie they watch, marginally (if at all) conscious of themselves as watcher, so too we lose ourselves in the contents of our life, rarely aware of our actual nature as the consciousness that is witnessing all this—much how we lose all awareness of ourselves as dreamer at night, lost completely in the 'reality' of the dream content.

The Egyptian Mysteries and the Second Death

As discussed in Chapter 1, an idea that crops up in many esoteric teachings is the idea of the 'second death'. This is connected to the view that a human is essentially a threefold structure: body (matter), soul (individuality), and spirit (formless consciousness). According to most esoteric doctrine, when a person dies their material body decomposes and is dispersed. Their subtler aspect (mind and spirit) then enters a type of 'in-between' dimension referred to in different ways—the Pyramid Texts of ancient Egypt called it the 'realm of Osiris'; Plutarch of 1st century C.E. Greece designated it as the domain of the Moon (or 'sublunary'); in Christian tradition it is 'purgatory'; in the *Tibetan Book of the Dead* it is called the *bardo* ('intermediate state'), and so forth. What most of these traditions agree on is that a person who has shed their physical body spends a period of time in this 'in-between' dimension undergoing various forms of purification (though according to Tibetan Buddhism, this really amounts to an elaborate dream-world in which we experience the momentum of our habits and various delusions). The 'second death' occurs when our time in this in-between realm is complete, and we pass on to the higher realms, which are sometime connected to the 'Celestial', or the Sun. (Some of these traditions have the essence of the person directly reincarnating into a new body on Earth without ever passing on to the 'higher' realms).

The idea behind initiation, or work on self, or creation of the Body of Light, is ultimately connected to the idea of experiencing the 'second death' in advance—*while still alive on Earth*. In so doing, the person can pass with greater ease through the intermediate realm after the death of the physical body, and so proceed to the Celestial realms of unobstructed consciousness, light, and freedom, bypassing needless suffering and struggle.

The ancient Egyptians in particular provided a comprehensive model of the soul of a person, viewing it as comprised of nine important aspects. These were called the *khat* (body), *ku* (reason), *khaibit* (shadow), *ab* (heart), *ba* (soul), *ka* (double), *sab* (spiritual body), *ren* (name), and *sekhem* (vital force).[20] In the context of our discussion, of greatest importance here is the *ka*, or double. In much of literature the 'double' represents a split-off part of a person, often little more than a characterization of Jung's 'shadow self', which embodies the denied and repressed elements of the individual's personality. In the esoteric wisdom traditions the 'double' points toward a higher ideal, that of the 'guardian angel', which is ultimately understood to be the higher self of the person. The Egyptians often depicted the *ka* as a second image of a king, hence the connection with it as a 'double'. According to myth, the *ka* of a person was breathed into them at birth, instilling their body with life and consciousness. (Compare that to the Biblical God who breathes life into Adam). The process of spiritual awakening may be likened to re-identifying with our inner reality, which is pure spirit, or pure formless consciousness.

What obstructs this process is identification with matter (form). Dr. Frankenstein and his monster have been thought to represent many things: everything from aggressive science minus a conscience, to the inner division—the Jekyll and Hyde split of the mad scientist and his creation—within a human being. In terms of esoteric teachings, however, they are good symbols of the resulting ruin and suffering that arises from ignorance of our inner spiritual nature. Victor Frankenstein sought to engineer a creation for his own purposes, but it was a material creation animated with electrical force, a poor copy of the process of spiritual creation that unfolds within us as we set our intention to realize our higher nature. His repugnance with the form of his own creation caused him to reject it. This rejection in turn triggered a series of destructive events that led to everyone's demise. It can all be seen as a powerful metaphor for what happens when we lose ourselves in concrete material form, oblivious to the subtle, the deep, and the higher. What Victor did to his creature and his creature in turn did to others, is what we do to ourselves when we fail to look beyond the surfaces of self, other, and universe—when we fail to recognize the inner light.

When we do begin to recognize the inner light, the formless nature of consciousness, it then becomes possible to see this same inner light everywhere we look. But it is necessary to recognize it within first.

Into my heart's night
Along a narrow way
I groped; and lo! the light,
An infinite land of day.
—Rumi

Chapter 15

A Brief History of Witchcraft

All witchcraft comes from carnal lust, which is in women insatiable.
—*Malleus Maleficarum* ('Hammer of the Witches'; published in 1486).[1]

The role of Witchcraft within the Western esoteric tradition has for some time been notoriously unclear. On the one hand, legitimate shamanic and pagan spiritualities have long existed, and continue to do so in modern forms. On the other hand, much of pre-20th century European 'witchcraft', and all the politics, theology, and persecutions surrounding it, was a complex social phenomenon that in large part appears to have been based on elaborate fabrications concocted by a combination of unchallenged beliefs, fear of authorities, economic purposes, and simple misogyny. The present chapter is undertaken to understand more clearly the psychodynamics of the relationship between Church and witchcraft, and between Inquisitor/priest/accuser and 'witch'. Further and arguably more important relationship dynamics, those of between Church and Satan, and Church and women, are also looked at.

As to what exactly a 'witch' is, or what the word implies, there are a broad range of views; indeed, the word is probably one of the most loaded in the English language. This chapter is not, however, a study of witches or witchcraft as a bona fide spiritual tradition (which it certainly is, at least in modern times),[2] but is rather an examination of the Church's persecution of witches and witchcraft during a gruesome phase of European history generally known as the 'Burning Times' (beginning around the 12th century CE, peaking from roughly from the mid-16th to the mid-17th centuries, and essentially ending by the 18th century). The word 'witch', when used herein, is often presented in quotation marks as scholarly research has demonstrated that many of those tried and executed, though convicted of being witches, were not in fact that; there is a valid argument that a majority of them were everyday Christians who happened to be in the wrong place at the wrong time. That the vast majority of them, witches or non-witches, were falsely convicted, or at the least unjustly tried, certainly by modern judicial standards, is more or less accepted at face value here.

According to the *Oxford Concise Dictionary of English Etymology* (1993 edition) the word 'witch' derives from the Old English terms *wicca* (a male sorcerer or wizard) and *wicce* (a female sorcerer or wizard). These were related to the Old English terms *wiccian*, meaning to 'practice magical arts', and *wiccecraeft* (witchcraft). The terms *wicca* or *wicce* are sometimes believed to derive from an older word meaning 'wise', although in fact it is the word 'wizard' that derives from the Old English *wiseard* ('wise one').[3] The word *wicce* is believed by most linguist scholars to derive from the term 'bend' or 'twist'. Some modern Pagans re-interpret this as a witch's 'shamanic ability' to bend or twist reality,[4] perhaps something along the lines of Dion Fortune's definition of magic: 'the art of causing changes to occur in consciousness in conformity with will.' This interpretation, though reasonable, appears to be a modern contrivance.

Modern Witchcraft, or 'Wicca' as it is now more commonly called by its practitioners, is a bona fide faith and has a clear recent history that can at least be traced back to the publication of Gerald Gardner's *Witchcraft Today* (1954), and more significantly, to the Egyptologist and anthropologist Margaret Murray's controversial landmark work *The Witch-cult in Western Europe* (1921). Beyond that the historical roots are obscure, and a subject of much debate. Indeed the history of the 'attempted history' of witchcraft is almost as interesting as any consideration of its actual roots.

The Roots of Persecution

Before considering the more recent and known history of witchcraft, and especially the witch-craze persecutions of the 15th through 18th centuries, it helps to have some understanding of the roots of the conflict between Church and witchcraft. Most believe this to begin with the infamous line from the Old Testament (Exodus, 22:18): *Thou shalt not suffer a witch to live* (King James Version). However, modern adherents of Neo-Pagan faiths sometimes forget that the title 'Witch' in current times implies something very different (at least for Pagans and other sympathizers) than it did in 1611 when the KJV Bible was produced, and more to the point, back when Exodus was written.

The Old Testament, of course, was not written in English, but Hebrew. Exodus 22:18 in Hebrew reads (transliterated with vowels), *M'khashephah lo tichayyah.* This means, essentially, 'you will not allow a *khashephah* to live.' A *khashephah* is a 'spell-caster'; a more currently accurate English term for it is probably 'sorcerer' or 'sorceress'. The 'spell-caster' referred to in the writing of Exodus was a *hostile* spell-caster, not the benign Goddess or Nature-worshipper of Neo-Pagan traditions. (And indeed, some recent editions of the Bible have replaced the Exodus 22:18 word 'witch' with 'sorceress', a trend followed by some modern historians such as Christopher Mackay, whose 2009 translation of the *Malleus Maleficarum*—see below—uses the terms 'sorcery' and 'sorcerer/sorceress' in place of 'witchcraft' and 'witch' throughout the entire text.) In older times, such malefic spell-casters were common (and often associated with poisoners), and found in many cultures (just as they are today, particularly in African or Caribbean nations). Just as commonly, their power was believed to be real and they were often hunted down.[5] Contrary to some popular views, the practice of witch-hunting, while largely eradicated from Western Europe by the late 18th century, still crops up occasionally in the world. As recently as 2008 eleven people in Kenya were accused of witchcraft and burnt to death,[6] and in Papua New Guinea, the execution of witches, often via burnings, is still done on occasion up to current times.[7]

The origin of the persecutions of witches on a mass scale that began in the early 14th century in Europe appears to be, at first glance, a study of chiefly two phenomena: misogyny, and 'magical thinking'. The first, hatred of women (deriving, presumably, from *fear* of them) was clearly one of the main underlying themes of the infamous polemic published in 1486 by two Dominicans, the German Inquisitor Heinrich Kramer (1430-1505) and the Swiss priest Jacob Sprenger (1437-1495), called the *Malleus Maleficarum* ('Hammer of the Witches'). Kramer—also known by his Latinized name Henricus Institoris—is believed by historians to have written most of the text. The book was commissioned by Pope Innocent VIII via his 1484 papal bull, and was heavily influential, going through dozens of editions, the last as recent as 1669.[8] It is a lurid manual of instruction for would-be witch hunters, describing witches and their way of life, including vivid depictions of their 'sabbats' with the Devil, and how they are to be dealt with. It contains more than its share of sweeping critiques and condemnation of women in general, concluding that women are easier prey for Satan because they are weaker both intellectually and physically, more credulous, and more prone to gossip (thus naturally recruiting others into their 'wickedness').

The persecution of 'heretics' did not begin with 15th century witches, however; it had earlier roots, most notably with the Cathars, a large and powerful semi-Gnostic sect that was persecuted by Pope Innocent III, culminating in the Albigensian Crusade of 1209–29 in which tens of thousands of Cathars (including women and children), most in southeastern France, were massacred. From the ashes of this Crusade was born the 'Holy Office of the Papal Inquisition', initiated by Pope Gregory IX in 1239. The job of this Inquisition was to suppress heretics. (The word 'heresy' derives from the Greek *hairetikos*, meaning 'able to choose'—a disturbing reminder of the Church's powers at that time to limit free will, or at the least, make attempts to exercise it in the realm of ideas, dangerous). The destruction of the Cathars was followed by the persecution and destruction (in 1312) of the Knights Templar, the powerful (though ultimately corrupt) Christian military order suspected of heretical beliefs. It had been just prior to that, in 1252, that Pope Innocent IV issued a papal bull authorizing torture as an Inquisitional tool (which some Knights Templar were subjected to), although in general, torture was not seriously and regularly used until the beginning of the witch persecutions in the late 15th century. (Torture did, however, remain outlawed in some countries, like England). The Inquisitions in general provided the intellectual and spiritual basis for the prosecution of witches, but over time ecclesiastical authorities became less involved in actual witch-hunts and trials. By the 16th century most witches were being tried and convicted by secular courts (coinciding with the general weakening of papal authority brought on by the Protestant Reformation). Witchcraft was recognized as a secular crime by the early 16th century, and this ultimately proved far more dangerous for suspected witches than the long arm of the Church. In fact, ecclesiastical authorities became increasingly cautious with witch-prosecutions (and reluctant to use torture), whereas local, secular courts were more prone to rash hunts, accusations, and convictions.

The main job of the *Malleus Maleficarum* had been to refute arguments that witches did not exist, and as mentioned, to petition the case for women being the main spawns of the Devil. Rossell Hope Robbins called the book, 'The most important and most sinister work on demonology ever written…opening the floodgates to the inquisitorial hysteria.'[9] The misogyny in the text is almost overwhelming, making any male philosophers throughout history who have been critical of the female mind (and there have been many) seem like feminists. This extract from the text is as good as any:

> What else is woman but a foe to friendship, an unescapable punishment, a necessary evil, a natural temptation, a desirable calamity, a domestic danger, a delectable detriment, an evil of nature, painted with fair colours! Therefore if it be a sin to divorce her when she ought to be kept, it is indeed a necessary torture; for either we commit adultery by divorcing her, or we

> must endure daily strife. Cicero in his second book of *The Rhetorics* says: The many lusts of men lead them into one sin, but the lust of women leads them into all sins; for the root of all woman's vices is avarice. And Seneca says in his *Tragedies*: A woman either loves or hates; there is no third grade. And the tears of woman are a deception, for they may spring from true grief, or they may be a snare. When a woman thinks alone, she thinks evil… but because in these times this perfidy is more often found in women than in men, as we learn by actual experience, if anyone is curious as to the reason, we may add to what has already been said the following: that since they are feebler both in mind and body, it is not surprising that they should come more under the spell of witchcraft.[10]

And so on, although the *Malleus* was not alone in such misogyny. The well-known and respected French philosopher Jean Bodin, author of the influential *On the Demon-Mania of Witches* (published in 1580), had declared that the heads of men are larger than women, and therefore they are more intelligent and prudent than women; and Pierre de Lancre, a 16th/17th century French judge and witch-hunter, had suggested that the Devil captures women more easily than men because women are 'naturally more imbecile'.[11] (And they had all long been preceded; as early as circa 200 CE the Church father Tertullian had maintained that women are more prone to the deceptions of demons). Such arguments may seem strange nowadays, but at the time they were taken very seriously because the cultural mindset was radically different. (Grasping cultural relativism is a key to understanding the witch-craze, because people think and experience reality in utterly different ways, depending on time, place, and cultural context). That said, it should be noted that while upward of 80 percent of tried and condemned witches in Western Europe were women (and often women over the age of 50, a fact that some historians suggest may be related to menopause and its psycho-social ramifications), this was not the case in some

Scandinavian countries, where a majority of those persecuted and killed were men (possibly because shamanistic traditions were strong in the north, and many Scandinavian shamans were male).

Added to the issue of misogyny, was that of 'magical thinking'. By this is not meant some esoteric or occult art, but rather a specific type of faulty thinking known in logic as the *post-hoc* fallacy. This is a confusing of causal linkages of events—in this case, the observation that event A comes before event B, therefore event A *must be* the cause of event B. The following small example sheds immediate light on the potential dangers of this kind of thinking:

> A woman in Scotland is burned as a witch for stroking a cat at an open window at the same time the householder finds his brew of beer turning sour.[12]

It was common for someone to make a casual observation of supposedly linked events (in the case above, the beer turning sour just as this poor woman happened to stroke her cat) and immediately assuming something sinister and *linked* by the events. Neighbors in areas that were prone to witchcraft-accusations would commonly become involved in petty disputes (as neighbors in all times have) in which to blame something on witchcraft was not an abnormal procedure. Such accusations, based in part on the *post-hoc* fallacy, become the basis of all superstition—most of which is harmless (such as the routines of many professional athletes)—but some of which occasionally deteriorates into the worst human folly and depravity. Most unjust persecutions and many wars were motivated by magical thinking, that is, by a failure to understand cause and effect at even a rudimentary level.

Additionally, there is a third apparent element; while not as significant as misogyny or magical thinking, it merits mention. It can be called the 'German factor'. After decades of tedious work examining trial records and related documents, scholars now have a fairly good idea of some of the statistics associated with the witch-hunt, from roughly 1300 to 1750. Current overall estimates run from approximately 35,000 to 65,000 'witches' killed, of whom between 17,000-26,000 were Germans—that is, over 40 percent of all those executed were German (many of these occurring during the so-called 'superhunts' of 1586-1639 in Western Germany). No other nation comes close to this percentage; most have significantly smaller numbers, with France (around 5,500, or about 10 percent) coming next, followed closely by Poland and Switzerland. Many countries, such as England, lost less than a thousand. In the case of England this amounts to an overall average of about one execution every four months, from 1450–1750, when most executions occurred (though the great majority occurred between 1560 and 1660).[13] Other countries, like Italy and Spain, had relatively rare bouts of witch-hysteria, and Eastern Europe was largely untouched by the witch-craze. Modern scholarship, based on meticulous research, thus informs us of two things: the number of witches killed during the Burning Times is much lower than was commonly assumed (as recently as in the 1970–80s); and Germans, followed distantly by the French, comprised the heavy majority. (Additionally, the term 'Burning Times' does not apply to England, where witches were hanged, not burned.[14] The more primitive form of execution, burning, was exclusive to the Continent, and on occasion, Scotland).

Those who watched the popular documentary put out in 1990 by the reputable National Film Board of Canada (*The Burning Times*), which featured a panel of modern neo-Pagans and Wiccans such as Merlin Stone and Starhawk and other sympathizers like the renegade Christian priest Matthew Fox, heard mention in the film of 'an upper figure of nine million witches' being killed during the Burning Times. That figure had been mentioned by Gerald Gardner in his *Witchcraft Today*,[15] and was repeated in Starhawk's highly influential 1979 publication *The Spiral Dance* (although in her 1989 revised edition, she allowed that the actual figure was 'between 100,000 and 9 million', with the upper figure being 'probably high'). Gardner in turn appeared to get this upper figure from Margaret Murray's *The*

Witch-cult in Western Europe. Back when Murray published her book (in 1921), scholarship on the matter of Witches and the Burning Times was scant. It appears that Murray got the 'nine million' figure from the 18th century German scholar Gottfried Voigt (1740–1791), who—starting from just forty-four confirmed executions in a small region of Germany—used a peculiar method of mathematical extrapolation to arrive at 'nine million' in a paper he published in 1784, a result now recognized as wildly inaccurate by a multiplication factor of over a hundred. That this figure has only been recently invalidated and the more accurate estimate of between 35,000 and 65,000 executed now widely accepted by scholars, is reflected in the number of neo-Pagans who still believe in a 'women's holocaust' that wiped out women on a scale similar to the Holocaust of World War Two (in which approximately six million men, women, and children, mostly Jews, lost their lives).

Naturally, 35,000 to 65,000 executions—many of them accompanied by grotesque forms of torture and many dying in agonizing pain—does not somehow mitigate the horror and depravity of the matter. If there is any value in recognizing the difference between nine million and 65,000 or 35,000, it is solely in historical accuracy, not in any lesser need to understand how such things come to be in the first place.

Anyone seeking to examine the relationship between Church and witchcraft ultimately ends up being faced with the realization that the deeper we look into the Church-witchcraft dynamic, the more witchcraft (real or not) vanishes. What is then revealed are three underlying relationships: the Church and Satan; the Church (male clergy) and women; and a third—and perhaps most surprising—women and women.

The Church and Satan/The Church and Women

The first is essential to examine for the simple reason that the main argument behind the Church's persecution of witches was that they were tools of the Devil—'instruments of darkness' as the historian

James Sharpe put it. They were means to an end, simply pawns in the Devil's plan to corrupt humanity. Accordingly, we need to take a look at the Church's ideas around Satan, and in particular, the ways in which Satan was believed to manifest in physical reality.

In the most basic sense, the whole existence of Satan, especially as a shadowy, conspiratorial figure, has its roots, as alluded to above, in a deeply flawed grasp of cause and effect, namely the post-hoc fallacy. However, the delusions that gripped the common accusations against witches went further than this particular logical error. The Devil became the sole causal factor behind all negative events—sickness, bad weather, ill fortune of all sorts. He was the ultimate scapegoat—witches were used as vehicles to punish as they provided a tangible face for the Devil.

Part of the problem lay in the fact that the nature of Satan himself was a matter of endless dispute amongst theologians and Church authorities going back to the 1st century CE. There were many competing theories and assumptions, and this can be seen in the various different guises of Satan in the Bible. In the Old Testament Satan appears to act purposefully, or as in the case of the Book of Job, as a 'tester' of humanity and an accomplice of God. But in the New Testament he seems to be out of control, or as historian Gerard Messadie put it, 'behaving like the demons of Oceania and Australia, doing everything willy-nilly. Everyone had come to believe himself threatened by a Devil who was as uncontrollable as a rabid dog.'[16] It was in the New Testament that the Devil came to associated with such things as leprosy, blindness, paralysis, epilepsy—in short, with illness itself—and, to boot, with ugliness and physical deformities as well. The Devil became the chief personification of evil fortune, and accordingly, a highly useful tool to wield against enemies—be they theological, political, or psychological in nature. And more specifically, this sort of Devil was needed as a pure contrast to aid in highlighting the divine purity of Jesus. The 'whiter' Jesus is, the more a purely 'blackened' oppositional factor is required. (And indeed, the Devil in 'witch's sabbats' was usually depicted as being cloaked in black). As the idea of divine incarnation is introduced—pure goodness—so does its opposite naturally leap into existence, in accordance with the inescapable laws of duality.

Yahweh of the Old Testament carries within him darker strains than Jesus does. Not that Jesus is without occasional aggression (ejecting the money-changers from the temples, cursing a fig tree, condemning the Pharisees, etc.), but he embodies the teaching of forgiveness—'love your enemies'—in a way that Yahweh certainly does not. In some ways Yahweh is a god of war. Because he is no example of stainless 'goodness', he does not require any counter-force of pure capricious evil, and this is why the Satan of the Old Testament does not have the nasty sting of Satan of the New Testament. As Jesus was introduced, evil was enhanced and given a darker and more gratuitous shade of malice.

In the first few centuries after Christ there was much theological hair-splitting around the nature of Satan and his army of demons, and the belief that there was more than one kind of evil spirit. At the council of Constantinople in 543, a canon was introduced that proclaimed there was, essentially, only one kind of demon. This narrowed the focus and made it easier to ascribe all evil events to this singular force of evil. Even science, and especially mathematics, was until the late 17th century suspected by many of being the work of the Devil, which was why Copernicus did not publish his work demonstrating that the Earth is not the center of the universe until on his deathbed, and why Galileo, as late at 1615, was forced to recant his confirmation of Copernicus's idea.

As the Dark Ages passed into the Middle Ages, the Devil took on an actual mythic form—generally that of a distorted version of the Greek god Pan, or the Roman god Faunus—complete with hooves, horns, general goat-like attributes, and a dark, wild, sexual look. The sexual element in his makeup was of major significance, not just because of the celibacy of many Catholic clergy, but also because of the purity and saintliness ascribed to Jesus. This purity always seemed to exclude his sexuality in such a way as to almost render him asexual. (Not to mention, he was held to have been brought into the world via a virgin birth). Accordingly, the Devil would naturally embody the polar opposite of all that, and this was exemplified in the belief in the existence of the notorious demonic 'Incubi', subordinates of the Devil, spirits that were alleged to visit women at night and make love to them in such a way as to incite wild orgasms. (The equivalent female demons, said to visit men at night, were called the 'Succubi').

In fact, when the historical records concerning the alleged gathering of witches—typically called 'sabbats'—is examined, it becomes clear that much of the psychological roots of it involved an inversion of Christian values—in effect, a type of religious psychopathology. Sabbats were reported to have generally involved witches gathering late at night in a wild place, in a meeting that was led by the Devil himself, generally in a black goat-like or dog-like form, dressed in black and seated on a black throne—perhaps best depicted by the famous Spanish painter Francisco Goya in his 1823 work *El Aquelarre* ('the Witch's Sabbat'). These meetings involved a great deal of sexuality, such as the witches being required to kiss the Devil's genitals and anus, and the whole gathering concluding with the Devil copulating with everyone present.[17] The blackness of the Devil, and rampant sexual energy, can all easily be seen as more of a direct peak into the contents of the repressed unconscious mind (of religious 'authorities', or of the common folk), than to any real ceremonies involving actual people. In that sense, Church and witchcraft or Church and women, becomes, more accurately, Church and Satan—or even more to the point, male clergy and the common folk and their own repressed sexuality. However, as we will see shortly, that dynamic was not the only one of import going on.

Women and Women

An important element to understand in the Church's claimed rationale for the witch-hunts was the idea of *maleficia*. This word (from the Latin *malitia*, 'ill will') was the Church's term for the 'evil spells' and assumed 'malefic influence' of 'witches'. The whole argument around the need to hunt them down and be rid of them was based on the belief that not only did they exist, but that they were actively involved in causing evil fortune to those around them (which included such things are crops, animals, and so on).

One thing need always be born in mind when attempting to understand some of the motives behind the witch-craze, as well as far earlier examples of the persecution of those thought to possess occult powers (or 'psychic' powers, as the more common modern term has it), and it is this: despite the obvious irrationalism of the witch-persecutions, it has been a long standing belief, found in almost all old cultures on Earth, that people possessing such powers—'sorcerers', for want of a better term—have always existed. (And certainly they have; 'spell-casters' claiming to be able to curse and bring misfortune, or even to administer poison, all usually for a price, have long been commonplace in most cultures). Here in our modern era of 'scientific enlightenment' and sophisticated technology we may have a hard time realizing to what extent this was (and still is, in many places) true. The advent of weapons, especially handguns, altered much of this—after all, what need is there to place hexes on enemies when you can simply shoot them? (Although it is interesting to note that the early muskets first used in Europe in the 15th century were thought by some to be tools of the dark arts, owing not just to their deadly power, but also to the sulfurous smell following their discharge).[18] James Frazer, in his *The Golden Bough,* describes many examples of how cultures prior to the Early Modern period made regular practice of guarding against malefic sorcery.[18] This is common in the East was well. Even Tibetan Buddhist monasteries, which traditionally (certainly prior to the mid-20th century annexation of Tibet by China) taught some of the most philosophically advanced material concerning the path of spiritual transformation, commonly have 'protector deities' called Dharmapalas, whose spiritual agency is involved in safeguarding the Dharma and the monks who practice it, from evil forces. The scholar Mircea Eliade also discusses the commonality of this practice within global shamanic tradition.[20] Norman Cohn, in his exhaustive study of the European witch-craze, provides many examples from direct historical records.[21]

The power of the mind in bringing about tangible effects from such beliefs—and especially for such beliefs to catch on, on a mass level—can never be underestimated. The anthropologist Claude Levi-Strauss once wrote:

> We understand more clearly the psycho-physiological mechanisms underlying the instances reported from many parts of the world by exorcism and the casting of spells. An individual who is aware that he is the object of sorcery is thoroughly convinced that he is doomed according to the most solemn traditions of his group. His friends and relatives share this certainty. From then on the community withdraws. Standing aloof from the accursed, it treats him not only as if he were already dead but as though he were a source of danger to the entire group.[22]

We include these mentions of the commonality of belief in 'malefic occult power' in this subsection on 'Women and Women', because what is not generally recognized is the extent to which women have been involved, historically, in not just being accused of using 'evil occult powers', but in *accusing other women* of evil occult powers.

A relatively recent, and uniquely American, version of this unfolded with the infamous Salem Witch trials that took place on the east coast of the United States from 1692–93. Space does not permit for an in depth look at this event,[23] but in brief, over a fourteen month span, twenty-nine people were convicted of witchcraft in three counties of Massachusetts (Essex, Suffolk, and Middlesex), though mostly centered on the town of Salem, in Essex. Of those, nineteen were eventually executed (all by hanging)—fourteen women, five men. The entire matter began with two young girls (aged nine and eleven) undergoing spontaneous bouts of hysteria (that resembled epilepsy, but that appeared to have been psychosomatic or deliberately enacted). This behavior soon 'spread' to several other young women in the communities. A doctor then diagnosed 'witchcraft' as the likely cause behind the strange behavior of the two young girls—that is, they had been 'hexed' by someone. The youngest of these girls, under pressure to point a finger, did so—first at a local black Caribbean slave girl who used to entertain them with stories—and then both young girls accused two other young women as well. All three of these women were then arrested (with the accusations of the young girls being backed up by others at this point). Under interrogation, the three 'admitted' to witchcraft.

Just a few days after this, four more women began showing signs (so they believed) of being afflicted by witchcraft. Over the next month, numerous other young women were accused, most by other women, of witchcraft—including a *four-year-old girl.* What is more extraordinary, this small child, after being accused of being a witch, was actually arrested, interrogated, and kept in prison for nine months. Although not executed, she went temporarily insane. In the end, dozens were accused, and a number of these were eventually hanged. What was significant was that 'spectral evidence' was often used, this being 'evidence' gained via visions or dreams, almost all of which was coming from the women. Although men were involved in the Salem trials, and some men were even convicted and hanged, the majority of the whole affair was precipitated by women (many young or teenage girls, although some older women were involved too) accusing other women.

Cases involving the factor of 'women against women' or exclusive female hysteria were not unique to Salem of 1692–93. Earlier cases abound, a spectacular example being sixteen Catholic nuns of Loudon, in western France, who in 1634 underwent spontaneous mass hysteria in such a fashion that all observing became convinced that they had been possessed by demons. A local priest (Urbain Grandier) was eventually convicted of witchery, and accordingly tortured and burned alive. (His actual crime had been that he'd had sexual relations with some of the nuns). Both the Salem and Loudon events received 20th century literary and Hollywood treatments; Salem via Arthur Miller's 1953 play, and the 1996 film (both called *The Crucible*); and Loudon via Aldous Huxley's 1952 historical novel *The Devils of Loudon*, and Ken Russell's 1971 film adaptation of Huxley's novel, called *The Devils*.

Salem and Loudon were only the high profile cases, however. Detailed historical records from small towns throughout Western Europe, mostly concerning the period of the 15th to 17th centuries, show many examples of villagers caught up in petulant quarrels, accusations, and counter-accusations—in part leveled by women against women—involving disputes over land, matrimonies, rents in arrear, and all the usual issues of conflict found in any small town. Many of these accusations involved *maleficia*, and with that, the accusation of 'witchcraft'. Many, if not most, ended in convictions and burnings.[24] (An excellent representative case study, brought out in 2009 by the American historian Thomas Robisheaux called *The Last Witch of Langenburg*, covers in exhaustive detail a drama that unfolded in the German town of Langenburg in 1672, in which the relations between villagers, and in specific, between women and women, was the actual driving force behind one of the last witch-panics of Europe).[25]

None of this is to propose that the early 13th century Inquisitions behind the original witch-craze itself was not a male-perpetuated phenomenon. It ultimately was, as was the barbaric culture of torture often used to extract confessions, which were then used to manipulate the accused into fingering accomplices. But when one studies the detailed histories compiled by such rigorous scholars as Diane Purkiss, Norman Cohn, Robin Briggs, Ronald Hutton, Brian Levack, or Thomas Robisheaux, one is left with the realization that neighbors accused other neighbors (including women accusing other women) of witchcraft far more commonly than is popularly realized today. This is emphasized by the fact that the countries in which the Inquisition was most entrenched (such as Italy and Spain) actually had relatively few witch-trials and executions. In other words, the witch-craze was a more local, secular, neighborly phenomenon than commonly thought.

Whence Witchcraft?

From all this arises a natural question, and one that has troubled historians for many years: Was there, in fact, any actual pre-20th century legitimately organized pagan tradition called 'witchcraft'? In answer to this, two extremes have arisen: the first, probably best exemplified by the eccentric Christian fundamentalist Montague Summers (1880–1948), is that not only is organized witchcraft both real and ancient, it is a tool of Satan and has only one purpose, that being to lead people astray from Christ and God. At the other end of the pole, we have scholars like Norman Cohn, Robin Briggs, and Rossell Robbins, who after exhaustive research and admittedly persuasive argument, conclude that most historical witchcraft—of the kind existing in any organized or even semi-organized fashion—is largely fantasy, based mostly on forged documents, pathological delusions, petulant and mean-spirited accusations, and livelihoods (sanctioned witch-hunters were, after all, paid for their services). Somewhere in the 'middle', we have many modern Wiccan and Neo-Pagans—perhaps best summarized by Margot Adler who wrote that 'the truth probably lies somewhere in between' the two poles just mentioned—most of whom subscribe to a version of Margaret Murray's ideas (see below).

As mentioned above, much of contemporary Witchcraft, Wicca, or Neo-Pagan traditions and networks can, without difficulty, trace their roots at least back to the 1950s and Gerald Gardner (1884–1964). Gardner claimed actual direct influence from underground groups—in specific a coven in southern England, that he called the 'New Forest coven'—that he said he had been initiated into in 1939. It was from this coven that Gardner claimed to derive authority to launch a modern day 'revival' of the Witchcraft faith. He further maintained that this coven was carrying on the tradition of an ancient witch-cult that derived from pre-Christian times, a type of original European shamanism, only one that had a fair degree of organization.

For years serious researchers tended to dismiss Gardner's 'New Forest coven'—its existence never corroborated by anyone—as simply a device to legitimize his creation of a 20th century Pagan tradition. Many writers have used this device in the past—that is, to fabricate a legendary teacher or secret society of teachers, through which to propagate a group of ideas. Examples of this in more recent times, of varying degrees of legitimacy, have included H.P. Blavatsky ('the Mahatmas'), William Wynn Wescott ('Fraulein Anna Sprengel, Secret Chief' for the Hermetic Order of the Golden Dawn), G.I. Gurdjieff (the 'Sarmoung Brotherhood'), T. Lobsang Rampa ('Tibetan masters'), Carlos Castaneda ('men of knowledge' don Juan Matus, don Genaro, and others), Kyriacos Markides ('Daskalos' and his circle of Cypriot Greek mystics), and Gary Renard ('ascended' masters).[26] The method, a type of *deux ex machina*, is clearly time-honored, and often works for how it is intended. It works in the same way that theatre, fictional literature, and the modern art form of cinema does, being based on the human ability to suspend disbelief and ascribe reality to something imaginary—a reality that easily goes beyond mere entertainment and can even become regarded as gospel truth that people will willingly kill or be killed for.

Gardner had been an English colonial bureaucrat and amateur anthropologist who spent many years in south-east Asia. In the late 1930s he made contact with a Rosicrucian order in southern England. It was from within this order that Gardner claimed he connected with a small group of people who in 1939 took him through an initiation that he identified as being of the tradition of witchcraft, and in particular of the type that had managed to survive underground for many centuries. Gardner further claimed that the leader of this group was a woman named Dorothy Clutterbuck, and that she was the 'High Priestess' of an actual coven of Witches in the New Forest area. Subsequent research has shown that Gardner was the sole source of the claim about Clutterbuck. Not only are there no corroborating sources, Clutterbuck's own diaries from that time make no mention of any sort of occult, let alone Witchcraft-related, activities. Further, there was a problem with Gardner's integrity concerning the matter of forgery. In 1946 he had claimed, to the members of the Folklore Society, to have doctorates from the universities of Singapore and Toulouse, claims later proven to be false.[27]

In May of 1947, Gardner, aged 62, met the controversial magus Aleister Crowley, himself 71 at the time and in the last year of his life. Gardner and Crowley became friends of sorts, and after several informal meetings, Crowley authorized Gardner to set up a branch of the Ordo Templi Orientis (OTO) in England (the fraternity that Crowley was head of, although it had become temporarily defunct in England at that time).[28] Crowley provided Gardner with papers containing information of specific rituals and teachings. Crowley gave Gardner the name 'Brother Scire' (which Gardner would later use as his 'Craft name') and initiated Gardner into the 7th degree of the OTO. Nothing however would come of this and Gardner never did begin an OTO lodge in England.

According to Wiccan lore, as first told by Raymond Buckland (one of the earliest initiates of Gardner's Wicca), in the 1940s Gardner began pressing 'Old Dorothy' Clutterbuck and her fellow Witches for permission to write a book about their existence and activities. The Witches allegedly declined, presumably because Witchcraft at that time was still illegal in England (and remained so until 1951). Eventually the New Forest Witches allowed Gardner to write about them, but only in veiled terms. This he did by writing the novel *High Magic's Aid*, which he published in 1949, under his OTO initiate name 'Brother Scire'. After the repeal of the last witchcraft laws two years later, Gardner claimed he again approached the coven and this time was granted, somewhat reluctantly, permission to write about them in a non-fictional form, which Gardner did with his 1954 book *Witchcraft Today*. Gardner felt it was important to write about the 'authentic Craft' before it disappeared altogether.[29] This, incidentally, was the same sentiment that gripped Israel Regardie when he broke his vows and published the 'knowledge lectures' and full rituals of the Golden Dawn in 1939.

According to the scholar Richard Kaczynski (and others, such as Leo Ruickbie and Ronald Hutton), Aleister Crowley's influence on Gardner and future Gardnerian Wicca had been considerable. Kaczynski remarks:

> Gardnerian Witchcraft, particularly in its earliest forms, is clearly derivative of Crowley. The symbolic great rite comes from the OTO's VI° ritual; the pagan catchphrase 'Perfect love and perfect trust' is drawn from 'The Revival of Magick' [a Crowley essay], and the Wiccan III° initiation—the highest in the Craft—is essentially a Gnostic Mass [a mystical rite written by Crowley in Moscow in 1913, based in part on the Eastern Orthodox Mass]. The pagan banishing [ritual] originates with the Golden Dawn [the organization that first trained Crowley], and the summoning of the Four Watchtowers [a Wiccan rite] is right out of John Dee's Enochian magic [a 16th century system taught in the Golden Dawn in the 1890s and practiced by Crowley in Africa in 1909]. And, for all of its evocative beauty, the Charge of the Goddess is largely a paraphrase of The Book of the Law [Crowley's main text, written in 1904]. Margot Adler reflects the prevalence of this opinion when she quotes a Wiccan priestess who wrote to her, 'Fifty percent of modern Wicca is an invention bought and paid for by Gerald Gardner from Aleister Crowley. Ten percent was 'borrowed' from books and manuscripts like Leland's text Aradia. The forty remaining percent was borrowed from Far Eastern religions and philosophies.'[30]

Gardner (as influenced by Crowley, the Golden Dawn, and others) may have been the practical force behind the creation of 20th century Wicca, and for this alone, many modern Wiccans hold him in considerable esteem. If nothing else he was resourceful and wise in a pragmatic fashion, in a way that allowed thousands to gain (or recover) a passion for some form of organized religion. However Gardner was not the main intellectual source of modern Wicca. That honor appears to go to Margaret Murray (1863–1963), and standing behind her, the figure of James Frazer (1854–1941) and in particular, his toweringly influential work *The Golden Bough* (first published in part in 1890, with additions from 1906–15, and then in full in 1922).

Murray was primarily an Egyptologist who spent eleven years as an assistant professor of Egyptology at the University College of London (1924–35). Her main accomplishment was developing her theory of a surviving Western European 'Witch-cult', one that for centuries had been persecuted by the Church, but that had managed to persist into the present day in a very low profile form. Over the decades since the publication of her work in 1921, she has been taken to task by numerous historians and scholars who cite her questionable scholarship, one practice of which involved Murray selectively deleting sections of records she was quoting in order to bolster her argument. The historian Norman Cohn, after a long study of her primary sources that she used for her thesis, concluded:

> Margaret Murray's knowledge of European history, even of English history, was superficial and her grasp of historical method was non-existent. In the special field of witchcraft studies, she seems never to have read any of the modern histories of the persecution...by the time she turned her attention to these matters she was nearly sixty, and her ideas were firmly set in an exaggerated and distorted version of the Frazerian mold.[31]

By 'Frazerian mold' Cohn was referring, of course, to James Frazer. Frazer's work *The Golden Bough* argued for the existence of a near universal 'fertility cult' involving the deification of a sacred king—and on occasion, the sacrifice of such a king.[32] A main part of Frazer's thesis was that age-old fertility rites are ultimately about the need to kill off the old spirit of Nature and then bring it back life—to resurrect it—in a form that was commonly that of worshipping and then killing (sacrificing) a sacred king.

He argued that world mythologies tend to consistently reflect this legend, which generally involves a solar deity or king marrying an Earth goddess. The king then dies at harvest time, only to be reborn in the spring time. (Note the connection there with Easter and the 'resurrection' of Jesus). The old religions were, thus, deeply intertwined with agriculture and the timing of the seasons. It was from this thesis that Margaret Murray developed her idea of an ancient, organized pagan faith that had survived the witch-craze, and whose rites and ceremonies had been simply misinterpreted by Church authorities and the common folk. The problem with her idea is that historical research has unearthed no evidence of organized paganism, in particular in the form of meetings called 'sabbats'. Moreover, all of the records used by Murray as evidence to support her thesis, contained fantastic imagery (witches flying to sabbats, the Devil copulating with the witches, babies being eaten, and so forth), the worst and most fantastic passages of which she was found to have selectively left out when quoting the records of them.[33]

And so the irony: Margaret Murray wrote a short Introduction to Gardner's landmark *Witchcraft Today*, endorsing the author's writings about an ancient and legitimate organized witchcraft, when she herself (with unwitting help from James Frazer) is likely the true 'High Priestess' and unintentional founder of modern Wicca. Indeed, there is a strong probability that the New Forest coven that Gardner claimed to have been initiated in, did in fact exist in some form, but that it had come into being only in the 1920s, basing its ideas on Murray's work. (The 1920s was an extraordinarily fertile decade for metaphysical teachings of all stripes, a sort of pre-World War Two precursor of the New Age movement that blossomed in the 1970s and 80s).

Two other sources bear mentioning: the American journalist and folklorist Charles Leland (1824–1903), who made an extensive study of Gypsies and in 1899 published *Aradia or the Gospel of the Witches*, a book known to have influenced some of the Wiccan rites created by Gardner half a century later. The other important literary figure was Robert Graves, especially via his influential *The White Goddess* (1948), a poetic work that outlined the idea of an overarching Goddess tradition found throughout history, in which feminine deities are connected to the Moon. Graves claimed to take Frazer's ideas outlined in *The Golden Bough*, and render them more detailed and explicit. *The White Goddess* has been panned by numerous critics for its questionable historical research—and Graves himself admitted it was primarily a poetic venture—but the book nonetheless remained a strong influence on many 20th century Pagans.

All valid historical criticism aside, there is bound to be some semblance of truth in the ideas best represented by Margaret Murray's work, because loosely organized spiritual traditions have existed for millennia, most of which can be categorized by the term 'shamanistic'. Medieval or Early Modern era sabbats and orgies involving 'the Devil' and thirteen 'witches' is indeed likely the product of fantasy or religious agenda—and organized witchcraft, along the lines of modern Wicca, in any form prior to the 1920s is indeed probably only wishful thinking—but the existence of shamanic and pagan traditions throughout history, if only in the form of the solitary 'cunning man', 'wise-woman', or sorcerer, is indisputable, and this would naturally include European cultures as well.

However, the distinction between legitimate shamanistic or pagan practices, and the idea of an organized spiritual tradition such as modern Wicca stretching back into antiquity, needs to be carefully understood. It is all too tempting to dismiss out of hand the stark historical work of scholars like Norman Cohn who find absolutely no evidence for anything like a pre-20th century European witchcraft, merely on the basis of what appears to be an egg headed approach lacking in experiential understanding. For example, in commenting on Cohn's work *Europe's Inner Demons*, the

20th century author and Pagan Margot Adler remarks:

> One of the problems with Cohn's argument is his limited conception of what is possible in reality. For example, he considers all reports of orgies to be fantasy...he is surprisingly ignorant of the history of sex and ritual. Orgiastic practices were a part in religious rites in many parts of the ancient world.[34]

That may be so, but it still does not prove the existence of organized witchcraft prior to the 20th century. Adler's only other significant criticism of Cohn, that he uses psychoanalysis in interpreting the possible roots of what he believes to be the fantasies at the heart of 'witch sabbats'—a psychoanalysis that she calls 'the most popular witchcraft religion of our day'—does not negate the meticulous historical research that he, and other scholars, undertook. The core issue remains: no historical evidence for a pre-20th century *organized faith* resembling modern Witchcraft has yet been found. The modern version of Witchcraft (Wicca) bears almost entirely late 19th and early 20th century influences: Margaret Murray, James Frazer, Charles Leland, Aleister Crowley, the Hermetic Order of the Golden Dawn, Robert Graves, and Gerald Gardner. To that, we can safely add Rosicrucianism and Freemasonry—the former an influence on both Gardner's 'New Forest coven' as well as on the Golden Dawn, and the latter an influence on both the Golden Dawn and Crowley.

Interpretation

The relationship between the Church and witchcraft was an extremely complicated phenomenon, involving religious, political, social, psychological, and economic elements. And these were only the large-scale factors. Added to that was the mix of human petulance and general capacity for mean-spiritedness of all sorts, as well as a depraved 'appetite' (there is no better word) for sadism, torture, and humiliation to unfathomable degrees. Alongside all that, it is important to realize, as Lucien Febvre once wrote, 'the mind of one age is not necessarily subject to the same rules as the mind of another age'.[35] Reality as we experience it is a mentally constructed, and that includes the powerful factor of cultural context. Humans move in groups, largely, and are prone to collective thinking and collective 'agreements'. For good or bad, we tend to go with the crowd, regardless of what direction the crowd is moving in.

What is striking to note is that of all the more recent primary influences on modern Wicca (mentioned above) all, with the exception of Murray, are male. The irony of this, and in particular of the patriarchal Freemasonry ancestral link with modern Wicca (via the Golden Dawn and Crowley), is marked, but perhaps understandable. When the Hermetic Order of the Golden Dawn was founded in England in 1888, it was done so by three Freemasons (William Woodman, William Wynn Westcott, and Samuel Mathers), partly in order to investigate esoteric teachings more deeply, but also partly to break the traditional Masonic gender barrier and grant women admission. The Golden Dawn, at its height in the late 1890s, did comprise around 35 percent female membership; some of the more prominent women involved were stage actress Florence Farr, theatre producer Annie Horniman, future Rider-Waite Tarot deck artist Pamela Coleman-Smith, scholar and author Evelyn Underhill, actress Sarah Allgood, and author, feminist, and Irish revolutionary Maud Gonne. All these women practiced the Golden Dawn version of ceremonial magic, with its roots in much older ritual magic—and just as certainly all these women would have been accused of consorting and fornicating with the Devil only a century or two earlier. (Not that late 19th century England was of equal tolerance compared to the early 21st century Western world—as mentioned, witchcraft remained illegal in England until 1951—but the 'craze' element involving witchcraft accusations, resulting hysteria, and vicious persecutions, had long since gone, at least from Europe and North America).

In looking at psychological interpretations, arguments can be mounted in support of the idea that the witchcraft persecutions were largely a matter of the repressed sexual energy of male religious authorities finding outlet in the depraved and licentious imagery of the Devil. And it is indeed reasonable to wonder, for example, at the sex lives of the two 'authorities' (Kramer and Spengler) who authored the lurid and influential *Malleus Maleficarum*. Arguments can also be mounted that the old occult idea that the female mind carries within it the seeds of chaos and the tendency toward interpersonal strife, and a far greater propensity toward the carnal, is valid; and that accordingly, women had a much greater hand in the witch-craze than assumed. All these gender issues, however, would seem to be a matter impossible to unravel in this case because of the lack of consistent records. But more to the point, gender issue here is ultimately a secondary concern (unpopular as that idea may seem to some). What is more useful to look at is the entire nature of the conflict inherent in religion, in specific its often confused relationship with the carnal.

The very image of the Devil in the standard descriptions and depictions of him, as he consorts with his witches in sabbats that invariably involve kinky sexuality, bears looking closely at—for example, the tradition of witches kissing the Devil's anus. This kiss was called the *osculum infame* ('kiss of shame') and was regarded as a key ritual of initiation during a sabbat. But why the anus? It is, in a sense, the part of the body that is the real 'forbidden fruit', more so than the genitals. The genitals may be feared, unconsciously, as the center of sexual power, but the anus is associated with elimination, waste, and dead matter (and thus, with death itself). It is the orifice of the body concerned with expelling the old and useless, and it is also the source of the worst smells. It is, in a sense, the 'hidden portal' and 'final taboo'.

The slang expression 'kiss my ass' is generally recognized as an insult, but what kind of insult in specific? From the *egocentric* perspective, it is one that involves, above all, humiliation—the rendering of the 'other' into an object. (Pornography, in its lowest light, operates in a similar mode). However, the one humiliating is not necessarily alone in actualizing their secret sadistic lusts—the one being humiliated may also be, to some degree, participating in a deeply repressed masochistic fantasy. And it is precisely this degree of repression that makes a 'forbidden zone' so potentially eroticized.

Caution, of course, is needed here—the violence against, and debasement of, women throughout the centuries cannot be blamed on some actualization of dark masochistic fantasies. However in order to glean some manner of insight from the witch-craze, and in particular to be able to apply this insight into our present lives, we need to look squarely into our more repressed desires—whether we be male or female. As Isaac Bashevis Singer once wrote, 'We are all black magicians in our dreams, in our fantasies, perversions, and phobias…'[36]

Looking into repressed desires, however, means *inner work*, in the most real sense of that term. Such work is rarely easy, in part because most of us know that to honestly and deeply face our secret and hidden fantasies is to uncover potentially powerful energies. Such power always carries within it the potential for bringing about significant changes in our life—the proverbial 'rocking the boat'. Most of us are creatures of habit, and most of us tend to equate significant change with stress. Accordingly, many people fear looking within in a deeply honest fashion, and as a result never penetrate to any depth of self-observation. The result is to live a life based more on superficial views, status quos, and accepting what is traditionally held to be true. In the case of the witch-craze, it is not hard to see how this type of psychological intransigence was a key element in keeping the whole (essentially crazy) matter going for centuries.

We live in an era where rationalism—at least as an ideal—rules, even if such rationalism amounts to little more than a need to demonstrate that one is not making false claims (as in the academic concern with citations). Much of the witch-craze was based on false claims, with the worst example being the 'spectral evidence' (as for example, in the Salem case, where one could claim that one had seen a ghost or non-physical demon accost someone, and on that basis, accuse someone of witchcraft). However what we tend to overlook, in this time of scientific materialism and high tech gadgetry, is that there is a great degree of vibrancy in living an embodied life, one in which all human subjective domains (for example, thinking, feeling, intuition, sensing) are in relative balance. In such a world, the unconscious mind may be said to interface more easily with the conscious mind, and thus myths, legends, superstitions, and even dreams carry more force. The gift of the so-called Age of Reason (beginning in earnest around 1700), had been to aid in dispensing with the more dangerous and troubling elements of an 'enchanted' life (and the ending of the witch-craze, by the 18th century, testifies in part to that). But there has also been a cost, and that is that most people are probably now less embodied—that is, live more through abstractions (and technology—just step into a modern Western café in current times, and see most young people lost in their laptops, smart phones, and the processing of information of whatever quality).

The point here is not to suggest that life during the witch-craze was somehow preferable to modern life; it certainly wasn't, except perhaps for all but the most incurable romantic. Most will happily take modern technological obsession, depression, boredom, and global terrorism over plague, rampant disease, malnutrition, religious and racial intolerance, grinding poverty, high infant and child mortality rates, and an average lifespan of 40 or 50 years, any day. However it was not *entirely* worse back then—the lack of sophisticated technology, the stronger relationship with the raw environment, the greater degree of worldly innocence, the greater need to actually *interact* with people and make powerful efforts to accomplish even simple things, doubtless meant a world where people were, in the main, more 'embodied' than now in our softer, more virtual society. We stress this point because it is all too easy to dismiss the Burning Times as an example of a primitive society in which absurd and dangerous superstitions were granted free reign, with terrible consequences. The casual assumption is that we are now beyond such things. In reality, however, our various psychopathologies have just assumed more varied and subtle forms.

While the story lines of the grand dramas of spiritual conflict played out throughout history—be that between Osiris and Set, or Jesus and Judas, or the Church and witchcraft—may be constantly changing, the underlying patterns remain. Executions of modern Witches may not be a present-time reality (at least in Europe or North America), but the essence of the inner dynamic of prejudice and lack of curiosity about different traditions is alive and well. Norman Cohn had hypothesized that part of the psychological roots of the more lurid aspects of the common beliefs about witches and their orgiastic sabbats lay in Christianity 'exalting spiritual values at the expense of the animal side of human nature', resulting in 'unconscious resentment against Christianity as too strict a religion and Christ as too stern a taskmaster.'[37] There is likely truth in that, but Cohn seems to apply this interpretation only to the common people (in this case, mostly women), and doesn't seem to include the religious clergy itself (mostly men).

The celibate priest or monk (of whatever tradition) is, in a sense, living an unnatural life, because he (and it is usually a he) is in a kind of war with himself, living in a perpetual state of repression. This repression will naturally seek outlets, and the Christian image of the Devil—a dark, hoofed, horned, freakish creature who requires women to kiss his anus (as well as his genitals)—can hardly be more than the outer face of repressed sexual energy and fantasy. He is, essentially, the celibate priest inverted, as much as he is the inversion of a whitewashed Jesus who enters the world via a virgin.

From this perspective, the priest and the Devil can be seen as two sides of the same coin. Cohn's view that the Devil and his sabbat—including orgies and the strange legend of witches 'eating babies', itself an echo of old Greek infanticide myths involving certain annoyed gods (such as Chronos/Saturn) attempting to eat their children—is a fantasy that is the product of the Christian-hating,

God-hating, and Jesus-hating frustrated public, probably carries some truth. But almost certainly the 'horny' Devil and his harem of nympho-maniacal 'witches' is equally so a product of male celibate ecclesiastical unconscious fantasy. Further, it is also reasonable to conjecture that the inclusion of the derriere as part of the 'diabolic' ritual is a suggestion of repressed homosexuality. That celibate priests and monks can readily enough become homosexually (or at the least, bisexually) oriented, is common knowledge.

The lesson we can glean from the witch-craze tragedy is on many levels, but certainly the issue of integrating our loftier, spiritual impulse with our earthy, animal nature, is at the forefront. The witch-craze was in part a sexual phenomenon—regardless of the many other realms of human concern it touched on (religious, social, economic), and regardless of the fact that most persecuted witches were no longer young women. At a superficial glance it may seem as if persecuting witches was a need of the Church to exert control over potentially dangerous usurpers, but looked at a bit closer the whole thing can be seen as both the Church's, and common person's, need to exert control over disowned 'shadow' elements from within. We generally seek to punish that which reminds us most uncomfortably about the part of ourselves that we have not come to terms with, and we often 'see' these disowned qualities in the world around us. That, ultimately, transcends the issue of gender. It is arguable that most people carry within the seeds of an Inquisitor, sadistic secular judge, or torturer—the capacity for intolerance, for unreasoned judgment, for sadistic dominance. And we equally carry within the seeds of both the Devil and the Church's 'witch'—the former as a darkened, shadowy, furtive expression of guilt, and the latter as a primal expression of lust, power, and the secret desire to rebel against authority. We also carry within us the ancient need to explain death, to assign cause to the unknown, to go on 'witch-hunts' in order to relieve ourselves of the burden of not knowing the cause of unforeseen negative circumstances—in short, to be victims, and to be righteous in that stance.

It is perhaps fitting that the modern Wiccan (Witch) practices a religion that is generally innocuous and concerned with healing and spiritual awakening; and above all with being attuned to that which is *natural*. The witch-craze and its shadowy archetypes was a manifestation of an unnatural internal split in the mind—the artificial disconnect between 'angel' and 'devil', between selflessness and self-centeredness. To be truly natural is to bring the two together, so as to move beyond both—beyond the limitations of being bloodless, self-sacrificing and self-loathing, and beyond the limitations of being crude, narcissistic, and driven by selfish impulse.

Chapter 16

Lycanthropy, Shapeshifting, and the Assumption of God-forms

The title of this book—*The Inner Light*—does not mean that matters of darkness are not addressed, and that is nowhere truer than in the current chapter. (Light itself means nothing without the contrast of the dark). Legends of humans who transform into animals (sometimes under disturbing circumstances) are very old. The main argument of this chapter is that these worldwide legends are ultimately a debased form of certain legitimate practices—sometimes known as 'metamorphosis' or by the more modern term 'shapeshifting'—within the ancient spiritual tradition known as 'shamanism'. These practices, in turn, are primitive versions of advanced mystical practices known in some Western esoteric traditions as the 'assumption of god-forms', and in certain Eastern traditions as 'deity yoga'. In terms of modern psychological views, the idea of the human who transforms into an animal (of whatever species) represents a good representation of the psychodynamics of the 'Shadow'. Arguably this element is as strong, or stronger, in so-called spiritual seekers, because the very striving for 'the light' carries the risk of bringing about an imbalance resulting from the denial of impulse and darkness.

Werewolves in Lore

The word 'werewolf' originates in the Old English terms *wer* ('man') and *wulf* ('wolf'); the word has been in use as far back as 1000 CE. The wolf throughout history has served as an intense mirror for human nature, doubtless because of its apparent 'dual' nature. On the one hand it has been associated with the antisocial and the disloyal, along with savage impulse, lack of conscience, and evil. On the other hand it has also been connected to bravery, loyalty, and the power of team-work, family, organization, or nation (the 'pack') to overcome obstacles. This is an obvious metaphor for human nature. What marks the psychology of the human being as much as anything is the division between the polarities of sublime wisdom and nobility of character, versus the capacity for self-centered destructive malice and sheer evil.

The earliest recorded mention of humans changing into wolves is from ancient Greek literature, in specific from the Balkan area known as Arcadia. Legend has it that this land was ruled by a king named Lycaon (circa 1500 BCE), who also promoted the worship of Zeus. (The Eastern timber wolf derives its scientific nomenclature—*Canis lupus Lycaon*—from this Greek legend). Lycaon's sons—according to some versions of the myth there were as many as fifty of them—like typical privileged offspring, were reportedly subversive and arrogant. The matter came to Zeus's attention who decided to monitor them 'undercover', disguised as a common worker. In a visit to Lycaon's house the undercover Zeus was fed a vile mix of flesh from a sacrificed human child and animal entrails (the purpose being to determine if the stranger was actually Zeus). Angered at the murder of the child, Zeus turned Lycaon into a wolf. Some versions of the myth have him turning all his sons into wolves as well; other versions have him killing the sons with a lightning bolt. (It is from this legend that the technical term for werewolfery, 'lycanthropy', derives).

From this myth we can see the coincidental nature of the association of the wolf with evil intent. At the simplest level, werewolf legends are in part a reflection of the reality of sharing a territory with a particular predator. Prior to the human depredations of wolves of the 20th century, the wolf was the dominant predator in Europe alongside Man. Predictably, it is from these lands that the werewolf legend has been strongest (such as in Scandinavia, for example). In India there has been the belief in the 'weretiger', in South America the 'werejaguar', in Japan the 'werefox', and in Africa the 'wereleopards' and 'werelions'. Belief in wereleopards was famously found among a group calling itself the Leopard Society—eighteen members of which were executed in Nigeria in 1946 for 'terrorizing' a town, in which up to two hundred victims appeared to have been mysteriously killed by man-leopards.[1] The matter of werelions came to light in a series of arrests in 1947 in Tanganyika (today part of Tanzania) in which close to seventy 'Lion Men' were accused of carrying out various acts of mayhem (including murder) while dressed up in lion skins and leaving wounds resembling marks from lion claws. These acts, some of which were ritualistic, were in some instances motivated by the ancient theme of blood-sacrifice, where the belief is that by a ritualistic killing certain merits will be achieved and blessings accorded from deities (such as good weather, crops, hunting, and other benefits).[2]

Werewolf killings have traditionally been of the lurid sort, often involving sexual depravities and the eating of human flesh (commonly of the young and/or female). Doubtless for a significant number of these cases the root of the matter was straightforward: mental illness (including hallucinations) and psychopathy.[3] However in cases where these stories are mere legend, or fabrications extracted under torture (common during the various witch-persecutions), the sources appear to be connected to old beliefs around the power, or other attributes, that can be obtained by consuming the flesh or blood of an enemy. (As far back as Plato this idea has been used as an allegory to warn about the likely end result: in *The Republic,* Socrates had forecast that any leader who plots to eliminate a political rival—for which he used the metaphor 'tasting human flesh'—will himself become a tyrant. As Nietzsche once wrote, 'be on your guard not to become the monster that you hunt!'). Other sources of the legend are clear, such as the Norse traditions of warriors dressing up in the skins of bears they had killed. These warriors, called *berserkers,* were renowned for a superhuman strength and fierceness in battle that was likened to a frenzied trance (hence the root of the word 'berserk'). From this it was easy to credit the warrior with the power of the beast he dressed up as.[4] ('Clinical lycanthropy' is the modern psychological term for one who believes that they actually *are* a 'werebeast').

Some of the classic roots of the werewolf legend can also be traced to the novel *Satyricon*, written by the Roman Gaius Petronius (27–66 C.E.), which was rendered into *Fellini's Satyricon*, an infamous 1969 film by the renowned Italian director Federico Fellini.[5] Petronius' *Satyricon* contains a chapter called *The Feast of Trimalchio*, centering on a wealthy and pretentious former slave who entertains his guests with lavish excess. During a particular feast he regales them with stories, one of which involves him and a companion who go out one night on a walk that takes them near a cemetery. While there, Trimalchio's companion suddenly disrobes, proceeds to urinate in a circle around them, turns into a wolf, and then runs off into the woods, howling as he goes. Trimalchio finds that the man's clothes have turned to stone. He then visits his mistress who tells him that a wolf just attacked their cattle, but was driven off with a pitchfork to the neck. Come morning Trimalchio returns home, only to find his companion suffering a pitchfork wound on his neck and being attended to by a doctor. He then concludes that the man is a *versipella* (werewolf). Rossell Hope Robbins noted that this story contains four essential elements of werewolf legend: nocturnal transformation, nudity, urination and/or related specific magical acts, and 'sympathetic wounding'.[6] The latter factor, the wounding of a wolf and the later capture of a human with a similar wound, was actually used as proof in European werewolf trials[7], the height of which corresponded roughly to the peak of the witch-hunting craze in the late 16th century.

The theme of 'sympathetic wounding' was central in one of the more renowned werewolf trials of that time, which occurred in the district of Poligny, France, in 1521. The story begins with a traveler passing through Poligny who is ambushed by a wolf. The traveler survives, trails the wolf, and ends up at a small house where he discovers a wounded man who is being treated by his wife. The traveler reports the wounded man—his name was Michel Verdung—to the authorities, who arrest him. Presumably under torture Verdung told an elaborate story that implicated another man, Pierre Bourgot. This man in turn made his own confession, which placed his 'dealings with the Devil' originating nearly twenty years before, in 1502. Bourget claimed that at that time, following a storm that had frightened off his sheep, he was confronted by three 'black horsemen', one of whom offered to help him in exchange for a vow of loyalty. Bourgot agreed, and to his relief his flock was soon found. In a subsequent meeting one of the horsemen revealed himself to be a disciple of the Devil, and extracted a further oath of obedience from Pierre, who consecrated this oath by kissing the horseman's left hand, which he described as black and ice cold. After a couple of years Pierre began to lose his connection with the Devil's disciple and appeared to be re-associating with the Christian faith again. Michel Verdung, another of the Devil's servants, set to work luring Pierre back into the satanic fold with promises of riches. Pierre then attended a sabbat, during which he was made to apply an ointment of some sort (a common theme in werewolf stories). Pierre then found himself turning into a wolf; with the aid of Michel Verdung he was able to revert to his human form. Confessions were extracted from Pierre Bourgot under torture. Amongst other lurid actions he admitted to killing children, which including eating at least two girls under the age of ten, and describing their taste as 'delicious'. He also claimed he fornicated with wolves. Bourgot, Verdung, and another 'werewolf', Philippe Mentot, were all tortured and then burned at the stake.[8]

Two more sordid examples are illustrative of probable psychopathic serial killers condemned as 'lycanthropes': those of Gilles Garnier and Peter Stubb. The former was a hermit who was declared a werewolf and executed in France in 1574. He had been accused of murdering and eating children. He confessed that he had been in the form of a wolf when he did these killings, and claimed to have often dragged his victim away with his 'fangs'. On one occasion Garnier was caught with one of his victims by some peasants who later agreed that he was in the shape of a wolf-man—body of a wolf, yet with his human face still recognizable. Garnier was forced to confess to making a pact with the Devil, convicted and burnt at the stake. (The actual story was that a wolf had killed some local children, and Garnier, starving, was caught scavenging the carcass of the child—which during that time easily became grounds for being accused of something more sinister than scavenging).[9] The latter story, concerning the German Peter Stubb, occurred near Cologne in 1589; at the time, it was one of the more famous werewolf trials in Europe. Stubb claimed to have a 'magic belt' that enabled him to transform into a powerful and ravenous wolf. Similar to Garnier he was accused of preying on women and young people, from as far back as 1561. He further claimed that throughout his nearly three decades of raping and killing he had been influenced by a 'succubus' (a female demon said to visit men at night; the male counterpart is called an 'incubus'). Stubb was tortured in the harshest fashion, then decapitated, then burned. Colin Wilson speculated that the cruelty of the torture may have resulted in fabricated confessions, which doubtless was often the case with so-called witches and lycanthropes.[10] However it seems more probable that this was an actual case of a 16th century schizophrenic serial killer.

There were a number of other relatively high profile trials involving alleged werewolves in Europe; most of these were in the late 16th century, and most occurred in France. It is not clear why there was a concentration of cases at that time in that part of the world—apart from the simple demographic fact that France was the most populated country in Europe throughout the Middle Ages and into the Early Modern era—but it may have been no more than the power of transmitted suggestion and mass-hysteria. (The fact that most witch-hunting took place in Germany and France, and that it was these two countries that saw the most accusations and trials concerning alleged werewolves as well, strengthens the likelihood that mass hysteria was at work).

One of the more infamous cases occurred later, in the late 18th century, when werewolf cases had become rare (most witch-trials had stopped by then as well). It concerned the 'Beast of Gévaudan', the name given for the alleged creature (or creatures) behind a series of killings between 1764 and 1767 in south-central France in the former province of Gévaudan (modern-day Lozère). Word about these killings traveled widely. The *London Magazine* of January 1765 reported, '...a detachment of dragoons [light cavalry] has been out six weeks after him. The province has offered a thousand crowns to any persons that will kill him.'[11]

During this three year stretch, in a mountainous area ranging over two thousand square miles, some two hundred attacks were allegedly made, resulting in at least sixty-four deaths, and possibly over a hundred. The creature or creatures making the killings was never clearly determined; various reports were made describing a vicious and foul-smelling beast that some thought resembled an African wildcat (lion, tiger, panther) or even a hyena. Reportedly it could leap to great heights, and had a large and deadly tail to accompany its lethal fangs. Most of the victims were children. The matter came to the attention of King Louis XV, who commanded small armies to track down the creature. Despite some two thousand wolves being shot, the army failed to find the culprits. Eventually an elderly hunter named Francois Antoine succeeded in killing a large animal that weighed 130 pounds and was some 32 inches high at the shoulder (consistent with the dimensions of a large male gray wolf). This animal was identified by some surviving victims as the culprit (it was subsequently stuffed and displayed for the king at Versailles). However, even after this cull, killings of dozens of people, some of whom were children, continued to be reported. Finally another hunter, fifty-nine year old Jean Chastel, succeeded in killing a creature in 1767. Upon opening its stomach, he discovered human remains. Shortly after this, the killings stopped. This story was rendered into a novel in 1936 by Abel Chevally (*La Bete du Gévaudan*), where it was embellished by adding the legend that a pious and praying Charest killed the 'evil beast' with two silver bullets (and hence the origin of the legend).[12] Later speculation is that this 'beast' was a wolf-dog hybrid, which can be larger and more aggressive than either of its parents (and less likely to fear humans).[13]

The eccentric English scholar and Christian fundamentalist Montague Summers, in his prodigiously researched work *The Werewolf in Lore and Legend*, wrote:

> ...belief in the werewolf by its very antiquity and its universality affords accumulated evidence that there is at least some extremely significant and vital element of truth in this dateless tradition, however disguised and distorted it may have become in later days by the fantasies and poetry of the epic sagas, roundel, and romance.[14]

Summers' motivation for uncovering this 'vital element of truth' may have been compromised by his Christian 'Devil-hunting' agenda, but there is a truth buried in his speculation, and indeed it lies at the basis of this chapter. The 'disguised truth' does not involve, however, anything as banal as actual men turning into berserk werewolves and committing atrocities under cold moonlight (although clearly, such atrocities occurred, regardless of their cause). The distorted idea detectable in werewolf legends that we are more interested in here concerns a bona-fide and ancient shamanistic tradition: shapeshifting.

Shapeshifting

'Shapeshifting' is a late 20th century term devised to describe ancient beliefs and practices found in most worldwide cultures. In its broadest sense it refers simply to the ability of a person to change their form, usually into the form of an animal, but it can also suggest a change into the form of any other entity, including human or imaginary creature.

Shapeshifting is a practice closely related to 'sympathetic' or 'imitative magic'. Probably the crudest form of this practice is the common act, frequently engaged in by protesting groups or crowds, of burning an effigy. In destroying the effigy it is believed that this will bring some sort of ill fate to the likeness of the effigy. Certain practices of what are sometimes categorized as black magic or sorcery are based on this, with the stereotype of the magician or sorcerer who sticks pins into a doll that represents an actual person. The more evolved form of this magic is based on the idea that by mimicking something, we can become more deeply attuned to it, thereby understanding it more fully, and, if desirable, even gaining some of its qualities.

According to this idea we can also—provided we have the clear intent—manipulate, control, or otherwise affect what we are imitating by first, establishing a 'resonance alignment' with it, and second, changing our own behavior in such a fashion that this change will cause the object of our focus to change in a similar fashion. (This is similar to certain behavioral practices called 'mirroring', something many good salespeople either know of, or do naturally. The idea is that if we adopt a person's mannerisms in a sufficiently subtle fashion, it can result in them feeling more relaxed and 'in tune' with us, which in turn may cause them to be more agreeable to buying our product. This is also similar to a psychotherapeutic tool called 'reality pacing', in which the therapist achieves a strong rapport with their client by deeply acknowledging their point of view, which in turn results in the client feeling 'understood', and in turn, more likely to be open to positive and constructive use of the therapy).

One of the oldest pieces of art work known, the approximately 14,000 year old 'Les Trois Freres' cave paintings in southern France, contains a particular rendering that has long been cause for deep speculation. The image has come to be known as 'The Sorcerer'. It depicts what appears to be a dancing man dressed up in a costume of sorts that seems to be a composite of different animals.

Alternately, is has been speculated that the image shows a man who has partially transformed into an animal, or who himself may simply be part animal. The main idea behind a 'shaman'—the modern term for a practitioner of primordial magic—dancing as an animal, or otherwise seeking to attune deeply to the spirit of an animal, is mainly so that the shaman can acquire some of its natural powers. These 'natural powers' can be understood in terms of subtle, psychological or spiritual aspects—the courage of a lion, the perspective of a hawk, the grandness of an eagle, the power of a tiger or bear, the gentleness of a deer, the cunning of a fox, and so on. They can also be seen in terms of simple physical qualities—physical power, strength, endurance, health, etc. In many worldwide shamanistic traditions, it is believed that the act of deliberately attuning to the spirit of a particular animal is to 'acquire' a guardian spirit (or sometimes called a 'totem' or 'power animal') based on the energies of the entire species represented by the animal. In other words, to acquire an eagle power animal is to tap into the collective power of Eagle; to acquire a bear power animal is to receive the help of Bear, and so on.

The technical term for shapeshifting is therianthropy (from the Greek *therion*, 'wild beast', and *anthropos*, 'human'). The term 'shapeshifting' is somewhat misleading, as the vast majority of shamanistic traditions dealing with this matter acknowledge that so-called shapeshifting is in fact an altered state of consciousness, and thus is a transformation of *perception*, not of form (which, in the shamanistic context, does not diminish the value and purpose of it). That said, the difference between 'shift in perception' and 'shift in form' was doubtless rarely understood and even now is not always openly clarified, no doubt in large part due to the common folk of past times believing in the physical reality of therianthropes of whatever sort. The anthropologist Michael Harner, in his popular work *The Way of the Shaman* (1982), reported how the belief in shapeshifting is widespread in shamanistic traditions the world over.[15] He mentions the pervasiveness of the belief in North, Central and South American Indian mythology, amongst Australian aborigines, Scandinavian Lapp (where werewolfery is especially prevalent), Siberians and the Inuit, throughout Africa, and so on. Harner's popularization of the shamanic traditions came closely on the heels of Carlos Castaneda's highly influential books, in some of which he described his own 'transformation' into a crow. In particular Castaneda went a long way toward conveying the importance of *perception* in experience, and of the meaning and purpose of altered states of consciousness. Both Harner and Castaneda had been preceded by the Romanian scholar Mircea Eliade, who in 1951 put out his landmark work *Shamanism: Archaic Techniques of Ecstasy*. This work went a long way toward shedding light on a key matter related to shapeshifting, and that is the question of the so-called 'familiar' or 'helping spirit'. The word 'familiar' relates to family-intimacy; in late 16th century Europe the word also came to be used to represent the 'evil helping spirit' of a witch or sorcerer. The historian James Sharpe noted,

> …the idea that a witch was usually assisted by a familiar in the shape of an animal constantly recurred in pamphlet accounts; indeed it was present in two of the first surviving pamphlets concerned with witchcraft, both published in 1566…[16]

It is ironic to note that the more astute scholars of that time held a view that discounted the possibility of actual shapeshifting, seeing it all rather as illusion or perceptual tricks—and yet at the same time, ascribed a *supernatural cause* to these illusions—namely, that they were the work of the Devil. In 1608 the Italian clergyman Francesco Guazzo published his *Compendium Maleficarum* (a 'study' of witches), in which he wrote:

> …As I have already said, no one must let himself think that a man can really be changed into a beast, or a beast into a real man; for these are magic portents and illusions…for the Devil, as I have

> said elsewhere, deceived our senses in various ways. Sometimes he substitutes another body, while the witches themselves are absent...and himself assumes the body of a wolf formed from the air and wrapped around him, and does those actions which men think are done by the wretched absent witch who is asleep.[17]

Werewolfery was impossible, and thus an illusion: but an illusion created by the Devil. It was a twisted synthesis of critical thinking and religious dogma.

Lurid and even erotic powers were ascribed to some 'familiar' spirits, such as the bizarre practice of sucking blood from the genitalia or the anus of the witch.[18] (As we saw in the previous chapter this was all seen as a variant of the belief, prevalent on continental Europe at that time, that the Devil had wild orgies with witches during late night ceremonies called 'sabbats'). However as legitimate shamanistic traditions bear out, the 'familiar' or 'helping spirit' is not seen as lascivious, let alone evil; on the contrary, it is generally regarded as a benevolent assistant, loyal, trustworthy, and able to instill helpful power into the shaman who invokes it.

Eliade defined three essential categories of 'spirits' within the shaman's world: 'familiars' or 'helping spirits'; 'tutelary spirits'; and 'divine or semi-divine beings'.[19] It is the first group, the 'helping spirits', which is of interest in the matter of shapeshifting.

A common theme in shamanic tradition is that of the shaman undergoing a key process of awakening (or 'illumination'), after which he must retreat to a wild and natural setting and obtain a helping spirit. This usually occurs via the shaman entering some sort of trance or altered state of consciousness (as via dance, drumming, meditation, hallucinogens, etc.). When the 'helping spirit' comes to him he enters into a deep communion with it, to the point of taking on some of its behavior and characteristics:

The spirits all manifest themselves through the shaman, making strange noises, unintelligible sounds, etc.[20]

The helping spirit is almost always the spirit-form of a particular animal. Eliade clarified that this process is not the same as 'possession', in that the shaman is acting willfully and voluntarily—and that if anything, the process is reversed, in that it is the shaman who is taking possession of the helping spirit. The helping spirit is of great importance to the shaman, as it represents the shaman's ability to navigate the 'bridge' between the physical dimension and the 'other worlds'. Many worldwide traditions feature legends of the 'psychopomp', the term for a spirit-guide who ushers the soul of a dead person to and through the Other Side, or even to become the new form of the deceased person.[21] Commonly this spirit-guide is in the form of an animal (e.g., the Egyptian jackal-god Anubis).

The 'tutelary spirit' is generally understood to be a guardian spirit of a very high order, and in some respects correlates to the idea of the 'Holy Guardian Angel' that is central to many schools of the Western esoteric tradition. This spirit is, in fact, the higher self of the person, but seen from the perspective of the personality it appears to be a distinct entity that 'guards' or 'oversees' the person's life. In describing beliefs among shamans of Siberia and Mongolia, Eliade writes:

> The tutelary animal of the Buryat shamans is called the *khubilgan*, a term that can be interpreted as 'metamorphosis' (from *khubilkhu*, 'to change oneself', 'to take on another form'). In other words, the tutelary animal not only enables the shaman to transform himself; it is in a manner his 'double', his alter ego. This alter ego is one of the shaman's 'souls', the 'life soul'.[22]

As Eliade astutely noted, the whole basis of the shaman's connection to the helping spirit relates to not just his ability to travel 'between worlds', but also to his ability to undergo 'death and resurrection' by overcoming the limitations of material existence. In short, the ability to shapeshift ultimately relates to the ability to conquer death by undergoing an initiation that thematically involves death itself. Not the death of simply the body, but the death of egocentric distortions and delusions brought about by excessive attachment to material form.

The Psychology of Familiars and Shapeshifting

To further increase our perspective on all this, it is helpful to briefly discuss the psychology of shapeshifting. Before doing so it should be clarified, however, that the traditional shaman is a metaphysical realist, in the sense of believing that the various dimensions and entities contacted actually exist outside of his or her own mind.[23] Any attempts at psychological interpretation in the matter of shamanic practices needs to be tempered with this understanding. That does not have to stop us, however, from looking at the big picture. Whether we regard something as 'outside' of our consciousness or not, we still have to come to terms with the lesson that the experience represents for us if we wish to understand ourselves better. This is true for any wishing to understand the underlying psychology of certain shamanistic practices.

First, to look at the obvious: the question of mental illness. As mentioned above in the discussions of some of the actual werewolf trials of Early Modern Europe, the cases that involved murders and other criminal depravities (as opposed to 'confessions' fabricated under pain of torture) were quite clearly examples of what today would be called psychopathy. There is, however, a 'milder' form of mental illness connected to mystical experiences, what the psychiatrist Roger Walsh called 'mystical experiences with psychotic features'. Walsh cited transpersonal psychologists Stanislav and Christina Grof who noted in their studying the cases of 'ordinary' people who underwent spiritual crises that their mystical experiences often involved themes such as great suffering (breakdown of some sort) and symbolic death, followed by 'rebirth', 'ascent and magical flight', and even 'communication with animals or animal spirits'. Walsh goes on to discuss a shamanic phenomenon of particular relevance to a chapter on werewolves, that being 'possession':

> Experiences of possession have been described throughout history and may be a major feature of the shamanic crisis. Today they may occur either spontaneously or in religious or psychotherapeutic settings. The experiences battling with or being overwhelmed by rage and hatred can be of hideous intensity. So powerful, repugnant, and alien do these emotions feel that they seem literally demonic, and the victim may fear he is engaged in a desperate battle for his very life and sanity.[24]

He goes on to point out, however, that the entire matter can be understood as a process of shedding an old self-image, i.e., a type of spiritual metamorphosis:

> Psychiatrist John Perry has described the renewal process as an experience of profound, all-encompassing destruction followed by regeneration…yet this destruction is not the end but rather is a prelude to rebirth and regeneration.[25]

The 'degraded' form of this process of shamanic death, regeneration, and rebirth is well symbolized by the dark, blindly destructive face of the werewolf—the end result of a tormented transformation into a powerful beast (in effect, possession), under moonlight. For the werewolf, the 'rebirth' never comes. There are only endless deaths (losing consciousness) and transformations which he has no ability to control. The German novelist Herman Hesse, in his 1927 novel *Steppenwolf,* about a man inwardly conflicted over the tug-of-war between his 'high, spiritual' side and his 'low, animalistic' side, described the process more in terms of social alienation, rejection of bourgeois values and mainstream mediocrity. This is an example of what Colin Wilson called an 'Outsider', one who instinctively seeks to move beyond the mediocrity of the masses, but in most cases lacks the guidance, or the ability to 'regenerate' and re-invent themselves in a fulfilling manner.

True shamanic practice involves voluntary intent in the matter of regeneration and rebirth. From the point of view of a person seeking (consciously or not) to become inwardly unified, integrated, a whole person, the ultimate spiritual purpose of associating with 'familiars' or the practice of shapeshifting is becoming more conscious of elements of one's own nature. The key, of course, is consciousness. We cannot integrate a part of our nature without first becoming aware of it. (As Gurdjieff said, we 'name the devil in order to route him out'). We cannot integrate our 'inner beast' and all the ways its energies become manifest, without first seeing and understanding something of the nature of this beast. In referring to the tale of the wizard Faust and the devil he conjures (Mephistopheles), C.G. Jung wrote:

> Mephistopheles is the diabolical aspect of every psychic function that has broken loose from the hierarchy of the total psyche and now enjoys independence and absolute power. But this can be perceived only when the function becomes a separate entity and is objectivated or personified…'[26]

Magical evocation—the classical practice of a wizard or magician standing in a circle fortified by Holy Names and 'raising a spirit' by calling it forth via various magical formulae—is essentially the ritualized equivalent of the shaman acquiring a helping spirit. (It goes without saying that the 'type' of spirit being raised, its disposition and qualities, can vary greatly). Seen from a psychological perspective, this represents 'calling forth' elements of the magician's psyche so that he can objectify them and begin to understand them. (In alchemy, this stage corresponds to necessary processes defined by various forms of separation, prior to recombining them). Of course, the magician or shaman will not always automatically understand how the 'spirit' ultimately reflects a quality or potential within the magician or shaman's own psyche. This point is crucial. The risk in 'evoking' parts of our nature to objective reality is that we may be so disturbed by what we see that we disown these parts, or worse, project them on to others, who then become our convenient scapegoats. (An idea that lies behind the notion of the magician or shaman evoking a spirit that proves to be too much for him to handle). The psycho-spiritual purpose of shapeshifting can be only one: to objectify parts of our nature, establish a relationship with them, and 're-absorb' them by owning and taking responsibility for their energies—which are, after all, *our* energies. In so doing we integrate their qualities. In so doing, we become more Whole.

The 'wolfman' is part of human nature—aggressive impulse, secretive and repressed, potentially destructive—for whatever causes. It has been commonly associated with masculine impulse, but it is alive and well in the feminine mind also, hinted at in its legendary connection with the lunar cycle (and menstrual process), and further shown in the traditional Moon card of the Tarot, which commonly features a dog howling at the Moon. Man or woman, we need not undergo a writhing and tormented transformation into a murderous beast under a full Moon—that is, we need not deny and repress our aggressive impulses, by becoming secretive or furtive about them. As Jung wrote:

> ...we have to expose ourselves to the animal impulses of the unconscious without identifying with them and without 'running away'; for flight from the unconscious would defeat the purpose of the whole proceeding. We must hold our ground, which means here that the process initiated by...self-observation must be experienced in all its ramifications and then articulated with consciousness to the best of understanding.[27]

Finally, it bears mentioning that a term from alchemy—antimony (an actual chemical element with the atomic number of 51)—referred to the hidden wild beast within, and was associated with the wolf in medieval alchemy texts. It particularly pointed toward the shadow element of the monk or priest, something that has become all too much a matter of common knowledge.

Deity Yoga and the Assumption of God-forms

If the brutal and twisted imagery of the werewolf—secretive, cursed, predatory, preying mostly on women and children, the ghoul of every Little Red Riding Hood's worst nightmare—represents some of the more degraded elements of imagination, then the esoteric practices known as the 'assumption of god-forms' and 'deity yoga' represent some of its most elevated. As suggested above, in psychological language the werewolf is a manifestation of the 'Shadow'. As with all Shadow-work the aim is not to run away from the energy, nor to indulge it, but rather to courageously face into it, embrace it, and transmute its powerful energies. In so doing, the vitality, creativity, and power of the Shadow are freed up, minus the secretiveness, hostility and aggression. Much as with a powerful 'problem child', we need to establish a profound level of relationship with this energy and ultimately take responsibility for the reality that it is not our 'feral child', it is rather *part* of us. (In general, this requires a deep level of honesty about our less desirable qualities).

Tibetan Buddhism, being a unique amalgam of rarefied Indian Buddhist metaphysics and earthy Tibetan shamanism, developed particular methods for working with and transforming some of the darkest and densest energies of the Shadow. Some of these practices are included in parts of what is usually termed 'deity-yoga', and they involve utilizing particular tutelary deities as *yidams* (the Sanskrit equivalent term is *Ishta-deva,* meaning 'deity that is desired and given reverence to'). A *yidam* is a celestial being that is the object of personal focus and devotion, either for a spiritual retreat, or as a life-long object of meditation.

In the Tibetan Buddhist pantheon many exalted deities are recognized, but three very important ones are Chenrezig, the lord of Compassion (known in India as Avalokiteshvara and in China as Kuan Yin); Manjushri, lord of Wisdom; and Vajrapani, lord of Power. These deities in turn all have a 'wrathful aspect'—for Chenrezig it is Mahakala; for Manjushri it is Yamantaka; and the wrathful face of Vajrapani (which usually goes by the same name). These 'wrathful deities' all appear, to one unaware of Tibetan Buddhist teachings, as simply demonic—fierce, ugly, threatening, often adorned with skulls and of a terrifying disposition. But the three just mentioned are not demons; they are expressions of 'active wisdom', 'active compassion', and 'active power', respectively. According to the teachings they exist in part to protect the *dharma* (Buddhist teachings), and any practitioner who calls on them, a protector/guide theme that is found in many worldwide spiritual mythologies. But there is a subtler, deeper teaching involved here, and it has to do with the 'taming' and integration of Shadow-energies. The fierce deities of Tibetan Buddhism can be thought of as masters of 'tough love', fearless and courageous, spiritual warriors ready to deal with the darkest faces of our egos. They do this not by beating these parts of our nature into submission, but rather by resonating with them, entering their worlds, speaking their language, so to speak, so as to acquire their trust. In so doing, they are then capable of guiding these parts of our darker nature back into the light of integrated awareness. In referring to Yamantaka, the wrathful aspect of Manjushri (lord of Wisdom), Buddhist psychologist Rob Preece wrote:

> Yamantaka gives the forces of the Shadow a symbol that hooks their energy and provides a channel and direction for their expression and transformation...he is able to harness their energy and embody their power consciously. The archetypal forces of the instincts and emotions held in the Shadow are given a channel through Yamantaka so that they can be brought into consciousness, transformed, and integrated...as the Shadow forces are transformed, their energy is not lost, but integrated into personal power.[28]

Preece also cited the vivid analogy of a gang of biker thugs gone out of control (representing our Shadow-elements that are disconnected and 'acting out', such as impulsive anger, tendencies toward depression, unhinged jealousy, etc.). He then asks how such thugs should correctly be 'put in their place', and suggests that it will not be effectively done by a mild-mannered sort, but most likely by one who resembled a biker-tough guy himself, and yet is really an advanced teacher. That is what a wrathful deity like Yamantaka represents: the highest expression of tough love.

However, the deeper point is to understand that the wrathful deities are not actually separate from us. They are elements of our own nature. The difference between them and a tormented creature like a werewolf is that they are using their power and aggression in the service of a higher purpose. The werewolf is the beast with no purpose, no reason for being; a furtive expression of repressed and distorted passion; at best, a twisted rebelliousness. When purpose is squashed, when there exists no other reason for being than serving someone else's agenda, then hostility breeds and seeks outlets.

The fundamental motivating force toward a higher purpose is compassion, precisely because 'higher purpose' always, without fail, involves playing a role in the awakening and evolution of the human species. Accordingly, compassion is cultivated with a view toward helping others develop and awaken to their true nature as beings of unlimited potential. The key quality in this compassion is *enthusiasm* (deriving from the Greek terms *enthousiasmos* and *entheos,* both of which relate to 'divine inspiration' and the idea of being ecstatically possessed by a divine being). The idea of merging with a divine being is ancient, and found within many world myths and wisdom traditions. It is very common in ancient Egyptian tradition but perhaps in ways that have not always been correctly interpreted, an idea that was developed by Jeremy Naydler in his work *Shamanic Wisdom in the Pyramid Texts.*[29] Naydler argued that ancient Egyptian writings preserved in the famous Pyramid texts are more than simple funerary arrangements or frivolous mythology, but are rather teachings describing the initiatic process of awakening to the divine on Earth, while alive, and not just in some after-life.

Naydler wrote:

> The role of the shaman as mediator between the 'nonordinary' reality of the spirit world and the ordinary reality of the sense-perceptible world is in many respects paralleled in ancient Egypt by the Egyptian king, whose role is similarly to act as mediator between worlds. Such important shamanic themes as the initiatory death and dismemberment followed by rebirth and renewal, the transformation of the shaman into a power animal, the ecstatic ascent to the sky, and the crossing of the threshold of death in order to commune with ancestors and gods are all to be found in the Pyramid Texts...[30]

The Western esoteric practice known as 'the assumption of Godforms' involves extensive usage of active imagination. This is done via the practice of visualizing in detail the particular god (usually Egyptian) chosen to unify with. As esoteric scholar Arthur Versluis wrote, in referring to ancient Egyptian practices of identifying with particular deities,

> ...to be the God, to not only mirror, but to attain complete identification with the God, with that state of consciousness, was the aim of initiatory ritual as such.[31]

The result is intended to develop the candidate's 'Body of Light', and ultimately, to change or transmute the Body of Light into the 'Body of God'. That is the ageless goal of both mysticism and high magic: union with the Source and transfiguration into infinite Light.

The Western esoteric practices of assuming Godforms are, of course, very similar to the Tibetan Buddhist practices of deity yoga mentioned above, although it should be pointed out that the Tibetan systems generally emphasize the necessity of developing compassion and understanding emptiness (the intrinsic formlessness of ultimate reality) prior to engaging the visualization work. There are also preliminary trainings in Western esoterica, but they relate more to the development of will and imagination rather than compassion and grasp of emptiness. Both approaches, however, are ultimately concerned with the highest possible usage of imagination as a tool to realize our divine potential.

Appendix I

Ancient Egypt, Hermeticism, Rosicrucians, and the Kybalion

The roots of the Western esoteric tradition lie mostly in the triangular relationship between the ancient Egyptians, Greeks and the Judeo-Christian tradition. Over time much of the Egyptian influence faded, to the extent that by the time of Christ the 'triangular' configuration of Egypt/Greece/Judeo-Christianity could be said to have been reduced to the twin influences of the Greek and Judeo-Christian minds; geographically, to that of Athens and Jerusalem. To these two key pillars of the Western mind we will turn shortly, but first a brief overview of the ancient Egyptian influence.

The 'Old Kingdom' phase of pharaonic Egypt ran from roughly 3100–2200 BCE, the period that saw the construction of most of Egypt's great architectural monuments.[1] In the study of Egyptian religion, of particular interest are the 'Pyramid Texts' (believed to have been written around 2350 BCE), parts of which eventually became by 1500 BCE the *Book of the Coming Forth by Day*, commonly known in current times as the *Egyptian Book of the Dead*.

Up until the 19th century conventional wisdom held that the finer accomplishments of Greek philosophical thought had its origins in Egypt, which was regarded as the older and wiser of the two cultures. This view, which held up for a long time, began to change in the late 19th century when some European scholars, making close studies of Egyptian writings, concluded that nothing of any profound level of sophistication in philosophical or spiritual thought could be found in ancient Egypt. That view gradually took over and held sway among most mainstream academic Egyptologists until around the middle of the 20th century. It still persists to a fair degree even now where ancient art and monuments are all that are known of ancient Egypt to most of the world. One academic in the 1930s wrote, 'The Egyptian mind was practical and concrete and concerned itself little or not at all with speculations regarding the ultimate nature of things...they never disentangled philosophy from the crudest theology'.[2] This summed up the prevailing view of the ancient Egyptians among the early 20th century historians: the Egyptians were practical, not philosophical people, and their spirituality was essentially primitive, based on animistic myths, legends, and preoccupation with externalized individual gods.

This view was colored by the Western academic filters of that time, which were influenced by several factors, among which were the ideas of evolution introduced by Darwin in the 19th century, yielding the general assumption that everything—including wisdom—evolves, and that therefore Greek wisdom must be superior to Egyptian as it came later. Western academia has also been given to exalt the scientific method, and thus to be inclined to see things in terms of the visible world and demonstrable effects only. When the writings of the Egyptian pyramid texts were translated they were seen as simply funerary spells, mumbo-jumbo that related to myth and legend and little else. However others, as early as the 1930s, saw these writings differently, such as when Israel Regardie was pointing out how the descriptions of the 'afterlife' dimensions in the Pyramid Texts corresponded closely to that of Hindu writings.[3]

Much of the writings of the Pyramid Texts were found inscribed on the walls of the pyramid of Unas, which is situated close to Zoser's Step Pyramid, in Saqqara, about twenty miles south of Giza (site of the Great Pyramid and Sphinx). The Step Pyramid is the oldest pyramid in Egypt and still in reasonable shape despite being built around 3100 BCE. The pyramid of pharaoh Unas, built around 2350 BC, is in ruins, but the interior lower chambers survive, the walls of which house the complicated hieroglyphs of the texts.

Most of these writings appear to be concerned with the transition of the dead pharaoh to the afterlife, and the complex process of navigation that that entails. Hence they were referred to by scholars as 'funerary texts'. As pointed out by Jeremy Naydler, these descriptions of the afterlife seem to correlate closely with shamanic visions and the inner investigations of Oriental cultures such as that of the yogis and mystics of India and Tibet.[4] In fact, much of the famous *Bardo Thodol,* or *Tibetan Book of the Dead,* describes states of consciousness and levels of reality that appear very similar to those described in the *Egyptian Book of the Dead,* which itself evolved from the Pyramid Texts. The *Egyptian Book of the Dead* is about 2,500 years older than the *Tibetan Book of the Dead* (which was written around 900 CE), and arose in a land far from Tibet, but held in common with the Tibetans a spirituality that embraced shamanistic elements. Mircea Eliade pointed out that one of the main symbols of religious myth throughout history has been an ascendant connection to a 'higher world', such as via the 'tree', 'ladder', 'bridge' or 'sacred mountain' that connects Earth with the heaven worlds. While most cultures are familiar with such an idea, only a small percentage of people have ever sought to make this journey to the 'higher world' *while still alive* (as opposed to waiting for the afterlife as promised by typical orthodox religion). In esoteric language one who seeks to make the journey to the 'higher world' while alive is an *initiate*. Part of this initiation is, of course, accompanied by the understanding that this 'higher world' is accessible via individual consciousness here and now.

Egyptian religion was, strictly speaking, monotheistic, in that it was based on the idea of one Source that created the universe, a universe that is deeply alive and spiritual. The many gods of the Egyptian pantheons were representations of the divine forces and qualities of the universe. Here we see the magical world view *par excellence*—the world is seen as spiritual in itself, to be embraced as such (as opposed to denied or renounced).

Egyptian writings indicated different 'worlds' or levels of reality: central of which were the *duat* (underworld; in modern occult terminology, the 'astral plane'; in modern psychological language, probably best defined as the 'collective unconscious'); and the *ahket* (the higher planes of illumination). We see in this simple division an essential feature of the esoteric teachings, reaching its later clearest culmination in Plato, Plotinus, and the Gnostics—the idea that reality is multileveled, corresponding in various ways to our inner being and levels of consciousness—and that these levels can be navigated and their 'secrets' revealed via a sufficient combination of intent and discipline.

Hermeticism

The term 'Hermeticism' derives from the name Hermes Trismegistus (Hermes 'Thrice-Blessed'—the origin of the term 'thrice blessed' is uncertain, though occasionally this is thought to be a reference to a tripartite nature of king, philosopher, and priest). This name is in turn deriving from the Greek god Hermes (known by the Romans as Mercury) and has come to also be associated with the older Egyptian deity known as Thoth, the god of wisdom, writing, magic, etc. Hermeticism has been characterized as a 'pagan form of Gnosticism', based on similar doctrines such as a divine trinity and the key role of the number seven in the unfolding of the cosmos (seven hierarchical levels or 'heavens', often corresponding to the seven classical 'planets,' Sun, Moon, Mercury, Venus, Mars, Jupiter, Saturn).[5]

Hermeticism arose out of the meeting of the two great Western cultures of antiquity, Egypt and Greece, mostly following the conquests of Alexander the Great in the early 300s BCE. The rational philosophy of the Greeks, led by Socrates, Plato, and Aristotle, met the esoteric spirituality of the Egyptian priesthoods, and the resulting cross cultural mix, influential in the Hellenized Mediterranean (roughly 300 BCE to 300 CE) and arising more or less parallel to Gnosticism and Neoplatonism, was a body of spiritual teachings and practices that eventually came to be loosely known as 'Hermetism' (and much later in the Middle Ages, as Hermeticism, the name more commonly given to it now, and that for the sake of simplicity we will use herein). The basic ideas of Hermeticism are consistent with most paths of perennial wisdom, those being a disciplined attempt to escape from the prison of the human condition, and awaken to (or *re*-awaken to) our innate association with the divine.

Hermeticism has been seen, especially by Renaissance scholars such as Marcilio Ficino, as deriving from the *prisca theologia,* a term that refers to a single universal wisdom tradition that existed in the ancient past and from which all wisdom traditions (and their exoteric forms, the organized religions) derive. *Prisca theologia* is different from *Philosophia perennis,* in that it views all subsequent derivations from the original universal wisdom teaching as degradations, whereas the perennial philosophy is more optimistic, maintaining that the pure wisdom traditions emerge from time to time to rejuvenate the spiritual condition of humanity.

In older times individual spiritual teachers or authors were rarely remembered or credited with anything, and thus most early Hermetic teachings and writings are attributed to the mythical Hermes Trismegistus. Few early Hermetic texts survive, possibly owing in part to the torching of the famous Alexandrian library, but some notable ones that did survive—all written roughly between 100 and 300 CE—are the *Corpus Hermeticum*, the Latin *Asclepius,* and the *The Eighth and Ninth Sphere* of the Coptic Hermetica. (The Renaissance scholars, such as Ficino and Pico della Mirandola, believed at the time that the Hermetic texts were much older, dating possibly even to pre-Mosaic times, which lent them a further aura of importance; it was only demonstrated in the 17th century that in fact they were composed after the time of Christ). All showed a marked Greek influence, but none could be classified as 'philosophy' in the strictest sense, because all hold to the importance of mystical or religious revelation as a means of arriving at a personal understanding of higher truths.[6]

This process of attaining to higher truth was usually described via an elaborate imagery of ascending through various levels (commonly seven) of the heavens to reach the Divine, a process that was understood to be fundamentally internal. In so doing, Man could also regain his control over the material universe, something he supposedly had lost in the 'fall'. The central difference between Hermetic and Christian doctrine lay in the central figure: Hermes Trismegistus was both the redeemer and the revealer of truth, not Jesus. (That said, the similarities between Hermes and Jesus are too many to list here; one interesting symbol they held in common was that of the Shepherd; some of the oldest Greek statues of Hermes depicted him in the company of rams or lambs.[7] Hermetic teaching was similar to Neoplatonism and Kabbalah in its regard of the material dimension as an opportunity to learn and grow, in contrast to more anti-cosmic traditions such as Gnosticism. It also holds in common with Zoroastrianism the idea that humanity not only has an opportunity to awaken but to participate in the transformation and redemption of the world. Hermetica was thus pre-eminently concerned with the empowerment of Man, and accordingly became a key precursor to 19th and 20th century 'New Thought' paradigms in which the purpose to life was understood to lie in the individual embodiment of divine status and the fulfilling of a role in the 'divine plan'. This greater purpose lay in contrast to a life based on subservient trust in an omnipotent power or a meaningless existence based on the mechanical results of blind cause and effect.

The *Corpus Hermeticum* is a group of fifteen books; the most renowned of these is the first, known as the *Poimandres* (sometimes transliterated as *Pymander*), a name that, according to recent scholarship, may be sourcing from the Egyptian words for 'the knowledge of Ra'.[8] The *Poimandres* is one of the more significant Hermetic texts in that it parallels other wisdom teachings that emphasize the pre-eminence of consciousness, which is usually symbolized by a primordial and supreme Light (the 'Clear Light' of Tibetan Buddhism, or the 'Ancient Lights' of the Zohar, or the pure Light of Jacob Boehme's *Aurora*).[9]

A key passage in the *Corpus Hermeticum* occurs in Chapter 11, titled 'Mind Unto Hermes':

> *Behold what power, what swiftness, you have! And can you do all of these things, and God not?*
>
> *Then, in this way know God; as having all things in Himself as thoughts, the whole Cosmos itself.*
>
> *If, then, you do not make yourself like unto God, you cannot know Him. For like is knowable to like alone.*
>
> *Make, then, yourself to grow to the same stature as the Greatness which transcends all measure; leap forth from every body; transcend all Time; become Eternity; and thus shall you know God.*
>
> *Conceiving nothing is impossible unto yourself, think yourself deathless and able to know all—all arts, all sciences, the way of every life.*
>
> *Become more lofty than all height, and lower than all depth. Collect into thyself all senses of all creatures—of fire and water, dry and moist. Think that you are at the same time in every place—in earth, in sea, in sky; not yet begotten, in the womb, young, old, and dead, in after-death conditions.*
>
> *And if you know all these things at once—times, places, doings, qualities, and quantities; you can know God.*[10]

We see in this the essential creed of the esoteric path, which is the idea that complete identification with the divine is not just possible but is the basis of the Great Work of inner transformation. This does, naturally, carry a shadow-element, something touched on in other parts of this book. Grandiosity and personality-inflation has always been the bane of the occultist or esoteric practitioner. There are, however, methodologies that work to prevent this, such as the various meditations given in Chapter 11. Additionally, a personality-typology system such as the Enneagram (mentioned in Chapter 10) can be very effective in undermining attempts of the ego-self to utilize esoteric teachings as a means to bolster its identity. That said, the Hermetic idea of 'like unto like' that underlies the idea of becoming like something in order to know it, is valid on many levels and also works to counteract the dogma of organized religion, and its stress on the need to be blindly subservient to the supreme authority of God; something that all too easily becomes degraded into the need to be unquestioningly obedient to secular masters.

One of the key Hermetic texts from the *Corpus*, called the *Tabula Smaragdina* or *The Emerald Tablet of Hermes*, has been translated many times and has long been considered a cornerstone of Hermetic philosophy. The following passages are a common translation of some lines from *The Emerald Tablet*:

1. *This is true and remote from all cover of falsehood:*
2. *Whatever is below is similar to that which is above. As above, so below. Through this the marvels of the work of one thing are procured and perfected.*
3. *Also, as all things are made from One, by the consideration of One, so all things were made from this One, by conjunction.*
4. *The father of it is the sun, the mother the moon.*
5. *The wind bore it in the womb. Its nurse is the earth, the mother of all perfection.*
6. *Its power is perfected.*
7. *If it is turned into earth, separate the earth from the fire, the subtle and thin from the crude and coarse, prudently, with modesty and wisdom.*
8. *This ascends from the earth into the sky and again descends from the sky to the earth, and receives the power and efficacy of things above and of things below.*
9. *By this means you will acquire the glory of the whole world, and so you will drive away all shadows and blindness.*
10. *For this by its fortitude snatches the palm from all other fortitude and power. For it is able to penetrate and subdue everything subtle and everything crude and hard.*
11. *By this means the world was founded*
12. *And hence the marvelous cojunctions of it and admirable effects, since this is the way by which these marvels may be brought about.*
13. *And because of this they have called me Hermes Trismegistus*

since I have the three parts of the wisdom and Philosophy of the whole universe.

14. *My speech is finished which I have spoken concerning the solar work.*[4]

Many mystery traditions and 'secret societies' have their roots in Hermeticism, which in general was very given to the idea of 'initiation'. Among the more prominent and influential of these 'secret' organizations were the Rosicrucians—a great irony, in that for the first century or so of their mention, they almost certainly did not even exist.

The Rosicrucians

Around the year 1610 a mysterious manuscript began circulating in Kassel, in present-day central Germany. It was published in 1614, called *Fama Fraternitatis RC* (Tradition of the Brotherhood of the Rosy Cross). The following year another publication appeared, called the *Confessio Fraternitatis RC* (Confession of the Brotherhood of the Rosy Cross). The first appeared in German, and told of a mysterious mystic named Christian Rosenkreuz ('Rose-Cross') whose long life allegedly spanned the 14th and 15th centuries, and who was said to have founded a brotherhood based on wisdom he had acquired from travels in the East. The second reiterated in forceful terms the messages transmitted in the first, which were the following: papal tyranny was to be overthrown, society itself to be radically reformed, and all of this to be based on profound and mysterious teachings rooted in the great wisdom traditions of the world. Rosenkreuz himself was the central myth, a great Adept who dedicated his life to healing the less fortunate, and teaching—those who were ready—the exalted wisdom of the ancients. As for when exactly Christian Rosenkreuz lived, the documents did not explicitly say, but a reference in the *Confessio* implied that he had been born in 1378 and lived for 106 years, suggesting that he died in 1484. The legend continues that his body then lay undiscovered in a vault, in a state of perfect preservation, for 120 years, until 1604.

Rosenkreuz's alleged life spanned the early part of the European Renaissance (generally recognized to have begun in Italy around the year 1400). The decades of the mid-14th century had been transformative, albeit due to devastating reasons, such as the Black Death that devastated much of Europe between the years 1346–1353. The plague was a bacterium that had originated in China and spread to the Mediterranean via the Silk Road; from there it engulfed most of Europe, including the British Isles, reducing the population by as much as 50 percent. The enormous suffering of this period led to major upheavals in European civilization, part of which involved a reshaping of philosophy and religious thought. The ideal of the Renaissance was about celebrating the power of individual creativity on Earth here and now, with less reliance on blind faith in doctrine or a promised beneficent afterlife for the pious.

Following the publications of the *Fama* and *Confessio*, a third document appeared in 1616, called *Chymische Hochzeit Christiani Rosencreutz anno 1459* (*The Chymical Wedding of Christian Rosenkreuz in 1459*). This document was of a markedly different style from the first two, and is generally recognized as an alchemical allegory (the word 'chymical' was the archaic term for alchemy). It concerns the visit of Christian Rosenkreuz to a mysterious castle, whereupon he witnesses and assists in the marriage of a king and queen. This work was originally written by Johann Valentin Andreae in 1604, though not initially published. It was then revised and published in 1616, immediately following the appearance of the first two documents.

Fama is Latin for 'talk, rumor, report, tradition,' and even 'gossip'. Most ideas are initially transmitted in such a fashion—the modern terms are 'meme', 'word of mouth' or 'going viral', something every astute advertising agency knows the power of. Some have suggested that *fama* in this case can also be understood simply as 'legend' or 'myth'[11] Either way, the whole idea was an expression of a deep desire to bring about a revolution in collective consciousness, to help people remember what really mattered in life, and of the need to discover and fulfill one's highest destiny. Christian Rosenkreuz was presented as a Christian mystic, an advanced Adept, allegiant to Christ—but he was not Christ himself. Rosenkreuz did not resurrect; he was rather perfectly preserved in a stasis. The idea of preservation after the death of the physical body is old, and found in many traditions, most notably in the mummification practices of ancient Egypt. There are even modern stories of particular spiritual teachers whose bodies seem to defy typical biological processes of decay following death.

The Rosicrucian mystical tradition, arising in the 17th century and later to become a strong influence on both Freemasonry and the late 19th century Hermetic Order of the Golden Dawn, was itself influenced by the Hermetic ideas. It bore a strong influence on 17th century esotericists such as the alchemist Michael Maier and the astrologer and physician Robert Fludd, and spawned numerous closed societies that operated on initiatory levels. One of the first of these was the German Order of Golden and Rosy Cross (founded in 1710 by the alchemist Samuel Richter), followed by a host of others such as the Societas Rosicruciana in Scotia (founded in Scotland in the mid-1800s), the Societas Rosicruciana in Anglia (founded in England in 1865), the Societas Rosicruciana in Civitatibus Foederatis (SRICF, founded in America in 1880), and the Ancient Mystical Order Rosae Crucis (AMORC, founded in 1915 in New York).

The Kybalion

Deserving mention here—if only for the good reflection it presents of many 20th century schools of alternative spiritual thought—is the slim volume called *The Kybalion*, first published in 1908 and claiming to source from ancient esoteric principles. It was famously attributed to 'Three Initiates', although subsequent research revealed that the author was almost certainly William Walker Atkinson (1862–1932), a one-time lawyer and later New Thought writer and editor. *The Kybalion* claimed to represent Hermetic principles of antiquity, but clearly drew influence from 19th century New Thought ideas.

Atkinson used several pseudonyms, one of which was 'Yogi Ramacharaka'. Atkinson's 1911 publication, *Fourteen Lessons in Yogi Philosophy and Oriental Occultism,* appears to have been a source for Carlos Castaneda, especially in the latter's second book, *A Separate Reality: Further Conversations with Don Juan* (1970), where Castaneda's mentor describes human 'auras' in a way that dovetails closely with those of Yogi Ramacharaka.[12] In *The Kybalion,* Atkinson listed seven 'hermetic principles'. They are listed below, with some critical remarks following in parentheses.

1. *The Principle of Mentalism.* The main idea here is consistent with philosophical Idealism, that being that mind is primordial and all pervasive. The added emphasis here is that this 'mind' is ultimately identical with 'spirit', and is alive, infinite, and supremely wise. All phenomena of the universe are understood to be a creation of universal mind. Accordingly it is assumed that one who masters this principle can cause changes in their life based on the correct usage of mental powers. (The potential weakness here is that the role of the unconscious mind is not acknowledged, an issue addressed by modern psychology and psychotherapy. One can work with mental intention all that one wants, but if one is divided inwardly, i.e., one's unconscious mind is holding too much conflicted and repressed material, nothing much will change outwardly, something like a vehicle with a running engine that goes nowhere because its parking breaks are engaged).

2. *The Principle of Correspondence.* The idea here is that reality consists of a series of correspondences between the immaterial and material worlds, a network of interdependence that when understood yields the secrets of nature and the ability to navigate reality in an effective manner. Much of this idea forms the basis of science, such as via direct observations and repeated experiments. (The potential weakness of this view is what is known as 'magical thinking', based on the *post-hoc* logical fallacy, the idea that because event 'A'

precedes event 'B', event 'A' *must be* the cause of event 'B'. This is, of course, the basis of superstition, and more dangerous views—much of the witch-trials were based on 'evidence' that essentially amounted to magical thinking; because a woman was observed doing *this*, or that *this and that* happened around her, it *must mean* that she is a witch, and so on. Conversely, this principle when used *properly* leads to the scientific method).

3. *The Principle of Vibration*. Atkinson here stated his view that all of existence is in a perpetual state of motion, vibrating, and never at rest. Understanding this principle is supposed to lead to an ability to control one's 'vibrations' and to 'conquer natural phenomena'. This principle addresses the development of the will. (It may be pointing toward discoveries in science, regarding the nature of energy and in particular the mysterious 'dark matter', that have not yet been realized).

4. *The Principle of Polarity*. The idea here is that everything carries a dual nature, even if not *immediately* apparent; all appearances have their opposite. The principle has profound implications on a psychological level, because it provides a means by which to convert 'hate' into 'love', for example; or 'impatience' into 'patience', and so on, made possible because the principle states that opposites are different only in terms of degree, and little else (hot can become cold, and cold can become hot, because they differ not intrinsically, but only in terms of degree). Atkinson does not comment on the idea of transcending duality, but is more concerned with the idea of balance, which is an echo of the essential principles of alchemy.

5. *The Principle of Rhythm*. This principle describes the universe as governed by a natural rhythmic process, something like a pendulum, perpetually swinging between opposite poles. It is claimed that a 'hermetic master' achieves freedom by mastering this principle; in effect, escaping the mechanical law of rhythm by 'using it', instead

of being 'used by it'. Atkinson describes the escape from this law by mastery of the somewhat nebulous 'Mental Law of Neutralization'. This is perhaps best understood by ideas from Gurdjieff and the Buddha, related to 'identification': we bounce from experience to experience unconsciously when we identify with things too strongly, in so doing forgetting our essential nature as the 'ground of being' that is witness to all, in contrast to getting blindly caught up in things. (Reincarnation is often used as a metaphor for this process of being subject to blind rhythm, in so doing identifying with body after body, buffeted along by blind causal forces of rhythm).

6. *The Principle of Cause and Effect.* Atkinson here attempts to tackle a famously thorny topic, declaring that 'all happens according to causal law', and that there is 'no such thing as chance'. The main theme stressed here by Atkinson is that of personal empowerment; how to become a 'causer' (as opposed to one merely shunted to and fro as little more than an effect of surrounding forces), an idea that was one of the main themes of the New Thought and mind-healing movements of the late 19th century. (This topic was once humorously characterized by the well-known 20th century seminar teacher Werner Erhard as 'either you are enrolling life, or life is enrolling you'. David Hume had appeared to come close to demolishing the notion of cause and effect, showing how we only observe 'constant conjunctions' of events, and never truly observe the causal event itself. In essence, however, he was showing that we can never be certain about the true cause of something, not necessarily that cause and effect is non-existent. Certain elements of quantum physics appear to argue something similar, but again, they are really only amounting to a declaration that exact causes escape detection, not necessarily that they do not exist. The whole matter remains something of a red herring, however. The rational mind sees things in terms of duality and causes. The meditative mind, or the 'supra-rational' domain, is not fixed on this, but rather sees in terms

of non-duality, non-local awareness, and simultaneity).

7. *The Principle of Gender*. Here Atkinson comments on the nature of polarity and duality as it expresses via gender. He maintains that this principle is the key behind all generation of life and creative force. He ends his remarks on it with a somewhat vehement denunciation of 'debased' practices and 'degraded' teachings that investigate this area. Presumably he was referring to 'left hand tantra' or the 'sex magick' of Paschal Beverley Randolph and others (as covered in Chapter 5). Given his magnanimous embrace of universal energies in the previous principles, this concluding moral instruction is somewhat curious, but was a natural reflection of the Victorian-Edwardian-Puritan imprint still strong in Anglo-American culture at that time.

Appendix II

The Fall of Man According to Eight Traditions

1. *Zoroastrianism*: For any interested in the history of Western esoteric ideas Zoroastrianism is an important tradition to understand. It originated with the Persian prophet Zarathustra (Zoroaster to the Greeks). His date of birth is uncertain, variously estimated to have been anywhere from 1200 to 550 BCE. There are sound arguments for Zoroastrianism being the first monotheistic tradition, as well as the first to posit an adversarial force of pure evil (*Angra Mainyu*) in opposition to the pure good of God (*Ahura Mazda*). In fact, the very word 'dualism' was first used in a religious context (in 1700 CE) to describe the Zoroastrian doctrine of the opposing spirits.[1] The primacy of Zoroastrianism is not disputed; earlier Egyptian pharaohs, like Akhenaton, may have hinted at monotheism, but Zoroaster's doctrine, featuring an absolute and supreme God, his chief prophet, and a singular adversary, lies at the roots of the three great Western religious traditions that followed (Judaism, Christianity, Islam). Two key points to understand with Zoroastrianism are those of dualism and progression. Consistent with a truly dualistic teaching, the dual forces of *Ahura Mazda* and his adversary *Angra Mainyu* are coeval, existing prior to anything else. Unlike non-dualistic teachings where 'evil' is generally presented as an illusion (essentially a bad dream to be awoken from) in a dualistic tradition it (along with good) is an intrinsic reality of the universe. However Zoroastrianism is also progressive in its spiritual doctrine, meaning that it prophesies that the evil of *Angra Mainyu* is destined to be overcome, and furthermore that it is the function of Man to rise up and aid in the transformation of the world via the great work of aligning with *Ahura Mazda*, the God of Light and Life (a progressive stance echoed later by Paul in the New

Testament, e.g., Romans 8:19–22, and by certain Alexandrian Hermetic texts of the early centuries CE). This is in contrast to the Eastern traditions that teach two essential paths in life: either abiding by the system and its laws, or withdrawing from it (the renunciate) and seeking to transcend all dualities and apparent opposites.[2] In general, Eastern paths have little concern with the actual transformation or evolution of the world.

From this, we see the influence of Zoroaster on the Western esoteric tradition, much of which is based on the idea of actively working to transform not just one's inner being, but one's outer domain as well, in contrast to the Eastern approach of passive self-observation and disengagement from the world. (There is of course an 'active' Eastern way as well, especially in the Mahayana Buddhist schools and their ideal of the Bodhisattva, but even there the emphasis is more on developing inner qualities such as compassion, in contrast to the Zoroastrian ideal of directly reforming the corruption of the world via personal engagement). In short, Eastern approaches emphasize that the world, such as it is, is not at issue and need not be reformed—it is only *we* that need wake up. The Western approaches (those rooted in dualism), influenced by Zoroaster, include the reformation of the world—its redemption—along with the personal transformation of the individual.[3]

2. *Plato and Plotinus*: Our mention of Plato's ideas here will be limited to the context of 'original separation' from source.[4] Plato maintained that the Source, being pure and whole, necessitated that any descent into division and matter involved degradation and a loss of purity. There are references throughout Plato's writings (sometimes voiced by Socrates) to the degraded nature of this material world and the need to return to the divine world. Plato taught a form of dualism that regarded the body (but not the world in general) as a negative. As to the creation of the world, Plato presented a viewpoint that allowed for both a positive and negative angle: in part the world exists because its architect (what he called the 'Craftsman') seeks to

replicate his perfection in the world. Yet in so doing corporeal matter inevitably interferes with God's intentions; evil arises from matter, stemming from a primal chaos that existed prior to the original creation, thus making possible a willful choice to oppose the good.

Of note here is to understand the old Delphi Oracle maxim 'know thyself'. For the early Greek pre-Socratics this adage pointed toward the idea of cultivating humility and staying within one's limits—'know thyself' meant, in a sense, 'recognize your limitations and guard against pride'. After Plato's influence the term came to mean 'know your true nature', which was understood to be divine. Thus 'know thyself' meant 'work on yourself to uncover the divine origin and essence of your nature'.[5] In this re-working of the idea, it was implied that there was a cosmic purpose to the separation from our divine source, that being to recover it and in so doing, become divinity manifest.

Plotinus (205-270 CE), the first 'Neo-platonist' (a term applied only much later|), developed and refined some of Plato's views. In keeping with Plato he had a natural distrust of material reality, regarding it as a lesser version of what was assumed to be the more subtle and rarefied worlds. Plotinus taught the idea of *ex deo* (out of God), in contrast to the Judeo-Christian doctrine of *ex nihilo* (out of nothing). The idea is of great significance; according to Plotinus, the existence of the world (and by extension, of the separate self of an individual) is an inevitable and natural consequence of the existence of God, which he called 'the One'. His view of the One was sophisticated in that he said that it was beyond all categories such as existence or non-existence, was not a 'thing', and nor was it the 'totality' of all things. This definition—a type of 'cannot be defined' definition—essentially points toward a view that transcends intellectual categorizing, placing it on a similar footing to some of the views of Advaita Vedanta or Zen Buddhism. Plotinus taught that the One naturally emanates from itself, leading to various descending and degrading levels or dimensions, resulting in the individual soul and at the bottom of it all, material reality. Although individuality and matter are to be transcended, they are not regarded as anything other than divine in origin, sourcing as they do from the One. Plotinus went to lengths to clarify this point, especially in his criticisms of the Gnostics of his time and their condemnation of material reality which they regarded as 'evil'. Plotinus did not argue that evil was not a reality—he believed it was, and that it was a manifestation of separation, which by nature is most pronounced at the level of the material dimension—but he maintained that this 'evil' was really nothing other than the 'fading out' of the light of the One. Evil he saw as natural to individuality: 'Since [individual souls] were clearly delighted with their own independence, and made great use of self-movement, running the opposite course and getting away as far as possible, they were ignorant even that they themselves came from that world [God, the One]'.[6]

3. *Judeo-Christian tradition*: The key text to be considered here is of course Genesis of the Old Testament, and in particular the figures of Adam, Eve, and the serpent. The essential point we begin with is the Judeo-Christian doctrine that God created Man and imbued him with free will. This was understood as necessary in order for God's children to be free agents and love by choice—for what value and depth can love have it is not freely chosen? And in particular, the love of God means little if it is not freely and consciously opted for. Man 'fell' in the Garden of Eden because Eve, followed by Adam, chose to rebel against God, thus exercising their God-given gift to think and function independently. Adam and Eve were not the original rebels, however—that fate fell to Lucifer, who challenged his spiritual Father and accordingly was cast out.

In the Old Testament, evil as an idea cannot properly be understood without also considering the idea of sin. The word 'sin' originated from the Hebrew word for 'missing the mark'. In particular it referred to committing an offence against God. The profane understanding of this refers to matters of conduct and behavior. The religious view points toward sin as a failure to follow the laws and doctrine of God. The deeper esoteric interpretation points toward the idea that sin is a failure to realize our spiritual potential.

The Old Testament specifies that in addition to individual sin there is also collective sin, those follies committed by our ancestors that we often must pay for. (For example, Jeremiah states that Israel can be attacked by its enemies owing to its collective sins). The idea of sin is closely connected to guilt, which ultimately is deriving from some form of idolatry. The deeper spiritual meaning is not difficult to see; to direct one's attention toward the distractions of this world—the 'lesser gods'—is inevitably to 'miss the mark' (sin), and thus to incur negative repercussions born out of spiritual ignorance. This deeper understanding was not generally put forth, however. Instead ideas like the 'scapegoat', a dumping ground for collective guilt, were offered, simply reinforcing the dualistic idea that solutions to distress lie in fixing or attacking something that is outside of us. And indeed the view that God alone (who is seen as forever outside of us) can offer forgiveness is central to the Old Testament.

The Old Testament views human nature as fundamentally negative, i.e., the human being is understood to incline naturally toward sin and often evil. When God, fed up with human iniquity, brings about the Flood, he nevertheless does not forsake humanity, and even vows never to repeat his punishment:

> And the LORD smelled a sweet savour; and the LORD said in his heart, I will not again curse the ground any more for man's sake; for the imagination of man's heart is evil from his youth; neither will I again smite any more every thing living, as I have done. (Genesis 8:21, KJV).

The origin of this 'evil in the heart' is understood as manifested in Adam and Eve's rebellion, although in point of fact the 'fall' story is generally quarantined in the Old Testament, almost never referred to apart from Genesis 3.[7]

Christian doctrine, as shaped by the apostle Paul, stresses one essential point: no human is capable of extracting themselves from the effects of Adam and Eve's sin. According to Paul, we can't get out of our flawed condition via our own individual will. We can only do this via the grace of Christ. Paul summarized the whole matter in Romans 8:1–4:

> There is therefore now no condemnation to them which are in Christ Jesus, who walk not after the flesh, but after the Spirit. For the law of the Spirit of life in Christ Jesus hath made me free from the law of sin and death. For what the law could not do, in that it was weak through the flesh, God sending his own Son in the likeness of sinful flesh, and for sin, condemned sin in the flesh: That the righteousness of the law might be fulfilled in us, who walk not after the flesh, but after the Spirit. (KJV)

There has been something of a trend in scholarly tradition over recent decades—assisted, naturally, by the spectacular discovery of Gnostic scriptures in Egypt (Nag Hammadi) in 1945 that had been secreted away for seventeen centuries—to promote the Gnostic view that the serpent of Genesis was actually a type of liberator and teacher, not a mere force of mischief or evil. In 1967 Paul Ricoeur had written, 'The harm that has been done to souls, during the centuries of Christianity, first by the literal interpretation of the story of Adam, and then by the confusion of this myth, treated as history, with later speculations, principally Augustinian, about original sin, will never be adequately told.'[8] The American literary critic Roger Shattuck argued that these words became the basis for many subsequent popularizations of the Gnostic view, such as in Elaine Pagels's works, but that in so doing an important element is obscured, that being that 'evil' is a demonstrable reality in our world—'always ready to tempt, to corrupt, to infect'.[9]

Shattuck cited the example of John Milton's famed *Paradise Lost* (written from 1658–64 when the poet was blind) as indicative of a thorough treatment of the very real lessons in Genesis. Milton elaborated greatly on the Biblical treatment of the rebellion of Lucifer/Satan, the war in heaven in which the Son of God (later to incarnate as Jesus Christ) defeats Satan and his army of rebellious angels, God's subsequent creation of the World, Eden, and Adam, followed by Adam's request for a mate and the creation of Eve, leading up to Satan's seduction of Eve (while in the form of a serpent), and the subsequent entry of 'sin' and 'death' into what had previously been Paradise. The end result is the human condition as we know it, although Milton made it clear that the human being's innate capacity for sin and evil stems from Satan's original rebellion, not from Eve's eating of the fruit as St. Augustine, the main architect of the original sin doctrine, had argued.

Milton depicted Satan as a master manipulator, utilizing rhetoric as well as Eve's vanity, to seduce her into eating the fruit of the forbidden Tree of Knowledge. His main and clinching argument—to which Eve ultimately capitulated—was that 'knowledge of good and evil' is the best protection *against* evil. In urging Eve to eat the fruit that God had expressly forbidden her to do, he assured her that 'ye shall not die', and added:

> *For such a petty Trespass, and not praise*
> *Rather your dauntless virtue, whom the pain*
> *Of Death denounced, whatever thing Death be,*
> *Deterred not from achieving what might lead*
> *To happier life, knowledge of Good and Evil;*
> *Of good, how just? of evil, if what is evil*
> *Be real, why not known, since easier shunned?* (IX, 693–699)

In short, evil can be best resisted when it is known and understood. Ergo, eat the fruit, know evil in contrast to good, and thereby be protected. Eve, convinced, eats; and in so doing, breaks her contract with God, her creator. Adam, distressed by what Eve has done, loves her so deeply that he cannot bring himself to forsake her, and so eats also even though he understands fully what will happen. Accordingly, his sin is greater because he eats the fruit knowing full well the consequences of his actions. Eve, however, was more the victim of seduction. That, at least, is the portrayal, initiating a view that the feminine is more prone to victimization and thus less accountable; and that the masculine is more prone to willful evil, i.e., defying one's conscience with full awareness of consequences—although in the case of Adam, it is framed in tragedy, since he does this out of fear of losing Eve.

In terms of straightforward psychology there is an element of absurdity in the Garden of Eden parable, in that God's pronouncement that *only* the Tree of Knowledge was forbidden immediately makes it obvious that this temptation will be impossible for Adam and Eve to ultimately resist. We humans are innately curious, and are compelled to explore the unknown and in particular, the so-called forbidden. Chaucer had summed it up in the 14th century when he wrote 'forbede us thyng, and that desiren we' (we desire that which is forbidden). Accordingly Adam and Eve can be seen as blameless, because God himself endowed them with the very trait—curiosity—that led to their fate.

Milton's epic poem was very influential, although his message has been interpreted in different ways—some have argued that his basic point was that the 'Fall of Man' was a great fortune, allowing for free will to be exercised in the service of spiritual righteousness, and that Satan's actions were simply part of God's plan. As Shattuck put it, 'Milton narrates a secular story about a legendary yet very human couple who move through four stages of knowledge: innocence, fancy or dream, experience, and wisdom. We can read *Paradise Lost* as a tale about the downward path to wisdom, a path that must lead through the experience of sin'.[10] Others have maintained that the rebellion was not part of God's plan, but was freely chosen by Adam and Eve, only because God granted them free will. But what seems undeniable, as Shattuck pointed out, is that there is a paradoxical element in the story that is essential: the twin admonishments of Genesis, 'thou shalt surely die' (God's warning not to eat the fruit) and 'your eyes shall be opened and ye shall be as gods, knowing good and evil' (the serpent's words) *both* carry weight and truth. The main message of Milton, however, is that we need to temper our curiosity and desire for knowledge with humility—'be lowly wise' (VIII, 173).[11]

The point to be noted here about the Biblical Garden of Eden myth (in contrast to Milton's version) is that it is ultimately based on the essential idea that the 'fall' is due to human disobedience, not to any pre-existing tendency toward evil (as manifest in Satan). This is closely connected to the Messianic tradition of Judaism, which in reality had a political basis, via its interest in establishing Israel as world leader. As Joseph Campbell remarked:

> The biblical view, placing the Fall within the frame of human history as an offence against its god, cuts out the wider reach of a challenge to the character of that god, denigrates the character of man, and fosters, furthermore, an increasingly untenable insistence on the historicity of its myth; while the other, cosmic view of the problem is actually symbolized philosophy, and, as later centuries would show, was to become one of the leading inspirations of every major spiritual threat to the hegemony of biblical literalism in the West.[12]

In the context of the Western esoteric tradition, Christian doctrine, as centered on the Nicene Creed ratified by Emperor Constantine in Nicaea in 325 CE and later 'original sin' doctrines formulated by St. Augustine, is ultimately antithetical to the idea of inner transformation brought about by personal effort. Quite simply, Christian doctrine maintains that evil is real, human nature is essentially corrupt, and our salvation lies in accepting Christ. This is in contrast to the esoteric paths (Gnostic, Hermetic, Kabbalistic, etc.) that instruct that we must not merely 'accept' Christ, we must literally *follow in his footsteps* (and other liberated ones) so as to replicate their self-transformation process ourselves.

4. *Gnosticism*: Gnostic myth and doctrine—deriving largely from four key figures, Basilides, Valentinus, Marcion, and Mani—is complex, and based on a group of basic myths. Gnostic traditions have been categorized by some scholars as mere inversions of orthodoxy (rejecting traditional interpretations of scripture, rejecting the body and the world, showing little interest in social engagement, etc.) but in fact they are more comprehensive than this. In general Gnosticism holds to three essential views: that the material dimension is seriously corrupted, that the 'true God' did not directly create the world, and that the world was created by an imperfect 'creator god' sometimes called the 'Demiurge'. The word derives from the Greek *demiourgos*, meaning 'craftsman' or 'architect', and was originally used by Plato to designate the lesser 'creator god' in contrast to the true God. Plato saw the Demiurge as fundamentally good in nature, though doomed to creating a flawed universe as he was fashioning it out of non-being. Because Gnostic teachings incline toward arch-dualism, the Demiurge was understood to be essentially malevolent in nature, which was thought to explain the imperfect nature of this world.

Basilides (100?–170? CE) was the first prominent Gnostic teacher. Similar to other legendary figures such as Pythagoras and Lao Tzu, almost nothing is known about his personal life, including his dates of birth or death. His ideas are known via criticisms of him by the early Church fathers Irenaeus and Hippolytus. Basilides posited a prime source that he saw as the uncreated true God. This God then projects twelve powers (in six pairs), the last two of whom (Sophia-Wisdom and Dynamis-Power) give rise to 365 powers called aeons, the last of which creates the world. The first of the 365 aeons, and leader of them, was called Abrasax, though the name is usually rendered as Abraxas. This figure was accorded significance by C.G. Jung, who in his Gnostic *Seven Sermons to the Dead* mentioned it numerous times as an important symbol of the unification of opposites:

> *God and devil are distinguished by the qualities fullness and emptiness, generation and destruction. Effectiveness is common to both. Effectiveness joineth them. Effectiveness, therefore, standeth above both; is a god above god, since in its effect it uniteth fullness and emptiness.*
>
> *This is a god whom ye knew not, for mankind forgot it. We name it by its name Abraxas. It is more indefinite still than god and devil…*
>
> *…Hard to know is the deity of Abraxas. Its power is the greatest, because man perceiveth it not. From the sun he draweth the summum bonum; from the devil the infimum malum; but from Abraxas life, altogether indefinite, the mother of good and evil.*
>
> *Smaller and weaker life seemeth to be than the summum bonum; wherefore is it also hard to conceive that Abraxas transcendeth even the sun in power, who is himself the radiant source of all the force of life.*
>
> *Abraxas is the sun, and at the same time the eternally sucking gorge of the void, the belittling and dismembering devil.*
>
> *The power of Abraxas is twofold; but ye see it not, because for your eyes the warring opposites of this power are extinguished.*[13]

The seven letters of Abraxas are sometimes thought to correspond to the seven celestials visible to the ancients (Sun, Moon, Mercury, Venus, Mars, Jupiter, Saturn), and the numeric value of his name thought to symbolize the 365 days of the year, thus denoting his universal quality.

Marcion (85?–160? CE), like Basilides, rejected elements of Christian doctrine as it had shaped up in the first century after Christ. Prime of these was his rejection of the Jewish Old Testament God, whom he believed was a punitive and jealous tribal deity rather similar to a typical Egyptian or Greek god that might be claimed by a given portion of a country and duly honored in its temples but that also had a vengeful streak that essentially made it a god of war. Along with Basilides, Marcion also held that Jesus was a redeemer and an emanation of the true God, but that his body was a 'material copy' of his spiritual body, and that his supposed suffering on the cross was therefore bogus. This idea that Jesus' body and earthly life was essentially a phantasm, and that he was never truly human in a conventional sense, is called 'docetism', and was condemned as heresy by the Nicaea council of 325 CE. There were two basic views of docetism: one that Jesus, being one and the same as God, could not truly be material nor capable of conventional suffering; the other was that Jesus was a mortal man whose human vehicle had been used by the 'Christ-spirit', entering him at baptism and leaving prior to the crucifixion. Marcion rejected much of biblical scripture but did accept parts of Luke's gospel. For his selective interpretations (not to mention his widespread influence) he was condemned as 'the devil's mouthpiece' and as 'assuming the role of the devil by saying everything contrary to truth' by the Church fathers Tertullian and Irenaeus.

The apocryphal Gnostic text *The Secret Book of John,* written around 150 CE, ascribes the creation of a particular power or entity named Ialdobaoth to the misguided actions of Sophia (the aeon of Wisdom), who sought to create, without 'higher authorization', a likeness of herself. The result was both unexpected and disturbing (a serpent with a lion's face), and Sophia rejected it. This entity, Ialdobaoth, is then equated with Yahweh, the God of the Old Testament. He then goes on to create 'Man in his image', but the Adam that he creates has form but no life. Sophia then tries to correct what she has begun, by tricking her 'son' Ialdobaoth (Yahweh) into transferring his spark of life into Adam. All of this leads to the complications depicted in the various myths of the Old Testament. The underlying message is that the Gnostics (who did not call themselves by this term, but rather thought of themselves as Christians who had the correct understanding) asserted that the Judeo-Christian doctrine stemming from the Old Testament was based on a fundamental misunderstanding, which was that the true God (dwelling in Pleroma) was not the creator of Man nor the material universe. It should be noted here that Sophia is part of the Godhead, and thus this 'original error' brought on by her actions occurs from within the Godhead.

Gnosticism deriving from *The Secret Book of John* is generally regarded as Sethian (as they argued that Seth was the only legitimate son of Adam and Eve), and of Jewish influence. The other significant Gnostic tradition is the more Christianized Valentinian line in which Ialdobaoth is regarded as a paradoxical entity, and less severe. In the Valentinian version, Sophia creates Ialdobaoth out of a profound desire to create like God, but out of ignorance creates something deeply flawed. She suffers remorse and grief over her actions, which God takes pity on and accordingly decides to create both the Holy Spirit and Christ in order to address the situation of Sophia's error and its vast consequences, as well as to comfort Sophia. Of course this whole model can be challenged (as it was by Plotinus) on the basis of the idea that any capacity for error in Sophia was created (or allowed for) by God, and thus all potentials (including that of error and darkness) are innate to the Source.

The essential Gnostic idea of the universe being a creation of a 'lesser god' is the reflection of an idea that is common in wisdom traditions: there is something basic in our nature that is given to going astray (as in the technical meaning of sin, 'missing the mark'). Different views differ on the degree of our responsibility in the matter, and what must be done to correct it, but most share the understanding that we must get out of a particular way of thinking and viewing reality that is based on our inherent tendency to distort matters and wander into ignorance and delusion.

5. *Manichaeism*: This was the religion founded by the Persian prophet Mani (216–276 CE). Although chiefly Gnostic, it also mixed in elements of Christianity, Judaism, Zoroastrianism and even Buddhism. It achieved some remarkable territorial successes and for many centuries was the chief rival of Christianity, prior to fading out around the 14th century. Manichaeism taught a radical dualism,

positing a powerful God of goodness and light who is yet not fully omnipotent, against a force of darkness that is essentially equal and opposite, a force that is identified with matter. For Mani, there was God and matter; the one wholly good and pure, the other impure, corrupt, and evil.

The essential Manichean myth went like this: There are two distinct realms, the Kingdoms of Light and Darkness. The Dark eventually becomes aware of the Light, and led by a force of greed and impulse, attacks it. The supreme God of Light, Ohrmazd, then calls forth the mother of life, who in turn calls forth the first human (also named Ohrmazd). This primal Man then challenges the forces of darkness in battle, and loses, although his loss is a type of Trojan Horse, done with a hidden purpose. In this 'loss' he undergoes a willing sacrifice of his inner light, which eventual becomes unbearable. He then prays to God to relieve him of his torment, and God responds by sending forth the 'living spirit' (later known as Mithra, in a sense synonymous with the Holy Spirit of Christian doctrine) and the mother of life, both of which extend to the primal Man. The operation succeeds and the Man returns to the divine realm. In so doing, however, the forces of Dark end up 'swallowing' light, which is used by the divine realms to create the celestial lights (Sun, Moon, galaxies, etc.). Later, Adam and Eve are created, but they are disconnected from their divine source and must be redeemed by the primal Man (Ohrmazd, now synonymous with Jesus). This is accomplished by Ohrmazd showing Adam the light locked within matter and his own being, and the way to liberate this light (a redeeming knowledge known as *gnosis*). In keeping with other Gnostic teachings, much of which appears to derive from Plato, Manichaeism taught that the material realm is corrupt and untrustworthy simply because it is transient; only the immaterial is of value because it is eternal and unchanging (evocative of the Buddha's teachings on impermanence).

6. *Kabbalah*: Some Kabbalistic traditions maintain that 'evil' and any

primeval 'Fall' associated with its origins is an intrinsic part of our learning process, not just mere illusion. One version of this was summarized by the 15th century philosopher and esoteric scholar Pico della Mirandola (1463–1494) when he wrote, among his 'Cabalistic Conclusions': 'The letters of the name of the evil demon who is the prince of the world are the same as those of the name of God—TETRAGRAMMATON—and he who knows how to effect their transposition can extract one from the other'.[14]

This alchemical notion is not just the 'extraction' of gold from lead, but more to the point is the idea that the dark side of life is not to be shunned or denied or naively ignored, it is rather is a key element on our journey toward the goal. The 'monsters' we encounter on our way are not mere annoying illusions or arbitrary demonic intrusions; they are 'testers' through which we forge our higher qualities. In fact, without these adversarial forces we would have no real means by which to attain to our higher actualizations. There is also a subtext to Pico's words, and it is this: good can be extracted from evil, but the reverse is also possible, evil arising from good. This is possible due to the two twin pillars of sanctimoniousness: vanity and pride. Good, if fascinated with itself and proud of its attainment, however subtly, has already birthed the conditions for its decline.[15]

There are Western esoteric schools of thought that parallel the Eastern view that evil is but a shadow of good, lacking inherent reality, and these derive from Plato, Plotinus, the Neoplatonists, and some Kabbalistic schools. In this view 'evil' results from estrangement from our source: in our very separation from this source we cannot receive all of its 'gifts', and from this condition evil arises as a negative reality, something like cold existing only because of an absence of heat.

Other Kabbalistic traditions, such as the *Sefirah Gevurah*, refer to evil as the 'left hand' of God, a reality that finds its manifestation in the world when the human capacity for judgment is disconnected from human compassion. Another, via the Shabbateans, argues that evil co-exists with good in the mind of God from the beginning, and is an unavoidable reality based on the perpetual struggle between active and passive forces—that which seeks to create, and that which seeks to sabotage creation via resistance to change.[16] (A fuller discussion of the Kabbalah can be found in Chapter 3).

7. *Sufism*: Sufism, being the mystical undercurrent of Islam, also derives from Mohammad and the Old Testament, but has an interesting and striking twist on the story of Satan and his rebellion against God. Put forth by the Sufi mystic Mansoor Al-Hallaj (857–922 C.E.), the story taught was that when God created Adam he commanded all living beings to bow down to him. All did as bidden, with the exception of Iblis (Satan). But the reason for Iblis's rebellion was not arrogance or willful discontent or jealousy of Adam; he rather refused to bow because he loved God so much he would subordinate himself to none other than God—even if God wished it. Mansoor himself was eventually executed for both his heretical views and certain political activities, but he well represented the mystical and occult stance toward the divine when he uttered the words 'anal-Haqq' ('I am the Truth'), suggesting a complete merging with the divine, in distinction to the Western orthodox view that a human being is forever subordinate to the one God.

8. *A Course in Miracles*: The mystical text scribed by Helen Schucman between 1965 and 1972 and known as *A Course in Miracles* (ACIM), is a fully non-dualistic teaching, similar to Eastern paths such as Advaita Vedanta and Buddhism. It posits that the Absolute is pure love, wisdom, and goodness, and being non-dual, has no opposite. Only in the realms of the ego-mind and the universe of apparent separation, does 'good' as we conventionally know it have an opposite: 'bad', or 'evil'. The idea, then, is to escape the realm of apparent duality and remember (or awaken to) our actual condition, which is perfect peace and Oneness. According to ACIM, the 'fall of Man' only occurred as an appearance and nothing more; that is, we

are entirely imagining that we are separate from God, when in fact we did not truly undergo this separation. As ACIM puts it,

> You are at home in God, dreaming of exile but perfectly capable of awakening to reality.

Caught in the throes of the vast illusion we find ourselves in, it is natural to pose the most difficult of all questions: how did we actually separate from our source? How did we fall asleep and accordingly come to suffer so profoundly? According to ACIM, asking this question is useless and does nothing but reinforce the illusion of the ego-mind's experience of separation. The question is fundamentally unanswerable, because it assumes that separation is a reality, when it is not. In that regard, ACIM's approach is essentially identical to that of Zen Buddhism in particular, wherein such questions—typically called 'koans'—are not directly answered, but are themselves destroyed by the fire of pure inquiry, i.e., the practical work of contemplation and/or meditation.[17]

Appendix III

The Chief Grimoires of Magic

The main sources for the following list of grimoires are A.E. Waite, *The Book of Ceremonial Magic: A Complete Grimoire* (New York: Citadel Press, 1970; first published in 1898); Richard Cavendish, *A History of Magic* (New York: Taplinger Publishing, 1977); Owen Davies, *Grimoires: A History of Magic Books* (Oxford: Oxford University Press, 2009); Joseph H. Peterson's excellent website www.esoteric archives.com; as well as the site www.sacred-texts.com and the antiquarian books site www.wierus.com. The order of presentation below is approximately chronological, from oldest to most recent. The grimoires are listed here for more than mere historical curiosity; they are a record of a different worldview, cultural artifacts predating (or in some cases coinciding with the beginning of) the scientific worldview. In some respects they are simply primitive attempts at science, and often were reflective of depressed economic eras in which men and women were driven to all sorts of ideas and efforts to achieve some means of control over Nature and their lives (the Spanish anthropologist Julio Caro Baroja referred to the grimoires as 'the last products of the Medieval mind'). The kind of magic associated with grimoires is usually classified by scholars as 'folk magic' or sometimes as 'demonic magic', and is considered to be polar opposite to the transcendent mysticism of a Pseudo-Dionysius the Areopagite, a St. John of the Cross, or a Jacob Boehme. However that is not entirely accurate, as several of the important grimoires do in fact contain disciplined instructions for achieving deep spiritual purification prior to consorting with the darker realms.

Although the grimoires below begin with the 3rd–4th century CE *Sepher ha-Razim*, they certainly have older roots, mainly in the Greco-Roman world of approximately 300 BCE–300 CE. As we have seen from our discussion in Chapter 4, religion and magic have traditionally overlapped and at times been essentially impossible to distinguish from each other (for example, both Christ and Moses were labeled *goetes* [sorcerers] by their critics, not just for polemical reasons, but because the legends associated with them were indistinguishable from those credited to magicians).[1] That said, a key element of both religion and magic has been belief in the power of the spoken word, and it was this—and in particular the usage of spiritual *names*—that most of the magical grimoires ultimately came to be based on. The roots of the tradition of spiritual power via the usage of names or words goes back to the Babylonians, Sumerians, and ancient Egyptians. In Kabbalism the term given to the 'Master of the Divine Name' was *Ba'al Shem*, the one who reputedly had secret knowledge of the Holy Names, including the Tetragrammaton. Even Socrates was recorded (by Plato) to have claimed that the power of a particular plant to heal would only work if certain special words were uttered at the same time:

> ...when he asked me if I knew the cure of the headache, I answered, but with an effort, that I did know. 'And what is it?' he said. I replied that it was a kind of leaf, which required to be accompanied by a charm, and if a person would repeat the charm at the same time that he used the cure, he would be made whole; but that without the charm the leaf would be of no avail.[2]

This usage of 'words of power' had several faces. The highest usages were for the alignment of one's soul with its divine source (as in the Eastern usage of the 'mantra'), and for healing or protection, as in the original usage of 'abracadabra' (see below). Lower forms involved using words of power for binding and controlling demons, and perhaps lowest of all was employing particular words for curses. (The most common form of Greco-Roman curse was the *defixio*, written down on a piece of wax or metal and placed somewhere underground. It was believed that the words had an instantaneous effect.[3] Doubtless in part because of the power of suggestion, many of these curses had results—most obviously if the target was made aware that they had been cursed). In general, however, the magical grimoires and the practitioners who used them were less concerned with affecting others than they were with advancing their own cause, either materially, or in more elevated cases, by contacting higher (angelic) guidance and furthering their spiritual development or large scale ambitions (the 16th century scholar-magician John Dee, and his efforts with his 'seer' Edward Kelley, being a good example).

Sepher ha-Razim: This work of Jewish magic is one of the oldest magical texts, generally dated to the 3rd or 4th century CE, thus predating major Kabbalistic works such as the Zohar and the Bahir. The book contains many of the essential elements of the grimoires that followed, including shamanistic practices such as healing, attacks on enemies, obtaining prophetic visions, and so forth, as well as the somewhat peculiar marriage of these rituals to the invocation of the Hebrew holy names of God. As with the *Book of Raziel* (see below) according to legend this book was conveyed by the archangel Raziel, in this case to Noah.

Ghayat al-Hakim (*The Aim of the Sage*): Originally written in Arabic (in Spain) somewhere between the years 1000 and 1150 CE, this famed grimoire was translated into Spanish around 1250, and shortly thereafter into Latin, after which it came to be known as *The Picatrix*. Deriving mostly from older Greek and Persian traditions, it was essentially a manual of astrological and 'astral' magic, including instructions for 'drawing down' the powers and energies of the stars and planets into talismanic symbols. It did not deal with demonology *per se*, but because some of its rituals involved animal sacrifices (doves and goats) it was denounced as a work of necromancy.

Sepher Raziel HaMalakh (*The Book of Raziel the Archangel*): An important medieval Jewish grimoire, probably written in the 13th century, and one of the foundational sources of some of the major grimoires to follow. This book—not to be confused with the 16th century grimoire called *Sepher Raziel* that was written by a Christian and based on standard Solomonic magic—had an influence on both Trithemius and Agrippa (see below), arguably the two most important Renaissance magi. According to the legend Raziel was an archangel who transmitted certain 'secret' teachings to Adam and Eve, after their expulsion from Eden, so they could return to their divine condition. (The name 'Raziel' itself means 'secrets of God'). Raziel had done this without permission and as such was considered a rebel by his fellow angels, and his book duly confiscated. (According to some legends it was later retrieved by God, however, and eventually found its way via Archangel Raphael to Noah, who used its information to build the ark). Raziel is the Jewish parallel of Prometheus, the Greek god who 'stole fire from heaven' to give to humans, in so doing incurring the wrath of Zeus. These myths lie behind the notorious and glamorous reputation of high magic, the idea that the individual can determine their own spiritual fate by independent acts of will (with all the Faustian perils included), though a deeper understanding of magic transcends these stereotypes.

Liber Juratus Honorii (*Sworn Book of Honorius*): This book, allegedly a compendium by a group of magicians attempting to save their teachings from being lost to the flames of Catholic book-burners, is recognized as one of the oldest medieval grimoires, probably written sometime during the 13th or early 14th century. Many magic grimoires acquired notorious reputations, but this one more than most, owing in part to its apparent 'Trojan Horse' method of transmitting its teachings on the means of controlling and using demons for personal gain. It did this by claiming that its practical demonology was sanctioned by the Church, proclaiming in an opening spiel, '...I give unto thee the Keys of the Kingdom of Heaven, and unto thee alone the power of commanding the Prince of Darkness and his angels...' (Subsequent Church authorities would use this spurious Church authorization as proof of the trickery of demons). The attribution of authorship to 'Honorius' has been speculated to apply to a semi-mythical medieval 'Honorius of Thebes' (mentioned also by Trithemius and Agrippa), a type of spokesperson for a secret group of magicians who later become conflated with the identity of a pope, either Honorius III (1148–1227), or even to the 'Dark Ages' Pope Honorius I (d. 638). The *Sworn Book of Honorius*, based on a conversation with an archangel named Hochmel (after the *sephira* Chokmah) and a sizeable ninety-three chapters long, is a key and influential grimoire, containing many of the basic elements of practical 'goetic' magic that were to appear in a host of grimoires to follow, the more important of which are listed below. Perhaps more significantly this grimoire touches on the whole area of the question of the usage of magic and sorcery within the Church, and even beyond that, to the essential questions about magic vs. divinity, including the nature of Christ and whether or not he was a magician himself (as discussed in Chapter 4).

Clavicula Salomonis (*The Key of Solomon*): The oldest extant manuscript of this famous grimoire seems to be the *Magic Treatise of Solomon*, originally written in Greek in 1572, although Waite and others speculated that the first version of the work was written sometime between 1350 and 1450. Undoubtedly it had its inspiration in apocryphal texts written over a thousand years earlier, such as *The Revelation of Adam* and *Testament of Solomon*. That said, no singular original version of the *Clavicula* is recognized by scholars, although the work itself was highly influential in the grimoire world and led to many derivative versions. The attribution to Solomon is of course spurious, and the book is not of a Jewish teaching or origin, despite its usage of Hebrew terms (the Hebrew translation of it only appeared in the 17th century; the earliest copies are in Greek). The essential feature of the demonological grimoire lay at the basis of this book, that being the command and control of lower spirits and structured manifestation practices (based on the cooperation of these spirits) allegedly leading to the fulfilment of personal wishes. A key element of the *Clavicula* is its religiously pious tone, and its insistence that the operator must invoke the presence of God (via the Hebrew Holy Names) and be ceremonially purged of 'self-recognized sin' (via confession). This focus on spiritual and psychological purification, prior to evoking the spirits, was to be even more strongly echoed in the grimoire of Abramelin.

The Sacred Magic of Abramelin the Mage: This book, supposedly written by one Abraham ben Simon (c. 1362-c. 1458), a Jewish writer from Worms (located in modern-day western Germany), features the story of Abraham traveling to Egypt where he allegedly encounters an Egyptian magician named Abramelin, and records the magician's teachings to his son Lamech. The book is internally dated to 1458, although there is some evidence that it may have been written a century earlier. The earliest extant version of the book in manuscript form is in German and was written down in 1608. The grimoire was made popular via S.L. Mathers' copy taken from a flawed version in a French library and first published in English in 1898. Subsequent research has established that older, more accurate versions were found in Germany (including such notable facts that the six-month retreat originally reported by Mathers, based on Abramelin's guidance, was in fact eighteen months).[4] Despite the apparent Kabbalistic tone of the book, some, including the Kabbalah scholar Gershom Scholem, believed that the author, Abraham of Worms, was 'not in fact a Jew', and that the German original was 'badly translated' *into* Hebrew, not from Hebrew. Scholem further claimed that the book showed a 'partial influence of Jewish ideas' but did not have 'any strict parallel in Kabbalistic literature'.[5] The essential basis of the Abramelin grimoire is the initial purification procedure (involving daily prayer and other austerities for a year and a half), followed by the direct experience of the 'Holy Guardian Angel', a title whose origin appears to lie with this grimoire, although there is evidence that Zoroastrians long before used a similar term. The Holy Guardian Angel is, essentially, the rarefied and awakened part of our nature (often called the 'true self'). The Abramelin grimoire is exceptional in its highly disciplined focus and insistence on the awakening of this higher spiritual principle and faculty, prior to working with lower orders of spirits. It has often been considered to be the grimoire *par excellence* of high magic, as opposed to the majority of grimoires which are concerned more with 'low magic' (the art of practical manifestation), and less with the structured practices of inner discipline needed to align with the higher nature of the soul. In this regard, the Abramelin grimoire is as much a teaching of mysticism as it is of magic. Ultimately however its concern is also practical, and its cosmology is consistent with Hermetic and Kabbalistic magical worldviews in which angels are thought to control demons who in turn control much of the world. Abramelin guides candidates into becoming 'Masters of Light' who, utilizing their ascetic training, can then control demonic forces with the aid of specific 'magic squares' specified and illustrated in the book. These allegedly allow for the magician to gain remarkable powers enabling him to obtain wealth, love, the ability to heal diseases or transform into an animal, and even to raise the dead. Some of the magic squares found in the book have been traced to the times of Charlemagne (via 8th century CE Carolingian bibles) and further back to 2nd century CE Roman villas in England.[6]

Le Grand Albert: This text first appeared in a Latin edition in 1493. It was mainly concerned with 'natural magic', including the usage of herbs, precious stones, ways to ward off diseases, usages of alchemy and physiognomy, and so forth. 'Albert' supposedly referred to Albertus Magnus (1200?-1280), the Catholic bishop who was learned in science, theology, and allegedly in certain occult arts, including astrology and alchemy. Almost certainly it was not written by

Albertus himself, despite the fact that some of his material was probably reproduced in the text. Later editions of this work became popular in 18th century France in particular.

The Heptameron: This work first appeared in 1496 and was attributed to the Italian philosopher and astrologer Peter d'Abano (1250–1316), but as with so many grimoires, this is generally recognized as another false attribution. This grimoire later appeared as an appendix in works attributed to Agrippa in the 16th century. It is in the tradition of medieval and Renaissance grimoires, being a manual of ritual and practical astrological magic.[7]

The Steganographia: This work was written by the important German abbot, cryptographer, and magus Johannes Trithemius (1462–1516) in 1499. It was widely distributed in manuscript form for many years but not printed until 1606. The fact that Trithemius was an abbot of a monastery and also was delving into the arcane arts was not exceptional, owing mostly to the fact that many Hermetic texts brought to light by Marcilio Ficino (1433–1499) via his Florentine Academy, though attributed to Hermes Trismegistus, were usually put together by Hellenistic Christians in the early centuries immediately after Christ and were thus not—at least initially—considered particularly troublesome for the Church.[8] *The Steganographia* was, however, placed on the list of books prohibited by the Catholic Church in 1609, three years after its publication. It was initially believed to be essentially a work of angel magic, utilizing codes in order to communicate with spirits and people in non-ordinary fashions. Over time however the book has been revealed to be mostly a form of cryptography, utilizing the 'magic work' as an elaborate cover, although Trithemius was, without question, concerned with occult sciences (he was, after all, one of Agrippa's chief mentors, and John Dee, himself deeply involved with angel magic, made a study of his work). Trithemius's last and posthumously published work, *Polygraphiae* (1518), is generally considered the first book on cryptology, the science of encoding and decoding messages. Many of Trithemius's ideas, especially those involving celestial, angelic, and natural magic, shaped in part by Albertus Magnus, Ficino, and Pico della Mirandola, were key influences on Agrippa.

De Occulta Philosophia (On Occult Philosophy): This work, a massive encyclopedia of magical lore written in 1510 by Agrippa, is probably the single most influential text ever composed on the arts of high and low magic. It was not published until 1533, apparently at the suggestion of Trithemius, who was one of Agrippa's main mentors. It was translated into English in 1651 as *Three Books of Occult Philosophy*. An excellent edition of the book was put out by Llewellyn, exhaustively edited and annotated by Donald Tyson, in 1993. Agrippa himself was a somewhat ambiguous figure; he wrote his work in his early 20s, but there are reports that near the end of his life he had condemned his own writings. (This was not uncommon among Renaissance-era mages, however, as they often had to maneuver carefully through the thickets of ecclesiastical intolerance).[9]

Fourth Book of Occult Philosophy: This is the notoriously disputed 'follow up' book to Agrippa's enormously influential *De Occulta Philosophia*. The *Fourth Book* was published in 1559 (over twenty years after Agrippa had died), and first translated into English in 1665. It was primarily concerned with practical magic (in contrast to Agrippa's *Three Books* which was largely theoretical), including the summoning of demons. Agrippa's alleged student Johann Weyer (see the following entry) dismissed the *Fourth Book* as pseudepigraphical, believing that it was beneath the quality of his teacher. Despite his protests the book became popular and was widely distributed among 16th and 17th century occultists, including John Dee, who carried around a copy with him during his sojourns on the Continent and his meetings with Emperor Rudolph and famed alchemists such as Michael Meier in Bohemia in the 1580s.

De Praestigiis Daemonum (*On the Deceptions of Demons*): This is not a grimoire *per se,* but rather a skeptical study of them that warrants mention here for its influence. Originally published by the Dutch proto-psychiatrist, physician, and demonologist Johann Weyer in 1563, it was a rebuttal of Kramer and Sprenger's 1486 witch-hunter's manual *Malleus Maleficarum.* Weyer's book also included a section on 'spells and poisons', reflecting the view that darker forms of sorcery were often thought to be associated with assassins and their art. In his 1577 edition of the book Weyer included an influential appendix called *Pseudomonarchia Daemonum* (*False Kingdom of Demons*), in which he listed sixty-nine demons (minus images of them or the sigils they were later associated with). This list (with the order mixed up), along with three other demons, re-appeared sometime later to comprise the seventy-two demons of the *Goetia* (see below). Weyer's source for the demonic hierarchy was a book called *Liber Officiorum Spirituum* (*The Book of the Offices of Spirits*), a copy of which was owned by Trithemius, who himself had taught both the famed alchemist Paracelsus as well as Cornelius Agrippa, the latter of whom was supposedly the teacher of Weyer. At any rate, the list of demons specified and popularized by the *Goetia* and *Dictionnaire Infernal* appear to derive from at least as far back as 1500, and probably much further. As for Weyer, his intentions in publishing his book were not always understood. Although he has been nominated as the founder of modern psychiatry (see Chapter 5), in part for his brave efforts to counter the barbaric witch-trials via his view that most 'witches' were innocent women suffering from mental illness, he did not doubt the reality and power of Satan or of his demons, and believed magicians to be deserving of prosecution and severe punishment. The efforts of Weyer were countered by authors such as Jean Bodin, whose *On the Demon-Mania of Witches* (1580) sought to maintain the orthodox view that witches were both real and complicit tools of Satan. Weyer's work was adapted by Reginald Scot in his *Discovery of Witchcraft* (1584). Scot used Weyer's work to argue further against the unjust treatment of witches, based on the essential point that they did not actually exist (as conceived of by the Church) and that all so-called 'magic acts' could be explained by arts of illusion and trickery. His book is often considered the first text on 'stage magic' ('legerdemain', or sleight of hand). King James I (1566–1625), a demonologist himself, added to the furor around the attempts of Scot and Weyer to demystify the so-called *maleficia* of witches, by ordering all copies of Scot's work burnt upon his accession to the English throne in 1603.

Clavicula Salomonis Regis (*The Lesser Key of Solomon*): The author of this famed demonology grimoire is unknown. The work, in a partly complete form, was mentioned by Reginald Scot in 1584, and exists in manuscript form in the British Museum in several editions dating to the mid-to-late 1600s, based in part on Weyer's *Pseudomonarchia Daemonum, The Steganographia* of Trithemius, earlier grimoires from the 14th century (including the *Sworn Book of Honorius*), and possibly material from much older Gnostic texts. The work has also been known as the *Lemegeton*, and more informally as *The Goetia*, although this latter word (Greek for 'sorcery') actually refers to only the first part of the book. In all the *Lemegeton* contains five books (some versions contain only four, omitting the last book, *Ars Notoria*): *Ars Goetia* (*The Art of Sorcery*); *Ars Theurgia Goetia* (*The Art of High Magic and Sorcery*); *Ars Paulina* (*The Art of Paul*), which is a reference to the apostle Paul; *Ars Almadel* (*The Art of the Almadel*), the 'almadel' being a wax tablet used for rituals; and *Ars Notoria* (*The Notable Art*), essentially a section of prayers deriving from much older texts. Although the notoriety of the *Lemegeton* is based on its representation of seventy-two demons and the means by which to contact and control them, it is not just a manual of sorcery, including as it does theurgical and religious practices. The seventy-two demons are thought by some to originate with the Kabbalistic idea of the *Shemhamphorasch* (the 'explicit' or 'interpreted' name, a reference to the Tetragrammaton), connected to Exodus 14:19–21, in which are found three verses each of seventy-two letters. It is believed by some

Kabbalists that when organized in a specific manner the letters reveal the names of seventy-two angels (or Names of God), and that further, if the symbolic sigils of these angels are reversed, the names of the seventy-two demons emerge.

Le Petit Albert: The 'little brother' of *Le Grand Albert*, this popular grimoire seems to have first appeared in France around 1668, with numerous reprintings over the next century. 'Albert' in this case apparently refers not to Albertus Magnus, but to a certain Albertus Parvus Lucius. *Le Petit Albert* was, as with Barrett's *The Magus* (see below), a composite of numerous previous writings, including possibly those of Paracelsus. This book was condemned and censored by the Catholic Church, which allegedly made its value on the 18th–19th century French 'black market' skyrocket. The book achieved a remarkable popularity in rural France, was at times compared to a type of 'farmer's almanac', was devoid of demonic conjurations, and was more concerned with the practical element of 'low magic' so as to cause desired changes in one's life. Perhaps its more infamous recipe concerned that of the so-called 'Hand of Glory', based on a type of necromancy that involved procuring the left hand of an executed man. This object could then allegedly confer certain powers of protection, as well as the ability to become invisible.

Grimorium Verum (*The True Grimoire*): This work was written sometime around 1750 in Italian, probably in Rome (with later French translations). Despite its lofty-sounding title, the authorship, as with so many related works, is unclear, even confusing. The book claims to have been translated from Hebrew by a certain 'Dominican Jesuit' called Plaingiere, and allegedly published in 1517 by an 'Alibeck the Egyptian'. A.E. Waite pointed out that a 'Dominican Jesuit' is an absurdity, suggesting the grimoire was written by a 'Jew or heretic'. The mid-to-late18th century was a time when Egyptian romanticism had gripped the European occult subculture (Court de

Gebelin had first introduced his notion of the Tarot cards deriving from Egyptian mystery teachings not long after *The Grimorium Verum* appeared), a possible influence behind the attribution to an Egyptian publisher. The *Grimorium Verum* was influenced by the *Clavicula Salomonis*, the *Lemegeton*, and Weyer's *Pseudomonarchia Daemonum*, and is in the usual tradition of evoking demons (many of the same ones found in the *Lemegeton*, including the very highest in the demonic hierarchy) for the purposes of personal gain, while at the same time emphasizing the standard Christian piety and need to invoke the heavenly hosts and the 'Most High' first. Nevertheless, S.L. Mathers, in his 1888 English edition of *The Key of Solomon*, dismissed the *Grimorium Verum* as 'full of evil magic' and warned the occult student to avoid it. (An excellent scholarly study of this grimoire was brought out by Joseph Peterson in 2007).[10]

The Grand Grimoire: Also known (in some later editions) as *Le Dragon Rouge* (*The Red Dragon)*, this notorious grimoire was written in Italian (with early French translations) sometime in the mid to late 18th century, with reprints into the 19th century. It often claims a date of 1521, but this is known to be false. The book is styled upon *The Sworn Book of Honorius* and *The Key of Solomon*, but is of a darker tone, centering on forming a Faustian pact with Lucifer (or his demonic 'Prime Minister Lucifuge Rofocale'). The subtitle of the grimoire makes clear its purpose: 'The art of controlling celestial, aerial, terrestrial, and infernal spirits. With the TRUE SECRET of speaking with the dead, winning whenever playing the lottery, discovering hidden treasure, etc.' The grimoire begins with a blend of prayer to God via Hebrew holy names, ascetic austerities (though mild in comparison to Abramelin), the sacrifice of a goat (which is straight out of Leviticus), and other oddities such as procuring four nails from the coffin of a child who has recently died—a probable echo of an old belief, mentioned by Apuleius, that fingers, noses, and nails from the cross of a crucified man possess great power. (Necromancy—the practice of utilizing dead people to contact other realms—has ancient animistic roots. Keith Thomas cited the case of a 14th century magician found carrying around the decapitated head of a Saracen that he had procured in Spain, 'within which he proposed to enclose a spirit that would answer his questions').[11] All this is followed by the construction of a magic circle and the summoning of 'Emperor Lucifer' to appear 'by the name of the great living God, his dear son and the Holy Ghost and by the power of Adonai, Elohim', etc. The book then descends into a number of rituals involving further animal sacrifice, including boiling a cat, cutting the throat of a young wolf, and decapitating a frog, elements that render it one of the baser grimoires and a true book of sorcery with roots in primitive shamanism. (Needless to say, its prime value lies in an anthropological history of ideas within cultural context, *not* as an instruction manual—although that said, it did in fact become a source of working material for some forms of Caribbean sorcery).

The Magus: Written by Francis Barrett and published in 1801, this work was essentially a compilation of previous texts, mostly *The Heptameron* and Agrippa's *De Occulta Philosophia*. Because it lacked original material it may be questioned why it is mentioned here, excepting for two reasons: it was very influential during a time when such writings had fallen out of vogue in many circles (owing mainly to the burgeoning scientific and industrial revolution); and it is a fact that most grimoires simply borrowed and/or modified from the contents of previous ones, so in that regard *The Magus* was not out of sorts.

The Sixth and Seventh Books of Moses: Despite occasional pretensions to antiquity, these are comparatively recent grimoires, probably first written in German in the 18th century, although the earliest known publication is dated to 1849 and the first English translation was in 1880. These books had some influence on African-American and Anglophone Caribbean occult traditions (such as Hoodoo, Voodoo,

Obeah, and Rastafarianism). The books purport to have been written by Moses (thus joining the standard pseudepigraphical tradition of grimoires) containing 'secret' occult lore that was allegedly hidden or removed from the Old Testament. In particular, the book derives its mythic power from the legend of the 'magical victories' of Moses over the Egyptian magicians, and how exactly he did this. The content is, as in all grimoires, concerned with the usage of occult means to gain personal advantages in one's life.

A concluding note on the word 'abracadabra'. No word has been more commonly cited (and lampooned) in many cultures down through the centuries as a reference to mundane forms of magic. It many ways it is the symbol of folk magic *par excellence*, having its apparent origins in amulets and attempts to ward off disease and the evil spirits that were thought to be the causes of such illnesses. Daniel Defoe, in his *Journal of the Plague Year* (1722) mentioned it, stating that the common belief ascribed the plague to demons and a recipe for warding it off to the practice of writing 'abracadabra' in the shape of a descending triangle. These beliefs had apparently been brought to Britain by the Romans; reference to 'abracadabra' was made by the Roman doctor Quintus Sammonicus in 208 CE in which he prescribed usage of the word, written down on paper and tied around the neck, as a device to cure fevers. One of the prescriptions involved wearing the charm around the neck for nine days followed by tossing it backward over the shoulder into a stream (from which probably derives the superstition of throwing salt over one's shoulder if it is accidentally spilled).[12] Multiple sources for the word have been speculated on, and while its origin is unknown, the most probable source appears to be Hebrew-Aramaic, in particular the expressions *ibra k'dibra* ('I create through my speech'); *abhadda kedkabhra* ('disappear like this word'); or *Abra kadavra* ('I will create with words').[13] The word has also been connected to the Gnostic god Abraxis. Aleister Crowley altered it slightly to 'Abrahadabra', replacing the central 'c' with an 'h', which he connected to the

Egyptian deity Horus, to the completion of the Great Work, and to the uniting of microcosm with macrocosm.[14] Mystical complexities aside, the central meaning of the word is clearly associated with creative force, and of the magician's ultimate challenge to seemingly *create something from nothing*—in so doing, replicating the creative power of God.

Appendix IV

A Note on the Tarot and Experiential Astrology

History of the Tarot

The word 'Tarot' derives from the Italian word *tarocco* (plural: *tarocchi*), the name that was used to refer to Tarot cards in the early 1500s in Italy; the name has been speculated to originate with the Taro river in northern Italy, consistent with some evidence that the cards were devised in a northern Italian town such as Milan, Ferrara, or Bologna.[1] Wilder speculation links the name to older cultures, such as Egypt, and even to the middle four letters in the name of the Phoenician goddess-become-demon Astaroth.[2] There is evidence that a close precursor of Tarot cards was used in Germany and Italy in the early 1400s, but at that time they were simply playing cards with trumps. The first definite reference to Tarot cards occurs in 1442, in Ferrara, northern Italy. The word *tarocco* does not appear in recorded literature until the year 1516. This word became 'tarot' (pronounced 'ta-ro') once the cards migrated from Italy to France; the French word has been used by the English-speaking world since then.

Although the Tarot is a relatively young esoteric system—much younger than astrology or alchemy—its origins are notoriously shrouded in mystery. What seems reasonably clear is that the cards were not initially a mystical teaching or occult system, but rather were originally simple gaming cards. Typical playing cards first appeared in Europe by at least 1377, the year a German monk mentioned them in an essay, although he added that their origins were unknown.[3] By 1397 playing cards had made such inroads in Paris that an edict was made disallowing people to use the cards on working days.[4] Some have speculated that playing cards had arrived in Europe in the late 1300s via Islamic Egypt. (There is earlier evidence for the existence of playing cards in Eastern cultures, such as China, Korea, and India, dating back to the 10th century, but again, the origins of these are also unknown). At any rate, the Tarot as we now know it almost certainly took form in the early 1400s in northern Italy.

One of the earliest known Tarot decks, and the most complete early deck still in existence, is the Visconti-Sforza deck (named for Francesco Sforza, the fourth Duke of Milan), which appears to have been painted by the artist Bonifacio Bembo (1420–1478) sometime around 1440 in Milan. In 1499 parts of northern Italy, including Milan, were conquered by the French. Evidence suggests that the Tarot gradually faded from Italy after this time, the cards being taken by the French where they eventually spread across France and Switzerland. The famous Marseilles deck subsequently appeared around the year 1500, a pack which to a large extent has remained the main style upon which modern decks have been based.[5]

If the early 15th century Tarot decks appear to have been artistic curiosities used mainly for recreational gaming purposes, by the late 18th century that began to change. It was in 1775 that the French pastor, Freemason and scholar Antoine Court de Gebelin (1719–1784) proposed that the deck was in fact an expression of older (especially Egyptian) myths and mystical ideas. He is the first known person to have referred to the Tarot as a tool for spiritual initiation and psychological insight. It may be hard to believe that in the three hundred and fifty years prior to him no one had hit upon this idea, but if they did it has not been found to be recorded anywhere. There are, however, definite historical references prior to the 18th century to the Tarot being merely a game, mentioned alongside chess. The tendency to 'retroactively romanticize' elements of the Western esoteric tradition has been present since the Renaissance, but especially since the 19th century and beyond. Games such as chess and those using playing cards such as the Tarot (as well as the Kabbalah) are highly susceptible to such romanticizing, owing to their elaborate symbolism. As Daniel O'Keefe had argued in *Stolen Lightning*,[6] his scholarly tome on magic, esoteric theory and practice (such as high magic) tend to be more recent lines of development arising *out* of organized religion (contrary to the stereotypical view that esoteric teachings must be older and therefore more valid).

The notion of an ancient Egyptian link to the origins of the Tarot came into fashion due mainly to the writings of Court de Gebelin, and these in turn set the tone for the esoteric interpretations of the Tarot that became so commonplace from the 19th century and on. Court de Gebelin believed that the Major Arcana (the twenty-two trump cards) were a pictorial representation of the 'Book of Thoth', the pseudepigraphical works (or works) ascribed to the Egyptian god of wisdom.[7] However there are some interesting ironies in this whole matter, resting on the fact that Court de Gebelin was operating under certain historical misconceptions. As mentioned, the period from the Renaissance up till Gebelin's time had a tendency to romanticize ancient cultures, particularly the Egyptian. This tendency itself had older roots, stemming from the period of approximately 100–300 CE, when the Greek mystics and scribes of that time, convinced that they themselves inhabited a relatively degraded era in history and that the ancient Egyptians had been custodians of great wisdom and powerful magic, ascribed their writings to Egyptian deities such as Thoth (or by his Greek name, Hermes). Books such as the *Corpus Hermeticum* were presented as teachings directly derived from Egyptian gods, and these in turn were believed by Renaissance scholars and magicians to be exactly that, when in fact these books had been written only in the immediate centuries after Christ. The other misconception that Court de Gebelin was operating under was that the first deck he saw, and upon which he based his Egyptian theories about the card's origins, was the French Marseilles deck. This deck however did not even accurately replicate the earlier Italian cards upon which it was based, let alone any ancient Egyptian system.[8] In 1799 (fifteen years after Court de Gebelin's death) the Rosetta Stone was discovered in Egypt by one of Napoleon's officers.

In 1822 the Egyptian hieroglyphs on the stone were transliterated by Francois Champollion. The Rosetta Stone included dual inscriptions in Greek and hieroglyphics, enabling scholars for the first time to understand the old Egyptian language. In so doing much was learned about ancient Egypt, but no evidence of Tarot cards or anything resembling them has been subsequently found. In addition, it bears mentioning that playing cards of any sort were originally designed on paper, and the ancient Egyptians did not use paper. It was rather the Chinese who invented paper (in the 2nd century CE), which bolsters the argument that playing cards were originally created by the Chinese.[9]

In the mid-19th century the French magus Eliphas Levi (1810–1875, born Alphonse Louis Constant)—who in many ways became the father of modern occult theory of the Tarot—developed an idea originally noticed by Court de Gebelin's associate the Comte de Mellet (and published in a 1781 volume of Gebelin's *Monde Primitif*), that the twenty-two letters of the Hebrew alphabet, as well as the twenty-two pathways linking the ten *sephirot* in the Kabbalistic Tree of Life, correspond in number to the twenty-two trump cards of the Tarot. While there is no historical evidence to suggest that the Tree of Life and the Tarot were created from a common source, the correlation between the two can nevertheless be seen as meaningful as both share universal ideas relating to personal and collective transformation. Some have argued, however, that the heavy emphasis on Kabbalistic correspondences to the Tarot has diminished the artistic merits and qualities deriving from the original Renaissance efforts of the first Tarot card creators. As Tarot scholar and artist Robert Place put it:

> At worst the collection of letters and numbers with their memorized meanings becomes more important than the pictures. Instead of letting the pictures unlock images in one's mind, they are ignored and one recites the correspondences from rote memory.[10]

Place's view, though valid as a counterbalance to the overemphasis on rote memorization, is not supported by traditional esoteric teachings that do in fact maintain that all the memorizing aids in attuning one's consciousness to specific qualities. The matter, as always, comes down to balancing inner tendencies, ultimately a subjective determination. Nevertheless Place's point is important because it highlights the fact that the original cultural context of when a tradition arises must never be lost sight of. The artists of 15th century Italy who created the first Tarot decks were not writing tomes linking them to Hebrew letters, and nor were they psychologizing their symbols.

Eliphas Levi had died in 1875; not long after, in 1888, the Hermetic Order of the Golden Dawn was founded in England by three Freemasons. This Order was based on graded initiations and combined many mystical teachings into a workable system for personal transformation. The system was based heavily on the Tree of Life, and its connections to both ritual and divination systems like the Tarot. They made one slight but significant adjustment to Levi's original correspondence list between the twenty-two trumps and the twenty-two Hebrew letters and pathways on the Tree of Life (which had been echoed by Gerard Encausse and Oswald Wirth), moving The Fool card from 21 to 0. That model has generally been used as the esoteric standard since then.

In 1910 Arthur Edward Waite, a former Golden Dawn initiate, designed and published his own deck, called the Rider-Waite deck (painted by Pamela Coleman-Smith; 'Rider' was the name of the publisher). This became the dominant deck for much of the 20th century and is still popular today, despite its somewhat simplistic design. In 1938 Aleister Crowley undertook to revise and improve upon the Rider-Waite deck. Crowley's deck, called the Thoth Tarot, was painted by Frieda Harris and given an initial limited edition printing (of low quality) in 1944. It was not given a proper printing and mass published until 1968, a number of years after the deaths of both Crowley and Harris. The Thoth deck is generally considered one of the most, if not *the* most, artistically accomplished and interesting of all modern decks, and is favored by many Tarot and esoteric practitioners for its rich and sophisticated symbolism. Crowley's deck also altered some of the names of the Major Arcana—The Magician became The Magus, Strength became Lust, Justice became Adjustment, Temperance became Art, Judgment became The Aeon, and The World became The Universe. While these alterations are accepted and used by those who prefer the Thoth deck, they have not been universally applied. Most modern decks still use the original Rider-Waite version of the Major Arcana cards.

The Purpose of the Tarot

Tarot cards have, traditionally, provoked many strong reactions from those who view and contemplate their symbols. Stuart Kaplan, in his exhaustive *The Encyclopedia of Tarot (Volume I)*, cites an interesting sermon given by a Franciscan monk in approximately 1470 in northern Italy. It is highly revealing, both of the religious mindset of the times, and of the provocative psychological power of the Tarot:

> Concerning the third class of games, that is trumps [tarot]. There is nothing so hateful to God as the game of trumps. For everything that is base in the eyes of the Christian faith is seen in trumps, as will be evident when I run through them. For trumps are said, so it is believed, to have been given their names by the Devil, their inventor, because in no other game does he triumph (with the loss of souls to boot) as much as in this one. In it not only are God, the angels, the planets and the cardinal virtues represented and named, but also the world's luminaries, I mean the Pope and the Emperor, are forced, a thing which is degrading and ridiculous to Christians, to enter into the game. For there are 21 trumps which are the 21 steps of a ladder which takes a man to the depths of Hell.[11]

What is interesting about the friar's sermon is how he reacts to the perceived 'degradation' of the pope and emperor owing to their inclusion in the deck (he also mentions God, though in fact there is no specific card for 'God' in the Tarot deck). He views both pope and emperor as individuals commanding a particular office. From our modern psychologized viewpoint we would tend to see him as committing an error in understanding; for surely in the context of the Tarot they are not individuals, they are *archetypes*. That is, 'Pope' (or 'Hierophant') and 'Emperor' or 'Empress' represent particular qualities and forces that affect things on both the macrocosmic level, i.e., politics, and the microcosmic level, that is, the psychological makeup of the individual who is using the cards to look into their own mind. However, back in the 15th century the 'psychologized' viewpoint was not there, or if so, only in rudimentary form. Much as the magicians of that time did not view the spirits they conjured as mere figments of their unconscious (or of any 'collective' unconscious), so too were figures such as those presented in the Tarot seen as nothing other than actual representations of real people and the real offices they held. For example, the Hanged Man card of the original 15th century Visconti-Sforza deck simply referred to a 'traitor' and his means of public execution. The Fool did not appear to be any romanticized symbol of Dionysius or Cernunnos or some notable archetype of spontaneous power. He was merely a ragged beggar, what in modern terms we would call a 'homeless person'. And perhaps most significantly of all, the Magician card referred more to a trickster-conjuror or mountebank who worked at a public stall in the village performing stage magic as a means of entertainment—not as some elevated magus or wizard who symbolized the higher self. And even the controversial 'Popess' card was likely a mischievous reference to a popular legend of the 14th and 15th centuries of a female pope who never existed, not to the exalted High Priestess or manifestation of the goddess that the modern version of this card grew into.

It is somewhat interesting, and perhaps ironic, that the history of the Tarot as a vehicle for esotericism and self-knowledge seems to begin with Court de Gebelin in the late 18th century—within a few years of when Immanuel Kant published his *Critique of Pure Reason*. Far as we know Kant did not consort with the Tarot, and Gebelin, if he knew of Kant, was unlikely to have been influenced by him. But Kant was the first Western philosopher to provide a clear and convincing explanation for why reason alone cannot penetrate to ultimate reality (or what he imagined to be 'outside' of the reach of reason). The esoteric tradition, of course, bases much of its central tenets on this understanding—that we need to resort to different modes of consciousness in order to grasp, or directly experience, transcendent realities. Symbolic systems such as the Tarot actually do have the ability to function as contemplative tools in which we can access different orders of consciousness, precisely because the symbols compel us to move beyond dualistic thinking. The original Tarot figures may have largely been commentaries, at times tongue-in-cheek, on the culture of their times (perhaps similar to modern day comics writers and artists). Nevertheless Tarot symbols certainly can be used as vehicles for psychological understanding—symbols of the unconscious mind, the hidden elements of personality. Even more, they can also function as devices to train the mind to move beyond dualistic rationality.

The stereotypical view of the Tarot (and other potential divinatory systems like astrology or the Norse runes), is that it is used for forecasting our future—most commonly, to suggest to people what they should or should not do with their lives. A whole industry has for a long time existed around this function of the cards in which 'psychics' of all stripes have offered up services for the purpose of guiding people into allegedly advantageous situations. While this approach is not baseless—it only takes common sense to see that the use of symbols, combined with intuition, sensitivity, and intelligence, can point out possible options or avenues of choice for most typical dilemmas—it is not the deepest use of symbols such as those found in the Tarot. From the point of view of one seeking insight and transformation, Tarot symbols are probably best understood as *archetypes*. The word derives from the Greek terms *arkhe* ('first') and *typos* ('model', or 'type'). An archetype is an original model upon which common themes and forms are based—for example, 'Hero', 'Mother', 'Wise Old Man', etc. Most people tend to commonly identify with archetypes, even to the point of seeking to actively emulate them so as to achieve something in (or with) their life. Archetypal symbols such as those found in the Tarot, like the Fool, or the Hermit, or the Lovers, are literally the stuff of dreams, as we commonly dream of such symbols at night in such a way as to embody them—for example, by 'playing the fool', or by shying away from things (hermit-like), or by connecting intimately with someone (lovers). Further, not only do we dream of such things, we also act them out in our daily lives, sometimes in ways that make us uncomfortable or lead to suffering, or in ways that help us to achieve some goal or simply just to enjoy our present reality as it is.

To use the Tarot as a tool for psychological or spiritual insight is to utilize its symbols as a means for seeing and understanding the nature of our mind. As *know thyself* is the underlying credo for the truth-seeker, it follows that a richly symbolic system like the Tarot can be a potential goldmine to aid on the path of self-discovery—provided we develop the skill to use it this way.

Tarot Literature

The 20th century saw an explosion in the popularity of the Tarot, and a proliferation of published decks of all conceivable stripes. The 21st century appears to be following the trend. Literature on the Tarot has followed closely behind the quantity of decks published, although the number of truly quality writings, of both the historical and theoretical kind, has been limited. At the top of the list must be *Meditations on the Tarot: A Journey into Christian Hermeticism*, written in the 1960s and first published in French in 1984. The author chose to remain anonymous, claiming that he did not want any personality to get in the way of the information provided in the book.[12] The subtitle indicates his Christian foundation, but his writing and scope of knowledge reveals a profoundly ecumenical spirit and a master of the perennial philosophy. His book is six hundred pages of dense text, and although devoid of any focus on divination or cartomancy, still makes most other works on the Tarot look simplistic in comparison. Aside from *Meditations,* the outstanding work in the field is Stuart Kaplan's *Encyclopedia of Tarot,* a monumental four volume series (published successively in 1978, 1986, 1990, and 2005). Two excellent additional works on the history of the tarot are Richard Cavendish's *The Tarot* (1975) and Robert M. Place's *The Tarot: History, Symbolism, and Divination* (2005). Also worthy of mention are Robert Wang's *The Qabalistic Tarot: A Textbook of Mystical Philosophy* (1983), Cynthia Giles' *The Tarot: History, Mystery, and Lore* (1994), and Rachel Pollack's *Seventy-Eight Degrees of Wisdom: A Book of Tarot* (2007). The works of Eliphas Levi, especially *Dogme et Rituel de la Haute Magie* (1855, translated into English by A.E. Waite in 1896 as *Transcendental Magic*), Waite's *The Pictorial Key to the Tarot* (1911), P.D. Ouspensky's chapter on the tarot in *A New Model of the Universe* (1913), and last but not least Aleister Crowley's *The Book of Thoth* (1944), are mainly of historical interest, but all contain plenty of insightful commentary on tarot symbolism that remains relevant.

Experiential Astrology

Probably the most glaring omission from this book has been the topic of astrology; indeed, as the oldest of all 'occult arts' it certainly deserves mention in a book on the Western esoteric tradition. Owing to space limitations the history and theory of astrology have been left out of this volume[13], however mention is made here of a somewhat unusual methodology of psycho-spiritual exploration and psychodrama known as 'experiential astrology'.

The method is straightforward. While it can be done in solitude, it works better with a group of any size, though ideally of eleven people. The idea is to choose one person's natal chart (the exact position of the planets of the solar system at the moment of their birth—this information and the corresponding chart can easily be accessed free of charge from the Internet), and then to 'lay out' the chart on the ground of a room big enough to contain ten cushions (or small chairs). The cushions or chairs should be arranged to roughly approximate the positions of the planets on the natal chart. Earth is in the middle of the chart, of course, as astrology is geocentric (as opposed to heliocentric—and no, that does not make astrology flawed from that basis, because from the point of view of where we reside on Earth, the planets do indeed appear to revolve around us. This counts because astrology is based pre-eminently on psychological perspective). A cushion or chair in the center of the circle represents Earth. The person whom the natal chart represents then sits on the central cushion or chair. If a group (of the ideal number of eleven) is present, the ten others then sit on the cushions or chairs representing the remaining eight planets plus the Sun and Moon. Once everyone is in position, the idea is to become mindful of one's bodily experience in the location one finds oneself in. Various communication exercises can then be undertaken, in which each 'planet' gets to communicate with other planets in the circle, noticing the particular thoughts and feelings that arise in relation to other planets. (A simple example process being, 'this is how I feel about you' or 'this is how I currently see you from this point of view', and so on, with emphasis given to intuitive, subjective communication delivered with straightforward honesty, along with willingness to hear communications from others without reactive or defensive replies). The person in the middle can participate or just observe other planets in dialogue with each other. The entire thing amounts to a type of psychodrama, and can easily lead to interesting and even profound insights as one allows oneself to embody the role of the planet one is playing. The process tends to work best if preconceived ideas about what a particular planetary energy or quality is 'supposed' to be do not interfere with one's spontaneous expressions. Participants in general should remain on their spot, so as to maximize the experience based on spatial location in relation to others in the room. (Needless to say, this process can also be enacted within one's mind, utilizing active imagination). Because astrology is pre-eminently about relationship (the geometric positioning of planets relative to each other—called the 'planetary aspects'—as well as to the earth and the 'background' stars, along with perceptual perspective (the positioning we find ourselves in when born, or at any given point in our lives), it tends to work well as an interactive, psycho-dramatic process.

Bibliography and Suggestions for Further Reading

For the more academically inclined, the best books on the history of magic are probably Lynn Thorndike's massive eight volume *A History of Magic and Experimental Science* (1923-58), followed by Keith Thomas, *Religion and the Decline of Magic* (1971), and Daniel O'Keefe, *Stolen Lightning: The Social Theory of Magic* (1983). Of the three, Thomas's is the most readable, but all made Herculean efforts, delving into the history and social meaning of magic with unsurpassed attention to detail. Also excellent (and more accessible) are Richard Cavendish's *The Black Arts* (1967) and *The History of Magic* (1975), Gareth Knight's *A History of White Magic* (2011, originally published in 1991 as *Magic and the Western Mind*), Owen Davies' *Grimoires: A History of Magic Books* (2009), and Nevill Drury's *Stealing Fire from Heaven* (2011). For the Kabbalah, Gershom Scholem's work (*The Kabbalah*, 1978), is unsurpassed as a reference work. For a more practical angle, Rabbi David Cooper's *God is a Verb* (1998) and Will Parfitt's *Kabbalah for Life* (2010) are excellent. For the 'hermetic' version, Dion Fortune's 1935 publication *The Mystical Qabalah* is the generally acknowledged classic. As a general history of philosophy, Bertrand Russell's *The History of Western Philosophy* (1945) is hard to beat, although one does have to bear in mind Russell's training as a mathematician and logician, and his concern with politics and activism. For the history of psychiatry and psychology, Henri Ellenberger's *The Discovery of the Unconscious* (1970) is magisterial. For a general 'history of ideas' accessibly written, excellent is Richard Tarnas's *The Passion of the Western Mind* (1991); also good, though more generalized, is Charles Van Doren's *A History of Knowledge* (1991). For an anthropological take on the roots of religion (including shamanism), Weston LaBarre's *The Ghost Dance* (1970) is outstanding. For histories of the Western esoteric tradition written by scholars and writers with a more sympathetic ear for the practical domains of esotericism, excellent are any works written by Frances Yates, Nicholas Goodrich-Clarke, Antoine Faivre, Wouter Hanegraaff, Joscelyn Godwin, Richard Smoley, Arthur Versluis, Richard Grossinger, and Nevill Drury. Although not covered in this book (I have written of him elsewhere), the Greek-Armenian mystic G.I. Gurdjieff (1872?-1949) is a key figure in modern Western esoterica; his ideas are best described in the classic work by P.D. Ouspensky, *In Search of the Miraculous* (1949). Also deserving mention is the magnum opus of the magician and poet Aleister Crowley, *Magick: Book Four, Liber ABA* (1930) especially the revised 1997 edition edited by Hymenaeus Beta. For alchemy, excellent are the works of Titus Burckhardt, Mircea Eliade, C.G. Jung, and Lawrence Principe, although these authors present anything but a unified view. For the theory of traditional Golden Dawn-styled magic, the writings of Israel Regardie and the Ciceros are best. For emphasis on the practical angle, Donald Michael Kraig's *Modern Magick* (1988, most recent revised edition 2010) is very effective, as are the works of Franz Bardon and R.J. Stewart. Teachings on the 'art of manifestation' are of course ubiquitous; outstanding in the field are the writings of David Spangler (one of the original teachers at Findhorn). The literature on Witchcraft is voluminous, but Ronald Hutton's *Triumph of the Moon: A History of Modern Pagan Witchcraft* (1999) is excellent, both scholarly and sympathetic. The best work from the point of view of an actual practicing modern Wiccan is Margot Adler's *Drawing Down the Moon* (1979, most recent revised edition 2006). The best purely historical analysis is probably Brian Levack's *The Witch-Hunt in Early Modern Europe* (1987, 1995, 2006), and the most original is Stuart Clark's *Thinking With Demons: The Idea of Witchcraft in Early Modern Europe* (1997). For Tantra and the various schools of Yoga, recommended are the works of Georg Feuerstein. For Tibetan Dream Yoga, consult Namkhai Norbu and Tenzin Wangyal Rinpoche, and for lucid dreaming, best are still the works of Steven LaBerge, along with Robert Waggoner's recent effort. For the 'out of body' state, the classics (and still the best, in this writer's opinion) are the works of Robert Monroe.

Agrippa, Henry Cornelius (Donald Tyson ed.), *Three Books of Occult Philosophy* (Llewellyn Publications, 1993).

Alexander, Franz G., and Selesnick, Sheldon T., *The History of Psychiatry: An Evaluation of Psychiatric Thought and Practice from Prehistoric Times to the Present* (Harper & Row, 1966).

Ankarloo, Bengt, and Clark, Stuart, eds., *Witchcraft and Magic in Europe: The Period of the Witch Trials* (University of Pennsylvania Press, 2002).

Assagioli, Roberto, *The Act of Will* (Penguin Books, 1980).

Bakan, David, *Sigmund Freud and the Jewish Mystical Tradition* (Schocken Books, 1965).

Beitchman, Philip, *Alchemy of the Word: Cabala of the Renaissance* (State University of New York, 1998).

Bennett, J.G., *The Masters of Wisdom* (Turnstone Press, 1982).

Bloom, Harold, *Where Shall Wisdom Be Found?* (Riverhead Books, 2004).

— , *Omens of Millennium* (Fourth Estate, 1997).

Bodin, Jean, *On the Demon-Mania of Witches* (CRRS Publications, 1995).

Bogdan, Henrik, *Western Esotericism and Rituals of Initiation* (State University of New York Press, 2007).

Briggs, Robin, *Witches & Neighbours: The Social and Cultural Context of European Witchcraft* (Viking, 1996; 2nd edition Blackwell, 2002).

Brunschwig, Jacques and Lloyd, Geoffrey E.R., *A Guide to Greek Thought* (Harvard University Press, 2003).

Burckhardt, Titus, *Alchemy: Science of the Cosmos, Science of the Soul* (Fons Vitae 1997).

Carroll, Peter J., *Liber Null & Psychonaut: An Introduction to Chaos Magic* (Samuel Weiser Inc., 1987).

Cavendish, Richard, *A History of Magic* (Taplinger Publishing, 1979).

— , *The Black Arts* (Perigee, 1983).

— , *The Tarot* (Michael Joseph Ltd., 1975).

Cicero, Chic, and Cicero, Sandra Tabatha, *The Essential Golden Dawn: An Introduction to High Magic* (Llewellyn Publications, 2003).

Clark, Stuart, *Thinking With Demons: The Idea of Witchcraft in Early Modern Europe* (Oxford University Press, 1999).

Cohn, Norman, *Europe's Inner Demons* (Paladin, 1976).

Conger, John P., *Jung and Reich: The Body as Shadow* (North Atlantic Books, 1988).

Conway, David, *Secret Wisdom: The Occult Universe Explored* (The Aquarian Press, 1987).

Cooper, Rabbi David, *God is a Verb: Kabbalah and the Practice of Mystical Judaism* (Riverhead Books, 1997).

Crowley, Aleister, *Magick: Book Four, Liber ABA* (Weiser Books, 1998).

— , *The Book of Thoth* (Samuel Weiser, 1992).

Davidson, Gustav, *A Dictionary of Angels: Including the Fallen Angels* (Macmillan Publishing Co., Inc., 1971).

Davies, Owen, *Grimoires: A History of Magic Books* (Oxford University Press, 2009).

Deslippe, Philip, ed., William Walker Atkinson's *The Kybalion* (Jeremy P. Tarcher/Penguin, 2011).

Drury, Nevill, *Stealing Fire from Heaven: The Rise of Modern Western Magic* (Oxford University Press, 2011).

Dunn, Patrick, *Magic, Power, Language, Symbol: A Magician's Exploration of Linguistics* (Llewellyn, 2008).

Durant, Will, *The Story of Philosophy* (Pocket Books, 1961).

Eliade, Mircea, *The Forge and the Crucible: The Origins and Structures of Alchemy* (University of Chicago Press, 1978).

— , *Shamanism: Archaic Techniques of Ecstasy* (Princeton University Press, 1974)

Ellenberger, Henri F., *The Discovery of the Unconscious: The History and Evolution of Dynamic Psychiatry* (Basic Books, 1970).

Flanagan, Owen, *Consciousness Reconsidered* (The MIT Press, 1992).

Fortune, Dion, *The Mystical Qabalah* (Weiser Books, 1998).

Freke, Timothy, and Gandy, Peter, *The Hermetica: The Lost Wisdom of the Pharaohs* (Piatkus Publishers, 1997).

French, Peter, *John Dee: The World of an Elizabethan Magus* (Ark Paperbacks, 1987).

Freud, Sigmund, *The Origins of Religion* (Penguin Books, 1990).

— , *The Basic Writings of Sigmund Freud* (Random House, 1938).

Feuerstein, Georg, *Tantra: The Path of Ecstasy* (Shambhala Publications, 1998).

Galdston, Iago (ed.), *Historic Derivations of Modern Psychiatry* (McGraw-Hill, 1967).

Godwin, David, *Light in Extension: Greek Magic from Homer to Modern Times* (Llewellyn, 1992).

Godwin, Joscelyn, *The Golden Thread: The Ageless Wisdom of the Western Mystery Traditions* (Quest Books, 2007).

Goodrick-Clarke, Nicholas, *The Western Esoteric Traditions: A Historical Introduction* (Oxford University Press, 2008).

Happold, F.C., *Mysticism: A Study and an Anthology* (Penguin Books, 1970).

Harrington, Anne, *The Cure Within: A History of Mind-Body Medicine* (W.W. Norton and Company, 2008).

Hauck, Dennis William, *The Emerald Tablet: Alchemy for Personal Transformation* (Penguin Arkana, 1999).

Hill, Napoleon, *Think and Grow Rich* (Fawcett Crest, 1960).

Hine, Phil, *Condensed Chaos: An Introduction to Chaos Magic* (New Falcon Publications, 1996).

Hoffman, Edward, *The Kabbalah Reader: A Sourcebook of Visionary Judaism* (Trumpeter Books, 2010).

Hoeller, Stephen A., *The Gnostic Jung and the Seven Sermons to the Dead* (Quest Books, 1994).

Holman, John, *The Return of the Perennial Philosophy: The Supreme Vision of Western Esotericism* (Watkins Publishing, 2008).

Horney, Karen, *Neurosis and Human Growth* (W.W. Norton and Company, Inc., 1991).

— , *The Neurotic Personality of our Time* (W.W. Norton and Company, Inc., 1964).

Hutton, Ronald, *The Triumph of the Moon: A History of Modern Pagan*

Witchcraft (Oxford University Press, 2001).

James, William, *The Varieties of Religious Experience* (Barnes and Noble Classics, 2004).

Johnston, Sarah Iles (ed.), *Ancient Religions* (Harvard University Press, 2007).

Jung, C.G., *Man and His Symbols* (Dell Publishing, 1962).

— , *Aion* (Princeton University Press, 1978).

— , *Mysterium Coniunctionis* (Princeton University Press, 1989).

Kaufman, Walter, *The Portable Nietzsche* (Penguin Books, 1982).

Kieckhefer, Richard, *Magic in the Middle Ages* (Cambridge University Press, 2000).

Kinney, Jay (ed.), *The Inner West: An Introduction to the Hidden Wisdom of the West* (Jeremy P. Tarcher, 2004).

Knight, Gareth, *A History of White Magic* (Skylight Press, 2011, originally published as *Magic and the Western Mind: Ancient Knowledge and the Transformation of Consciousness,* Llewellyn Publications, 1991).

LaBarre, Weston, *The Ghost Dance: The Origins of Religion* (Dell Publishing, 1972).

LaBerge, Stephen, and Rheingold, Howard, *Exploring the World of Lucid Dreaming* (Ballantine Books, 1990).

Layton, Bentley, *The Gnostic Scriptures* (Doubleday, 1995).

Levack, Brian P., *The Witch-Hunt in Early Modern Europe* (Longman, 1995).

— , *The Devil Within: Possession and Exorcism in the Christian West* (Yale University Press, 2013).

Lisiewski, PhD, Joseph C., *Ceremonial Magic and the Power of Evocation* (New Falcon Publications, 2006).

Luck, George, *Arcana Mundi: Magic and the Occult in the Greek and Roman Worlds* (John Hopkins University Press, 1985).

Mackay, Christopher S., *The Hammer of Witches: A Complete Translation of the Malleus Maleficarum* (Cambridge University Press, 2011).

Mathers, S.L. MacGregor, editor, *The Key of Solomon the King* (Dover

Publications, 2009).

— ,translator, Crowley, Aleister, editor and introduction by, *The Goetia: The Lesser Key of Solomon the King*, (Ordo Templi Orientis, 1997).

— , translator, *The Book of the Sacred Magic of Abramelin the Mage*, (Dover Publications, 1975).

Maxwell-Stuart, P.G., *The Chemical Choir: A History of Alchemy* (Continuum Books, 2008).

McDonald, Kathleen, *How to Meditate: A Practical Guide* (Wisdom Publications, 2005).

McIntosh, Christopher, *The Rosicrucians: The History, Mythology, and Rituals of an Esoteric Order* (Samuel Weiser, 1997).

Messadié, Gerard, *A History of the Devil* (Kodansha International, 1996).

Metzinger, Thomas, *The Ego Tunnel: The Science of the Mind and the Myth of the Self* (Basic Books, 2009).

Moore, Robert (Red Hawk), *Self Observation: The Awakening of Conscience* (Hohm Press, 2009).

Murphy, Joseph, *The Power of Your Subconscious Mind* (Prentice Hall Press, 2008).

Naydler, Jeremy, *Shamanic Wisdom in the Pyramid Texts: The Mystical Tradition of Ancient Egypt* (Inner Traditions, 2005).

Needleman, Jacob (editor), *The Sword of Gnosis: Metaphysics, Cosmology, Tradition, Symbolism* (Arkana, 1986).

O'Brien, Elmer, *Varieties of Mystic Experience* (Mentor-Omega, 1965).

O'Keefe, Daniel Lawrence, *Stolen Lightning: The Social Theory of Magic* (Vintage, 1983).

Ouspensky, P.D., *In Search of the Miraculous: Fragments of an Unknown Teaching* (Harcourt Brace Jovanovich, Inc., 1949).

Palmer, Helen, *The Enneagram: Understanding Yourself and the Others in Your Life* (HarperSanFrancisco, 1988).

Patterson, William Patrick, *Voices in the Dark: Esoteric, Occult, and Secular Voices in Nazi-Occupied Paris 1940-1944* (Arete Communications, 2000).

Pilkington, Roger, *Robert Boyle: Father of Chemistry* (John Murray, 1959).

Plato, *The Republic* (Dover Publications, 2000).

— ,*The Last Days of Socrates* (Penguin Books, 2003).

Plotinus, *The Enneads* (Penguin Classics, 1991).

Ponce, Charles, *The Game of Wizards: Psyche, Science, and Symbol in the Occult* (Penguin Books, 1975).

Preece, Rob, *The Wisdom of Imperfection: The Challenge of Individuation in Buddhist Life* (Snow Lion, 2006).

Principe, Lawrence M., *The Secrets of Alchemy* (University of Chicago Press, 2013).

Reich, Wilhelm, *Character Analysis* (Farrar, Straus, and Giroux, 1990).

Robbins, Rossell, *The Encyclopedia of Witchcraft and Demonology* (Crown Publishers, 1959).

Russell, Bertrand, *The History of Western Philosophy* (Touchstone, 1972).

Russell, Jeffrey Burton, *Witchcraft in the Middle Ages* (Cornell University Press, 1972).

Scholem, Gersholm, *Kabbalah* (Penguin Books, 1978).

— , *Alchemy and Kabbalah* (Spring Publications, 2006).

Seligmann, Kurt, *Magic, Supernaturalism, and Religion* (Pantheon Books, 1971).

Smoley, Richard, and Kinney, Jay, *Hidden Wisdom: A Guide to the Western Inner Traditions* (Penguin Arkana, 1999).

Smoley, Richard, *Forbidden Faith: The Gnostic Legacy from the Gospels to The DaVinci Code* (HarperSanFrancisco, 2006).

— , *The Dice Game of Shiva: How Consciousness Creates the World* (New World Library, 2009).

Spangler, David, *Everyday Miracles: The Inner Art of Manifestation* (Bantam Books, 1996).

St. John of the Cross, *The Collected Works of St. John of the Cross* (ICS Publications, 1991).

Stewart, R.J., *Advanced Magical Arts* (Element Books, 1989).

Sullivan, Lawrence E. (ed.), *Hidden Truths: Magic, Alchemy, and the*

Occult (Macmillan, 1989).

Tarnas, Richard, *The Passion of the Western Mind* (Ballantine Books, 1991).

Tenzin Wangyal Rinpoche, *The Tibetan Yogas of Dream and Sleep* (Snow Lion, 1998).

Thomas, Keith, *Religion and the Decline of Magic* (Charles Scribner's Sons, 1971).

Van den Broek, Roelof and Hanegraaff, Wouter, *Gnosis and Hermeticism: From Antiquity to Modern Times* (State University of New York Press, 1998).

Van Doren, Charles, *A History of Knowledge* (Ballantine Books, 1991).

Versluis, Arthur, *The Philosophy of Magic* (Arkana Paperbacks, 1986).

— , *Magic and Mysticism: An Introduction to Western Esotericism* (Rowman and Littlefield, 2007).

Visser, Frank, *Ken Wilber: Thought As Passion* (State University of New York Press, 2003).

Yates, Frances, *The Rosicrucian Enlightenment* (Routledge & Kegan Paul, 1972).

— , *Giordano Bruno and the Hermetic Tradition* (University of Chicago Press, 1991).

— , *The Occult Philosophy in Elizabethan England* (Routledge & Kegan Paul, 1979).

Waggoner, Robert, *Lucid Dreaming: Gateway to the Inner Self* (Moment Point Press, 2009).

Waite, Arthur Edward, *The Book of Ceremonial Magic: A Complete Grimoire* (Citadel Press, 1970).

Wapnick, Kenneth, *Love Does Not Condemn: The World, the Flesh, and the Devil According to Platonism, Christianity, Gnosticism, and* A Course In Miracles (Foundation for *A Course In Miracles*, 1989).

Washburn, Michael, *Transpersonal Psychology in Psychoanalytic Perspective* (State University of New York Press, 1994).

Watts, Alan, *Psychotherapy East and West* (Vintage Books, 1975).

Webb, James, *The Occult Establishment* (Open Court, 1976).

Wellbeloved, Sophie, *Gurdjieff: The Key Concepts* (Routledge, 2003).

West, John Anthony, *The Serpent in the Sky: The High Wisdom of Ancient Egypt* (Quest Books, 1993).

Wilber, Ken, *A Brief History of Everything* (Shambhala, 1996).

— , *Eye to Eye: The Quest for the New Paradigm* (Shambhala, 1996)

— , *Integral Psychology: Consciousness, Spirit, Psychology, Therapy* (Shambhala, 2000).

— , *Integral Spirituality* (Integral Books, 2006).

Wilson, Colin, *The Occult* (Grafton Books, 1972).

Notes

Introduction

1. C.G. Jung, *Psychology and the East* (New Jersey: Princeton University Press, 1978), p. 16.
2. Ibid., p. 112.
3. Ibid., p. 113.
4. Alan Watts, *Psychotherapy East and West* (New York: Vintage Books, 19[illegible]), pp. 101–102.
5. Ibid., p. 107.
6. The famed—and infamous—20th century magician Aleister Crowley once summed it up as 'magic is the practice of communicating with divine intelligences, and mysticism that of becoming One with them.'

Chapter 1: The Essence of the Western Esoteric Path

1. Eckhart Tolle, *A New Earth* (New York: Dutton, 2005), pp. 117–118.
2. Joseph Campbell, *The Masks of God: Oriental Mythology* (New York: Penguin Books, 1982), pp. 13–15.
3. Zen Buddhism, for example, has the term *makyo*, meaning 'the devil in phenomena', which refers to the various forms of trickery and illusion that the mind tends to fall prey to when we deepen our meditation practice. The implicit assumption is that 'the devil' or all forms of perceptual distractions or temptations leading to folly are ultimately mere illusion, mental traps to be avoided, overcome via the power of focussed intention on ultimate truth only. Similarly, Tibetan Buddhism, via one of its foundational texts *Bardo Thodol* (*The Tibetan Book of the Dead*), teaches that in the 'afterlife' realms we encounter all sorts of frightful entities that are in fact nothing more than projections of our own minds.
4. For more on the following [illegible] see [illegible] and [illegible], *The [illegible] [illegible]ld*

Religions (New York: HarperCollins, 1991), pp. 95–96.

5. It should never be forgotten, however, that these models are theoretical and, for the active seeker of wisdom, of less significance than the practical inner work of encountering, engaging, and understanding one's mind.
6. Mircea Eliade, *Myth and Reality* (New York: Harper Torchbooks, 1975), pp. 79–81.
7. Ibid., p. 88.

Chapter 2: Introduction to Spiritual Alchemy

1. Lawrence M. Principe, *The Secrets of Alchemy* (Chicago: University of Chicago Press), 2013.
2. Mary Anne Atwood, *A Suggestive Inquiry into Hermetic Mystery* (Yogi Publication Society, reprint of 1918 edition), p. 162. The book had something of a bizarre history. After publishing it in 1850 at age thirty-two, Atwood (named Mary South at the time) was, strangely, advised by her father Robert South (whose vast library she had grown up with and which was the source for her research) to burn all copies, as he surmised that the book gave away too many of the esoteric secrets of alchemy. Mary Anne obliged, but a few copies escaped the flames.
3. Principe, *The Secrets of Alchemy*, pp. 144–146. The historian Keith Thomas pointed out that many of the medieval alchemists had been monks, including the well known Augustinian, George Ripley, and he argued that 'the transmutation of metals was secondary to the main aim, which was the spiritual transformation of the adept'. It is an interesting point of debate, however, as to whether a monk practices alchemy for spiritual purposes, or to discover new powers of 'natural magic', i.e., science. See Keith Thomas, *Religion and the Decline of Magic* (New York: Charles Scribner's Sons, 1971), pp. 269-271.
4. Ibid., p. 17. It can be added here that it has been shown, in modern times, that gold *can* be formed by a nuclear bombardment of Mercury, which stands next to gold on the

periodic table (79 to 80), but this is obviously possible via modern science instruments only.

5. James Hannam, *God's Philosophers: How the Medieval World Laid the Foundations of Modern Science* (Australia: Allen & Unwin, 2010), p. 131.
6. P.G. Maxwell-Stuart, *The Chemical Choir: A History of Alchemy* (London: Continuum Books, 2008), p. 1; p. 19.
7. One of the more concise histories of Western alchemy is Mircea Eliade's *The Forge and the Crucible,* originally published in French in 1956, first English translation by Rider and Company in 1962.
8. Principe, *The Secrets of Alchemy,* p. 13.
9. For those interested in practical laboratory alchemy, a good primer to begin with, in addition to Principe's more theoretical *The Secrets of Alchemy,* is Brian Cotnoir's *The Weiser Concise Guide to Alchemy* (Weiser Books, 2006).
10. Rudolf Bernoulli, *Spiritual Development as Reflected in Alchemy and Related Disciplines;* from *Spiritual Disciplines: Papers from the Eranos Yearbooks,* edited by Joseph Campbell (New York: Bollingen Foundation, 1985), pp. 308–309.
11. Julius Evola, *The Hermetic Tradition: Symbols and Teachings of the Royal Art* (Rochester: Inner Traditions International, 1995), p. xi.
12. Catherine MacCoun, *On Becoming an Alchemist: A Guide for the Modern Magician* (Boston: Trumpeter Books, 2008), p. 164.
13. Mircea Eliade, *The Forge and The Crucible: The Origins and Structures of Alchemy* (Chicago: University of Chicago Press, 1978), p. 153.
14. Charles Ponce, *The Game of Wizards: Psyche, Science, and Symbol in the Occult* (Harmondsworth: Penguin Books, 1975), pp. 181–182.
15. Empedocles, in his *Fragments,* refers to the elements as sun, earth, sky, and sea.
16. *Empedocles of Acragas: Fragments,* www.abu.nb.ca/courses/grphil/EmpedoclesText.htm, accessed April 4, 2012.

17. Eliade, *The Forge and The Crucible*, p. 79.
18. Titus Burckhardt, *Alchemy: Science of the Cosmos, Science of the Soul* (Louisville, Kentucky: Fons Vitae, 2006; originally published by Walter Verlag-Ag, 1960), p. 95.
19. Ibid., p. 140.
20. Mark Haeffner, *The Dictionary of Alchemy: From Maria Prophetissa to Isaac Newton* (London: The Aquarian Press, 1991), p. 225.
21. Principe, *The Secrets of Alchemy*, pp. 123–124.
22. Karen-Clair Voss, *Spiritual Alchemy*; from *Gnosis and Hermeticism: From Antiquity to Modern Times*, edited by Roelof van den Broek and Wouter J. Hanegraaff (Albany, NY: State University of New York Press, 1998), pp. 160–161.

Chapter 3: Essentials of the Kabbalah

1. Gershom Scholem, *Kabbalah: A Definitive History of the Evolution, Ideas, Leading Figures and Extraordinary Influence of Jewish Mysticism* ((New York: Meridian Books, 1978), p. 3.
2. Harold Bloom, *Kabbalah and Criticism* (New York: Continuum, 1983), pp. 15–16.
3. www.etymonline.com/index.php?term=topaz
4. Scholem, *Kabbalah*, p. 376; and Harold Bloom, *Kabbalah and Criticism* (New York: Continuum, 1983), pp. 20–21.
5. Harold Bloom: *Omens of Millennium: The Gnosis of Angels, Dreams, and Resurrection* (London: Fourth Estate, 1997), p. 45.
6. Scholem, *Kabbalah*, p. 10.
7. Ibid., p. 11.
8. Brian Easlea, *Witch-hunting, Magic, and the New Philosophy: An Introduction to Debates of the Scientific Revolution 1450–1750* (Sussex: The Harvester Press Limited, 1980), pp. 97–98.
9. Mircea Eliade and Ioan P. Couliano, *The HarperCollins Concise Guide to World Religions* (San Francisco: HarperCollins, 1991), p. 179.
10. Ibid., p. 43.

11. Dion Fortune asserts that it is the names of these ten archangels that are the key to ceremonial magic, and that their debased remnants became the notorious 'barbarous names of evocation' to be pronounced by the magician while evoking and conjuring. See Dion Fortune, *The Mystical Qabalah* (San Francisco: Red Wheel/Weiser, 2000), p. 23.
12. Scholem, *Kabbalah*, pp. 101–104.
13. Ibid., p. 106.
14. Ibid., p. 123.
15. Ibid., pp. 196–197.
16. www.telegraph.co.uk/news/worldnews/1577958/Medici-philosophers-mystery-death-is-solved.html (accessed December 22, 2012).
17. Scholem, *Kabbalah*, p. 198.
18. Ibid., p. 203.
19. Gershom Scholem, *Kabbalah and Alchemy* (Putnam: Spring Publications, 2006, originally published in German in the Eranos Yearbook, 1977). Scholem wrote this book early in his career, then revised it near the end of his life. It is a slim volume, but crammed with historical detail. Scholem's works, similar to those of Mircea Eliade, require close attention and often multiple reads, but are second to none in scholarly rigor.

Chapter 4: Angels, Demons, and the Abyss

1. Hugh Thompson Kerr Jr., Ed., *A Compend of Luther's Theology* (Philadelphia: The Westminster Press, 1963), p. 3.
2. Lon Milo DuQuette, *Low Magick*, Llewellyn Publications, 2010.
3. George Luck, *Arcana Mundi: Magic and the Occult in the Greek and Roman Worlds* (Baltimore: John Hopkins University Press, 1985), p. 163.
4. Ibid., p. 164.
5. Bentley Layton, *The Gnostic Scriptures* (New York: Doubleday, 1995, p. 61.
6. www.gnosis.org/naghamm/origin.html (accessed December 6,

2012).

7. Keith Thomas, *Religion and the Decline of Magic* (New York: Charles Scribner's Sons, 1971), pp. 68–69.
8. Ibid., pp. 27–50.
9. Morton Smith, *Jesus the Magician* (San Francisco: Harper & Row, 1978), p. 69. The book was reissued in 1998 with a new subtitle, *Charlatan or Son of God?*
10. Those are, of course, the ideal viewpoints. Both mysticism and magic have been subject to extreme corruption; the former by using it to merely escape the world and evade responsibility, and the latter by using it to attempt to gain power and wealth solely for their own sake.
11. Thomas, *Religion and the Decline of Magic*, p. 269.
12. As a psychological exercise, the traditional Goetic diagram of the Solomonic circle and 'Triangle of Art', with the Triangle appearing at the 'top', can be inverted, so as to more pointedly depict the relation of the Triangle of Art to the Conscious Self (i.e., 'below' it). The demonic energies bear a connection to the Kabbalistic idea of the 'Pit', a zone of ruin and decay usually placed below *Malkuth* on the Tree of Life. There is also a symbolic connection with Mars. There is a legend from Jewish demonology that all demons derive via patrimony from the ambiguous archangel Samael, who is characterized as the 'soul of the planet Mars' and the 'guardian angel of Esau', as well as the 'angel of Edom'. (Scholem, *Kabbalah*, p. 321.) In Hebrew 'Edom' means 'red', and Esau, the older son of the Biblical Isaac, was described as 'born red'. (Genesis 25:25: *And the first came out red, all over like an hairy garment; and they called his name Esau.* (KJV). Samael was connected to the 'sin of Rome', and in general appears to be another name for Lucifer, the serpent, Satan, and the Gnostic Ialdobaoth (who is, ironically, also associated with Yahweh by the Gnostics). All of this can, from one perspective, be regarded as elaborate symbolism pointing toward the energies of the masculine 'magician shadow-self'

and its need to be integrated into conscious life.

13. Ronald Hutton, *The Triumph of the Moon: A History of Modern Pagan Witchcraft* (Oxford: Oxford University Press, 1999), p. 67.
14. G.R. Evans, *Augustine on Evil* (Cambridge: Cambridge University Press, 1982), pp. 112–132.
15. Ibid., pp. 116-117.
16. See Keith Dowman, *The Sky Dancer* (London: Penguin Arkana, 1991).
17. Sarah Iles Johnston, *Ancient Religions* (Cambridge: Harvard University Press, 2007), pp. 140–142.
18. The story is recounted in Mark 3, Luke 11, and Matthew 12.
19. Brian P. Levack, *The Devil Within: Possession and Exorcism in the Christian West* (New Haven: Yale University Press, 2013), p. 273, n. 6. Even more difficult to explain away are the various miracles attached to the disciples, for e.g., those recounted in the Acts of the Apostles
20. Smith, *Jesus the Magician*, p. 83. The full text of *Origen contra Celsus* can be found online, for e.g., www.earlychristian-writings.com/text/origen161.html (accessed December 13, 2012).
21. David Bakan, *Sigmund Freud and the Jewish Mystical Tradition* (New York: Schocken Books, 1965), p. 232.
22. Ibid., pp. 232–233.
23. Gustav Davidson, *A Dictionary of Angels: Including the Fallen Angels* (New York: Macmillan Publishing, 1971), p. 261. This book, written in the 1960s, remains far and away the best source for angelology lore, a massive compendium, painstakingly researched.
24. From the scientific perspective, Einstein of course vividly demonstrated the interdependence of space and time via his Special and General Theories of Relativity.
25. For a good discussion of this, see J. Daniel Gunther, *Initiation in the Aeon of the Child: The Inward Journey* (Lake Worth: Ibis Books, 2009), pp. 127–139.

26. For a clear overview of the idea of the 'Holy Guardian Angel' in the context of Crowley's writings, see www.erwinhessle.com/writings/pdfs/The_Holy_Guardian_Angel.pdf (accessed December 19, 2012).

Chapter 5: Psychotherapy and the Western Esoteric Tradition

1. Alan Watts, *Psychotherapy East and West,* (New York: Vintage Books, 1975 edition), pp. 2–3.
2. George Mora, M.D., *From Demonology to the Narrenturm,* from *Historic Derivations of Modern Psychiatry,* Iago Galdston, Ed. (New York: McGraw-Hill, 1967), p. 50. Also Franz G. Alexander and Sheldon T. Selesnick, *The History of Psychiatry: An Evaluation of Psychiatric Thought and Practice from Prehistoric Times to the Present* (New York: Harper and Row, 1966), pp. 86–88.
3. www.esotericarchives.com/solomon/weyer.htm#lectoris, accessed September 3, 2012.
4. Henri Ellenberger, *The Discovery of the Unconscious: The History and Evolution of Dynamic Psychiatry* (New York: Basic Books, 1970), pp. 53–57.
5. Henri Ellenberger, *The Evolution of Depth Psychology,* from *Historic Derivations of Modern Psychiatry* (New York: McGraw-Hill Inc., 1967), p. 164. This technique is well known to modern practitioners of alternate healing therapies stemming from the 1960s human potential movement, such as bioenergetics, 'Primal Therapy', and 'Rebirthing'.
6. Ibid, p. 170.
7. Alexander and Selesnick, *The History of Psychiatry,* pp. 98–99.
8. Eli Zaretsky, *Secrets of the Soul: Social and Cultural History of Psychoanalysis* (New York: Alfred A. Knopf, 2004), pp. 18–19.
9. Ibid., p. 20.
10. Ellenberger, *The Discovery of the Unconscious,* pp. 199–200.
11. Ibid, pp. 168–169.
12. Ibid., p. 277.

13. Anthony Flew, *An Introduction to Western Philosophy: Ideas and Argument from Plato to Sartre* (London: Thames and Hudson, 1971), p. 465.
14. *The Encyclopedic Dictionary of Psychology*, Rom Harré and Roger Lamb, Ed. (Cambridge: The MIT Press, 1983), p. 224.
15. Ibid., p. 223.
16. Rollo May, *Existence* (New York: Basic Books, 1958), pp. 18–19.
17. www.etymonline.com
18. *The Oxford Companion to Philosophy* (New York: Oxford University Press, 1995), p. 300.
19. Morton Hunt, *The Story of Psychology* (New York: Anchor Books, 2007), p. 218.
20. Ibid., p. 217.
21. Maurice Charlton, from *Psychiatry and Ancient Medicine*, from *Historic Developments of Modern Psychiatry*, pp. 14–15.
22. Sigmund Freud, *Collected Papers, IV*, ed. James Strachey (London: Hogarth Press, 1950–1952), p. 437.
23. Ibid, p. 451.
24. Harold Bloom, *Omens of Millennium* (London: Fourth Estate, 1997), p. 120.
25. Ellenberger, *The Discovery of the Unconscious*, p. 331.
26. Alexander and Selesnick, *The History of Psychiatry*, p. 173.
27. Margot Adler, author of *Drawing Down the Moon*, one of the few reasonably good studies of Neo-paganism written by a pagan, is Adler's granddaughter.
28. C.G. Jung, *Flying Saucers: A Modern Myth of Things Seen in the Skies* (New York: MJF Books, 1978).
29. Joseph Campbell, editor, *The Portable Jung* (New York: Penguin Books, 1976), p. 59: 'Probably none of my empirical concepts has met with so much misunderstanding as the idea of the collective unconscious.'
30. Ibid., p. 59–60.
31. John G. Benjafield, *Psychology: A Concise History* (Don Mills: Oxford University Press, 2012), pp. 47–48.

32. www.britannica.com/EBchecked/topic/496351/Wilhelm-Reich (accessed February 7, 2013).
33. www.omnibehavioralhealth.com/pdf/delphi_poll.pdf (accessed September 18, 2012).

Chapter 6: Tantra and the Fundamentals of Sex Magick

1. Georg Feuerstein, *Tantra: The Path of Ecstasy* (Boston: Shambhala Publications, 1998), p. 8.
2. Mary Scott, *Kundalini in the Physical World* (London: Penguin Arkana, 1983), p. 16.
3. Feuerstein, *Tantra: The Path of Ecstasy,* p. 1.
4. Philip Rawson, *The Art of Tantra* (London: Thames and Hudson, 1992), p. 17.
5. Arthur Avalon (Sir John Woodroffe), *The Serpent Power: The Secrets of Tantric and Shaktic Yoga* (New York: Dover Publications, 1974, first published in 1919), p. 27.
6. Scott, *Kundalini in the Physical World,* p. 16.
7. Feuerstein, *Tantra: The Path of Ecstasy,* p. xiii.
8. Rawson, *The Art of Tantra,* p. 24.
9. Ibid., p. 24.
10. Feuerstein, *Tantra: The Path of Ecstasy,* p. 231.
11. Ibid., p. 233; compare with Titus Burckhardt, *Alchemy: Science of the Cosmos, Science of the Soul,* p. 140.
12. Joscelyn Godwin, Christian Chanel, John P. Deveney, *The Hermetic Brotherhood of Luxor: Initiatic and Historical Documents of an Order of Practical Occultism* (York Beach: Samuel Weiser Inc., 1995), pp. 40–41.
13. Ibid., p. 41. This is arguably the best description for the process underwent by such well-known late 20th century 'mediums' as Helen Schucman (who wrote *A Course in Miracles* via dictating information from a 'Voice' that claimed to be Jesus), and Jane Roberts, who 'channeled' the presence and thoughts of the incorporeal 'higher dimensional' entity called Seth.
14. Ibid., p. 45.

15. I have written about Crowley in a previous work of mine, *The Three Dangerous Magi: Osho, Gurdjieff, Crowley* (O-Books, 2010). The most comprehensive biography of Crowley is Richard Kaczynski's *Perdurabo* (North Atlantic Books, 2010).
16. Hugh Urban, www.esoteric.msu.edu/VolumeV/Unleashing_the_Beast.htm, accessed November 22, 2012.
17. Ibid.
18. Bentley Layton, *The Gnostic Scriptures* (New York: Doubleday, 1995), p. 199.
19. Ibid., pp. 206–207.
20. Ibid., p. 210.
21. For this, and a good discussion on the philosophy of Crowley's sex magick in contrast to Tantra, see Gordan Djurdjevic, *Aries: The Journal for the Study of Western Esotericism,*10.1 (2010), 85–106, available online.

Chapter 7: Philosophy and the Western Esoteric Tradition

1. Practically every paragraph in this chapter could be footnoted. To save the reader some tedium, the following sources were drawn upon: Will Durant, *The Story of Philosophy* (Pocket Books, 1961); Richard Tarnas, *The Passion of the Western Mind* (Ballantine Books, 1991); Anthony Flew, *An Introduction to Western Philosophy* (Thames and Hudson, 1971); *The Oxford Companion to Philosophy* (Oxford University Press, 1995); *Free Will: Readings in Philosophy*, Derk Perebroom, ed. (Hackett Publishing, 1997); *Philosophy Through Its Past*, Ted Honderich ed. (Penguin Books, 1984); *Nineteenth-Century Philosophy*, Patrick Gardner, ed. (The Free Press, 1969); Bertrand Russell, *The History of Western Philosophy* (Simon and Schuster, 1972); Ken Wilber, *Eye to Eye: The Quest for the New Paradigm* (Shambhala, 1996); *Gnosis and Hermeticism* (van den Broek and Hanegraaff, ed., State University of New York, 1998).
2. This is a vast topic and only a basic appraisal can be made here. The interested reader can consult some of the works of Arthur

Lovejoy (1873–1962, founder of the field of intellectual history known as the 'history of ideas'), Meyer Abrams (still alive at one-hundred years old as of this writing in early 2013), and contemporary writers such as Richard Tarnas, Antoine Faivre, Richard Smoley, Joscelyn Godwin, Nicholas Goodrich-Clarke, Wouter Hanegraaff and Ken Wilber.

3. Rene Descartes (1596–1650) was a seminal influence on modern philosophy (as well, of course, on science and mathematics). His famous expression *cogito ergo sum* ('I think therefore I am') gave expression to the notion that only our conscious experience of this moment can truly be confirmed to be 'real'. (Soren Kierkegaard, 'father' of existentialism, pointedly challenged this by suggesting that Descartes had got it backward; it was not that thought validated being, but rather that the very arising of thought validated that *being* already existed, a position that Eastern mysticism accords with). Descartes famously advocated a dualistic basis for viewing reality in which the mind is distinct from the body and mechanical laws of Nature (similar in some ways to Aristotle's views); this in turn became a key philosophical basis to the objective study of matter and the scientific revolution.

Baruch Spinoza (1632–1677), a Dutchman of Jewish-Portuguese descent, was perhaps as much a mystic as a philosopher. His famous expression, 'I hold that God is imminent, and not the extraneous, cause of all things. All is in God; all lives and moves in God' is usually recognized as the most definitive proclamation of pantheism, the idea that God is found immanently in Nature, not as something separate from it. This position is sharply anti-anthropocentric. Issues such as 'why is there evil in the world?' are resolved via the understanding that these are smaller human projections onto a reality rendered confusing only because we assume that we are somehow separate from it. (Spinoza was here pointedly disagreeing with Descartes, who held that mind and matter *are* distinctly separate). Spinoza points out that our great dilemmas in life are really a function of our immaturity; like a child, we expect the universe to conform to our self-centered agendas, when in fact a much vaster design is operating of which we are only a part of, equal to all else. Accordingly, he taught a form of determinism; but not one that amounted to a hopeless despair at having no real free will, thus giving us licence to be irresponsible. He rather taught that all acts and circumstances find their source in God, which lends a much deeper meaning to existence. Our feelings of alienation are arising only from our self-centered belief that we have nothing to do with the existence we find ourselves immersed in. Spinoza was also notable for his benevolent and humble character, which appeared to be very consistent with his lofty principles. His behavior was evidently congruent with what he taught, something that is more uncommon than typically assumed.

4. There is some evidence that certain interpretations (or more accurately, misinterpretations) of Fichte's views ultimately contributed to serious problems on a socio-political level. His assertion that the Self is all that is real easily became confused with the idea that only the ego-self is real, which in turn became degraded into the idea that the German self (ego) was superior (Fichte had written earlier essays on German nationalism, following the defeat to Napoleon at the battle of Jean in 1806). See Bertrand Russell's section on Fichte in his *The History of Western Philosophy*. Russell was notoriously anti-metaphysical, but he was more politically astute than most philosophers and thus his comments on Fichte merit consideration.

5. It has been observed, especially by Arthur Lovejoy, that there were so many diverse forms of 'Romanticism' (not to mention those influenced by nation) that it was better to refer to a 'Romantic period' rather than to a Romanticism *per se*. See Hanegraaff, *Gnosis and Hermeticism*, p. 239.

6. John Holman, *The Return of the Perennial Philosophy* (London:

Watkins Publishing, 2008), pp. 11-14.

7. Will Durant, *The Story of Philosophy* (Washington: Pocket Books, 1961), p. 300.

Chapter 8: Transcendentalism, New Thought, New Age

1. *The Quimby Manuscripts*, edited by Horatio W. Dresser (Secaucus: The Citadel Press, 1961), p. 351.
2. Ibid., p. ix, and www.phineasquimby.com/biography.html (accessed August 21, 2011).
3. *The Quimby Manuscripts*, p. ix.
4. Ibid., p. x.
5. Ibid., p. 15.
6. www.ppquimby.com/nletters/july2012.htm (accessed August 21, 2011).
7. www.phineasquimby.com/biography.html (accessed August 25, 2011).
8. Robert David Thomas, *With Bleeding Footsteps: Mary Baker Eddy's Path to Religious Leadership* (New York: Alfred A. Knopf, 1994), p. 102.
9. http://phineasquimby.wwwhubs.com (accessed February 28, 2013).
10. http://warrenfeltevans.wwwhubs.com (accessed August 25, 2011).
11. Thomas, *With Bleeding Footsteps*, p. 91.
12. Ibid., pp. 100–101.
13. A good summary of this controversial matter can be read at http://marybakereddy.wwwhubs.com (accessed September 3, 2011).
14. The term 'Christian Science', though commonly associated with Eddy, was not first coined by her, but rather by Rev. William Adams in 1850 in his work *The Elements of Christian Science*. See *The Encyclopaedic Sourcebook of New Age Religions* (Prometheus Books, 2004), p. 67.
15. www.religioustolerance.org/cr_sci.htm (accessed September 3,

2011).

16. Gail Harley, *Paradigms of New Thought Promote the New Age*, from *The Encyclopaedic Sourcebook of New Age Religions*, p. 69.
17. For this section on the New Age I draw mainly from Wouter J. Hanegraaff's excellent essay *The New Age Movement and the Esoteric Tradition*, found in *Gnosis and Hermeticism: From Antiquity to Modern Times* (pp. 359–382); as well as Nevill Drury's *Wisdom Seekers: The Rise of the New Spirituality* (O-Books, 2011).
18. This matter was commented on in a 2012 publication by Julia Assante (*The Last Frontier: Exploring the Afterlife and Transforming Our Fear of Death*), in which the author remarks that we are ignorant of the 'non-time' nature governing 'other worlds' because we are trapped in a progressively linear, evolutionary mindset, which is blamed mostly on Darwin, and to a lesser extent Freud and Marx—although curiously, the author appears not to note that Zoroastrian, Hermetic, Gnostic, and Neoplatonic cosmologies, developed two millennia before Darwin, were all based on ideas of a progressive spiritual evolution that is part of the 'return to Source'.

Chapter 9: The Fundamentals of Spiritual Psychology (Part I)

1. To read directly from the source, recommended are Wilber's *A Brief History of Everything* (Shambhala Publications, 1996) and *The Marriage of Sense and Soul: Integrating Science and Religion* (Random House, 1998); as well as Washburn's *Transpersonal Psychology in Psychoanalytic Perspective* (State University of New York Press, 1994). For more layman friendly treatments, Frank Visser's *Ken Wilber: Thought As Passion* (State University of New York Press, 2003) or Brad Reynold's *Where's Wilber At?: Ken Wilber's Integral Vision in the New Millennium* (Paragon House, 2006) can be consulted.
2. Wilber discusses this idea in more than one of his books. A thorough discussion of it can be found in his *Eye to Eye: The*

Quest for the New Paradigm (Boston: Shambhala Publications, 1996), pp. 198–243.

3. Alexander and Selesnick, *The History of Psychiatry*, p. 25.
4. Gurdjieff's year of birth is a notoriously contentious topic among students of his life. James Moore argued for 1866, William Patrick Patterson and John Bennett for 1872, and Jeanne de Salzmann for 1877. I give my own reasons for favoring 1872 in my work *The Three Dangerous Magi* (O-Books, 2010).
5. For a good representation of the Gurdjieff-purist view and accompanying criticism of modern Enneagram teachers, see William Patrick Patterson's *Taking With the Left-Hand* (Arete Publications, 2008).
6. A.H. Almaas is the pen-name of A-Hameed Ali, a prolific author and founder of the 'Diamond Approach' psycho-spiritual system. For the following section on the 'Holy Ideas' and the nine Enneagram types, I rely mostly on Almaas's *Facets of Unity: The Enneagram of Holy Ideas* (Boston: Shambhala Publications, 2002), and Naranjo's *Ennea-type Structures: Self-Analysis for the Seeker* (Nevada City: Gateways/IDHHB, Inc., 1990).
7. Naranjo, *Ennea-Type Structures*, p. 142.
8. I explore some of these issues in my book *Rude Awakening: Perils, Pitfalls, and Hard Truths of the Spiritual Path* (Washington: Changemakers Books, 2012).
9. Thomas, *Religion and the Decline of Magic*, p. 225.
10. Robert Moore, *Facing the Dragon: Confronting Personal and Spiritual Grandiosity* (Wilmette: Chiron Publications, 2003), p. 203.
11. Sigmund Freud, *Totem and Taboo*, from *The Origins of Religion* (London: Penguin Books, 1990), p. 136.
12. Ibid., p. 136.
13. Ibid., p. 144.
14. For Tart's complete essay, see Charles T. Tart, *Transpersonal*

Psychologies: Perspectives on the Mind from Seven Great Spiritual Traditions (New York: HarperCollins, 1992), pp. 61–111.

Chapter 10: The Fundamentals of Spiritual Psychology (Part II)

1. In some ways solipsism may appear similar to non-duality, but this is misleading, as non-duality is based on the direct experience of wholeness, whereas solipsism is founded on deep doubt. From this it has been reasoned by some that a truly solipsist position must also doubt the existence of one's own subjective consciousness, as well as doubting the existence of everything else—and that further, the only means of confirming one's own self would be via others, impossible to do so since these 'others' have already been dismissed as unreal.
2. For a good overview of this, see Ken Wilber, *Integral Spirituality* (Boston and London: Integral Books, 2006), pp. 119–141.
3. Ibid., pp. 136–137.
4. For an excellent discussion on this see Richard Smoley, *The Dice Game of Shiva: How Consciousness Creates the World* (Novato: New World Library, 2009), pp. 63–85.
5. The American spiritual teacher Ram Dass once humorously remarked, 'The yoga of relationship is the biggest stinker of them all'.

Chapter 11: Meditation and Self-Realization

1. Hume, *A Treatise of Human Nature* (1739).
2. Owen Flanagan, *Consciousness Reconsidered* (Cambridge: The MIT Press, 1992), pp. 177–182. Flanagan draws openly and substantially from William James in this chapter. His most recent work is the provocatively titled *The Bodhisattva's Brain: Buddhism Naturalized* (MIT Press, 2011).
3. Thomas Metzinger, *The Ego Tunnel: The Science of the Mind and the Myth of the Self* (New York: Basic Books, 2009), pp. 8, 208. Some of Metzinger's lucid lectures can be viewed on YouTube (as of early 2013).

4. Peter J. Carroll, *Liber Null & Psychonaut* (Samuel Weiser Inc., 1987), p. 164. *Liber Null* was originally published in 1978, *Psychonaut* in 1982, and both merged in the 1987 publication. Carroll, along with Ray Sherwin, are the founders of post-modern Chaos Magic, although they certainly had past inspirations they drew upon, most notably Austin Osman Spare and to a lesser extent Aleister Crowley. *Liber Null* is a concise and lucid essay on practical magic, remarkable in that Carroll wrote it in his early 20s, reminiscent of other precocious esotericists such as Pico della Mirandola, Cornelius Agrippa, Israel Regardie, and Manley Palmer Hall, all of whom wrote important and influential works about the Western esoteric tradition while in their early 20s.
5. This meditation is from the Tibetan Buddhist tradition, but has universal applicability. See Geshe Kelsang Gyatso, *Mahamudra Tantra: The Supreme Heart Jewel Nectar, an Introduction to Meditation on Tantra* (Glen Spey: Tharpa Publications, 2005), pp. 130–139.
6. Carroll, *Liber Null & Psychonaut*, p. 17.

Chapter 12: Magic and Manifestation

1. George Luck, *Arcana Mundi: Magic and the Occult in the Greek and Roman Worlds* (Baltimore: John Hopkins University Press, 1986), p. 61.
2. Gareth Knight, *Magic and the Western Mind: Ancient Knowledge and the Transformation of Consciousness* (St. Paul: Llewellyn Publications, 1991), p. 3.
3. Good examples of this idea as presented in modern fiction and film, were the early writings of Carlos Castaneda and his ideas of 'seeing' and 'stopping the world'; and the Wachowski brothers' *Matrix* films, where the task of the heroes was to 'unplug' from the 'virtual' world that had been constructed by a computer (with the virtual reality being, of course, a good metaphor for mass social constructs of reality).

4. A good source for related exercises of training the will can be found in Roberto Assagioli's *The Act of Will* (New York: Penguin Books, 1980), pp. 36–45.
5. This was first used by the American guru Adi Da Samraj (born Franklin Jones, 1939–2008). See his autobiography *The Knee of Listening*, a fascinating chronicle of the awakening process.
6. A good practical manual for engaging such practices is Donald Michael Kraig's *Modern Magick* (Llewellyn Publications, most recent edition 2011) or Franz Bardon's *Initiation into Hermetics* (Merkur Publishing, 2007). For more abstract inner practices, R.J. Stewart's *Advanced Magical Arts* (Element Books, 1989) is useful.
7. For more on this, see Phil Hine's *Condensed Chaos: An Introduction to Chaos Magic* (Tempe: New Falcon Publications, 1996), pp. 80-87.

Chapter 13: Inner Planes Work: Lucid Dreaming, Dream Yoga, Astral Travel

1. Carlos Castaneda (1925–1998), was a Peruvian-American writer who had a marked influence on young North American seekers, particularly of the 1970s-80s. He claimed to have met and been trained by an old but powerful Yaqui Indian *brujo* (shaman, or 'sorcerer' as he translated it), and subsequently documented this apprenticeship, and the teaching he later developed on his own, through twelve books. Castaneda's first four works, published between 1968 and 1974, are often recognized as his best. However they were also shown, via the incisive analysis of Richard DeMille (*Castaneda's Journey*, 1976; *The Don Juan Papers*, 1980), and Daniel Noel (*Seeing Castaneda*, 1976) to have been almost certainly fictional accounts, despite his claims to the contrary. Nevertheless his works contain plenty of legitimate teachings and valid techniques of transformation, even though he seems to have followed in the old tradition of attributing these teachings to a fictional master and

storyline, or at the very best a semi-factual one much embellished.

2. This stage used to be divided into two separate stages, 3 and 4; as of 2008 the American Academy of Sleep Medicine decided to discontinue the stage 4 category.
3. For a full description of these processes see Stephen LaBerge and Howard Rheingold, *Exploring the World of Lucid Dreaming* (New York: Ballantine Books, 1990). Also excellent is Robert Waggoner's *Lucid Dreaming: Gateway to the Inner Self* (Moment Point Press, 2009).
4. The evidence is that many experiences involving what are retroactively interpreted as 'intrusive entities' occur during this phase—everything from the so-called 'incubi' and 'succubi' of medieval lore, to the 'extraterrestrials' of the late 20th century 'abduction' literature. Whether these intrusive experiences all involve some meta-level of objective reality, or simple hallucinations, has of course been long debated.
5. LaBerge, *Exploring the World of Lucid Dreaming*, p. 41.
6. The following is adapted from the website www.dreamviews.com
7. See the writings of the Tibetan Dzogchen master Namkhai Norbu, especially *Dream Yoga and the Practice of Natural Light* (Ithaca: Snow Lion Publications, 1992).
8. For a fleshed out discussion of this, see Tenzin Wangyal Rinpoche, *The Tibetan Yogas of Dream and Sleep* (Ithaca: Snow Lion Publications, 1998), especially pp. 114–115; and Namkhai Norbu, *Dream Yoga and the Practice of Natural Light*, pp. 45–64.
9. Waggoner, *Lucid Dreaming*, pp. 276–277.
10. Mark Stavish, *Between the Gates: Lucid Dreaming, Astral Projection, and the Body of Light in Western Esotericism* (San Francisco: Weiser Books, 2008), p. 60.
11. Norbu, *Dream Yoga and the Practice of Natural Light*, p. 73–83.
12. If we recall the Jedi Knights of George Lucas's *Star Wars* fables, they had an ability to control matter with their minds. Lucas

got his ideas from Joseph Campbell, who was in turn influenced by Vedanta and Tibetan Buddhism. The Jedi Knights were basically Hollywood CGI versions of juiced-up Shaolin monks.

13. www.near-death.com/experiences/evidence01.html (accessed February 14, 2013).
14. www.sawka.com/spiritwatch/an.htm (accessed March 21, 2013).
15. For those interested in pursuing the matter of astral traveling, the following are some of the classics in the field as well as some of the better recent offerings: Sylvan Muldoon, *The Projection of the Astral Body* (1929); Oliver Fox, *Astral Projection: A Record of Research* (1939); Robert Monroe, *Journeys Out of the Body* (1971), *Far Journeys* (1985), and *Ultimate Journey* (1994); William Buhlman, *Adventures Beyond the Body* (1996); Robert Bruce, *Astral Dynamics* (1999); Albert Taylor, *Soul Travel* (2000); John Magnus, *Astral Projection* (2005); and Mark Stavish, *Between the Gates* (2008).

Chapter 14: The Body of Light

1. Mary Shelley, *Frankenstein: or, The Modern Prometheus* (London: Penguin Classics, 1985), pp. 47–48.
2. Ibid., p. 60.
3. The word 'galvanism' was taken from the discoverer of bioelectricity, Luigi Galvani, who in 1791 first published his study showing how nerve cell signals passed to muscles are electrical in nature. The modern term, electrophysiology, is the study of the electrical properties of living cells.
4. Nevill Drury, *Stealing Fire from Heaven: The Rise of Modern Western Magic* (New York: Oxford University Press, 2011), p. 3.
5. Shelley, *Frankenstein*, pp. 57–58.
6. Ibid., p. 87.
7. Ibid., p. 88.
8. Ibid., p. 89.

9. Ibid., p. 90.
10. Ibid., p. 95.
11. Ibid., p. 96.
12. Ibid., p. 97.
13. Martin Tropp, *Mary Shelley's Monster: The Story of Frankenstein* (Boston: Houghton Mifflin, 1976), p. 56.
14. Gershom Scholem, *Kabbalah* (New York: Meridian, 1978), p. 353.
15. Ibid., p. 352.
16. *The BFI Companion to Horror*, edited by Kim Newman (London: Cassell, 1996), p. 122.
17. Dolores Ashcroft-Nowicki, *The Ritual Magic Workbook: A Practical Course in Self-Initiation* (New York: Red Wheel/Weiser, 1998), p. 153.
18. Shelley, *Frankenstein*, p. 105.
19. Harold Bloom, *Bloom's Modern Critical Views: Mary Shelley* (Philadelphia: Chelsea House Publishers, 1985), p. 2.
20. There is not always a general consensus among Egyptology scholars about the precise meanings of these terms. I am here following Arthur Versluis, generally recognized as one of the more eminent scholars in the field of the philosophy of magic. See Arthur Versluis, *The Egyptian Mysteries* (New York: Arkana, 1988), pp. 52–53.

Chapter 15: A Brief History of Witchcraft

1. www.malleusmaleficarum.org. The Dover edition of this important and infamous book, first published in 1971, translated and introduced by the eccentric fundamentalist Montague Summers, is probably the best known modern version. It deserves to be surpassed by Christopher Mackay's 2009 annotated translation (*The Hammer of Witches*, Cambridge University Press), recognized by many scholars as the best version produced to date.
2. Modern Witchcraft (Wicca) and related neo-Pagan faiths are

comparatively popular here in the early 21st century, and as such there are innumerable books available explaining the tradition from the point of view of a modern Wiccan, neo-Pagan, or sympathetic writer. A majority of these are practically oriented, simplistic, and lack any historical perspective on their subject. Probably the best one written by an actual practitioner was by Margot Adler (granddaughter of the famed psychologist Alfred Adler), called *Drawing Down the Moon* (Boston: Beacon Press, originally published in 1979, appearing in revised editions in 1986, 1996, and 2006). A number of excellent scholarly historical treatments of the subject of pre-20th century witchcraft appeared in the mid-to-late 20th century and into the early 21st century, by authors such as Rossell Robbins, Norman Cohn, Jeffrey Burton Russell, Diane Purkis, Robin Briggs, Brian Levack, R. Kieckhefer, James Sharpe and Stuart Clark. One of the better more recent ones is Ronald Hutton's *The Triumph of the Moon: A History of Modern Pagan Witchcraft* (Oxford University Press, 1999). Hutton in particular deserves recognition for the exceptional balance he achieved between scholarly rigor in dealing with historical witchcraft and intelligent sympathy toward modern neo-paganism and Wicca.

3. *Oxford Concise Dictionary of English Etymology* (Oxford: Oxford University Press, 1993), p. 543.
4. See John Michael Greer, *The New Encyclopedia of the Occult* (St. Paul: Llewellyn Publications, 2005), pp. 516–517.
5. See http://www.proteuscoven.org/proteus/Suffer.htm, accessed June 30, 2010
6. www.reuters.com/article/idUSL21301127, accessed June 30, 2010.
7. www.cnn.com/2009/WORLD/asiapcf/01/08/png.witchcraft/index.html, accessed July 6, 2010.
8. Rossell Hope Robbins, *The Encyclopedia of Witchcraft and Demonology* (New York: Crown Publishers, 1959) p. 337.
9. Ibid., p. 337.

10. See *The Hammer of Witches*, Mackay's translation (Cambridge Press, 2011 edition), pp. 162-173.
11. Robin Briggs, *Witches and Neighbours: The Social and Cultural Context of European Witchcraft* (New York: Viking, 1996), p. 259. The authors of the *Malleus* claimed scriptural legitimacy from the apocryphal *The Book of Ecclesiasticus*, also known as *The Wisdom of Sirach*, which includes lines such as 'there is no head worse than the head of a snake, and there is no anger surpassing the anger of a woman' (25:22-23). Regarding Bodin's remark about the relative size of male-female heads, one is tempted to evoke the image of Immanuel Kant, perhaps one of the most intelligent humans ever to have lived—all five feet tall and with a presumably small head.
12. Robbins, *The Encyclopedia of Witchcraft and Demonology*, p. 4.
13. These numbers are from an exhaustive work by Ronald Hutton of Bristol University, available online at www.summer lands.com/crossroads/remembrance/current.htm (accessed July 1, 2010). For Witchcraft trials in England, including records of executions and carefully compiled numbers, A.D.J. Macfarlane, *Witchcraft in Tudor and Stuart England* (Harper & Row, 1970) can be consulted. For statistics of trial records and executions on the Continent, Brian Levack, *The Witch-Hunt in Early Modern Europe* (Longman, 1995, and Pearson, 2006) is well regarded by most serious historians of the witch-craze. Levack calculated, based on close examination of trial records and statistical analysis, that there were about 110,000 prosecutions and a maximum of 60,000 executions in Europe overall (1995 edition, pp. 21-26).
14. James Sharpe, *Instruments of Darkness: Witchcraft in England 1550–1750* (London: Penguin Books, 1997), p. 111.
15. Gerald Gardner, *Witchcraft Today* (New York: Magickal Childe Publishing, 1991), p. 35. (Originally published in England by Rider & Co., 1954).
16. Gerard Messadie, *A History of the Devil* (New York: Kodansha

America Inc., 1997), p. 255.

17. Norman Cohn, *Europe's Inner Demons* (Frogmore: Paladin, 1976), pp. 101–102. The sabbat itself (according to Gershom Scholem) did have a parallel in 13th century CE Jewish lore, where according to the Zohar there were 'mountains of darkness' frequented at night by sorcerers to study black magic under the rebel angels Aza and Azael. See Scholem, *Kabbalah*, p. 184.
18. Jack Kelly, *Gunpowder Alchemy, Bombards, & Pyrotechnics: The History of the Explosive that Changed the World* (New York: Basic Books, 2004), p.32.
19. James Frazer, *The Golden Bough* (London: Papermac, 1991 edition), for example, pp. 194–195.
20. Mircea Eliade, *Shamanism: Archaic Techniques of Ecstasy* (Princeton University Press, 1974 edition), p. 508.
21. Cohn, *Europe's Inner Demons*, pp. 239–252.
22. Claude Levi-Strauss, *Magic, Witchcraft, and Curing* (edited by John Middleton; Garden City: The Natural History Press, 1967), p. 23.
23. For a good concise article on the Salem Witch trials, see Robbins, *The Encyclopedia of Witchcraft and Demonology*, pp. 429–448. A more updated and detailed work is Frances Hill's *A Delusion of Satan: The Full Story of the Salem Witch Trials* (Da Capo Press, 1995). Credible sources can also be found online.
24. See Cohn, *Europe's Inner Demons*, pp. 225–255.
25. Thomas Robisheaux, *The Last Witch of Langenburg* (New York: W.W. Norton and Company, 2009).
26. Most of these are fictitious (despite the claims of their authors), although some carry allegorical value, particularly Gurdjieff's Sarmoung.
27. Greer, *The New Encyclopedia of the Occult* (St. Paul: Llewellyn Publications, 2005), pp. 108–109, and 188.
28. There appears to be some scholarly disagreement over the nature of this 'empowerment' bequeathed by Crowley to

Gardner. Crowley's biographer Richard Kaczynski claims that the empowerment was authentic, but John Michael Greer questions this, saying the 'OTO Charter' appears to have been written in Gardner's hand, and contains a grammatical error—'Do what thou wilt shall be the Law' rather than the correct 'Do what thou wilt shall be the whole of the Law'—an error that Greer believes Crowley would never have made. (See Greer, Ibid., p. 188). That noted, it is possible, even likely, that Crowley *was* dictating to Gardner and the latter simply wrote Crowley's words down inaccurately. Crowley frequently dictated to others—the entirety of his *Diary of a Drug Fiend* and large parts of his *Confessions* were dictated to his 'Scarlet Women' at the time.

29. See Raymond Buckland's Introduction to Gerald Gardner's *Witchcraft Today* (New York: Magickal Childe Publishing, 1991), p. v.
30. Richard Kaczynski, *Perdurabo: The Life of Aleister Crowley* (Tempe, New Falcon Publications, 2002), p. 448. As a long standing member of Crowley's OTO organization and a Crowley biographer, we can grant Kaczynski a certain inevitable bias, but his research is hard to refute when the facts he mentions are chased down.
31. Cohn, *Europe's Inner Demons*, p. 109. For Cohn's entire (and convincing) demolition of Murray's thesis, see pp. 108–120.
32. For Crowley aficionados, Frazer's ideas around the 'sacrificed' or 'dying king' appear to have been a major influence on Crowley's ideas around the 'Osirian Age', previous to what he believed to be the current 'Aeon of Horus', begun in 1904 as heralded by his *The Book of the Law*. Crowley was known to have made a serious study of Frazer.
33. Cohn, p. 117. The only possibly scholarly support for Murray's now generally discredited thesis came from Carlo Ginzburg, whose 1966 publication *The Night Battles* focused on an obscure shamanistic sect in the Italian province of Friuli, circa 1600 CE,

called the *benandanti,* who claimed that they 'battled evil witches' at night, in trance-state, via what modern occult lingo would call the 'astral plane' (or 'dream-time', etc.), and later, under pressure from authorities, confessed to being witches themselves. Historians tend to discount the validity of the *benandanti* as supporting any idea of organized witchcraft, however, as their practices were largely visionary, and did not imply actual physical meetings such as 'sabbats' or any sort of legitimate outer organization. See Carlo Ginzburg, *The Night Battles: Witchcraft and Agrarian Cults in the Sixteenth & Seventeenth Centuries* (English translation, Penguin Books, 1983), and Brian P. Levack, *The Witch-Hunt in Early Modern Europe* (London: Longman, 1995), pp. 19-20.

34. Adler, *Drawing Down the Moon* (1986 edition) p. 52.
35. Bengt Ankarloo and Stuart Clark, *Witchcraft and Magic in Europe: The Period of the Witch Trials* (Philadelphia: University of Pennsylvania Press, 2002), p. viii. Stuart Clark also put it very well when he wrote, in reference to grasping the collective mind of the era of the witch-trials, '...a different notion of language will have to be considered—in particular, that it should not be asked to follow reality, but to constitute it'. That is to say, we cannot simply and blanketly apply the present-time construct of our cultural and personal reality to that of the peoples of times past if we wish to understand them. See Clark, *Thinking With Demons: The Idea of Witchcraft in Early Modern Europe* (Oxford: Oxford University Press, 1999), p. 6.
36. Isaac Bashevis Singer, back cover blurb to Richard Cavendish's *The Black Arts* (New York: A Perigee Book, 1983).
37. Cohn, p. 262.

Chapter 16: Lycanthropy, Shapeshifting, and the Assumption of God-forms

1. This story is complex and ultimately involves decidedly less arcane issues such as inter-tribal rivalries, resistance to British

rule, and the usual matters of corruption in an unstable society following the turmoil of the Second World War. See David Pratten's *The Man-Leopard Murders: History and Society in Colonial Nigeria* (Indian University Press, 2007).

2. Gordon Wellesley, *Sex and the Occult* (London: Souvenir Press, 1973), pp. 66–67.
3. This idea was explored as far back as 1865, by the clergyman/scholar Sabine Baring-Gould, in his intelligent and comprehensive study *The Book of Were Wolves*.
4. Rossell Hope Robbins, *The Encyclopedia of Witchcraft and Demonology* (New York, Crown Publishers), 1959, p. 325.
5. Fellini underwent Jungian analysis and in part credited Jung's ideas on archetypes and the anima/animus as influential on his film.
6. Ibid, p. 325.
7. Barry Holstun Lopez, *Of Wolves and Men* (New York: Scribner, 1978), p. 234.
8. Robbins, *The Encyclopedia of Witchcraft and Demonology*, p. 537.
9. Lopez, *Of Wolves and Men*, pp. 240–241.
10. Colin Wilson, *The Occult* (New York: Vintage Books, 1973), p. 440.
11. Montague Summers, *The Werewolf in Lore and Legend* (Mineola: Dover Publications, 2003), p. 235. Originally published in 1933 as *The Werewolf*.
12. Robert Jackson, *Witchcraft and the Occult* (Devizes, Quintet Publishing, 1995) p. 25. The entire story of the 'Beast of Gevaudan' was made into a successful (and reasonably well done) big budget movie in France in 2001 called *Brotherhood of the Wolf*.
13. Lopez, *Of Wolves and Men*, pp. 70–71.
14. Summers, *The Werewolf in Lore and Legend*, p. 1.
15. Michael Harner, *The Way of the Shaman* (New York: Bantam Books, 1982), pp. 73–83.
16. James Sharpe, *Instruments of Darkness: Witchcraft in England*

1550–1750 (London: Penguin Books, 1997), p. 71.

17. Francesco Maria Guazzo, *Compendium Maleficarum* (New York: Dover Publications, 1988), p. 51. Guazzo drew some of his material from the notorious witch-hunter Nicholas Remy.
18. Sharpe, *Instruments of Darkness*, pp.73–74.
19. Mircea Eliade, *Shamanism: Archaic Techniques of Ecstasy* (Princeton University Press, 1974; originally published in French in 1951), p. 88.
20. Eliade citing Webster, Ibid, p. 92.
21. Ibid, p. 93.
22. Ibid, pp. 94–95.
23. Roger Walsh, *The Spirit of Shamanism* (Los Angeles: Jeremy P. Tarcher Inc., 1990), p. 115.
24. Ibid, p. 95.
25. Ibid, p. 95.
26. C.G. Jung, *Psychology and Alchemy* (Princeton University Press, Bollingen Series, 1980), p.69.
27. Ibid, pp. 145–146.
28. Rob Preece, *The Psychology of Buddhist Tantra* (Ithaca: Snow Lion Publications, 2006), p. 187.
29. Jeremy Naydler, *Shamanic Wisdom in the Pyramid Texts: The Mystical Tradition of Ancient Egypt* (Rochester: Inner Directions, 2005).
30. Ibid, p. 15.
31. Arthur Versluis, *The Egyptian Mysteries* (London: Arkana, 1988), pp. 117–118.

Appendix I: Ancient Egypt, Hermeticism, Rosicrucians, and the Kybalion

1. There is a well known argument that the Sphinx is much older, possibly over seven thousand years old, and some science has been employed to back this up. The matter is, of course, disputed, though most mainstream Egyptologists reject the 'older Sphinx' hypothesis, maintaining that it was carved

around 2500 BCE. For the Sphinx-as-much-older argument, see Robert Schoch, *Voices of the Rocks*, 1999; or John Anthony West, *Serpent in the Sky*, 1993.

2. T. Eric Peet, *The Present Position of Egyptological Studies* (Oxford: Oxford University Press, 1934), p. 18.
3. Regardie, *The Tree Of Life: An Illustrated Study in Magic*, p 82.
4. For more on this see Jeremy Naydler's *Shamanic Wisdom in the Pyramid Texts* (Inner Traditions, 2005). The book was Naydler's PhD thesis and is well grounded in references. His book achieves something remarkable, a synthesis of scholarly rigor and metaphysical insight; all the more so in a field polarized by either dry scholarship or unfounded New Age imaginativeness.
5. John Holman, *The Return of the Perennial Philosophy: The Supreme Vision of Western Esotericism* (London: Watkins Publishing, 2008), p. 7.
6. Roelof van den Broek, *Gnosticism and Hermeticism in Antiquity*, from *Gnosis and Hermeticism: From Antiquity to Modern Times*, Roelof van den Broek and Wouter J. Hanegraaff, editors (Albany: State University of New York Press), 1998, p. 5.
7. www.gnosis.org/library/grs-mead/TGH-v2/th203.html, accessed February 28, 2013.
8. R. van den Broek and Cis van Heertum, editors, *Poimandres to Jacob Böhme: Gnosis, Hermetism and the Christian Tradition* (Brill Academic Publishers, 2000), p. 47.
9. Versluis, *The Philosophy of Magic*, p. 11.
10. www.gnosis.org/library/grs-mead/TGH-v2/th223.html, accessed February 28, 2013.
11. Colin Wilson's Foreword to Christopher McIntosh's *The Rosicrucians: The History, Mythology, and Rituals of an Esoteric Order* (York Beach: Samuel Weiser Inc., 1997), p. ix.
12. This had been noted by Richard DeMille in his *Carlos Castaneda: The Power and the Allegory* (Santa Barbara: Capra Press, 1976), pp. 94–95.

Appendix II: The 'Fall' According to Eight Traditions

1. Ibid., p. 95.
2. Joseph Campbell, *The Masks of God: Occidental Mythology* (New York: Penguin Books, 1976), p. 190.
3. A relevant example of an early 21st century Western spiritual teaching that speaks to this is Andrew Cohen's model of 'evolutionary enlightenment'. The very idea that enlightenment can be 'evolutionary' (progressive) is thoroughly Western, and very much influenced by early 19th century Romanticism, although Cohen also includes a non-dualistic emphasis.
4. The famous allegory known as 'Plato's Cave' perhaps best sums up the ideas of his that proved to be most impactful on the Western esoteric tradition. Briefly this can be summarized as follows. In the fable, a group of prisoners live in a cave that is closed off from the world. They sit facing a wall. Behind them is a big fire, and between the fire and the people a series of objects are placed by puppeteers. These objects cast a shadow on the wall of the cave that the people are looking at. All they can see are the shadows. As a result, they conclude that the shadows are the actual thing. Using this metaphor, Plato reasoned that a person who begins waking up to reality becomes aware that the shadows appearing on the wall are in fact caused by the combination of the light from the fire and the objects between the fire and the people. The firelight is simply casting shadows of the objects onto the wall. Thus the awakening person becomes directly aware of the *cause* of things (the firelight and the objects), as opposed to only witnessing *effects* (the shadows). But Plato takes the analogy deeper. In the story one of the prisoners is taken outside of the cave, where he becomes aware of the existence of the Sun as the source of all light. Plato here takes the Sun as symbolic of the 'Form of Goodness', the archetype of divine light. The man who has left the cave also now sees that the objects in the cave were merely copies of deeper realities, living forms that exist outside the

cave, such as a living dog, whereas in the cave there had been only a facsimile of a dog, and so forth The objects in the cave owe their existence to the 'real things' outside of the cave upon which they are based. The fire in the cave owes its existence to the Sun, much like all that we perceive in reality owes its existence to the Form or archetype of Goodness and light. The final piece to Plato's allegory is that the person who escapes from the cave and into the light of reality has a moral obligation to return to the cave and attempt to help others escape. He may in fact be ignored, or worse, killed by the cave dwellers, who will likely feel threatened by his 'crazy' ideas of a greater reality outside of the cave, but it remains his duty to try to reach them anyway. Plato's allegory foreshadowed early 20th century ideas in Freudian psychoanalysis concerning 'projection', the process of seeing things in our world (including other people) that are in fact located in our own minds. Plato described the source of all appearances as the 'Form of the Good' and implies that it is outside of us, but the view can just as easily be taken that this resides deep in our own soul, as the undiscovered part of our nature. Ignorance of this undiscovered part of us causes us to misunderstand reality, much as psychological projection causes us to misperceive things and imagine things to be 'out there' that are in fact no more substantial than shadows. An important point in Plato's thought is that our knowledge of the highest levels of reality is *a priori* knowledge; that is, it is *independent of experience*, in particular our physical senses. This spiritual knowledge our birthright; it is recoverable via self-understanding, pure reason, and insight. Such a view lies at the very basis of the esoteric traditions, being that we hold within us the key to a profound understanding of reality, and that our very makeup as human beings endows us with the faculties to rise to the highest levels of the sublime and the good. Plato wrote in *The Republic*, 'When the soul is firmly fixed on the domain where truth and reality shine resplendent it apprehends and knows them and appears to possess reason, but when it inclines to that region which is mingled with darkness, the world of becoming and passing away, it opines only and its edge is blunted, and it shifts its opinions hither and thither, and again seems as if it lacked reason'.

5. Eliade and Couliano, *The HarperCollins Concise Guide to World Religions*, p. 116.
6. Plotinus, *Enneads*, V.1.1.
7. Hans Schwartz, *Evil: A Historical and Theological Perspective* (Ohio: Academic Renewal Press, 2001), p. 50.
8. Paul Ricoeur, *The Symbolism of Evil* (New York: Harper and Row, 1967), p. 239.
9. Roger Shattuck, *Forbidden Knowledge: From Prometheus to Pornography* (New York: St. Martin's Press, 1996), p. 53.
10. Ibid., p. 73.
11. Ibid., pp. 75–76.
12. Joseph Campbell, *The Masks of God: Occidental Mythology* (New York: Penguin Books, 1976), p. 208.
13. C.G. Jung, *Septem Sermones ad Mortuous*: II, III.
14. A summary of Pico's *Kabbalistic Conclusions* can be found in A.E Waite's *The Holy Kabbalah*, Mineola: Dover Publications, 2003), pp. 445–451. Waite's work was originally published in 1929.
15. Philip Beitchman, *Alchemy of the Word: Cabala of the Renaissance* (Albany: State University of New York Press, 1998), pp. 67-68.
16. Gershom Scholem, *Kabbalah* (New York: Meridian Books, 1978), pp. 122–128.
17. For a good and comprehensive study on the theology and psychology of ACIM as contrasted to the great Western wisdom traditions, see Ken Wapnick, *Love Does Not Condemn: The World, the Flesh, and the Devil According to Platonism, Christianity, Gnosticism, and* A Course in Miracles (Roscoe: Foundation for *A Course in Miracles*, 1989), pp. 111–112. Wapnick's work, though written from the point of view of an editor, follower and main

promoter of *A Course in Miracles*, is a good historical summary of the inner psychology of the main Western wisdom traditions.

Appendix III: The Chief Grimoires of Magic

1. Sarah Iles Johnston, *Ancient Religions* (Harvard University Press, 2007), p. 141.
2. Plato's *Charmides*. See http://classics.mit.edu/Plato/charmides.html (accessed March 14, 2013). The whole relationship between science and magic is clarified in part via how the two traditions view the nature of words and language. Magic tends to regard particular language and words as intrinsically sacred and powerful, whereas for science they are more the product of human consensual agreement, mere constructs with no meaning beyond what we have assigned to them. See Stuart Clark, *Witchcraft and Magic in Europe* (University of Pennsylvania Press, 2002), pp. 156-157.
3. Johnston, *Ancient Religions*, p. 143.
4. See Georg Dehn and Stephen Guth, *The Book of Abramelin: A New Translation* (Nicolas Hayes Inc., 2006). Dehn and Gruth's version corrects several errors found in Mathers's version.
5. Gershom Scholem, *Kabbalah* (New York: Meridian Books, 1978), p. 186.
6. Richard Cavendish, *The Black Arts* (New York: Perigree Books, 1983), pp. 128-129.
7. The controversial modern magician and physicist Joseph Lisiewski, a sharp critic of post 19th century ceremonial magic and a practitioner and teacher of what he characterizes as 'Old Magic', considers *The Heptameron* pre-eminent as a working manual.
8. David Kahn, *The Codebreakers: The Story of Secret Writing* (New York: Macmillan Publishing, 1967), p.131.
9. Owen Davies, *Grimoires: A History of Magic Books* (Oxford: Oxford University Press, 2009), p. 48.

10. Joseph H. Peterson, *The Grimorium Verum* (CreateSpace Independent Publishing Platform, 2007).
11. Keith Thomas, *Religion and the Decline of Magic* (New York: Charles Scribner's Sons, 1971), p. 230. For the matter of the alleged power of nails from the crosses of crucified men, see Richard Kieckhefer, *Magic in the Middle Ages* (Cambridge: Cambridge University Press), p. 36.
12. Cavendish, *The Black Arts*, pp. 126-127.
13. Craig Conley, *Magic Words: A Dictionary* (San Francisco: Weiser Books, 2008), p. 66.
14. Crowley's ideas on this word can be found in several of his works, especially *Magick: Book 4*, and *777 and Other Qabalistic Writings*.

Appendix IV: A Note on the Tarot and Experiential Astrology

1. Michael Dummett, *The Visconti-Sforza Tarot Cards* (New York: George Braziller Inc., 1986), p. 6.
2. Richard Cavendish, *The Tarot* (London: Michael Joseph Ltd., 1975), p. 9.
3. Ibid., p. 11.
4. Ibid., p. 11.
5. Dummett, *The Visconti-Sforza Tarot Cards*, p. 9.
6. Daniel O'Keefe, *Stolen Lightning: A Social Theory of Magic* (Vintage Books, 1983).
7. Stuart Kaplan, *The Encyclopedia of Tarot, Volume I* (Stamford: U.S. Games Systems Inc., 1978), p. 12.
8. Cynthia Giles, *The Tarot: History, Mystery, and Lore* (New York: Fireside, 1992), pp. 23–25.
9. Robert M. Place, *The Tarot: History, Symbolism, and Divination* (New York: Jeremy P. Tarcher, 2005), p. 9.
10. Ibid., p. 73.
11. Kaplan, *The Encyclopedia of Tarot, Volume I*, p. xvi.]
12. His name was Valentin Tomberg (1900–1973), a Russian-German lawyer who had once been a member of Rudolf

Steiner's Anthroposophical Society. He later converted to Catholicism.

13. For the reader interested in the deeper understandings of Western astrology, the works of Steven Arroyo, Liz Greene, Dane Rudhyar, and particularly Richard Tarnas's *Cosmos and Psyche* can be consulted.

Index

Aaron, 110, 115
Abaddon, 121
Abraxas, 488-489
A Course in Miracles, 22, 50, 222, 237, 330, 383, 494, 532, 543, 566-567
abracadabra, 338, 497, 510
Abraham, 62, 66
Abraham of Worms (Abraham ben Simon), 122, 501
Abraxas, 488-489
Abyss, 76-77, 108, 113, 121, 124, 332
Adam, 65, 68, 80, 83-84, 89, 94, 108, 230, 397-398, 409, 482-486, 490-492, 494, 499-500, 547
Adler, Alfred, 140, 150-151, 251, 542, 556
Adler, Margot, 427, 430, 434, 525, 542, 556
Adonai, 68, 80, 509
Agrippa, Henry Cornelius, 88, 127, 336-337, 391-392, 394-395, 405, 499-500, 503-505, 509, 526, 551
albedo, 57-59
alchemy, 1, 12, 28-59, 63, 74, 89, 100, 116, 126, 152, 176, 178, 213, 238-239, 245, 273, 303, 336, 340, 388, 391, 394, 396, 405, 457-458, 473, 476, 502, 512, 525-528, 530-531, 535-537, 562, 566
Alexander the Great, 36, 93, 467
analytical meditation, 328
Andreae, Johann Valentin, 473
angels, 45, 62, 65-68, 74, 90, 96, 106, 115-117, 120, 239, 241, 248, 275, 485, 499-500, 502, 507, 517, 537-538, 540, 558
anger work (psychological), 300-302
antichrist, 97
antimony (alchemy), 29-30, 458
antinomianism, 281-282
Apollo, 121
Appollyon, 121
Aquinas, Thomas, 115, 191, 201, 394-395
archangels, 64-67, 72, 117, 119-120, 122, 538
Aristotle, 35, 39, 43-44, 47, 135, 143, 206, 213, 247, 283, 467, 545
Assagioli, Roberto, 2, 8, 103, 140, 155, 244-245, 353, 368, 552
Assiah, 72
Astaroth, 95, 512
astral, 106, 247, 385, 400-401, 466, 498, 552-554, 560
astral projection, 352, 383-384

astrology, 13, 62, 126, 152, 268, 336, 388, 394
Atkinson, William Walker, 208, 295, 474-478
Atwood, Mary Anne, 28-29, 535
Atziluth, 72
Augustine, St., 105-108, 124, 211, 370, 485, 487, 540
Aurobindo, Sri, 8, 352
Babylon, 43, 65, 119, 334, 497
Bailey, Alice, 236-237
Ba'al Shem, 497
Beelzebub, 93, 95, 111
Berkeley, George (Bishop), 188, 191-192, 195-196, 202, 217
Bible, The, 8, 40, 65-66, 101, 117-118, 197, 227-228, 237, 282, 355, 413, 420, 502
Binah, 76-77, 81, 85, 89
bioenergetics, 162, 541
Black Death, 98, 473
Bloom, Harold, 62, 149, 407, 537, 542, 555
Body of Light, 40, 332, 386, 388, 394, 398-401, 409, 462, 553-554
Boehme, Jacob, 206, 469, 496, 563
Bohm, David, 238
Book of the Sacred Magic of Abramelin the Mage, the, 122, 346, 501-502, 567
Boyle, Robert, 37, 135
Briah, 72
Bruno, Giordano, 178
Buddha, Gautama, 9, 79, 168, 247, 262, 321, 325, 327, 338, 344, 477, 492
Buddhism, 3, 57, 105, 124-125, 168, 170, 174, 239, 333, 346, 355, 376, 400, 409, 459-460, 469, 481, 491, 494-495, 534, 550, 554, 571
Burckhardt, Titus, 28, 32, 45, 525, 537, 543
calcination, 49-51, 54, 58, 303
Calvinism, 215, 228, 230
cambion, 66
Carroll, Peter, 327, 330
Castaneda, Carlos, 370, 372, 428, 452, 475, 551-552, 563
catharsis (psychological), 131, 143, 323, 342
Cayce, Edgar, 236-237
Chaldean Oracles, 335
Cherubim, 63, 116
Chesed, 77-78, 81, 85, 89
Chokmah, 75-77, 81, 85, 89, 500
Christ, Jesus, 12-13, 25, 35, 57, 69, 83, 87-89, 94, 108-112, 117-118, 177-178, 184-185, 213, 222, 225, 227-228, 231, 236, 241, 247, 279, 303, 331-332, 334, 400-401, 421, 427, 439, 464, 468, 474, 484-485, 487, 489-491, 497, 500, 503, 514

Christianity, 57, 64, 70, 87, 94, 112, 121, 184, 211-212, 226, 237, 241, 355, 400, 402, 439, 464, 479, 484, 491, 566
Christian Science, 217, 223, 226, 229, 231-234, 547
Chymical Wedding, 473
Circe, 333
Clavicula Salomonis (Greater Key of Solomon), 68, 500, 508
Clavicula Salomonis Regis (Lesser Key of Solomon; see Goetia)
Cloud of Unknowing, The, 332
coagulation (alchemy), 40, 57, 60
Confessio Fraternitatis, 472
conjunction (alchemy), 54-55, 59
Coptic, 36, 94, 468
Corpus Hermeticum, 468-472, 514
Court de Gebelin, Antoine, 12, 89, 513-515, 519
Cramer, Malinda, 233-234
Crowley, Aleister, 122, 173, 181-184, 239, 327, 429-430, 434-435, 511, 516-517, 521, 525, 534, 541, 558-559, 568
da'ath, 76
dark night of the soul, 11, 56, 332
de Leon, Moses, 70, 74
Dead Sea Scrolls, 65
decision exercise, 350
Dee, John, 103, 490, 498, 503-504
demon(s), 9, 66, 68, 74, 84, 93-96, 99-101, 103-106, 109-112, 114, 127, 132, 173, 183, 239, 280, 416, 420-422, 425, 438, 447, 460, 493, 497-502, 504-508, 510, 512, 538-539
demonology, 1, 91, 93, 95, 104, 106, 127, 148, 415, 497-502, 505-506, 531, 539, 541, 556-558, 561
Descartes, Rene, 128, 135, 188, 190-191, 196-197, 202, 283, 313, 545-546
Devil, the, 19, 23, 97-99, 106, 114, 118, 126, 128, 148-149, 414-416, 419-422, 426, 432-433, 435-436, 439-440, 446-447, 449, 452-453, 457, 489-490, 517, 540, 557, 566
dissolution (alchemy), 40, 51-52, 54, 58
distillation, 56, 59
Dominions, 116
dragon, 30
Dragon Rouge (see *Grand Grimoire*)
Dresser, Julian, 225
dualism, 22-23, 41, 94, 121, 331, 479-480, 488, 491
duat, 41, 368, 466
eagle, 64, 116, 451

Eddy, Mary Baker, 217, 222-223, 225-227, 229-232, 234, 547
ego, 2, 3, 6-9, 18-27, 40, 50-52, 54-55, 58-59, 66, 77-79, 81-82, 90, 107, 114, 121-124, 129, 146-148, 150, 155, 157, 172, 175, 183, 186, 204, 211, 216, 245-246, 250-270, 276-278, 281, 284, 286-288, 291-292, 295, 305-306, 312, 325-328, 331, 334, 338, 340, 342, 344, 347, 352, 364, 380, 388, 403, 454-455, 460, 470, 494-495, 546, 550
Egypt/Egyptian/Egyptology, 12, 25, 35-36, 40, 92-93, 95-96, 106, 109-112, 178, 213, 280, 333-334, 336, 368, 400, 405, 408-409, 412, 431, 454, 461-462, 464-467, 469, 474-475, 479, 484, 489, 497, 501, 507-508, 510-515, 555, 562-563
Ein-Sof, 70-72, 74
Eliade, Mircea, 26, 28, 209, 424, 452-454, 466, 525, 534-538, 558, 562, 566
Elohim, 65, 76, 509
Emerald Tablet, the, 471-472
Emerson, Ralph Waldo, 205, 215-217
Empedocles, 43-44, 213, 536
Enneagram, 2, 254-269, 470, 530, 549
Enoch, 63, 65-67, 69, 116-117, 119
Enochian, 430
Erhard, Werner, 236, 477
Esalen, 156, 165-166
Essenes, 65
Evans, Warren F., 225-226, 236, 547
Eve, 398, 482-484, 486, 491-492, 499
Evola, Julius, 28, 32, 37, 536
existentialism, 135, 138-142, 168, 545
exorcism, 93, 110, 127-129, 529, 540
Ezekiel, 63
Fall, the, 21, 24, 479-495
Fama Fraternitatis, 472
Faraday, Anne, 369
Ferguson, Marilyn, 237
fermentation, 55-56, 59
Fichte, Johann Gottlieb, 3, 16, 132, 135, 203-205, 217, 341, 546
Ficino, Marcilio, 14, 87, 336, 468, 503-504
Flanagan, Owen, 3, 22, 326-327, 527, 550
Fludd, Robert, 474
Fortune, Dion, 4, 239, 412, 524, 538
Fox, Oliver, 384, 554
Frankenstein, 389-394, 397, 399, 402, 404-407, 410, 554-

555
Frazer, James, 280, 423, 431-434, 559
Freemasonry, 182, 434-435, 474
Freud, Anna, 156-157
Freud, Sigmund, 2, 20, 25, 32, 59, 113-114, 127, 133-135, 138, 142-157, 179, 203,245, 250-251, 278-280, 289, 323, 353, 526, 528, 540, 542, 548-549, 565
Gabriel (Archangel), 65-66, 80, 117, 119, 122
Gardner, Gerald, 412, 418, 427, 430, 434, 537, 559
Gassner, Johann, 127-129
Gebser, Jean, 8, 161
Geburah, 77-78, 81, 89
Genesis, book of, 8, 63, 66-67, 69-70, 116, 230, 398, 482-485, 487, 539
Gikatilla, Joseph, 74
Gnosticism, 3, 23-24, 35-36, 62, 64, 73, 83, 184-185, 231, 236, 467, 469, 488, 491, 532, 563, 566
Goetia, 333-334, 505-506, 530
gold (alchemy), 28, 30, 32-36, 38-40, 49, 58, 63, 89, 100, 340, 493, 535
Golden Bough, The, 280, 423, 431, 433, 558
Golden Calf, 115
Golden Dawn (see Hermetic Order of the Golden Dawn)
Golden and Rosy Cross, Order of, 474
Golden Rule, the, 202, 355
golem, 394, 396-398, 401, 404
Grand Grimoire (*Dragon Rouge*), 508-509
grandiosity, 175, 187, 276-278, 281-282, 470, 549
Great Chain of Being, 120, 247-250
Greece/Greek, 9-12, 30, 35-36, 43, 46-47, 57, 67-68, 80, 82, 93-95, 101, 104, 111-112, 115, 121-122, 129, 143, 153, 165, 178, 188, 193, 207, 213, 221, 241, 254, 281, 284, 291, 333, 336, 345, 351, 358, 390, 400, 403, 406, 408, 414, 421, 428, 439, 443, 451, 461, 464-465, 467-469, 479, 481, 488-489, 498-500, 506, 514-515, 520, 525, 538, 551
Green, Celia, 369
grimoire, 68, 91, 95, 97-99, 102, 105, 108, 237, 496-510, 524, 527, 532, 567
Grof, Stanislav, 163-164, 166
Guenon, Rene, 28, 32, 37, 209
Gurdjieff, G.I., 2, 25, 156, 164, 206, 226, 236, 254-255, 270, 282, 306, 328, 342, 351, 364, 383, 400, 402, 428, 457, 477, 525, 532, 544, 549, 558

Hanegraaff, Wouter, 238, 525, 532, 537, 544-546, 548, 563
Hegel, Georg Wilhelm, 24, 135, 139, 203, 205-207, 217, 352
henosis, 9, 345
Heraclitus, 43, 57, 206, 213
Hermes, 37, 58, 471, 514
Hermes Trismegistus, 137, 467-469, 471, 503
Hermetic Order of the Golden Dawn, 12, 102, 122, 180, 208, 309, 364, 428, 430, 434-435, 474, 516, 525, 527
Hermeticism, 24, 35, 62, 102, 153, 178, 208, 236, 241, 467-472, 520, 532, 537, 544, 546, 548, 562-563
Hesse, Herman, 456
Hildegard of Bingen, 332
Hinduism, 170-171, 238, 355
Hitchcock, Ethan Allan, 28
Hod, 79-80
holarchy, 248
holons, 248
Holy Guardian Angel, 1, 104, 108, 113, 120-124, 327, 345-346, 399, 454, 502, 541
Holy Spirit, 82-83, 232, 346, 491-492
homunculus, 326, 394-399
Hopkins, Emma Curtis, 232-234
Horney, Karen, 146, 154-155
Hume, David, 125, 135, 188, 192-194, 196-197, 200, 202, 278, 316, 325-326, 477, 550
Ialdobaoth, 184, 490-491, 539
Iamblichus, 106, 213, 335-336
Iblis, 494
Identification, 18, 21, 33, 50, 77, 115, 123-124, 172, 175, 253, 256, 260, 273-274, 278, 296, 305-306, 325, 332, 342, 346, 363, 410, 462, 470, 477
Imagination, 81, 92, 136, 178, 188, 190, 209, 285-286, 290, 334, 339, 340-343, 345, 390, 392, 459, 462-463, 483, 523
Inquisition, 126, 414-415, 426
Integral Psychology, 165, 244-245, 247, 250
Islam, 70, 97, 119-120, 403, 479, 494, 512
Jabir ibn Hayyan, 36, 47
James, William, 142, 144, 217, 224, 244, 325, 550
Janet, Pierre, 142, 150-151
Janov, Arthur, 154, 162-164
John (gospel), 325, 331
Judaism, 61, 65, 67, 69, 83, 88, 112, 119, 121, 355, 403, 479, 487, 491,
Julian the Chaldean, 335
Jung, Carl Gustav, 2, 5-8, 19-20, 24, 28, 30-32, 37-38, 48, 55, 103, 126, 137, 143, 146, 150-151-153, 155, 163, 172, 239-240, 245, 251, 282, 291,

297, 353, 368, 409, 457-458, 488, 525, 534, 542, 561-562, 566
Jupiter, 398, 467, 489
Kabbalah, 1, 3-4, 24-25, 61-89, 133, 149, 155, 178, 213, 241, 245, 469, 492, 494, 501, 513, 524, 537-539, 555, 558, 566-567
Kant, Immanuel, 3, 125, 135, 188, 194-206, 213, 215, 217, 245, 304, 325, 335, 341, 519, 557
Kelley, Edward, 498
Kempis, Thomas à, 332
Kether, 25, 89, 178
Kierkegaard, Soren, 135, 139, 213, 545
Klein, Melanie, 153, 156-157
Koran, 119
Kramer, Joseph (Henricus Institoris) , 414, 436, 505
Kybalion, 208, 295, 474-475, 562
LaBerge, Steven, 369, 374, 377, 384, 525, 553
Laing, R.D., 163-164
Lemegeton (see Goetia)
Levi, Eliphas (Alphonse Louis Constant), 88, 512, 515-516
lion, 30, 48, 56, 64, 116, 443-444, 448, 451, 490
Locke, John, 125, 135-136, 187-192, 194-196, 198, 202, 209
Lovejoy, Arthur, 249, 545-546
Lowen, Alexander, 157, 162
lucid dreaming, 368-385, 525, 552-553
Lucifer, 120, 406, 482, 485, 508-509, 539
Luke (gospel), 111, 130, 490, 540
Luria, Isaac, 71, 81, 85-86, 337
Luther, Martin, 90, 97, 281-282, 538
lycanthropy, 442-449, 560
Magic(k), 1-2, 12, 31, 41, 64-66, 68-69, 87, 91, 97-104, 106, 109-113, 122, 126-127, 129, 152, 161, 178-188, 209, 237, 239, 241, 277-281, 293, 327, 331-367, 388, 391, 396-397, 399, 405, 408, 412, 430, 435, 445, 447, 450-452, 455, 457-458, 462, 467, 475, 478, 496-511, 514, 517-518, 521, 524-525, 534-540, 543, 544, 549, 551-552, 554-555, 558, 560, 563, 567-568
Magnus, Albertus, 336, 391-392, 394, 502, 504, 507
Maharshi, Ramana, 269, 325
Maier, Michael, 474
Maimonides, 119-120
Malkuth, 25, 73-74, 77-78, 80-81, 83, 85, 539
Malleus Maleficarum, 106, 127, 411, 413-415, 436, 505

Manichaeism, 22, 491-492
manifestation, 1, 10, 38, 41, 55, 68, 71, 75, 91, 150, 228, 231, 294, 331-367, 382, 501-502, 525, 551-552
Mansoor, Al-Hillaj, 494
Mark (gospel), 111, 400, 540
Mars, 467, 489, 539
Maslow, Abraham, 126, 141, 151, 155, 161, 166, 244
Mathers, Samuel Liddell MacGregor, 89, 122, 435, 501, 508, 567
materia prima, 39, 43
Matthew (gospel), 40, 93, 111, 229, 303, 355, 405, 540
May, Rollo, 141, 151, 154, 161-162, 542
meditation, 1, 13, 20, 31, 55, 71, 171, 202, 204, 253, 270, 273, 312-330, 334, 337, 339, 342, 343, 345-347, 353, 365-366, 380, 453, 459, 470, 495, 534, 550-551
Meister Eckhart, 332
Mercury (alchemy), 47-48, 55, 58-59, 176-177, 467, 489, 535
Merkabah, 63-65, 69, 116
Merlin, 66
Mesmer, Franz, 127-132, 143, 145, 180, 213, 215, 217, 219-220
mesocosm, 248, 352, 361
metanoia, 221, 230, 234
Metatron, 63, 66-67, 75, 116
Metzinger, Thomas, 3, 22, 326-327, 550
Michael (archangel), 65-66, 80, 95, 110-111, 116-118, 122
Milton, John, 404, 406, 484-487
Mirandola, Giovanni Pico della, 86, 336, 468, 493, 504, 551
Mithras, 67
Mohammad, 119, 494
Monroe, Robert, 384, 526, 554
Moon, 55, 379, 409, 433, 449, 456, 458, 467, 471, 489, 492, 522, 525, 540, 542, 556, 560
Moses, 62, 66, 70, 88, 106, 109-110, 115, 118-119, 497, 509-510
Muldoon, Sylvan, 384, 554
Muir, John, 215
mysticism, 11-12, 16, 25, 32, 61, 63-66, 69-70, 73, 102, 124, 152, 208, 216, 238, 241, 278, 331-337, 462, 496, 502, 534, 537, 539, 545
Nazis, 65, 213, 303
Neoplatonism, 3, 24, 62, 84, 87, 208, 213, 216, 245, 337, 467, 469
Netzach, 79, 81, 85
New Age, 1, 53, 160, 164, 167, 169, 174, 213, 215, 226, 236-241, 253, 291, 307, 432, 547-548, 563

New Testament, 82, 93, 111, 116-117, 120, 405, 420-421
New Thought, 1, 130, 208, 213, 215-236, 241, 291, 307, 469, 474, 477, 547-548
Nietzsche, Friedrich, 125, 135, 138-139, 203, 210-213, 444
nigredo, 57-59, 64
Nile, 36, 110
Noah, 65-66, 498-499
non-dualism (or non-duality), 22-23, 75, 202, 253, 258, 331, 355, 371, 377, 403, 478, 550
occultism, 12-13, 97, 208, 394, 404, 475, 543
Odysseus, 333
Old Testament, 58, 63, 65, 70, 75, 94, 116-117, 120-121, 280, 397, 402, 413, 420-421, 482-483, 489-490, 494, 510
Orage, A.R., 236
Ohrmazd, 492
Orr, Leonard, 164, 323
Osiris, 25, 40, 67, 333, 400, 408, 439
Ouspensky, P.D., 226, 254, 521, 525
Paracelsus, 36, 47, 129, 391-392, 394-397, 405, 505, 507
Patterson, Charles Brodie, 235
Perennial Philosophy, 14, 87, 165, 468, 521, 546, 563
Perls, Fritz, 141, 156, 166, 381
Peter (apostle), 40, 112, 400
Philosopher's Stone, 35, 38, 49, 55, 57-59
Piaget, Jean, 157
Picatrix, 498
Plato, 12, 14, 22, 35, 43-44, 46, 72-73, 77, 80, 87, 93, 106, 120, 133, 147, 196, 206, 212-213, 217, 222, 247, 368, 395, 444, 467, 469, 480-481, 488, 492-493, 497, 564-567
Plotinus, 12, 14, 71-72, 87, 120, 133, 149, 188, 213, 216-217, 247, 467, 480-482, 493, 566
Poimandres, 469, 563
Potentates, 117
pre-trans fallacy, 250-254
Primal Therapy, 154, 162-163, 541
Principalities, 117, 248
Principe, Lawrence, 29-30, 32, 525, 535-537
Proclus, 213
projection (psychological), 51, 91, 133, 145-146, 149, 157, 224, 273-274, 278, 280, 288-291, 309-310, 314, 344, 534, 545, 565
Prometheus, 207, 389-391, 406-407, 499, 547, 554, 566
Protestant Reformation, 97, 281, 415
Pseudo-Dionysius the Areopogite, 115-117, 332, 496
Psychology, 1-2, 16, 21, 37, 91,

107, 125-126, 130-133, 142, 146, 151-157, 160-161, 163-166, 183, 204-206, 240, 244-311, 353, 443, 455, 475, 486, 524, 534, 541-542, 548, 550, 562, 566-567
Psychotherapy, 1-2, 5, 8, 20, 26, 85, 91, 125-166, 179, 210, 212, 239, 248, 252, 270, 273, 309, 312, 475, 534, 541
Puyseger, Jacques, 130
Pythagoras, 43, 87, 213, 488
Qliphoth, 83-86, 115
quicksilver (see Mercury)
Quimby, Phineas, 130, 145, 215, 217-232, 234, 547
Qumran, 65
Raguel (archangel), 66, 117
Rank, Otto, 153-154, 160, 162, 164, 323
Raphael (archangel), 66, 79, 117, 122, 499
reaction-formation, 145, 157, 272
rebirthing, 163-164, 322-323, 541
Reich, Wilhelm, 130, 155-160, 162, 179, 543
reincarnation, 69, 238-239, 477
REM (rapid eye movement) sleep, 371, 378
Remiel (archangel), 66
Renaissance, 14, 64, 87, 97, 100, 104-105, 108, 164, 178, 239, 396, 468, 473, 499, 503-504, 513-515, 566
repression (psychological), 133, 138, 144-145, 150, 156-157, 172, 273, 289, 299, 309, 315, 437, 439
resistance (psychological), 26, 90-91, 105, 145, 266, 324, 347-348, 361-362, 494
Reuchlin, Johann, 88-89, 336
Revelation, Book of, 117-118, 121
Ripley, George, 30, 535
Roberts, Jane, 237, 239, 543
Rogers, Carl, 126, 141, 151, 154, 160-161, 166
Romanticism, 135-137, 150, 187-188, 206-209, 213, 507, 546, 564
Rosarium Philosophorum, 29, 58
Rosenkreuz, Christian, 472-474
Rosetta Stone, 514-515
Rosicrucianism, 12, 37, 182, 208, 281, 428, 434, 464, 472-474, 562-563
rubedo, 57-59
Rudolph, Emperor, 504
Salem, 424-426, 438, 558
salt, 47-48, 51, 510
Samael (archangel), 120, 539
Saraqael (archangel), 66
Satan, 9, 67, 69, 78, 93, 116, 120-121, 406-407, 411, 414, 419-422, 427, 485-487, 494,

505, 539, 558
Saturn, 40, 439, 467, 489
Schelling, Friedrich, 3, 24, 132-133, 135, 137-138, 203, 205-206, 217
Scholem, Gershom, 61, 89, 397, 501, 524, 537-539, 555, 558, 566-567
Schopenhauer, Arthur, 135, 138-139, 194, 203, 210-211, 272, 307
Schucman, Helen, 237, 494, 543
Secret Book of John, 490-491
Self-realization, 1, 3-4, 9, 23, 33, 38-39, 60, 91, 124, 134, 154-155, 201-202, 312-338, 550
Self-remembering, 313-315, 319, 383
Sepher ha-Bahir, 69, 73, 84
Sepher ha-Razim, 496, 498
Sepher Yetzirah, 69, 73-74
Sepher Zohar, 69, 70, 73, 83-84, 469, 498, 558
sephira (*sephirot*), 69, 71-81, 83, 85, 89, 174, 247, 500, 515
Seraphim, 45, 115-117
sex magick, 1, 167, 178-186, 478, 543-544
Shaddai, 80, 88
Shadow, the (psychological), 1, 23, 52-53, 56, 91, 100, 103, 105, 152, 239, 248, 258, 276, 282, 291-292, 296-299, 307, 344, 347, 409, 440-442, 458-460, 470, 539
Shakti, 76, 158, 169, 172, 176-177, 334, 543
shamanism, 293, 428, 442, 452, 459, 509, 524, 558, 562
shapeshifting, 442, 449-453, 455, 457-458, 560
Shekhinah, 82-83
Sheldrake, Rupert, 238
Shelley, Mary, 389-390, 394, 398-399, 401, 406, 554-555
Shelley, Percy, 391, 406-407
Shemhamphorasch, 506
sigil, 183, 366, 505, 507
Silberer, Herbert, 32
silver (alchemy), 34-35, 38-39, 58, 89
Smith, Morton, 100, 109, 112, 539
Societas Rosicruciana, 474
Socrates, 72, 122, 134, 213, 325, 344, 444, 467, 480, 497
solipsism, 286, 550
Solomon, King, 94-97, 105, 110-111, 279, 499-500
solve et coagula, 39-41, 49, 57, 238
sorcery, 110, 112, 181, 276, 279-280, 333, 413, 423-424, 450, 500, 505-506, 509
Spare, Austin Osman, 327, 366, 391, 551
Spinoza, Baruch, 125, 133, 188, 207, 545-546

spiritization (alchemy), 56
Sprenger, Jacob, 414, 505
Stoics, 213
St. John of the Cross, 332, 496
St. Teresa of Avila, 332
Sufi/Sufism, 22, 25, 47, 70, 180-182, 256, 494
sulphur (alchemy), 47-48, 55, 58, 177
Sun, 30, 40, 45, 55-56, 84, 119, 280, 409, 467, 471, 489, 492, 522, 536, 564-565
suppression (psychological), 157, 272-273
Tabula Smaragdina (see Emerald Tablet)
Tantra, 1, 35, 54, 167-186, 307, 334, 363, 478, 525, 543-544, 551, 562
Taoism, 35, 71, 125, 141, 182, 355
Tarot, 12, 56-57, 62, 74-80, 89, 126, 241, 344, 435, 458, 508, 512-521, 568
Tart, Charles, 165, 244, 282
Tetragrammaton, 67-68, 72, 75, 88, 493, 497, 506
thaumaturgy, 351, 353, 363-364
Theosophy, 7, 12-13, 180, 245
theurgy, 177, 333-335
Thomas (Gnostic gospel), 112, 346
Thomas, Keith, 97, 509, 524, 535, 539, 568
Thoreau, Henry David, 215
Thoth, 41, 467, 514, 516-517, 521
Tibet/Tibetan, 6, 9, 41, 57, 92, 105, 152, 168, 170-171, 174, 291, 346, 369, 374, 376-377, 380, 400, 409, 423, 428, 459-460, 462, 466, 469, 525, 534, 551, 553-554, 571
Tibetan Book of the Dead, 152, 377, 409, 466, 534
Tibetan Book of the Great Liberation, 6
Tiphareth, 78-81, 85
Tolle, Eckhart, 18-19, 534
Torah, 70, 88, 119
Traditionalists, 32, 37, 209
Transcendentalism (philosophy), 205, 215-216, 236, 547
transmutation (alchemy), 33, 38, 45, 535
Transpersonal Psychology, 125, 155, 163, 165, 244, 282-283, 548
Tree of Life, 25, 69, 71, 73-75, 79, 81, 83, 85, 89, 116, 174, 515-516, 539, 563
Trithemius, Johann, 336, 499-500, 503-506
unio mystica, 331
Upanishads, 331, 333
Uriel (archangel), 66, 117, 122
Valentine, Basil, 29

Vedanta, 3, 7, 71, 75, 125, 149, 172, 203, 216, 333, 370, 481, 494, 554, 571
Venus, 467, 489
Vivekananda, Swami, 217
Waite, A.E., 89, 496, 507, 521
Washburn, Michael, 8, 244, 246
Watts, Alan, 6-8, 125, 166, 534, 541
werewolf, 442-449, 452-453, 455-456, 459, 461
Weyer, Johann, 95, 127, 148, 504-506, 508
Whitman, Walt, 215
Wicca, 412, 418, 427, 429-435, 441, 525, 555-556
Wilber, Ken, 2, 8, 157, 161, 165, 187, 201, 238, 244-247, 249-251, 291, 297, 352, 544-545, 548, 550
Wilhelm, Richard, 5, 42
Wilson, Colin, 447, 456, 561, 563
Witchcraft, 98, 127, 219, 411-441, 452, 505, 525, 555-561, 567
Woodroffe, John (Arthur Avalon), 169, 543
wolf, 30, 442-443, 445-449, 453, 458, 509, 561
Yahweh, 65-68, 121, 402, 421, 490, 539
Yesod, 80-81, 85
YHWH, 67-68, 76, 79, 110
yidam, 459
Yoga, 4-7, 79, 104, 125, 164, 168-169, 171, 182, 240, 323, 335, 346, 364, 368-369, 374, 376-377, 381, 442, 459, 462, 525, 543, 550, 552-553
Zen, 7-8, 124, 141, 168-169, 204, 291, 320-321, 333-334, 338, 481, 495, 534, 571
zimzum, 71, 85, 337, 364
Zohar (see *Sepher-Zohar*)
Zoroaster, 102, 479-480
Zoroastrianism, 22, 65, 94, 119-120, 469, 479-480, 491
Zosimos, 30

Acknowledgments

An author is mostly a visionary who at best can transmit his vision to a computer monitor (and print it out if he feels ambitious). Behind his name is a small army of people who help bring his ideas and writing (such as they are) to the tangible reality we know as a book. My thanks to the team at Axis Mundi Books who magically turned my keystrokes into this book: John Hunt, Trevor Greenfield, Krystina Kellingley, Nick Welch, Stuart Davies, Maria Maloney, Catherine Harris, Mary Flatt, and Lucya Szachnowski. Many thanks to Gareth Knight, Will Parfitt, R.J. Stewart, Gordan Djurdjevic, Donald Michael Kraig, Owen Davies, and Richard Grossinger for reviewing and in some cases commenting on the manuscript. My appreciation also to the staff of the Vancouver Central Library.

An additional personal note here. Despite long being aware of (since the mid-1970s) and sporadically studying and practicing the teachings of the Western esoteric tradition, from about 1980 to 2005 I had been heavily oriented toward, and immersed in, Eastern teachings. I traveled to India and Nepal twice, stayed in Indian ashrams and Tibetan Buddhist monasteries, studied and practiced for many years under a prominent guru, underwent initiations and instructions in Tibetan and Zen Buddhism, and even conducted satsang gatherings myself in the Advaita Vedanta tradition in the early 2000s. Then in 2006 following a series of personal losses I passed through a mild depression that lasted the better part of a year (despite the fact that I kept up a busy travel schedule during that time, conducting many seminars in cities around the world). Despite trying all sorts of ways to snap out of it, nothing worked. One day I was rummaging through my personal library and decided to pick up a book I'd purchased in 1999 but had not yet seriously read. It was Donald Michael Kraig's *Modern Magick*. I decided to read it thoroughly and undertake the exercises in his eminently practical book. Around that time I traveled to England and journeyed with a friend to Stonehenge, Avebury, and Glastonbury. I still remember practicing the Lesser Banishing Rituals of the Pentagram and Hexagram while standing atop the Glastonbury Tor, in mythical Arthurian territory, under a clear blue sky amidst a brisk wind. Within a few weeks of this my mental funk lifted. It was then that I began a serious reappraisal of the Western esoteric tradition, realizing as I did that it contained so many hidden gems of teachings and that moreover, it was designed for the Western psyche. Above all it is the practicality within this tradition, along with its richly creative elements, that is so potentially (and actually) helpful for inner well-being.

About the Author

P.T. Mistlberger was born in Montreal in 1959. He is a writer, researcher, transpersonal therapist, and seminar leader who since 1987 has privately coached individuals and run transformational workshops and training programs in numerous cities around the world. He is the author of three previous works, *A Natural Awakening* (2005), *The Three Dangerous Magi* (2010), and *Rude Awakening* (2012). He is based in Vancouver, Canada, and can be contacted via www.ptmistlberger.com or pmistlberger@yahoo.com

Axis Mundi Books provide the most revealing and coherent explorations and investigations of the world of hidden or forbidden knowledge. Take a fascinating journey into the realm of Esoteric Mysteries, Magic, Mysticism, Angels, Cosmology, Alchemy, Gnosticism, Theosophy, Kabbalah, Secret Societies and Religions, Symbolism, Quantum Theory, Apocalyptic Mythology, Holy Grail and Alternative Views of Mainstream Religion.